FORMAL ONTOLOGY IN INFORMATION SYSTEMS

Frontiers in Artificial Intelligence and Applications

FAIA covers all aspects of theoretical and applied artificial intelligence research in the form of monographs, doctoral dissertations, textbooks, handbooks and proceedings volumes. The FAIA series contains several sub-series, including "Information Modelling and Knowledge Bases" and "Knowledge-Based Intelligent Engineering Systems". It also includes the biennial ECAI, the European Conference on Artificial Intelligence, proceedings volumes, and other ECCAI – the European Coordinating Committee on Artificial Intelligence – sponsored publications. An editorial panel of internationally well-known scholars is appointed to provide a high quality selection.

Volume 209

Recently published in this series

Vol. 208. G.L. Pozzato, Conditional and Preferential Logics: Proof Methods and Theorem Proving
Vol. 207. A. Bifet, Adaptive Stream Mining: Pattern Learning and Mining from Evolving Data Streams
Vol. 206. T. Welzer Družovec et al. (Eds.), Information Modelling and Knowledge Bases XXI
Vol. 205. G. Governatori (Eds.), Legal Knowledge and Information Systems – JURIX 2009: The Twenty-Second Annual Conference
Vol. 204. B. Apolloni, S. Bassis and C.F. Morabito (Eds.), Neural Nets WIRN09 – Proceedings of the 19th Italian Workshop on Neural Nets
Vol. 203. M. Džbor, Design Problems, Frames and Innovative Solutions
Vol. 202. S. Sandri, M. Sànchez-Marrè and U. Cortés (Eds.), Artificial Intelligence Research and Development – Proceedings of the 12th International Conference of the Catalan Association for Artificial Intelligence
Vol. 201. J.E. Agudo et al. (Eds.), Techniques and Applications for Mobile Commerce – Proceedings of TAMoCo 2009
Vol. 200. V. Dimitrova et al. (Eds.), Artificial Intelligence in Education – Building Learning Systems that Care: From Knowledge Representation to Affective Modelling
Vol. 199. H. Fujita and V. Mařík (Eds.), New Trends in Software Methodologies, Tools and Techniques – Proceedings of the Eighth SoMeT_09
Vol. 198. R. Ferrario and A. Oltramari (Eds.), Formal Ontologies Meet Industry
Vol. 197. R. Hoekstra, Ontology Representation – Design Patterns and Ontologies that Make Sense

ISSN 0922-6389

Formal Ontology in Information Systems

Proceedings of the Sixth International Conference (FOIS 2010)

Edited by

Antony Galton

University of Exeter, United Kingdom

and

Riichiro Mizoguchi

Osaka University, Japan

IOS Press

Amsterdam • Berlin • Tokyo • Washington, DC

ISBN 978-1-60750-534-1 (print)
ISBN 978-1-60750-535-8 (online)
Library of Congress Control Number: 2010923730

Publisher
IOS Press BV
Nieuwe Hemweg 6B
1013 BG Amsterdam
Netherlands
fax: +31 20 687 0019
e-mail: order@iospress.nl

Distributor in the USA and Canada
IOS Press, Inc.
4502 Rachael Manor Drive
Fairfax, VA 22032
USA
fax: +1 703 323 3668
e-mail: iosbooks@iospress.com

PRINTED IN THE NETHERLANDS

Formal Ontology in Information Systems
A. Galton and R. Mizoguchi (Eds.)
IOS Press, 2010

Preface

Ontology began life in ancient times as a fundamental part of philosophical enquiry concerned with the analysis and categorisation of what exists. In recent years, the subject has taken a practical turn with the advent of complex computerised information systems which are reliant on robust and coherent representations of their subject matter. The systematisation and elaboration of such representations and their associated reasoning techniques constitute the modern discipline of formal ontology, which is now being applied to such diverse domains as artificial intelligence, computational linguistics, bioinformatics, GIS, knowledge engineering, information retrieval, and the Semantic Web. Researchers in all these areas are becoming increasingly aware of the need for serious engagement with ontology, understood as a general theory of the types of entities and relations making up their respective domains of enquiry, to provide a solid foundation for their work.

The conference series *Formal Ontology in Information Systems* (FOIS) is intended to provide a meeting point for researchers from these and other disciplines with an interest in formal ontology, where both theoretical issues and concrete applications can be explored in a spirit of genuine interdisciplinarity. FOIS began with the first meeting in Trento, Italy, in June 1998, which was followed by meetings in 2001, 2004, 2006, and 2008. The current, sixth FOIS conference is being held in Toronto, Canada, during 11-14 May 2010. In our call for papers, we solicited contributions from a wide range of areas important to the development of formal ontologies:

Foundational Issues

- Kinds of entity: particulars vs universals, continuants vs occurrents, abstracta vs concreta, dependent vs independent, natural vs artificial
- Formal relations: parthood, identity, connection, dependence, constitution, subsumption, instantiation
- Vagueness and granularity
- Identity and change
- Formal comparison among ontologies
- Ontology of physical reality (matter, space, time, motion, ...)
- Ontology of biological reality (genes, proteins, cells, organisms, ...)
- Ontology of artefacts, functions and roles
- Ontology of mental reality and agency (beliefs, intentions and other mental attitudes; emotions, ...)
- Ontology of social reality (institutions, organizations, norms, social relationships, artistic expressions, ...)
- Ontology of the information society (information, communication, meaning negotiation, ...)

- Ontology and Natural Language Semantics, Ontology and Cognition

Methodologies and Applications

- Top-level vs application ontologies
- Ontology integration and alignment; role of reference ontologies
- Ontology-driven information systems design
- Ontology-based application systems
- Requirements engineering
- Knowledge engineering
- Knowledge management and organization
- Knowledge representation; Qualitative modeling
- Computational lexicons; Terminology
- Information retrieval; Question-answering
- Semantic web; Web services; Grid computing
- Domain-specific ontologies, especially for: Linguistics, Geography, Law, Library science, Biomedical science, E-business, Enterprise integration, ...

Out of 71 papers submitted to FOIS-2010, 28 were selected for inclusion in the final programme, covering both the foundational issues and more application-oriented topics. Every submission was reviewed by at least two (and in almost every case by three) experts from the Programme Committee, together with a number of extra reviewers as listed below.

Many people have contributed to the success of FOIS-2010. First and foremost, of course, are the authors who responded to the call for papers, without whom there would have been no FOIS. We would like to thank the members of the Programme Committee for undertaking the reviewing work to a tight deadline, as well as the additional reviewers whose help was solicited where necessary. We are particularly grateful to our three invited speakers, Francis Jeffry Pelletier, John Bateman, and Alan Rector, whose contributions in themselves range across the whole spectrum of ontology from philosophical foundations to applications. We would like to thank the Conference Chair, Nicola Guarino, and the local chairs, Michael Grüninger and Chris Welty, for their indispensible handling of organizational aspects of the conference. Finally we must acknowledge the support of the newly-formed International Association for Ontology and its Applications, which from 2010 has taken over the general oversight and management of FOIS.

February 2010

Antony Galton
Riichiro Mizoguchi

Conference Organization

Organising Committee

Conference Chair	
Nicola Guarino	ISTC-CNR, Trento, Italy
Programme Chairs	
Antony Galton	University of Exeter, UK
Riichiro Mizoguchi	Osaka University, Japan
Local Organisation Chairs	
Michael Grüninger	University of Toronto, Canada
Chris Welty	IBM Research, Hawthorne, USA

Programme Committee

Bill Andersen	Ontology Works, Inc., USA
John Bateman	University of Bremen, Germany
Brandon Bennett	University of Leeds, UK
Stefano Borgo	ISTC-CNR, Trento, Italy
Joost Breuker	University of Amsterdam, The Netherlands
Paul Buitelaar	National University of Ireland, Galway
Roberto Casati	CNRS-EHSS, Paris, France
Werner Ceusters	University of Buffalo, USA
Matteo Cristani	University of Verona, Italy
Ernest Davis	New York University, USA
Maureen Donnelly	University of Buffalo, USA
Martin Dörr	Foundation for Research and Technology, Greece
Carola Eschenbach	University of Hamburg, Germany
Jérôme Euzenat	INRIA, Grenoble, France
Christiane Fellbaum	Princeton University, USA
Roberta Ferrario	ISTC-CNR, Trento, Italy
Antony Galton	University of Exeter, UK
Aldo Gangemi	ISTC-CNR, Rome, Italy
Pierdaniele Giaretta	University of Verona, Italy
Pierre Grenon	Open University, UK
Michael Grüninger	University of Toronto, Canada

Nicola Guarino	ISTC-CNR, Trento, Italy
Udo Hahn	Jena University, Germany
Jerry Hobbs	University of Southern California, USA
Ken Kaneiwa	National Institute of Information and Communications Technology, Kyoto, Japan
Werner Kuhn	University of Münster, Germany
Terry Langendoen	University of Arizona, USA
Alessandro Lenci	University of Pisa, Italy
Leonardo Lesmo	University of Torino, Italy
Claudio Masolo	ISTC-CNR, Trento, Italy
William McCarthy	Michigan State University, USA
Chris Menzel	Texas A & M University, USA
Simon Milton	University of Melbourne, Australia
Riichiro Mizoguchi	Osaka University, Japan
Philippe Muller	University of Toulouse III, France
John Mylopoulos	University of Toronto, Canada
Natasha Noy	Stanford University, USA
Daniel Oberle	SAP Research, CEC Karlsruhe
Leo Obrst	The Mitre Corporation, USA
Maria Teresa Pazienza	University of Rome, Italy
David Randell	University of Birmingham, UK
Alan Rector	University of Manchester, UK
Riccardo Rosati	University of Rome, Italy
Guus Schreiber	University of Amsterdam, The Netherlands
Johanna Seibt	University of Aarhus, Denmark
Michael Sintek	DFKI GmbH, Kaiserslautern, Germany
Barry Smith	University of Buffalo, USA
John Sowa	Vivomind Intelligence Inc., USA
John Stell	University of Leeds, UK
Veda Storey	Georgia State University, USA
Achille Varzi	Columbia University, New York, USA
Laure Vieu	CNRS-IRIT, Toulouse, France
Chris Welty	IBM Research, Hawthorne, USA

Additional Reviewers

Diego Calvanese, Gianluca Colombo, Robin Cooper, William Duncan, Laura Hollink, Edmund Kazmierczak, Chris Keen, Patrick Maué, Manuel Moeller, Alessandro Oltramari, Alexander Paar, Dimitris Plexousakis, Simon Scheider, Patrice Seyed, Willem van Hage, Özgür Özçep

Contents

Applications I

Ontology Building

Biomedical and Chemical Ontologies I

Products and Functions

Verification and Evaluation

Invited Talks

Formal Ontology in Information Systems
A. Galton and R. Mizoguchi (Eds.)
IOS Press, 2010

doi:10.3233/978-1-60750-535-8-3

Ontological Lessons from the Semantics of Mass and Count Nouns

Francis Jeffry PELLETIER
University of Alberta, Canada

Abstract

Mass terms are those such as 'water', 'computer software', 'advice', and 'knowledge'. They are contrasted with count terms such as 'person', 'computer program', 'suggestion', and 'belief'. Intuitively, mass terms refer to "stuff" while count terms refer to "objects". Since mass terms refer to stuff, they (but not count terms) allow for measurement: 'a liter of water', 'three CDs worth of computer software', 'too much advice', 'many books worth of deep knowledge'. Since count terms refer to objects, they (but not mass terms) allow for counting, quantifying and individuating: 'a person', 'three computer programs', 'each suggestion', 'that belief of his'.

The presumed fact that mass nouns are not true of individuals has seemed to some to show that traditional logical theory is inadequate as a medium for their semantic representation. It has seemed implausible to represent 'Snow is white' as $\forall x(\mathsf{Snow}(x) \rightarrow \mathsf{White}(x))$, since there are no plausible values for x. (What could be the value of x in 'For each x, if x is snow then x is white'?) In turn, this has been the driver for the use of mereological-based approaches to the semantics of mass terms. ('Mereology' is here to be understood widely to include not only classical mereology, but a range of approaches that share some features with the classical mereology.)

Further philosophical problems traditionally associated with mass terms include distinguishing mass from count terms (is it a syntactic or semantic distinction?), deciding the extent of the classification (does it include more than noun phrases?), describing the semantic underpinnings of mass terms (since they are not true of individuals, how can a model theory be developed?), and explaining the ontology presupposed by mass terms *vs* count terms.

Alongside these concerns, there is the meta-philosophical question of the extent to which the linguistic practices of a language can be used as evidence for how those speakers view reality, or indeed, what reality is. It is this issue, as applied to the question of the ontology presupposed by mass terms *vs* count terms, that I wish especially to address.

I am going to restrict my attention to the category of nouns and noun phrases, even though some writers have noted parallels between count terms and event-verbs and between mass terms and process-verbs. Others have noted how aspectual distinctions sometimes mirror the mass/count distinction in nouns: one can eat dinner for an hour (eating dinner is mass-like; and the temporal modification is not punctual), but it seems nonsensical to eat a dinner for an hour (eating a dinner is count-like, but this does not happily combine with non-punctual temporal modification). Some writers have argued that some adjectives can be classified as count or mass: for instance, 'triangular' might be count, 'watery' might be mass. I think many of my observations within the nominal domain might carry over to these other categories, but I don't wish to argue for that here.

Throughout the recent history of philosophical and linguistic reflections on the mass/count distinction, there have been skeptics who disparage the attempt to make the distinction carry any semantic weight or philosophical importance. Such skeptics point to the fact that the same meaning can be count in one language but mass in another, even in very closely related languages. Furthermore, some languages, especially the Sino-Japanese-Korean ones, have been argued to assign mass to all lexical nouns. There are also some Amerindian languages that seem to have no mass/count distinction at all. The skeptics also point to pairs of terms within one language where one is count and the other mass, yet they seem to designate very similar items of reality—for instance, 'brownie' vs. 'baklava'—or sometimes even the same item of reality—for instance, 'this suggestion' vs. 'this advice'. (Or, to consider a more philosophically relevant example: 'belief' is a count term while 'knowledge' is a mass term. Yet we commonly think that what is one and the same thing can be a belief of Sandy's but knowledge of Kim's; and that before Kim had enough evidence to make it be knowledge, it was a belief of Kim's.) Still others, myself included, have argued that (almost?) all nouns can be employed in both a mass and a count manner, showing that some very fancy footwork is required in order to give a reasonable semantic and ontological accounting for this.

I too am a skeptic about the viability of using the mass/count distinction to draw any firm metaphysical/ontological conclusions. However, I am not a skeptic about the individual/stuff distinction—it is just that I don't think it parallels the mass/count distinction. And I want to describe some ways that one might take to de-couple the two.

One way I want to proceed is to cast doubt on the assignment of mass/count to lexical nouns, and I will argue instead for the view that they should be assigned only at the level of noun phrases. (Following the suggestions made by Keith Allen (1980).) But in addition to these syntactic moves, we need to deal with the semantic consequence of (what I presume to be) the fact that every noun is sometimes used in a count manner and sometimes in a mass manner. Solutions in the literature postulate a number of 'conversion functions' or 'coercions' that will convert the meaning of 'chicken' (+count) to the meaning of 'chicken' (+mass). I think these are all misguided, and wish to give a plausible replacement account.

Formal Ontology in Information Systems
A. Galton and R. Mizoguchi (Eds.)
IOS Press, 2010

doi:10.3233/978-1-60750-535-8-5

Ontological diversity: the case from space

John A. BATEMAN [1]
Faculty of Linguistics and Literary Sciences &
SFB/TR8 Spatial Cognition Research Center
University of Bremen, Bremen, Germany

Abstract The situated interpretation of natural language concerning space, spatial relationships and spatial activities is a complex problem spanning contributions from several disciplines. Space plays a central role in many theories of cognition and the spatial language observed in actual contexts of use is extremely flexible. In our work on spatial representations of all kinds, principles drawn from ontological engineering play a central role. Moreover, we have been led to augment those principles in particular ways: most specifically with respect to ontological modularity, ontological heterogeneity, and multiple ontological levels or strata. In the presentation accompanying this position statement, I give an overview of our work on space and the ontologically-relevant conclusions that we have drawn. I also suggest that these conclusions are relevant for ontological work in general, and not just for that concerned with spatial issues.

Keywords. Spatial language, spatial ontology, ontological modularity, ontology design, qualitative spatial representation, natural language processing, natural language semantics.

Introduction

The starting point for the discussion here will be the problem of providing a semantics for spatial expressions as they occur in natural languages in natural interactions. As we shall see, this leads us fairly directly to several ontologically-based accounts and to approaches that are usefully related to ontological engineering. The analysis and formalization of the meaning of spatial expressions represents an extremely active area of research at this time; there are detailed studies of spatial language use in contexts ranging over formal semantic interpretations, psychological studies, human-machine interaction, dialogue analysis, computational modeling and many more. Several extensive overviews of the field are available [2]. Much is now known about the factors contributing to spatial language use and the kinds of abstractions that will need to find a place in any complete account and yet, despite these advances, there remain significant problems in relating spatial expressions to their intended interpretations in context. In particular, the very notion of the 'meaning' of spatial expressions and terms in natural languages is still approached from a variety of diverging perspectives.

[1]The financial support of the Deutsche Forschungsgemeinschaft (DFG) through the Collaborative Research Center on Spatial Cognition (SFB/TR 8) is gratefully acknowledged for the work reported in this paper, as well as the substantial contributions of my co-workers in all the areas addressed—particularly: Joana Hois, Oliver Kutz, Till Mossakowski, Robert Ross and Thora Tenbrink.

One consequence of this is that there is no generally accepted approach to providing spatial interpretations of natural spatial expressions in context. The approaches proposed within individual perspectives do not generalize well to cover other areas of application. For example, interpretations of spatial language for guiding autonomous robots look very different from formal semantic constructions of spatial interpretations, and both of these are quite distinct from the interpretations employed for geographic information systems or dialogic spatial assistance systems. We can explain many of these differences in the following way. Almost regardless of theoretical position taken towards the linguistic system, spatial language presents a particularly close point of contact between the abstract system of language and its contextualized use. Spatial language is closely associated with issues of embodiment, with mental imagery, and many other non-linguistic capabilities and there is good psychological and neurocognitive evidence that spatial descriptions activate an entire range of spatial processing routines, simulations and diverse mental model constructions that do not lie within the linguistic system itself. It is probably because of this that we find an unusually broad range of proposals for spatial semantics that take their lead primarily from *non-linguistically* motivated considerations—including *ontological* approaches of various kinds.

Providing a natural language semantics directly in terms of a non-linguistic external representation is, however, more problematic than might have been thought from the perspective of ontology. From that perspective, it is natural that fundamental issues of space and spatial organisation stand centre-stage and are considered independently of considerations of how any particular natural language might talk about space. Varzi gives an explicit warning that any other approach is seriously flawed; as he argues concerning the use made of linguistic data when thinking of ontology:

> "There is, in fact, no way of telling what sorts of things there are given the sorts of things we say. But neither is there a complete gap between our words and the world out there. It's just that that bridge must be built from below, as it were: ontology comes first, and depending on what we think there is, we must attach a meaning to what we say. Going the other way around is wishful thinking." [35]

The problem with this view is that it assumes an overly simple relationship between the kinds of abstractions and their organisation that appear in natural language expressions and those that might be motivated 'purely' on ontological grounds. If language served simply to recapitulate more deeply anchored spatial organisations, all would be well; but this theoretical assumption appears to be inaccurate. In fact, each domain is responsible for different kinds of tasks and construes space in its own ways. As a consequence, the semantics underlying linguistic usage tend to cross-cut and redefine distinctions that have been motivated solely in terms of space.

The positions adopted have direct consequences for how well theoretical treatments meet the challenge of accounting for spatial language semantics. Whereas it is possible for limited areas of language use to draw up detailed accounts of how natural language terms relate to non-linguistic spatial representations or ontologically-motivated organisations, actual natural language usage tends to frustrate attempts to produce fully general models. There are a number of responses to this, perhaps the most frequently observable being a marginalization of the cases that 'do not fit'. This is reminiscent of earlier argumentation in linguistics that marginalized much of linguistic behavior to 'mere' performance. However, when our aim is to explain how spatial language works in general, this manoeuvre is not available to us.

The most frequently occurring non-linguistic descriptions of linguistic spatial semantics are: accounts based on Euclidean geometry, accounts based on various flavours of qualitative spatial calculi, accounts based on field potentials, and accounts based on ontological organisations motivated primarily by non-linguistic considerations. All of these share the same basic problem: they attempt to impose on linguistic spatial semantics organisations that are not natural to that semantics. In contrast, I consider it necessary to address these issues by starting at both ends: we cannot rely on an ontology of space to provide all the necessary detail, or even the appropriate organization, for the construals of space required for natural language semantics. There is likely to be a correlation, or at least the possibility of an interrelation, but this cannot only be built 'from below'. We also need to characterize in detail the semantic contributions of linguistic spatial descriptions and only then relate this semantics to contextualized geometric (or other) specifications of locations. Capturing this multi-stratal organisation within an ontological framework then itself sets interesting requirements for ontological modeling.

The paper is organised as follows. First, I give some brief examples of the different approaches to proposing treatments of space and describe some of the difficulties that they face when considered as general approaches for capturing spatial semantics. Second, I sketch the rough outlines of a framework motivated by principles of ontological engineering that, we claim, takes us closer to being able to capture the full flexibility of human language usage concerning space and spatially embedded activities and objects.

1. Treating space

There are several approaches that assume that an appropriate semantics for linguistic expressions concerning space will relate linguistic expressions to regions of three-dimensional space. These assume a close relationship between linguistic semantics and Euclidean geometry. The motivation is that we can clearly characterise any spatial information we choose drawing on a geometric foundation. Early approaches in this vein include the very well known work of Herskovits [15], which provides an extensive range of examples of spatial language in English illustrating the extreme diversity in interpretation that typically is required. Despite this diversity, Herskovits attempts to preserve a generally geometric interpretation, construed as the 'ideal' meaning of a spatial term, by assuming a variety of 'sense shifts' and degrees of 'tolerance'. It is then the regions to which geometric relations apply that vary rather than the relations themselves.

Several more recent frameworks assume a similarly geometric ideal meaning. This is often independent of particular linguistic theories or frameworks that might be adopted. For example, a broadly model-theoretic framework using universal syntactic phrase structure is developed in a series of papers by Kracht [22,23], while a rather different angle is taken within a combinatory categorial grammar (CCG) framework by Francez and Steedman [13]. Despite their differences, some rather similar problems arise. We can see this by focusing very closely on just where the semantics of spatial expressions enter into the two accounts.

For Kracht, the semantics of spatial terms is characterised in terms of *parameterized neighborhoods*, that is, time-dependent areas of three-dimensional space. This means that the semantics of *in*, for example, is a function that requires an object x and a time t and which produces the set of regions that are contained in the inside of x at that time t. For Francez and Steedman, the semantics of sentence-modifying spatial expressions serves to restrict the spatial extents of the events being modified to some specified sub-regions of those provided by the expressions themselves. The modifications involved are defined in terms of what Francez and Steedman term 'shift-functions'. The role of a shift function is to take some spatial region and to modify, or 'shift', this to produce another region related in some particular specified way to the originating one. Remaining with *in*, therefore, the corresponding shift function restricts some original spatial region to a proper subpart of that region. Both accounts are actually more concerned with achieving a workable view of compositionality, so that the semantics of more complex spatial expressions can be derived from the semantics of the parts, than with characterizing the spatial commitments involved. As a consequence, relatively little detail is provided concerning the spatial relationships themselves.

This is a pity in that it makes it possible to overlook just how flexible some of the spatial relationships will need to be made to cover normally occurring spatial language. Francez and Steedman suggest for their shift functions that "some are easy" [13, p394], such as those for temporal *after* and *before* (which they relate to particular temporal sub-intervals); whereas others, such as *behind*, "we will not even try to describe ... in words." [13, p395]. But this is important since the entire architecture rests on the ability of these shift-functions to pass on sensible and appropriate restrictions that are well behaved during composition. Reliance on a Euclidean space for defining potential spatial relationships actually opens up a considerable gap between language usage and the semantics being proposed. The compositionality achieved relies crucially on the identification of appropriate time-bound regions in space and is therefore tied closely to geometric views of the spatial world.

Kracht himself notes the need to move away from precise geometric relations in a similar vein to Herskovits' account above. However, his proposals are limited to considering language as 'vague' or fuzzy—a common position when starting from a formal characterisation rather than language. In fact, linguistic and non-linguistic accounts appear to be focusing on very different kinds of relationships. The differences in regions involved with such alternatives as 'the water is in the jar', 'the crack is in the jar', 'the bird is in the tree', 'the chair is in the corner' (and the many more examples listed by Herskovits) are not adequately construed as one simply being a less exact version of one of the others. Kracht also notes these difficulties and is forced to describe his own characterization of localisers as an 'approximation' that does not match up with intuitions concerning the semantics of these expressions at several points [22, p191].

The next logical move away from semantics based on geometry is to consider spatial semantics in terms of qualitative spatial representations, particularly qualitative spatial calculi [10,4,9]. Qualitative spatial calculi such as the well known Region Connection Calculus (RCC: [29]), the double cross calculus (DCC: [14]) or the 9^{+}-intersection [24] have all been proposed at various times as candidates for the semantics of linguistics spatial expressions. Interesting for us, however, is the fact that this often suggests alternatives that are *not in competition* with one another. That is, sometimes it is appropriate to use a semantics involving orientation, such as the double-cross calculus, sometimes it is more appropriate to use a semantics that involves regions. There are no qualitative spatial calculi that stand as convincing proposals for *all* of the kinds of spatial relationships that we need to cover when addressing spatial language.

Moreover, the fit between natural language and these calculi is often far from good: in studies participants often do not make the distinctions required by the more discriminating 8-relation RCC-8 as reliably as they do when using the 5-relation RCC-5 [30]. However, RCC-5 is a rather inexpressive calculus which does not go far towards providing a semantics for natural spatial language. What is worse, more expressive calculi that explicitly attempt to combine properties available in individual calculi generally have exceedingly poor complexity behavior. When combining, for example, orientation with size constraints it is very easy to tip the scales towards extreme intractability. So here also there is no direct path to a general spatial linguistic semantics.

Finally, we can consider approaches popular in robotics involving probability fields that take a rather different perspective on what serves as an appropriate semantics for spatial expressions; a recent and well developed exemplar of this direction is that of Kelleher and colleagues [21]. Field potential formalizations build on the observation that many linguistic spatial terms appear to identify general directions or areas rather than precise orientations. For example, 'to the left of X' picks out a general direction towards the left but is not restricted to a 90° angle. Use of projective terms therefore suggests a *graded applicability structure*, whereby one direction may be a 'best' exemplar (a 'focal axis') but other directions are also acceptable to the extent that they approximate this best case. This can be captured by defining for each projective relation a probability field that reflects the likelihood of application of a term given a particular spatial position. The spatial expression 'in front of X' can then be seen as generating a field of potential applicability around the object X such that areas near to and towards the designated front of that object are assigned higher probabilities than other parts of the field.

Although such graded probabilities of locations often match quite well with applicability judgements made by speakers, there remain some difficult issues. The most significant problem is the basic question of just how the potential field relevant for a particular communicative situation is to be determined. Potential fields need to be parameterized in various ways (e.g., by being stretched or relaxed according to relative size and orientation [39], with respect to potential distractors [21], and according to the selected reference frame), but the precise motivations for that parameterization are often context specific or *ad hoc*. This is exactly analogous to the problems with the Euclidean approaches mentioned above: just as it was unclear what regions are called for, here it is equally unclear just what kind of field is appropriate.

2. Treating space and its linguistic construal

Whereas the approaches described above consider the spatial world independently of language, there is also a growing range of approaches that consider more carefully just what distinctions spatial language is relying upon or constructing. In these approaches, the regularities observable with respect to spatial language can themselves be used to suggest abstract characterizations of space that differ in important ways from those inherited from Euclidean geometry. Concentrating instead on the commitments that linguistic expressions bring for construals of space opens up possibilities for variation that an early imposition of relations expressed via geometry renders difficult.

Two proposals made with respect to quite different spatial areas give a good indication of how this can be approached and so will be used as examples here. Eschenbach [12] and Zwarts [40] both choose not to relate linguistic expressions to regions in three-dimensional space directly, but instead attempt to specify abstract algebraic structures that capture just what is involved in linguistic spatial expressions in their own right. These algebraic structures then serve as constraints on further contextualization, which may well involve three-dimensional regions, but do not necessarily do so.

The two layers of description introduced by Eschenbach are the following: on the one hand, there is a direct contribution of the common or "core" linguistic semantics of a spatial term, which is constant across contexts, and, on the other hand, there are the concepts that are required to contextualize these terms [12, p339]. In this framework, an *abstract* 'geometric' structure is imposed on the *concrete* spatial situation, depending on the 'reference frame' that applies. As an example, *in front of* is commonly used in three situations:[2] with an intrinsic reference frame in which the reference object's intrinsic sides are used as basis for the establishment of a spatial direction, with a relative reference system, where the observer's line of vision is used as an origin for reference, and thirdly, with a motion trajectory providing its own perspective on the objects. In all cases, use of *in front of* (and related terms such as *behind*) are treated in terms of half-lines: i.e., in order to cover the semantics of these terms it is necessary to assume an 'ontology' that consists at least of half-lines. In contrast to this, consideration of the terms *right* and *left* require a minimal commitment to half-planes. The algebraic structures motivated linguistically for these expressions therefore differ. Although opinions may vary concerning whether these particular representations are the correct interpretations of the linguistic terms considered or not [34], the two-level architecture of the approach moves us significantly towards being able to deal with the flexibility of interpretation required. The structures defined provide precisely the abstractions that are necessary for assigning a semantics to the corresponding expressions and no more: over-commitment to any particular geometric regions is therefore avoided.

In Zwarts' account, we also find a level of abstract algebraic specification motivated primarily by linguistic phenomena, but here focused specifically on *paths*. Zwarts' approach is also interesting in that it illustrates how quite diverse linguistic phenomena can be drawn upon in order to triangulate the abstract linguistic spatial distinctions necessary. In particular, he shows how there is an interaction between the properties of paths expressed in a variety of natural language expressions and considerations of verbal aspect and telicity. Two components of this account are particularly relevant to our concerns here.

First, Zwarts makes it clear that spatial language as such appears to commit to certain idealizations away from the concrete details of time-dependent locations in three-dimensional space. While this fact is generally accepted, approaches differ in their responses to it. Kracht, for example, builds the time-dependence into his formalization at a very basic level; Francez and Steedman similarly allow time and spatial contextual arguments to pervade the semantics of linguistic expressions. In contrast to this, Zwarts follows Talmy [33] and others in assuming that this time-dependence is inherent to the view of space that language constructs and so should no longer appear freely in corresponding semantics: i.e., the linguistic semantics generalises away from this variance. Zwarts ac-

[2]Eschenbach's account is actually of German lexemes, in this case, the preposition *vor*; this is not relevant for the immediate discussion, however.

cordingly builds this relativism into his account by describing only the spatial relationships that persist over time rather than the specific and possibly changing extensional locations carrying them.

Second, Zwarts points out that it is not the extensional set of points on a path that determines whether it be considered telic or atelic; any given path may be picked out by linguistic expressions of both kinds. For example, for a given set of points lying along a river between some origin and a house, each of the following phrases might be appropriate [40, Example 11, p746]:

The car drove …	(1) into the valley (*for hours)	[telic]
	(2) towards the house (for hours)	[atelic]
	(3) across the border (*for hours)	[telic]
	(4) along the river (for hours)	[atelic]

The conclusion here is clear: "this shows that (a)telicity is a property of a *description* of objects, not of the objects themselves." [40, p746]. I suggest that this is in fact the appropriate stance to take with *all* linguistic expressions: we need to account for the regularities underlying the *descriptions* that language(s) allow us, and in certain respects, require us to build. And this cannot be presumed to simply follow from characterizations of space independent of language.

3. Embedding within an ontologically-motivated framework

There appear to be many areas of spatial language where minimally necessary algebraic structures for explaining regularities in linguistic phenomena can be sought. The approach we are developing builds further on the two-level decomposition of spatial semantics and interpretation that this entails by allowing linguistically-motivated abstract algebraic structures to play the role of plug-and-play ontology modules in the manner first proposed for space in Bateman and Farrar [5].

Ontology modules of this kind are specified as theories within the language we use for all of our ontological work: the Common Algebraic Specification Language, CASL [28]. CASL is a specification language for first-order logic theories with strong structuring mechanisms and good tool support. The structuring mechanisms are important for us since we particularly want to avoid the distinct spatial modules interfering with one another—we already know that combinations of spatial calculi can readily lead to computational complexity explosions and so caution is advisable. We are also currently planning to make increasing use of other spatially-relevant theories of space specified in CASL, including a broad range of qualitative spatial calculi [37]. Several examples of using structured specifications for spatial representations are given in Bateman *et al.* [3].

In order to bring together the information provided in the distinct spatial ontology modules, we are exploring a range of 'loose coupling' techniques, drawing on work such as $\mathcal{E}$-Connections [25,11], distributed description logics [31] and modular ontologies in general [32]. This involves several design decisions concerning the construction of an ontological framework over all.

First, because the distinct spatial theories are maintained separately, we also need mechanisms for deciding just which theories are going to be selected for use when. For this, we adopt a *linguistically-motivated* ontology, called the Generalized Upper Model (GUM: [6]), originally developed for use within the Penman natural language generation system but now extended within our work to apply equally for both automatic natural language generation and analysis. We have produced a spatial extension of GUM axiomatized to lie within the description logic of the Semantic Web Ontology language, $\mathcal{SROIQ}$ [20], since this level of expressivity is widely relied upon in natural language processing technology. The ontology as a whole accordingly has a structural backbone based on the class-subclass relationship, and a collection of constraints on possible roles and their fillers. Both the classes making up the backbone and the roles defined over these classes are motivated throughout by distinguishable patterns of grammatical behavior—in this sense, the ontology is 'linguistically motivated'. In our work so far we have focused specifically on grammatical evidence from English and German; our semantics is accordingly limited in this respect and extensions to consider other languages offer an obvious direction for future work.

Our efforts to date have focused particularly on capturing spatial relations: that is, the semantics of utterances where distinct entities are brought into a spatial configuration with particular, more or less precisely specified relations holding between them. These relations can involve both static relations of relative location, distance, overlap, containment, etc. and dynamic relations where entities move with respect to each other. The precise motivation and contents of this linguistically-motivated spatial ontology are set out at length elsewhere [16]; the ontology plus documentation and examples is freely available online.[3]

The GUM spatial extension formalizes spatial language in terms of two primary concepts: GeneralizedLocation and SpatialModality. The concept GeneralizedLocation is used to provide a common semantics for any linguistic expression of a 'place'—including prepositional phrases, adverbials, nominals and other spatially-relevant constituents when used in appropriate grammatical contexts. Moreover, a GeneralizedLocation does not yield a place directly, but instead *constructs* a place on the basis of a combination of a specified entity, or reference object, and some specified set of 'modes of anchoring and hosting' [7] of places adopted with respect to the reference object. These latter are grouped together under the single concept SpatialModality; in our account, this category holds the majority of linguistic 'spatial' relationships offered by a language. The categories beneath SpatialModality, together with their interrelationships and mutual constraints, are motivated solely on the basis of grammatical evidence.

A GeneralizedLocation in our sense may then be considered formally as a one-place predicate that 'locates' its argument. The precise placement of that argument is *constrained* by the specification of a particular subclass of SpatialModality. This can be shown in an expression of the form:

$$\lambda x.\textsc{Loc}(x, P_{\textit{spatial-modality}}(R))$$

where R is the reference object (e.g., the 'desk' in 'in front of the desk', the 'tree' in 'in the tree', etc.) and Loc a predicate of co-location. This assumes a standard compositional semantics with phrase-internal detail omitted for current purposes. The above expression then says that some entity x co-locates with some 'location' that must be derived from the reference object R in the manner identified by the given spatial modality $P_{\textit{spatial-modality}}$.

This formalization shows considerable similarities to that originally proposed by Bierwisch and Wunderlich [8,38]; there are also relations to be drawn out with Kracht's

[3] http://www.ontospace.uni-bremen.de/ontology/stable/GUM-3-space.owl

view of location expressions and Francez and Steedman's shift-functions as discussed above. In our case, however, there is no commitment to any geometric interpretations of either the reference object or the location constructed with reference to that reference object. Particular subtypes of SpatialModality instead refer to particular domains of algebraic formalization along the lines seen in the approaches of Eschenbach and Zwarts.

The way in which this 'ontological' organisation is used is then as follows. Individual grammatical expressions and lexical items concerned with expressing spatial semantics are linked with one or more configurations drawn from the GUM spatial extension. These constructs are themselves linked to abstract spatial theories that, in principle, could be drawn from quite diverse accounts. Within a particular context of use, a given linguistic expression may call for the activation of several distinct spatial theory areas, each even relying possibly on different logics. These are then the areas that are candidates for being related for further inferences to flow.

In one of our experimental approaches to loose coupling, discussed in more detail by Hois and Kutz [18,19], an extension of $\mathcal{E}$-Connections is employed to directly link GUM categories and relations within external spatial calculi—in particular, with the double cross calculus (DCC) of [14] and the 9^+-intersection of [24]. The basic notion behind $\mathcal{E}$-Connections is that a mapping is defined between selected entities of two ontologies: this mappings allows for information to be exchanged along the paths defined by the mappings while still maintaining the ontologies as distinct. This therefore isolates the informational content of each ontology, preventing unwarranted inferences or even inconsistency from arising due to conflicting modeling requirements in the two ontologies. A graphical characterization of this approach is suggested in Figure 1 for some of the GUM spatial modalities for horizontal projective terms (left/right, front/back, etc.) and the corresponding relations of DCC. Spatial reasoning can be pursued on the right-hand side of the connection using dedicated spatial tools [36], whereas purely linguistic commitments are maintained on the left-hand side of the connection.

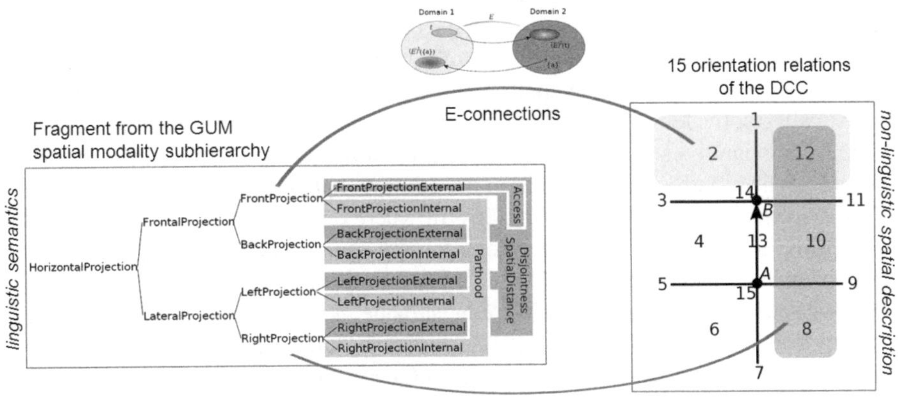

Figure 1. Selected $\mathcal{E}$-connections between linguistic semantics and non-linguistic spatial descriptions (simplified and adapted from Hois and Kutz [19])

An alternative approach to loose coupling that we are also now pursuing considers directly attaching to each category of the GUM spatial backbone a dedicated abstract spatial theory representing the minimal *semantic* commitments entered into by the category; examples of such theories were given above from Eschenbach and Zwarts. The connection between the linguistic abstract spatial semantics and non-spatial semantics is then also followed using an extended $\mathcal{E}$-connection approach, but in this case the theory on the linguistic side has naturally become far richer. Further research will be needed to discover the precise merits or problems of the two approaches; some exploratory discussion is presented in Bateman *et al.* [1].

4. Discussion and Conclusions

The discussions of the previous sections and the work they are based upon strongly suggest that it is crucial to pull the relative contributions of linguistic semantics and non-linguistic models of space apart in order to appropriately characterise and capture the full flexibility of natural spatial language. Moreover, to provide such a characterization, we can apply certain principles from ontological engineering and the solutions proposed there for dealing with space and with ontology design. In particular, within our work on space more generally we have found a clear need for ontological 'multiperspectivalism' and modularity [3,17]. Formal research on space has revealed many distinct characterizations, each with its own benefits and drawbacks, and these cannot be sensibly reduced to one common foundation. We accordingly adopt an ontology architecture that provides a library of spatial theories, each with their own entities and relations.

We then see no need to restrict this modular heterogeneous approach purely to the spatial domain. When we consider language, it appears beneficial also to see linguistic spatial construals as subject to an *additional layer* of ontological information that formalizes the 'semantic commitments' entered into by any linguistic construction. We term this a *linguistically-motivated ontology* because its organization is motivated solely by grammatical and lexical evidence involving the natural usage of spatial expressions. It is therefore specifically tailored to the requirements of spatial language, which also makes it particularly well suited for natural language processing in information systems. The linguistically-motivated ontology takes on the task of mediating between linguistic form and contextualized interpretation, just as other ontological perspectives on space take up other tasks. Although several approaches to processing spatial language now rely on linguistically-motivated classifications of linguistic utterances in this way, they generally provide a comparatively limited range of relevant abstractions due, on the one hand, to task and application restrictions and, on the other, to appeals to narrower ranges of linguistic evidence [26,27]. Finally, regardless of where one stands on the issue of whether this organisation is genuinely an 'ontology' or not, established principles of ontological engineering have also been applied beneficially to improve modeling consistency.

Once separations of this nature have been made, it is necessary to establish mechanisms by which specifications of linguistic semantics can be related suitably with non-linguistic specifications and for distinct spatial theories to be related to one another. And here, again, we can apply results from within formal ontological engineering. Current approaches to ontological *structuring*, *modularity* and *heterogeneity* are producing a range of techniques for bringing together distinct representations so that reasoning can proceed across potentially incompatible bodies of knowledge. This is also ideally suited to the situation that has been painted here concerning natural language and its interpretation. The spatial theories, and linguistic semantic configurations, are loosely coupled according to the demands of individual communicative situations.

The experiences we have gained in working with lattices of smaller scale ontology modules, each fully specified as a formal theory, has convinced us that this offers a very general architecture for ontology work. In our current research, therefore, we are exploring its use in other domains, including web service provision, engineering processes and ambient assisted living.

References

[1] John Bateman, Thora Tenbrink, and Scott Farrar. The Role of Conceptual and Linguistic Ontologies in Discourse. *Discourse Processes*, 44(3):175–213, 2007.

[2] John A. Bateman. Situating spatial language and the role of ontology: issues and outlook. *Linguistics and Language Compass*, forthcoming 2010.

[3] John A. Bateman, Stefano Borgo, Klaus Lüttich, Claudio Masolo, and Till Mossakowski. Ontological Modularity and Spatial Diversity. *Spatial Cognition and Computation*, 7(1):97–128, 2007.

[4] John A. Bateman and Scott Farrar. Spatial ontology baseline. SFB/TR8 internal report I1-[OntoSpace]: D2, Collaborative Research Center for Spatial Cognition, University of Bremen, Germany, 2004.

[5] John A. Bateman and Scott Farrar. Towards a generic foundation for spatial ontology. In Achille C. Varzi and Laure Vieu, editors, *Formal Ontology in Information Systems: Proceedings of the Third International Conference on Formal Ontology in Information Systems (FOIS-2004)*, pages 237–248, Amsterdam, 2004. IOS Press.

[6] John A. Bateman, Renate Henschel, and Fabio Rinaldi. Generalized Upper Model 2.0: documentation. Technical report, GMD/Institut für Integrierte Publikations- und Informationssysteme, Darmstadt, Germany, 1995.

[7] Brandon Bennett and Pragya Agarwal. Semantic Categories Underlying the Meaning of 'Place'. In Stephan Winter, Matt Duckham, Lars Kulik, and Benjamin Kuipers, editors, *Spatial Information Theory: Proceedings of the 8th international conference (COSIT-2007, Melbourne, Australia)*, number 4736 in Lecture Notes in Computer Science, pages 78–95. Springer, 2007.

[8] Manfred Bierwisch. On the grammar of local prepositions. In Manfred Bierwisch, W. Motsch, and I. Zimmermann, editors, *Syntax, Semantik, und Lexikon: Rudolf Ruzicka zum 65. Geburtstag*, pages 1–65. Akademie Verlag, Berlin, 1988.

[9] A G Cohn and J Renz. Qualitative Spatial Representation and Reasoning. In F. van Harmelen, V. Lifschitz, and B. Porter, editors, *Handbook of Knowledge Representation*, pages 551–596. Elsevier, Oxford, 2007.

[10] A.G. Cohn and S.M. Hazarika. Qualitative spatial representation and reasoning: an overview. *Fundamenta Informaticae*, 43:2–32, 2001.

[11] Bernardo Cuenca Grau, Bijan Parsia, and Evren Sirin. Combining OWL Ontologies Using $\mathcal{E}$-Connections. *Journal of Web Semantics*, 2006.

[12] Carola Eschenbach. Geometric structures of frames of reference and natural language semantics. *Spatial Cognition and Computation*, 1(4):329–348, 1999.

[13] Nissim Francez and Mark Steedman. Categorial grammar and the semantics of contextual prepositional phrases. *Linguistics and Philosophy*, 29:381–417, 2006.

[14] C. Freksa. Using orientation information for qualitative spatial reasoning. In A. U. Frank, I. Campari, and U. Formentini, editors, *Theories and methods of spatio-temporal reasoning in geographic space*, volume 639 of *LNCS*, pages 162–178. Springer, Berlin, 1992.

[15] Annette Herskovits. *Language and Spatial Cognition: an interdisciplinary study of the prepositions in English*. Studies in Natural Language Processing. Cambridge University Press, London, 1986.

[16] J. Hois, Thora Tenbrink, R. Ross, and J. Bateman. The Generalized Upper Model spatial extension: a linguistically-motivated ontology for the semantics of spatial language. SFB/TR8 internal report, Collaborative Research Center for Spatial Cognition, University of Bremen, Germany, 2008. V. 3.0.

[17] Joana Hois, Mehul Bhatt, and Oliver Kutz. Modular ontologies for architectural design. In R. Ferrario and A. Oltramari, editors, *Formal Ontologies Meet Industry*, pages 66–77. IOS Press, Amsterdam, 2009.

[18] Joana Hois and Oliver Kutz. Counterparts in Language and Space - Similarity and $\mathcal{S}$-Connection. In Carola Eschenbach and Michael Grüninger, editors, *Proceedings of the International Conference on Formal Ontology in Information Systems (FOIS)*, pages 266–279, Amsterdam, 2008. IOS Press.

[19] Joana Hois and Oliver Kutz. Natural Language meets Spatial Calculi. In Christian Freksa, Nora S. Newcombe, Peter Gärdenfors, and Stefan Wölfl, editors, *Spatial Cognition VI: Learning, Reasoning and Talking about Space*, number 5241 in Lecture notes in Artifiicial Intelligence, pages 266–282. Springer, 2008. International Conference, Spatial Cognition 2008, Freiburg, Germany.

[20] Ian Horrocks, Oliver Kutz, and Uli Sattler. The Even More Irresistible SROIQ. In *In Proceedings of the 10th International Conference on Principles of Knowledge Representation and Reasoning (KR 2006)*. AAAI Press, 2006.

[21] John D. Kelleher and Fintan J. Costello. Applying computational models of spatial prepositions to visually situated dialog. *Computational Linguistics*, 35(2):119–149, June 2009.

[22] Markus Kracht. On the semantics of locatives. *Linguistics and Philosophy*, 25:157–232, 2002.

[23] Markus Kracht. Directionality selection. In Patrick Saint-Dizier, editor, *Linguistic Dimensions of the Syntax and Semantics of Prepositions*, pages 101–114. Springer, Berlin, 2006.

[24] Yohei Kurata and Max Egenhofer. The 9^{+}-intersection for topological relations between a directed line segment and a region. In B. Gottfried, editor, *1st Workshop on Behaviour Monitoring and Interpretation, KI 2007*, pages 62–76, 2007.

[25] O. Kutz, C. Lutz, F. Wolter, and M. Zakharyaschev. $\mathcal{E}$-Connections of Abstract Description Systems. *Artificial Intelligence*, 156(1):1–73, 2004.

[26] Michael Levit and Deb Roy. Interpretation of spatial language in a map navigation task. *IEEE Transactions on Systems, Man and Cybernetics*, 37(3):667–679, 2006.

[27] Inderjeet Mani, Janet Hitzeman, J. Richer, D. R. Harris, R. Quimby, and B. Wellner. SpatialML: Annotation Scheme, Corpora, and Tools. In *Proceedings of the 6th International Conference on Language Resources and Evaluation (LREC'08)*, Marrakech, Morocco, 2008.

[28] Peter D. Mosses, editor. *CASL Reference Manual.* Number 2960 in LNCS. Springer, Berlin, 2004.

[29] D.A. Randell, Z. Cui, and A.G. Cohn. A spatial logic based on regions and connection. In *Proceedings of the 3rd. International Conference on Knowledge Representation and Reasoning*, pages 165–176, San Mateo, 1992. Morgan Kaufmann.

[30] Reinhold Rauh, Cornelius Hagen, Markus Knauff, Thomas Kuss, Christoph Schlieder, and Gerhard Strube. Preferred and alternative mental models in spatial reasoning. *Spatial Cognition and Computation*, 5(2-3):239–269, 2005.

[31] Luciano Serafini, Alex Borgida, and Andrei Tamilin. Aspects of Distributed and Modular Ontology Reasoning. In *Proceedings of the Nineteenth International Joint Conference On Artificial Intelligence* , pages 570–575, Edinburgh, Scotland, 2005. International Joint Conferences on Artificial Intelligence.

[32] Heiner Stuckenschmidt, Christine Parent, and Stefano Spaccapietra, editors. *Modular Ontologies: Concepts, Theories and Techniques for Knowledge Modularization*, volume 5445 of *Lecture Notes in Computer Science.* Springer, 2009.

[33] Leonard Talmy. How language structures space. In H.L. Pick and L.P. Acredolo, editors, *Spatial Orientation: Theory, Research, and Application*, pages 225–282. Plenum Press, New York, 1983.

[34] Thora Tenbrink. *Space, time, and the use of language: An investigation of relationships.* Mouton de Gruyter, Berlin, 2007.

[35] Achille C. Varzi. From language to ontology: beware of the traps. In M. Aurnague, M. Hickmann, and L. Vieu, editors, *The Categorization of Spatial Entities in Language and Cognition*, volume 20 of *Human Cognitive Processing*, pages 269–284. John Benjamins Publishing Company, Amsterdam, 2007.

[36] Jan Oliver Wallgrün, Lutz Frommberger, Diedrich Wolter, Frank Dylla, and Christian Freksa. Qualitative spatial representation and reasoning in the SparQ-toolbox. In Thomas Barkowsky, Markus Knauff, Gerard Ligozat, and Dan Montello, editors, *Spatial Cognition V: Reasoning, Action, Interaction*, number 4387 in Lecture Notes in Computer Science, pages 39–58. Springer, Berlin, Heidelberg, 2007.

[37] Stefan Wölfl and Till Mossakowski. CASL specifications of qualitative calculi. In Anthony G. Cohn and David M. Mark, editors, *Proceedings of Spatial Information Theory: International Conference, COSIT 2005*, number 3693 in LNCS, pages 200–217, Berlin, 2005. Springer.

[38] Dieter Wunderlich. How do prepositional phrases fit into compositional syntax and semantics? *Linguistics*, 29:591–621, 1991.

[39] A. Yamada, T. Nishida, and S. Doshita. Figuring out most plausible interpretation from spatial descriptions. In *Proceedings of the 12th International Conference on Computational Linguistics (COLING-88)*, pages 764–769, 1988.

[40] Joost Zwarts. Prepositional aspect and the algebra of paths. *Linguistics and Philosophy*, 28(6):739–779, 2005.

Formal Ontology in Information Systems
A. Galton and R. Mizoguchi (Eds.)
IOS Press, 2010

doi:10.3233/978-1-60750-535-8-17

Knowledge Driven Software and "Fractal Tailoring": Ontologies in development environments for clinical systems

Alan RECTOR
School of Computer Science, University of Manchester, UK

Abstract. Ontologies have been highly successful in applications involving annotation and data fusion. However, ontologies as the core of "Knowledge Driven Architectures" have not achieved the same influence as "Model Driven Architectures", despite the fact that many biomedical applications require features that seem achievable only via ontological technologies – composition of descriptions, automatic classification and inference, and management of combinatorial explosions in many contexts. Our group adopted Knowledge Driven Architectures based on ontologies to address these problems in the early 1990s. In this paper we discuss first the use cases and requirements and then some of the requirements for more effective use of Knowledge Driven Architectures today: clearer separation of language and formal ontology, integration with contingent knowledge, richer and better distinguished annotations, higher order representations, integration with data models, and improved auxiliary structures to allow easy access and browsing by users.

Keywords. Ontology based systems, Model driven architecture, OWL

1. Introduction

In the past fifteen years, the notion of "ontology" has gone from being an obscure "O" word to almost a synonym for "good". Everybody thinks, and is often told, that they need ontologies. At the same time ontologies have, on the one hand, become dissociated from other forms of knowledge representation and, on the other hand, been taken by some to be all of knowledge representation. Specialist ontology languages have been developed, and have, to a considerable degree, displaced work on broader knowledge environments. The characteristics of ontology languages, particularly OWL, are often taken as defining "ontologies".

These trends have served some applications well but others less well. Ontologies have been widely used for annotation, as the basis for terminologies, and sometimes for schema and data fusion, document enrichment and semantic discovery.

Our requirements are different. We wish to build "Knowledge Driven Architectures" analogous to "model driven architectures" (MDA) but based around core "ontologies". Our group shares the interest of the Model Driven Architectures community in software based on a foundation of declarative knowledge. However, to avoid combinatorial explosions and achieve indefinite levels of "fractal tailoring," it requires logical composition, automatic classification, and a framework for managing defaults and exceptions. This was the motivation for our group's successful early use of ontologies in PEN&PAD [1, 2] and GALEN [3]. We have still only been able to achieve this combination of features using description logics and the related "ontological" methods.

However, perhaps because our requirements are different, we still often find ourselves too often building bespoke environments rather than working with off-the-shelf, preferably open-source, tools, and frequently find ourselves working around, rather than with, standards for ontologies and ontology languages. In the remainder of this paper, we first set out key aspects of our use cases and then identify a number of the issues that limit the usefulness of current systems for our purposes.

2. Our use cases: Building Complex Clinical Systems

Developing successful clinical information systems has been notoriously difficult. Scaling up isolated successes to sustainable wide scale use has rarely proved successful. We believe there are five key problems:

1. *Combinatorial explosions* – of terms, codes, guidelines, protocols, and patients' problems. Any one condition may occur in many locations, grades, types, and be caused by many different etiologies; patients come with many different combinations of conditions; health care institutions with many different combinations of resources.
2. *Fine-grained specialization in healthcare delivery* – so that, combined with doctors' resistance to "one-size-fits-all" solutions, systems are required for myriad specialist niches. This leads to the need for *"fractal tailoring"* of almost every aspect of systems, a requirement that conventional software engineering techniques have been unable to meet.
3. *Variability and legacy of medical language* – so that information is communicated telegraphically, and words' use in practice often does not conform to their literal meanings.
4. *Rapid evolution and high variability of medical knowledge and practice* – in both place and time, so that any fixed solution will be have only limited impact.
5. *Myriad independently developed systems*– to meet the myriad specialist niches so that standards are essential for interworking and intercommunication.

It has not proved possible to build systems flexible enough to address these issues without declarative knowledge representations and knowledge driven approaches in which ontologies play a crucial role.

Our fundamental approach is based on

1. *Compositional systems of descriptions* – so that not all possible entities need be enumerated
2. *Fractal tailoring* – so that information can be expressed in its most general form to "fail safe" and yet be specialized to any degree required by specialty, subspecialty, user, task, and patient situation.
3. *Language independenc*e – so that the same system can be used with many different natural languages and cultures with a minimum of adaptation and translation.

We shall focus on five issues and show later how they combine to achieve the above three aims.

1. The separation of language and the symbolic system that constitutes the logical ontology.
2. *Representation of the background knowledge* in clinical systems, only the core of which is "ontological"
3. *Binding of structural and ontological knowledge*
4. *Representation of higher order and meta knowledge*
5. *Human comprehensibility*

3. Our Approaches

3.1 Ontology and language in information systems

We draw a sharp distinction between the symbolic systems – often described as "models' – and the language used to label those symbols. The validity for the information systems as we build them depends solely on the symbol system. Communication with the humans about the interpretation of that behaviour depends on the language for labeling, or more generally for interpreting, those symbols. For example, whether we label the main bone in the lower extremity the "femur", "thigh-bone", "fémur," or "combcsontra" – it will be a long bone, part of the lower extremity, have an anatomical neck, and fractures of the anatomical neck will typically be fixated by pins, etc. (using the same symbols labeled in whatever language).

This seems trivial, but Separating linguistic information from the symbolic system / logical model has four important consequences:

1. It allows for separate description of linguistic and logical/ontological phenomena.
2. It allows the language and ontology to evolve independently. Minor spelling and other errors are common, and even major changes over time and regional differences in language not infrequent. The software and symbolic ontology need to be insulated from such purely linguistic changes.
3. It allows language generation techniques to produce human understandable language from the formal descriptions in the ontology language. GALEN showed this to be particularly important for quality assurance and acceptance by those less familiar with the formal system.
4. It allows arguments about language and terms to be separated from arguments about the logical / ontological substance. For example, whether "neoplasm" implies "malignant tumour" or just "tumour"[1] has changed over the last two decades. Arguments over the words have been fierce, but nobody has questioned the need for a way to refer to categories for each of "benign tumour", "malignant tumour", and "benign or malignant tumour" nor about their organization in a subsumption hierarchy, nor about their clinical significance. The argument has been almost purely about words. Similarly, few question the need for some top root entity in our representations, The

---

[1] more properly "proliferation", since one must include diffuse proliferations such as leukemias.

effect of the labeling of this node in the symbol system on the behaviour of the rest of the system is almost always nil. However, whether it should be called "Top", "Thing", "TopThing", "Concept" or "Category" has occasioned not a little heated debate and occasional disparagement (*e.g.* Smith 2004 [4]), most of it irrelevant to our use of "ontologies" in information systems.

A "Terminology" in our usage is the association of a symbolic system of descriptions and a language layer for communicating those descriptions. The separation of language and content is an old requirement most dramatically stated in Cimino's desiderata [5] for "non-semantic identifiers" – i.e. meaningless symbols as their prime identifiers – a practice now followed by virtually all ontologies or terminologies in widespread use in biomedicine.

Work on the formal relationship between formal symbolic ontologies and language seems to us surprisingly sparse. There is some work on the relation of ontologies and language *e.g.* Hahn [6, 7] and Bateman [8] and some work on the generation of language from description logics [9, 10, 11], but the field seems surprisingly limited. There is now an urgent demand to be able to generate pseudo natural language from expressions in representations such as SNOMED[2] and the NCI Thesaurus and to use natural language techniques to enrich and even compile ontologies.

Finally, logical ontologies combined with literal interpretations of language can lead to errors. For example, in early versions of GALEN, "heart valve" was simply defined as a valve in the heart, and logically subsumed prosthetic valves and various fetal structures that act as valves as well as the four great valves, which are normally the intended clinical meaning of "heart valves". More seriously, in general usage, "Heart disease" includes not only diseases of the heart itself, but also diseases of the covering of the heart ("pericardium"), which is a separate organ clearly distinguished embryologically. To get the clinically relevant answers to "All heart diseases" requires notion of functional association, which is lacking in both the Foundational Model of Anatomy [3] and SNOMED [12]. To match clinical usage, the system must represent that, in standard clinical usage, the English language phrase "heart disease" covers more than the logical category "diseases of the heart."

3.2 Background knowledge: What can be said, what is necessarily true, what can be assumed, and what must be taken into account as fact.

One way of describing the fundamental goal of knowledge driven systems is that their behaviour should depend on declaratively represented background knowledge rather than procedural coding to meet each possible situation. Another is to say that they should interact with their human users on the basis of similar background assumptions. The system should be able to make inferences from "obvious" facts such as that the heart is part of the circulatory system, extremities exist in roughly mirror-imaged pairs, and that pneumonia occurs in the lung, etc.

Either definition requires the representation of extensive background knowledge. However, background knowledge comes in several different forms which are too often conflated, in no small measure because no single environment provides a common framework and syntax that makes it easy to use each appropriately.

---

[2] http://www.ihtsdo.org/

[3] http://sig.biostr.washington.edu/projects/fm/FME/

3.2.1 Ontological or necessary knowledge and logical composition.

The ontological, or necessary, information forms the skeleton of the background knowledge in the form of a logical system of descriptions. It serves four functions:

1. To specify the entities and relations about which there is information to be conveyed.
2. To organize the entities and descriptions into "kind-of" or "subsumption" lattice.
3. To represent the universal characteristics of those entities and relations– those things that are either true by definition or by necessity.
4. To specify what can, and cannot, be sensibly said about those entities and relations.

From these four functions, we gain two key components for our architecture:

1. *An index* of the entities and relations inferred from their to their logical relations
2. *Compositional rules* i.e. how descriptions of new entities can be composed, what descriptions are consistent, which tautologous, and where new description fit in the hierarchical index of kinds. For example, from the fact that lungs are organs we can derive that they can be punctured, and that a "punctured lung" is sensible. From the fact that pneumonia necessarily occurs in lungs, we can derive that "Pneumonia of the lung" is tautologous. It is simply impossible to enumerate everything that might be of interest in biomedical applications, and attempts to do so rapidly lead to absurdities such as the "exploding bicycle". [4]

Ontological knowledge today is most commonly captured in description logics, most often the W3C standard otology language, OWL-DL[5]. The systems we work with all come equipped with one or more reasoners that infer the subsumption hierarchy and check consistency. Such reasoners may be thought of as "terminology compilers" and are essential to our applications: it is simply not possible to manage manually the massively interconnected networks of descriptions and relations needed by clinical systems.

Such description logic based systems serve the functions 1) - 3) above well. They perform function 4) less well. In fact, as standard, they perform the converse – they specify what *cannot* be sensibly said – i.e. what relations amongst entities are inconsistent or "unsatisfiable." What can be said can only be determined as that which is not unsatisfiable. Unless the constraints in the ontology are fully complete, this will be over inclusive. Furthermore, standard reasoners support no simple query for 4), so that the result must be obtained by exhaustive testing to eliminate the impossible, which can be massively inefficient. In short, ontologies as we currently express them are good at ruling out complete nonsense such as "friendly thyroids" but poor at helping us say what might actually be said of thyroids. This is sometimes called the

[4] The number of codes for bicycle accident in related Read ICD terminologies went from eight in 1980, to 80 in the early 1990s, to 587 in the 1999 Australian Clinical modification, including such items as *"V31.22 Occupant of three-wheeled motor vehicle injured in collision with pedal cycle, person on outside of vehicle, nontraffic accident, while working for income"* Jeremy Rogers, personal communication 1999.

[5] Now OWL-DL-2, see http://www.w3.org/TR/owl2-overview/

problem of "sanctioning" from the construct used to deal with this problem in the early description logic GRAIL from the GALEN project [13].

Note that, contrary to the way in which some realist philosophers formulate their criteria for "ontologies" in their sense for their purposes, it is essential that "ontologies" in "knowledge driven information systems" be able to describe entities whether or not they exist in the "real world". Indeed, it is often necessary to describe entities precisely to say that they do not exist. For example, an ontology can describe "metastatic basal cell carcinoma", and may need to do so as part of an information system, precisely to say that, by contrast to all other carcinomas, they have never been observed to occur. Equally, the information system must be able to express that, despite all previous experience, one such has been discovered and to describe it.

This is completely in keeping with the standard logical form used to represent ontologies. In all formal logical languages for ontologies, all statements in the ontology are of the form "All Xs…". It is a well known feature of logic that expressions of the form "All Xs…" do not imply the existence of any Xs, only that if there are Xs, then they must satisfy the given condition.

Confusion might have been less had the common name for the artifacts in information systems now called "ontologies" been taken to be something like "system of descriptions". However, as in the medical domain itself, language evolves for historical reasons, and its historical evolution is a fact we have to live with. We should not allow the evolution of the use of the world "ontology" as it has come to be used in information systems to obscure the fundamental requirements for the artifacts in our information systems now called "ontologies."

3.2.2 Contingent and typical knowledge

Whatever definition is used, ontological knowledge is universal. Its characteristic is that all statements are of the form "All Xs …". This is true whether we are dealing with binary relational languages such as OWL or larger fragments of first order logic, or even higher order logic.

Most background knowledge is contingent: i.e. of the form "Most Xs…" "Some Xs…", "There are Xs that…", etc. Consider a seemingly simple question such as "What are the causes of pneumonia" which might appear equally on an undergraduate medical school exam or as part of the process of determining the value set for causes of pneumonia on a data entry form or decision support system. While it is difficult to rule out, absolutely, any micro-organism from causing pneumonia, a standard list of headings "bacterium, virus, yeast, parasite" with a similar short list under each subheading is what is expected for most purposes. Furthermore, even if we take the archetypical cause – the bacterium pneumococcus – it is true neither that all pneumococci cause pneumonia nor the converse. It is not true even true that all pneumococci have the "disposition" to cause pneumonia; many are "non-pathogenic." The best we can say in standard ontology languages is that there is a class of pneumococci that cause (or have the disposition to cause) pneumonia – which is true if and only if there is also a class of pneumonia caused by pneumococcus (although none of the standard reasoners deliver this inference automatically or simply).

The ontology can provide a framework for contingent knowledge, but the contingent knowledge itself can be expressed at best indirectly within the ontology itself. The authors have argued elsewhere [14] that, if we are going to use ontological forms, then the best formal answer to what causes pneumonia is a list of the form

"Bacteria that cause some Pneumonia", "Virus that causes some Pneumonia" etc. Such expressions can be used safely in further inference, and suitable user interaction software can strip off the parts that appear redundant to the user.

However, is even this appropriate? If the ontology is about what is universal, then what is contingent ought to be expressed in some other way, using the ontology but going beyond it. A major problem is that we lack a convenient formalism and environment that covers both contingent and universal knowledge.

Note that using first order logic does not address this problem adequately. Intrinsically, first order logic provides only a simple existential qualification to which is usually taken to capture the notions of "some", although even this is at variance with common linguistic usage. However, the information we need to answer the question "What causes pneumonia" is really, "What commonly causes pneumonia?" A commonly used alternative to using existential quantifiers to get the effect of "generally" or "may" in ontology languages is to create pairs of properties systematically– *e.g.* "*may_cause*" and "*causes*". All variants of this method suffer from various defects. In particular they are not reciprocal; even if the relation "*may_cause*" is symmetric, we cannot conclude that if "(all) pneumococcus *may_cause* some pneumonia" that "(all) pneumonia *may_be_caused_by* some pneumococcus". Yet, our expectation is that "If A *may_cause* B, then "B *may_be_caused_by* A".

We distinguish three cases:

1. *Categorical facts about what generally happens* – the case of causes of pneumonia
2. *Defaults with exceptions* – how to express the general knowledge that most birds fly, or most patients with cardiovascular disease should have their data collected with a given protocol
3. *Probabilistic or uncertain knowledge* – more specific knowledge about the probabilities, typically in medicine, that one condition is caused by another, e.g. that the link between a positive HIV test and HIV infection is X%, or that 70% of male patients with acute abdominal pain have appendicitis.

All three are important to biomedical applications. As discussed above, *categorical facts* about what generally happens form the basis for many question answering and user input systems.

Defaults and exceptions apply wherever there are complex networks of facts that form interacting contexts. In the decision support systems, they are important for assigning actions and treatments according to context, *e.g.* that beta-blockers are generally strongly contraindicated in asthma but certain subclasses of beta-blockers may be used "with caution." A safe default value is required, even if it is often overridden in specific contexts. In data capture systems they important for assigning "value sets" to fields according to context. For example, the default value set for "loudness" may be "loud, medium, soft, inaudible", but when applied to heart murmurs, the value set is "Grade_I…Grade_VI". Requirements from users include complete replacement of value sets, addition to existing value sets, and deleting of specific values – all while maximizing re-use.

The fundamental requirement for defaults and exceptions is that they allow systems to be built so that they "fail soft" – i.e. work safely with a minimum of information, but can be tailored to any degree through any number of stages to meet any degree of sub sub …sub specialization. This is what we refer to as "*fractal tailoring*".

There is no general logically complete and computationally tractable solution to reasoning with defaults. However, collecting the set of most specific values for a given property according to the standard Touretzky criterion [15] provides a set of candidate solutions. If the ontology is well normalized [16], this set is almost always a singleton. Although provision must always be made for resolving the conflicts that cannot be ruled out, this method provides a quick, easily implemented, and well tested mechanism that, in practice, covers the majority of cases. In the author's opinion, ignoring or abandoning this heuristic, has been a major step backwards in the use of knowledge based systems and ontologies in clinical medicine, and perhaps other fields.

Probabilistic knowledge is very different and required for decision support or suggestions as well as aspects of "intelligent interfaces". Exact probabilities are rarely critical in our applications (and the statistics to support them are rarely available). However, approximations for updating belief that behave consistently with probability theory are important. Most obviously, we need to be able to attach "updating strengths" to causal or evidential links – roughly likelihood ratios and the likelihood ratio of the inverse – so as to be able to say that "X is good evidence for Y if present" or "X is good evidence against Y if absent" or both. Bayesian networks have made enormous strides in the past two decades, and there are several proposals for combining probabilities with ontologies [17-20]. However, given that probabilistic knowledge is clearly not universal, and clearly uses numerical calculations rather than logical inference in its implementation, is integration the most appropriate path? Or would hybrid systems exploiting the complementary relation between two forms of reasoning be more promising? For example, one might imagine systems in which the ontology indexed updating strengths and Bayesian calculations (or approximations to them) performed the actual updating of beliefs.

3.2.3 Facts and databases

Facts ought to be simple: relations between two or more individuals, *e.g.* that a particular drug is licensed for use in a particular disease, that the ID number for this product is NNNN, that the topic of this trial is breast cancer. The difficulty for ontology languages and systems is that most facts of importance are compiled in closed world databases, where negation as failure is intrinsic to correct interpretation. By contrast, the "facts" or "A-Boxes" of most ontology languages are open world and take negation to mean proven falsehood. Because most large fact bases in biomedicine come from closed world databases, large open world description logic "A-boxes" are rarely appropriate. For example, if there is no product with ID NNNN in a drug database, then there is no such product. If it is there, but there is no entry that says it is licensed for the treatment of asthma, then it is not licensed for the treatment of asthma. No further inference is needed; a demand for further proof leads to wrong, possibly dangerous, answers.

A common pattern is of an open world schema or ontology describing the categories for a closed world database of facts. There is much work on large A-Boxes for OWL. There appears to be much less work and few off-the-shelf solutions for systems combining OWL T-boxes with standard closed world databases even though this combination frequently appears to be appropriate.

3.3 Meta data and annotation

It comes as something of a shock to many ontology implementers that, in many applications, users regard the meta-data and annotations as the core of the system. To the users, the ontology is often little more than a skeleton for those annotations. It is regrettable that most knowledge representation and ontology systems provide a single mechanism for annotation and meta data, even though there are numerous different categories of meta data and annotation that play very different roles in systems:

1. *Comments and guidelines* as to what the entities in the ontology are supposed to mean and how they are expected to be used. Simple names or "descriptions"[6] are rarely enough, and in any complex ontology, further information is required.
2. *Editorial information and provenance* on which both the credibility and the maintenance of the ontology depend.
3. *"Schemas" for the ontology.* Curiously, while databases have long emphasized the schema, ontologies have not. There is much work on universal upper ontologies, but little work on describing the specific domain level ontologies in ways that make it easy for users to comprehend them.
4. *Information to software* about how different entities in the ontology are to be used, additional information to support "sanctioning" and other issues of use, information on how entities are combined into patterns, access to "attached procedures" for calculations, etc. At its richest, such metadata forms a major extension to the reasoning mechanisms as proposed by Parsia.[7]

3.4 Higher order statements

Metadata and annotations should not be confused with higher order statements, even though in many of our ontology languages, higher order statements can only be expressed as annotations.

Consider the statement: "Whales are an endangered species." It is neither a statement about "All whales", nor an annotation on the information about whales, nor an annotation on the symbols in the knowledge representation itself. It is a statement about "Whales" qua class or species. Likewise, it is difficult to deal with aggregate notions such as the average value of a test or the prevalence of a condition – *e.g.* "Swine Flu" - except by treating that entity "Swine Flu" as a first class object in its own right. That is, we need to be able to express higher order information about "Swine Flue" itself as opposed to first order information about "All instances of swine flu". There are tricks, *e.g.* creating a class for "cases of swine flu" of or a "dependent continuant" for "Swine Flu", but none has been demonstrated to be satisfactory.

OWL and related reasoners support only first order reasoning and reject any ontology with higher order statements. Therefore, we are faced with a trilemma. We either give up reasoner support completely or give up higher order statements or resort to tricks. "Punning" is a compromise in the new OWL-2 standard but still limited. There are but proposals for greater integration either through "rich annotations" layered implementations [21], but none are widely available. This needs to be rectified. To

---

[6] what typically appears in the Dublin Core dc:description. (See http://dublincore.org/)

[7] http://code.google.com/p/owl1-1/wiki/RichAnnotations

meet requirements, systems need to allow higher order knowledge to be represented and queried while still allowing full inference with the first order component.

3.5 Binding of Ontology to Data Models

Most information systems are specified in terms of "data models" that are really templates of fields and value sets. Such template-based data models' behaviour is precisely opposite of that of ontologies and description logics. Description logics are sets of axioms that restrict what can be said. The more that is known, the more the domain is restricted and the less can be said. By contrast, in information systems, whether specified by UML (at least in practice) or object oriented models, are templates. Nothing can be said until there is a place for it in the template. Hence, the more you know, the more can be said – *i.e.* in UML parlance, the more associations and attributes apply.

A special requirement for meta knowledge is in using ontologies to provide the titles and value sets for fields in information systems. Space does not permit repeating the arguments made elsewhere [22], that when entities from ontologies are used in data models the classes from the ontology should be treated as individuals in the data model – *i.e.* that the information about how to use them in data model is metadata about the class in the ontology artifact rather than first order information about the members of that class in the ontology domain. Treating data structures and ontology classes at the same level leads, inevitably, to absurdities such as a "person with a missing blood pressure." Rigorously synergistic methodologies and environments for binding ontologies and data structures remains a major challenge.

4. Human navigable hierarchies: Thesauri, classifications, and other artifacts that are not ontologies.

4.1 SKOS and knowledge organization systems

Ontologies are frequently unintuitive to navigate for domain experts. Upper level entities are regarded as just "noise". Doctors are interested in disorders, anatomic structures, findings, etc. These categories have long histories even if often the topic of much dispute. Furthermore, even distinctions that they would agree with in theory they do not use in practice – *e.g.* the difference between "breast cancer" and "breast tumor".

Each domain will differ, but two key distinctions are pervasive in clinical systems:

1. Between entities that can be present or absent and those that can be normal or abnormal
2. Between those than can be directly observed or measured and those that must be inferred.

The first distinction might be derived from the ontology – those entities that can be normal or abnormal are those that are always present – mainly qualities or parts of the body or its parts – *e.g.* heart rate, heart valve, skin colour, etc. Those that can be present or absent are disorders or abnormal structures – fractures, bruises, tumors, diabetes, dementia, etc. – roughly parts and dependent continuants in BFO's language.

The second distinction is more subject to arguments. Most clinicians would agree that the "blood pressure" was an observable finding and "hypertension" an "disorder" arrived at by judgment. However, whether "elevated blood pressure" should be a judgment or an "observable" is far from clear.

Equally awkward, most clinicians expect clinical entities to be organized according to how they are traditionally collected and reported in clinical histories and physicals, organized according to nested sections rather than any logical notion of subsumption. Similarly, most information systems expect entities to be defined by their position in a data model, which is typically a containment structure – often today an XML schema – which again depends on containment rather than subsumption.

We can imagine two solutions to these problems:

1. Formal tricks, so that the primary organization is along the doctors expected lines and the ontological categories are provided as additional characteristics (restrictions in OWL). This can work up to a point, although it always risks creating inconsistencies.
2. An entirely separate Knowledge Organisation System over the clinically significant entities in the ontology. The most obvious candidate for such organisation is the new W3 standard SKOS[8]. This seems a safer solution.

In fact, providing a separate "browsing view" of the ontology based on non-logical principles seems critical to user acceptance in many situations. Ideally, the non-logical view would be systematically linked to the ontology – *e.g.* by combining subsumption, partonomy, and causality with annotations as to which entities in the ontology should be "hidden" in the browsing view. However, in other situations, it may be necessary to construct such a view entirely independently just because that is the way users expect it.

5. Summary: Requirements for Environments for Ontology Driven Applications

The only means we know to meet the range of requirements for clinical information systems require Knowledge Based Architectures with "ontologies" at their core. The key criteria are that the ontology support the information to be conveyed and the computational operations that need to be performed on that information. The key values of using ontologies are in supporting:

1. *Composition of descriptions* so that not everything that has to be described need be enumerated.
2. Automatic Indexing and "Fractal tailoring" with defaults with exceptions.

Essential to the effective functioning of ontologies for these purposes are:

1. Clear separation of language and symbolic knowledge
2. Clear understanding of the binding between the axiom-based ontology and the template-based data models that use the symbols from that ontology.
3. Auxiliary information to make the ontology comprehensible and usable by human authors, software engineers and other users.

Ultimate solutions to formal integration of all relevant forms of reasoning are beyond current technology, probably beyond possibility. However, heuristic integration has proved possible in many cases. We suggest it as a "grand challenge" to the "ontologies" community to develop, test, and refine the generic heuristics needed

---

[8] http://www.w3.org/TR/2009/CR-skos-reference-20090317/

for hybrid systems to realize the potential of ontology driven software to achieve the flexibility, maintainability, and usability needed by future information systems, whether in biomedicine or elsewhere.

References

[1] W. A. Nowlan, Kay, S., Rector, A. L., Horan, B., and Wilson, A. 1991. PEN&PAD: A multi-lingual patient care workstation based on a unified representation of the medical record and medical terminology. Medical Informatics Europe (MIE-91). 1043-1048.

[2] A. L. Rector, Glowinski, A. J., Nowlan, W. A., and Rossi-Mori, A. 1995. Medical concept models and medical records: An approach based on GALEN and PEN&PAD. *Journal of the American Medical Informatics Association* 2:19-35. (reprinted in JH van Bemmel and A T McCray, *Medical Informatics Yearbook 1996* pp 225-241).

[3] A. L. Rector and Rogers, J. E. 2006 Ontological and practical issues in using a description logic to represent medical concept systems: Experience from GALEN. In *Reasoning Web*, P. Barahona, F. Bry, E. Franconi, N. Henze, and U. Sattler,Eds Springer-Verlag.

[4] B. Smith 2004. Beyond concepts: Ontology as reality representation. Formal Ontology in Information Systems (FOIS 2004).

[5] J. J. Cimino 1998. Desiderata for controlled medical vocabularies in the twenty-first century. *Methods of Information in Medicine.* 37, 4-5, 394-403.

[6] U. Hahn and Romacker, M. 1999. An integrated model of semantic and conceptual interpretation from dependency structures. COLING 2000 - Proceedings of the 18th International Conference on Computational Linguistics. 1, 271-277.

[7] U. Hahn, Romacker, M., and Schulz, S. 2000. medSynDiKATe: Design considerations for an ontology-based medical text understanding system. AMIA 2000 - Proc Annual Symposium of the American Medical Informatics Association. . 330-334.

[8] J. A. Bateman 1993. Ontology construction and natural language. Intl Workshop on Formal Ontology. 83-93.

[9] R. H. Baud, Rassinoux, A.-M., and J.-R, S. 1991. Knowledge representation of discharge summaries. Third European Conference on Artificial Intelligence in Medicine. 173-184.

[10] J. C. Wagner, Rassinoux, A.-M., Baud, R. H., and Scherrer, J.-R. 1994. Generating noun phrases from a medical knowledge representation. Twelfth International Congress of the European Federation for Medical Informatics, MIE-94. 218-223.

[11] D. Scott and Power, R. 2001 Generating textual diagrams and diagrammatic texts,. In Cooperative Multimodal Communication, H. Bunt and R.-J. Beun,Eds Springer-Verlag.

[12] C. Rosse and Mejino, J. L. V. J. 2003. A reference ontology for biomedical informatics: the Fondational Model of Anatomy. *Journal of Biomedical Informatics.* 36, 478-500.

[13] A. L. Rector, Bechhofer, S., Goble, C. A., Horrocks, I., Nowlan, W. A., and Solomon, W. D. 1997. The GRAIL concept modelling language for medical terminology. *Artificial Intelligence in Medicine.* 9, 139-171.

[14] A. Rector, Stevens, R., and Drummond, N. 2008. What causes pneumonia? The case for a standard semantics for "may" in OWL. Owl Experiences and Directions (OWLEd 2008). www.webont.org/owled/2008/papers/owled2008eu_submission_14.pdf.

[15] D. S. Touretzky. 1986 *The Mathematics of Inheritance Systems.* Morgan Kaufmann.

[16] A. Rector 2003. Modularisation of domain ontologies Implemented in description logics and related formalisms including OWL. Knowledge Capture 2003. 121-128.

[17] Z. Ding and Yun, P. 2004. A probabilistic extension to ontology language OWL. 37th Hawaii International Conference on System Sciences (2004).

[18] P. Klinov. 2008 Pronto: A non-monotonic probabilistic description logic reasoner. In The Semantic Web: Research and Applications, Springer Verlag.

[19] P. Klinov and Parsia, B. 2009. On improving the scalability of checking satisfiability in probabilistic description logics. International Conference on Scalable Uncertainty Management (SUM-2009). Springer LNCS 5785/2009, 138-149.

[20] D. Koller, Levy, A., and Pfeiffer, A. 1997. P-Classic: a tractable probabilistic description logic. Fourteenth National Conference on Artificial Intelligence(AAAI-97). 390-397.

[21] J. Z. Pan, Horrocks, I., and Schreiber, G. 2005. OWL FA: A metamodeling extension of OWL DL. Proc International workshop on OWL: Experiences and Directions (OWL-ED2005).

[22] A. Rector, Qamar, R., and Marley, T. 2009. Binding ontologies and coding systems to electronic health records and messages. *Applied Ontology.* 4, 1, 51-69.

Fundamentals

Formal Ontology in Information Systems
A. Galton and R. Mizoguchi (Eds.)
IOS Press, 2010

doi:10.3233/978-1-60750-535-8-31

Foundations for an Ontology of Environment and Habitat

Brandon BENNETT [1]
School of Computing, University of Leeds, Leeds, UK

Abstract. The paper examines the semantics of the terms 'environment' and 'habitat' and presents a semi-formalised ontological framework in which these concepts are related to the spatial and material structure of the world. Since habitats are essentially associated with lives and behaviour of animals and plants the framework incorporates an abstract model of an organism. This enables the spatial extensions of habitats to be characterised in terms of the possible 'life trajectories' of organisms constrained by the physical properties of a geographic region and by the biological requirements for their survival.

Keywords. Environment, Habitat

1. Introduction

The words 'environment' and 'habitat' are key terms used to describe the world. There is presently an increasing need for us to tackle issues relating to changes in the environment and loss of habitat; but, in order for a computational information system to provide functionality that will help us classify and visualise the world in terms of these concepts, we need a precise model of their semantics. Here we face fundamental problems: What is an environment? What is a habitat?

An extensive ecological literature has developed informal theories for describing and classifying environments and habitats. Such analysis dates back at least to [9] and later [7], who introduced ideas such as the ecological *niche* of an animal, which have played a key role in subsequent theorising [11, 21]. However, as regards the development of formal ontologies, relatively little attention has been given specifically to environment and habitat. A mereological theory of the concept of *niche*, intended to serve as a basic notion in ontologies of ecology and habitat has been developed in [19] and [20]. Their treatment focusses mainly on the expressing topological constraints on a relation $\mathsf{N}(x, y)$, read as 'x is a niche of (entity) y'. More general requirements of ecological ontologies were investigated in [8] and [14]. Issues specifically relating to representation of the *niche* concept were further examined in [15] and [16].

Ecological concepts are perceived as being difficult to pin down and geographic ontology development has already encountered huge problems in establishing robust semantic models of seemingly more straightforward concepts [13, 6]. Many of these problems appear to be rooted in deep philosophical problems concerning the meanings of

---

[1]Email: `B.Bennett@leeds.ac.uk`

geographic and ecological terminology [22, 4]. Despite these difficulties, the EnvO environmental ontology network [1] has recently made some progress in constructing an ontology covering a wide range of environmental concepts, which is primarily intended for supporting annotations for data and samples collected by researchers in the biological, medical and environmental sciences.

As the foundation of our theory, we assume a formal language capable of describing geometrical properties and 'matter types' (see Sec. 3.5 below), which could in principle be given a fully formal model-theoretic semantics along the lines of [2]. The more abstract ecological concepts with which we are here concerned could then be axiomatised relative to these spatial and material primitives.[2] Our aim at this stage of development is not to give a fully axiomatised ontology, but rather to identify the types of entity that should be present in an ontology of 'environment' and 'habitat' and analyse the relational dependencies between them. Nevertheless, a certain amount of formalism will be presented to illustrate how a more rigourous theory could be constructed.

The structure of the paper is as follows: in the next section we consider some general problems of ambiguity and indeterminism confronting the formalisation of precise ontologies that seek to describe the semantics of natural language terminology. Our aim is to motivate an approach in which a term may be characterised by a combination of a number of distinct though strongly correlated modes of definition. In Section 3 we outline a background theory of space, time and material entities, that will underpin our subsequent analysis. Section 4 examines the nature of geographic regions, giving a semantics in terms of more basic spatial and material concepts. In Section 5 we analyse the term 'environment', identifying three different ways in which the concept can be defined and examining the relationships between them. Section 6 discusses the formal treatment of the concept of the *ecological niche* of a species and shows how this can be used to derive the *potential habitat* of the species. Finally, Section 7 is our conclusion.

2. Conceptual Ambiguity and Modes of Definition

In order to develop an ontology, we need to establish interpretations of the key terms that are sufficiently precise that we can, at least approximately, characterise their relationship to the world and to the meanings of other conceptual terms. This will enable us to specify a structure of conceptual relationships and axiomatise semantic constraints on these relationships. To achieve this we often need to disambiguate distinct senses that are conflated by the variegated usages of natural language terminology.

Even where a natural language term seems unambiguous, when we try to pin down its semantics we often find that there are a number of different ways that the term could be defined. A typical example would be the case of an artifactual physical object such as a cup. Some might argue that the concept referred to by the word 'cup' is best defined by means of material and geometrical properties, whereas others might say that a satisfactory definition must be formulated in terms of the intended purpose of the artifact. This

[2] We presume that since they are essentially determined by configurations of matter environmental concepts are definiable from spatial and material primitives. However, concepts related to 'habitat' are likely to be difficult to define since they depend on biological phenomena, which have an extremely complex dependence on physical properties. Thus it is likely to be expedient to treat certain biological concepts as additional primitives.

phenomenon is discussed in some detail in [3], which introduces the idea that a term can have multiple *modes* of definition.

It should be understood that the notion of distinct modes of definition does not mean simply that there are different ways of defining the same thing. The possibility of giving different but necessarily equivalent definitions applies to all terms even they are completely unambiguous; whereas, with terms affected by mode ambiguity there are alternative definitions that are not strictly equivalent. For instance, in the case of 'cup', there could be objects whose material, geometric (and indeed functional) characteristics satisfy any reasonable materialistic definition of 'cup', and yet the object was not intended to be used as a cup (it might not even be an artifact).

The question immediately arises as to why a language should employ terms that have multiple distinct meanings. How are they interpreted? And, how are the different senses related? We suggest that the meanings of a term according to different modes of definition are related by being *naturally correlated*. Such correlation occurs because the physical laws of the universe and the particular properties of our world ensure that in ordinary circumstance the different modes of definition characterise concepts that (although logically distinct) are highly interdependent. A particular form of this interdependence, dubbed *exemplar clustering* is discussed in [3]. This refers to the fact that, because of the physical constraints of the world, the examples found in nature that satisfy a given concept definition constitute only a limited sample of the range of logically possible instances of the concept. Moreover, these examples will often share properties that are not necessary consequences of the definition itself. Because of this 'clustering' of exemplars it can often turn out that two logically distinct concepts have in reality exactly (or almost exactly) the same set of instances (see [12, part 6]). E.g., we might define the term 'bicycle' either as a physical object with certain material and kinematic properties, or alternatively as a type of artifact constructed by intelligent agents for a particular purpose. Because it is highly unlikely that an object with the physical characteristics of a bicycle could occur naturally, without intelligent design and construction, both definitions would apply equally to the same class of real objects. Nevertheless, the two definitions are logically distinct because it is possible, albeit vanishingly unlikely, that an object with the physical form of a bicycle could arise from some freak natural process.[3]

In the current paper we propose a more general notion, which includes exemplar clustering as a special case. By *natural correlation* we mean any interdependence between defined concepts that arises from those conditions of reality that are predominant in the actual world, although they are not strictly logically or physically necessary. For this to occur, the concepts need not have the same instances, but the instances of one concept must determine or partially determine the instances of the other and vice versa.

Returning to the questions about how and why multiple modes should arise in natural language semantics, we can explain this as follows. In the case of clustering of exemplars, we see that, for nearly all practical purposes, the instances to which a term can be applied are the same irrespective of the mode of definition that is adopted. Hence it is not surprising that the same term is used to cover the different modes. With respect to language learning and interpretation it is almost impossible to distinguish the alternative meanings since these processes are conditioned primarily by reference to actual examples rather than abstract definitions.

[3]In the terminology of [3], a bicycle-like object of this kind is called an *artifable* as opposed to an artifact.

Regarding the more general case of natural correlation, where one aspect of reality is interdependent with another, information about one aspect will imply information about another. Hence, when a term is used to refer to one aspect, a person interpreting the term is likely to think of the other correlated aspects. Since the term evokes consideration of several aspects, it is not surprising that they all become part of its meaning, albeit an ambiguous meaning that moves between different senses. (E.g. a political party may be identified either as a set of doctrines, an institutional organisation or a group of people.)

3. Background Theories

Despite their subtlety, it is clear that concepts of environment and habitat are interpreted in relation to properties of the physical world. Hence, any satisfactory ontology explaining the meanings of these terms will also make reference to concepts of space, time, matter and physical objects. The ontology presented here assumes a background theory that is largely the same as that proposed in [2], although somewhat simplified. However, it should be possible to adapt the central parts of our formalisation that deal with environment and habitat to work with other ontologies of space and matter. In the rest of this section we give a concise overview of the main elements of our background theory.

3.1. Space

We take a classical Cartesian view of space, modelling it as a set of points $S = \{\ldots, p_i, \ldots\}$, over which a primitive function $\mathsf{d}(p_1, p_2)$ gives the Euclidean distance between points p_1 and p_2. We also assume that the standard topological notions of open and closed sets and of regularity are defined in the usual way. We assume that space is characterised by a reference frame that is fixed in relation to the Earth. Thus for the purpose of this paper we ignore the Earth's rotation and its motion in space.

The predication $\mathsf{Reg}(r)$ asserts that r is a *(purely) spatial region* — a part of the universe considered only in terms of its spatial extent and geometrical properties. We shall also refer to lines, surfaces and volumes. These can be considered as subsets of the domain of spatial regions. For convenience, we introduce a function $\mathsf{surf}(r)$ which maps any regular 3-dimensional region to its surface.[4] We envisage that a mereo-topological language such as that of [18], would be used to specify qualitative relationships between spatial regions. Since such theories are now well-known, we do not go into details here.

3.2. Time and Spatio-Temporal Regions

We model time as an ordered set of points. No particular assumptions are made about the nature of this set and its ordering, although we have in mind a continuous linear ordering. A *convex temporal interval* is the closed set of all time points between and including a beginning and an ending time point.

We shall also sometimes want to refer to spatio-temporal regions. Such a region can be modelled as a set of pairs $\langle p, t\rangle$ consisting of a spatial and a temporal point, meaning

[4] surf is a partial function over the domain of regions. We note that while notationally convenient, partial functions can be tricky to handle in a formal system and would probably be best avoided in a fully formal extension of the framework presented here.

that the spatial point is within the region at time t. We allow that the surf function be applied to a spatio-temporal volume to yield a spatio-temporal surface.

3.3. Physical Regions

A *physical region* is a part of the universe considered both as spatially extended and as possessing material and dynamic characteristics. We assume there is a 1-to-1 correspondence between spatial and physical regions and to formalise this relationship we introduce two functions $\mathsf{phys}(r)$, mapping spatial region r to a physical region and $\mathsf{ext}(\rho)$, mapping physical region ρ to its purely spatial extension.

Although we allow physical regions of any dimensionality (even irregular regions of mixed dimension), we will typically be interested in 3-dimensional physical volumes and 2-dimensional orientable physical surfaces. A physical surface is manifest in the physical entities (chemical molecules, photons) and forces (gravity, electro-magnetism) that impinge upon or cross the surface. For present purposes, we will not need to construct explicit models capturing all the details of physical surfaces, but we suggest that they might be modelled by means of vector fields. We write $\mathsf{surf}(\rho)$ to denote the physical surface enclosing a regular physical volume ρ (i.e. $\mathsf{surf}(x)$ is a spatial surface if x is a spatial volume but a physical surface when x is a physical volume).

oriented physical surfaces, are physical surfaces considered as viewed from one particular side. By orienting a surface we can describe properties such as the direction of heat flow across a surface. We may model an oriented surface as a pair consisting of a surface and a triple of three points on the surface given in clockwise order.

We also include spatio-temporal physical regions, which are just temporally indexed versions of ordinary physical regions.

3.4. Individual Physical Objects

We use the term *individual* to refer to an object that persists in time in accordance with certain identity criteria [10]. This means that spatial and physical extensions of an individual depend on a time parameter. We represent these extensions using the functions $\mathsf{ext}(i, t)$ and $\mathsf{phys}(i, t)$. The *trajectory* $\mathsf{traj}(i)$ of an individual i is a spatio-temporal volume, whose spatial extension varies continuously (in the topological sense) over time and is self-connected at each moment in time. Also, its spatial extension is non-empty at every time point within a durative convex temporal interval $\mathsf{span}(i)$, and is empty at every other time point. The physical region $\mathsf{phys}(\mathsf{traj}(i))$ will be abbreviated as $\mathsf{life}(i)$.

3.5. Matter Types

A distinctive feature of the proposed ontology is that, following [2], we place emphasis on the ontological category of *matter type*. These correspond to the referents of natural language *mass nouns* (e.g. 'water', 'wood', 'grass'), which differ from *count nouns* (aka common nouns) in respect of their individuation criteria. A count noun refers to a set of individual objects and not to any proper sub-parts of these individuals; whereas a mass noun refers to a continuous expanse of stuff and to any portion of that stuff. A coarse classification of physical matter is given by dividing it into three general matter types: **solid**, **liquid** and **gas**. For present purposes we shall not go much beyond this, although a fully fledged environmental ontology would clearly require a detailed classification.

We assume that matter types form a lattice structure so that for every pair there is a union $\mathbf{m}_1 \sqcup \mathbf{m}_2$, which refers to the sum of matter of either type (e.g. $\mathbf{fluid} = \mathbf{liquid} \sqcup \mathbf{gas}$, and an intersection $\mathbf{m}_1 \sqcap \mathbf{m}_2$ (e.g. $\mathbf{liquid} \sqcap \mathbf{metal}$), which refers to matter that manifests the characteristics of both matter types. In the latter case where the characteristics of $\mathbf{m}_1$ and $\mathbf{m}_2$ are not found together in any portion of matter, $\mathbf{m}_1 \sqcap \mathbf{m}_2$ will refer to the empty (or non-existent) matter type $\mathbf{m}_\perp$.

We adopt Quine's suggestion for the semantics of mass nouns, which is that they function similarly to proper nouns, in that they refer to a unique individual [17]. This individual is manifested by that part of the physical universe consisting of the sum of all regions exhibiting particular (typically physical) characteristics associated with the meaning of the mass noun.[5] Tnder this analysis, the denotation of the mass term 'water' would be the physical totality of all water in the universe. This semantics means that mass noun symbols are subject to the same semantic functions as individual constants, so we can refer to $\mathsf{ext}(\mathbf{m}, t)$, $\mathsf{phys}(\mathbf{m}, t)$ and $\mathsf{traj}(\mathbf{m})$.

As well as giving a plausible (or at least seemingly consistent) account of the semantics of typical mass nouns referring to types of physical substance (such as water, sand, wood etc.), the Quinean approach also seems to be well suited to apply to environmentally related mass-noun-like terms such as 'rainforest'. Thus, this term would refer to the totality consisting of all physical regions occupied by rainforest.

In fact we shall use the word *totality* in a technical sense. Let $\phi(r)$ be a property of regions — i.e. a formula with a free region variable r. Then the term $\mathsf{totality}_r[\phi(r)]$ denotes the largest region r^* satisfying $\phi(r^*)$. More precisely:

$$(r^* = \mathsf{totality}_r[\phi(r)]) \equiv_{def} (\phi(r^*) \wedge \forall r'[(\phi(r') \wedge \mathsf{Part}(r^*, r')) \rightarrow r^* = r'])$$

The subscript r in the operator $\mathsf{totality}_r$ is used to indicate the variable in $\phi(r)$ relative to which the totality is derived. This is needed in case $\phi(r)$ contains additional variables other than r. This notation does not take us beyond first-order logic, since the definiens is a standard first-order formula.

4. Geographic Regions and their Properties

In this section we define a certain kind of geometric entity that will be taken to correspond to 'geographic regions'. Thus, according to our semantics, any term referring to a geographic region will have such an entitiy as its denotation. It should be noted that the particular formalism presented here is by no means the only possibility, and may not be the best. But it does demonstrate how complex geographic entities and properties can be defined using set theory and geometry from a relatively limited base of primitives.

Informally, one might define a geographic region to be a part of the Earth's surface, perhaps satisfying some further conditions. However, since the Earth is in many places covered by water or other non-rigid substances such as mud or sand, there is some indeterminism as to what actually counts as its surface. Further ambiguity arises due to the presence of overhangs and cavities. Yet another complication is that, in many contexts, a geographic region is not treated as a mathematical surface of zero thickness but more like a 3-dimensional volume that can contain material objects such as trees or buildings.

[5] This semantics is adopted primarily for technical simplicity.

4.1. Interpretation of Geographic Regions

Because of the ambiguities just noted, we define a precise class of entities, which will constitute the domain geographic regions in our formal semantics. We call these entities *geo-regs*, and write $\mathsf{GeoReg}(\rho)$ to assert that ρ is an entity of this kind.

Geo-scientists often describe regions on the Earth in terms of their coordinates relative to a *reference ellipsoid*, a mathematical idealisation of the surface of the planet.[6] In our ontology we take the surface of the Earth's reference ellipsoid as a primitive entity, denoted by 'res'. We write cres to refer to the point at the centre of res. We can use res to define identity criteria for geographic regions. First we introduce a primitive function $\mathsf{resProj}(\rho)$, mapping each geo-reg to a regular closed subsurface of res. Intuitively $\mathsf{resProj}(\rho)$ consists of all those points on res that lie above or below or are coincident with some point that is considered to be within the physical region ρ, along a line passing through the centre of the reference ellipsoid.

A necessary and sufficient identity criterion for geo-regs is that two geo-regs are identical if and only if they have the same projection onto the reference ellipsoid:

$$\forall \rho\rho'[\mathsf{GeoReg}(\rho) \rightarrow ((\rho = \rho') \leftrightarrow \mathsf{resProj}(\rho) = \mathsf{resProj}(\rho'))$$

Whereas $\mathsf{resProj}(\rho)$ is a purely spatial region, geographic regions are more naturally thought of as being a kind of physical region. But given the difficulty, mentioned above, of identifying what should count as the Earth's surface, it is not obvious what should be considered as the spatial extension of a geo-reg. In fact, this is not really a substantive issue: since geo-regs are already a technical construct, we can make any reasonable stipulation, as long as it fits in with the rest of our ontology. For definiteness, we make the following stipulation, which, although somewhat arbitrary, is fairly easy to work with: the purely spatial extension $\mathsf{ext}(\rho)$ of a geo-reg ρ is a regular closed subset of space including all those points that are less than 10,000 km from cres and lie on any half-line originating at cres and passing through any point of $\mathsf{resProj}(\rho)$. The physical region ρ itself is then given by $\rho = \mathsf{phys}(\mathsf{ext}(\rho))$. The constant $\mathsf{maxGeoReg}$ will be used to denote the 10,000 km radius ball of physical space that is centred at the centre of the Earth (this is the maximal geo-reg entity).[7]

Clearly, those points of a geo-reg that lie within the Earth's core or way off in the exosphere are not relevant to most descriptions of geographic regions. However, including them in the formal denotation of a geo-reg will not cause any harm, since, whenever we want to represent anything specific about a geographic region, we can employ functional operators that map geo-reg entities to other more limited kinds of physical region. Some of these will be explored in the following subsections.

4.2. Geographic Surfaces

We shall often want to refer to certain types of surface that occur within the extension of a geo-reg. Surfaces of interest can often be described in terms of the vertical ordering of matter types within a geo-reg. Hence we define:

[6]Several different reference ellipsoids have been proposed. We assume that some standard has been adopted.

[7]The particular shape and size of $\mathsf{maxGeoReg}$ do not matter as long as it definitely includes any point that is incident with any of Earth's geographic regions and excludes points incident with any other celestial body.

- $\mathsf{GeoAbove}(p_1, p_2) \equiv_{def} (\mathsf{d}(p_1, \mathsf{cres}) > \mathsf{d}(p_2, \mathsf{cres}))$
- $\mathsf{GeoBelow}(p_1, p_2) \equiv_{def} (\mathsf{d}(p_1, \mathsf{cres}) < \mathsf{d}(p_2, \mathsf{cres}))$

We can now define the *global upper surface* of a given matter type **m** to be the surface of those points furthest from the centre of the Earth that have points of matter type **m** immediately below them:

$$\mathsf{globalUpperSurface}(\mathbf{m}) =_{def}$$
$$\{p \mid p \in \mathsf{ext}(\mathsf{maxGeoReg}) \wedge \forall q[\mathsf{GeoAbove}(q,p) \rightarrow \neg(q \in \mathbf{m})] \wedge$$
$$\exists p'[\mathsf{GeoBelow}(p',p) \wedge \forall q[\mathsf{GeoAbove}(q,p') \wedge \mathsf{GeoBelow}(q,p) \rightarrow (q \in \mathbf{m})]]\}$$

Thus, $\mathsf{globalUpperSurface}(\mathbf{solid})$ denotes the upper surface of the solid mater of the Earth, while $\mathsf{globalUpperSurface}(\mathbf{solid} \sqcup \mathbf{liquid})$ refers to what we might call the cartographic surface of the Earth, which incorporates the surfaces of both water bodies and (non-submerged) land-forms. We define:

$$\mathsf{cartSurf} =_{def} \mathsf{globalUpperSurface}(\mathbf{solid} \sqcup \mathbf{liquid})$$

The cartographic surface of a given geographic region ρ is then simply given by $\mathsf{cartSurf}(\rho) = \rho \cap \mathsf{cartSurf}$.

From any geographic surface s we can derive the geo-reg within which it is situated. The term $\mathsf{geoReg}(s)$ denotes the minimal geo-reg that contains all points of s.

We will often be interested in the properties of the cartographic surface, such as the distinction between land surface and water surface. Rather than defining these directly, it will be useful to define the concept of the *exposed surface* of a matter type **m**. This is that part of the upper surface of **m**, such that all points above it are within the **gas** matter type (i.e. it is the upper surface separating **m** from the Earth's atmosphere):

$$\mathsf{exposedSurface}(\mathbf{m}) =_{def} \{p \mid p \in \mathsf{globalUpperSurface}(\mathbf{m}) \wedge$$
$$\forall p'[\mathsf{GeoAbove}(p',p) \rightarrow (p' \in \mathbf{gas})]\}$$

It is then simple to define:

- $\mathsf{landSurface} =_{def} \mathsf{exposedSurface}(\mathbf{solid})$
- $\mathsf{waterSurface} =_{def} \mathsf{exposedSurface}(\mathbf{water})$
- $\mathsf{landReg} =_{def} \mathsf{geoReg}(\mathsf{landSurface})$
- $\mathsf{waterReg} =_{def} \mathsf{geoReg}(\mathsf{waterSurface})$

4.3. Deriving Regions from Surface Point Properties

One method of defining geographic regions is to identify those regions such that all points on their cartographic surface satisfy some particular property. For example, we might want to identify hot regions by specifying a minimum temperature for their surface points. To this end we define the operation $\mathsf{RSSPP}_p[\rho, \phi(p)]$, to be read as 'region ρ satisfies surface point property ϕ':

$$\mathsf{RSSPP}_p[\rho, \phi(p)] \equiv_{def} \forall p[(p \in \mathsf{cartSurf}(\rho)) \rightarrow \phi(p)]]$$

We can also define the *totality* (i.e. the largest region) satisfying a surface point property ϕ by:

$$\mathsf{tsspp}_p(\phi(p)) =_{def} \mathsf{totality}_\rho[\mathsf{RSSPP}_p(\rho, \phi(p))]$$

5. Environment

As the reader may have inferred from the discussion in Section 2, our view is that the terms 'environment' and 'habitat' are significantly affected by mode ambiguity. Hence, rather than try to give a single definition characterising the semantics of 'environment' we begin by identifying aspects of environment corresponding to different modes of identification. We shall then look into the natural correlations between these modes, which will give a more comprehensive picture of the meaning of the natural language term 'environment'. We begin with three aspects that we consider to be of primary significance:

- Immediate Environment: the factors that affect a particular *subject* by directly impacting the subject's outer surface,
- Affective Environment: collection of objects and/or quantities of substance identified relative to a given *subject*, such that these objects each contribute to and jointly determine the immediate environment of the subject,
- Local Environment: the physical region proximal to the subject (this is vague as the degree of proximity is unspecified — the local environment of an organism could be related to the range over which it can move during one day),
- Global Environment: a physical totality characterised in terms of physical characteristics that determine a range of immediate environments that are possible within the region of that totality.

The informal definitions of *immediate* and *affective* environment refer to a *subject* relative to which the environment is determined. The subject would typically be a living organism. However, we allow that the subject might also be an inanimate object. Fig 1 illustrates the distinctions we are making. The diagram shows a lizard situated in a rocky desert environment. Various elements of its affective environment are shown (the sun, the local atmosphere, gravity and the rock on which it is standing). These elements together determine the lizard's immediate environment, which is the inward oriented physical surface within which the creature is enclosed.

5.1. Immediate Environment

The concept of an organism's *immediate environment* plays a key role in our analysis. We define the immediate environment of an organism to be the *inward oriented physical surface* that encloses the organism. Across this surface come a variety of physical entities/stimuli: chemicals, photons, forces etc. Clearly these will have an effect on the organism, and different species of organism will be adapted to functioning in different kinds of environment. We can consider the immediate environment of an organism either at a single point in time, or over some period (up to its whole life). Hence, our ontology contains two types of entities corresponding to *instantaneous immediate environments* and *temporally extended immediate environments*.

For obvious reasons we do not normally describe the environment of an organism in terms of a surface of impacting forces/chemicals. This would be too detailed and

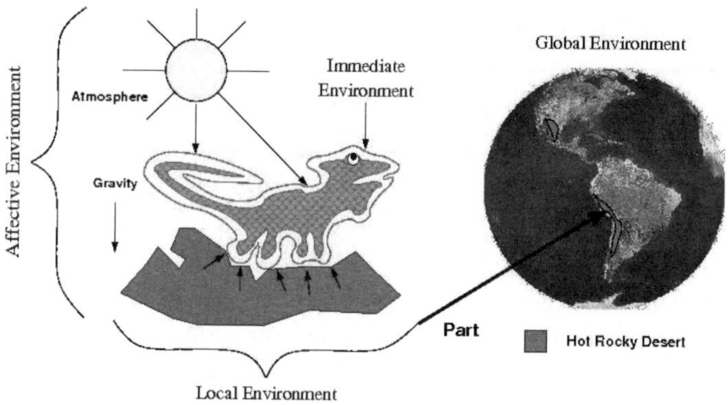

Figure 1. Four Modes of Environment: Immediate, Affective, Local, Global.

complicated to be practical. Instead descriptions of environment usually rely on the fact that the immediate environment is largely determined by objects and forces in the vicinity of the subject and by average properties that hold in the region where it is located.

5.2. *Affective Environment*

In describing a subject's environment, we typically look beyond the animal's skin to the terrain, vegetation, weather conditions etc. in which it lives. These factors will determine typical or average properties (or ranges of variation) of its immediate environment.

The affective environment of a subject consists of a collection of entities and quantities of material which affect the subject in some way. These entities can be of a variety of forms, including forces and fluid media as well as physical objects and their surfaces. Some of the main categories of affecting entities are the following:

- the atmosphere or fluid in which the subject exists,
- the sun,
- objects and matter constituting the surface upon which the subject resides,
- objects and their surfaces contributing to the visual perception of the subject,
- gravitational force (or material objects contributing to gravity local to the subject).

Our current model of affective environments is rudimentary. We suggest that an affective environment may be characterised by an *effect function*, which specifies the degrees to which each object in the universe has some effect on the subject's immediate environment. Each of the modes of affectation listed above would involve particular laws by which properties of the affecting objects govern the way that they will affect the immediate environment of any subject in their vicinity.

5.3. *Local Environment*

Intuitively, the local environment of a subject is a physical region within which the subject is located. But how large should this region be? One idea is that it should be large enough to include all those objects that have some affect on the subject. But if we were to include all effects (such as gravity) this would take in the whole universe. To counter this, one might propose to include only the region comprising objects that have a sufficiently strong effect on the subject, but then 'local environment' would be a somewhat redundant concept as it would be completely determined by the affective environment.

Our suggestion is that, the local environment is indeed closely related to the affective environment, but also involves a distinction between local and non-local effects. Since, gravity acts approximately uniformly over the Earth's surface it is not considered as contributing to the local environment. The sun and atmosphere would be discounted for similar reasons. Since the criteria for identifying a local environment are unclear, it may be that this concept should be further dissected into more precise modes. However, for present purposes the main thing that we require is that a local environment is a physical region that is proximal to the subject. For instance we could just take it to be a geographic region whose surface is a disc of some fixed radius (say 100m) centred on the subject.

5.4. Global Environment

According to the immediate, affective and local approaches to characterising environment, the notion of environment is associated with a subject (usually an organism) upon which the environment acts. Nevertheless, there are many contexts in which it is common to use the term 'environment' without specifically indicating any particular subject. Thus, we might describe the Sahara desert as a harsh environment without mentioning a particular organism or species that is to be found there. In fact we can describe an environment even where there are no organisms present: "The surface of Venus is an extremely harsh environment, which is incompatible with life (as we know it)."

For many purposes the subject need not be specified, since within a geographic region that is uniform in relevant characteristics, all organisms will tend to experience similar immediate environments. Of course this will depend to some extent on the particular behaviour of the organisms. Moreover, this observation also begs the question as to what characteristics are 'environmentally relevant'. But given that we have a more or less precise definition of *immediate environment*, we can characterise environmentally relevant characteristics as those properties of a geographic region that impose constraints on the possible immediate environments that can be experienced within that region. Typical characteristics of this kind would be the average temperature or humidity of a region.

We propose to represent global environments as special kinds of matter type (albeit ones that can refer to rather heterogeneous portions of matter). Hence, in its global sense, a term such as 'rainforest' will be treated as of the same logical type as 'wood'. So, under this analysis the semantics of "This area is rainforest" would be analogous to "This chair is wood". As was explained in Section 3.5, we model matter types as individual constants referring to the physical region that includes the totality of regions satisfying given conditions. For example, the term 'desert' might be defined as a region satisfying conditions regarding its temperature and precipitation. Since these conditions related to measurements made at surface points of a putative desert region, we can employ the $\mathsf{tsspp}_p[\phi(p)]$ function, introduced above, to provide a concise definition:

$$\mathbf{desert} = \mathsf{tsspp}_p[(\mathsf{avTemp}(p) > 15°C) \wedge (\mathsf{avPrecip}(p) < 20mm \text{ per month})]$$

Since 'desert' is a vague term, there are no standardly agreed thresholds for the levels of temperature and precipitation that constitute desert. Such, vagueness is intrinsic to many environmental terms. Addressing this issue is beyond the scope of the current paper, but the *standpoint semantics* approach proposed in [5] might be used.

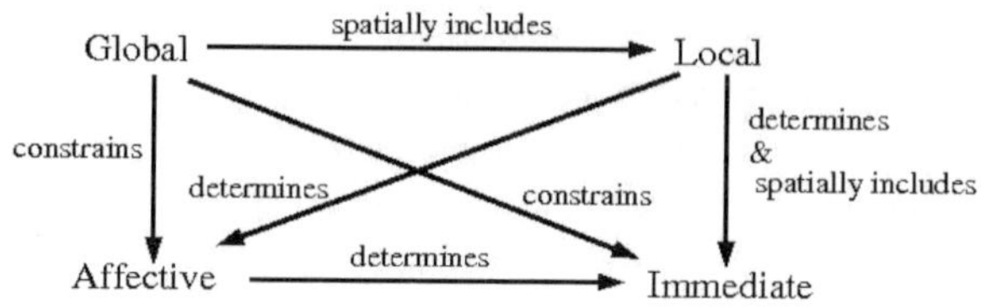

Figure 2. Interactions between the four modes.

5.5. *Interaction Between Different Modes*

The modes of identification for environments are highly interconnected because of exemplar clustering and other forms of natural correlation. Interaction among modes is illustrated in Figure 2. The conditions that define a global environment induce restrictions on what kinds of affective environment can satisfy those conditions and hence indirectly constrain the immediate environment. The spatial extension of the global environment includes the local environment. The affective environment fully determines the immediate environment (but not vice versa). The local environment also fully determines both the affective and immediate environments, because if we are given a specific physical region of the world centred on the subject, we can determine conditions at that location.

6. Species, Niches and Habitats

Whereas the concept of environment can be used without reference to any particular life form, it is apparent that the term 'habitat' is tpically used to refer to aspects of the world that are intimately related to living things. Hence, before attempting to explain the semantics of habitat we first examine the nature of species and organisms, focusing especially on characteristics that govern their interaction with environmental conditions.

The most established approach is *Niche Theory* [11, 21], where the niche of a species is modelled as a hyper-volume in a space of environmental parameters. This represents the space of possible conditions under which a species can survive (or thrive). The parameters used to characterise a niche may include complex factors such as predation and temporal behaviour patterns. However, many significant parameters relate to environmental properties that can be represented in terms of an accptable range of some physical measurement (e.g. temperature). Within our framework, a niche described in terms of such parameters can be represented as a conjunction of predicates, which (leaving aside certain granularity issues) can be evaluated at each point of a geographic region.

6.1. *Formal Specification of 'Potential Habitat'*

Suppose the environmental niche constraints for species s are specified by a geographic point predicate $\mathsf{Niche\_pred}_s(p)$ (and we ignore other factors such as predation), then, using our definition from section 4.3, the geographic region that the species could potentially inhabit will be given by

$$\mathsf{potential\_habitat}(s) \;=\; \mathsf{tsspp}_p(\mathsf{Niche\_pred}_s(p))\,.$$

We can regard this as a possible way to formally stipulate the *habitat* of species s. According to this mode of specification, a habitat is a type of *global environment* (in the sense of 5.4), where the defining predicate is derived from the niche parameter constraints of the species. However, it must be realised that 'habitat' is deeply affected by mode ambiguity (as discussed in section 2 above). Hence, this is one among several naturally correlated, but logically distinct ways of defining habitat.

6.2. Modes of Habitat

The term 'habitat' appears to be subject to even more mode ambiguities than 'environment'. The conditions under which an individual organism lives or could live are naturally correlated with the average conditions to which a species is adapted. Hence, there is a mode ambiguity between an organism focused interpretation and an interpretation in relation to a species. There is also a deep ambiguity as to whether the concept of habitat relates to the the location of actual, typical, or possible life trajectories.

We identify the following principal mode ambiguities in the meaning of 'habitat':

- 'Habitat' may be interpreted either as a kind of *global environment* (as per the formal specification given above), or in terms of an organism's *affective environment* (i.e. a collection of objects which have some effect on the organism). (It seems less natural to conceive of a habitat in terms of a local or immediate environment).
- 'Habitat' may be applied to an individual organism or to a species. (It is also possible that one considers an individual in relation to the habitat of its species — e.g. 'This caged polar-bear is not in its natural habitat'.)
- 'Habitat' may refer to the actual environment where an individual or species occurs (its geographic range), or to environments that are typical of a species, or to possible environments that are survivable by an organism/species (potential habitat), or perhaps to environments in which an organism/species is likely to thrive.

As yet, we have only formalised one sense of 'habitat' by the predicate $\mathsf{potential\_habitat}(s)$. But we believe that the primitives and structures identified in our examination of geographic regions, environments and organisms provide a good basis for an constructing ontology within which the other modes could be defined explicitly.

7. Conclusion

In this preliminary investigation we have applied a particular approach to elucidating the meanings of the terms 'environment' and 'habitat'. We have picked apart a range of possible interpretations and examined the relationships that tie these together. Although many details have been glossed over, we believe that the framework provides a useful starting point for a more comprehensive treatment and for the development of a fully formal ontology. As well as contributing to understanding the specific problems that arise in the environmental domain, we believe that the approach is more generally applicable to semantic analysis across a wide range of domains.

Among the many directions in which this work coult be extended, the following seem to be particularly important: a) development of a theory of granularity that takes into account the scale-dependent aspects of concepts relating to environment; b) modelling of the phenomenon of vagueness which is pervasive in the meanings of geographic and environmental concepts; c) more detailed consideration of temporal aspects of environment and habitat; d) elaboration of how one can use models of the characteristics of organisms and species in order to derive information about their habitats.

Acknowledgements

I would like to thank Norman Morrison, Chris Mungall, Michael Ashburner, Dawn Field and all involved in the EnvO environmental ontology network for introducing me to the fascinating complexities of this domain.

References

[1] The EnvO environment ontology network. `http://environmentontology.org`.
[2] B. Bennett. Space, time, matter and things. In C. Welty and B. Smith, editors, *Proceedings of the 2nd international conference on Formal Ontology in Information Systems (FOIS'01)*, pages 105–116, Ogunquit, 2001. ACM. `http://www.comp.leeds.ac.uk/qsr/pub/bennett-fois01.pdf`.
[3] B. Bennett. Modes of concept definition and varieties of vagueness. *Applied Ontology*, 1(1):17–26, 2005.
[4] B. Bennett and P. Agarwal. Semantic categories underlying the meaning of 'place'. In *Spatial Information Theory: proceedings of the 8th international conference (COSIT-07)*, volume 4736 of *Lecture Notes in Computer Science*, pages 78–95. Springer, 2007.
[5] B. Bennett, D. Mallenby, and A. Third. An ontology for grounding vague geographic terms. In C. Eschenbach and M. Gruninger, editors, *Proceedings of the 5th International Conference on Formal Ontology in Information Systems (FOIS-08)*. IOS Press, 2008. `http://www.comp.leeds.ac.uk/qsr/pub/Bennett08fois.pdf`.
[6] S. Durbha, R. King, V. Shah, and N. Younan. A framework for semantic reconciliation of disparate earth observation thematic data. *Computers and Geosciences*, In Press, Available On-Line, 2008.
[7] C. S. Elton. *Animal ecology,*. New York,Macmillan Co.,, 1927.
[8] F. T. Fonseca, J. Martin, and M. A. Rodríguez. From geo- to eco-ontologies. In *GIScience '02: Proceedings of the Second International Conference on Geographic Information Science*, pages 93–107, London, UK, 2002. Springer-Verlag.
[9] J. Grinnell. The niche-relationships of the California thrasher.
[10] A. Gupta. *The Logic of Common Nouns: an investigation in quantified modal logic*. Yale University Press, New Haven, 1980.
[11] G. Hutchinson. Concluding remarks. In *Proceedings of the Cold Springs Harbor symposium on quantitative biology*, volume 22, pages 415–427, 1957.
[12] H. Kamp. Two theories about adjectives. In E. Keenan, editor, *Formal Semantics of Natural Language*. Cambridge University Press, Cambridge, England, 1975.
[13] M. Kavouras, M. Kokla, and E. Tomai. Comparing categories among geographic 0ntologies. *Computers and Geosciences*, 31(2):145–154, 2005.
[14] C. M. Keet. Factors affecting ontology development in ecology. In *Proceedings of Data Integration in Life Sciences (DILS-05)*, volume 3615 of *LNCS*. Springer, San Diego, 2005.
[15] C. M. Keet. Representations of the ecological niche. In *Third International Workshop on Philosophy and Informatics (WSPI2006)*. IFOMIS Reports, Saarbrucken, Germany, May 2006.
[16] D. Pennington. Representing the dimensions of an ecological niche. In *Proceedings 5th International Semantic Web Conference (ISWC'06) Workshop: Terra Cognita 2006 – Directions to the Geospatial Semantic Web*, Athens, Georgia, November 2006.
[17] W. V. O. Quine. *Word and Object*. MIT Press, 1960.
[18] D. A. Randell, Z. Cui, and A. G. Cohn. A spatial logic based on regions and connection. In *Proc. 3rd Int. Conf. on Knowledge Representation and Reasoning*, pages 165–176, San Mateo, 1992. Morgan Kaufmann.
[19] B. Smith and A. C. Varzi. The niche. *Nous*, 33(2):198–122, 1999.
[20] B. Smith and A. C. Varzi. Surrounding space: The ontology of organism-environment relations. In *Theory in Biosciences*, pages 139–162, 2002.
[21] J. Vandermeer. Niche theory. *Annual Review of Ecology and Systematics*, 3:107–132, 1972.
[22] A. Varzi, editor. *Topoi: special issue on the philosophy of geography*, volume 20(2). Kluwer, 2001.

Formal Ontology in Information Systems
A. Galton and R. Mizoguchi (Eds.)
IOS Press, 2010

doi:10.3233/978-1-60750-535-8-45

Towards Ontological Correctness of Part-whole Relations with Dependent Types

Richard DAPOIGNY [1], and Patrick BARLATIER
LISTIC/polytech'Savoie, Domaine Universitaire,
Po. Box 80439, 74944 Annecy le vieux cedex, France

Abstract. Generally, part-whole relations are modeled using fragments of first-order logic(FOL) and difficulties arise when meta-reasoning is done over their properties, leading to reason outside the logic. Alternatively, classical languages for ontological reasoning such as Description Logics + Logic Programming lack of expressive formal foundations resulting in ambiguous interpretations of relations. Moreover, they show some difficulties to prove that a given meta property is logically correct. In order to address these problems, we suggest a formal framework using a dependent (higher-order) type theory such as those used in program checking and theorem provers (e.g., Coq). All properties of part-whole relations are formalized through abstract constructs called parameterized specifications (p-specifications). We detail their content and explain how they are suitable to build an ontology of formal properties that can be further used for reasoning about higher-order properties.

Keywords. Formal ontology, dependent types, part-whole relation, p-specifications

Introduction

Despite the amount of methodologies and languages proposed in order to design ontologies, the validation of ontologies continues to be an unsolved problem [1]. Ontology validation checks the absence of errors (consistency) of an ontology. This aspect is crucial in ontology modeling and rarely solved with simple First Order Logic (FOL) based languages (e.g., to reason about the transitivity of relations). In a large ontology, maintaining consistency without automatic mechanisms is a considerable challenge and the limited expressive power of FOL might result in reasoning problems that are known to be undecidable [2]. Furthermore, in [3], the authors has developed a theory of parthood, component-hood, and containment relations in FOL with description logics (DLs). They conclude that DLs are not appropriate for formulating complex inter-relations between relations.

We restrict here the spectrum of ontological validation to part-whole relations. While the specific ontological nature of part-whole relations has been widely studied [4,5,6] and

[1]Corresponding Author: Richard Dapoigny, LISTIC/polytech'Savoie, Domaine Universitaire, Po. Box 80439, 74944 Annecy le vieux cedex, France

integrated within knowledge modeling formalisms, these relations are only considered within the restricted framework of set theory with first-order logic. A number of problems and limitations has emerged from this assumption [7]. Challenging topics include (i) the differences that appear in parthood relations between classes and parthood relations between instances (ii) resolving the issues around the relation of the parthood relation (i.e., the non-differentiation among the roles that parts play within the structure of a whole) (iii) whether the inheritance property holds for parthood relations.

Since the justification of the validity of many structuring choices can only be made on ontological grounds there is a need to investigate an expressive theory underpinned on strong logical foundations. With respect to this requirement, type theory appears as a powerful candidate. More precisely, this paper addresses the above difficulties through a constructive type theory termed Knowledge-based Dependent Type Theory (K-DTT) that provides a highly expressive representation of ontological structures while maintaining tractability. This formal system is designed to act both as a proof system (above constructive logic) and as a typed functional programming language (typed λ-calculus) with a high-level of expressiveness. The novel contribution of the paper is to suggest a formal theory with dependent types (i.e., types depending on objects) able to guarantee the ontological correctness of properties focusing on part-whole relations. It relies on the parameterized specification of properties of part-whole relations resulting in a formal ontology of these specifications. Dependent types are used because (i) the judgments-as-types principle allows specifications to be represented as types, with their proofs represented as objects of those types and (ii), dependency allows a type checker to connect proofs and the data the proofs prove something about.

1. Formal Foundations

1.1. Type Theory and Ontologies

Most ontologies in the area of knowledge representation philosophically refer either to the ontological realism or to the cognitively-oriented approach. We would maintain neutrality in this regard and claim that the theory presented here can be used for realist ontologies which are based on the Aristotelian notion of universals as well as for conceptualist ontologies based on the notions of concepts[2] which are formed through meaning. All scenarios in the following will refer to the ontology of particulars suggested in DOLCE (Descriptive Ontology for Linguistic and Cognitive Engineering).

Formal ontologies make a distinction between universals and particulars characterized by means of instantiation (unlike universals, particulars are entities that cannot have instances). In [8], the authors argue for a top-level ontology of universals containing concepts whose instances are universals. Since types correspond to the result of a categorization procedure, they have a natural adequacy with universals. According to the Aristotelian conception of universals, types are justified in the sense that there are no uninstantiated universals just as there are no untyped objects. We assume that types are intensional entities and that there exists a mapping between concepts and types in which types represent concepts, but not all types describe concepts (e.g., they can describe relations). As underlined in [10], in a foundational ontology there should be no negative or

[2]Concepts refer to abstract representations of certain aspects of entities that exist in a domain.

disjunctive concepts. Furthermore, a model for concepts must be intensional [11]. These constraints are fully assumed in K-DTT.

1.2. Type Theory as a Logic

The core paradigm of dependent type theory is that correct typing corresponds to provably correct models. Typing also provides typical software engineering principles such as modularization and data abstraction. The logical background uses a constructive type theory with polymorphism and functional dependency [9]. We have extended this theory to K-DTT with subsumption and inductive types that are useful for knowledge representation. By itself, logic is ontologically neutral, but the combination of logic with an ontology provides a language that can express relationships about the entities in the domain of interest. Type theory makes use of the so-called Curry-Howard isomorphism stating that propositions are seen as types while proofs are seen as objects. It establishes an "equivalence" between a computation system (i.e., a lambda-calculus) and a (intuitionistic) logical theory. Type theory has explicit proof objects which are terms in an extension of the typed lambda-calculus while at the same time, provability corresponds to type inhabitation[3]. Proofs in a computational setting can be the result of a database lookup, the existence of a function performing a given action or the output of a theorem prover, given assumptions about entities, properties or constraints. A proof is built up of premises, and using different contexts, the same assertion can have different meanings. The higher-order logic will be used (i) to validate relation properties (e.g., transitivity) through p-specifications and (ii) to restrict the search space of these properties by quantification over lower level categories.

1.3. Type Theory as Computation

Three levels of stratification are available, a sort level (for type universes), a type level and an object level (proof objects). The theory comprises an infinite hierarchy of predicative type universes denoted $Type_0$, $Type_1$, ... and an impredicative universe noted $Prop$[4]. The universes $Type_i$ are the universes for data types while $Prop$ is the universe for logic. The hierarchy is cumulative, that is, $Type_i$ is contained in $Type_{i+1}$ for every i. A universe is seen as a type that is closed under the type-forming operations of the calculus. Since impredicativity exists only for $Prop$, $Type_i$ may contain only types from universes $Prop$, $Type_0$, ..., $Type_{i-1}$ while $Prop$ may be constructed with types from $Prop$, $Type_0$, ..., $Type_i$, ... $Type_0$ denote the sort of basic types or data structures and relates to domain ontologies, $Type_1$, the type of basic types, $Type_2$, the type of types of basic types used in upper-level ontologies and $Prop$, the sort of propositions (for logic). Every type that belongs to a universe is considered as an object of upper universes. The resulting universe of a dependent type is the maximum universe between $Type_0$, and the universe of its components. For example, if PD denote the type of perdurants, then $eating, reading, ChemicalReaction$ are such perdurants while at the same time denoting types themselves. Therefore, $eating, reading, ChemicalReaction$ reside in $Type_0$ whereas the collection of these types, i.e., PD is in $Type_1$.

[3] A proposition is true iff its set of proofs is inhabited.

[4] The fact that $Prop$ is impredicative, means that one can quantify over propositions to form a new proposition.

1.3.1. Representing Knowledge with Dependent Types

What is generally termed classes, concepts or universals in ontologies will be denoted by types in K-DTT, whereas individuals (instances), are called proof objects or simply objects when no confusion occurs. The building blocks of K-DTT are terms and the basic relation is the typing relation. The context is a finite sequence[5] of expressions of the form $x_i : T_i$ where x_i is a variable and T_i a type. The context $\Gamma \triangleq x_1 : T_1; \ldots; x_n : T_n$ in a judgment $\Gamma \vdash x : T$ contains the prerequisites necessary for establishing the statement $x : T$ meaning that the term x has type T. We call x an inhabitant of T, and we call T the type of x. For instance, the universal "heart" in $heart : Type_0 \vdash x : heart$ gives the proof (is instanced by): $x = John'sHeart$ while $heart : Type_0$ asserts that "heart" is a well-formed type. Notice that the relation of instantiation (between an instance and its universal) corresponds here to the process of type inhabitation and is clearly distinct from the relation of subsumption (between a less general and a more general universal) which is defined with subtyping (see next subsection). Generally, types are dependent types by contrast with non-dependent types which are called ground types.

The characteristic feature of dependent type theories is that they allow a type to be predicated on a value. That property make them much more flexible and expressive than conventional type systems [12]. K-DTT admits two dependent types, the dependent product or Π-type and the dependent sum or Σ-type. The non-dependent versions of these types are respectively noted $\rightarrow$ (functions) and $\times$ (non-dependent pair). Given two types A and B, the type forming operation for the dependent sum type (or Σ-type) of $B(x)$ is expressed as $\Sigma x : A.B(x)$, x ranging over A. When B is a predicate over A, it expresses the subset of all objects of type A satisfying the predicate B. Proof objects for dependent sums are pairs in which the second component depends on the first. They can be nested to model properties, relations or constraints. For instance, the situation in which a patient has a shaft of femur fracture, is described with the sum type:

$$\Sigma x : Patient\ .\ \Sigma y : ShaftOfFemur\ .\ hasFractureOf(x, y)$$

A proof for this Σ-type[6] is given for example by the (nested) pair $\langle P12737, \langle P12737 - F19, q_1\rangle\rangle$ indicating that for the patient identified as $P12737$, with a shaft of femur referred to as $P12737 - F19$, q_1 is a proof of $hasFractureOf(P12737, P12737 - F19)$. The proved pairs express the subset of patients having a fracture of the shaft of femur. In each pair s, appropriate rules [9] extract the first and the second component with the respective functions $\pi_1(s)$ and $\pi_2(s)$. In the above example, with $s = hasFractureOf(P12737, P12737 - F19)$, we get $\pi_1(s) = P12737$ and $\pi_2(s) = \langle P12737 - F19, hasFractureOf(\pi_1(s), P12737 - F19)\rangle$. Since $\pi_2(s)$ is itself a pair, we get: $\pi_1(\pi_2(s)) = P12737 - F19$.

Given two arbitrary types A and B, the dependent product of $B(x)$ noted $\Pi x : A.B(x)$, where x ranges over A, models (dependent) functions whose output type may vary according to the input. Any proof of the input x of type A yields a proof of $B(x)$. For instance, to represent the fact that a cell has a membrane, one introduces:

$$\Pi x : Cell\ .\ hasMembrane(x)$$

[5] The sequence is ordered because any type in the sequence may depend on the previous variables.

[6] A sum type is proved iff all its components are proved. A proof of the $hasFracture$ predicate exists only iff the previously proved objects $Patient$ and $ShaftOfFemur$ are related in the database.

in which $hasMembrane$ is a predicate (i.e., a function $Cell \rightarrow Prop$) which for each instance x (e.g., $cell1276$) of the type $Cell$ yields a proof object (e.g., $hasMembrane(cell1276)$) for the proposition. Since it means that all cells have a membrane, Π-types also express the universal quantification ∀. Mixing dependent types allows for more complex relations. For example, let us consider the medical condition (mc) ureterolithiasis where a person has stones in the ureter. Obstruction of the ureter by the kidney stones causes a renal colic attack which results in an intense pain. To express that if a person suffers from an ureterolithiasis, then he has pain with it, one will write:

$$\Pi x : Person\ .\ \Pi y : (\Sigma mc : ureterolithiasis\ .\ hasMedicalCondition(x, mc))\ .\ hasPainWith(x, \pi_1(y))$$

Notice that the quantification (Πy) is over a subset of persons, i.e., the persons having an ureterolithiasis. It results that (i) we get a better precision than mere ∀ quantification and (ii) it decreases the search space from a computing perspective. A binary part-of structure can be easily described with a sum type. Given two types T_1 and T_2, $PartOf$ is a predicate of type $T_1 \rightarrow T_2 \rightarrow Prop$ with the type definition:

$$\Sigma x : T_1\ .\ \Sigma y : T_2\ .\ PartOf(x, y)$$

This is a syntactic structure and its semantics is given by parameterized specifications (cf section 2) or appropriate rules. The logical consistency[7] of the core theory has been demonstrated and the decidability property has been deduced as a corollary [13].

1.3.2. Subtyping

For non-dependent types, i.e., ground types, the basic subtyping relation (Sub) allows to replace a type A with a type A' in any term provided that $A \leq A'$.

$$\frac{\Gamma \vdash M : A \quad \Gamma \vdash A' : Type \quad A \leq A'}{\Gamma \vdash M : A'}\ (\mathsf{Sub}) \qquad (1)$$

According to this rule, a given term may have several types. However, it can be shown that whenever a term is typeable, it has a uniquely determined principal type. This principal type is the minimum type of the term with respect to the conversion rule and relatively to a given context. For ground types, subtyping expresses intensional subsumption. For example, if we consider the types $sensor$ and $device$, we can assert that $sensor \leq device$, since a sensor corresponds to a more precise information than a device. In such a way, the relation of instantiation (e.g., $x : A$) is clearly separated from the relation of subsumption occurring between types (e.g., $A \leq A'$).

Relations and concepts are described with sum-types. However, argument types of sum types can be sum types themselves, giving rise to nested sum types. Two terms M and N are called convertible, written as $M \simeq N$, if they can be transformed into one another by repeated applications of reductions [9].

$$\frac{\Gamma \vdash M : A \quad \Gamma \vdash A' : Type \quad A \simeq A'}{\Gamma \vdash M : A'}\ (\mathsf{conv}) \qquad (2)$$

[7] For a type theory, the logical consistency is identified with termination.

Lemma 1 *[9] The subtyping relation is a partial order over terms with respect to conversion.*

The subtyping rule subsumes the conversion rule. The following meta-theoretic property introduced as a corollary will be useful for our purpose:

Corollary 2 *[9] The relation $\leq$ is the smallest partial order over terms with respect to conversion such that:*

if $A \leq A'$ and $B \leq B'$, then $\Sigma x : A \,.\, B \leq \Sigma x : A' \,.\, B'$

1.4. Type Theory as a Higher-order Logic

The usual logical operators of the internal higher order logic of the type theory can be expressed using the (dependent) product. For example, the logical implication $A \supset B$ is expressed with the non-dependent product $A \rightarrow B$ while the logical conjunction $A \,\&\, B$ and the negation $\neg A$ are respectively written $\Pi R : Prop \,.\, (A \rightarrow B \rightarrow R) \rightarrow R$ and $A \rightarrow \bot$. In the following, we make use of the standard (high-order) notations to facilitate comprehension. In addition, a notion of propositional equality is introduced. The propositional equality [14] complies to the Leibniz principle which says that two objects of the same type A are propositionally equal if and only if they are indistinguishable from each other with respect to all their logical properties.

$$(a =_A a') \triangleq \forall P : A \rightarrow Prop \,.\, (Pa) \rightarrow (Pa')$$

2. Formalizing Specifications

The terminology introduced in this paper for types is fully compatible with DOLCE's formal ontology [15]. In order to formally characterize the ontological distinctions between part-whole relations, their properties, such as transitivity, must be clarified [11]. For this purpose, in K-DTT specifications [9] appear as an appropriate tool since they can compute the logical consistency of modeling decisions made by the modeler about the relations. Type theory allows for the so-called "meta" reasoning but without leaving the internal higher-order logic. For that purpose, a specification of some data structure is provided as the left member of a Σ-type, whereas the right member introduces the properties (i.e., the axioms) that the structure is supposed to fulfill.

Definition 1 *(Specification) A specification Sp consists of a pair $\langle Struc[Sp], Pr[Sp]\rangle$ whose objects are (i) a type $Struc[Sp]$ of any Sp-structure and (ii) a predicate $Pr[Sp]$ over $Struc[Sp]$ specifying the axioms that the realization of such a specification should satisfy, with $i : N$, a natural number, $i \geq 0$.*

$$Sp \triangleq \langle Struc[Sp], Pr[Sp]\rangle, \;\; Struc[Sp] : Type_i \,, \;\; Pr[Sp] : \; Struc[Sp] \rightarrow Prop$$

In such a way, the computational contents (the structure type of the specification) is separated from the axiomatic requirements (correctness proofs).

Definition 2 *(Consistent specification) A specification Sp is consistent if there exists an object r of type $Struc[Sp]$ such that $Pr[Sp](r)$ is provable.*

2.1. Operations on Specifications

We introduce the $Fusion$ and the $Extent$ operators on specifications as follows.

Definition 3 *(Fusion) Given two specifications S and S' having the same structure, i.e., $S_J \equiv Struc[S] \simeq Struc[S']$, the $Fusion$ specification is defined with:*

$$\begin{aligned} Struc[Fusion(S,S')] &\triangleq S_J \\ Pr[Fusion(S,S')](z) &\triangleq Pr[S](z) \ \& \ Pr[S'](z) \end{aligned}$$

for any z of type S_J.

Definition 4 *(Extension) Given a specification S, E_S an extent of that structure, i.e., $E_S : Struc[S] \rightarrow Type$, and Pr_S, a predicate over the extended structure, the $Extent$ specification is defined with:*

$$\begin{aligned} Struc[Extent(S, E_S, Pr_S)] &\triangleq \Sigma x : Struc[S] \,.\, E_S(x) \\ Pr[Extent(S, E_S, Pr_S)](z) &\triangleq Pr[S](fst(z)) \ \& \ Pr_S(z) \end{aligned}$$

for any z of type $Struc[Extent(S, E_S, Pr_S)]$.

2.2. Specification of Part-of relations

Definition 5 *A binary relation Rel between types is expressed with a sum type having these types as arguments and whose extension consists of all the proofs for that relation.*

$$Rel \triangleq \sum [\, T : Type_i,\ T' : Type_i,\ R : T \rightarrow T' \rightarrow Prop \,] \tag{3}$$

The idea is to introduce a specification whose structure is general enough to encompass most problems that appear in formal ontologies, i.e., a generic binary relation. Then, the second part of the specification embed some properties that the binary relation is supposed to fulfill. However, in order to make these specifications more general, we define the notion of parameterized specification. A parameterized specification, or p-specification for short, of a binary relation is a function which, when applied to its arguments returns a p-specification that resides (at least) in $Type_2$:

$$\lambda T : Type_i . \lambda T' : Type_i . \lambda R : T \rightarrow T' \rightarrow Prop \,.\, Sp(T, T', R)$$

Now, we are able to complete the p-specification of a part-of structure using the Rel structure[8]. Let us consider the part-of relations sharing at least the constraints of Ground mereology, i.e., the part-of relation is a partial order that is reflexive, antisymmetric and transitive [7]. We have also to consider the proper part-of relation that is irreflexive, asymmetric and transitive. The p-specifications $Trans$, $Refl$, $Antsym$ and $ITrans$ with the obvious meanings are given by the following definitions (T will denote the common type in sum types):

[8]The p-specifications are higher-order since they take relations as arguments and polymorphic since they are quantified over arbitrary types T and T'.

- Trans(T,T',R):

$$Struc[Trans(T,T',R)] \triangleq Rel$$

For any binary structure r of type $Struc[Trans(T,T',R)]$:

$$Pr[Trans(T,T',R)](r) \triangleq \begin{array}{l} \forall u : r, u' : r(u) \ . \\ (sec(sec(u)) =_{Prop} sec(sec(u'))) \supset \\ (R(fst(u), fst(sec(u))) \ \& \\ R(fst(u'), fst(sec(u'))) \supset \\ R(fst(u), fst(sec(u')))) \end{array}$$

with $fst()$ and $sec()$ the functions extracting respectively the first and the second argument of a pair[9]. Notice that the axiom first checks for the equality of predicates in the relation.

- Refl(T,T',R): For any binary structure re of type $Struc[Refl(T,T',R)]$:

$$\begin{array}{ll} Struc[Refl(T,T',R)] \triangleq & Rel \\ Pr[Refl(T,T',R)](re) \triangleq & \forall u : re \ . \ (fst(sec(u)) =_T fst(u)) \supset \\ & \qquad R(fst(u), fst(u)) \end{array}$$

- Antsym(T,T',R): For any binary structure ra of type $Struc[Antsym(T,T',R)]$:

$$\begin{array}{ll} Struc[Antsym(T,T',R)] \triangleq & Rel \\ Pr[Antsym(T,T',R)](ra) \triangleq & \forall u : ra \ . \ R(fst(u), sec(fst(u))) \ \& \\ & \qquad R(sec(fst(u)), fst(u)) \supset \\ & \qquad (fst(u) =_T fst(sec(u))) \end{array}$$

The p-specifications $ITrans(T,T',R)$ (intransitivity) and $IRefl(T,T',R)$ (irreflexivity) are similar and will not be detailed here. It is easy to see that compound p-specifications can be added, based on the common structure $z : Rel$ in a p-specification denoted POR (for partial order relation) with z having the same meaning as above:

$$\begin{array}{ll} POR(T,T',R) & \triangleq Fusion(Refl(T,T',R), Trans(T,T',R), Antsym(T,T',R)) \\ Struc[POR(T,T',R)] \triangleq & Rel \\ Pr[POR(T,T',R)](z) \triangleq & Pr[Refl(T,T',R)](z) \ \& Pr[Trans(T,T',R)](z) \\ & \& \ Pr[Antsym(T,T',R)](z) \end{array}$$

Alternatively, a non-transitive relation[10] is described with the p-specification $z : Asym(T,T',R)$ (asymmetry) resulting from the p-specifications:

$$\begin{array}{ll} Asym(T,T',R) & \triangleq Fusion(IRefl(T,T',R), Antsym(T,T',R)) \\ Struc[Asym(T,T',R)] \triangleq & Rel \\ Pr[Asym(T,T',R)](z) \triangleq & Pr[IRefl(T,T',R)](z) \ \& \ Pr[Antsym(T,T',R)](z) \end{array}$$

An intransitive relation is described with a p-specification called ITR such that:

$$\begin{array}{ll} ITR(T,T',R) & \triangleq Fusion(Asym(T,T',R), ITrans(T,T',R)) \\ Struc[ITR(T,T',R)] \triangleq & Rel \\ Pr[ITR(T,T',R)](z) \triangleq & Pr[Asym(T,T',R)](z) \ \& \ Pr[ITrans(T,T',R)](z) \end{array}$$

[9]They are the implementation of respective operators π_1 and π_2.

[10]Neither transitive nor intransitive.

We easily introduce in a similar way the specification $IRT(PT, PT, PPartOf)$ (proper-part-of specification) by first introducing the asymmetric (therefore irreflexive) and transitive p-specification:

$$IRT(T, T', R) \triangleq \ Fusion(Asym(T, T', R), Trans(T, T', R))$$
$$Struc[IRT(T, T', R)] \triangleq \ Rel$$
$$Pr[IRT(T, T', R)](z) \triangleq \ Pr[Asym(T, T', R)](z) \ \& \ Pr[Trans(T, T', R)](z)$$

In [7] the authors argue that for different types of part-whole relations, different categories of entity types have to be related. Extending that assumption, we claim that successive distinctions between the relations can be made according to (i) the categories of the entity type participating in the relation and (ii) the formal properties that the type of part-of relation satisfies. Types are able to constrain the scope of individuals that appear within relations and to satisfy case (i), whereas case (ii) is addressed with p-specifications. Nevertheless, we adopt their taxonomy in which a first principal distinction is made between mereological and meronymic $part - of$ based on their transitivity property: the mereological part-of relation is transitive while the meronymic is not necessarily. For that purpose, we introduce in $Type_1$ the part-of specification denoted $POR(PT, PT, PartOf)$ while the meronymic part-whole ($mpart - of$) specification is referred to as $NTR(PT, PT, MPartOf)$. The latter admits, in its generic form, no transitive information. Argument types involved in part-whole structures include the categories of entities extracted from the DOLCE foundational ontology (e.g., PT for particulars, ED for endurants, POB for physical objects, etc.). All these categories belong to the universe $Type_1$ and satisfy the (Sub) subtyping rule: $ED \leq PT$, $PED \leq ED$, $POB \leq PED$, etc. Then it follows that the specifications are related to their respective p-specifications with the typing assertions:

$$POR(PT, PT, PartOf) \ : \ POR(T, T', R) \ \text{transitive PartOf}$$
$$NTR(PT, PT, MPartOf) : \ Asym(T, T', R) \ \text{non} - \text{transitive meronymicPartOf}$$
$$IRT(PT, PT, PPartOf) \ : \ IRT(T, T', R) \ \text{intransitive properPartOf}$$
$$ITR(PT, PT, MPartOf) \ : \ ITR(T, T', R) \ \text{intransitive meronymicPartOf}$$

For specifications another operation called subsumption extends the subtyping to the structure part of specifications while preserving the axiomatic part.

Definition 6 *(Subsumption of specifications) A specification $S(T_1, T_2, R)$ subsumes a specification $S'(T_1', T_2', R')$, i.e., $S'(T_1', T_2', R') \leq S(T_1, T_2, R)$, iff the following conditions are satisfied:*

(i) $Struc[S'(T_1', T_2', R')] \leq Struc[S(T_1, T_2, R)]$ *according to corollary (2)*
(ii) $\forall z' : Struc[S'(T_1', T_2', R')] \ . \ Pr[S'(T_1', T_2', R')](z') \supset Pr[S(T_1, T_2, R)](z)$

where z stand for objects of type $Struc[S(T_1, T_2, R)]$. As a consequence, a given specification can be extended and re-used in further specifications. This aspect is crucial for applying (p-)specifications to ontologies.

Definition 7 *A binary relation $R \triangleq \Sigma x : T_1 \ . \ \Sigma y : T_2 \ . \ P(x, y)$ subsumes a relation $R' \triangleq \Sigma x : T_1 \ . \ \Sigma y : T_2 \ . \ P'(x, y)$, i.e., P subsumes P' if the following rule holds:*

$$\Pi x : T_1 \ . \ \Pi y : T_2 \ . \ P'(x, y) \rightarrow P(x, y) \tag{4}$$

Lemma 3 *Given two specifications S and S' such that $Struc[S'(T'_1, T'_2, P')] \triangleq \Sigma x : T'_1 \,.\, \Sigma y : T'_2 \,.\, P'(x, y)$, $Struc[S(T_1, T_2, P)] \triangleq \Sigma x : T_1 \,.\, \Sigma y : T_2 \,.\, P(x, y)$, $T'_1 \leq T_1 \leq PT$, $T'_2 \leq T_2 \leq PT$ and P subsumes P', then $Struc[S'(T'_1, T'_2, R')] \leq Struc[S(T_1, T_2, R)]$.*

Proof. From corollary 2, we get $\Sigma x : T'_1 \,.\, \Sigma y : T'_2 \,.\, P'(x, y) \leq \Sigma x : T_1 \,.\, \Sigma y : T_2 \,.\, P'(x, y)$. Then applying rule (4) to the right member of this subtyping assertion, we obtain $\Sigma x : T'_1 \,.\, \Sigma y : T'_2 \,.\, P'(x, y) \leq Struc[S]$. □

As a consequence, if a specification S subsumes a specification S', then S' must satisfy all the axioms of S.

3. Working with Specifications

3.1. Exploiting the Axiomatic Part of Specifications

Let us consider a proof of a (transitive) part-of relation is given by checking its structure type $Struc[POR(PT, PT, PartOf)]$. Since this relation follows the specification $POR(PT, PT, PartOf)$, it is assumed to be transitive. Then, let us consider the pairs σ and σ' extracted from a knowledge base with the judgments:

$$\Gamma \vdash \sigma \;: (\Sigma x : Valve.\Sigma y : CarEngine.\ PartOf(x, y))$$
$$\Gamma \vdash \sigma' : (\Sigma x : CarEngine.\Sigma y : Car.\ PartOf(x, y))$$

These terms are of type $Struc[POR(PT, PT, PartOf)]$ since $CarEngine : POB$, $Valve : POB$, $Car : POB$ and since we have $POB \leq PED$, $PED \leq ED$ and $ED \leq PT$. Applying lemma (3) and provided that the specification $POR(PT, PT, PartOf)$ subsumes $POR(POB, POB, PartOf)$, the latter inherits the properties of former. The terms σ and σ' satisfying the structure of the specification $POR(PT, PT, PartOf)$ should satisfy the predicate of transitive relations $Pr[Trans(PT, PT, PartOf)](r)$ with r being the respective types of σ or σ'. If we obtain from the database the respective proof objects for σ and σ': $\langle ValveL1, \langle MyCarEngine, p_1\rangle\rangle$ and $\langle MyCarEngine, \langle MyCar, p_2\rangle\rangle$ with p_1 and p_2 the respective proofs of $PartOf(ValveL1, MyCarEngine)$ and $PartOf(MyCarEngine, MyCar)$. From axiom $Pr[Trans(PT, PT, PartOf)](r)$, the premises are proved $(fst(sec(\sigma)) =_{CarEngine} fst(\sigma') = MyCarEngine)$ then it yields a proof for $PartOf(ValveL1, MyCar)$ since we have simultaneously $PartOf(fst(\sigma), fst(sec(\sigma)))$ (with proof $PartOf(ValveL1, MyCarEngine)$) and $PartOf(fst(\sigma'), fst(sec(\sigma')))$ (with proof $PartOf(MyCarEngine, MyCar)$). Notice that since all structures and axioms are checked with concrete data (proof objects), then the realization of part-whole specifications depends entirely on objects.

3.2. Mereological Specifications

Let us consider the relation "involved in", whose domain is constrained to perdurants PD with $PD \leq PT$ and whose predicates are such that $PartOf$ subsumes $InvolvedIn$. Introducing a specification $involved - in$ such that $Struc[POR(PT, PT, PartOf)]$ subsumes $Struc[involved - in]$, we can assume from definition 6 that their specifications are also in the subsumption relation: $involved - in \leq POR(PT, PT, PartOf)$ and then, all properties of the specification POR apply with their argument types. For example, the data type $\Sigma x : Chewing.\Sigma y : Eating.InvolvedIn(x, y)$ is of type $\Sigma x : PD.\Sigma y : PD.InvolvedIn(x, y)$, then it satisfies the specification $involved - in$ and all its predicates are fulfilled.

Let us turn now to the "contained in" relation. It appears from [7] that it can be seen as an extension of the spatial part of relation described by the predicate $SpPartOf$ having two arguments of type region (R). From the ontology of particulars, we have $R \leq A$, $A \leq PT$ with R for region and A for abstract. Due to the transitivity of the subtyping relation, we derive $R \leq PT$. Then, provided that $PartOf$ subsumes $SpPartOf$, we introduce a specification $space - PO$ with:

$$Struc[space - PO] \triangleq \sum [R : Type_1, \quad SpPartOf : R \rightarrow R \rightarrow Prop\,]$$

such that: $Struc[space - PO] \leq Struc[POR(PT, PT, PartOf)]$. Then, the specification $POR(PT, PT, PartOf)$ subsumes the specification $space - PO$ and lemma 3 applies to them. The "contained in" relation requires a specification $contained - in$ that can be seen as an extension of the $space - PO$ specification with:

$$\begin{aligned} Struc[contained - in] &\triangleq \sum \begin{bmatrix} Spo : & Struc[space - PO], \\ has\_3D : ED \rightarrow Spo \rightarrow Prop \end{bmatrix} \\ Pr[contained - in](s) &\triangleq Pr[space - PO](fst(s)) \;\&\; Pr3D(s) \end{aligned}$$

for any s of type $Struc[contained - in]$ and for any binary structure z of type $Struc[contained - in]$, where sp abbreviates $Spo[s]$:

$$Pr3D(s) \triangleq \begin{array}{l} \forall u : sp\ \exists w, z : ED\ .\ has\_3D(w, fst(u))\ \& \\ \qquad\qquad\qquad\qquad has\_3D(z, fst(sec(u))) \supset \top \end{array}$$

The same definition applies to the specification $located - in$:

$$\begin{aligned} Struc[located - in] &\triangleq \sum \begin{bmatrix} Spo : & Struc[space - PO], \\ has\_2D : ED \rightarrow Spo \rightarrow Prop \end{bmatrix} \\ Pr[located - in](s) &\triangleq Pr[space - PO](fst(s)) \;\&\; Pr2D(s) \end{aligned}$$

with $Pr2D$ deduced from $Pr3D$ by substituting has_3D with has_2D.

3.3. Meronymic Specifications

Due to a lack of space, we describe only the relation "participates in" involving the predicate $ParticipatesIn$. The domain of $Struc[participates - in]$ is constrained to endurants ED and perdurants PD and it is a subtype of $MPartOf$ [7], then:

$$\Sigma x : ED.\Sigma y : PD.ParticipatesIn(x, y) \leq \Sigma x : PT.\Sigma y : PT.MPartOf(x, y)$$

Since the relation is intransitive, it requires the specification $ITR(PT, PT, MPartOf)$. Introducing the specification $participates - in$, it follows that: $Struc[participates - in] \leq Struc[ITR(PT, PT, MPartOf)]$. From definition 6, we deduce that the specification $ITR(PT, PT, MPartOf)$ subsumes the specification $participates - in$ and that all properties of the ITR specification can be applied. For example, let us consider

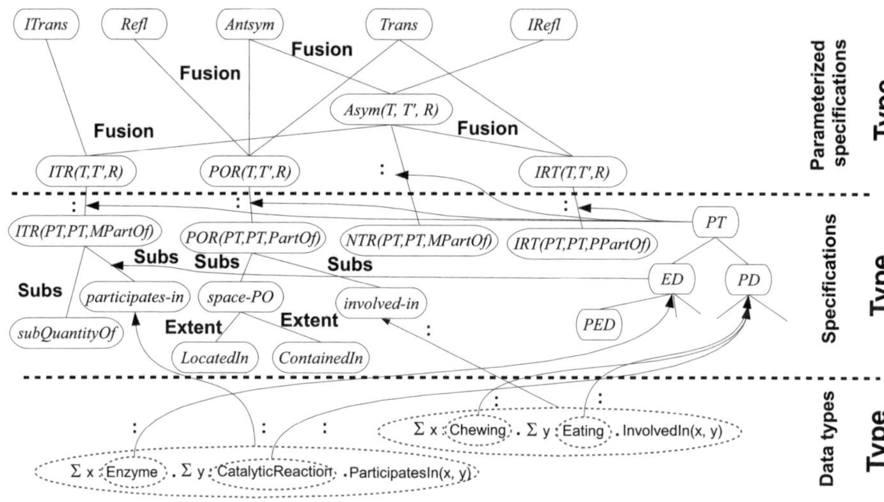

Figure 1. An excerpt of the formal ontology of part-whole p-specifications.

the enzyme (endurant) that participates in a catalytic reaction (process). This is described with of a sum type:

$$(\Sigma x : Enzyme \,.\, \Sigma y : CatalyticReaction \,.\, ParticipatesIn(x, y))$$

with $ParticipatesIn : Enzyme \rightarrow CatalyticReaction \rightarrow Prop$. This sum type is also of type $\Sigma x : ED.\Sigma y : PD.ParticipatesIn(x, y)$ since $Enzyme : ED$, $CatalyticReaction : PD$ and $ParticipatesIn : ED \rightarrow PD \rightarrow Prop$. The structure $\Sigma x : ED.\Sigma y : PD.ParticipatesIn(x, y)$ as a structure of a specification belongs to the universe $Type_1$. Specifications of $Type_1$ characterize data types of $Type_0$. The structure $\Sigma x : ED.\Sigma y : PD.ParticipatesIn(x, y)$ belongs to $Type_1$ because (i) some of its components belong to $Type_1$ and (ii) $Prop : Type_0$ is a valid judgment. Notice the polymorphism applied to the predicate $ParticipatesIn$ since its type is $ParticipatesIn : Enzyme \rightarrow CatalyticReaction \rightarrow Prop$ or one of its super-type: $ParticipatesIn : ED \rightarrow PD \rightarrow Prop$.

The formalization described so far results in a formal ontology of specifications for part-whole relations that is a formal version of the taxonomy given in [7] whose fragment is given on figure 1. Arrows labeled ":" denote "is-of-type" judgments while "subs" links address subsumed (p-)specifications. Arrows from the hierarchy of particulars to links between p-specifications correspond to instantiation of parameters. The design of the ontology of p-specifications in $Type_2$ and $Type_1$ is above the ontology designer's responsibility while the conceptualization problems in $Type_0$ concerns the user's part.

3.4. Example of Scenario

Let us consider an ontological fragment having the DOLCE categories (types) ED and PD that are subtypes of PT. It follows that $ED \leq PT$ and $PD \leq PT$. Then, if a user adds types Car and $CarChassis$ such that $Car : ED$ and $CarChassis$:

ED, he may suggest a part-of relation where $CarChassis$ is a part of Car. Since $Car : ED$, $CarChassis : ED$ and $ED \leq PT$, the structure of the specification $POR(PT, PT, PartOf)$ is satisfied, which means that it is logically correct to speak of part-of relation between $CarChassis$ and Car. In addition with $\sigma_1 \triangleq \Sigma x : CarChassis.\Sigma y : Car.PartOf(x, y)$, it is possible to automatically derive the inverse relation with the rule: $\Pi z : \sigma_1.HasPart(fst(sec(z)), fst(z))$.

Suppose now that the user tries to apply the $involved - in$ relation with the types Car and $CarChassis$ as in $\Sigma x : CarChassis.\Sigma y : Car.InvolvedIn(x, y)$. The type checking will reject such an assertion since Car and $CarChassis$ are not of type PD.

Another problem arises when arguments of a given relation are more general than those of its parent relation (highest in the hierarchy) [7]. For example, if the user has specified arguments of the respective type PD and PT for $PartOf$ and $involved - in$. In addition, he declares Car and $CarChassis$ as being of type PT, i.e., $CarChassis : PT$ and $Car : PT$. Therefore, we get a situation where the ontology of specifications expects that the following equation holds:

$$\Sigma x : PT.\Sigma y : PT.InvolvedIn(x, y) \leq \Sigma x : PD.\Sigma y : PD.PartOf(x, y)$$

Applying the corollary 2, it requires that $PT \leq PD$, which is contradictory to the DOLCE ontology of particulars. Then, the current configuration is logically inconsistent.

When a new specification (in $Type_1$) is introduced, this specification must fulfill some constraints (e.g., an intransitive relation is irreflexive). For instance, if the designer defines a $subquantity - of$ specification that is intransitive, then its p-specification (in $Type_2$) must be also irreflexive. Therefore, the choice could be $ITR(PT, PT, MPartOf)$ subsuming $subquantity - of$. An instance of the specification $subquantity - of$ is created and inserted into the knowledge base. By propagating this instance upwards in the ontology of specifications (see fig. 1), an instance of the p-specification $ITrans(T, T', R)$ is created, and the proofs of the desired property (i.e., intransitivity and irreflexivity) can be read off. As a consequence, if a $Type_1$-specification inherits of a specification which generates an incoherence at the $Type_2$ level, then either a constraint in $Type_2$ is relaxed (e.g., intransitivity) or the $Type_1$-specification is moved across the ontology until it inherits from correct properties.

4. Conclusion

Our primary motivation has been to provide a basis for the formal representation of properties of part-whole relations. The main idea is that, like an ontology of particulars, an ontology of p-specifications can be designed as well. Important topics have been addressed such as: (i) differentiation between $partOf$ and meronymic relations through p-specifications, (ii) $partOf$ relations can be unambiguously identified through their p-specifications while restricting the arguments of the relation for different types of part-whole relations and (iii) the unifying logical theory is able to provide the logical consistency of the user-defined structures. For that purpose, all constructors have computational support in a functional language. Horizontal inter-relations between the parts of a whole are also possible through p-specifications but are not explained here (see for example [16] for more details). Alternatively, p-specifications could help the automatic alignment of concepts by restricting the amount of possibilities due to the enhanced precision they offer. Nevertheless, the additional expressiveness upon enabling proper representation of part-whole properties comes at a cost of greater difficulty during the modeling stage since most people are not aware of type theory. One can go around this difficulty by providing guidance through a question answering process, decision diagrams, and drop-down boxes to facilitate selecting the appropriate relation and constraints. This is part of further work. Alternatively, an ongoing work includes the extension of an existing algorithm that has implemented dependent types for context-based reasoning [17].

References

[1] Keijzer A. and van de Keulen M., Information Integration - the process of integration, evolution and versioning, *Technical report*, no. 05-58, Centre for Telematics and Information Technology (CTIT), (2005).

[2] Baader F., Calvanese D., MCGuinness D., Nardi D. and Patel-Schneider P., *The Description Logic Handbook*. Cambridge University Press, 2003.

[3] Bittner T. and Donnelly M.: Computational ontologies of parthood, component hood, and containment, *Procs. of the Nineteenth International Joint Conference on Artificial Intelligence*, 382–387, (2005).

[4] Gerstl P. and Pribbenow S., Midwinters, end games, and body parts: a classification of partŰwhole relations. *Int. Journal of Human-Computer Studies*, **43**, 865–889, (1995).

[5] Artale A., Franconi E., Guarino N. and Pazzi L., Part-whole relations in object-centered systems: An overview. *Data & Knowledge Engineering*, **20**, 347–383, 1996.

[6] Varzi A. C., Spatial Reasoning and Ontology: Parts, Wholes, and Locations. *Handbook of Spatial Logics*, 945–1038, (2007).

[7] Keet C. M. and Artale A., Representing and reasoning over a taxonomy of partŰwhole relations. *Applied Ontology*, **3**, 91–110, (2008).

[8] Guarino N. and Welty C., A Formal Ontology of Properties. *in R. Dieng and O. Corby (Eds.): EKAW 2000*, LNAI 1937, 97–112, (2000).

[9] Luo Z., Computation and Reasoning. *International series of Monographs on Computer Science*, **11**, (1994).

[10] Bunge M.: Ontology I: The Furniture of the World. *Treatise on Basic Philosophy*, **3**, D. Reidel Publishing, (1977).

[11] Guizzardi G., Ontological foundations for structural conceptual models. *PhD Thesis*, Telematica Institute, Twente University, the Netherlands. (2005).

[12] McKinna J., Why dependent types matter, *SIGPLAN Not.*, **41**(1), (2006).

[13] Luo Z., An extended Calculus of Constructions. *PhD thesis*, University of Edimburgh, (1990).

[14] Lambek J. and Scott P.J., Introduction to higher order categorical logic. *Cambridge Studies in Advanced Mathematics*, (1994).

[15] Masolo C., Borgo S., Gangemi A., Guarino, N. and Oltramari, A. Ontology Library, *WonderWeb Deliverable D18 (ver.1.0, 31-12-2003)*, (2003).

[16] Dapoigny R. and Barlatier P., Towards an Ontological Modeling with Dependent Types: Application to part-whole Relations, *Procs. of the 28th International Conference on Conceptual Modeling*, LNCS 5829, 145–158, (2009).

[17] Barlatier P. and Dapoigny R., A Theorem Prover with Dependent Types for Reasoning about Actions. In *Frontiers in Artificial Intelligence and Applications (ECAI/STAIRS'08 Procs.)*, **179**, 12–23, (2008).

Formal Ontology in Information Systems
A. Galton and R. Mizoguchi (Eds.)
IOS Press, 2010

doi:10.3233/978-1-60750-535-8-59

Goals in a Formal Theory of Commonsense Psychology

Jerry R. HOBBS and Andrew GORDON
University of Southern California, Marina del Rey, California

Abstract.
In the context of developing formal theories of commonsense psychology, or how peole think they think, we have developed a formal theory of goals. In it we explicate and axiomatize, among others, the goal-related notions of trying, success, failure, functionality, intactness, and importance.

Keywords. Goals, commonsense psychology, commonsense reasoning, intention

Introduction

While robots today are capable of remarkable physical action, their capabilities in simulating or interpreting human cognitive behavior is considerably more limited. In this paper, we present a step toward resolving this problem in the form of an inferential theory of human goals, authored in first order logic. This theory is part of a larger effort to formalize a broad range of commonsense inferences related to human psychology [17], and supplements previously published reports on theories of human memory and emotions [9,18]. These papers describe the empirical grounding of this work in linguistic data and in people's descriptions of their strategies [8]. The set of concepts surrounding the idea of a goal turned out to be among the most important areas of commonsense psychology. Goals are central not just in our work but traditionally in the philosophy of mind, in psychology, and in work in artificial intelligence on belief-desire-intention (BDI) models of agents.

Section 1 of this paper briefly reviews some of the vast literature in this area, especially in psychology. In Section 2 we present succinctly the notational and ontological background required to get an enterprise like this off the ground. In Sections 3 through 8 we explicate and axiomatize the concepts of goal and a number of significant concepts that depend on goals.

1. The Psychology of Goals

One of the predominant themes in our research is to underscore the difference between cognitive models and inferential theories. In developing an inferential theory of human goals, our aim is not to characterize the actual cognitive mechanisms in which goals affect human behavior. Instead, our interest is in characterizing the commonsense infer-

Corresponding Author: Jerry R. Hobbs, Information Sciences Institute, University of Southern California, Marina del Rey, California; E-mail: hobbs@isi.edu.

ences that people make when they are thinking about their own goals and those of others. We are less interested in the way people actually think than in the way people think they think. These non-scientific models of mental states and processes are historically and often pejoratively referred to as naive psychology or folk psychology. But the proper characterization of these inferential theories is itself a scientific endeavor. Our efforts may be as relevant to the engineering of human-computer systems as psychological models of human cognition. Given the relevance of cognitive models of human goals to inferential theories of goals, we highlight some trends in the psychology of goals.

Eccles and Wigfield [3] review the historical progression of theories of human motivation beginning with Atkinson's [1] expectancy-value theory, which proposes that motivation and effort are the combined result of people's expectations of success and the value that they attach to that success. Following Atkinson, Weiner [25] proposed attribution theory, which emphasized an individual's interpretations of their achievement outcomes in motivation over motivational dispositions or actual outcomes. Weiner's model defines achievement attributions, including ability, effort, task difficulty, and luck, along the three dimensions of locus of control, stability of causes, and controllability of causes. Contemporary theories within these traditions are the subject of a recent edited volume on the psychology of goals [21].

A separate line of psychology research has focused on characterizing the goals that are the target of individual's achievement attributions. Ford and Nichols [5,6] characterized 24 types of achievement goals, ranging from within-person goals of happiness and intellectual creativity to person-environment goals of social responsibility and material gain. To develop a more all-encompassing taxonomy of human goals, Chulef et al. [2] identified 135 achievement goals in previous research on developing comprehensive categories, including Murray's list of 44 variables of personality [22], Rokeach's 18 instrumental and 18 terminal values [23], and 56 goals from the study of Wicker et al. [26]. They then developed a hierarchical organization of 135 goals by having different populations of subjects sort these these goals into conceptually similar groups.

2. Notational and Ontological Background

In order to deal with a domain as complex as commonsense psychology, including goals, one must build up a great deal of conceptual and notational infrastructure and make a large number of warranted but highly controversial decisions about representation. We have done that, and we cite the relevant papers below as appropriate. In this presentation of the necessary background, we do not present the arguments in favor of our decisions; the interested reader can consult the references. Citations of the appropriate literature in these areas occur there as well. It is important to note that while we are driven in our theory construction by the need to capture concepts that occur in the data we analyzed, the theories themselves cannot follow that data slavishly, but must be constructed in as workable and elegant fashion as possible.

The concepts we introduce in the background theories and the commonsense psychology theories are often not *defined*, but are rather *characterized*, by richly axiomatizing the concept and thereby constraining the possible interpretations of the corresponding predicate. For example, we do not attempt to define `cause`, but we do encode its defeasible transitivity and make it available for expressing causal knowledge in many specific domain theories.

The domain of discourse is the class of possible individual entities, states, and events. They may or may not exist in the real world, and if they do, it is one of their properties, expressed as `(Rexist x)`. (Throughout this paper we use a subset of the notational conventions of Common Logic.) In a narrowly focused inquiry it is often most perspicuous to utilize specialized notations for the concepts under consideration. But our view is that in a broad-based effort like ours, this is not possible, and that it can be avoided by sufficient judicious use of reification.

For example, we treat sets as first-class individuals. Moreover, sets are taken to have "type elements", whose principal feature is that their properties are inherited by the real elements of the sets [13,16].

The term "eventuality" is used to cover both states and events [11,14]. Eventualities like other individuals can be merely possible or can really exist in the real world. We can speak of the "arguments" of eventualities or the participants in the states or events. The expression `(arg* x e)`, for example, says that `x` is a direct argument of `e` or an `arg*` of an eventuality argument of `e`. We have axiomatized a theory of time [19], and eventualities can have temporal properties. Thus, `(atTime e t)` says that eventuality `e` occurs at time `t`.

Eventualities are very finely individuated. For example, Pat's flying to Toronto and Pat's going to Toronto are two different eventualities. However, they are closely related by a relation we call `gen` (for "generates"). The principal property of this relation is that if `(gen e1 e2)` and `e1` really exists, then so does `e2`. It says that Pat's going occurs by virtue of the fact that Pat's flying occurs; the flying constitutes the going.

Eventualities can have type elements of sets as their arguments, and when they do, they are eventuality types. An `instanceOf` relation relates eventuality types and tokens. A notational convention we use is that whereas the expression `(p x)` says that predicate `p` is true of `x`, the expression `(p' e x)` says that `e` is the eventuality of `p` being true of `x`. The relation between the primed and unprimed predicates is given by the axiom schema

```
(forall (x)
   (iff (p x)(exist (e)(and (p' e x)(Rexist e)))))
```

We have posted our development of a number of the necessary background theories at [16]. They include, in addition to theories of sets, eventualities, and time, a theory of composite entities, or things made of other things, a theory of change of state, and a theory of causality (cf. also [15]). The key distinction in the theory of causality is between the monotonic notion of a "causal complex", which includes all the eventualities that need to happen or hold for the effect to occur, and the nonmonotonic or defeasible notion of "cause", which is the context-dependent eventuality which is viewed somehow as central in the causal complex. The principal properties of a causal complex are that if the whole complex really exists, then so does the effect, and that every eventuality in the causal complex is relevant to the effect in a sense that can be made precise. Elements of a causal complex other than the cause are said to "enable" the effect. (The use of the concept of "cause" is sometimes taken to be controversial, but it is so pervasive in commonsense reasoning it seems to us indispensible in this enterprise.)

Agents have beliefs. We take the objects of belief to be eventualities. Because eventualities are very finely individuated, there is a straightforward translation between talking of belief in an eventuality and belief in a proposition. Thus, the expression `(believe a e)` can be read as saying that agent `a` believes the proposition that eventuality `e` really exists. We have developed but not published our treatment of belief, but our use of the predicate here should be obvious and unproblematic.

Mutual belief figures in several places below. The chief inferences associated with mutual belief are that if a set `s` of agents mutually believes `e`, then they mutually believe they mutually believe it, and every member of `s` believes it.

Any treatment of commonsense knowledge requires a mechanism for defeasibility. We are assuming in our work that a system using weighted abduction would be applied to the set of axioms. We indicate the defeasibility of a rule by including the conjunct `(etc)` in the antecedent of implications. It is really an abbreviation of a predication unique to that axiom of the form `(etc-i x y ...)`. It can be thought of as the negation of the abnormality predicates in circumscription [20]. It should be straightforward to translate these indications of defeasibility into the formalisms required by other adequate approaches to nonmonotonicity.

3. Goals, Subgoals, and Plans

Human beings are intentional agents. We have goals, we develop plans for achieving these goals, and we execute the plans. We monitor the executions to see if things are turning out the way we anticipated, and when they don't, we modify our plans and execute the new plans. The concept of a goal is central to this formulation.

A theory of goals and planning can be applied not just to people but also to other entities that can be conceived of as agents, such as organizations and complex artifacts. In fact, it is a not uncommon cognitive move among people to attribute such agency even to natural phenomena like trees, volcanos and hurricanes. Anything that seems to exploit and manipulate the causal structure of the world as a means toward some supposed end can be and often is viewed as a planning mechanism.

The key concept in modeling intentional behavior is that of an agent `a` having some eventuality type `e` as a goal. The expression `(goal e a)` says that eventuality `e` is a goal of agent `a`. Normally, `e` will be an eventuality type that can be satisfied by any number of specific eventuality tokens, but it is entirely possible in principle for an agent to have an eventuality token as a goal, where there is only one satisfactory way for things to work out. We won't belabor the distinction here.

Agents know facts about what causes or enables what in the world, in most cases, facts of the form

```
(forall (e1 x)
   (if (p' e1 x)
       (exist (e2)(and (q' e2 x)(cause e1 e2)))))

(forall (e1 x)
   (if (p' e1 x)
       (exist (e2)(and (q' e2 x)(enable e1 e2)))))
```

That is, if `e1` is the eventuality of `p` being true of some entities `x`, then there is an eventuality `e2` that is the eventuality of `q` being true of `x` and `e1` causes or enables `e2`. Or stated in a less roundabout way, `p` causes or enables `q`.

The agent uses these rules to plan to achieve goals, and also uses them to infer the goals and plans of other agents. A plan is an agent's way of manipulating the causal properties of the world to achieve goals, and these axioms express causal properties.

We will work step by step toward a characterization of the planning process. The first version of the axiom we need says that if agent a has a goal e2 and e1 causes e2, then a will also have e1 as a goal.

```
(forall (a e1 e2)
   (if (and (goal e2 a)(cause e1 e2))(goal e1 a)))
```

This is not a bad rule, and certainly is defeasibly true, but it is of course necessary for the agent to actually believe in the causality, and if the agent believes a causal relation that does not hold, e1 may nevertheless be adopted as a goal. The causal relation needn't be true.

```
(forall (a e0 e1 e2)
   (if  (and (goal e2 a)(cause' e0 e1 e2)(believe a e0))
        (goal e1 a)))
```

We can say furthermore that the very fact that a has goal e2 causes a to have goal e1. We do this by reifying the eventuality g2 that e2 is a goal of a's, and similarly g1. (The e's in this axiom are the eventualities of having something; the g's are the eventualities of wanting it.)

```
(forall (a e0 e1 e2 g2)
   (if (and (goal' g2 e2 a)(cause' e0 e1 e2)(believe a e0))
       (exist (g1)(and (goal' g1 e1 a)(cause g2 g1)))))
```

That is, if agent a wants e2 and believes e1 causes e2, that wanting will cause a to want e1. (The belief is also in g1's causal complex, but that would not normally be thought of as the cause: Why do you want e2? Because I want e1.)

Note that while the antecedent and the consequent no longer assert the real existence of having the goal (i.e., g2 and g1), if we know that g2 really exists, then the real existence of g1 follows from the properties of "cause".

Note also that the predicate goal reverses causality. For example, because flipping a light switch causes a light to go on, having the goal of the light being on causes one to want to flip the switch.

The eventuality e1 is a "subgoal" of e2 for a, and we can encode this in the axiom.

```
(forall (a e0 e1 e2 g2)
   (if (and (goal' g2 e2 a)(cause' e0 e1 e2)(believe a e0))
       (exist (g1)
          (and (goal' g1 e1 a)(cause g2 g1)(subgoal e1 e2 a)))))
```

Finally, this axiom is not always true. There may be many ways to cause the goal condition to come about, and the mystery of the agent's free choice intervenes. The axiom is only defeasible. We can represent this by means of an "et cetera" proposition in the antecedent.

```
(forall (a e0 e1 e2 g2)
   (if (and (goal' g2 e2 a)(cause' e0 e1 e2)(believe a e0)(etc))
       (exist (g1)
          (and (goal' g1 e1 a)(cause g2 g1)(subgoal e1 e2 a)))))
```

That is, if agent a has a goal e2 (where g2 is the eventuality of wanting e2) and a believes e1 causes e2, then defeasibly this wanting e2 will cause a to want e1 as a subgoal of e2 (where g1 is the eventuality of wanting e1).

A similar succession of axioms can be written for enablement.

In the STRIPS terminology of Fikes and Nilsson [4], the enabling conditions are the prerequisites of the plan operator, and the cause is the body.

The "subgoal" relation is a relation between two goals, and implies the agent's belief that the subgoal is in a causal complex for the goal.

```
(forall (e1 e2 a)
   (if (subgoal e1 e2 a)
       (and (goal e2 a)(goal e1 a)
            (exist (e3 e4 e5 s)
               (and (causalComplex' e3 s e2)(member' e4 e2 s)
                    (and' e5 e3 e4)(believe a e5))))))
```

In lines 5-6 of this axiom, e3 is the proposition that s is a causal complex for e2, e4 is the proposition that e2 is a member of s, e5 is the conjunction of these two propositions, and that's what agent a believes.

The "subgoal" relation is transitive.

```
(forall (e1 e2 e3 a)
   (if (and (subgoal e1 e2 a)(subgoal e2 e3 a))
       (subgoal e1 e3 a)))
```

It will be useful below to state that if one believes he or she has a goal, then defeasibly he or she really does have the goal. Though not always true, we are usually pretty reliable about knowing what we want.

```
(forall (e e1 a)
   (if (and (goal' e e1 a)(believe a e))
       (Rexist e)))
```

However, it is possible for an agent to have a goal without knowing it.

Goals do not have to be directly achievable by actions on the part of the agent, but successful plans have to bottom out in such actions or in states or events that will happen or hold at the appropriate time anyway.

4. Kinds of Goals

The most central cluster of goal-related concepts we discovered was a set of 27 concepts that characterized variations in the types of goals that people pursue, for example, "knowledge goals" as indicated by expressions such as "desire to understand, "curious", "curiosity", "inquisitive", and "nosiness". All of these types of goals can be defined in the machinery we have built up here and in our background theories. For example, a goal of knowing something, important because most actions have knowledge prerequisites, can be defined in our framework by the axiom

```
(forall (e a)
   (iff (knowledgeGoal e a)
        (exist (e1) (and (goal e1 a)(know' e1 a e)))))
```

Similarly, you can have a goal to envision a situation in a certain manner, a goal to plan in a certain manner, or a goal to execute a plan in a certain manner.

Using our theory of time, we are also able to define goals to preserve situations, violations of such goals, goals that persist over time, goals that are achieved by a particular time, goals that are not achieved by some particular time, and goals that are never achieved. We are able to define conflicting goals and auxilliary goals that may be given up in the face of conflicts.

Individual persons are not the only kind of intentional agent. Sufficiently complex devices of various sorts can be viewed as intelligent agents. So can collectives of agents, whether collectives entirely of people, or assemblages of people and devices. These collectives can have goals. For example, General Motors has the goal of selling cars. They can devise plans for achieving goals. General Motors' plan involves manufacturing and marketing cars. These plans must bottom out in the actions of individual persons or devices, or in things that will be true at the appropriate time anyway.

For example, we can have a plan to get your car started by pushing it a short distance to the top of a hill and then letting it pick up speed on the downhill side until it is fast enough that you can pop the clutch. This plan bottoms out in my individual action of pushing on the back of the car and your individual action of pushing on the frame of the open left door. Of course these actions have to be synchronized, but these are properties of the individual actions. The plan also bottoms out in the event of the car rolling down the hill from the top. This is something that will happen anyway at the appropriate time, and doesn't have to be carried out by any member of the collective.

A shared or collaborative goal is a goal where the agent having the goal is a collective (cf. [24,12]). Moreover, the members of the collective mutually believe the collective has the goal.

```
(forall (e s e1)
   (iff (sharedGoal' e e1 s)
        (exist (e0)
           (and (goal' e0 e1 s)(mb s e0)(gen e e0)
                (forall (x)(if (member x s)(agent x)))))))
```

Since mutual belief implies belief and since if you believe you have a goal then you do really do have the goal, it follows that the individual members of s have e1 as a goal.

We can similarly define competitive goals and adversarial goals.

5. Trying, Succeeding, and Failing

When we try to bring about some goal, we devise at least a partial plan to achieve it, including subgoals of the original goal which are actions on our part, and we execute some of those subgoals. Moreover, our executing those actions is a direct result of our having those actions as subgoals. We can take this as a definition of "trying".

```
(forall (e a e1)
   (iff (try' e a e1)
        (exist (e0 e2 e3 e4)
           (and (goal e1 a)(subgoal' e3 e2 e1 a)
                (instanceOf e4 e2)(Rexist' e0 e4)
                (agentOf a e4)(cause e3 e0)(gen e e0)))))
```

In this definition, e is the eventuality of an agent a trying to do e1. The eventuality (or eventuality type) e1 is a goal of a's; it's what a tries to do. The eventuality type e2 is a subgoal of e1, and a is the agent in action e4 which is an instance of e2. In the expression (Rexist' e0 e4), e0 refers to the actual occurrence or execution of the action e4 by a. The expression (cause e3 e0) says that a's having the subgoal e2 causes a to actually do e2. The expression (gen e e0) says that the actual doing (e0) constitutes the trying (e). That is, a tries to do e1 exactly when a executes a subgoal e2 of e1 precisely because it is a subgoal.

For example, suppose you want to pass a course. An important subgoal would be to study for the final. If you study for the final precisely because it will help you pass the course, then you are trying to pass the course.

It follows that if you try to do something e1, then you perform some action or actions in a causal complex whose effect is an instance of e1.

```
(forall (a e1)
   (if (try a e1)
       (exist (s e2 e3)
          (and (instanceOf e3 e1)(causalComplex s e3)
               (member e2 s)(agentOf a e2)(Rexist e2)))))
```

This is not sufficient as a definition of trying. The causal role of having e2 as a subgoal is necessary in the definition of try. Suppose Pat wants to meet Chris. One way for that to happen is for them to run into each other someday. Now Pat is driving to the grocery store where Chris, unbeknownst to Pat, is currently shopping. Pat's driving to the grocery store is an element of a causal complex leading to the two of them meeting. But we wouldn't say that Pat's driving to the grocery store constitutes an attempt to meet Chris. That wasn't his intent in driving.

We can talk about trying and failing at a seemingly executable action, as in "He tried to lift his arm." But we are refining the granularity and viewing the action as a composite, e.g., in which the first subaction is willing the motion.

Note that this explication of trying allows for an agent to try to achieve conflicting goals. The student who studies for a final and then goes out drinking the whole night before the final may be doing just that.

To succeed at some goal is to try to do it and to have that trying cause the goal to actually occur.

```
(forall (e a e1)
   (iff (succeed' e a e1)
        (exist (e0 e2 e3)
           (and (try' e2 a e1)(instanceOf e3 e1)(cause e2 e3)
                (Rexist' e0 e3)(gen e e0)))))
```

Here, e2 is the attempt, e1 is ultimate goal, e3 is the specific instance of e1 that occurs, e is the success in achieving the goal, and e0 is the actual occurrence of the instance of the goal. The expression (gen e e0) says that the actual occurrence e0 constitutes the event e of succeeding.

Succeeding implies trying. The converse, sadly, is not true.

To fail at some goal is to try to do it and for it not to actually occur.

```
(forall (a e1)
   (iff (fail a e1)
        (and (try a e1)
             (not (exist (e2)
                     (and (instanceOf e2 e1)(Rexist e2)))))))
```

There is space between succeeding and failing. One can try to achieve something and that something can come about but not because of one's efforts. In that case, the agent has lucked out, rather than having succeeded. So a student who studied for the final but nevertheless got a 0 on it, but passed the course because the professor gave everyone an A as a political protest, wouldn't be said to have succeeded at passing the course.

6. Functionality

Complex artifacts are generally constructed for some purpose. Some real or hypothetical agent has a goal in mind, and the artifact achieves that goal. Cars, for example, have at least the purpose of moving us from place to place. The structure of complex artifacts typically reflects a plan to achieve the goal, where the various components are involved in some subgoal. For example, the steering wheel of a car is involved in the subgoal of having the car go in particular directions. We will call such a subgoal the functionality of the component. Organizations and their components can be analyzed similarly.

In fact natural objects can too, if we associate a hypothetical agent having as a goal the normal behavior the natural object tends to engage in. We can stipulate that the "goal" associated with a tree is to grow and reproduce, and we can analyze the structure of the tree as an instantiation of a plan to achieve that goal. We can then talk about the function of the various parts of the tree. We can even view volcanos, for example, as composite entities with the "goal" of erupting, and talk about the functions of its parts to this end.

In general, almost any composite entity can be associated with a goal by some hypothetical agent, and where components are causally involved with the behavior of the whole, we can view the relation between an action by the component and the behavior of the whole as a "subgoal" relation. We can then define the functionality of the component as that "subgoal" relation.

Plans to achieve goals are just a way of exploiting the causal structure of the world to achieve some end, so "goal talk" can be imported into any domain where the manipulation or exploitation of causal structure is involved.

A composite entity that goes through changes can be viewed as having as a goal some element or subset of those changes. We will define that "goal" as the functionality of the whole. We call this predicate `functionality0` because it is absolute functionality, not the functionality of a component relative to the behavior of the whole.

```
(forall (x e)
   (if (and (compositeEntity x)(changeIn' e x))
       (iff (functionality0 e x)
            (exist (e2 e3 a))
               (and (goal' e2 e a)(agent' e3 a)(imply e3 e2)))))
```

Line 2 says that `x` is a composite entity and `e` is one of `x`'s behaviors. Under these conditions, `e` is a functionality of `x` if and only if there is some possible agent `a` whose existence would imply that `e` is a goal of `a`'s. The roundabout formulation in line 5 is a way of allowing hypothetical agents. In any positive modality in which `a` exists, `a` will have goal `e`.

If a component has some property or engages in some behavior that is in a causal complex for the functionality of the composite entity as a whole, we can say that property or behavior is the functionality of the component with respect to the `functionality0` of the whole.

```
(forall (e1 y e x)
   (iff (functionality e1 y e x)
        (exist (s)
           (and (functionality0 e x)(causalComplex s e1)
                (member e1 s)(arg* y e1)(componentOf y x)))))
```

The expression (functionality e1 y e x) says that e1 is the functionality of y with respect to behavior e by composite entity x, of which y is a component. Because of the close connection between the subgoal relation and causal complexes, functionality can be viewed as a close analog of the subgoal relation.

A component is "intact" if it is able to fulfill its functionality. That is, there are no properties of the component that would cause the functionality not to occur.

```
(forall (x)
   (iff (intact x)
        (forall (e1 y e)
           (if (functionality e1 y e x)
               (not (exist (e2 e3)
                       (and (arg* y e2)(not' e3 e1)
                            (cause e2 e3)))))))))
```

7. Thriving

It is formally convenient to assume that agents have one plan that they are always developing, executing, monitoring and revising, and that that plan is in the service of a single goal. We will call this goal "Thriving".

```
(forall (a)
   (if (agent a)
       (exist (e)(and (goal e a)(thrive' e a)))))
```

More specific goals arise out of the planning process using the agents' beliefs about what will cause them to thrive.

The main reason for positing this top-level goal is that now instead of worrying about the mysterious process by which an agent comes to have goals, we can address the planning problems of what eventualities the agent believes cause other eventualities, including the eventuality of thriving, and of what alternative subgoals the agent should choose to achieve particular goals. We are still left with the problem of when one goal should be given priority over another, but this is now a plan construction issue.

We will not attempt to say what constitutes thriving in general, because there are huge differences among cultures and individuals. For most of us, thriving includes staying alive, breathing, and eating, as well as having pleasurable experiences. But many agents decide they thrive best when their social group thrives, and that may involve agents sacrificing themselves. This is a common view in all cultures, as seen in suicide bombers, soldiers going into battle in defense of their country, and people risking death to rescue accident victims. So thriving does not necessarily imply surviving.

Similarly, a man may decide that he is in so much pain that the best way to thrive is to kill himself. In contrast, a religious ascetic may decide that the best way to achieve the long-term goal of eternal life is to live in pain.

A good theory of commonsense psychology should not attempt to define thriving, but it should provide the materials out of which the beliefs of various cultures and individuals can be stated in a formal manner.

8. Importance

In [16] we define scales in terms of partial orderings. Many scales, including the scale of importance, cannot be defined precisely, but constraints can be placed on their partial ordering. That is what we will do here.

A concept, entity or eventuality is more or less important to an agent depending on its relation to the agent's goals. The "more important" relation is thus a partial ordering that depends on the agent.

```
(forall (x1 x2 a)
   (if (moreImportant x1 x2 a)(and (neq x1 x2)(agent a))))
```

The expression (moreImportant x1 x2 a) says that something x1 is more important than something else x2 to agent a. We place no constaints on the things x1 and x2 whose importance is being measured. They can be anything.

The "more important" relation is, at least defeasibly, transitive.

```
(forall (x1 x2 x3 a)
   (if (and (moreImportant x1 x2 a)(moreImportant x2 x3 a))
       (moreImportant x1 x3 a)))
```

An agent proceeds through the world by continually developing, executing and modifying a plan to achieve the top-level goal "To Thrive", All of the agent's actions can be seen as subgoals in this plan; when the actions are dysfunctional, we can see them as part of a plan based on false beliefs about what will result in thriving. A plan can be thought of as a tree-like structure representing the subgoal relation. The higher a goal is in a plan, the more important it is, because of the greater amount of replanning that has to be done if the goal is not to be achieved. So the first constraint we can place on the importance scale is that it is consistent with the subgoal relation.

However, this is a bit tricky to specify because an eventuality can be a subgoal of a number of different higher-level goals in the same plan, and we do not want to say an eventuality is of little importance simply because one of its supergoals is of little importance. So we first need to define the notions of an "upper bound supergoal" and a "least upper bound supergoal". An eventuality e1 is an upper bound supergoal of e2 if it is a supergoal of all of e2's immediate supergoals. More precisely, any supergoal of e2's must either be e1, be a subgoal of e1, or be a supergoal of e1. It will be convenient to define the upper bound for a set of subgoals.

```
(forall (e1 s a)
   (iff (ubSupergoal e1 s a)
        (and (agent a)(goal e1 a)
             (forall (e2) (if (member e2 s)(subgoal e2 e1 a)))
             (forall (e2 e)
                 (if (and (member e2 s)(subgoal e2 e a))
                     (or (subgoal e e1 a)(eq e e1)
                         (subgoal e1 e a)))))))
```

The expression (ubSupergoal e1 s a) says that e1 is an upper bound supergoal of all the goals of agent a in set s. Lines 3-4 specify the conditions on the arguments of the predicate. The predicate holds if and only if any eventuality e which is a supergoal of a member e1 of s is either a subgoal of e1, e1 itself, or a supergoal of e1.

A goal e1 is a least upper bound supergoal if it is an upper bound supergoal and a subgoal of all other upper bound supergoals.

```
(forall (e1 s a)
   (iff (lubSupergoal e1 s a)
        (and (ubSupergoal e1 s a)
             (forall (e)
                (if (ubSupergoal e s a)
```

```
                    (or (eq e e1)(subgoal e1 e)))))))
```

Because every goal is ultimately in the service of the top-level goal "To Thrive", every goal has a least upper bound supergoal.

Now we can say that if eventuality e1 dominates eventuality e2 on every path in the agent's plan that includes e2, then e1 is more important than e2. Every reason for wanting e2 is in the service of e1.

```
(forall (s e1 e2 a)
   (if (and (singleton s e2)(lubSupergoal e1 s a))
       (moreImportant e1 e2 a)))
```

More generally,we can say that the least upper bound supergoal of a set of goals is more important than the whole set, since all the members of the set are in the service of the supergoal.

```
(forall (s e a)
   (if (lubSupergoal e s a)(moreImportant e s a)))
```

An agent's goals are important. So are eventualities that affect the agent's goals. Importance doesn't care about polarity; if passing a course is important to you, so is not passing the course. Thus, we define an eventuality as "goal-relevant" to an agent if its existence implies the existence or nonexistence of one of the agent's goals.

```
(forall (e a)
   (iff (goalRelevant e a)
        (exist (e1)
           (and (goal e1 a)
                (or (imply e e1)
                    (exist (e2)(and (not' e2 e1)(imply e e2))))))))
```

The "goal consequences" of an eventuality are those goals of the agent's whose existence or nonexistence is implied by by the eventuality.

```
(forall (s e a)
   (iff (goalConsequences s e a)
        (forall (e1)
           (iff (member e1 s)
                (and (goal e1 a)
                     (or (imply e e1)
                         (exist (e2)
                            (and (not' e2 e1)(imply e e2))))))))))
```

Then we can say the importance of an eventuality depends on the importance of its goal consequences. The first of the following axioms says that if something x is more important than the goal consequences of eventuality e, then it is more important than e. The second axiom says the opposite.

```
(forall (x s e a)
   (if (and (moreImportant x s a)(goalConsequences s e a))
       (moreImportant x e a)))
```

```
(forall (x s e a)
   (if (and (moreImportant s x a)(goalConsequences s e a))
       (moreImportant e x a)))
```

In a more complete theory of importance, we would relate the importance of an eventuality to its effect on the likelihood of the agent's goals obtaining or not.

The importance of an entity depends on the importance of its properties and of the events it participates in. Thus, we define the set of "goal-relevant properties".

```
(forall (s x a)
   (iff (grProps s x a)
        (forall (e)
           (iff (member e s)
                (and (arg* x e)(goalRelevant e a))))))
```

The expression `(grProps s x a)` says that the set `s` of properties of `x` are relevant to a goal of `a`'s.

The next two axioms say that the importance of an entity depends on the importance of its goal-relevant properties.

```
(forall (s x a)
   (if (and (moreImportant x1 s a)(grProps s x2 a))
       (moreImportant x1 x2 a)))

(forall (s x a)
   (if (and (moreImportant s x1 a)(grProps s x2 a))
       (moreImportant x2 x1 a)))
```

To summarize, `x1` is more important than `x2` to `a` if `x2` is, or affects something that is, or has properties that affect something that is, in the service of `x1`. Note that there may be other properties constraining the `moreImportant` relation, but this one at least is among the most significant.

9. Summary

In this paper we have developed a formal treatment of an agent's goals. We have shown how a variety of goal-relevant concepts that arise in natural language and in strategic planning can be explicated in terms of this. Moreover, we have provided at least a first pass at axiomatically characterizing such concepts as trying, succeeding, failing, functionality, intactness, and importance. These concepts are critical in modeling human behavior and also in the development of more human-like computational agents.

Acknowledgments

This research was supported in part by the Office of Naval Research, under Contract No. N00014-09-1-1029 and Contract No. NOOO14-09-C-0613.

References

[1] Atkinson, J. (1964) *An introduction to motivation*, Princeton, NJ: Van Nostrand.

[2] Chulef, A., Read, S., and Walsh, D. (2001) A hierarchical taxonomy of human goals. *Motivation and Emotion* 25(3):191-232.

[3] Eccles, J. and Wigfield, A. (2002) Motivation beliefs, values, and goals. *Annual Review of Psychology* 2002(53):109-32.

[4] Fikes, R., and Nilsson N. (1971) STRIPS: A new approach to the application of theorem proving to problem solving, *Artificial Intelligence*, 2: 189-208.

[5] Ford, M. (1992) *Human motivation: Goals, emotions, and personal agency beliefs*. Newbury Park, CA: Sage.

[6] Ford, M. and Nichols, C. (1987) A taxonomy of human goals and some possible application. In M. Ford and D. Ford (Eds.) *Humans as self-constructing living systems: Putting the framework to work*, pp.289-311. Hillsdale, NJ: Erlbaum.

[7] Gordon, A. (2002) The Theory of Mind in Strategy Representations. *Proceedings*, Twenty-fourth Annual Meeting of the Cognitive Science Society (CogSci-2002), George Mason University, Aug 7-10. Mahwah, NJ: Lawrence Erlbaum Associates.

[8] Gordon, A. (2004) *Strategy Representation: An Analysis of Planning Knowledge*. Mahwah, NJ: Lawrence Erlbaum Associates.

[9] Gordon, A. and Hobbs, J. (2003) Coverage and Competency in Formal Theories: A Commonsense Theory of Memory. *Proceedings*, 2003 AAAI Spring Symposium on Logical Formalizations of Commonsense Reasoning, Stanford University, March 24-26, 2003.

[10] Gordon, A., Kazemzadeh, A., Nair, A., and Petrova, M. (2003) Recognizing Expressions of Commonsense Psychology in English Text. *Proceedings*, 41st Annual Meeting of the Association for Computational Linguistics (ACL-2003) Sapporo, Japan, July 7-12, 2003.

[11] Hobbs, J. (1985) Ontological promiscuity, *Proceedings*, 23rd Annual Meeting of the Association for Computational Linguistics, Chicago, Illinois: 61-69.

[12] Hobbs, J. (1990) Artificial intelligence and Collective intentionality, in P. Cohen, J. Morgan, and M. Pollack, *Intentions in Communication*, Cambridge: MIT Press: 445-460.

[13] Hobbs, J. (1995) Monotone decreasing quantifiers in a scope-free logical form, in K. van Deemter and S. Peters (Eds.), *Semantic Ambiguity and Underspecification*, CSLI Lecture Notes No. 55, Stanford, California: 55-76.

[14] Hobbs, J. (2003) The logical notation: Ontological promiscuity, `http://www.isi.edu/ hobbs/disinf-tc.html`

[15] Hobbs, J. (2005) Toward a useful concept of causality for lexical semantics, *Journal of Semantics*, 22: 181-209.

[16] Hobbs, J. (2005) Encoding commonsense knowledge, `http://www.isi.edu/ hobbs/csk.html`.

[17] Hobbs, J. and Gordon, A. (2005) Encoding Knowledge of Commonsense Psychology. 7th International Symposium on Logical Formalizations of Commonsense Reasoning. May 22-24, 2005, Corfu, Greece.

[18] Hobbs, J. and Gordon, A. (2008) The Deep Lexical Semantics of Emotions. Workshop on Sentiment Analysis: Emotion, Metaphor, Ontology and Terminology (EMOT-08), 6th International conference on Language Resources and Evaluation (LREC-08), Marrakech, Morocco, May 27, 2008.

[19] Hobbs, J. and Pan F. (2004) An ontology of time for the Semantic Web, *ACM Transactions on Asian Language Information Processing*, 3(1): 66-85.

[20] McCarthy, John, (1980) "Circumscription: A Form of Nonmonotonic Reasoning", *Artificial Intelligence*, 13: 27-39.

[21] Moskowitz, G. and Grant, H. (Eds.) (2009) *The psychology of goals*. New York: The Guilford Press.

[22] Murray, H. (1938) *Explorations in personality*. New York: Oxford University Press.

[23] Rokeach, M. (1973) *The nature of human values*. New York: Free Press.

[24] Searle, J. (1990) Collective intentions and actions, in P. Cohen, J. Morgan, and M. Pollack, *Intentions in Communication*, Cambridge: MIT Press: 401-416.

[25] Weiner, B. (1985) An attributional theory of achievement motivation and emotion. *Psychological Review* 92:548-73.

[26] Wicker, F., Lambert, F., Richardson, F., and Kahler, J. (1984) Categorical goal hierarchies and classification of human motives. *Journal of Personality* 52(3):285-305.

Formal Ontology in Information Systems
A. Galton and R. Mizoguchi (Eds.)
IOS Press, 2010

doi:10.3233/978-1-60750-535-8-73

Revisiting the Ontological Square

Luc SCHNEIDER [1]
Institute for Formal Ontology and Medical Information Science, Universität des Saarlandes, Saarbrücken, Germany

Abstract. Considerations regarding predication in ordinary language as well as the ontology of relations suggest a refinement of the Ontological Square, a conceptual scheme used in many foundational ontologies and which consists of particular substrates as well as their types on the one hand and particular attributes as well as their types on the other hand. First, the distinction between particulars and universals turns out to be one of degree, since particulars are merely the least elements in the subsumption hierarchy. Second, relations may be analysed in terms of roles as ways of participating in events. In consequence, the Logic of the Ontological Square proposed in [1,2] has to be revised accordingly.

Keywords. Universals, particulars, substrates, attributes, relations, predication, attribution, subsumption, foundational ontologies, higher-order logic

1. Introduction

1.1. Motivation

In my [1,2] I discuss a four-categorial scheme that is recurrent in foundational ontologies, namely the so-called Ontological Square. This scheme consists of particular substrates as well as their types on the one hand and particular attributes (features) as well as their types on the other hand. For the purposes of this study it is sufficient to think of substrates as any bearers of features, be they qualities, realisable traits such as dispositions, functions or roles, or relations. I would like to remain neutral as to whether (particular) substrates are perdurants or endurants, i.e. whether they have temporal parts or not.[2]

This paper revisits the Ontological Square as well as my prior attempts to provide a logical calculus that is based on the intuitions underpinning Aristotelian substrate-attribute ontology. I will start with considerations on predication in ordinary language which are mainly due to Jonathan Lowe [4,5]. Though these considerations support an Aristotelian view of ontology, they also suggest that the distinction between particulars and universals boils down to a difference of degree: particulars as their own infimae species are merely the lowest elements in the subsumption hierarchy. A further major difference with the assays of four-category ontology in [1,2] is a neo-Aristotelian analysis

---

[1]Institute for Formal Ontology and Medical Information Science, Universität des Saarlandes, Po. Box 151150, D-66041 Saarbrücken, Germany; E-mail: luc.schneider@ifomis.uni-saarland.de.

[2]Some authors, such as McCall and Lowe [3], actually argue that endurantism and perdurantism are equivalent accounts of persistence through time and change.

of relations in terms of relational attributes or roles, more precisely in terms of roles as ways of participating in events.

All this considerations suggest a considerable revision of the Logic of the Ontological Square (LoOS), a system of higher-order logic proposed in [1,2], a revision which will be described in the second part of this paper.

1.2. Subsumption, attribution and exemplification

According to the conventional view of predication, an elementary proposition consists in the application of a predicate expressing a universal attribute to one or several terms that denote particular substrates. The underlying ontology, which Smith [6] calls *fantology*, but could also be appropriately named the *Ontological Diagonal*, is a bi-categorial scheme that combines repeatable attributes with non-repeatable substrates :

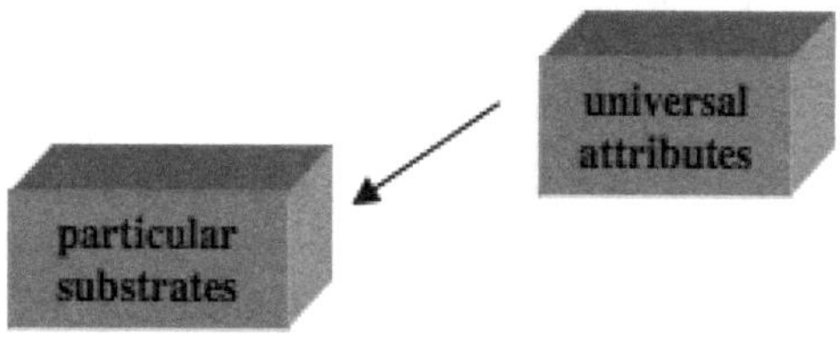

Figure 1. The Ontological Diagonal

However, E. J. Lowe [4] rightly points out that predication in natural languages is richer than the one in classical predicate logic. Indeed, we need to distinguish between the copula of subsumption and the copula of attribution. The copula of subsumption (“is a” or "are") combines terms denoting particulars or universals with terms denoting universals:

- This (particular organism) is a bacterium.
- Staphylococci are bacteria.

Ordinary language and traditional logic do not differentiate between cases in which the subsumee refers to a particular and those cases in which the subsumee denotes a universal. Thus, it seems arbitrary to draw a distinction between the instantiation of universals by particulars and the subsumption of universals by other universals.

The copula of attribution (“is” or “are”) also combines terms denoting particulars or universals with terms referring to universals:

- This (particular organism) is unicellular.
- Bacteria are unicellular.

Contrary to the conventional view, ordinary language and traditional logic allow for universal predicates applying to terms denoting universals. This generic attribution is not to be confused with second-order predication: it pertains to generic features of kinds or types of substrates.

At this point it becomes obvious that it is erroneous to conflate the distinction between substrates and attributes with that between particulars and universals. Indeed, there seem to be two sorts of general terms: those referring to universal substrates or kinds and those denoting universal attributes. It seems convenient to distinguish between generic attribution and what should be properly called *exemplification*, which holds between attribute universals and particular substrates.

Now, the use of aspects in English may indicate that "exemplification" actually covers two distinct ties between universal attributes and particular substrates:

1. This (portion of) gold melts at 1064,18°C.
2. This (portion of) gold is melting at 1064,18°C.

Indeed, while the present simple in (1) expresses a *dispositional* exemplification, the present continuous in (2) suggests an *occurrent* exemplification [5]. (1) affirms that a certain portion of gold has the disposition to melt at 1064,18°C, while (2) describes the actual occurrence of this portion of gold melting at 1064,18°C. Lowe (ibid.) suggests that the distinction between dispositional and occurrent exemplification can be explained, if one assumes that besides generic attribution on the level of universals, there is also specific attribution on the level of particulars. Thus, *dispositional* exemplification holds between a particular substrate and a universal attribute iff the latter is a generic attribute of a substantial universal which is instantiated by the former. E.g. since Melting-at-1064,18°C is an attribute of Gold, the portion under investigation dispositionally exemplifies Melting-at-1064,18°C, even without presently doing so. *Occurrent* exemplification holds between a particular substrate and a universal attribute iff the former has a trope that instantiates the latter. E.g. our portion "occurrently" exemplifies Melting-at-1064,18°C, iff it is the substrate of a particular instance of melting at 1064,18°C.

1.3. A four-category ontology

The considerations above suggest a four-fold classification of the denizens of reality, namely into particular substrates (*objects*) as well as universal substrates (*kinds*) on the one hand and particular attributes (*tropes*) as well as universal attributes (*properties*) on the other hand. This categorial scheme, which has been read into Aristotle's *Categories* (more precisely lines 1a20–1b10) by Ackrill [7], Villemin [9] and Angelelli [8], is commonly referred to as the "Ontological Square":

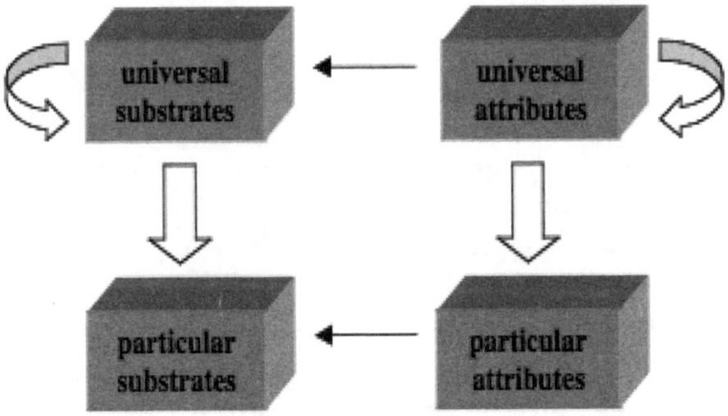

Figure 2. The Ontological Square

The Ontological Square is structured by two ontological ties or nexus, namely *subsumption* (indicated by thick arrows in Figure 2) and *attribution* (indicated by thin arrows in Figure 2). This Aristotelian four-category ontology has recently been defended by Barry Smith [10,6], Jonathan Lowe [5] and myself [1,2]; as such it can be said to underly two major foundational ontologies, namely DOLCE [11] and BFO [12].

In the version of the Ontological Square described above, subsumption applies to particulars and universals indifferently. Thus, each particular turns out to be its own infima species. This view has not only been shared by Leibniz [13][3], but is also akin to the assimilation of set-theoretical *urelements* to their singleton sets in Quine's system ML [14, par. 25].

Given that each particular or *instance* is its own infima species, there are no "bare" particulars the only *raison d'être* of which is to be bearers of their attributes (*pace* Bergmann [15]). Indeed, all particulars, whether objects or tropes, are – as infimae species of themselves – members of the subsumption hierarchy just like universals. Subsumption, however, is a tie between quiddities, i.e. essences. Thus, the distinction between an entity and its essence is only notional.

Another consequence is that the universal-particular distinction is not an absolute divide, as has been pointed out by MacBride [16], but only a matter of degree: particulars are merely the least elements in the subsumption hierarchy. Of course, this does not mean that this dichotomy is vacuous, as Ramsey [17] has contended. Indeed, in order to account for the difference between occurrent and dispositional exemplification it is mandatory to distinguish generic attribution between universals and specific attribution between particulars. Furthermore, attribution between particulars and that between universals differ inasmuch as particular attributes or tropes are bearer-specific, i.e. each trope, e.g. a particular redness, is the attribute of exactly one object, e.g. a particular rose.

It is often maintained that ties such as attribution or subsumption are no addition to being, that they are grounded by their terms [18, p. 12]. There is no room here to discuss this stance in detail, but suffice it to point out that if the terms of a tie were bare particulars, the thesis in question would entail that subsumption and attribution hold of their terms as a brute fact. The view that ties supervene on their terms is nonetheless much less counterintuitive if the terms are quiddities. Now, in the ontological framework presented here, there are no bare particulars, since all entities, universals and instances alike, are quiddities. The ties of subsumption and attribution may then be explained in terms of affinities between essences, just like chemical bonds in molecules are based on the valences of their constituent atoms.

1.4. Relations in the Ontological Square

In [1,2], I have taken the standard account of relations as being fundamentally characterised by order and arity simply for granted. However, Kit Fine [19, pp. 2 ff] forcefully argues that this account according to which relations apply to their relata in a specific order is flawed. In order to show this, one just needs to appeal to the trivial fact that each binary relation, e.g. *Loves*, has its converse, e.g. *Loved-By*. Now, the assertion that John loves Mary is true in virtue of John loving Mary or Mary being loved by John. It seems plausible that John's loving Mary and Mary's being loved by John are descriptions of the same states of affairs. But could the same states of affairs be constituted by two distinct relations ? It would seem not. But then, which one of the two relations is the more basic, in the sense of being constitutive of the states of affairs, and which one is derived ?

[3] "...ce que S. Thomas asseure sur ce point des anges ou intelligences (quod ibi omne individuum sit species infima) est vray de toutes les substances..." [13, chap. ix]

This conundrum seems to have a plausible solution, namely positionalism, i.e. the view that relations do not entail any specific order, but have positions or argument-places to be filled by their terms. Thus the Loving-Relation would have two positions: one for the Lover and one for the Beloved [19, pp. 10 ff]. But positionalism seems to fails to account for relations which obviously do not have qualitatively distinct argument-places, so-called *neutral relations* such as the Sibling-relation [19, pp. 17 ff].

Now, it seems to me that, *pace* Fine, there is a variant of positionalism which even works for neutral relations. Indeed, assume that positions are actually particulars, namely *tropes*: thus, in the case of neutral relations, they may be qualitatively identical, but nonetheless quantitatively distinct. Of course, this would presuppose that we reify relations and view them as objects with respect to which other objects can have roles. Relations would turn out to be tantamount to *occurrents* in which other objects, including other occurrents, may participate in. Such an account is akin to the event-based analysis of predication in natural language as it has been proposed by Davidson [20] and developed by Parsons [21].

Therefore, besides attribution, there is yet another tie between attributes and substrates, namely the tie of being a role in some substrate, which I will call *relation*. Since there are role-universals such as *Agent* or *Recipient*, there is a generic as well as a specific form of relation: e.g. the occurrent-kind *Loving* has three generic roles, namely *Experiencer* and *Patient* or *Theme*. Thus roles, whether universals or particulars, are basically extrinsic attributes or relational attributes, which is, after all, perfectly Aristotelian.

The remainder of this article presents the revised Logic of the Ontological Square, LoOS$^+$, its axiom system as well as its metatheory. As detailed in [2], LoOS$^+$ is a copula logic rather than a predicate logic, copulae being uninterpreted operators that form sentences out of terms denoting substrates and attributes alike. Hence a copula calculus is distinguished from Fregean predicate calculus by the fact that categoremata or lexemes and syncategoremata or grammemes are strictly separated.

2. The formal system LoOS$^+$

2.1. The Language of LoOS$^+$

2.1.1. Signature of LoOS$^+$

LoOS$^+$ contains four sorts of variables, respectively constants:

- *kind variables*: $x_k, y_k, z_k, x_k{}', y_k{}', z_k{}', x_k{}'', y_k{}'', z_k{}'', \ldots$
- *kind constants*: $a_k, b_k, c_k, a_k{}', b_k{}', c_k{}', a_k{}'', b_k{}'', c_k{}'', \ldots$
- *property variables*: $x_p, y_p, z_p, x_p{}', y_p{}', z_p{}', x_p{}'', y_p{}'', z_p{}'', \ldots$
- *property constants*: $a_p, b_p, c_p, a_p{}', b_p{}', c_p{}', a_p{}'', b_p{}'', c_p{}'', \ldots$
- *object variables*: $x_o, y_o, z_o, x_o{}', y_o{}', z_o{}', x_o{}'', y_o{}'', z_o{}'', \ldots$
- *object constants*: $a_o, b_o, c_o, a_o{}', b_o{}', c_o{}', a_o{}'', b_o{}'', c_o{}'', \ldots$
- *trope variables*: $x_t, y_t, z_t, x_t{}', y_t{}', z_t{}', x_t{}'', y_t{}'', z_t{}'', \ldots$
- *trope constants*: $a_t, b_t, c_t, a_t{}', b_t{}', c_t{}', a_t{}'', b_t{}'', c_t{}'', \ldots$

Kind and property terms are referred to as *universal terms*, while object and trope terms are called *instance terms*. Furthermore, kind and object terms are referred to as *substrate terms*, while property and trope terms are called *attribute terms*.

Sans serif letters (with or without subscripts or superscripts) are used as schematic variables or constants in the meta-language. The letters t, t', t'', etc. (with or without subscripts or superscripts) stand for any terms. In particular, x_i, $\mathsf{x}_i{}'$, $\mathsf{x}_i{}''$, etc., a_i, $\mathsf{a}_i{}'$, $\mathsf{a}_i{}''$, etc., t_i, $\mathsf{t}_i{}'$, $\mathsf{t}_i{}''$, etc. respectively stand for variables, constants and terms of the sort i.

LoOS$^+$ contains seven formal predicates or copulae:

1. subsumption between substrates: "SB_s" (read: "subsumes"),
2. subsumption between attributes: "SB_a" (read: "subsumes")),
3. attribution between universals: "AT_u" (read: "(is an) attribute of"),
4. attribution between instances: "AT_i" (read: "(is an) attribute of"),
5. relation between universals: "RE_u" (read: "(is a) role in") ,
6. relation between instances: "RE_i" (read: "(is a) role in"),
7. identity ("=").

Functional terms can be introduced as definite descriptions, which in turn can be introduced by implicit definition in the usual manner (see below).

2.1.2. Well-formed formulae of LoOS$^+$

The logical constants of LoOS$^+$ are negation ($\neg$), implication ($\rightarrow$) and the universal quantifier ($\forall\mathsf{x}$); brackets are used to delimit the scope of these operators. All other logical constants (conjunction $\wedge$, disjunction $\vee$, equivalence $\leftrightarrow$, and the existential quantifier $\exists\mathsf{x}$) are defined. The lower-case greek letters ϕ, ψ and ξ are used as schematic variables for formulae. Well-formed formulae (wff) of LoOS$^+$ are recursively defined as follows:

1. if t is a kind term and t' any substrate term, then $\ulcorner \mathsf{t}\,\mathsf{SB}_s\mathsf{t}' \urcorner$ is a wff;
2. if t is a property term and t' any attribute term, then $\ulcorner \mathsf{t}\,\mathsf{SB}_a\mathsf{t}' \urcorner$ is a wff;
3. if t is a property term and t' a kind term term, then $\ulcorner \mathsf{t}\,\mathsf{AT}_u\mathsf{t}' \urcorner$ is a wff;
4. if t is a trope term and t' an object term, then $\ulcorner \mathsf{t}\,\mathsf{AT}_i\mathsf{t}' \urcorner$ is a wff;
5. if t is a property term and t' a kind term, then $\ulcorner \mathsf{t}\,\mathsf{RE}_u\mathsf{t}' \urcorner$ is a wff;
6. if t is a trope term and t' an object term, then $\ulcorner \mathsf{t}\,\mathsf{RE}_i\mathsf{t}' \urcorner$ is a wff;
7. if t_i and t_i' are terms of the same sort i, then $\ulcorner \mathsf{t}_i = \mathsf{t}_i' \urcorner$ is a wff;
8. if ϕ and ψ are wffs, then so are $\neg(\phi)$ and $(\phi \rightarrow \psi)$;
9. If ϕ is a wff and x is any variable, then $\ulcorner \forall\mathsf{x}(\phi) \urcorner$ is a wff.

I shall omit parentheses where this does not lead to confusion. In particular formulae like $\ulcorner \forall\mathsf{x}(\forall\mathsf{y}(\phi)) \urcorner$ will be shortened to $\ulcorner \forall\mathsf{x}\forall\mathsf{y}(\phi) \urcorner$.

If x is a variable occurring in a well-formed formula ϕ, then x is *bound* by $\forall\mathsf{x}$ within $\forall\mathsf{x}(\phi)$, except in subformulae of the form $\forall\mathsf{x}(\psi)$. Any variable x that is not bound in a formula ϕ is *free in* ϕ. A term t is *free in* ϕ iff t is a constant or a variable that is free in ϕ. in A formula ϕ with no free variables is called a *closed formula* or a *sentence*. If ϕ is any formula, and t_1 a term occurring free in ϕ, then $\phi^{\mathsf{t}_2}_{\mathsf{t}_1}$ is the result of substituting one or more occurrences of t_1 in ϕ with occurrences of t_2.

Definite descriptions can be defined as a special sort of quantifiers [22, p. 173], i.e., for any sort i, any formula ϕ containing the sole free variable x_i:

Definition 1. $[\iota\mathsf{x}_i\phi]\psi(\iota\mathsf{x}_i\phi) \equiv_{df} \exists\mathsf{y}_i\,\forall\mathsf{z}_i\,((\phi^{\mathsf{z}_i}_{\mathsf{x}_i} \leftrightarrow \mathsf{z}_i = \mathsf{y}_i) \wedge \psi(\mathsf{y}_i))$ [4]

[4]This definition has the apparent flaw that it may be the case that $\ulcorner[\iota\upsilon\phi(\upsilon)]\psi(\iota\upsilon\phi(\upsilon)))\urcorner$ is false, while $\ulcorner\forall\upsilon\psi(\upsilon)\urcorner$ is true. However, no inconsistencies arise, since the axioms and rules for the quantifiers operate on the level of the basic language where all defined terms are resolved into their defining terms.

2.2. The Deductive System of $LoOS^+$

2.2.1. Logical axioms and inference rules

The logical axioms and inference rules of LoOS^+ are those of standard predicate logic with identity. For any formulae ϕ, ψ or ξ, the axioms of LoOS^+ are as follows:

Axiom 1. $\phi \rightarrow (\psi \rightarrow \phi)$

Axiom 2. $(\phi \rightarrow (\psi \rightarrow \xi)) \rightarrow ((\phi \rightarrow \psi) \rightarrow (\phi \rightarrow \xi))$

Axiom 3. $(\neg\phi \rightarrow \neg\psi) \rightarrow (\psi \rightarrow \phi)$

Axiom 4. (For any sort i, for any formula ϕ, variable x_i and term t_i occurring free in ϕ)

$\forall \mathsf{x}_i\, \phi(\mathsf{x}_i) \rightarrow \phi(\mathsf{t}_i)$

Axiom 5. $\forall \mathsf{x}\, (\mathsf{x} = \mathsf{x})$

Axiom 6. $\forall \mathsf{x}\, \forall \mathsf{y}\, (\, \mathsf{x} = \mathsf{y} \rightarrow (\phi \leftrightarrow \phi^{\mathsf{y}}_{\mathsf{x}}))$

A formula ϕ is *derivable in $LoOS^+$* from a set of formulae Δ ($\Delta \vdash_{LoOS^+} \phi$) iff there is a finite sequence of formulae $\phi_1, \ldots, \phi_n$ such that $\phi = \phi_n$ and, for any $i \leq n$, ϕ_i is in Δ, and is either an axiom of LoOS^+ or such as to follow from previous members of the sequence by one of the following inference rules.

Rule 1. (For any formulae ϕ and ψ:) From ϕ, $\phi \rightarrow \psi$ infer ψ

Rule 2. (For any formulae ϕ and ψ and any variable x that does not occur free in ϕ or in any of the premisses in the derivation:)

From $\phi \rightarrow \psi(\mathsf{x})$ infer $\phi \rightarrow \forall \mathsf{x}\, \psi(\mathsf{x})$

2.2.2. Axioms of predication

The axioms specific to LoOS^+ are those that pertain to the six copulae. I adopt a minimal characterisation of the different modes of predication, in particular I deliberately leave out any existence claims. The latter already belong to metaphysics proper and are thus beyond the scope of formal logic as formal ontology.

Subsumption between substrates resp. attributes is antisymmetric and transitive.[5]

Axiom 7. $\forall \mathsf{x}\, \forall \mathsf{y}\, (\, (\mathsf{x}\, \mathsf{SB}_s \mathsf{y} \wedge \mathsf{y}\, \mathsf{SB}_s \mathsf{x}\,) \rightarrow \mathsf{x} = \mathsf{y}\,)$

Axiom 8. $\forall \mathsf{x}\, \forall \mathsf{y}\, \forall \mathsf{z}\, (\, (\, \mathsf{x}\, \mathsf{SB}_s \mathsf{y} \wedge \mathsf{y}\, \mathsf{SB}_s \mathsf{z}) \rightarrow \mathsf{x} \mathsf{SB}_s \mathsf{z}\,)$

Axiom 9. $\forall \mathsf{x}\, \forall \mathsf{y}\, (\, (\mathsf{x}\, \mathsf{SB}_a \mathsf{y} \wedge \mathsf{y}\, \mathsf{SB}_a \mathsf{x}\,) \rightarrow \mathsf{x} = \mathsf{y}\,)$

Axiom 10. $\forall \mathsf{x}\, \forall \mathsf{y}\, \forall \mathsf{z}\, (\, (\, \mathsf{x}\, \mathsf{SB}_a \mathsf{y} \wedge \mathsf{y}\, \mathsf{SB}_a \mathsf{z}) \rightarrow \mathsf{x} \mathsf{SB}_s \mathsf{z}\,)$

[5]The formation rules are enough to ensure that the terms on both sides of the respective copula are of the right sort.

Properties are inherited downwards the subsumption hierarchy. In other words, properties of the subsumer should also be properties of the subsumee. Note that this axiom is meant to act as a constraint both on attribution (between universals) and on subsumption (between kinds): in case of doubt, either the attribute under consideration is not a property of the subsumer or subsumption does not hold.

Axiom 11. $\forall x \forall y \forall z\, ((x\, \mathsf{AT}_u y \wedge y\, \mathsf{SB}_s z) \rightarrow x \mathsf{AT}_u z)$

A trope is an attribute of at most one object.

Axiom 12. $\forall x \forall y \forall z\, ((x\, \mathsf{AT}_i y \wedge x\, \mathsf{AT}_i z) \rightarrow y = z)$

Just like properties, roles are inherited downwards the subsumption hierarchy. In other words, roles in the subsumer should also be roles in the subsumee. Again, this axiom is meant to act as a constraint both on relation (between universals) and on subsumption (between kinds): in case of doubt, either the attribute under consideration is not a role in the subsumer or subsumption does not hold.

Axiom 13. $\forall x \forall y \forall z\, ((x\, \mathsf{RE}_u y \wedge y\, \mathsf{SB}_s z) \rightarrow x \mathsf{RE}_u z)$

A trope is a role in at most one object.

Axiom 14. $\forall x \forall y \forall z\, ((x\, \mathsf{RE}_i y \wedge x\, \mathsf{RE}_i z) \rightarrow y = z)$

Given the parallelism between the axioms for attribution and relation, I should point out that I leave it open whether a substrate can have an attribute that is a role with respect to the same substrate. (Universals) of self-regulatory processes come immediately to mind as an example, since it would seem that the latter have the role of regulators with respect to themselves.

Note that every axiom of predication is the universal quantification of a conditional with a conjunction of atomic formulae in the antecedent and an atomic formula in the consequent. This means that each axiom could be replaced by an inference rule having the conjuncts of the antecedent as premisses and the consequent as the conclusion.

3. Meta-theory of LoOS$^+$

3.1. A model for LoOS$^+$

A LoOS$^+$ model is akin to a first-oder model for standard second-order logic [24]. Indeed, a model $\mathfrak{M}$ of LoOS$^+$ is a quadruple $\langle \mathfrak{U}, \mathfrak{u}, \mathfrak{p}, \mathfrak{I} \rangle$ such that:

1. $\mathfrak{U}$ is a is a non-empty set called *universe of entities*
2. $\mathfrak{u}$ is a function from the interval $[0, 7]$ into the powerset of $\mathfrak{U}$ such that:
   (a) $\mathfrak{u}(0) \subset \mathfrak{U}$ is a non-empty set called *universe of kinds*;
   (b) $\mathfrak{u}(1) \subset \mathfrak{U}$ is a non-empty set called *universe of properties*;
   (c) $\mathfrak{u}(2) \subset \mathfrak{U}$ is a non-empty set called *universe of objects*;
   (d) $\mathfrak{u}(3) \subset \mathfrak{U}$ is a non-empty set called *universe of tropes*;
   (e) $\mathfrak{u}(4) \subset \mathfrak{U}$ is a non-empty set called *universe of universals*;
   (f) $\mathfrak{u}(5) \subset \mathfrak{U}$ is a non-empty set called *universe of instances*;

(g) $\mathfrak{u}(6) \subset \mathfrak{U}$ is a non-empty set called *universe of substrates*;
(h) $\mathfrak{u}(7) \subset \mathfrak{U}$ is a non-empty set called *universe of attributes*;
(i) $\mathfrak{u}(0) \cup \mathfrak{u}(1)$ is a partition of $\mathfrak{u}(4)$;
(j) $\mathfrak{u}(2) \cup \mathfrak{u}(3)$ is a partition of $\mathfrak{u}(5)$;
(k) $\mathfrak{u}(0) \cup \mathfrak{u}(2)$ is a partition of $\mathfrak{u}(6)$;
(l) $\mathfrak{u}(1) \cup \mathfrak{u}(3)$ is a partition of $\mathfrak{u}(7)$;
(m) $\mathfrak{u}(4) \cup \mathfrak{u}(5)$ is a partition of $\mathfrak{U}$;
(n) $\mathfrak{u}(6) \cup \mathfrak{u}(7)$ is a partition of $\mathfrak{U}$;

3. $\mathfrak{p}$ is a function from the interval $[0, 5]$ into the powerset of $\mathfrak{U} \times \mathfrak{U}$ such that:

(a) $\mathfrak{p}(0) \subseteq \mathfrak{u}(0) \times \mathfrak{u}(6)$ is antisymmetric and transitive;
(b) $\mathfrak{p}(1) \subseteq \mathfrak{u}(1) \times \mathfrak{u}(7)$ is antisymmetric and transitive;
(c) $\mathfrak{p}(2) \subseteq \mathfrak{u}(1) \times \mathfrak{u}(0)$ is such that for any $\mathrm{i} \in \mathfrak{u}(1)$, and any $\mathrm{i}', \mathrm{i}'' \in \mathfrak{u}(0)$, if $\langle \mathrm{i}, \mathrm{i}' \rangle \in \mathfrak{p}(2)$ and $\langle \mathrm{i}', \mathrm{i}'' \rangle \in \mathfrak{p}(1)$, then $\langle \mathrm{i}, \mathrm{i}'' \rangle \in \mathfrak{p}(2)$;
(d) $\mathfrak{p}(3) \subseteq \mathfrak{u}(3) \times \mathfrak{u}(2)$ is such that for any $\mathrm{i} \in \mathfrak{u}(3)$, there is at most one $\mathrm{i}' \in \mathfrak{u}(2)$, such that $\langle \mathrm{i}, \mathrm{i}' \rangle \in \mathfrak{p}(3)$;
(e) $\mathfrak{p}(4) \subseteq \mathfrak{u}(1) \times \mathfrak{u}(0)$ is such that for any $\mathrm{i} \in \mathfrak{u}(1)$, and any $\mathrm{i}', \mathrm{i}'' \in \mathfrak{u}(0)$, if $\langle \mathrm{i}, \mathrm{i}' \rangle \in \mathfrak{p}(4)$ and $\langle \mathrm{i}', \mathrm{i}'' \rangle \in \mathfrak{p}(1)$, then $\langle \mathrm{i}, \mathrm{i}'' \rangle \in \mathfrak{p}(4)$;
(f) $\mathfrak{p}(5) \subseteq \mathfrak{u}(3) \times \mathfrak{u}(2)$, such that for any $\mathrm{i} \in \mathfrak{u}(3)$, there is at most one $\mathrm{i}' \in \mathfrak{u}(2)$, such that $\langle \mathrm{i}, \mathrm{i}' \rangle \in \mathfrak{p}(5)$;

4. $\mathfrak{I}$ is a function called *interpretation* on $\mathfrak{M}$ such that:

(a) for each kind constant a_k, $\mathfrak{I}(\mathsf{a}_k) \in \mathfrak{u}(0)$;
(b) for each property constant a_p, $\mathfrak{I}(\mathsf{a}_p) \in \mathfrak{u}(1)$;
(c) for each object constant a_o, $\mathfrak{I}(\mathsf{a}_o) \in \mathfrak{u}(3)$;
(d) for each trope constant a_t, $\mathfrak{I}(\mathsf{a}_t) \in \mathfrak{u}(4)$;

5. $\mathfrak{M}$ is assumed to be faithful to the axioms for identity.

An *assignment on* $\mathfrak{M}$ is a function $\mathfrak{A}$ from the set of variables into $\mathfrak{U}$ which assigns to each kind variable an element of $\mathfrak{u}(0)$, to each property variable an element of $\mathfrak{u}(1)$, to each object variable an element of $\mathfrak{u}(2)$, and to each trope variable an element of $\mathfrak{u}(3)$. For any assignments $\mathfrak{A}$, $\mathfrak{A}'$ and any variables x, $\mathfrak{A} \simeq_{\mathsf{x}} \mathfrak{A}'$ means "$\mathfrak{A}$ agrees with $\mathfrak{A}'$ on every variable except possibly x". The *denotation relative to the interpretation* $\mathfrak{I}$ *and the assignment* $\mathfrak{A}$ is the function $\mathfrak{D}_{\mathfrak{I},\mathfrak{A}}$ such that, for any term t, $\mathfrak{D}_{\mathfrak{I},\mathfrak{A}}(\mathsf{t}) = \mathfrak{I}(\mathsf{t})$ iff t is a constant, and $\mathfrak{D}_{\mathfrak{I},\mathfrak{A}}(\mathsf{t}) = \mathfrak{A}(\mathsf{t})$ iff t is a variable.

The *satisfaction* relation between a model $\mathfrak{M}$ for LoOS$^+$, an assignment $\mathfrak{A}$ on $\mathfrak{M}$ and a formula ϕ of LoOS$^+$ ($\mathfrak{M}, \mathfrak{A} \models \phi$) can be defined as follows[6]:

$\models 1$ $\mathfrak{M}, \mathfrak{A} \models \neg\phi$ iff $\mathfrak{M}, \mathfrak{A} \not\models \phi$;
$\models 2$ $\mathfrak{M}, \mathfrak{A} \models \phi \rightarrow \psi$ iff $\mathfrak{M}, \mathfrak{A} \not\models \phi$ or $\mathfrak{M}, \mathfrak{A} \models \psi$;
$\models 3$ $\mathfrak{M}, \mathfrak{A} \models \forall \mathsf{x}\, \phi(\mathsf{x})$ iff for all assignments $\mathfrak{A}'$ such that $\mathfrak{A}' \simeq_{\mathsf{x}} \mathfrak{A}$, $\mathfrak{M}, \mathfrak{A}' \models \phi(\mathsf{x})$;
$\models 4$ for any terms t, t', $\mathfrak{M}, \mathfrak{A} \models \mathsf{t} = \mathsf{t}'$ iff $\mathfrak{D}_{\mathfrak{I},\mathfrak{A}}(\mathsf{t}) = \mathfrak{D}_{\mathfrak{I},\mathfrak{A}}(\mathsf{t}')$.
$\models 5$ for any terms t, t', $\mathfrak{M}, \mathfrak{A} \models \mathsf{t}\,\mathsf{SB}_s\mathsf{t}'$ iff $\langle \mathfrak{D}_{\mathfrak{I},\mathfrak{A}}(\mathsf{t}), \mathfrak{D}_{\mathfrak{I},\mathfrak{A}}(\mathsf{t}') \rangle \in \mathfrak{p}(0)$;
$\models 6$ for any terms t, t', $\mathfrak{M}, \mathfrak{A} \models \mathsf{t}\,\mathsf{SB}_a\mathsf{t}'$ iff $\langle \mathfrak{D}_{\mathfrak{I},\mathfrak{A}}(\mathsf{t}), \mathfrak{D}_{\mathfrak{I},\mathfrak{A}}(\mathsf{t}') \rangle \in \mathfrak{p}(1)$;
$\models 7$ for any terms t, t', $\mathfrak{M}, \mathfrak{A} \models \mathsf{t}\,\mathsf{AT}_u\mathsf{t}'$ iff $\langle \mathfrak{D}_{\mathfrak{I},\mathfrak{A}}(\mathsf{t}), \mathfrak{D}_{\mathfrak{I},\mathfrak{A}}(\mathsf{t}') \rangle \in \mathfrak{p}(2)$;

[6] Note that copulae are not treated as interpreted "predicates".

$\models 8$ for any terms t, t', $\mathfrak{M}, \mathfrak{A} \models \mathsf{t}\,\mathsf{AT}_i\mathsf{t}'$ iff $\langle \mathfrak{D}_{\mathfrak{I},\mathfrak{A}}(\mathsf{t}), \mathfrak{D}_{\mathfrak{I},\mathfrak{A}}(\mathsf{t}')\rangle \in \mathfrak{p}(3)$;
$\models 9$ for any terms t, t', $\mathfrak{M}, \mathfrak{A} \models \mathsf{t}\,\mathsf{RE}_u\mathsf{t}'$ iff $\langle \mathfrak{D}_{\mathfrak{I},\mathfrak{A}}(\mathsf{t}), \mathfrak{D}_{\mathfrak{I},\mathfrak{A}}(\mathsf{t}')\rangle \in \mathfrak{p}(4)$;
$\models 10$ for any terms t, t', $\mathfrak{M}, \mathfrak{A} \models \mathsf{t}\,\mathsf{RE}_i\mathsf{t}'$ iff $\langle \mathfrak{D}_{\mathfrak{I},\mathfrak{A}}(\mathsf{t}), \mathfrak{D}_{\mathfrak{I},\mathfrak{A}}(\mathsf{t}')\rangle \in \mathfrak{p}(5)$;

A set S of formulae is satisfied by a model $\mathfrak{M}$ and an assignment $\mathfrak{A}$ on $\mathfrak{M}$, iff the latter satisfy every member of S. A formula ϕ is *valid* iff for every model $\mathfrak{M}$ and assignment $\mathfrak{A}$ on $\mathfrak{M}$, $\mathfrak{M}, \mathfrak{A} \models \phi$. An inference rule is *sound* iff every model $\mathfrak{M}$ and assignment $\mathfrak{A}$ on $\mathfrak{M}$ that satisfy its premisses also satisfy its conclusions.

3.2. Soundness

Theorem 1. *Every theorem of LoOS$^+$ is valid.*

Proof. Inspection of the axioms and inference rules of LoOS$^+$ suffices to show its soundness. The logical axioms of LoOS$^+$ are valid and the inference rules of LoOS$^+$ are sound in virtue of clauses $\models 1$ to $\models 3$. Clause $\models 4$ grounds the validity of Axioms 5 and 6, given the assumption that $\mathfrak{M}$ is faithful to the axioms for identity.

Regarding the validity of the axioms of predication, we observe that the conditions 3(a)-(f) on the model-theoretical counterparts of the copulae are direct translations of the axioms. Thus establishing the validity of the axioms of predication is straightforward. Indeed, axioms 7 and 8 are valid in virtue of clause $\models 5$ and subclause 3(a) of the definition of a model for LoOS$^+$. Similarly, Axioms 9 and 10 are valid in virtue of clause $\models 6$ and subclause 3(b) of the definition of a model for LoOS$^+$. Axiom 11 is valid because of clause $\models 7$ and subclause 3(c) of the definition of a model for LoOS$^+$. Clause $\models 8$, together with condition 3(d) of the definition of a model for LoOS$^+$, guarantees the validity of Axiom 12. Axiom 13 is valid because of clause $\models 9$ and subclause 3(e) of the definition of a model for LoOS$^+$. Axiom 14 is valid in virtue of clause $\models 10$, together with subclause 3(f) of the definition of a model for LoOS$^+$. □

3.3. Completeness

First some definitions. A set S of formulae is *AX-consistent* (i.e. axiom-consistent) if, and only if there is no formula ϕ such that $S \vdash_{LoOS^+} \neg(\phi \rightarrow \phi)$ (indeed, $\phi \rightarrow \phi$ is a theorem of LoOS$^+$)[7]. A set of formulae S is *maximally AX-consistent* if, and only if S is AX-consistent and for every formula ϕ, either $\phi \in S$ or $\neg\phi \in S$. A set of LoOS$^+$-formulae S is *normal*, iff for any sort i, if $\exists \mathsf{x}_i\, \phi(\mathsf{x}_i) \in S$, then there is at least one constant a_i such that $\phi(\mathsf{a}_i) \in S$.

Theorem 2. *Every valid formula of LoOS$^+$ is a theorem of LoOS$^+$.*

Since the proof runs as as for the completeness of LoOS, it suffices to establish Lemma 1 and Lemma 2 below.

Lemma 1. *Each AX-consistent set is a subset of a maximally AX-consistent normal set.*

[7] The notion of derivability expressed by "$\vdash_{LoOS^+}$" involves not only the logical axioms and inference rules, but also the axioms of predication.

Proof. The assumption is that the signature of LoOS$^+$ contains denumerably many constants for each sort; otherwise it should be extended in such a manner that it is. The set of LoOS$^+$-constants will serve as a set of so-called *witnesses*. Let us assume that the formulae of extended LoOS$^+$, as well as its constants, are enumerated separately. Given any AX-consistent set of formulae S, one constructs a cumulative sequence of sets S_i in the following way:

$S_0 = S$
$S_{n+1} = S_n \cup \{\exists \mathsf{x}_j\, \phi(\mathsf{x}_j) \rightarrow \phi(\mathsf{a}_j)\}$ if the n+1-th formula is of the form $\exists \mathsf{x}_j\, \phi(\mathsf{x}_j)$, a_j being the first constant of sort j that does not appear either in S_n or in $\exists \mathsf{x}_j\, \phi(\mathsf{x}_j)$;
otherwise: $S_{n+1} = S_n$

Let S' be the union of all S_i: by induction it can be shown that every S_i is AX-consistent, and hence also S'. S' can be extended to a both normal and maximally AX-consistent set S^* as follows (enumerating anew the formulae not used up in the previous steps):

$S_0^* = S'$
$S_{n+1}^* = S_n^* \cup \{\phi\}$ if the n+1-th formula ϕ is such that $S_n \cup \{\phi\}$ is AX-consistent; otherwise:
$S_{n+1}^* = S_n^*$

S^* is the union of the S_i^*. □

Now, it can be shown that, since S^* is a maximally AX-consistent set, the following statements hold:

S*1 for all terms t, t', if $\ulcorner \mathsf{t\,SB}_s\mathsf{t}' \urcorner \in S^*$ and $\ulcorner \mathsf{t}'\mathsf{SB}_s\mathsf{t} \urcorner \in S^*$, then $\ulcorner \mathsf{t} = \mathsf{t}' \urcorner \in S^*$;
S*2 for all terms $\mathsf{t}, \mathsf{t}', \mathsf{t}''$, if $\ulcorner \mathsf{tSB}_s\mathsf{t}' \urcorner \in S^*$ and $\ulcorner \mathsf{t}'\mathsf{SB}_s\mathsf{t}'' \urcorner \in S^*$, then $\ulcorner \mathsf{tSB}_s\mathsf{t}'' \urcorner \in S^*$;
S*3 for all terms t, t', if $\ulcorner \mathsf{t\,SB}_a\mathsf{t}' \urcorner \in S^*$ and $\ulcorner \mathsf{t}'\mathsf{SB}_a\mathsf{t} \urcorner \in S^*$, then $\ulcorner \mathsf{t} = \mathsf{t}' \urcorner \in S^*$;
S*4 for all terms $\mathsf{t}, \mathsf{t}', \mathsf{t}''$, if $\ulcorner \mathsf{t\,SB}_a\mathsf{t}' \urcorner \in S^*$ and $\ulcorner \mathsf{t}'\mathsf{SB}_a\mathsf{t}'' \urcorner \in S^*$, then $\ulcorner \mathsf{t\,SB}_a\mathsf{t}'' \urcorner \in S^*$;
S*5 for all terms $\mathsf{t}, \mathsf{t}', \mathsf{t}''$, if $\ulcorner \mathsf{t\,AT}_u\mathsf{t}' \urcorner \in S^*$ and $\ulcorner \mathsf{t}'\mathsf{SB}_s\mathsf{t}'' \urcorner \in S^*$, then $\ulcorner \mathsf{t\,AT}_u\mathsf{t}'' \urcorner \in S^*$;
S*6 for all terms $\mathsf{t}, \mathsf{t}', \mathsf{t}''$, if $\ulcorner \mathsf{t\,AT}_i\mathsf{t}' \urcorner \in S^*$ and $\ulcorner \mathsf{t\,AT}_i\mathsf{t}'' \urcorner \in S^*$, then $\ulcorner \mathsf{t}' = \mathsf{t}'' \urcorner \in S^*$;
S*7 for all terms $\mathsf{t}, \mathsf{t}', \mathsf{t}''$, if $\ulcorner \mathsf{t\,RE}_u\mathsf{t}' \urcorner \in S^*$ and $\ulcorner \mathsf{t}'\mathsf{SB}_s\mathsf{t}'' \urcorner \in S^*$, then $\ulcorner \mathsf{t\,RE}_u\mathsf{t}'' \urcorner \in S^*$;
S*8 for all terms $\mathsf{t}, \mathsf{t}', \mathsf{t}''$, if $\ulcorner \mathsf{t\,RE}_i\mathsf{t}' \urcorner \in S^*$ and $\ulcorner \mathsf{t\,RE}_i\mathsf{t}'' \urcorner \in S^*$, then $\ulcorner \mathsf{t}' = \mathsf{t}'' \urcorner \in S^*$;

Proof. We first note that S* is deductively closed, i.e.

DC $\mathrm{S}^* \vdash_{LoOS^+} \phi$ iff $\ulcorner \phi \urcorner \in \mathrm{S}^*$.

Indeed, if $\mathrm{S}^* \vdash_{LoOS^+} \phi$, then $\mathrm{S}^* \nvdash_{LoOS^+} \neg\phi$ (by consistency), hence $\ulcorner \neg\phi \urcorner \notin \mathrm{S}^*$, and thus $\ulcorner \phi \urcorner \in \mathrm{S}^*$ (by maximality).

We then observe that S*1 and S*3 are of the form (1a), S*2, S*4, S*5 and S*7 are of the form (1b), and S*6 as well as S*8 are of the form (1c):

(1a) for any t, t', if $\ulcorner \phi(\mathsf{t}, \mathsf{t}') \urcorner \in S^*$ and $\ulcorner \psi(\mathsf{t}', \mathsf{t}) \urcorner \in S^*$, then $\ulcorner \xi(\mathsf{t}, \mathsf{t}') \urcorner \in S^*$
(1b) for any $\mathsf{t}, \mathsf{t}', \mathsf{t}''$, if $\ulcorner \phi(\mathsf{t}, \mathsf{t}') \urcorner \in S^*$ and $\ulcorner \psi(\mathsf{t}', \mathsf{t}'') \urcorner \in S^*$, then $\ulcorner \xi(\mathsf{t}, \mathsf{t}'') \urcorner \in S^*$
(1c) for any $\mathsf{t}, \mathsf{t}', \mathsf{t}''$, if $\ulcorner \phi(\mathsf{t}, \mathsf{t}') \urcorner \in S^*$ and $\ulcorner \psi(\mathsf{t}, \mathsf{t}'') \urcorner \in S^*$, then $\ulcorner \xi(\mathsf{t}', \mathsf{t}'') \urcorner \in S^*$

The respective conditionals, namely:

(i) $\ulcorner(\phi(\mathsf{t},\mathsf{t}') \wedge \psi(\mathsf{t}',\mathsf{t})) \rightarrow \xi(\mathsf{t},\mathsf{t}')\urcorner$
(ii) $\ulcorner(\phi(\mathsf{t},\mathsf{t}') \wedge \psi(\mathsf{t}',\mathsf{t}'')) \rightarrow \xi(\mathsf{t},\mathsf{t}'')\urcorner$
(iii) $\ulcorner(\phi(\mathsf{t},\mathsf{t}') \wedge \psi(\mathsf{t},\mathsf{t}'')) \rightarrow \xi(\mathsf{t}',\mathsf{t}'')\urcorner$

are such that instances of (i) follow from axiom 7 respectively 9, instances of (ii) follow from axiom 8, 10, 11 or 13 and instances of (iii) follow from axiom 12 or 14, by eliminating all quantifiers through successively using axiom 4 and rule 1.

Now, in virtue of **DC** (the deductive closure of S^*), all the axioms are in S^*. Hence all instances of the form (i), (ii) or (iii) are LoOS*-derivable from S^*, and thus, by **DC**:

(2a) for any t,t', $\ulcorner(\phi(\mathsf{t},\mathsf{t}') \wedge \psi(\mathsf{t}',\mathsf{t})) \rightarrow \xi(\mathsf{t},\mathsf{t}')\urcorner \in S^*$
(2b) for any $\mathsf{t},\mathsf{t}',\mathsf{t}''$, $\ulcorner(\phi(\mathsf{t},\mathsf{t}') \wedge \psi(\mathsf{t}',\mathsf{t}'')) \rightarrow \xi(\mathsf{t},\mathsf{t}'')\urcorner \in S^*$
(2c) for any $\mathsf{t},\mathsf{t}',\mathsf{t}''$, $\ulcorner(\phi(\mathsf{t},\mathsf{t}') \wedge \psi(\mathsf{t},\mathsf{t}'')) \rightarrow \xi(\mathsf{t}',\mathsf{t}'')\urcorner \in S^*$

Now suppose, by hypothesis, that

(3a) $\ulcorner\phi(\mathsf{t},\mathsf{t}')\urcorner \in S^*$ and $\ulcorner\psi(\mathsf{t}',\mathsf{t})\urcorner \in S^*$
(3b) $\ulcorner\phi(\mathsf{t},\mathsf{t}')\urcorner \in S^*$ and $\ulcorner\psi(\mathsf{t}',\mathsf{t}'')\urcorner \in S^*$
(3c) $\ulcorner\phi(\mathsf{t},\mathsf{t}')\urcorner \in S^*$ and $\ulcorner\psi(\mathsf{t},\mathsf{t}'')\urcorner \in S^*$

In virtue of **DC**, the respective conjunctions will be in S^*, hence:

(4a) $\ulcorner\phi(\mathsf{t},\mathsf{t}') \wedge \psi(\mathsf{t}',\mathsf{t})\urcorner \in S^*$
(4b) $\ulcorner\phi(\mathsf{t},\mathsf{t}') \wedge \psi(\mathsf{t}',\mathsf{t}'')\urcorner \in S^*$
(4c) $\ulcorner\phi(\mathsf{t},\mathsf{t}') \wedge \psi(\mathsf{t},\mathsf{t}'')\urcorner \in S^*$

Now, again by **DC**, (2a) and (4a) imply (5a), (2b) and (4b) imply (5b), while (2c) and (4c) imply (5c):

(5a) $\ulcorner\xi(\mathsf{t},\mathsf{t}')\urcorner \in S^*$
(5b) $\ulcorner\xi(\mathsf{t},\mathsf{t}'')\urcorner \in S^*$
(5c) $\ulcorner\xi(\mathsf{t}',\mathsf{t}'')\urcorner \in S^*$

which concludes the proof of S^*1 to S^*8. □

Lemma 2. *Every maximally AX-consistent normal set has a model.*

Proof. Let S^* be a maximally AX-consistent set constructed as described above. A model $\mathfrak{M}^* = \langle \mathfrak{U}^*_s, \mathfrak{u}^*, \mathfrak{p}^*, \mathfrak{I}^* \rangle$ for S^* can be devised in the following manner.

The *identity class* of a term t is the equivalence class of terms t' such that $\ulcorner \mathsf{t} = \mathsf{t}' \urcorner \in S^*$. Let then $\mathfrak{u}^*(0)$ be the set of identity classes of kind terms, $\mathfrak{u}^*(1)$ the set of identity classes of property terms, $\mathfrak{u}^*(2)$ the set of identity classes of object terms, and $\mathfrak{u}^*(3)$ the set of identity classes of trope terms; $\mathfrak{u}^*(4)$ to $\mathfrak{u}^*(7)$, as well as $\mathfrak{U}$ are then constructed bottom-up from the previous sets as required. The interpretation $\mathfrak{I}^*$ of a constant a is its identity class; similarly the assignment $\mathfrak{A}^*$ for a variable x is the identity class of x. The definition of the denotation $\mathfrak{D}^*_{\mathfrak{I}^*,\mathfrak{A}^*}$ relative to $\mathfrak{I}^*$ and $\mathfrak{A}^*$ is straightforward.

Furthermore, for any terms t, t', I stipulate:

1. $\langle \mathfrak{D}^*_{\mathfrak{I}^*,\mathfrak{A}^*}(\mathsf{t}), \mathfrak{D}^*_{\mathfrak{I}^*,\mathfrak{A}^*}(\mathsf{t}') \rangle \in \mathfrak{p}^*(0)$ iff $\ulcorner \mathsf{t}\,\mathsf{SB}_s\mathsf{t}' \urcorner \in S^*$; by S^*1 and S^*2; $\mathfrak{p}^*(0)$ satisfies condition 3(a) in the definition of a model of LoOS$^+$;
2. $\langle \mathfrak{D}^*_{\mathfrak{I}^*,\mathfrak{A}^*}(\mathsf{t}), \mathfrak{D}^*_{\mathfrak{I}^*,\mathfrak{A}^*}(\mathsf{t}') \rangle \in \mathfrak{p}^*(1)$ iff $\ulcorner \mathsf{t}\,\mathsf{SB}_a\mathsf{t}' \urcorner \in S^*$; by S^*3 and S^*4, $\mathfrak{p}^*(1)$ satisfies condition 3(b) in the definition of a model of LoOS$^+$;

3. $\langle \mathfrak{D}^*_{\mathfrak{I}^*,\mathfrak{A}^*}(\mathsf{t}), \mathfrak{D}^*_{\mathfrak{I}^*,\mathfrak{A}^*}(\mathsf{t}')\rangle \in \mathfrak{p}^*(2)$ iff $\ulcorner \mathsf{t}\,\mathsf{AT}_u \mathsf{t}' \urcorner \in S^*$; by S*5, $\mathfrak{p}^*(2)$ satisfies condition 3(c) in the definition of a model of LoOS$^+$;
4. $\langle \mathfrak{D}^*_{\mathfrak{I}^*,\mathfrak{A}^*}(\mathsf{t}), \mathfrak{D}^*_{\mathfrak{I}^*,\mathfrak{A}^*}(\mathsf{t}')\rangle \in \mathfrak{p}^*(3)$ iff $\ulcorner \mathsf{t}\,\mathsf{AT}_i \mathsf{t}' \urcorner \in S^*$; by S*6, $\mathfrak{p}^*(3)$ satisfies condition 3(d) in the definition of a model of LoOS$^+$;
5. $\langle \mathfrak{D}^*_{\mathfrak{I}^*,\mathfrak{A}^*}(\mathsf{t}), \mathfrak{D}^*_{\mathfrak{I}^*,\mathfrak{A}^*}(\mathsf{t}')\rangle \in \mathfrak{p}^*(4)$ iff $\ulcorner \mathsf{t}\,\mathsf{RE}_u \mathsf{t}' \urcorner \in S^*$; by S*7, $\mathfrak{p}^*(4)$ satisfies condition 3(e) in the definition of a model of LoOS$^+$;
6. $\langle \mathfrak{D}^*_{\mathfrak{I}^*,\mathfrak{A}^*}(\mathsf{t}), \mathfrak{D}^*_{\mathfrak{I}^*,\mathfrak{A}^*}(\mathsf{t}')\rangle \in \mathfrak{p}^*(5)$ iff $\ulcorner \mathsf{t}\,\mathsf{RE}_i \mathsf{t}' \urcorner \in S^*$; by S*8, $\mathfrak{p}^*(5)$ satisfies condition 3(f) in the definition of a model of LoOS$^+$.

That $\mathfrak{M}^*$ together with assignment $\mathfrak{A}^*$ satisfies S^* can be shown by induction on the degree of the formulae in S^*. More precisely, what one needs to show is that for every ϕ, $\mathfrak{M}^*, \mathfrak{A}^* \models \phi$ iff $\phi \in S^*$. This has first to be established for atomic formulae, where seven subcases have to be distinguished:

1. ϕ is of the form $\ulcorner \mathsf{t} = \mathsf{t}' \urcorner$: by construction of $\mathfrak{D}^*_{\mathfrak{I}^*,\mathfrak{A}^*}$, $\mathfrak{D}^*_{\mathfrak{I}^*,\mathfrak{A}^*}(\mathsf{t}) = \mathfrak{D}^*_{\mathfrak{I}^*,\mathfrak{A}^*}(\mathsf{t}')$ iff $\ulcorner \mathsf{t} = \mathsf{t}' \urcorner \in S^*$. Therefore, by $\models$ 4, $\mathfrak{M}^*, \mathfrak{A}^* \models \mathsf{t} = \mathsf{t}'$ iff $\ulcorner \mathsf{t} = \mathsf{t}' \urcorner \in S^*$.
2. ϕ is of the form $\ulcorner \mathsf{t}\,\mathsf{SB}_s \mathsf{t}' \urcorner$: by construction of $\mathfrak{p}^*(0)$, $\langle \mathfrak{D}^*_{\mathfrak{I}^*,\mathfrak{A}^*}(\mathsf{t}), \mathfrak{D}^*_{\mathfrak{I}^*,\mathfrak{A}^*}(\mathsf{t}')\rangle \in \mathfrak{p}^*(0)$ iff $\ulcorner \mathsf{t}\,\mathsf{SB}_s \mathsf{t}' \urcorner \in S^*$. Thus, by $\models$ 5, $\mathfrak{M}^*, \mathfrak{A}^* \models \mathsf{t}\,\mathsf{SB}_s \mathsf{t}'$ iff $\ulcorner \mathsf{t}\,\mathsf{SB}_s \mathsf{t}' \urcorner \in S^*$.
3. ϕ is of the form $\ulcorner \mathsf{t}\,\mathsf{SB}_a \mathsf{t}' \urcorner$: by construction of $\mathfrak{p}^*(1)$, $\langle \mathfrak{D}^*_{\mathfrak{I}^*,\mathfrak{A}^*}(\mathsf{t}), \mathfrak{D}^*_{\mathfrak{I}^*,\mathfrak{A}^*}(\mathsf{t}')\rangle \in \mathfrak{p}^*(1)$ iff $\ulcorner \mathsf{t}\,\mathsf{SB}_a \mathsf{t}' \urcorner \in S^*$. Thus, by $\models$ 6, $\mathfrak{M}^*, \mathfrak{A}^* \models \mathsf{t}\,\mathsf{SB}_a \mathsf{t}'$ iff $\ulcorner \mathsf{t}\,\mathsf{SB}_a \mathsf{t}' \urcorner \in S^*$.
4. ϕ is of the form $\ulcorner \mathsf{t}\,\mathsf{AT}_u \mathsf{t}' \urcorner$: by construction of $\mathfrak{p}^*(2)$, $\langle \mathfrak{D}^*_{\mathfrak{I}^*,\mathfrak{A}^*}(\mathsf{t}), \mathfrak{D}^*_{\mathfrak{I}^*,\mathfrak{A}^*}(\mathsf{t}')\rangle \in \mathfrak{p}^*(2)$ iff $\ulcorner \mathsf{t}\,\mathsf{AT}_u \mathsf{t}' \urcorner \in S^*$. Thus, by $\models$ 7, $\mathfrak{M}^*, \mathfrak{A}^* \models \mathsf{t}\,\mathsf{AT}_u \mathsf{t}'$ iff $\ulcorner \mathsf{t}\,\mathsf{AT}_u \mathsf{t}' \urcorner \in S^*$.
5. ϕ is of the form $\ulcorner \mathsf{t}\,\mathsf{AT}_i \mathsf{t}' \urcorner$: by construction of $\mathfrak{p}^*(3)$, $\langle \mathfrak{D}^*_{\mathfrak{I}^*,\mathfrak{A}^*}(\mathsf{t}), \mathfrak{D}^*_{\mathfrak{I}^*,\mathfrak{A}^*}(\mathsf{t}')\rangle \in \mathfrak{p}^*(3)$ iff $\ulcorner \mathsf{t}\,\mathsf{AT}_i \mathsf{t}' \urcorner \in S^*$. Thus, by $\models$ 8, $\mathfrak{M}^*, \mathfrak{A}^* \models \mathsf{t}\,\mathsf{AT}_i \mathsf{t}'$ iff $\ulcorner \mathsf{t}\,\mathsf{AT}_i \mathsf{t}' \urcorner \in S^*$.
6. ϕ is of the form $\ulcorner \mathsf{t}\,\mathsf{RE}_u \mathsf{t}' \urcorner$: by construction of $\mathfrak{p}^*(4)$, $\langle \mathfrak{D}^*_{\mathfrak{I}^*,\mathfrak{A}^*}(\mathsf{t}), \mathfrak{D}^*_{\mathfrak{I}^*,\mathfrak{A}^*}(\mathsf{t}')\rangle \in \mathfrak{p}^*(2)$ iff $\ulcorner \mathsf{t}\,\mathsf{RE}_u \mathsf{t}' \urcorner \in S^*$. Thus, by $\models$ 9, $\mathfrak{M}^*, \mathfrak{A}^* \models \mathsf{t}\,\mathsf{RE}_u \mathsf{t}'$ iff $\ulcorner \mathsf{t}\,\mathsf{RE}_u \mathsf{t}' \urcorner \in S^*$.
7. ϕ is of the form $\ulcorner \mathsf{t}\,\mathsf{RE}_i \mathsf{t}' \urcorner$: by construction of $\mathfrak{p}^*(5)$, $\langle \mathfrak{D}^*_{\mathfrak{I}^*,\mathfrak{A}^*}(\mathsf{t}), \mathfrak{D}^*_{\mathfrak{I}^*,\mathfrak{A}^*}(\mathsf{t}')\rangle \in \mathfrak{p}^*(5)$ iff $\ulcorner \mathsf{t}\,\mathsf{RE}_i \mathsf{t}' \urcorner \in S^*$. Thus, by $\models$ 10, $\mathfrak{M}^*, \mathfrak{A}^* \models \mathsf{t}\,\mathsf{RE}_i \mathsf{t}'$ iff $\ulcorner \mathsf{t}\,\mathsf{RE}_i \mathsf{t}' \urcorner \in S^*$.

For the inductive step, assume that it has been shown that $\mathfrak{M}^*$ is a model for all formulae of S^* up to, but not including, degree n. Formulae of degree n will be of one of the forms $\neg\phi$, $\phi \wedge \psi$, $\forall \mathsf{v}(\phi)$. The subproofs for each of these three cases runs as for a calculus of standard (many-sorted) predicate logic. In particular, as shown above, axioms 7 to 14 are contained in S^* in virtue of the deductive closure of S*, and, since $\mathfrak{M}^*$ by construction is faithful to these axioms, they will also be true in $\mathfrak{M}^*$. □

Acknowledgements. The author would like to thank three anonymous referees for their comments and suggestions.

References

[1] L. Schneider, The Ontological Square and its Logic, .in C. Eschenbach, C. and M. Gr§ninger (eds.), *Formal Ontology in Information Systems: Proceedings of the Fifth International Conference (FOIS 2008)*, Amsterdam, Berlin, Oxford, Tokyo, Washington/DC, IOS Press, 2008, pp. 36–48.
[2] L. Schneider, The Logic of the Ontological Square, *Studia Logica* **91**(1), 2009, pp. 25–51.
[3] S. McCall and E.J. Lowe, The 3D/4D Controversy: A Storm in a Teacup, *Noûs* **40**, 2006, pp. 570–578.
[4] E. J. Lowe, *Kinds of Being. A Study of Individuation, Identity and the Logic of Sortal Terms*, Oxford, Blackwell, 1989.

[5] E. J. Lowe, *The Four Category Ontology. A Metaphysical Foundation for Natural Science*, Oxford, Oxford University Press, 2006.
[6] B. Smith, Against Fantology, in M. Reicher and J. Marek (eds.), *Experience and Analysis*, Vienna, öbv&htp, 2005, 153–170.
[7] J. L. Ackrill, *Aristotle's Categories and De Interpretatione*, Oxford, Oxford University Press, 1963.
[8] I. Angelelli, *Studies on Gottlob Frege and Traditional Philosophy*, Dordrecht, Reidel, 1967.
[9] J. Vuillemin, *De la logique à la théologie. Cinq études sur Aristote*, Paris, Flammarion 1967.
[10] B. Smith, On Substances, Accidents and Universals: In Defence of a Constituent Ontology, *Philosophical Papers* **26** (1997), 105–127.
[11] A. Gangemi, N. Guarino, C. Masolo, A. Oltramari and L. Schneider, Sweetening Ontologies with DOLCE, in A. Gomez-Perez and V. R. Benjamins (eds.), *Knowledge Engineering and Knowledge Management. Ontologies and the Semantic Web. Proceedings of the 13th International Conference (EKAW 2002), LNCS 2473*, Heidelberg, Springer, 2003, pp. 166–181.
[12] P. Grenon and B. Smith, SNAP and SPAN, Towards Dynamic Spatial Ontology, *Spatial Cognition and Computation* **4**, 2004, 69–104.
[13] G. W. Leibniz, *Discours de métaphysique, Čdition Lestienne*, Paris, Vrin, 1962.
[14] W. V. Quine, *Mathematical Logic*, Harvard, Harvard University Press, 1951.
[15] G. Bergmann, *Realism: A Critique of Brentano and Meinong*, Madison/WI, University of Wisconsin Press, 1967.
[16] F. Macbride, The Particular-Universal Distinction: A Dogma of Metaphysics ?, *Mind* **114**, 2005, pp. 565 – 614.
[17] F. P. Ramsey, Universals, *Mind* **34**, 1925, pp. 401– 417.
[18] D.M. Armstrong, *A World of States of Affairs*, Cambridge, Cambridge University Press, 1997.
[19] K. Fine, Neutral Relations, *The Philosophical Review* **109**, 2000, pp. 1–33.
[20] D. Davidson, The Logical Form of Action Sentences, in his *Essays on Actions and Events*, Oxford, Oxford University Press, 1980, pp 105–148.
[21] PARSONS, T., *Events in the Semantics of English: A Study in Subatomic Semantics*, Cambridge/MA, MIT Press, 1990.
[22] WHITEHEAD, A. N., and B. RUSSELL, *Principia Mathematica to *56*, Cambridge, Cambridge University Press, 1962.
[23] A. Church, *Introduction to Mathematical Logic*. Princeton, Princeton University Press, 1956.
[24] S. Shapiro, *Foundations without Foundationalism: A Case for Second-Order Logic*, Oxford, Oxford University Press, 1991.

Quality and Quantity

Formal Ontology in Information Systems
A. Galton and R. Mizoguchi (Eds.)
IOS Press, 2010

doi:10.3233/978-1-60750-535-8-89

Founding properties on measurement

Claudio MASOLO
Laboratory for Applied Ontology, ISTC-CNR, Trento, Italy

Abstract. Taking for granted an ontological standpoint independent of any empirical or epistemological perspective, philosophical theories of properties are actually quite rarely adopted in the knowledge representation community. The theory of *qualities* introduced in the DOLCE-CORE ontology [4] allows for representing different viewpoints on the world in a unified framework but it does not refer to any process used in empirical or epistemic investigations. In this paper, I will found the theory of qualities on the measurement theory proposed in [8]. In this new perspective, the stability of properties is not assumed a priori but it is founded on the stability of specific (physical) objects: the measurement systems and standards.

Keywords. ontology, theory of properties, theory of qualities, measurement, empirical and epistemic foundations

Introduction

The nature of properties, how objects have properties, and how objects change through time, are fundamental issues not only in logic and philosophy, but, more generally in science. Most philosophical theories take for granted the *objectivity* (independence from cognition) and the *stability* (independence from time) of properties. These assumptions often reflect a *realistic* viewpoint on properties that some philosophers of science (see, for example, [32]) claim to be very important for clarifying the metaphysics of *measurement*. This realistic view is often opposed to *operationalism* or *conventionalism* (see [33] for a short survey) that consider properties as created by the application of measurement operations or conventions.

In this paper, I propose a framework that accounts for the empirical and epistemic foundation of properties. Being neutral with respect to the realistic vs. operationalistic controversy, my framework, differently from philosophical theories of properties, has no *explanatory power*. It does not explain what exists in reality to make possible (what are the *truth-makers*) for an object to have a property. It just analyzes how properties can be *ascribed* to objects on the basis of an *epistemic theory of measurement*, in particular, the one introduced in [17,8]. There exist different positions relative to the role of epistemology in measurement. Following [17], measures can be seen as: (1) "inherent properties of the measured things", a quite pure ontological perspective; (2) "the results of operations that preserve the relations observed among measured things", here observations introduce an epistemic component; (3) "the results of operations recognized as adequate for their goal of obtaining information of measured things", where the epistemic dimension becomes central. In all these views, properties can be *associated* to measures by assuming a general schema exemplified by: an object has the property of 'being 1m long' if and only if the result of its length measurement is *1m*. Objective facts "that trascend particular methods of measuring it" [32] are not denied at priori but in my approach, as in cases (2) and (3), they do not play any role in establishing the objectivity and the stability of measures (and therefore properties). How objects can be measured in a communicable and inter-subjective way, and how they can be diachronically compared, will be explained by relying on the objectivity and stability of *measurement systems* and *measurement standards* without any reference to the truth-makers necessary for objects to have specific measures. While disappointing from a purely ontological perspective, the ontological 'neutrality' of the proposed approach allows its application to a variety of domains without excluding possible refinements to account for specific applicative or ontological needs. I will support this generality by providing an explicit interpretation of both the *theory of qualities* introduced in the DOLCE ontology [19] (later modified in [18] and [4] to account for different epistemic point of views) and the *theory of social concepts* proposed in [20] in terms of this general framework.

Philosophical, empirical, and cognitive approaches to properties

Universalism (see [1] for an overview) claims that properties are *universals*, i.e. immutable entities wholly present in each one of their *instances*. *Trope Theory* (see [6] for an overview) introduces *tropes*, individualized properties that *inhere* in single objects.[1] Properties reduce to equivalent classes of (exactly) *resembling* tropes. Even though, for example, two apples have the same color property, their color tropes, the redness of the first apple and the redness of the second one, are numerically distinct entities. *Resemblance Nominalism* (see [26]) rejects both universals and tropes. By means of a *resemblance* relation directly defined on objects, it is not necessary to refer to properties because "what makes it true that a particular has a property is that it resembles other particulars" ([26], p.57). Properties are then devoid of any ontological relevance, however they can be at least *associated* to classes of resembling objects.

In all these theories, properties are independent from time and they form an objective and stable *framework*.[2] However, to diachronically compare objects, to take into account possible changes in objects, or, more generally, to analyze the expression 'the object a has the property P at time t' one has to clarify not only how *properties* persist through time but also whether and how *objects* persist. *Endurantism* (see [2] for a recent defense) claims that the *whole* a can exist at different times, therefore the 'has' relation needs to be temporally qualified specifying at what time a has the property P: 'a has-at-t P'. This position has been criticized because it excludes the possibility for objects to have properties *simpliciter*, independently of any temporal specification [16]. *Perdurantism* (see [15] and [29]) commits to the existence of temporal slices of objects, i.e. at every time t at which it exists, a has a different temporal slice, a-at-t. Therefore, 'a has P at t' because 'a-at-t has P'. *Stage Theory* (see [11]) denies the persistence of objects: *stages*, i.e. objects with an instantaneous existence, are the only true ontological entities. Common-sense persisting objects are the result of a conceptual construction that collects together similar stages. While, from an ontological point of view, Perdurantism and Stage

[1] I use the term *object* as synonymous of (the more technical) *particular* or *individual*.

[2] This is evident in the case of Universalism, while in Trope Theory and Resemblance Nominalism it follows from the purely ontological nature of the *resemblance* relations.

Theory have different commitments, their analyses of 'a has P at t' both predicate the property P on an instantaneous part of a (the temporal slice or the stage).

Some theories of properties commit to specific theories of persistence. Trope Theory relies on a generalization of the Stage Theory where tropes are not necessarily instantaneous but cannot change. For example, the change in color of a is explained by a trope *substitution*: the old color trope is substituted with a (non exactly resembling) new one. Therefore 'a has P at t' if and only if, at t, there exists a trope member of P (a set of resembling tropes) that inheres in a. In Resemblance Nominalism, the resemblance relation is a (non temporally qualified) transtemporal binary relation, i.e. it may apply both synchronically and diachronically. Differently from tropes, objects can change through time, therefore Resemblance Nominalism defines resemblance only on instantaneous slices of objects, i.e. it commits to Perdurantism.[3]

On the one hand, Universalism is not committed to a specific theory of persistence but it is founded on the quite abstract notion of universal that seems very difficult to relate to empirical theories. On the other hand, Trope Theory and Resemblance Nominalism are based on resemblance relations that, by means of their intuitive connection with *similarity* relations, offer a 'handle' to cognitive science and measurement theories, but they commit to stages, tropes, or temporal slices.

In Universalism, Trope theory, and Resemblance nominalism, properties are independent of any conceptualization of the world, thus necessarily objective. Vice versa, empirical and epistemic perspectives do not rely on this aprioristic objectivity. Following [17], *evaluation*, e.g. personal judgment or estimation, can be distinguished from *measurement* on the basis of the objectivity and the communicability of the results of measurement. To ground the objectivity, it is necessary to specify how a community of subjects can *share* a point of view on reality, i.e. how this community is able to measure (or at least classify) objects in a uniform and communicable way. In this context, I prefer to use the term *inter-subjectivity* instead of *objectivity*. In the following I will ground the inter-subjectivity on empirical and epistemic approaches. This grounding allows for a non absolutist and scientific interpretation of objectivity.

In cognitive science, inter-subjectivity is often implicitly assumed. Humans share the same cognitive system, therefore they (communities of them) also share a (basic) system of categories and a categorization mechanism. *Prototype Theory* (see [23] for a brief introduction) reduces *categorization* to judgments of *similarity* between the objects under analysis and the *prototypes*, i.e. shared archetypal examples of objects belonging to a category. It focuses on the reduction of similarity to more basic notions and not on what grounds inter-subjectivity. For example, in *featural* (*set-theoretical*) *models* [34], an object is represented by a set of features, and the similarity between two entities is expressed as a (linear) combination of the measure of the common and distinctive features. Or, in *geometrical* (*spatial*) *models*, an object is represented by a point in a multidimensional space, and the similarity between two objects is represented by the distance between the points that represent them. More specifically, the approach called *Multidimensional Scaling* (MDS) (see [14] for a review) derives a spatial representation typically starting from one or more matrices of *proximity* (subjective) judgments and "MDS techniques work backward to discover both the number and the nature of the stimulus attributes or dimensions that were used to make those judgments, and to estimate the loca-

[3]Resemblance Nominalism faces other difficult problems, like, for example the co-extensionality of properties. [26] discusses in details these problems and proposes some solutions to them.

tions of the stimuli along those dimensions" [14]. The MDS approach aims at finding the dimensions, the scales, and the distance that are able to 'explain' the collected empirical data but points (and features) are implicitly assumed as inter-subjective. In addition, as in the case of Resemblance Nominalism, similarity judgments are not relative to a specific aspect of the objects under analysis. In [10], Goodman claims that generic similarity judgments do not make sense, an entity is similar to another one only with respect to a specific dimension of comparison. This position undermines the MDS approach because it presupposes that the dimension of comparison must be known *before* any similarity judgment and not vice versa. By accepting Goodman's view, one needs to make explicit what a dimension is and how the dimension, as well as the similarity judgments, can be shared. Cognitive theories become close to scientific ones where the dimensions and their structures "are tightly connected to the *measurement methods* employed to determine the values on the dimensions in experimental situations" ([9], p.21).

In the following I will propose an analysis of the expression 'a has P at t' based on an epistemic measurement theory that identifies specific dimensions of comparisons without presupposing any aprioristic inter-subjectivity. In addition, it does not require stages, slices, tropes or individual qualities and, in fact, neither properties that, however, can be *associated* to the internal states of (calibrated) measurement systems. My analysis assumes the form 'a has P-at-t' already discussed in [35].[4] Later, it will be clear why I cannot assume the stability of properties a priori, however, as stated in [35], to seriously take into account this analysis, the *similarity* between P-at-t and P-at-t', two different properties, needs to be explained.[5] I will found this *similarity* on the stability of a framework of *objects*: the measurement systems and the measurement standards.

(Epistemic) theories of measurement

Representational Measurement Theory (RMT) (see [31]) is one of the best known measurement theories. According to RMT, measurement consists in building a mapping from an *empirical relational structure* to a *numerical relational structure* such that the relations among numbers *represent* the empirical relations among objects. More formally, measurement consists in building a *homomorphism*[6] (also called *scale*) ϕ from an *empirical* structure $\mathcal{E} = \langle D, R_1, \ldots, R_n \rangle$ (where D is a set of empirical objects and R_i are empirical relations on D) to a *numerical* structure $\mathcal{N} = \langle N, S_1, \ldots, S_n \rangle$ (where N is a set of numbers and S_i are relations on N) coupled with (1) a *representation theorem* that states that the axioms in $\mathcal{E}$ are preserved by ϕ in $\mathcal{N}$; and (2) a *uniqueness theorem* that establishes the permissible transformations $\phi \to \phi'$ that yield homomorphisms into the *same* numerical structure [31]. Given an empirical structure $\mathcal{E}$ regulated by specific (empirical) laws encoded by axioms, measurement aims at finding a unique (i.e. up to a class of transformations) scale into a numerical structure $\mathcal{N}$ that represents $\mathcal{E}$.

[4]In [35] such form is considered as a notational variant of 'a has-at-t P'. In the following I will argue against this equivalence.

[5]Notice that perdurantism faces a similar difficulty regarding the link between a-at-t and a-at-t', two different objects. This difficulty is usually solved adopting some notion of (spatio-temporal) continuity.

[6]ϕ is an homomorphism from $\langle D, R_1, \ldots, R_n \rangle$ to $\langle M, S_1, \ldots, S_n \rangle$ iff (i) $\phi : D \to M$ and (ii) ϕ maps R_i to S_i, $i = 1, \ldots, n$, i.e. $R_i(x_1, \ldots, x_m)$ iff $S_i(\phi(x_1), \ldots, \phi(x_m))$. Note that ϕ can map different empirical objects to the same number, i.e. it individuates sets of empirical objects that are ϕ equivalent.

RMT defines a notion of measurement in precise mathematical terms, but, as stated in [8], this notion is so abstract that in practice it is not used in empirical contexts (and, in particular, in physical metrology). One problem of RTM regards the nature of the empirical structure. The relations and the axioms (corresponding to physical laws) in this structure are the result of an abstractive process that is not considered in RMT. Taking the empirical structure as given, RTM moves to a lower level of abstraction the problem of founding measurement on empirical procedures or methods without solving it.

[8] proposes an alternative general model of measurement that addresses the empirical foundation of measurement by giving a central role to *measurement systems* (MSs). Roughly speaking, an MS is a system – a (physical) object describable by a set of states discernible in empirical terms – able to interact with the *system under measurement* (SUM) and "provided with instructions specifying how such interaction must be performed and interpreted" [8]. The output of the interaction between an MS and an SUM is a piece of (symbolic) information.

Following [8], an MS is formally represented by the tuple $\langle m, \mathcal{E}, \kappa, \mathcal{S}, \lambda \rangle$ where:[7]

- m is a (physical) object (the *support* of the MS).
- $\mathcal{E} = \langle U, R_1, \ldots, R_n \rangle$, the *empirical structure*, describes m in terms of the potential interactions with objects. U is the set of the *empirically discernible* states of all possible complex systems resulting from the interaction of any object $o \in O$ (the domain of objects) with m (noted by $m \bullet o$). R_i are relations among states in U, i.e. they are observable relations among the internal states of the complex systems. U and the R_i empirically anchor, respectively, the symbols and the relations in the symbolic (numerical) structure. Notice that $\mathcal{E}$ refers to potential interactions with objects, i.e., by abstracting from specific objects, it depends only on the (physical) structure of m.
- $\kappa\colon O \to U$ is the *interaction* function that associates to an object $o \in O$ the internal state of the complex system $m \bullet o$, i.e. it specifies, in terms of internal states in U, what the interaction of an object with m yields. The elements of U induce a partition on objects: $o \approx o'$ iff $\kappa(o) = \kappa(o')$, i.e. U gives the *resolution* of m. Similarly, each R_i induces a relation on objects: $R_i^O(o_1, \ldots, o_n)$ iff $R_i(\kappa(o_1), \ldots, \kappa(o_n))$. Therefore, differently from RMT, the empirical structure is determined by the (physical) structure of the MS that *induces* a structure on objects (by interacting with them) i.e. an MS (and the measurement procedure) provides a specific point of view on the reality.
- $\mathcal{S} = \langle V, S_1, \ldots, S_n \rangle$, the *symbolic structure*, is necessary to abstract from the internal states of the complex system. It translates (i) the internal states in U into symbols in V that can be used to communicate inter-subjectively; and (ii) each relation R_i between states into a relation S_i between symbols. Notice that, differently from RMT, $\mathcal{S}$ is not necessarily a *numerical* structure.
- $\lambda\colon U \to V$, the *symbolization* function, is a *one-to-one* function between U and V, such that $R_i(u_1, \ldots, u_n)$ iff $S_i(\lambda(u_1), \ldots, \lambda(u_n))$. Note that λ is an isomor-

[7] I omit here the set-up and reset procedures, i.e. I assume that the MS is always ready to correctly interact with an SUM. In addition, I do not address other important properties of MSs like (i) *selectivity*, i.e. measures must be related only to the objects under measurement and not to the environment in which they are situated (measurement must be independent from environment conditions as much as possible); or (ii) *invasivity*, i.e. in the measurement process, the MSs must interact with objects without changing them (at least with respect to the dimension under measurement).

phism, i.e. $\mathcal{S}$ contains the whole information in $\mathcal{E}$ but in a *communicable* and *manipulable* form. $\lambda \circ \kappa$ is an homomorphism that associates symbols (relations among symbols) to objects (relations among objects induced by an MS).

Summing up, in this model of measurement, the relations on objects are not assumed but they are induced by the structure of the MS and by the way its support interacts with the objects. Therefore, in addition to determining a symbolic structure, an MS selects a dimension along which the objects are measured and how objects compare with respect to this dimension. I.e., an MS sets a perspective on the world, the way one looks at the objects and what one can catch about them (the collectible *data*). This view places the MSs at the core of an epistemological foundation of measurement and allows for a simple position: "measurements are evaluations performed by means of measuring system" ([17], p.28). In general, an MS rests on the basis of a *theoretical framework* that needs to be validated from an empirical standpoint. However, an MS can also be linked to different theories, it can survive the change of the background theoretical framework, and the same theory can be associated to different measurement systems. In addition, according to the previous model, an MS has a unique support during its whole life. A different conception that allows the MSs to change their supports through time is possible[8] but I will not consider it in this paper.

To have *inter-subjective* measures that "convey the same information to different observers" ([17], p.28), MSs need to be *calibrated.* Calibration is based on *measurement standards* (mST), i.e. a set of reference objects, with a *conventionally* associated symbolic structure. [8] does not formalize mSTs. In this paper, I represent an mST by a tuple $\langle R, \mathcal{R}, \alpha \rangle$, where:

- R is the set of reference objects;
- $\mathcal{R} = \langle M, S_1^M, \ldots, S_n^M \rangle$ is a symbolic structure;
- $\alpha \colon R \to M$ is a one-to-one function that conventionally assigns to each object in R a symbol in M. In this case too, each S_i^M *induces* a relation on R.[9]

The MS $\langle m, \mathcal{E}, \kappa, \mathcal{S}, \lambda \rangle$ is calibrated with respect to the mST $\langle R, \mathcal{R}, \alpha \rangle$, iff (i) $\mathcal{S} = \mathcal{R}$, i.e. the MS has the same symbolic structure as the mST, and (ii) for each $r, r_1, \ldots, r_n \in R$, $\lambda(\kappa(r)) = \alpha(r)$ and $S_i(\lambda(\kappa(r_1)), \ldots, \lambda(\kappa(r_n)))$ iff $S_i^M(\alpha(r_1), \ldots, \alpha(r_n))$, i.e. measuring the reference objects in R with the MS under calibration, one obtains the same results established in the mST. Because both α and λ are one-to-one functions, $|R| = |U|$, i.e. the resolution of the MS is reducible to the reference objects.[10] Notice that, for a structurally integral MS, the calibration process reduces to the *tuning* of the λ function (that at this point can be seen as the composition of a physical and a tuning function). Two MS, m_1 and m_2, are *aligned* iff there exists an mST s, such that both m_1 and m_2 are calibrated with respect to s. Measurement standards together with the notion of alignment allow to abstract from single MSs, i.e. given an mST s, all the systems calibrated with respect to s are equivalent from the point of view of measurement, even if, physically, they can differ.

[8]One can recognize the classical problems linked to the *constitution* of objects (see [25] for an overview).

[9]Here I assume the S_i^M relations as given, but they could also be linked to a reference MS by convention.

[10]There are some calibration procedures that do not need to test the MS with all the objects it is able to resolve. For example, in the case of temperature, one can set the 0°C and the 100°C and check the linearity of the MS. This is very important from the practical point of view, but it does not conceptually change the scenario and it introduces the problem of checking, in the example, the linearity of the MS.

Sketching an empirical theory of properties

Given an mST s with symbolic structure $\langle M, S_1^M, \ldots, S_n^M \rangle$, it is possible to associate to each $s_p \in M$ a property P: 'a has P' (or 'a is an *instance* of P') if and only if there exists an MS $\langle m, \mathcal{E}, \kappa, \mathcal{S}, \lambda \rangle$ calibrated with respect to s such that $\lambda(\kappa(a)) = s_p$. First of all, note that according to this definition, 'a has P' only if it has been measured producing the result s_p. The definition can be generalized by introducing a potential aspect, i.e. 'a has P' if it *could* interact with the MS producing the result s_p. I don't consider this option because it moves away from a pure empirical approach and it seems to involve the difficult notion of *disposition* (see [22]). Second, different properties (e.g. properties associated to non-aligned MSs) can in principle have the same instances, i.e. properties are not *extensional*. The *intensions* of properties are linked to the MSs, the mSTs, and the procedures of measurement and calibration. Third, by means of the S_i^M relations, the mST s and the calibrated MSs individuate not only a set of properties but also how they are structured. Fourth, the properties that correspond to symbols cannot be further refined, they represent the *resolution* of the MSs calibrated with respect to s. In philosophy, these properties are called *determinate* properties (see [13,12]) and they are distinct from more general properties called *determinable* properties. Let us assume that 'being scarlet' and 'being crimson' are determinate properties. 'Being red' is a determinable property because it is the generalization of 'being scarlet', 'being crimson', etc., i.e. to be red an object needs to be scarlet, or crimson, etc. Coming back to the mSTs, *determinable* properties correspond to *sets* of symbols, i.e. 'a has the (determinable) property Q' iff there exists an MS $\langle m, \mathcal{E}, \kappa, \mathcal{S}, \lambda \rangle$ calibrated with respect to s such that there exists an $s \in S_q \subseteq M$ (S_q is the set of symbols of s associated to Q) such that $\lambda(\kappa(a)) = s$.[11]

Moving now to the analysis of the form 'a has P at t', I already observed that both theories of properties and theories of persistence need to be considered. Unsurprisingly, measurement theories rely on positions quite close to philosophical ones. [8] assumes that a is a *state* of an object, i.e. what an object is at a specific time. The notion of state is not further analyzed, thus it is not clear if states are similar to temporal slices or to more abstract entities like *states of affairs*. RTM has an even more obscure position that, in any case, seems very similar to the previous one. Cognitive sciences often refer to *stimuli* (like sounds, visual inputs, etc.) that abstract from objects by considering just the input of the human sensory system. However, stimuli too can have different properties at different times, therefore, as in the case of objects, one has to refer to how stimuli are at specific times. [7] defines a *wide sense* of measurement: "a process of empirical, objective assignment of symbols to attributes of objects and events of the real world, in a such way to represent them, or to describe them" ([7], p.41). According to this definition, measurement concerns the assignment of symbols to *attributes* of objects that seem quite close to *tropes* or to a generalization of them (see the *qualities* in the DOLCE approach described below).

I will show that giving a central and *referential* role to mSTs and MSs the existential commitment to temporal slices, states, tropes, or stimuli can be avoided by assuming objects as *direct subjects* of measurement. In this view, what objects under measurement are and how they can be recognized, selected, observed, measured, and re-identified through time are central questions. Admittedly, I have no definite answers, only few ob-

[11] To have a uniform representation, determinate properties can be associated to *singletons*.

servations. First of all, note that committing to temporal slices, states, or tropes, one still faces the problem of recognizing, selecting, and measuring them. Second, to account for change, one has to refer to persistent objects even though they are just conceptual constructions instead of real entitites. My approach requires the capability of re-identifying objects through time without committing to their ontological nature and to the way they persist. Third, in classical mechanics, observations and measures are attributed to *particles* that can be seen as a kind of objects. Particles constitute more complex *systems* the states of which are represented in multi-dimensional spaces. Classical mechanics does not directly refer to 'mesoscopic or macroscopic objects'. However, these objects can be mathematically reconstructed (and re-identified through time) from the representations of the systems without committing to their ontological nature [21].[12] Four, in cognitive science, the concept of object individuation, identification, and persistence across time, space, occlusion, property change, and loss of cohesion have been deeply studied starting from experience-dependent constructivist approaches to approaches that assume innate representation mechanisms for objects (see [27] for a recent review). In addition, some psychological theories of persistence have been linked to philosophical ones (in particular endurantism and perdurantism) [28]. Five, an MS selects the kind of entities it is able to interact with, therefore the nature of objects the MS can measure is (at least partially) determined by it.

Let us now consider how the form 'a has P at t' can be analyzed in terms of measurement just committing to objects. Assuming instantaneous processes of measurement, each measure (that can be seen as a *datum* or *observation* about an object) is collected by using an MS at a precise time. Given an MS $\langle m, \mathcal{E}, \kappa, \mathcal{S}, \lambda \rangle$, $[t](\lambda(\kappa(a)) = s_p)$ represents the fact that m and a interacted at t with the result s_p, i.e., $[t]$ is a sort of temporal operator that indicates *when* a has been measured.[13] From these premises, 'a has P at t' can be reduced to the following statement: given an mST s with symbolic structure $\langle M, S_1^M, \ldots, S_n^M \rangle$ such that P is associated to the symbol $s_p \in M$, there exists an MS $\langle m, \mathcal{E}, \kappa, \mathcal{S}, \lambda \rangle$ calibrated, *at* t, with respect to s, such that $[t](\lambda(\kappa(a)) = s_p)$. Objects can be diachronically compared by examining the measures collected at different times by MSs calibrated with respect to the same mST. For example, if m and m' are two MSs calibrated with respect to s, respectively, at t and t', then, from $[t](\lambda(\kappa(a)) = s_p)$ and $[t'](\lambda'(\kappa'(b)) = s_p)$, one can conclude that a and b share the property P.[14] Despite its apparent triviality, this conclusion relies on important additional hypotheses about the stability of mSTs and MSs. First of all, in the previous analysis, the property P is associated to a symbol of an mST that, by definition of mST, identifies a (physical) reference object. The diachronic alignment of the MSs relies on the calibration, at different times, with respect to *the same* mST. Therefore, the change (across time) of the reference objects that constitute an mST can invalidate this alignment. Second, the interaction and symbolization functions of an MS depend on the (physical) structure of the support m

[12]Things are more complex in the case of quantum mechanics.

[13]In an MS, a symbol corresponds to an internal state of the complex system resulting from the interaction between the support of the MS and the measurand. However, from an empirical point of view, one does not need to define what states or configurations are. It is enough to be able to observe (or measure), *at a specific time*, some characteristics of the complex system, i.e. states can be reduced to observations (or measures).

[14]I assume here the stability (through time) of symbols and natural laws.

that can change across time.[15] Therefore MSs too can change. If an mST s is stable, then by (diachronically) calibrating an MS with respect to s one makes sure that the MS is stable (at least for what concerns its measurement capacities). However, even though the measurement is instantaneous, from an empirical perspective it is very hard to assume that (i) all the MSs are re-calibrated every time they are used, and (ii) that the calibration and the measurement can be synchronically performed. These observations make clear that to diachronically compare objects one must rely on the stability of mSTs and MSs.[16] Once the mSTs are considered as *reference systems*, i.e., systems that are stable by *assumption*, and the MSs are assumed to be stable (at least from the calibration to the measurement), then the comparison between the state of $m \bullet a$ and the state of $m' \bullet b$ (where m and m' are the supports of two diachronically aligned MSs) depends exclusively on a and b. One can then conclude that two objects share a property but this conclusion relies on a framework of objects assumed to be stable.[17]

[3] discusses two alternative methods to diachronically tune systems. To align measures taken at different times, one method maximizes the stability of the objects, i.e. it assumes that the world is quite stable, the other one maximizes the stability of the structure of the measures, i.e. it assumes that the MSs are quite stable. On one hand, similarly to the previous analysis, these methods too assume the stability of objects or MSs. However, they are less precise because different tunings can maximize the stability of objects or MSs. On the other hand, by relying on the availability, at every time t, of the measures of every object a that exists at t with respect to any dimension that makes sense for a, they are unusable when, at each time, one has a partial knowledge of the world.

From an ontological perspective, in absence of the stability of the mSTs and the MSs, the fact that two objects measure the same does not imply any similarity between them. The identity of measures could be caused by a misalignment of the MSs used to collect these measures. If properties are associated to symbols of mSTs that identify reference objects, then properties do not depend only on symbols (that are assumed to be stable here) but on reference objects too because these objects are essential for the calibration process that makes possible the diachronic comparison of objects. In this perspective, a property can change accordingly to the referent object to which it is associated. Therefore one has to assume that, at t, a property depends on how the referent object identified by the symbol associated to P is at t. In principle, properties can change at every time and the *similarity* between 'P-at-t' and 'P-at-t'' is founded on the similarity (stability) of the reference object identified by the symbol associated to P. Instead of re-identifying objects on the basis of a stable framework of properties, here we are 're-identifying' properties on the basis of a stable framework of objects. But, on what empirical evidences can the stability of mSTs and MSs be grounded? To empirically justify the stability of an mST, one needs to diachronically compare its reference objects (at least along some dimensions). To do that one needs other mSTs and MSs, the stability of which, in turn, needs to be founded. It is evident that this approach suffers a circularity or infinite regression problem, very frequent at the foundational level. Instead of considering one

[15] To explicitly represent this dependence one has to analyze the temporal operator considered in the form $[t](\lambda(\kappa(a)) = s)$. For example, it is possible to add a temporal parameter to the λ and κ functions or to consider λ and κ as functions that individuate a function at every time. I don't consider this interesting aspect here.

[16] Statistical analysis on relative changes of calibrated MSs helps in discovering needs for system re-calibration, but does not solve the theoretical problem.

[17] Again, the approaches that commit to states, temporal slices, or tropes suffer the same problems.

single mST (or MS), one can consider the global framework that includes all the mSTs and the MSs. The stability of this global framework can be founded only on the stability of the mutual relationships between its components, and the mutual relationships are measured by the global framework itself. Changes are always relative to a framework, but once the global one is considered, then they represent the maximal resolution possible for an observer. Still, the global framework could be changing in absolute terms, i.e. the observer could ascribe the same property to objects that, in absolute ontological terms, do not share anything. However, even though an observer disposes of the whole data collected by the global framework, (s)he cannot detect this dissimilarity.

In the following, I will assume that all the mSTs and the MSs are stable. In this way the calibration too is stable and diachronic comparisons are always possible.

Qualities and measurement

In this section I will link one of the theories of qualities discussed in [18] (that avoids individual qualities) with the measurement theory above introduced.

DOLCE [19] adopts a theory of qualities that relies on the notions of (*individual*) *quality*, *quality kind*, and *space* (*of qualities*). Individual qualities, e.g. 'the color of my car', 'the weight of John', *inhere* in their unique hosts, but, differently from tropes, they can change. While tropes are individualizations (with respect to the host) of a *determinate* property (e.g. 'being 1m long', 'being 1g heavy'), individual qualities are individualizations of *determinable* properties that correspond to specific dimensions of comparison (e.g. 'being colored', 'being shaped') represented by quality kinds, i.e. properties that collect the individual qualities relative to the same dimension. Each space is associated to a unique quality kind. The determinate properties relative to the dimensions individuated by quality kinds are represented by the *atomic regions* of the spaces associated to these kinds.[18] These regions can be organized in taxonomies, or in more complex geometrical ways. DOLCE-CORE [4] extends DOLCE by allowing several spaces, in general with different structures motivated by epistemic or empirical considerations, to be associated to the same quality kind. An object can have only one individual quality of a specific kind, that, at a given time, can be *located* in different spaces (associated to such kind). In [18], the theory called ES avoids individual qualities by adopting a *location* relation directly defined on objects.[19] $\mathsf{L}(r, o, t)$ stands for 'the region r is the *location* of the object o at time t'. Regions correspond to properties therefore 'o has P at t' can be analyzed as: at t, the object o is located in the region r_P (where r_P corresponds to the property P). Here again several spaces can be associated to the same dimension of comparison (e.g. color, weight, etc.). While in DOLCE and DOLCE-CORE the quality kind allows to individuate all the spaces relative to the same dimension, in ES, to cluster all the regions that represent properties relative to the same dimension (*generalized spaces*), an additional primitive is required. I think that generalized spaces can be 'simulated', in measurement terms, by clustering mSTs (and MSs), however here I don't consider this aspect.

ES assumes a finite number of mutually disjoint spaces noted with SP_i. In each space a *classical extensional mereology* (see [5,30]) is assumed. Here I have no space for

[18] Determinable properties are represented by non-atomic regions.

[19] ES considers *endurants* (persons, cars, etc.) but excludes *perdurants* (events, processes, etc.). I follow this simplification, even though I think that the following results can be adapted to the case of perdurants.

taking into account this aspect therefore I consider all the regions as 'atomic'.[20] Finally, the primitive $\mathsf{EX}(o, t)$ stands for 'the object o *exists* at time t'. As already said, I do not address here the problem of persistence of objects, therefore I do not provide any epistemic interpretation of the primitive EX, I just assume to (empirically) know at what times an object exists. In addition, differently from ES, I consider only temporal instants. These moves simplify the formal framework without reducing its conceptual relevance.

Summing up, I consider a theory with the following extra-logical vocabulary: $\textsc{ob}$ (object), $\textsc{tm}$ (time), $\textsc{sp}_1, \ldots, \textsc{sp}_n$ (spaces), EX (existence), L (location). This is a general theory that represents properties abstracting from empirical, epistemic, or conceptual considerations. I will provide an interpretation of this theory in terms of *measurement structures*. A measurement structure, is a structure $\langle O, T, S, F, EX\rangle$ where O is a set of 'objects', T is a set of 'times', S is a set of 'symbols', F is a set of (*calibrated*) *measurement frameworks* (MFs), and $EX \subseteq O \times T$. A (calibrated) measurement framework $\mathcal{M}_i$ is a couple $\langle \mathsf{s}_i, M_i^*\rangle$ where s_i is an mST, and M_i^* is a set of MSs calibrated[21] with respect to s_i such that the supports of the MSs in M_i^* and the reference objects in s_i belong to O, and $M_i \subseteq S$, where M_i is the set of symbols of s_i.[22] A measurement structure of dimension n is a measurement structure such that $|F| = n$.

At this point the interpretation function $\mathcal{I}$ becomes trivial (a theory that assumes n spaces $\textsc{sp}_1, \ldots, \textsc{sp}_n$ is interpreted in a measurement structure of dimension n or greater):

(*a*) $\textsc{ob}^{\mathcal{I}} \subseteq O$;

(*b*) $\textsc{tm}^{\mathcal{I}} \subseteq T$;

(*c*) $\textsc{sp}_i^{\mathcal{I}} \subseteq M_i$ (the set of symbols of the mST s_i in an MF of F);

(*d*) $\mathsf{EX}^{\mathcal{I}} \subseteq EX$;

(*e*) $\mathsf{L}^{\mathcal{I}} \subseteq S \times O \times T$ and
$\langle r, o, t\rangle \in \mathsf{L}^{\mathcal{I}}$ iff there exists an MS $\langle m, \mathcal{E}, \kappa, \mathcal{S}, \lambda\rangle$ belonging to some M_i^* (in one measurement framework) such that $[t](\lambda(\kappa(o)) = r)$.[23]

According to (*c*), the regions of the space $\textsc{sp}_i$ correspond to the symbols of the mST s_i. All the MSs calibrated with respect to s_i have the same symbols, therefore the regions of the space $\textsc{sp}_i$ correspond to the symbols of the MF $\mathcal{M}_i$. This introduces a correspondence between spaces and MFs. Structural relations among regions belonging to a space are then mapped to structural relations among symbols in the corresponding MF (that all the MSs in it share). According to (*e*), at t, an object is located in a region of a space $\textsc{sp}_i$ if and only if there is an MS belonging to the M_i^* in the MF associated with $\textsc{sp}_i$ that, at t, interacted with the object giving as result the symbol associated to the given region. This makes clear in which sense spaces represent an empirical point of view. However, note that the correspondence between regions and symbols is valid only by rejecting non atomic regions. As said, symbols correspond only to determinate

[20] ES is compatible also with non-atomic spaces, i.e. it accepts the existence of determinable properties that are not partitioned by determinate properties. From both the conceptual and empirical point of views, I find this option quite debatable.

[21] Remember that the calibration is assumed to be stable.

[22] Every MS calibrated with respect to an mST s has the same symbols of s, therefore all the MSs belonging to M_i^* have the same symbols of s_i (a subset of S).

[23] Note that one needs to ensure that $[t](\lambda(\kappa(o)) = r)$ implies that both m and o exist at t. This constraint does not really regard the interpretation function but the notion of MS.

properties while non atomic regions correspond to determinable properties because they have atomic parts (in the case of an atomic space) that, in turn, correspond to determinate properties. This means that the parthood relation cannot be associated to a structural relation between symbols. If needed, as already observed, the interpretation function can be modified by associating *sets of* symbols to regions and the (set-theoretical) *inclusion* relation to the parthood relation. Alternatively, one can add some conventions in the measurement frameworks: an mST determines both the conventional symbols assigned to the reference objects and the conventional symbols assigned to the sets of reference objects. In this case, the parthood relation can be associated to the inclusion relation between sets of reference objects conventionally associated to symbols.

Let us now discuss, in the light of the given interpretation, the main axioms proposed in [18] and [4].

a1 $\mathsf{L}(r, o, t) \wedge \mathsf{L}(r', o, t) \wedge \mathrm{SP}_i(r) \wedge \mathrm{SP}_i(r') \rightarrow r = r'$

a2 $\mathsf{EX}(o, t') \wedge \exists r(\mathsf{L}(r, o, t) \wedge \mathrm{SP}_i(r)) \rightarrow \exists r'(\mathsf{L}(r', o, t') \wedge \mathrm{SP}_i(r'))$

a3 $\mathsf{EX}(o, t) \rightarrow \bigvee_i(\exists r(\mathsf{L}(r, o, t) \wedge \mathrm{SP}_i(r)))$

(a1) states that, in a given space and at a given time, the location of an object is unique. In the interpretation, the premises in (a1) imply that, in the MF associated to SP_i, there exist $\mathsf{m} = \langle m, \mathcal{E}, \kappa, \mathcal{S}, \lambda \rangle$ and $\mathsf{m}' = \langle m', \mathcal{E}', \kappa', \mathcal{S}', \lambda' \rangle$ such that $[t](\lambda(\kappa(o)) = r)$ and $[t](\lambda'(\kappa'(o)) = r')$. But m and m′ are in the same MF, thus they are aligned and, by definition of alignment, $r = r'$. Nevertheless, note that, from an empirical standpoint, this means that two MSs can be used at the same time to measure the same object, i.e. objects can simultaneously interact with different MSs (of the same kind). If needed it is easy to exclude this situation. (a2) states that if, at a given time, an object is located in a specific space, then it is located in this space at every time at which it exists. This seems ontologically but not empirically plausible. The fact that o has been measured at t does not imply that o has been measured (relatively to the same dimension) at every time at which it exists. Similarly in the case of (a3): it is possible that at a specific t, o has not been measured in any way. Axioms (a2) and (a3) make evident that the empirical theory does not presuppose a complete information about the world.[24]

[24] takes into account the cognitive processes underlying classification and measurement by extending the theory of qualities in DOLCE with the notions of *absolute magnitude* (human independent and objective value), *perceived magnitude* (subjective mental entity evoked by the interaction with objects) and *communicable symbol* (entity that allows the communication of a perceived magnitude). The theory proposed in [24] aims at understanding the *cognitive* foundations of measurement. This important aspect is left for future work.

Perspectives: concepts and measurement

The proposed measurement theory can also provide an interpretation of the theory of *social concepts* introduced in [20] and simplified in [4]. In this theory, concepts depend on communities of agents, who, by some sort of *social conventions*, create, make use of, communicate about, *define*, and accept them. These social conventions are represented

[24] This is the kind of information on which the methods proposed in [3] rely.

by *descriptions* that (i) are created by agents, (ii) are encoded in some 'public' (formal or informal) language, (iii) need to have at least a (but, in general, several) physical support, and (iv) are accepted by agents. Both concepts and descriptions are in time. $\mathsf{DF}(c, d)$ stands for 'the concept c is defined by the description d'. Objects can be classified by concepts, $\mathsf{CF}(c, o, t)$ stands for 'the objects o, as it is at t, is classified by the concept c'. I propose the following interpretation function $\mathcal{I}$ that maps the extra-logical vocabulary OB (object), TM (time), CN (concept), DS (description), DF (definition), CF (classification) into the measurement structures previously introduced:

(*a*) $\textsc{ob}^{\mathcal{I}} \subseteq O$;
(*b*) $\textsc{tm}^{\mathcal{I}} \subseteq T$;
(*c*) $\textsc{cn}^{\mathcal{I}} \subseteq S$;
(*d*) $\textsc{ds}^{\mathcal{I}} \subseteq F$;
(*e*) $\mathsf{DF}^{\mathcal{I}} \subseteq S \times F$ and $\langle c, \mathcal{M}_i \rangle \in \mathsf{DF}^{\mathcal{I}}$ iff $c \in M_i$ (the set of symbols of $\mathcal{M}_i$);
(*f*) $\mathsf{CF}^{\mathcal{I}} \subseteq S \times O \times T$ and
$\langle c, o, t \rangle \in \mathsf{CF}^{\mathcal{I}}$ iff there exists an MS $\langle m, \mathcal{E}, \kappa, \mathcal{N}, \lambda \rangle$ such that $[t](\lambda(\kappa(o)) = c)$.

According to this interpretation, concepts are associated to symbols of MFs (condition (*c*)), and descriptions are associated to MFs (condition (*d*)). In general, an MF determines a (complex) symbolic structure, therefore, by (*e*), a description can define several (structured) concepts. This holds also for (mathematical, scientific, philosophical) *theories* in which the primitive notions are usually characterized by the way they are interrelated. Second, an MF $\mathcal{M}_i$ can be seen as the maximal collection of the physical supports of a description. One may think it would be more appropriate to map a description to the theory behind the $\mathcal{M}_i$. As already observed, this theory does not always exist. In addition, different theories can be associated to the same MF (different theories at different times, or different theories associated to different, but aligned, MSs in the same MF). Theories are then not essential neither to define MFs nor the 'meaning' of the symbols, i.e., for measurement, the *operative* side seems more important than the theoretical one. This allows also to clearly establish the temporal extensions of descriptions and concepts, even though a deeper analysis of the persistence conditions of MSs, mSTs, and MFs is required.[25] The interpretation of CF (condition (*f*)) is very similar to the one of L. Spaces can thus be seen as networks of social concepts the acceptance and sharing of which can be grounded on calibration and alignment. The question whether this interpretation is compatible with the axioms in [20] and general enough to account for all kinds of social concepts, e.g. abstract concepts or concepts defined in terms of temporal or modal relations, is left for future work.

Acknowledgments. I really appreciated the comments of Emanuele Bottazzi, Silvia Gaio, Laure Vieu, and the anonymous reviewers. Unfortunately I have not been able to answer all their interesting and deep questions.

References

[1] D. M. Armstrong. *Universals: An Opinionated Introduction*. Westview Press, 1989.

[25] For example, I don't see any problem in accepting that some of the MSs in an MF are substituted in time.

[2] L. R. Baker. *The Metaphysics of Everyday Life*. Cambridege Univerity Press, 2007.
[3] S. Borgo and C. Masolo. Qualities in possible worlds. In B. Bennett and C. Fellbaum, editors, *Proceedings of the 4th International Conference on Formal Ontology in Information Systems (FOIS-06)*, pages 250–261. IOS Press, 2006.
[4] S. Borgo and C. Masolo. Foundational choices in DOLCE. In S. Staab and R. Studer, editors, *Handbook on Ontologies*, pages 361–381. Springer Verlag, 2nd edition, 2009.
[5] R. Casati and A. C. Varzi. *Parts and Places*. MIT Press, Cambridge, MA, 1999.
[6] C. Daly. Tropes. In D.H. Mellor and A. Oliver, editors, *Properties*, pages 140–159. Oxford University Press, Oxford, 1997.
[7] L. Finkelstein. Widely, strongly and weakly defined measurement. *Measurement*, 34:39–48, 2003.
[8] A. Frigerio, A. Giordani, and L. Mari. Outline of a general model of measurement. *Synthese*, Published online: 28 February 2009.
[9] P. Gärdenfors. *Conceptual Spaces: the Geometry of Thought*. MIT Press, Cambridge, 2000.
[10] N. Goodman. Seven strictures on similarity. In N. Goodman, editor, *Problems and Projects*. The Bobbs-Merrill Co, 1972.
[11] K. Hawley. *How Thing Persist*. Clarendon Press, Oxford, UK, 2001.
[12] I. Johansson. Determinables as universals. *The Monist*, 83(1):101–121, 2000.
[13] W. E. Johnson. *Logic*, volume 1. Cambridge University Press, Cambridge, 1921.
[14] S. S. Jones and L. M. Koehly. Muldimensional scaling. In G. Keren and C. Lewis, editors, *A Handbook for Data Analysis in the Behavioral Sciences*, pages 95–163. Lawrence Erlbaum Associates, 1993.
[15] D.K. Lewis. Counterpart theory and quantified modal logic. *The Journal of Philosophy*, 65:113–126, 1968.
[16] D.K. Lewis. *On the Plurality of Worlds*. Basil Blackwell, Oxford, 1986.
[17] L. Mari. Epistemology of measurement. *Measurement*, 34:17–30, 2003.
[18] C. Masolo and S. Borgo. Qualities in formal ontology. In P. Hitzler, C. Lutz, and G. Stumme, editors, *Foundational Aspects of Ontologies Workshop at KI 2005*, pages 2–16, Koblenz, Germany, 2005.
[19] C. Masolo, S. Borgo, A. Gangemi, N. Guarino, and A. Oltramari. Wonderweb deliverable d18. Technical report, CNR, 2003.
[20] C. Masolo, L. Vieu, E. Bottazzi, C. Catenacci, R. Ferrario, A. Gangemi, and N. Guarino. Social roles and their descriptions. In *Ninth International Conference on the Principles of Knowledge Representation and Reasoning*, Whistler Canada, 2004.
[21] P. Mittelstaedt. Cognition versus constitution of objects: From Kant to modern physics. *Foundations of Physics*, 39:847–859, 2009.
[22] S. Mumford. *Dispositions*. Clarendon Press, 2003.
[23] D.N. Osherson and E. E. Smith. On the adequacy of propotype theory as a theory of concepts. In E. Margolis and S. Laurence, editors, *Concepts: Core Readings*, pages 261–278. MIT press, 1999.
[24] F. Probst. Observations, measurements and semantic reference spaces. *Applied Ontology*, 3(1-2):63–90, 2008.
[25] M. Rea, editor. *Material Constitution*. Rowman and Littlefield Publishers, 1996.
[26] G. Rodriguez-Pereyra. *Resemblance Nominalism. A Solution to the Problem of Universals*. Clarendon Press, Oxford, 2002.
[27] L. R. Santos and B. M. Hood. Object representation as a central issue in cognitive science. In B. M. Hood and L. R. Santos, editors, *The Origins of Object Knowledge: The Yale Symposium on the Origins of Object and Number Representation*. Oxford Univeristy Press, 2009.
[28] B. J. Scholl. Object persistence in philosophy and psychology. *Mind & Language*, 22(5):563–591, 2007.
[29] T. Sider. *Four-Dimensionalism. An Ontology of Persistence and Time*. Clarendon Press, Oxford, 2001.
[30] P. Simons. *Parts: a Study in Ontology*. Clarendon Press, Oxford, 1987.
[31] P. Suppes, D. M. Krantz, R. D. Luce, and A. Tversky. *Foundations of Measurement*, volume I - Additive and Polynomial Representations. Academic Press, 1971.
[32] C. Swoyer. The metaphysics of measurement. In J. Forge, editor, *Measurement, realism, and objectivity.*, pages 235–290. D. Reidel, 1987.
[33] J. D. Trout. Measurement. In W. H. Newton-Smith, editor, *A companion to the philosophy of science*, Blackwell Companions to Philosophy, chapter 40, pages 265–276. Blackwell Publishers, 2000.
[34] A. Tversky. Features of similarity. *Psychological Review*, 84:327–352, 1977.
[35] A. C. Varzi. Riferimento, predicazione, e cambiamento. In C. Bianchi and A. Bottani, editors, *Significato e ontologia*, pages 221–249. Franco Angeli, Milano, 2003.

Formal Ontology in Information Systems
A. Galton and R. Mizoguchi (Eds.)
IOS Press, 2010

doi:10.3233/978-1-60750-535-8-103

On the Representation of Quantities and their Parts in Conceptual Modeling

Giancarlo GUIZZARDI
Ontology and Conceptual Modeling Research Group (NEMO)
Computer Science Department, Federal University of Espírito Santo (UFES), Brazil
gguizzardi@inf.ufes.br

Abstract. In a series of publications, we have employed ontological theories and principles used to evaluate and improve the quality of conceptual modeling grammars and models. In this article, we continue this work by providing an ontological interpretation and sound modeling guidelines for a traditionally neglected notion in the conceptual modeling literature, namely, the representation of types whose instances are quantities (amounts of matter, masses). Here, we analyze different alternatives for the adequate representation of quantities as well as their parts in conceptual models. Moreover, we advance a number of metamodeling constraints that can be incorporated in a UML 2.0 metamodel extension, thus, allowing for the suitable representation of these notions.

Keywords. Conceptual Modeling, Real-World Semantics, Representation of Quantities

Introduction

In recent years, there has been a growing interest in the application of *Foundational Ontologies*, i.e., formal ontological theories in the philosophical sense, for providing real-world semantics for conceptual modeling languages, and theoretically sound foundations and methodological guidelines for evaluating and improving the individual models produced using these languages.

In a series of publications, we have successfully applied ontological theories and principles to analyze a number of fundamental conceptual modeling constructs ranging from Roles, Types and Taxonomic Structures, Part-Whole Relations, Relationships, Attributes, Weak Entities and Datatypes, among others [1-4]. In this article we continue this work by addressing a representation problem which has been traditionally neglected not only in the literature of conceptual modeling but also in existing ontological analysis of conceptual modeling grammars. We focus here on the representation of *quantities* (amounts of matter, masses). Existing proposals for modeling quantities in conceptual modeling deal exclusively with the representation of a *quantitative measure* aspect of quantities (e.g., [5, p.36]). However, as we argue in this article, there are many modeling situations in which this approach does not suffice. For this reason, we need a modeling approach for explicitly dealing with the complementary *numerical identity* aspect.

The contributions of this article are two-fold. Firstly, we conduct an ontological analysis of the notion of quantities and explore alternative manners in which these entities could be adequately represented in conceptual models. Our criteria of adequacy here include fundamental requirements for conceptual modeling which includes that the types representing quantity universals in a conceptual model have only instances which are determinate, i.e., which obey determinate *principles of identity*. Moreover, we also consider a fundamental requirement that conceptual models including quantity types should be satisfiable by finite data populations. As a result, we advocate for a specific interpretation to the notion of quantities and a specific proposal for their representation.

Secondly, given the specific proposed ontological interpretation for quantities, we explore the nature of a parthood relation involving quantities and their subparts. We then explicitly define this relation both in terms of its traditional mereological meta-properties (e.g., transitivity, extensionality) but also in terms of two additional characteristics which are fundamental for conceptual modeling, namely, *shareability* and *essentiality*. As an additional result connected to this second contribution, we present a number of metamodeling constraint that can be used for the implementation of a UML[1] modeling profile for representing quantities and their subparts.

The remainder of this article is organized as follows. Section 1 briefly reviews a number of aspects related to part-whole theories which are germane to the purposes of this article. Section 2 revisits the notion of principle of identity and its connection to sortal universals. The section also briefly explores the connection between identity and the notion of *homeomerosity* for the case of quantities, as both notions are later shown to play an important role in evaluating representation alternatives. Section 3 analyzes three different alternative solutions for representing quantities in conceptual modeling. Section 4 elaborates on the representation of a specific type of parthood relation between quantities and their subparts. Finally, section 5 presents some final considerations.

1. A Review of Part-Whole Theories

1.1. Mereological Theories

In practically all philosophical theories of parts, the relation of proper parthood (symbolized as <) stands for a strict partial ordering, i.e., an asymmetric and transitive relation, from which irreflexivity follows:

$$\forall x\ \neg(x < x) \tag{1}$$
$$\forall x,y\ (x < y) \rightarrow \neg(y < x) \tag{2}$$
$$\forall x,y,z\ (x < y) \wedge (y < z) \rightarrow (x < z) \tag{3}$$

These axioms amount to what is referred in the literature by the name of *Ground Mereology (M)*, which is the core of any theory of parts. Taking reflexivity (and antisymmetry) as constitutive of the meaning of 'part' implies regarding identity as a limit case of parthood. In this spirit, an *improper part of* relation (≤) can be defined as:

$$(x \leq y) =_{def} (x < y) \vee (x = y) \tag{4}$$

[1] The Unified Modeling Language (UML) is a *de facto* standard for software and data engineering (http://www.uml.org/). A modeling profile is a built in mechanism in UML to create specialized versions of the language.

The axioms (1-3) define the minimal (partial ordering) constrains that every relation must fulfill to be considered a partOf relation. Although necessary, these constraints are not sufficient, i.e., it is not the case any partial ordering qualifies as a parthood relation. Some authors [6], require an extra axiom termed the *weak supplementation principle* (5) as constitutive of the meaning of part and, hence, consider (1-3) plus (5) (the so-called *Minimal Mereology* (MM)) as the minimal constraints that a mereological theory should incorporate.

$$\forall x,y\ (y < x) \rightarrow \exists z\ (z < x) \wedge \neg overlap(z,y) \tag{5}$$

An extension to MM has then been created by strengthening the supplementation principle represented by (5). In this system, (5) is thus replaced by the following stronger supplementation axiom:

$$\forall x,y\ \neg(y \leq x) \rightarrow \exists z\ (z \leq y) \wedge \neg overlap(z,x) \tag{6}$$

Formula (6) is named the *strong supplementation principle*, and the theory that incorporates (1-3), (5) and (6) is named *Extensional Mereology (EM)*. A known consequence of the introduction of axiom (6) is that in EM, we have that two objects are identical iff they have the same (proper) parts, a mereological counterpart of the *extensionality principle* (of identity) in set theory.

A second way that MM has been extended is with the aim to provide a number of closure operations to the mereological domain. As discussed, for example, in [6,7], theories named *CMM (Closure Minimal Mereology)* and *CEM (Closure Extensional Mereology)* can be obtained by extending MM and EM with the operations of *Sum*, *Product*, *Difference* and *Complement*. In particular, with an operation of sum (also termed *mereological fusion*), one can create an entity which is the so-called *mereological sum* of a number of individuals.

1.2. Problems with Mereology as a Theory of Conceptual Parts

Mereology has shown itself useful for many purposes in mathematics and philosophy [6,7]. Moreover, it provides a sound formal basis for the analysis and representation of the relations between parts and wholes regardless of their specific nature. However, as pointed out by [8,9] (among other authors), it contains many problems that make it hard to directly apply it as a theory of conceptual parts. As it shall become clear in the discussion that follows, on one hand the theory is too strong, postulating constraints that cannot be accepted to hold generally for part-whole relations on the conceptual level. On the other hand, it is too weak to characterize the distinctions that mark the different types of conceptual part-whole relations.

A problem with ground mereology is the postulation of unrestricted transitivity of parthood. As discussed in depth in the literature [1,10], there many cases in which transitivity fails. In general, in conceptual modeling, part-whole relations have been established as non-transitive, i.e., transitive in certain cases and intransitive in others.

The problem with extensional mereologies from a conceptual point of view arises from the introduction of the strong supplementation principle and, consequently, of formula (6) which states that objects are completely defined by their parts. If an entity is identical to the mereological sum of its parts, thus, changing any of its parts changes the identity of that entity. Ergo, an entity cannot exist without each of its parts, which is the same as saying that all its parts are *essential parts*. Essential parthood can be defined as a case of *specific constant dependence* (*existential dependence*) between individuals, i.e., x is an essential part of y iff y cannot possibly exist without having that specific individual x as part [6]. As discussed in depth in [2], essential parthood plays a fundamental role in conceptual modeling. However, while some parts of objects represented in conceptual models are essential, not all of them are essential. The failure to acknowledge that can be generalized as the failure of classical mereological theories to take into account the different roles that parts play within the whole. As discussed in [4,11], a conceptual theory of parthood should also countenance a *theory of wholes*, in which the relations that tie the parts of a whole together are also considered.

From a conceptual point of view, the problem with the theory of General (Classical) Extensional Mereology is related to the existence of a sum (or fusion) for any arbitrary non-empty (but non-necessarily finite) set of entities. Just as in set theory one can create a set containing arbitrary members, in GEM one can create a new object by summing up individuals that can even belong to different ontological meta-categories. For example, in GEM, the individual Θ created by the sum of Noam Chomsky's left foot, the first act of Puccini's Turandot and the number 3, is an entity considered as legitimate as any other. As argued by [9], humans only accept the summation of entities if the resulting mereological sum plays some role in their conceptual schemes. To use an example cited there: the sum of a frame, a piece of electrical equipment and a bulb constitutes an integral whole that is considered meaningful to our conceptual classification system. For this reason, this sum deserves a specific concept in cognition and name in human language. The same does not hold for the sum of bulb and the lamp's base. Once more, we advocate that a theory of conceptual parthood must also comprise a theory of wholes.

According to Simons [6], the difference between purely formal ontological sums and, what he terms, *integral wholes* is an ontological one, which can be understood by comparing their existence conditions. For sums, these conditions are minimal: the sum exists just when the constituent parts exist. By contrast, for an integral whole (composed of the same parts of the corresponding sum) to exist, a further *unifying condition* among the constituent parts must be fulfilled. A unifying condition or relation can be used to define a closure system in the following manner. A set B is a closure system under the relation R, or simply, R-closure system iff

$$\mathbf{cs}\ \langle \mathbf{R}\rangle\ \mathbf{B} =_{\mathbf{def}} (\mathbf{cl}\ \langle \mathbf{R}\rangle\ \mathbf{B}) \wedge (\mathbf{con}\ \langle \mathbf{R}\rangle\ \mathbf{B}) \quad (7)$$

where **(cl ⟨R⟩ B)** means that the set B is closed under R (R-Closed) and **(con ⟨R⟩ B)** means that the set B is connected under R (R-Connected). R-Closed and R-Connected are then defined as:

$$\mathbf{cl}\ \langle \mathbf{R}\rangle\ \mathbf{B} =_{\mathbf{def}} \forall \mathbf{x}\ (\mathbf{x} \in \mathbf{B}) \rightarrow ((\forall \mathbf{y}\ \mathbf{R}(\mathbf{x},\mathbf{y}) \vee \mathbf{R}(\mathbf{y},\mathbf{x}) \rightarrow (\mathbf{y} \in \mathbf{B})) \quad (8)$$

$$\mathbf{con}\ \langle \mathbf{R}\rangle\ \mathbf{B} =_{\mathbf{def}} \forall \mathbf{x}\ (\mathbf{x} \in \mathbf{B}) \rightarrow (\forall \mathbf{y}\ (\mathbf{y} \in \mathbf{B}) \rightarrow (\mathbf{R}(\mathbf{x},\mathbf{y}) \vee \mathbf{R}(\mathbf{y},\mathbf{x})) \quad (9)$$

An integral whole is then defined as an object whose parts form a closure system induced by what Simons terms a *unifying* (or *characterizing*) *relation* R.

Besides modal meta-properties such as generic or specific dependence of parts, conceptual modeling theory of parthood must also recognize additional modes in which something can be a part of a whole. One of these notions of great importance is the so-called *(non-)shareability* (or *exclusiveness*) of parts [4]. This distinction is reflected, for instance, in UML as the distinction between the aggregation relation (represented as a hollow diamond) and a composition relation (represented as a black diamond). In a nutshell, an individual x of type A is said to be an non-shareable (proper) part of another individual y of type B (symbolized here as $<_{NS}(x,A,y,B)$) iff y is the only B that has x as part:

$$<_{NS}(x,A,y,B) =_{def} instanceOf(x,A) \land instanceOf(y,B) \land (x<y) \land (\forall z\ instanceOf(z,B) \land (x < z) \rightarrow (y = z)) \quad (10)$$

Finally, in a seminal article entitled *"A taxonomy of part-whole relations"*, Winston & Chaffin & Herrmann [12] (henceforth WCH), propose an account of the notion of parthood by elaborating on different ways that parts can related to a whole. This study led to a refinement on the formal relation of parthood by distinguishing the six types of meronymic relations. This taxonomy has been later refined by [8] demonstrating that the six linguistically-motivated types of part-whole relation proposed give rise to only three distinct ontological types, namely: (a) *subquantity-quantity* (e.g., alcohol-wine) – modeling parts of an amount of matter; (b) *member-collective* (e.g., a specific tree – the black forest) – modeling a collective entity in which all parts play an equal role w.r.t. the whole; (c) *component – functional complex* (e.g., heart-circulatory system, engine – car) - modeling an entity in which all parts play a different role w.r.t. the whole, thus, contributing to the functionality of the latter.

2. Homeomerosity and Identity related to Quantities

In [13], van Leeuwen shows an important syntactical difference in natural languages that reflects a semantical and ontological one, namely, the difference between common nouns (CNs) on one side and arbitrary general terms (adjectives, verbs, mass nouns, etc...) on the other. CNs have the singular feature that they can combine with determiners and serve as argument for predication in sentences such as:

(i) (exactly) five mice were in the kitchen last night;
(ii) the mouse which has eaten the cheese, has been in turn eaten by the cat.

In other words, if we have the patterns *(exactly) five X...* and *the Y which is Z....*, only the substitution of X,Y,Z by CNs will produce sentences which are grammatical. To see that, we can try the substitution by the adjective *Red* in the sentence *(i): (exactly) five red were in the kitchen last night.* A request to 'count the red in this room' cannot receive a definite answer: Should a red shirt be counted as one or should the shirt, the two sleeves, and two pockets be counted separately so that we have five reds? The problem in this case is not that one would not know how to finish the counting but that one would not know how to start since arbitrarily many parts of a red thing are still red.

The distinction between the grammatical categories of CNs and arbitrary general terms can be explained in terms of the ontological categories of *Sortal* and *Characterizing universals* [14] (also termed *mixin types* in the object-orientation literature [3]), which are roughly their ontological counterparts. Whilst the latter supply only a *principle of application* for the individuals they collect, the former supply both a principle of application and a *principle of identity*. A principle of application is that in accordance with which we judge whether a general term applies to a particular (e.g. whether something is a Person, a Dog, a Chair or a Student). A principle of identity supports the judgment whether two particulars are the same, i.e., in which circumstances the identity relation holds. By supplying a principle of identity and individuation, a sortal can also supply a principle of counting: counting depends on identity since to count correctly one cannot count *the same* individual twice.

The statement that we can only make identity and quantification statements in relation to a Sortal amounts to one of the best-supported theories in the philosophy of language, namely, that the identity of an individual can only be traced in connection with a Sortal Universal, which provides a *principle of individuation* and *identity* to the particulars it collects [13]. The Sortal supplying these principles is named a Substance Sortal [13] or a *Kind* [3]. In [3], the authors advocate an equivalent stance for a theory of conceptual modeling by defending that: (i) among the conceptual modeling counterparts of general terms (classifiers), only constructs that represent substance sortals (kinds) can provide a principle of identity and individuation for its Instances; (ii) every individual in a conceptual model must be an instance of a sortal.

One difference between subquantity-quantity and the other two types of parthood is that the relata of this relation always belong to the category of *amounts of matter* (masses, quantities), while in the component-functional complex and member-collective they are *Substantials* (or *Objects*) [4]. Quantities (such as water, sand, sugar, martini, wine, etc.) lack both *individuation* and *counting principles*. For this reason, the general terms which are linguistically represented by mass nouns (the linguistic counterpart of amounts of matter) cannot be used to substitute X, Y and Z in the aforementioned sentence patterns. A substitution for, for example, water in sentence (i) is not viable, since arbitrarily many parts of water are still water. Likewise, a success in the substitution by water in (ii) depends on the possibility of determining the referent and judge identity statements of individual quantities of water. What exactly should be that referent?

Before answering this question we should call attention to the notion of *homeomerosity*, which is used both by the WCH taxonomy and by [8] to distinguish subquantity-quantity relations from the other two types aforementioned. Traditionally, homeomerosity means that an individual only has parts which are of the same kind [15]. This is clearly not the case for all amounts of matter, as the Gin-Martini case demonstrates. However, one can still say that every subquantity of Martini is again Martini and that although Martini is composed of Gin, Gin is itself “homeomerous” in this more liberal sense. This line of reasoning seems to suggest that homeomerosity is equated with infinite decomposability, i.e., for every subquantity of Martini there is always a subquantity of Martini, and the same holds for quantities of Gin. Some authors (e.g., [15]), nonetheless, admit the existence of quantities of type K having K-atoms, i.e., individuals of type K that have no parts of the same type K. Examples include concrete mass terms such as ‘furniture’, ‘cutlery’ or ‘crowd’. These allegedly exemplars of quantities are definitely not homeomerous, not even in the more liberal sense. For example, there are parts of a crowd, namely individual persons, which are not a crowd themselves and which are not homeomerous in any meaningful sense. What can be said in this case is that these aggregates have a uniform structure and, in parity with [8], we consider them as examples of *member-collective* parthood instead.

One could also consider homeomerosity to simply mean that an aggregate can merely have some parts of the same kind while having other parts of other kinds. However, if this were to be the case one could not use it as a meta-property to differentiate subquantity-quantity from member-collective. Notice that examples of "homeomerous" parts in this sense can be easily found for member-collective: a crowd can be part of a larger crowd; a forest can be part of larger forest. Since WCH do not consider member-collective to be homeomerous, they would have to agree that quantities should be considered necessarily infinitely divisible in subquantities of the same kind.

Now, an important question that comes to the mind is how we should represent in conceptual models the types whose instances are quantities in the sense just mentioned? As we have discussed in depth in [3,13], in order to be able to make viable references to general terms which are not count nouns (mass terms, adjectives, verbs) they first must be nominalized. A nominalization of a mass noun, verb or an adjective promotes the shift to the category of count nouns (e.g., the fall of Jack, a lump of clay), hence, allowing for the representation of the corresponding (nominalized) sortal type. An important question that then arises is: what is the best nominalization of mass terms so that they can be satisfactorily represented in conceptual models as sortal types? In the next section, we investigate three candidate nominalization/representation alternatives.

3. On the Representation of Quantities in Conceptual Modeling

3.1. Quantities as Mereological Sums

In order to investigate the representation alternatives let us take the example of a portion of wine which could be differentiated from other portions of wine by the year and source vineyard. What is the meaning (and implied principle of individuation) of a universal whose instances are portions of wine?

A first possibility is to consider the referent of the expression "the portion of wine" as a mereological fusion of all subportions of wine that constitutes it. This approach is standard in philosophy and [6] suggests that quantities are probably the best case of application of the Classical Extensional Mereologies (CEM), since practically all objections raised against the CEM for the purpose of conceptual modeling can be safely lifted in the case of quantities and their parts. Nonetheless, and still from a philosophical point of view, the first problem with this conception of quantities is whether it is at all possible to have a principle of identity for portions of wine in this sense [15,16]. A mereological principle of identity in this case prescribes that portion of wine A is equal to portion of wine B iff they have the same parts. However, since the parts of A and B are also portions of wine, to decide if A and B have the SAME parts one has to decide about the identity of the parts, and the parts of the parts, leading to an infinite regress, since, by assumption, quantities are infinitely divisible. One could derive some synchronic information about identity by saying that two quantities are different if they do not occupy the same region of space. However, this cannot be used as a diachronic principle of identity. Alternatively, one could say that a quantity A in t_1 is not the same quantity as B in t_2 if they have different properties such as volume or weight (still assuming the mereological principle). Nonetheless, the fact that B in t_2 has the same volume or weight as A in t_1 can only account for the sameness of the quantities in a very loose sense, meaning the same measure. In other words, in this case, the relation between A and B is one of equivalence, not one of *numerical identity*.

In conceptual modeling, there are a number of situations in which dealing only with qualitative identity of masses does not suffice. For instance, one might be interested in tracking the persistence of a quantity of a certain liquid which has been poisoned, or, in a chemical experiment, it could be important to track the change of properties in the very SAME persisting quantity. For this reason, contra [8], who proposes that "quantities are arbitrary pieces of the whole as long as they are properly characterized by the quantitative measure", we advocate that a treatment of masses in conceptual modeling must deal explicitly with the case of numerical identity.

However, there is still a bigger problem with this idea from a conceptual modeling stance. Figure 1 depicts the representation of a portion of Wine universal in the sense just mentioned. In this specification, the idea is to represent a certain portion of wine as the mereological sum of all subportions of wine belonging to a certain vintage. As it can be noticed, since every portion of wine is composed of subportions of wine, the cardinality of the part-whole relation cannot be specified in a finite manner. The same holds for every cardinality constraint for associations involving portions of wine. As discussed, for instance in [17], *finite satisfiability* is a fundamental requirement for conceptual models which are intended to be used in areas such as Databases and Software Engineering.

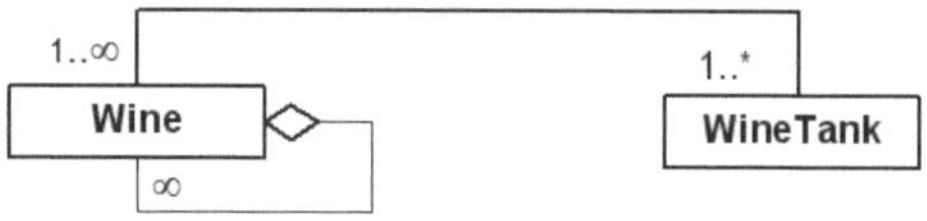

Figure 1. Representing Quantities as Mereological Sums.

Furthermore, "homeomerous" entities represented in this manner can induce to representation errors in the presence of other shareability constraints. For example, figure 2 presents an exact copy of a UML class diagram from [18][2] that symbolizes a Fractal (perhaps the prototypical example of homeomerous form). The intention of the authors seems to be to represent that a fractal, i.e., the rendering of one iteration step of an IFS (Iterated Function Series), is part of only one instance of the infinite recursion of this function. In other words, a part of an instantiation of a *Julia Series* is not a part of another instantiation of the same fractal form, or part of an instantiation of the *Mandelbrot Series*. However, that is not what is represented in the model. The model states that every instance of a fractal (i.e., every iteration of an IFS) is part of only one other fractal. This is clearly mistaken: the nth iteration of an IFS is part of all previous iterations of the same fractal. This problem is far from being specific to Fractals. In fact, for all homeomerous entities, with the exception of the maximal sum of subquantities, all other parts of quantity are necessarily part of innumerable other quantities of the same kind.

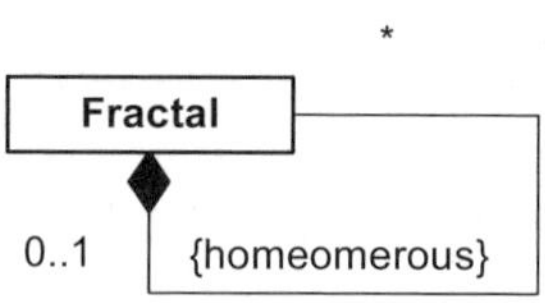

Figure 2. Mistaken Representation of homeomerous parts with non-sheareability (from [19]).

[2] The tagged value {homeomerous} in the picture is a proposal of [18] and it is present in the original article.

3.2. Quantities as the Identificationally Dependent on Objects

For the purpose of conceptual modeling, there is still one further philosophical argument invalidating the modeling alternative discussed in the previous section. According to [19], masses are *identificationally dependent* of substantials that are instances of sortal universals. As he put it: "The formal concepts 'amount', 'part' and 'stuff', like 'mass' and 'matter', are formed 'on the back of' [19, p. 191] the formal concept '(material) thing' or '(material) object'. There is no mass, except the mass of a certain object. There is no stuff except the stuff a certain thing consists of". This is to say that individuating a quantity depends on the definite descriptions used for referring, which succeeds only when the referent can be individuated by an object type, i.e., it is the water in the bathtub, the clay that constitutes the statues, a cube of sugar, that can be referred to, not just some water, some clay, or some sugar. Moreover, quantities have no criteria for when they constitute a whole of some sort (unity criteria), except in cases in which we derive those criteria from objects that are only identifiable via sortals. This view is also supported by Quine in [20], who proposes that every occurrence of a quantity expression having the form "The K", "The same K" (where K is a concrete quantity type) is really a masked reference to a *portion* of K to which an ordinary sortal type applies. Alternatively formulating, as Quine puts it: "[in these situations, always] some special individuation standard is understood from the circumstances". This perspective gives rise to a second option of representation for the wine/wine tank example, as depicted in figure 3.

Figure 3. Representing Quantities as *Identificationally Dependent* on Objects.

There are a number of observations that can be made about figure 3. In this second option for nominalization of quantities, Wine means the maximal content of a Wine Tank. Likewise, the referent of a portion of clay means whatever quantity of clay constitutes a given statue, which is in turn individuated by the principle of identity supplied by the sortal Statue. In this representation, there is no longer a problem for the specification of cardinality constraints between portion of wine and wine tank: every wine tank has as its content one single definite portion of wine. Additionally, since wine portion means the maximal content of a wine tank, it is not the case that this concept is homeomerous, i.e., there is no part of a portion of wine which is itself a portion of wine (otherwise, it would not be the maximal content). Thus, there is no problem with infinite cardinalities, infinite divisibility and, hence, the model can in principle be finitely satisfiable. Moreover, portion of Wine becomes a type supplying genuine principles of individuation, counting and identity: it is always determinate if two portions of wine are identical and it is always determinate how many portions of wine there are.

Now, what is the nature of the relation R between a quantity of Wine and WineTank in figure 3? It is more than a relationship of spatial containment. Notice that if the identity of the quantity is defined by its container than relation R becomes one of existential dependency. Take the statue/lump of clay example. If A is the same lump of clay as long as it constitutes the same statue B, A would have a complete life-time dependency to B. For instance: (a) if a piece of B is removed, B is still the same statue and so is A still the same lump of clay, since it still constitutes the same statue; (b) If the form of B is altered, B ceases to exist and so does A, since it no longer constitutes the same statue. In summary, in this second alternative nominalization, we have to arrive at the counter-intuitive conclusion that a quantity in this sense has properties which are more akin to the notion of *moment* (*trope*) than that of substantial (object) [4].

3.3. Quantities as Maximally Self-Connected Objects

Although this second alternative contains important advantages over the first one from a conceptual modeling point of view, it leads to a problematic consequence. The problem is implied exactly by the *rigid specific dependence* relation between a quantity in this sense and its container. As put by [21], a sentence such as the "same K" (where K is a quantity universal) should be understood in a such way that **x is the same K as y iff x is some K, y is some K, and (x = y),** or, as discussed in [3,13], in statements of identity, the relata must instantiate the same kind, i.e., the same rigid sortal supplying their principle of identity. In parity with [15, 21], we consider as meaningful a sentence such as "the sugar that was in that cube is the same sugar as the one in this lump". However, if this is the case, which kind of individuation and identity principle should be applied to x and y, that of cubes or of lumps?

A third nominalization alternative that solves this problem is presented as follows. This last option relies on the notion of *piece* discussed by Lowe in [16]. According to Lowe, a piece of a quantity K is a maximally self-connected object constituted by portions of K (portions in the first sense discussed in 3.1). Following Lowe, by maximal self-connected portion of K we mean the following: (i) *connected*, in the sense that every part of it is spatially connected to every other part of it by a series of spatially contiguous parts; (ii) *maximal*, in the sense that it is not a proper part of any larger connected part of stuff of the same kind K. One should notice that this relation of (spatially contiguous) connection is transitive: if x is connected to y by a series of spatially contiguous parts, and if y is connected to z in the same sense, we have that x is spatially-contiguously connected to z.

Like in the second nominalization alternative, a quantity of K in this sense is an instance of a type supplying definite individuation, identity and counting principles. Moreover, it is not homeomerous, however it can still be composed of other quantities K' in the same sense of quantity (see figure 4). Moreover, in this case, it is still convenient to consider all parts of quantity as essential: a specific quantity of Wine is composed by that specific quantity of Alcohol. Finally, this representation alternative also does not contain the infinite regress problems mentioned for the first case.

Now, differently from the second alternative, the dependence relation between a quantity and its container is a generic not a specific one. For this reason we can state that for the same maximally self-connected quantity of wine, there can be several "container phases". This idea is represented in the (incomplete) model of figure 4. A vintage is an (substantial) object constituted by (possibly many) quantities of wine. It is, however, not a quantity since it can be scattered over many quantities. Moreover, it is not necessary for its constituent quantities to be essential: even if the quantity of wine now stored in a certain tank is destroyed, we still have numerically the same vintage. We, therefore, propose the use of this third alternative for the nominalization of quantities and their representation in conceptual models. From now on, we shall use the term *quantity of matter K* or *objectified portion of matter K* to refer to a *piece of K* in the Lowe's sense aforementioned, and use the stereotype «quantity» to symbolize a (sortal) type whose instances are quantities in this sense.

In the first representation alternative, quantities have very minimal existence conditions and can hardly be said to constitute integral wholes. In the second representation alternative, a genuine characterizing or unifying relation can be defined creating an integral whole. However, this relation is an external one, creating a specific dependence to a container object. Moreover, in this second alternative, a quantity resembles more a moment than an object, becoming identificationally and existentially dependent on its container. In the third representation choice, quantities are object-like integral wholes, unified by an intrinsic and again genuine unifying relation of spatially contiguous maximal self-connectedness.

Finally, we can summarize many points of the argument carried out in this section by using an example proposed by [21]. If a sentence such as "Heraclitus bathed in some water yesterday and bathed in the same water today" is true then for some suitable substituends of x and y we have that: (a) x is a quantity of water and Heraclitus bathed in x yesterday; (b) y is a quantity of water and Heraclitus bathed in y today; (c) x = y. However, (c) when interpreted as (d) "the water Heraclitus bathed in yesterday = the water Heraclitus bathed in today" requires that: (e) there is exactly one x such that x is a quantity of water and Heraclitus bathed in x both yesterday and today. But, if quantity is interpreted in the first sense discussed in 3.1, there are not one but infinitely many particulars that would satisfy (a), (b) and (d) without satisfying (c). The same does not hold for the second and third senses.

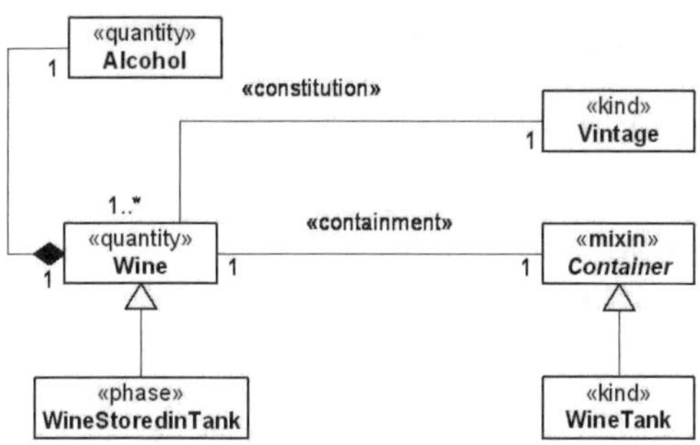

Figure 4. Representing quantities as maximally-self-connected portions

4. Representing parts of a Quantity: the subQuantityOf relation

We can now define the *subQuantityOf* as a part-whole relation holding between *quantities* in the technical sense explained in the previous section. As depicted in figure 5 below, we decorate here the standard UML symbol for composition with a Q to represent this relation.

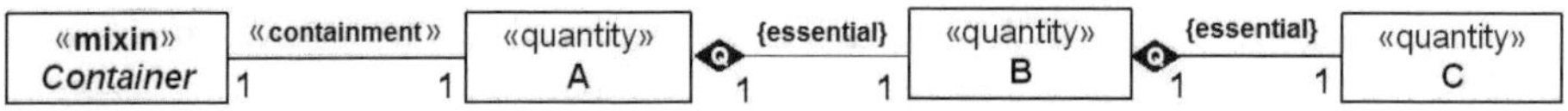

Figure 5. Part-Whole relations among Quantities.

Let us take the quantities A, B and C represented in this figure. We can show that for any A, B, C, the part-whole relation (C < A) holds as a result from the transitivity (C <

B) and (B < A). The argumentation can be developed as follows: if A is a quantity then it is a maximal portion of matter unified by the characterizing relation of self-connectedness. That is, any part of A is connected to any other part of A. If B is part of A then B is connected to all parts of A. Likewise, if C is part of B then C is connected to all parts of B. Since (as previously discussed) this notion of spatially contiguous connection is transitive, then we have that C is connected to all parts of A. Thus, since A is unified under self-connection, C must be part of A (otherwise the composition of A would not be a closure system, see definition in section 2). Therefore, we conclude that for the case of quantities, transitivity always holds. Another way to examine this situation is by inspecting A at an arbitrary time instant t. We can say that all parts of A are the quantities that are contained in a certain region of space R (i.e. a topoid[3]). Since A is an objectified matter, than the topoid R occupied by A must be self-connected. Therefore, if B is part of A then B must occupy a sub-region R', which is part of R. Likewise, if C is part of B, it occupies a region R'', part of R'. Since spatial part-whole relations are always transitive [22], we have that R'' is part of R, and if C occupies R'', then it is contained in R. Ergo, by definition, C is a part of A.

As discussed in section 3.3, a type stereotyped as « quantity » in this work stands for a maximally-connected-amount-of-matter. Since a quantity is maximal, it cannot have as a part a quantity of the same kind. For the same reason, a *subQuantityOf* relation is always non-shareable. For example, take a case in which this relation holds between a quantity of alcohol *x* and a quantity of wine *y*. Since y is self-connected it occupies a self-connected portion of space. The same holds for x. In addition, the topoid occupied by x must be a (improper) part of the topoid occupied by y. Now suppose that there is a portion of wine z (different from y) such that x is a subQuantityOf z. A consequence of this is that z and x overlap, and since they are both self-connected, we can define a portion of wine w which is itself self-connected. In this case, both z and x are part of w and therefore, they are not *maximally-self-connected-portions*. This contradicts the premises that x and z were quantities. Hence, we can conclude that the *subQuantityOf* relation is always non-sharable. Furthermore, since every part of a quantity is itself a quantity, subQuantityOf must also have a cardinality constraint of *one and exactly one* in the subquantity side. Take once more the alcohol-wine example above. Since alcohol is a quantity (and, hence, maximal), there is exactly one quantity of alcohol which is part of a specific quantity of wine.

Also as discussed in section 3.3, quantities are mereologically invariant, i.e., the change of any of its parts changes the identity of the whole. In other words, all *subQuantityOf* relations are essential parthood relations (see relations tagged with {essential} in figure 5). Therefore, since quantities are extensional entities, the *weak supplementation axiom* (4) defined to hold for all part-whole relations can be replaced by the adoption of the *strong supplementation axiom* for the case of this relation.

The axiomatization of the *subQuantityOf* relation thus includes the basic axioms of any mereological theory, namely, irreflexivity, anti-symmetry and transitivity of the proper-part relation. But also the *strong supplementation axiom* and the *extensionality principle*. Moreover, it includes the exclusive parthood and the essential parthood axioms. In other words, the axiomatization of this relation is the one of *Extensional Mereology (EM)*, with non-shareable and essential parts. That means that two quantities are the same iff they have the same parts, and no two instance of the same quantity kind overlap.

---

[3]A Topoid is a region of space with a certain mereotopological structure.

We summarize the results of these sections in a proposal that can be incorporated in a UML profile for representing subQuantityOf relations (table 1). Since a profile is constituted by syntactical constraints and, since UML conceptual models are always defined at the type level, the meta-properties of irreflexivity, anti-symmetry and transitivity (at instance level) cannot be captured by profile constraints. We have included a constraint to guarantee weak supplementation for these relations taking in consideration the type-level nature of the diagrams, i.e., taking into consideration the minimum cardinality constraints of all subQuantityOf relations connected to the same type representing a whole. Finally, one should notice that the diagrams of figure 4 and 5 do not obey this constraint and should be interpreted as (incomplete) model fragments.

Table 1. Metamodel Constraints for a UML profile for modeling Quantities and the subQuantityOf relation

Metaclass	**Description and Concrete Syntax**
«quantity» A	A «quantity» represents a sortal whose instances are *quantities*. Examples are those stuff universals that are typically referred in natural language by mass general terms (e.g., Gold, Water, Sand, Clay).
subQuantityOf	subQuantityOf is a proper parthood relation between two quantities. Examples include: (a) alcohol is part of Wine; (b) Plasma is part of Blood; (c) Sugar is part of Ice Cream; (d) Milk is part of Cappucino. We propose the icon 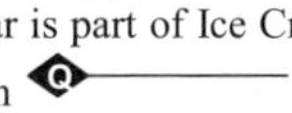 to represent this relation.

Meta-Properties of subQuantityOf

Irreflexivity, Asymmetry, Transitivity and Strong Supplementation (Extensional Mereology).

Constraints for subQuantityOf

1. The classes connected to both association ends of this relation must represent universals whose instances are *quantities*, i.e., they must be either stereotyped as «quantity» or be a *subtype* of a class stereotyped as «quantity»;
2. This relation is always non-shareable (always represented with the black diamond notation in UML);
3. All entities stereotyped as «quantity» are extensional individuals and, thus, all parthood relations involving quantities are marked with the tagged value **{essential}** representing an essential parthood relation. As a consequence, the association end connected to the part must be immutable;
4. The maximum cardinality constraint in the association end connected to the part must be one;
5. <u>Weak Supplementation:</u> Let U be a universal whose instances are wholes and let $\{C_1 \ldots C_2\}$ be a set of universals related to U via aggregation relations. Let $lower_{Ci}$ be the value of the minimum cardinality constraint of the association end connected to C_i in the aggregation relation. Then, we have that

$$\left(\sum_{i=1}^{n} lower_{Ci}\right) \geq 2;$$

5. Final Considerations

The development of suitable foundational theories is an important step towards the definition of precise real-world semantics and sound methodological principles for conceptual modeling languages. In this paper, we conduct an ontological analysis to investigate the proper representation of types whose instances are quantities, as well as the representation of parthood relations involving quantities. As result, we were able to provide not only a sound ontological interpretation for the notion of quantity types, but also one that satisfies two fundamental modeling requirements: determinate numerical identity for their instances; finite satisfiability for conceptual models representing quantity types and subQuantityOf relations. In addition, the results advanced here contribute to the definition of concrete engineering tools for the practice of conceptual modeling. In particular, the metamodel extensions and associated constraints proposed can be implemented using available UML metamodeling tools in a straightforward manner (as demonstrated in [23]). This extended UML metamodel, in turn, can be directly employed by automated tools to support the development of conceptual models which are sensible to the ontological notions discussed here. Finally, the representation for the notion of quantity and subQuantityOf put forth here have been employed successfully in an industrial case study in the domain of petroleum and gas [24] to model notions such as specific quantities of *Reservoir Rock* and its subparts (specific subquantities of Water, Gas and Oil) as well as the participation of quantities in events such as Petroleum Production and Transportation.

References

[1] Guizzardi, G. The Problem of Transitivity of Part-Whole Relations in Conceptual Modeling Revisited, 21st Intl. Conf. on Advanced Information Systems Engineering (CAISE'09), The Netherlands, 2009.
[2] Guizzardi, G. Modal Aspects of Object Types and Part-Whole Relations and the de re/de dicto distinction, 19th Int.l Conf. on Advanced Inf.Systems Engineering (CAISE'07), Trondheim, 2007.
[3] Guizzardi, G.; Wagner, G.; Guarino, N.; van Sinderen, M. An Ontologically Well-Founded Profile for UML Conceptual Models, 16th Intl. Conf. on Advanced Information Systems Engineering (CAiSE'04), Latvia, 2004.
[4] Guizzardi, G., Ontological Foundations for Structural Conceptual Models, Telematica Institute Fundamental Research Series, The Netherlands, 2005.
[5] Fowler, M. Analysis Patterns: Reusable Object Models, Addison-Wesley, 1997.
[6] Simons, P.M. 'Parts. An Essay in Ontology', Oxford: Clarendon Press, 1987.
[7] Varzi. A.C.: 'Parts, wholes, and part-whole relations: The prospects of mereotopology'. Journal of Data and Knowledge Engineering, 20:259–286, 1996.
[8] Gerstl, P. and Pribbenow, S., Midwinters, End Games, and Bodyparts. A Classification of Part-Whole Relations, Intl. Journal of Human-Computer Studies 43: 865-889, 1995.
[9] Pribbenow, S. 'Meronymic Relationships: From Classical Mereology to Complex Part-Whole Relations', The Semantics of Relationships, R.Green and C. A. Bean (ed.), Kluwer Academic Publishers, 2002.
[10] Vieu, L.; Aurnague, M. Part-of Relations, Functionality and Dependence, Categorization of Spatial Entities in Language and Cognition. Amsterdam: John Benjamins, 2007.
[11] Gangemi, A., Guarino, N., Masolo, C., and Oltramari, A 'Understanding top-level ontological distinctions', Proceedings of IJCAI 2001 , Workshop on Ontologies and Information Sharing, 2001.
[12] Winston M.E.; Chaffin R.; Herrman D. A taxonomy of part-whole relations, Cognitive Science, 1987.
[13] Van Leeuwen, J.: Individuals and sortal concepts : an essay in logical descriptive metaphysics, PhD Thesis, University of Amsterdam (1991).
[14] Strawson, P. F.: Individuals. An Essay in Descriptive Metaphysics. London-N.York: Routledge (1959).
[15] Zimmerman, D. W. 'Theories of Masses and Problems of Constitution', Philosophical Review, 1995.
[16] Lowe, E.J. Entity, Identity and Unity, Erkenntnis 48: 191–208, Kluwer Academic Publishers, 1998.
[17] Cadoli, M., Calvanese, D., De Giacomo, G. & Mancini, T. Finite satisfiability of UML class diagrams by constraint programming. Workshop on CSP Techniques with Immediate Application, 2004
[18] Saksena, M.; France, R. B.; Larrondo-Petrie, M. 'A Characterization of Aggregation', in Proceedings of the 5th International Conference on Object-Oriented Information Systems (OOIS'98), September 1998.
[19] Wandinger, N. 'Masses of Stuff and Identity', Erkenntnis 48: 303–307, Kluwer Academic Pub., 1998.
[20] Quine, W.V.O. 'Word and Object', MIT Press, Cambridge, 1960.
[21] Cartwright, H. M. 'Heraclitus and the Bath Water'. Philosophical Review 74, 1965.
[22] Johansson, I. 'On the Transitivity of the Parthood Relations', in H. Hochberg and K. Mulligan (eds.) Relations and Predicates, ontos verlag, Frankfurt 2004, pp.161-181, 2004.
[23] Benevides, A.B.; Guizzardi, G. A Model-Based Tool for Conceptual Modeling and Domain Ontology Engineering in OntoUML,11th Intl. Conf. on Enterprise Information Systems (ICEIS), Milan, 2009.
[24] Guizzardi, G.; Lopes, M.; Baião, F.; Falbo, R. On the importance of Truly Ontological Representation Languages, Intl. Journal of Information Systems Modeling and Design, IGI-Global, 2010 (forthcoming).

Formal Ontology in Information Systems
A. Galton and R. Mizoguchi (Eds.)
IOS Press, 2010

doi:10.3233/978-1-60750-535-8-117

Affordances as Qualities

Jens ORTMANN [a,1] and Werner KUHN [a]
[a] *Institute for Geoinformatics, University of Münster, Germany*

Abstract. Affordances elude ontology. They have been recognized to play a role in categorization, especially of artifacts, but also of natural features. Yet, attempts to ontologize them face problems ranging from their presumed subjective nature to the fact that they involve potential actions, not objects or properties. We take a fresh look at the ontology of affordances, based on a simple insight: affordances are perceived by agents and may lead to actions, just like qualities are perceived and may lead to observations. We understand perception as a process invoking a quale in an agent. This quale can then be expressed as an action, if it stems from an affordance, or as an observation, if it stems from an other quality. Thus, we see affordances as qualities of the environment, perceived and potentially expressed by agents. We extend our recently proposed ontology of observations to include affordances and show how the parallel between observations (producing values) and affordances (producing actions) provides a simple and powerful ontological account of both.

Keywords. Affordance, Observation, Ontology, Quality, Quale, Action

1. Introduction

Humans judge their environment according to the actions it affords. A river affords swimming and fishing; a house affords protection from wind, precipitation and cold; a chair affords sitting; and a knife affords cutting, vegetables as well as oneself. These affordances determine activities in our lives, ranging from the mundane to spatial planning. Yet, they have received limited attention from information system ontologists. Even though their existence and their importance for categorization has been acknowledged, foundational ontologies and domain ontologies still rest on ontological principles largely developed in ancient Greece, long before the advent of ecological psychology. Affordances are not only perceptual phenomena (depending on perception and influencing behavior), but also *real* action possibilities [38]. This circumstance led Sanders to state that "affordances are ideal primitives for general ontology"[28, p. 103]. Even if one does not want to go that far, it is unfortunate that ecological psychology, which originated the notion of affordance [7], so far enters ontology only through the idea of a niche [34,33]. Affordances are not treated explicitly in ontology and sometimes even get conflated with objects.

From the applied perspective of geographic information systems (GIS), ontologies would benefit from including affordances, given that they are what the environment offers its inhabitants [7]. Yet, information system ontologies typically rest on allocentric

[1]Corresponding Author: Jens Ortmann, Institute for Geoinformatics, Westfälische Wilhelms-Universität Münster, Weseler Strasse 253, D-48151 Münster, Germany; E-mail: jens.ortmann@uni-muenster.de

semantic reference frames [25], with the implicit or explicit assumption that the conceptualizations they specify are agent-independent. For application areas with standardized terminologies (e.g. the *Terminologia Anatomica* in medicine [43]) or relying on conventional technical sensor observations, an allocentric reference frame may be sufficient. For many applications at mesoscopic scales [31] and involving human activities [16], however, the human understanding of an environment is important. Humans share the same physical environment, but perceive it differently. For example, a person in a wheelchair perceives curbstones and stairs differently from a person that can walk; the person in a wheelchair perceives an obstacle, where other people just perceive a step they can climb. An ornithologist perceives and categorizes birds differently from an untrained observer. Such differences are a particular challenge, as well as a chance, for GIS applications: how to integrate information about the same environment, provided by different communities with varying backgrounds [21], possibly distributed all over the planet [3]. The chance for science and society at large is to benefit globally from information provided locally, increasingly also in the form of volunteered geographic information [8].

It is widely accepted that humans do not objectively perceive environmental properties or objects. Perception is determined by interaction capabilities [40,9,41]: humans (and animals) perceive what they can do. We follow Turvey's view that an affordance is a quality of the environment that exhibits a mutual relation to a quality of an agent [38], giving rise to agent behavior [9,37]. Such a view is fully compatible with Gibson's original definition:

> The affordances of the environment are what it offers the animal, what it provides or furnishes, whether for good or ill. [...] I mean by [affordance] something that refers to both the environment and the animal in a way that no existing term does. It implies the complementarity of the animal and the environment. [7, p. 127]
>
> [A]n affordance is neither an objective property nor a subjective property; or it is both if you like. An affordance cuts across the dichotomy of subjective-objective. [...] It is both physical and psychical, yet neither. [7, p. 129]

In this paper, we present an account of affordances for information system ontologies, focusing on their role in perception, observation, and action. The relational nature of affordances suggests to model the environment based on ontologies of its qualities [13, 25] and of human and technical observers [18]. The environment and the observing agent span the space for affordances, which link these two ontological efforts.

Our view of affordances as qualities is not new. For example, Vieu et al. [39] discuss the closely related (but simpler) idea of capacities:

> The notion of capacity is taken from Cummins [...] and characterizes the dispositions [...] or behaviors a physical endurant is able to express, independently of any agent, even in the specific case of artefacts. Capacities are a type of DOLCE individual *qualities* possessed by elements in (at least) categories Amount of Matter, Non-agentive Physical Object, and Physical Artefact. [39, p. 125]

The abstraction of capacities from agents, however, leaves out a key ingredient of affordances. A pen, for example, only has the capacity to write or to fit a hand for humans or humanoid agents. Affordances can be seen as extensions of capacities (including an explicit agent), and as qualities at the same time. A key contribution of our work is this explicit modeling of agents. With it comes a connection to the ontology of perception and observation and the inclusion of inanimate observers, covering the affordance notion used in robotics [26].

Our formal account of affordances builds on the definition by Turvey [38]. We add the formal link to observations as well as to actions based on them. Our formalization uses the functional language Haskell[2], because our primary goal is understanding and modeling, rather than encoding for machine reasoning. In addition to its higher order modeling power, Haskell offers the advantage of an executable model of an ontology, which serves for testing during development. Once an agreement has been reached on a particular ontological model, expressing it in any ontology encoding language (such as OWL) is straight-forward. As we are more interested in human understanding than in machine reasoning at this point, we provide a UML visualization of some key concepts.

The remainder of this paper reviews a recently proposed ontology of observations (in section 2), discusses its extension to include affordances (in section 3) and illustrates the ideas through the prototypical affordance example of stair climbing (in section 4), before presenting the formalization (in section 5) and concluding with open questions and plans for future work (in section 6).

2. Observations

Observations link information to reality and provide the building blocks of all conceptualizations. As such they ground communication and relate data in information systems to the world and to its observers. Yet, basic ontological questions like "what can be observed" or "how do observations relate to entities in reality?" cannot yet be answered today, neither by providers nor by users of observation data [23]. With sensor observations becoming ubiquitous and major societal decisions (concerning, for example, climate, security, or health) being taken based on them, an improved understanding of observation as the source of information has become imperative. Many current research issues in information science and the social web (for example, concerning quality, trust, and reputation) also require an improved understanding of observation processes and results. The point of this paper is, furthermore, to show that an adequate ontology of observations can also help to understand affordances.

The ontology of observation has been hindered by, among other factors, the idea that measurement instruments are objective reporters of a mind-independent state of the world. This commonly held view neglects the fact that instruments are built and calibrated by human beings. Neither the choice of the observed entity, nor the quality assigned to it, nor its link to a stimulus, nor the value assignment to the quality are mind-independent. All of them involve human conceptualizations, though these are clearly more amenable to grounding and consensus than anything else in an information system.

Our observation ontology[3] specifies observations as processes and defines the semantics of their results by the qualities, endurants, perdurants, and abstracts involved. It generalizes from technical and human sensors [8] to observing agents in general. This generalization of observation and sensing behavior, where people, devices, sensor systems and sensor networks can all observe, has been shown to simplify and improve software architectures in the sensor web area [1,35]. Based on Gibson's ecological psychol-

[2]For more information on Haskell and to download the free compilers and interpreters visit http://www.haskell.org (last accessed: 14.2.2010)

[3]published in [18], available in revised and simplified form from http://musil.uni-muenster.de/publications/ontologies (last accessed: 14.2.2010)

ogy [7], we have published a first account of how observations relate to endurants and perdurants in [29], and extended it in [30].

We adopt DOLCE's four top level categories of particulars [20]: endurants, perdurants, abstracts, and qualities (which can be physical, temporal, or abstract). Endurants, for example lakes, participate in perdurants, for example storms. Qualities inhere in particulars, with physical qualities inhering in physical endurants and temporal qualities inhering in perdurants. For example, a temperature quality inheres in an amount of matter, such as an amount of air, and a duration quality inheres in an event, such as a storm. Quality universals shall be admitted, so that a quality can be abstracted from multiple instances to a quality type (e.g., air temperature) and even further to a quality kind (e.g., temperature). Observations result from detectable changes in the environment (stimuli), which involve endurants and perdurants, and have values as results, which stand for qualities inhering in these endurants and perdurants.

As in [25], an observation process is seen as invoking first a "quale", i.e., an analog signal in an observer's mind or technical sensor. This notion of quale is slightly different from that in [19], but in line with the one in philosophy of mind[4]: it denotes a quality experience by an observer and is not abstracted from the carrier of the quality. The red of the rose experienced by an observer belongs to the rose as well as to the observer; it cannot be abstracted from either. Thus, observation involves firstly the production of a quale and secondly its symbolization - a sequence of impression and expression.

The core concepts in our observation ontology are those of quality, stimulus, agent, quale, and value. They have been chosen and defined with the goal to remain as compatible as possible with existing observation and measurement standards as well as with the literature (such as [42]) and with ordinary language.

A **quality**, physical or temporal, can be observed. Examples are the temperature of an amount of air (physical) or the duration of an earthquake (temporal). The choice of a quality bearing entity (say, of an air mass surrounding a thermometer or an earthquake) gives a rough account of the spatial or temporal resolution of an observation.

Since qualities as such cannot be detected (how would information about them enter an observer?), a **stimulus** is needed, generating the analog signal in the observer. It can be defined as a "detectable change in the internal or external environment" of an observer[5] or as a "physical or chemical change in the environment that leads to a response controlled by the nervous system"[6]. Examples of stimuli are the heat energy flowing between an amount of air and a thermometer or the seismic waves of an earthquake. Stimuli need to have well-defined physical or chemical relationships to the observed qualities.

We adopt the term **agent** from artificial intelligence:

> An agent is anything that can be viewed as **perceiving** its environment through **sensors** and **acting** upon the environment through **effectors**. [27, p. 31]

This notion of agent allows us to talk about humans, other animals, sensors with display or actuating capabilities, and robots.

Our conceptualization of observation processes, thus, involves two steps performed by agents. First, they generate a **quale** for the observed quality from stimuli. Second, they express the quale by symbols standing for the observation **value**. This account makes the

---

[4] for a good overview, see http://en.wikipedia.org/wiki/Qualia (last accessed: 14.2.2010)

[5] http://en.wikipedia.org/wiki/Stimulus_(physiology) (last accessed: 14.2.2010)

[6] http://www.emc.maricopa.edu/faculty/farabee/BIOBK/BioBookglossS.html (last accessed: 14.2.2010)

elements determining the semantics of observation values explicit: the reference to what is being observed and the symbolization of the result. It is consistent with the definitions of observations in standards for sensors and for geographic information, such as OGC's Observations and Measurements standard ("An Observation is an action with a result which has a value describing some phenomenon."[2]) or OGC's Reference Model ("An observation is an act associated with a discrete time instant or period through which a number, term or other symbol is assigned to a phenomenon."[24]).

Some examples of technical and human agents taking a variety of observations shall illustrate the notions. Each example identifies an observing agent, the observed quality, stimulus, signal, and value.

A **thermometer** measures the temperature of an amount of air using heat flow as stimulus. The heat expands an amount of gas by some amount, which is the signal that gets converted to a number of degrees on the Celsius scale.

A **sonar** measures water depth of a lake, generating sound waves as stimulus, and converting the time until they return from the ground (signal) into a distance value.

A **CCD camera** observes its visible environment using sunlight reflected from surfaces as stimulus. It integrates the received radiation intensity per spectral band at each of its pixels over some time interval (signal), and returns an image as value.

A **weather station** reports a type of weather by combining temperature, pressure, and humidity measurements (each of them a signal) and returning an aggregated value.

A **sailor** observes wind speed by watching the frequency and size of ripples on the sea (stimulus) and reporting a Beaufort number (value) expressing her impression of wind force.

A **nomad** reports the presence of water in a desert well by observing reflected sunlight (stimulus), getting the impression that there is some water, and sending a text message from his cell phone signifying "water available"[12].

A **doctor** observes a patient's mood by talking to the patient and describing her impressions (qualia) obtained from the patient's behavior (stimulus).

3. Affordances

The idea underlying the notion of affordances goes back to ecologist J. von Uexküll, who stated that sensory impression is overridden by the capabilities for interaction ("Das Wirkmal löscht das Merkmal aus", [40, p.27]). This eminent insight gave rise to a new paradigm for understanding environments of humans and animals. Possibilities for interaction started to be seen as individually different, following not only environmental characteristics, but also physical and biomechanical capabilities of humans and animals. The experience and exploration of the environment became subjective, together with the underlying and resulting conceptualizations. The coupling between sensors and actuators at the psychological level has meanwhile also been found by neuroscientist at the physiological level [14]. Sensory impressions as well as motor expressions are processed in close proximity in the brain. However, this insight has so far not been exploited in ontologies of agents and their environments.

Addressing this omission, we now address two questions that remained open in our past theory of observation [18]. The first is "what can be perceived?" We now suggest not only that agents perceive qualities, but that **affordances are qualities**. Affordances are complemented by an agent's capability to act on them [40,7,38], just like other qualities are complemented by an agent's capability to observe them. Secondly, we ask "what is the result of perceiving qualities, including affordances?". In analogy to the behavior of producing observation values, we introduce actions into the observation ontology, as behavior afforded to agents by environments. Perceiving any quality, thus, can be seen as producing an action potential, whether for expressing an observation value or for acting in the environment.

A tenet of ecological theories is that there can be no environment without agents and no agent without an environment; environment and agent imply each other [10,40,7]. The notion of "fitness" describes this dependance: an animal *fits* into an environment if the environment affords living to the animal and survival to its whole species, i.e., if the environment affords nourishment, protection, mating and breeding. Applied to the level of species instead of individuals, this set of livability affordances forms the ecological niche [7,34,33]. Gibson assumes an environment that is shared across animals [7], and his remarks on this topic allow the conclusion that only animals of the same species share an environment. Von Uexküll provides a stricter view of the environment, distinguishing also between agents of different age [40]. The correspondence he assumes between agent and environment even allows for a solipsist interpretation. However, for a general theory of observations in information systems, assuming a private environment is not practical. Therefore, we adapt the notion of niche as described in [34,32,33]. The environment as the niche is the physical world surrounding the agent into which it fits according to its sensors, actuators, requirements and possibilities.

A first formal definition of affordances was provided by Turvey, more than two decades after Gibson's coining of the term [38]. Turvey matched affordances, as properties of the environment, with effectivities, as the corresponding properties of the agent:

> Let W_{pq} (e.g., a person-climbing-stairs system) = $j(X_p, Z_q)$ be composed of different things Z (e.g., a person) and X (e.g., stairs). Let p be a property of X and q be a property of Z. Then p is said to be an affordance of X and q the effectivity of Z (i.e., the complement of p), if and only if there is a third property r such that
>
> (i) $W_{pq} = j(X_p, Z_q)$ possesses r
> (ii) $W_{pq} = j(X_p, Z_q)$ posseses neither p nor q
> (iii) Neither Z nor X posseses r. [38, p. 180]

In this definition the thing X is part of the environment of the agent Z, and the affordance is a dispositional property. Turvey's definition is fully compatible with Gibson's notion and the underlying system view of agents in environments particularly acknowledges von Uexküll's insights. Affordances are, thus, qualities of objects in the environment of an agent. This does not require that affordances must be perceived, nor that they can only be perceived by the agent [7,22]. Affordances can be said to exist independently of perception and one can distinguish perceived from hidden affordances [6].

As a first conclusion on the ontological nature of affordances, we can, thus, say that affordances are those qualities that emerge from fitting a quality of an object in the environment to a quality of an agent. For example, the climbability of a step for a person emerges from the mutual relation that the riser height of a step exhibits with the person's leg length (cf. Section 4). Here, we focus on physical affordances, i.e. affordances that depend on physical qualities in the environment complemented by an agent's physical qualities. An agent's physical, physiological or biomechanical quality enables controlled movements of his body or of parts of his body as well as other actions. However, the notion of affordance and our approach to its formalization covers any qualities in the environment of an agent, including those of social or mental objects.

Perceiving affordances generates possibilities for action. Thus, the quale invoked in an agent when perceiving an affordance allows the agent to act upon it. To execute an action, the agent's intention has to complement the affordance [37]. At any given time, there are countless affordances in the environment for the agent, but the number of actual interactions is limited and most affordances are not acted upon. All the pencils and books on your desk afford grabbing, but you will not grab them all or even any. In a theatre, all seats afford sitting, but you will normally only sit on one of them. Life is a continuous perception-action-perception cycle, characterized by conscious and unconscious choices about which affordances are perceived and, among these, which are acted upon.

4. Example: Climbing Stairs

To motivate the example of stair climbing, we emphasize again the determining impact of the human motor system on perception. The observable quality in our example, i.e., climbability, is the physical quality of a step that human actuators can perceive and act upon based on their abilities. The mode of perception can be visual, haptic or even ultrasonic, resulting in potentially different judgments of action (climbing) possibilities.

Among the first and most prominent experiments on the perception of affordances are those conducted by W.H. Warren [41]. Warren investigated the perception of the affordance to climb stairs. Stair climbing is a trivial everyday activity that most people do not even think about. However, it becomes important in environments of small children and elderly or handicapped people (cf. [15]). The configuration of this agent-environment system is quite simple. Warren showed that stair climbability can be modeled with two qualities only, namely the person's leg length L and the riser height R of the stairs. The climbability affordance can then be derived from the ratio of the values for these qualities. For young adults, Warren's experiments suggest that ratios of $R/L < 0.88$ realize the affordance. This result complies with predictions from biomechanical models. The other result, more relevant to a theory of perception of affordances, was that subjects could easily select, from a set of pictures, the stairs with a maximum climbable height as well as those with an optimal height for them.

Clearly, Warren's model of stair climbability is only a coarse approximation to reality and one can easily think of further pairs of environmental and agent properties to include, such as tread depth and foot length, or stability and weight. Yet, his results show two important things about the perception of affordances. First, he proved that humans perceive affordances, and that this perception indeed depends on the perceiver's physical abilities. Second, the invoked quale is not a boolean value but a gradual analog signal. Humans can distinguish the most energy-efficient climbability and the least climbable step. It seems likely that humans also distinguish categories of climbing difficulty.

5. Extending the Observation Ontology by Affordances

We now present the extensions to the observation ontology [18] that support the perception of an environment with affordances and implement the example from Section 4.

Listing 1: The Haskell type `Climbability`.

```
class (QUALITIES affordance physicalEndurant, PHYSICAL_ENDURANTS
    physicalEndurant) => AFFORDANCES affordance physicalEndurant

data PHYSICAL_OBJECTS step => Climbability step = Climbability step
instance QUALITIES Climbability Step
instance AFFORDANCES Climbability Step
```

Listing 2: The Haskell type `Height`.

```
data PHYSICAL_OBJECTS step => Height step = Height step
instance QUALITIES Height Step
```

The observation ontology already introduced technical sensors and persons as observing agents. It was written as an algebraic specification in Haskell and continues to serve as both, an ontological specification and a simulation for development and testing. We add the specifications for perceiving affordances and provide the functionality to simulate afforded actions. We will refer to Haskell code[7] in the text using capital true type fonts like `OBSERVATIONS` for Haskell type classes, normal true type fonts like `Climbability` for data types, and lower case true type fonts like `perceive` for operations and individuals. For readers not familiar with Haskell, and for better comprehensibility in general, we provide diagrams of the core parts of the ontology in the Unified Modelling Language (UML). We first introduce the upper-level type classes of the ontology and then the extensions to account for perceptions and actions. After that we state our ontological commitments and show how they are specified in Haskell.

The observation ontology is aligned to the foundational ontology DOLCE with its four top-level notions of *endurants*, *perdurants*, *qualities* and *abstracts*. The expressiveness of Haskell allows us to use language constructs to differentiate the main DOLCE top-level categories. Endurants are implemented as data types of kind *, with an identity. Perdurants are implemented as types of kind *->*, i.e. functions defined for endurance. Qualities, as dependent entities, are modeled as constructor functions applied to their host, i.e., to the entity the quality inheres in. Haskell offers a higher level notion of "class", namely that of type class. A type class unites all types (or tuples of types) sharing some behavior. For example, we define the type class QUALITIES for all tuples of entities and functions returning a certain quality of them. The usual notion of "class" in ontologies is captured by a Haskell data type.

We introduce `AFFORDANCES` as subclass of `QUALITIES` and model climbability as a type of `AFFORDANCES` which inheres in a `Step`. The constructor of `QUALITIES` requires a quality like climbability to be defined with its host. The implementation of `AFFORDANCES` and `Climbability` is shown in Listing 1. For comparison, we provide the code for `Height` in Listing 2, which is of type `QUALITIES`.

Agents perceive qualities of their environment through stimuli. Consequently, the class `STIMULI` provides the `perceive` behavior, which is by virtue of its signature a DOLCE perdurant. Perceive relates a quality inhering in an entity to an agent and

[7]The current Haskell specification and simulation can be downloaded from http://musil.uni-muenster.de/publications/ontologies/ (Last accessed: 14.2.2010)

Listing 3: The Haskell class STIMULI.

```
class (QUALITIES quality entity , AGENTS agent)
        => STIMULI quality entity agent where
        perceive :: quality entity -> agent -> agent
```

Listing 4: The Haskell implementation of perceiving height and climbability.

```
instance STIMULI Height Step Person where
        perceive (Height step) person = person{pQuale = riserHeight step}

instance STIMULI Climbability Step Person where
        perceive (Climbability step) person =
        person {pQuale = (riserHeight step) / (legLength person)}
```

Listing 5: The Haskell implementation of the classes OBSERVATIONS and ACTIONS.

```
class STIMULI quality entity agent => OBSERVATIONS quality entity agent
    where
        observe :: quality entity -> agent -> agent

class (AFFORDANCES affordance physicalEndurant , STIMULI affordance
    physicalEndurant agent) => ACTIONS affordance physicalEndurant agent
    where
        act :: affordance physicalEndurant -> agent -> agent
```

generates a quale in the agent. Listing 3 shows the class STIMULI. Each pair of a quality type and agent type instantiated to the type class STIMULI gets its own implementation of the perceive-function, modeling how the quality affects the agent. An agent has a field, such as pQuale for persons, whose value changes as a result of perception. When a person perceives the height of a step, a height quale is invoked, i.e. written into its pQuale field. When a person perceives the climbability affordance of a step, a quale standing for an action potential is written into the same field. In accordance with Warren [41], this quale is a ratio between the leg length of the observer and the height of the stair. The implementation of perceiving height and climbability is shown in Listing 4.

The perception of stimuli by itself does not yet result in a symbol or action. A subsequent phase can express an observation value or an action. Thus, observation as well as action require a preceding perception. We model this dependency by the observe and act functions calling perceive and then determining a value or action from the quale. They are the behavior provided by the classes OBSERVATIONS and ACTIONS, respectively. An action naturally requires the perception of an affordance, instead of any quality, as shown in Listing 5. The example of the climb action resulting from the perceived climbability affordance is given in Listing 6. The action requires an affordance of a physical endurant, the Climbability of a Step, and it requires an actor, the agent Person. The action is modeled by comparing the perceived climbability quale to the maximal ratio affording climbability. If a step is perceived to be climbable, the actor expresses an action, i.e., climbs the step. The observation of height works analogously. It expresses a perceived height quale in the intrinsic semantic reference system of the observer, distinguishing "low" from "high" by the observer's physical capabilities

Listing 6: The Haskell implementation of acting on climbability and observing height.

```
instance ACTIONS Climbability Step Person where
        act (Climbability step) person =
        if (pQuale (perceive (Climbability step) person)) < 0.88
        then person {pStep = step} else person

instance OBSERVATIONS Height Step Person where
        observe (Height step) person =
                person {pValue =
                if (pQuale (perceive (Height step) person)) /
                        (legLength person) < 0.26
                then  "low" else "high"}
```

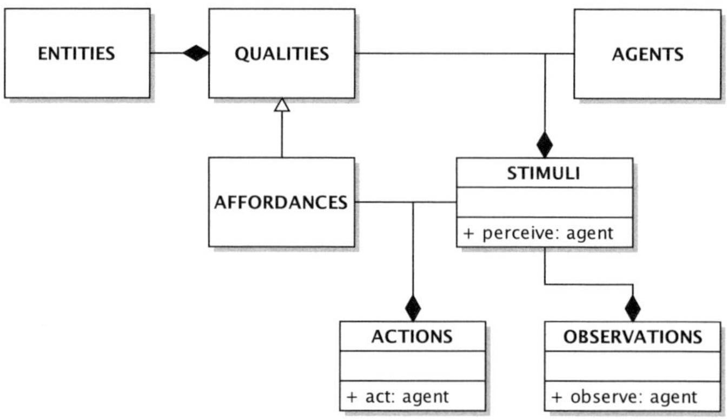

Figure 1. UML class diagram showing the alignment of the STIMULI, OBSERVATIONS and ACTIONS classes to DOLCE. We use composition arrows to denote existential dependence between classes.

(and using the threshold of 0.26 determined by Warren). The specifications of acting on climbability and observing height are given in Listing 6.

Figure 1 shows the core Haskell classes modeling the processes of perception and observation. The "components" (used here for participants) of stimuli are qualities inhering in entities and agents perceiving the qualities. The class STIMULI provides the perceive behavior that sets the quale of the agent. The OBSERVATIONS class provides the observe behavior that sets the observed value for the observing agent. Likewise, the ACTIONS class provides the act behavior (cf. Listing 3). The classes OBSERVATIONS and ACTIONS are associated with STIMULI, as an observation or action requires the perception of a stimulus. AFFORDANCES are a subclass of QUALITIES, the act behavior can only be executed on the perception of a type of AFFORDANCES. The qualities and the affordance we have implemented are shown in Figure 2. These qualities participate in the process of perception and invoke a quale in the perceiving agent.

With this account of perception and observations/actions we have completed a model of interacting perception and action. Though there remains a lot of work to do, the current state of the ontology provides a reasonably stable account of the perception and observation of qualities and affordances by humans and technical sensors. The remainder of this section summarizes our main ontological claims. We state each claim, give an explanation or justification for it, and reference the corresponding specification in Haskell.

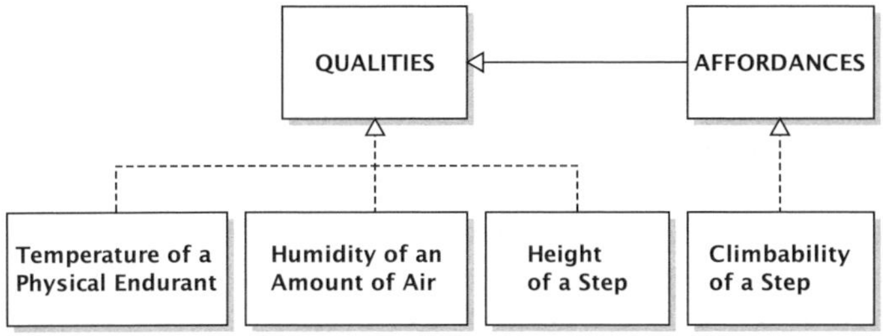

Figure 2. UML class diagram showing the modeled qualities, including the affordance of climbability.

Affordances are qualities. This claim follows directly from Turvey's definition of affordances [38] introduced in Section 3. Surprisingly, however, it has not been exploited in ontology yet. The class `AFFORDANCES`, (cf. Listing 1) provides the specification how to write an affordance in Haskell. `Climbability` implements this specification.

Affordances are perceptibles. The theories of perception by von Uexküll [40] and Gibson [7] directly imply that affordances are what humans and animals can perceive [36]. Affordances are perceptible because they are required to guide action. They are qualities that suggest a certain action to an agent. Even though their perception and use naturally requires an agent, affordances exist independently of perception [7,22,6] and before they are perceived. An example of this is given in the implementation of the perception of climbability (cf. Listing 4).

Agents perceive qualities through stimuli. Perception is realized through stimuli, i.e., changes in the environment of an agent. Not the quality per se, but the stimulus invokes a quale in the agent. Ontologically, a stimulus (as change in the environment) is a perdurant. The quality perceived (which can be an affordance) and the agent who perceives both participate in the stimulus. This is expressed in the `STIMULI` class with its two parameters for `perceive`, as shown in Listing 3.

Perception of affordances leads to possible actions. The perception of an affordance invokes a quale, which stands for an action possibility. Actions require the perception of an affordance, and every perception of an affordance leads to a possible action. However, not every possible action has to be executed. Therefore the `perceive` operation returns a quale and does not cause a change of the environment. The quale can then be acted upon, for example as an action climbing the step. In the same way, regular qualities lead to the possibility to express a symbol. This is captured by the specifications of stimuli in Listing 4.

Agents act on perceived affordances. The execution of an action follows the perception of an affordance. This is in line with Stoffregen [37], who explains the occurence of an action as the complementation of a perceived affordance with an intention to act. Even though we did not deal with intentions in our ontology, the preceding of perception to action is specified in the `act` function, which calls the `perceive` function. Necessarily this also means that the `ACTIONS` class assumes the `STIMULI` class. Of course, the actions considered here are only those traceable to affordances.

Agents observe perceived qualities. Analogous to acting, agents can express a value as a result of observing a regular quality. We define (following OGC) observation as resulting in a value. The expression of a value requires a quale which is obtained by perception. It can also be interpreted as an illocutionary act [5], but this unification is a topic for future work.

6. Conclusion

We have presented an approach to "ontologize" affordances. Extending an observation ontology that generalizes observation to human and technical sensors, we showed how a twist on observation results allows for capturing observations of regular qualities as well as actions realizing affordances. This led to an ontological account of perception and action in terms of affordances and other qualities. Humans perceive their environment according to their capabilities, i.e., they perceive affordances. Since affordances naturally connect an agent to an environment, we have specified affordances as qualities of the environment of an agent. Thereby we have anchored perceptions in the environment and in the agent's individual qualities. We have then modeled observations as the expression of a perceived quality and introduced actions as expressions of perceived affordances. Using Haskell as ontology modeling and specification language, we have shown that integrating affordances into an observation ontology founded on DOLCE is possible and beneficial. We agree with Sanders [28] in that affordances are at least valuable and beneficial primitives for ontologies and worth considering for information system ontologies.

The presented work suggests several directions for future work, in addition to the previously mentioned generalization of actions to include observations as speech acts. For one, we have focused so far on physical affordances, but the generalization to social affordances appears to be a straightforward extension to the specification. Humans do not only live in physical, but also in social environments. An extended theory distinguishing physical and social affordances, as for example in [11], will also help to improve and extend the observation ontology.

We will explore how the theory and its model can simulate whole cycles of action and perception. An isolated observation is rare and multiple observations are typically happening in parallel and sequentially, with afforded actions leading to new observations, which in turn lead to observable changes. The current ontology presents an ideal starting point for this exciting research direction, as its functional style allows for concatenations of the specified processes.

In previous work, the second author formalized the relation between spatial affordances and image schemas [17]. Connecting that theory to the perception-based formalization of affordances presented here will allow for relating the categorizing role of affordances to observed qualities. This might eventually lead to ontologies that refrain entirely from a priori specifications of types (kinds) and support instead an ad hoc computation of classifications based on observed qualities. Given that consensus on observable qualities is more easily achievable than consensus on object classifications, such an approach has the potential to improve semantic interoperability considerably.

Finally, the ontology assumes precise observations for now. In reality, most observations are imprecise and can only give uncertain accounts of environments. This affects affordances just like regular qualities. If we see a door, we cannot be sure that we can open it. This example also points to so-called false affordances [6]. A theory for perception-based probabilistic reasoning is presented in [44] and appears to supply the necessary mechanisms to account for uncertainty in observation ontologies. The seed for dealing with spatial, temporal, and thematic resolution has already been planted through the explicit modeling of quality bearers and through our work on semantic datums [29]. An additional perspective on this issue is [4], suggesting to specify qualia as convolutions of stimuli over space and time, which would produce resolution and uncertainty measures at once.

Acknowledgements

This work has been funded through the International Research Training Group on Semantic Integration of Geospatial Information by the DFG (German Research Foundation), GRK 1498.

References

[1] A. Bröring, K. Janowicz, C. Stasch, and W. Kuhn. Semantic challenges for sensor plug and play. In J.D. Carswell, A. S. Fotheringham, and G. McArdle, editors, *Web and Wireless Geographical Information Systems, 9th International Symposium, W2GIS 2009, Maynooth, Ireland, December 2009. Proceedings*, volume 5886 of *Lecture Notes in Computer Science*, pages 72 – 86, Berlin Heidelberg, 2009. Springer.

[2] S. Cox. OGC Implementation Specification 07-022r1: Observations and Measurements. Technical report, Open Geospatial Consortium, 2007.

[3] M. Craglia, M.F. Goodchild, A. Annoni, M. Camara, G. amd Gould, W. Kuhn, D.M. Mark, I. Masser, D.J. Maguire, S. Liang, and E. Parsons. Next-generation Digital Earth. A position paper from the Vespucci Initiative for the Advancement of Geographic Information Science. *International Journal of Spatial Data Infrastructure Research*, 3:146–167, 2008.

[4] A. U. Frank. Scale Is Introduced in Spatial Datasets by Observation Processes. In R. Devillers and M. Goodchild, editors, *Spatial Data Quality From Process to Decision, St. John's, Newfoundland and Labrador, Canada*, pages 17 – 29. CRC Press, 05.– 08. July 2009.

[5] H. Fujisaki. *Speech perception, production and linguistic structure*, chapter Modelling the process of fundamental frequency contour generation, pages 313–328. IOS Press, 1992.

[6] W.W. Gaver. Technology affordances. In *Proceedings of the SIGCHI conference on Human factors in computing systems: Reaching through technology*, pages 79–84. ACM New York, NY, USA, 1991.

[7] J.J. Gibson. *The ecological approach to visual perception*. Lawrence Erlbaum, Hillsdale, NJ, 1979.

[8] M.F. Goodchild. Citizens as sensors: the world of volunteered geography. *GeoJournal*, 69(4):211–221, 2007.

[9] H. Heft. Affordances and the body: An intentional analysis of Gibson's ecological approach to visual perception. *Journal for the theory of social behaviour*, 19(1):1–30, 1989.

[10] E. Husserl. *Ideen Zu Einer Reinen Phänomenologie Und Phänomenologischen Philosophie: Zweites Buch*. Kluwer Academic Publishers, Dordrecht, The Netherlands, 1991. Originally published in 1952 by Martinus Nijhoff, The Hague, The Netherlands.

[11] K. Janowicz and M. Raubal. Affordance-based similarity measurement for entity types. In S. Winter, M. Duckham, L. Kulik, and B. Kuipers, editors, *Spatial Information Theory: 8th International Conference, COSIT 2007, Melbourne, Australia, September 19-23, 2007, Proceedings*, volume 4736 of *Lecture Notes in Computer Science*, pages 133 – 151. Springer, Berlin, 2007.

[12] E.H. Jürrens, A. Bröring, and S. Jirka. A human sensor web for water availability monitoring. In *OneSpace 2009 - 2nd International Workshop on Blending Physical and Digital Spaces on the Internet, Berlin, Germany, 2009, Proceedings*, 2009.

[13] E. Klien, F. Probst, and M. Nientiedt. Category Membership Evaluation for Geographic Entities - Ontological Foundations and Implementation. *International Journal of Geographical Information Science*, submitted.

[14] E. Koechlin, C. Ody, and F. Kouneiher. The architecture of cognitive control in the human prefrontal cortex. *Science*, 302(5648):1181–1185, 2003.

[15] B. Krieg-Brückner, B. Gersdorf, M. Döhle, and K. Schill. Technik für senioren in spe im bremen ambient assisted living lab. In *2. Deutscher AAL-Kongress 2009*, Berlin-Offenbach, 2009. VDE.

[16] W. Kuhn. Ontologies in support of activities in geographic space. *International Journal of Geographical Information Science*, 15(7):613–631, 2001.

[17] W. Kuhn. An Image-Schematic Account of Spatial Categories. In S. Winter, M. Duckham, L. Kulik, and B. Kuipers, editors, *Spatial Information Theory: 8th International Conference, COSIT 2007, Melbourne, Australia, September 19-23, 2007, Proceedings*, volume 4736 of *Lecture Notes in Computer Science*, pages 152 – 168. Springer, Berlin, 2007.

[18] W. Kuhn. A functional ontology of observation and measurement. In K. Janowicz, M. Raubal, and S. Levashkin, editors, *Third Workshop on Geosemantics (GeoS 2009), Mexico City, 3-4 December 2009*, volume 5892 of *Lecture Notes in Computer Science*, pages 26–43, Berlin Heidelberg, 2009. Springer.

[19] C. Masolo and S. Borgo. Qualities in formal ontology. In *Foundational Aspects of Ontologies (FOnt 2005) Workshop at KI*, pages 2–16, 2005.

[20] C. Masolo, S. Borgo, A. Gangemi, N. Guarino, and A. Oltramari. Wonderweb deliverable D18 ontology library (final). *ICT Project*, 33052, 2003.

[21] P. Maué and J. Ortmann. Getting across information communities: Embedding semantics in the SDI for the Amazon. *Earth Science Informatics*, 2(4):217 – 233, December 2009.

[22] C. F. Michaels. Affordances: Four points of debate. *Ecological Psychology*, 15(2):135, 2003.

[23] H. Neuhaus and M. Compton. The Semantic Sensor Network Ontology. In *AGILE Workshop: Challenges in Geospatial Data Harmonisation*, 2009.

[24] G. Percivall, C. Reed, L. Leinenweber, C. Tucker, and T. Cary. OGC Reference Model. Technical report, Open Geospatial Consortium, 2008.

[25] F. Probst. Observations, measurements and semantic reference spaces. *Applied Ontology*, 3(1-2):63–89, 2008.

[26] E. Rome, J. Hertzberg, and G. Dorffner. *Towards Affordance-Based Robot Control: International Seminar Dagstuhl Castle, Germany, June 2006, Revised Papers*, volume 4760 of *Lecture Notes in Computer Science*. Springer, Berlin Heidelberg, 2008.

[27] S.J. Russell, P. Norvig, J.F. Canny, J. Malik, and D.D. Edwards. *Artificial intelligence: a modern approach*. Prentice Hall Englewood Cliffs, NJ, 1995.

[28] J.T. Sanders. An ontology of affordances. *Ecological Psychology*, 9(1):97–112, 1997.

[29] S. Scheider, K. Janowicz, and W. Kuhn. Grounding geographic categories in the meaningful environment. In K.S. Hornsby, C. Claramunt, M. Denis, and G. Ligozat, editors, *Spatial Information Theory: 9th International Conference, COSIT 2009, Aber Wrac'h, France, September 2009, Proceedings*, volume 5756 of *Lecture Notes in Computer Science*, pages 69–87, Berlin Heidelberg, 2009. Springer. Conference on Spatial Information Theory (COSIT) 2009, Aber Wrac'h (Centre de la Mer), France.

[30] S. Scheider, F. Probst, and K. Janowicz. Constructing Bodies and their Qualities from Observations. Accepted to the 6th International Conference on Formal Ontology in Information Systems (FOIS 2010), Toronto, this Volume.

[31] B. Smith. Ontologie des Mesokosmos. Soziale Objekte und Umwelten. *Zeitschrift für philosophische Forschung*, 52(4):522–541, 1998.

[32] B. Smith. *Life and motion of socio-economic units*, chapter Objects and their environments: From Aristotle to ecological ontology, pages 79–97. Taylor & Francis, 2001.

[33] B. Smith. Toward a Realistic Science of Environments. *Ecologial Psychology*, 21(2):121–130, 2009.

[34] B. Smith and A.C. Varzi. The Niche. *Noûs*, 33(2):214–238, 1999.

[35] C. Stasch, K. Janowicz, A. Bröring, I. Reis, and W. Kuhn. A stimulus-centric algebraic approach to sensors and observations. In Niki Trigoni, Andrew Markham, and Sarfraz Nawaz, editors, *GeoSensor Networks. Third International Conference, GSN 2009 , July 13-14, 2009 Proceedings*, volume 5659 of *Lecture Notes in Computer Science*, pages 169–179, Berlin Heidelberg, 2009. Springer.

[36] T.A. Stoffregen. Affordances and events. *Ecological Psychology*, 12(1):1–28, 2000.

[37] T.A. Stoffregen. Affordances as properties of the animal-environment system. *Ecological Psychology*, 15(2):115–134, 2003.

[38] M.T. Turvey. Affordances and prospective control: An outline of the ontology. *Ecological Psychology*, 4(3):173–187, 1992.

[39] L. Vieu, S. Borgo, and C. Masolo. Artefacts and Roles: Modelling Strategies in a Multiplicative Ontology. In *Proceeding of the 2008 conference on Formal Ontology in Information Systems: Proceedings of the Fifth International Conference (FOIS 2008)*, pages 121–134. IOS Press, 2008.

[40] J. von Uexküll and G. Kriszat. *Streifzüge durch die Umwelten von Tieren und Menschen: ein Bilderbuch unsichtbarer Welten*. Rowohlt, Hamburg, 1956.

[41] W.H. Warren. Perceiving affordances: Visual guidance of stair climbing. *Journal of Experimental Psychology: Human Perception and Performance*, 10(5):683–703, 1984.

[42] J.G. Webster. *The measurement, instrumentation and sensors handbook*. Springer, 1999.

[43] I. Whitmore. *Terminologia Anatomica, International Anatomical Terminology*. Thieme, Stuttgart, 1998.

[44] L.A. Zadeh. Toward a perception-based theory of probabilistic reasoning with imprecise probabilities. *Journal of statistical planning and inference*, 105(1):233–264, 2002.

Formal Ontology in Information Systems
A. Galton and R. Mizoguchi (Eds.)
IOS Press, 2010

doi:10.3233/978-1-60750-535-8-131

Constructing Bodies and their Qualities from Observations

Simon SCHEIDER [a,1], Florian PROBST [b] and Krzysztof JANOWICZ [c]
[a] *Westfälische Wilhelms-Universität Münster, Germany*
[b] *SAP Research CEC Darmstadt, Germany*
[c] *The Pennsylvania State University, USA*

Abstract. The principle challenge for information semantics lies in the degrees of freedom to interpret symbols in terms of thoughts and experiences which leads to incompatible views on the world. Consequently, incompatible information ontologies and interpretations of the described data will remain. Even though there is usually a common experiential ground, it stays often unknown to users of semantically annotated data. This *symbol grounding problem* is a bottleneck of information semantics, which remains largely unsolved in ontological practice. In this paper, we suggest – in the spirit of Jeremy Bentham – to introduce formal primitives which are directly grounded in inter-subjective experience, and which serve to expose and construct complex qualities in information ontologies.

Keywords. Ontology of qualities, Symbol grounding, Ontology and observation

Introduction

By developing ontologies to describe and query data, members of an information community aim at reconstructing the intended interpretation in terms of their own experiences. In previous work we argued that this requires *grounding*, i.e., relating the meaning of primitives in a theory to observations [1,2]. The so-called *symbol grounding problem* [3] states that declarative semantics expressed in terms of formal symbols give rise to an infinite regress. Formal theories alone cannot account for the sources of ambiguity in semantic interpretation, like indeterminacy of empirical theories, unintended domains and indistinguishability of reference [1]. We suggest that one way out of this regress cycle is to establish a primitive operational language of reproducible observations as a social fact. Such an approach parallels the idea of *embodied semantics* [4].

In this paper, we propose to trace formal ontologies about qualities and objects back to observation processes. In this, we follow an idea of Jeremy Bentham, that *fictive (reified)* entities in a language can be explained by deconstructing them into perceptibles. We argue that, on the one hand, the arbitrariness of reifications is a major source for ambiguity and hence limited interoperability between information ontologies (Section 1.1). On the other hand, a common experiential ground is often available in terms of universal

[1]Corresponding Author: Simon Scheider, Institute for Geoinformatics, Westfälische Wilhelms-Universität Münster, Germany; E-mail: simon.scheider@uni-muenster.de.

perceptive operations, whose existence is empirically supported (Section 1.2). We sketch a general theory for grounding objects and qualities in *reproducible observation procedures*, e.g. in order to support ontology mappings or to annotate data about qualities (in Section 2). Using a small number of perceptual primitives, we describe use cases that are commonly considered as challenging for information ontologies, the cases including *n-ary qualities*, *temporal object properties*, and the problem of how to keep track of *object identity in time* (Section 3).

Note that in discussing the problems of fictions in information ontologies, we do not suggest that they are not useful, or that the existence of fictive entities should be epistemologically questioned. Instead, we argue that for semantic engineering purposes [5], it is helpful and often possible to to relate these fictions to a common experiential ground.

1. Related Work

In this section we introduce background readings relevant for the understanding of our following argumentation.

1.1. Bentham's Fictions and the Arbitrariness of Reifications

The *Theory of Fictions* [6] published in 1815 by Jeremy Bentham is a noteworthy contribution to the problem of language semantics, which inspired Ogden in his treatment of the meaning triangle [7]. Bentham states that individual percepts, such as those of bodies, can be used to expose the meaning of *language fictions*. Language fictions are linguistic creations of the mind that cannot be directly observed, but depend on other perceivable entities. Bentham's treatment of language is a treatment of names, i.e., nouns and their compounds which denote particular entities in thought. For instance, the sentence *the color of this body is red* denotes three mental entities, a body, its color quality, and a thing called redness. According to Bentham, such entities can either be *real* or *fictitious* [6].

Real entities are the ones whose existence is non-disputable by the speakers of a language. But what does this mean in practice? This class mainly consists of *perceptibles* including *bodies* (physical entities) in the first place, as well as *individual percepts* like e.g., *pain* and *pleasure*.

In contrast, the existence of fictions is posited by a speaker because they are useful for communication. Fictions serve as language proxies for real entities and often depend on their existence. For example, redness depends on the existence of a concrete color percept and on the perceived part of the surface of a body. Without those it would not be sensible to talk about redness as an existing entity – this is related to Peirce's *Thirdness*. For Bentham, reifications of quality values are therefore fictions in the same sense as the entities denoted by the nouns *motion, cause, action* or the legal fictions *obligation* and *right*. All these existentially depend on other directly perceivable entities [6].

According to Bentham's theory, qualities are second order (unary) fictions since they can inhere in arbitrary entities – fictive or real. In principle all kinds of entities can have qualities ([6], page 27 f.). Qualities and the abstractions of their values, however, are not perceivable themselves. Abstracted quality values like redness are fictive entities, while qualities, like color, are again abstracted from them. Bentham similarly reckoned all sorts of *aggregations* (whether collections or classes) among the fictions [6]. We argue therefore that Bentham's fictions are what modern logicians such as Quine [8] would have called *reified logical entities*. Furthermore, Quine rightly suggested that such reifications can change the underlying *ontological commitment* of a theory [8], because reified entities are values of existentially quantified variables, and therefore have to be added to the domain of interpretation.

Similar to Bentham's suggestions how to sidestep fictions[2], Quine suggests that unnecessary (fictive) names can be avoided by introducing predicates which rephrase them as descriptions. For instance, to avoid talking of a fictive particular *Pegasus* as an existing entity, we can refer to it as *the winged horse captured by Bellerophon*. And to avoid talking of *classes or universals* as existing things, e.g., humanity, we can introduce a predicate like 'being human' which accounts for its instances.

Quine concludes that these reifications are arbitrary to a large extent [8]. Any reification or deconstruction of the sort described above is a substantial change of the theory, since the domain of discourse expands or shrinks. Consequently, such degrees of freedom in modeling the real world tend to produce non-interoperable ontologies. There cannot be one-to-one correspondence between semantic domains if the underlying ontological commitments differ. Many ontologies are affected by this arbitrariness of reification which is one reason for incompatible top level ontologies. For instance, Neuhaus et al. [9] argue for the existence of universal entities and reified quality values such as 'universal sphericity'. They introduce generic dependence relations among particulars and their instantiated universals which exactly match with Bentham's ideas of existential dependence. Additionally, they reify a layer of quality fictions orthogonal to this one, building an 'ontological square': quality values inhere in other particulars, like in *the particular red of this apple*, and instantiate quality universals like *redness*. Other ontologies such as DOLCE [10], exclude reified universals like *appleness* in their domain of discourse. In another paper, the authors demonstrate that there are many possible more or less reified formalizations of an ontology of qualities with roughly equal expressiveness [10]. In previous work we have demonstrated that 'grouping' quality values in value ranges such as 'redness' can be necessary in order to account for the complex dimensional relationships between objects and their qualities [11]: 3-dimensional rivers have a non-atomic water depth value that is a class of actual atomic water depths. Bateman thus rightly argues [12] for a flexible *layered ontological framework*, which can account for the granularities of different views on space.

Most of such ontological variations are useful and plausible by themselves. But it is their arbitrariness which puts a burden to reach semantic agreement. In their attempt to construct a linguistically and cognitively plausible theory, the authors in a way just illustrated that language and thought are indeterminate, creative, and full of (useful) fictions. But this is exactly the reason why semantic ambiguities exist in the first place.

1.2. Are there Universal Perceptive Operations?

In the following paragraphs, we review empirical evidence for the existence of appropriate human operations that are at everyone's disposal for interpreting qualities and objects. It is essential for a grounding theory that observations can be reproduced indepen-

[2]Compare pages 86 ff. in [6].

dently of who performs this interpretation. One further important requirement is that this can be done independently from other mental concepts or beliefs. The experiences have to emerge spontaneously, i.e., as a result of drawing the attention to externally triggered functions, or of performing some other simple operation, without presupposing certain conceptual or even socially influenced processing steps. In short, they must be based on some *preconceptual mechanism* which can be expected to be *universal*; compare chapter 4 in [13].

Attentional Moments We begin by stating the identity of a moment in which a human focuses his attention on a certain signal from the environment. We assume with v. Glasersfeld[3], that there is a pulsed attentional process in the human cortex that produces *discrete* mental entities on the very lowest level of conscious perception [16], and stores them in memory as a temporal sequence[4]. It is well known that the focus of attention can be shifted by an observer in a scene independently from the stimulus, and that this shift has an intermittent 'sampling' character [17,15]. We furthermore assume that each one of these stored attentional moments may or may not be *focused on some neural event* in the organism. By 'focused' we "intend no more than that an attentional pulse is made to coincide with some other signal (from the multitude that more or less continuously pervades the organism's nervous system) and thus allows it to be registered" [15]. If the pulsing attention is *focused on some external sensory-motor signal*, it produces a constant flow of *conscious experience*, into which those signals are 'encoded'. This encoded information is respresented in our theory as *perceptual relations among attentional moments*; see Section 2. Other mental operations are then available to construct abstract entities from this flow of consciousness. In a very similar way, Barsalou suggested that *perceptual symbols* on an abstract conceptual level are encoded as records of neural states in the sensory-motor regions stored in long-term memory [4].

Identifying Objects and Surfaces Mainstream philosophy of the mind says that *objects* (in general: particulars) are constructed from more primitive 'point-like' percepts of *qualities* using conceptual reasoning and the application of knowledge[5]. Likewise, cognitive scientists predominantly tend to think that experience is based on the projection of point-like stimuli, e.g. visual pixels on the retina, and the application of concepts, e.g. 'object-identification' predicates that were *derived from what we know* about those objects[6]. But such a view gives rise to the epistemological puzzles that concepts imply other concepts in infinite regress, and of how to explain that humans can share knowledge although concepts (especially fictions) cannot universally be expected.

A remarkable exception are Gestalt psychologists such as Wolfgang Köhler [19]. He realized that the perception of objects in its most general sense is not an epistemic issue, but the result of an unconscious, dynamic self-distributed process, which is hardwired into the system, and which spontaneously cuts out units from the signal input which correspond to circumscribed surfaces of the environment. One classical example

[3]H. v. Glasersfeld developed a 'pulse' model for the mental construction of unities, pluralities and number out of sensory raw material, see chapter 9 in [14] or [15].

[4]Although the question of whether conscious perception is discrete or not is in principle still open, there is much psychophysical evidence for its discreteness [16].

[5]See for example Strawson's influential idea of *feature-placing* [18].

[6]See for example traditional research in attentional studies [17], or the 'mental imagery' debate, chapter 4.5 in [13].

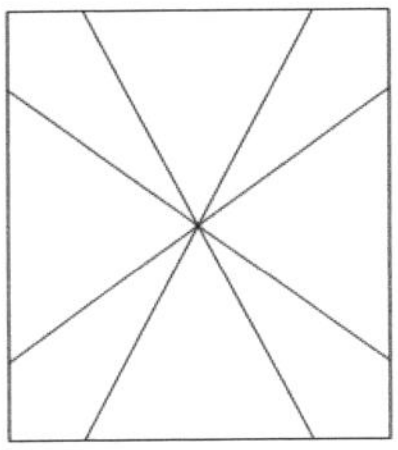

Figure 1. Slender x or thick cross? Adapted from Köhler [19].

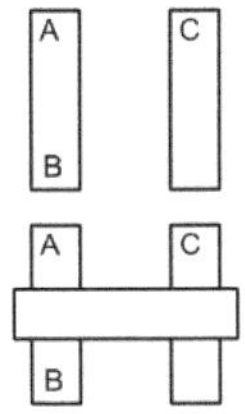

Figure 2. 'Same object advantage' in attentional spread [17].

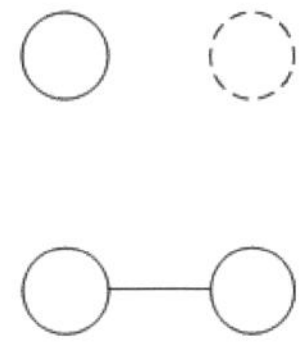

Figure 3. The effect of 'simultanagnosia', see text for details.

is depicted in Figure 1, which can either be perceived as a slender x or a thick cross – but not both at the same time, even though the information in the figure does not preclude this. Based on these insights, Gibson considered this autonomous apparatus for surface individuation an ecological constraint for the development of the visual system in the human environment [20].

There is recent empirical evidence for such a mechanism evolving from studies of object-based focal attention [17]. Same object advantages for example were demonstrated in target detection games. If attention is drawn to one end A of the bar-like object depicted in Figure 2, then *same object targets*, e.g., a sudden luminance decrement at B, can be detected faster than targets at C with exactly the same distance. The effect is stable even if the bars are partially occluded by another bar. There is an automatic spread of attention along the outlines of what humans perceive as an object, which takes into account its partial occlusion, its topological connectedness, and is symmetric and transitive. Further evidence for this mechanism is provided by the *Balint* syndrome, which is an object-based perceptual disorder that restricts attention to only one such object at a time (*Simultanagnosia*). While these patients are typically unable to see two separate discs simultaneously on a screen (see upper half of figure 3), they are perfectly able to see a single dumbbell (see lower half of figure 3), which suddenly appears when the two discs are connected by a line [17]. Pylyshyn therefore has recently [13] argued for the existence of spontaneous visual indices, called FINSTs, that are preconceptually available to refer to object surfaces, and that enable humans *to track* up to 4 such moving objects in a complex dynamic scene without any decrease in performance. This means that the same mechanism is also responsible for keeping object identity in time and under perspective change[7].

Identifying Locations, Directions and Length It is essential to understand that object and surface detection operations are crucial for all other perceptive operations that can be performed. Attentional studies show that relative mereological parts of objects as well as locations in the background environment can be identified [17]. But there is also recent evidence for a neurological mechanism underlying the construction of locations relative to the perceived object surfaces. Burgess [22] and others studied neurons in mammals, e.g., rats, that identify places (called *place cells*). These neurons fire in response to other cells (called *boundary vector cells*), that detect surfaces at a certain allocentric direc-

[7] We furthermore assume that this mechanism decides whether a strongly connected body stays the same if he loses parts, e.g. if he breaks. The mechanism therefore cannot be restricted to mere topological properties, compare [21].

tion and distance (see Figure 4). Allocentric means that the firing of all these cells is independent of an egocentric reference frame, but depends on external landmark objects and surfaces [22]. If a rat comes across a place defined relative to the walls of a box, the cell will fire regardless of the direction of approach. In addition to these low level mechanisms, there are also those higher-level measurement operations available that we ordinarily think of when speaking about the geometry of the environment. Humans are commonly able to reproduce steps into a given direction and of a given length, which is a prerequisite for building up geographic reference systems. In this way, they are able to indicate the meaning of a location by outlining and pointing at regions relative to the environment's surface layout. Furthermore, humans have an equilibrium sense for detecting whether their body is in upright direction, and are also able to detect *verticality* of directions using any kind of physical perpendicular.

Identifying Shapes and Colors In the study of Kay and McDaniel [23], the authors suggested that there are 6 different types of color-sensitive opponent cells for detecting the primary colors blue, yellow, red, green, black and white. Each of these fire with a certain probability that can be modeled by a fuzzy membership function of measured wavelengths and intensities. By using the fuzzy set intersection, the non-primary colors orange, purple, pink, brown and grey could be derived, whereas fuzzy set union could account for broader color categories as cool and warm. Using this mechanism, the 11 so called *focal colors* and their unions can be reconstructed, which are known to be of universal significance as basic color terms in every human language. Even though the theory has been criticized and modified with regards to its claims about natural language color terms, the basic insight, that a universal neurophysiological mechanism of primary color detection exists which forms the semantic basis for most color terms of most natural languages, remains valid [24]. Although this operation is universally and autonomously available, its uncertainty is apparent because primary colors are prototypes and the color boundaries are fuzzy.

The construction of object-based qualities like shape is a more complex case which seems to involve the construction of body parts, as well as perceiving their geometric configuration using direction and distance detectors. We stick to the principle idea of Marr and Nishihara [25], that shape recognition involves a process of retrieving, storing, and comparing complex shape descriptions of bodies. These could e.g. be descriptions of oriented cylindrical body parts, consisting in the lengths of such parts and the object centered orientation angles between their natural axes (all of these can be constructed using the available operations and an extraction mechanism) [25]. The underlying operation could be physically realized as an unconscious neurological mechanism, but could also be consciously reconstructed by measurements. In either case, if such shape descriptions are compared allowing for tolerance ranges, this automatically induces equivalence classes on them, which constitute abstract shape values. Identification of shapes is also uncertain, since it depends on the shape resolution and tolerance levels which are arbitrary to a certain extent (compare the discussion in [25]).

2. Bodies and Qualities as Reifications using Perceptive Operations

In this work, we argue that one of the main problems of ontologies lies in their choice of primitives which, to a certain degree, is always arbitrary. This arbitrariness is a con-

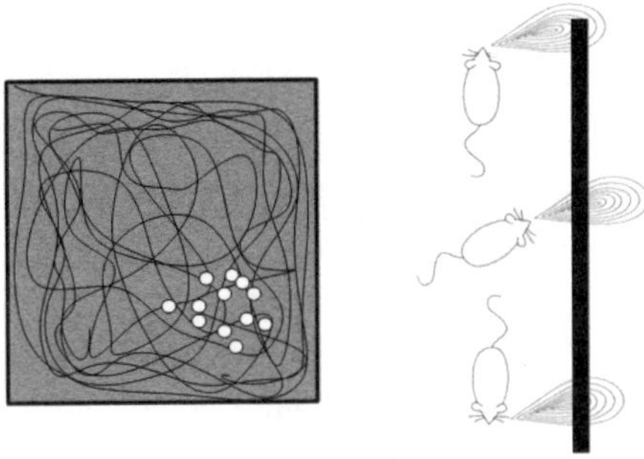

Figure 4. Place cell firing (white dots) of a rat tracked in a box (left). Principle of boundary vector cells (right). Adapted from Burgess [22], see text for details.

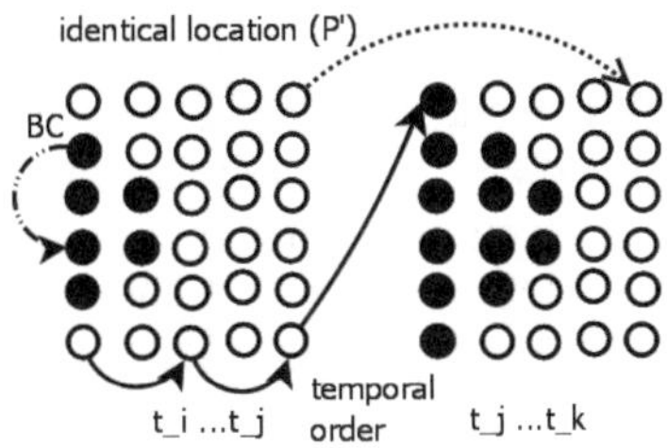

Figure 5. Principle of constructing temporal snapshots of bodies from foci of attention and location identifiers for two time intervals, see Section 2.4 for details.

sequence of the presence of language fictions [6]. In this section, we describe a formal theory of *personal perceptive capabilities*, which are at everyone's disposal in order to reconstruct bodies and their qualities. We begin with discussing the general idea of how to reconstruct certain kinds of fictions using identity criteria based on *equivalence relations*.

2.1. Identity Criteria for Abstract Classes, Qualities and Bodies

The importance of *identity criteria (IC)* for ontology engineering has been widely recognized [26]. In this section we argue that *identity criteria* are in fact an essential source for exhibiting the observable semantic plane of ontologies.

To state *true identity* ($=$) of two things in an ontology is a very fundamental semantic constraint, which influences the resolution of the described world into indistinguishable chunks, i.e., the ontology's *granularity*. This was recognized by Quine, who proposed a mechanism of *conceptual abstraction* based on indistinguishability; his *maxim of identification of indiscernibles* [27]. Quine claimed that any two-place predicate expressing an *equivalence relation* R could express identity relative to some sufficiently impoverished theory [27]. If, in this impoverished theory, two R-equivalent things become *indiscernible* with respect to the theory's terms (i.e., they satisfy Leibniz' criterion[8]), then the theory can always be *re-interpreted into a different (more abstract) domain* such that R just means $=$, and equivalent names are *identified* with one and the same thing. For example, "if one has a language in which one speaks of persons and in which persons of the same income are indistinguishable, the predicates of the language may be reinterpreted so that the predicate which previously expressed having the same income comes now to express identity. The universe of discourse now consists of income groups, not people" [29]. This is Quine's proposal of how abstract things, e.g. 'classes', but also 'objects' and 'qualities', come into being [27]. At the same time it indicates how *identity criteria* can be constructed for them: An individual in the second interpretation, an income group, is an *equivalence class* of R in the first interpretation. Similarly, suppose we have a theory about body parts containing arms, legs, and an equivalence relation R meaning 'related

[8] *Leibniz identity* is the criterion that requires indistinguishability of properties for identical things in a theory [28].

to the same body'. If arms and legs become indistinguishable in this theory, we can reinterpret R as $=$, resulting in a more abstract theory about whole bodies. And again, the R equivalence classes of body parts provide an identity criterion for bodies. In the same way, universal quality values like 'redness' can be abstracted from individual patches of red [27]. So identical things in a more abstract (coarse-grained) theory can be expressed as *equivalence classes* in a fine-grained theory. Williamson [30] called this mechanism of identification a *two-level criterion of identity*.

It can be seen that a chain of such entities of increasing coarseness is just a special case of a reification chain in the sense of Section 1.1, namely a chain of *aggregation or quality fictions*. In this case, however, the abstractions, e.g., income levels, are expressed *on the same language level* as their constituting more concrete entities, e.g., persons, using different names. Furthermore, the identity relation on abstract entities is then *definable* in terms of equivalence classes of lower level entities. The relevance of these considerations lies in the fact that they support the following hypothesis: The primitives for conceptual construction could be *equivalence relations, denoting outputs of preconceptual perceptive operations*, that account for the identities of various more abstract concepts in question[9]. Such an enterprise is readily confronted with the standard objections to previous attempts of 'extensional abstraction of qualities', like for example Carnap's *Aufbau* [31], which was based on an abstract *resemblance relation* among percepts. But unlike such philosophical attempts, our approach is modal, since it is based on perceptual neuron states, and it is properly grounded, so philosophical puzzles about the proper specification of the resemblance relation do not arise. The problem of *coextensionality of attributes*[10] can be accounted for by assuming that the output of each operation is a *relation involving a mental entity standing for that operation itself*. For reasons of simplicity, we left this straightforward modification out of the formalism.

In order to demonstrate the usefulness of our idea, we introduce the following 8 primitive perceptive relations[11] $\leq_T$, BC, P', $=_L$, OnL, $VertAln$, $=_{Color}$ and $=_{Shape}$ in a *first-order theory*, denoting outputs of perceptive operations on a *finite domain* D. The subdomain F of this theory together with *true identity* and a *reification operator* is introduced in the next subsection. In the remainder of this section, we will step-by-step add more abstract subdomains to D that can be *reified from* F using the primitive relations above, and discuss their identity criteria in terms of equivalence classes in F.

2.2. Identity of Foci of Attention and the Reification Operator

We start with the core domain of interpretation called *foci of attention* (F), consisting of the pulsed attentional moments of a human observer explained in Section 1.2. These moments already come with a natural identity relation: Perceiving time just means to perceive a temporal partial order relation $\leq_T$ on these pulses, from which identity $=_T$ can be derived. Because we assume that attentional moments are indivisible for an observer, this relation accounts for *true identity in* F. Furthermore, since the observer has stored

---

[9]The reified entities standing for equivalence classes were called *unities* in ontological frameworks like in [26], but the authors did not discuss identity criteria based on them.

[10]The problem of distinguishing between two qualities that happen to inhere in the same individuals

[11]The choice of these primitives builds on the discussion in Section 1.2 and allows to deconstruct the examples in Section 3, but the list is definitely not exhaustive and may have to be supplemented for other application areas.

attentional moments in memory, he is able to perform abstraction computations on them. For this purpose, we introduce a *reification operator schema* $[x]^{\Phi}_{R} : D \rightarrow \mathit{ReifiedEntity}$, where x denotes a particular element, e.g. a single attentional focus, of a subset of the domain of interpretation D. This subset is denoted by the predicate wild-card Φ. R is any *partial equivalence relation* on D. The function produces a reified entity for that R-equivalence class in the Φ-subdomain that contains x, given that x is in the ranges of both predicates. Otherwise it throws the *default exception*, which is supposed to be a special $\mathit{ReifiedEntity}$. We will omit R or Φ if we do not restrict the reification to a particular relation or subset of the domain. The domain of our theory, D, consists of the elements of F as well as of all reified entities constructed in the following. *True identity* in this theory is then defined based on the reificiation operator and the temporal relation:

$$e_1 = e_2 \leftrightarrow \begin{cases} e_1 =_T e_2 & \text{for } e_1, e_2 \in F \\ \exists x.[x]^{\Phi}_{R} = e_1 \wedge [x]^{\Phi}_{R} = e_2 & \text{otherwise} \end{cases} \tag{1}$$

2.3. Identity of Bodies and Surfaces

What is sometimes called the *individuation of a body in time and space* in the philosophical literature, can be conceived as an equivalence class of a *partial equivalence relation* on F. The relation is called *body-connected* (BC). It practically solves the philosophical problem of *object identity in time* by detecting whether two foci of attention focus on the same surface individuated by the spontaneous unifying mechanism discussed in Section 1.2, which is itself based on spatio-temporal continuity[12]. In this way, humans are spontaneously able to 'cut out' those parts or regions in the flow of conscious experience which correspond to the same body or the same surface *irrespective of its other perceived qualities*. The underlying operation cuts out e.g. just those parts of the visual field which correspond to Gibson's [20] 'solid angles in the ambient optical array', that is the surface patches in the perceivable environment. The relation has to be a *partial* equivalence relation (so it is not reflexive), because not all foci of attention are focused parts of bodies: there are also the empty gaps of space between them, which are sometimes called the *ground* for a *figure (resp. body)*, or the *medium* for its locomotion [20]. For the individuation of media, complementary operations can be assumed based on locomotion types and *affordances*[13].

2.4. Identity of Loci of Attention and Locations

A 'place', as Bentham conceived it [6], is a space for a body that is identified with reference to another (constant) body or surface, and which can therefore -in the same way as a body- be continually identified in time[14]. The identity of places must be constructed in reference to some surface, since there is no way of determining an absolute location in

[12]This mechanism of course does not account for identity across long intervals of spatial absence, which is a limit in the present outline of the theory.

[13]Compare the approach taken in [2]. Although we do not focus on media and affordances in this paper, they are essential for grounding complex conventional categories like doors or road networks [32]

[14]Note that we use the notion 'place' only in the sense of 'location', i.e. denoting a particular identifiable part of the environment.

space and time[15]. Note that this reference can be any body surface, and that locations can be parts of bodies or the empty space between them. For example, a location could be identified as a part of a body with respect to its own surface, i.e. as a relative location on it. For reasons of simplicity, we assume that we have another primitive equivalence relation P' for identifying *locations among attentional moments* (not a partial one this time, since every element of the domain F of attentional moments is focused on some location, and therefore the relation is reflexive). P' on F gives rise to equivalence classes of foci of attention, which can be reified as *smallest perceivable locations of the environment*, e.g. as $[x]_{P'} = l$. We call these reified abstractions *loci of attention* L, so for each P'-equivalence class in F we have exactly one element in L, and P' provides an identity criterion for identity on L as defined in Equ. 1.

Every equivalence relation on F, denoted by the wild-card R, implies a corresponding equivalence relation on L by virtue of P', denoted by the definition schema $[R]_{P'}$.

$$x[R]_{P'}y \leftrightarrow \exists a, b.[a]_{P'} = x \wedge [b]_{P'} = y \wedge aRb. \tag{2}$$

$$BodyAt(x_i, x_j) = [[x_i]_{P'}]_{[BC]_{P'}}^{\lambda l.(\exists x.[x]_{P'}=l \wedge x_i \leq_T x \leq_T x_j)} \tag{3}$$

Using the relation BC in this schema, we can now reify *bodies* as entities *representing classes of loci* for each one of a sequence of time intervals $1, ..., i, ..., n$. The expression $BodyAt(x_i, x_j)$ produces exactly that body for the time interval i with endpoints x_i and x_j, on which the attention is focused at x_i. Now it is possible to perceive *movements of this body* by calculating the differences among the classes $1, ..., i, ..., n$ on L for successive time intervals, in which the attention is focused on this body (Figure 5).

Arbitrary locations G can be constructed in a very similar way as *classes in* L, giving rise to an *extensional mereology*: With a wild-card $R' : L \times L$, let us refer to *all possible equivalence relations on loci of attention* in the perceivable environment[16]. Then every relation R' partitions the loci into equivalence classes. Just call the entities reified from these classes *locations* in domain G, and define a 'part-of' relation P such that each reification has all sublocations in its class as parts. It can be shown that G together with the so defined P operator satisfy a finite atomic version of extensional mereology (compare [33])[17]. The identity criterion for identity on G is then just given as an extensionality criterion on L: All locations made of the same loci of attention are identical.

2.5. *Identity of Direction and Distance, and the Perception of Geometry*

Let us call every pair of foci of attention an attentional *step*. Then we assume that there is a quaternary relation $=_L$ for perceiving equal length of two steps, e.g. $ab =_L cd$, where a, b, c, d are foci. With $[=_L]_{P'}$, we denote the reified version of this relation for the domain L. The operator realizes an equivalence relation on steps, which gives rise to the reification of *abstract lengths*: each equivalence class of steps can thus be associated with

[15]Even if we use a *spatial reference system*, this system is logically anchored in and therefore presupposes the identity of concrete places. Such an anchor place is a necessary part of a so called *geodetic datum* for a mathematical ellipsoid representing the earth surface.

[16]These are finitely many because our domain is finite.

[17]For reasons of space, we leave out the formal details here (assuming that these can be added if needed).

exactly one length. Furthermore, we have a primitive $OnL(x, y, z)$ for the perception of *collinearity* and *succession* of the two steps (x, y) and (y, z), that is, of whether both steps follow each other 'on a straight line'. Now we can define whether the length of the step x, y is smaller than that of another step q, z:

$$yx \leq_L qz \leftrightarrow \exists x'.OnL(y, x, x') \wedge yx' =_L qz \tag{4}$$

It is well known that from just these two primitives, pointless versions of a 3-dimensional Euclidean geometry can be constructed, if the domain is considered to be *continuous*[18]. Since the domain F (and likewise L) is neither *continuous* nor *dense*, but *finite*, we implicitly assume an analogous discrete 3-dimensional geometric structure in which the set of loci are 'equally spaced', like in a raster[19]. In this paper, we will not discuss any formal details of an appropriate geometry, but rather sketch the opportunities these operators offer. For example we can define a discrete notion of a *surface locus x of a body y*, following the converse idea of *isolation* in *discrete topology*, by requiring for all neighborhoods of this surface locus x, that, if they contain other loci, one of them must be not part of the body y:

$$\begin{aligned} Surface(x, y) \leftrightarrow \exists x_1, x_2.BodyAt(x_1, x_2) = y \wedge P(x, y) \wedge \\ \forall z.(z \neq x \rightarrow \exists z'.(xz'[\leq_L]_{P'} xz \wedge \neg P(z', y))) \end{aligned} \tag{5}$$

Additionally, we assume a primitive relation $VertAln(x, y)$, which detects whether the step x, y is vertically aligned with gravity.

2.6. Identity of Surface Qualities

As Gibson [20] recognized, surfaces are at the very heart of perception. They account for the individuation of bodies as well as for locating all sorts of their surface qualities. We denote the conscious operation of identifying two individual foci of attention by the universal color detection mechanism of Section 1.2 with the primitive equivalence relation $=_{Color}$. The identification of two shape descriptions (see Section 1.2), that were derived from two reified bodies for two time intervals, by the binary relation $=_{Shape}$. This last relation ranges over reified bodies, the first one over foci of attention[20].

3. Applications

The Withering Flower Representing a withering flower is a challenge for every ontology that presupposes a Leibniz-style identity criterion [28], because the flower changes all its perceivable qualities during withering very radically, e.g. shape, position, color, and odor. It might even lose some parts and still maintains its identity. The BC rela-

[18] See for example [34], and compare the approach taken in [35]. Note that many weaker geometries, e.g. topology, are definable with these primitives.

[19] The authors currently work on a discrete version of the theory about the *meaningful environment*, first outlined in [2], for this purpose. A version of such a finite space was e.g. described by Suppes [36].

[20] We suggest that each operation example stands for one of two general kinds: the first one could be called 'field-based', the second one 'object based'.

tion allows to decide whether a focused part of the flower is part of the same particular thing at another moment, regardless of any qualities. It is thus possible to individuate the flower bodies $flower_1 = BodyAt(x_n, x_m)$ and $flower_2 = BodyAt(x_i, x_j)$. If we pick out two foci x_1 and x_2 of the respective flower intervals that focus on a certain locus l on the blossom surface, i.e. $[x_1]_{P'} = [x_2]_{P'} = l$[21] with $Surface(l, flower_1)$ and $Surface(l, flower_2)$, we can check whether the perceived blossom colors are equal, $x_1 =_{Color} x_2$, that is, whether the flower has faded or not between the two time intervals. We can also express the flower's changing shape by checking $flower_1 =_{Shape} flower_2$.

The Far Side of The Moon Since the far side of the moon is always occluded from the viewpoint of the earth surface, the general layout of the moon surface was unknown until the Lunik 3 satellite managed to orbit around it and took the first photographs in 1959. Before 1959, the surface quality of the moon (e.g. its color and texture) in an astronomic ontology would have had no groundable meaning. Also, from a logical point of view, the far side could not be identified by its properties, and therefore the common Leibniz-identity criterion fails again. Observers are sure to photograph the moon only if they realize a continuous movement of the satellite to the far side. This movement is an interval in F, during which observers (or the engineers calculating the orbiting curve) must be able to constantly keep the identity of the moon surface while traveling in space. This can only be done by an independent mechanism like BC.

Distances vs. Widths of two Bodies Suppose we have to decide whether an armchair c fits between two cupboards cb_1 and cb_2. The width of the armchair is a unary quality inhering in an object, which is ordinarily dealt with in information ontologies. But the distance between the cupboards is a binary quality which inheres in two objects, and therefore cannot be attributed to one object. We first have to construct an operation $Horiz(x, y)$ which denotes horizontal steps, definable from the primitive $VertAln$ and the geometry of Section 2.5 [22]. Then we can define the width quality of the armchair c by the length of the largest horizontal attentional step that starts and ends at the armchair's surface:

$$Diam(x, y, c) \leftrightarrow Horiz(x, y) \wedge Surface([x]_L, c) \wedge Surface([y]_L, c) \quad (6)$$

$$Width(c) = (x, y) \leftrightarrow Diam(x, y, c) \wedge (\forall w, z.Diam(w, z, c) \rightarrow xy \geq_L wz) \quad (7)$$

Similarly, the distance between the cupboards cb_1 and cb_2 is the length of the smallest step connecting their surfaces:

$$Range(x, y, cb_1, cb_2) \leftrightarrow Horiz(x, y) \wedge Surface([x]_L, cb_1) \wedge Surface([y]_L, cb_2) \quad (8)$$

$$\begin{aligned} Dist(cb_1, cb_2) = (x, y) \leftrightarrow Range(x, y, cb_1, cb_2) \wedge \\ (\forall w, z.Range(w, z, cb_1, cb_2) \rightarrow wz \geq_L xy) \end{aligned} \quad (9)$$

It is now possible to check whether $Dist(cb_1, cb_2) \geq_L Width(chair)$.

[21] P' is used here to identify equivalent parts of the flower *relative to its own body*.

[22] For this purpose, we need to fix a *reference vertical*, i.e. a series of vertically aligned foci, for example at one edge of a cupboard. On each focus of this vertical we can construct a plane which lies perpendicular to the vertical. We can then assert $Horiz(x, y)$ if x and y lie in one of these planes.

4. Conclusion

In this work, we introduced a list of primitives for a logical theory that can be used to ground ontologies and datasets about objects and qualities in universal perceptive operations. We demonstrated that the mechanism of logical reification of fictive entities using identity criteria (based on equivalence classes evolving from these primitives) helps to deal with some examples that are commonly concerned as challenging for ontologies. We have also provided empirical support for the view that these primitives are based on preconceptual, concept independent and universal mechanisms, being at the disposal of most human beings, and therefore enabling a common semantic plane.

As our approach is in an early stage, several questions remain open. First, universality in a physiological or ecological sense, i.e., in the sense of sharing common dispositions for the proposed operations, is only a necessary prerequisite in order to reach semantic agreement. The principal challenge for semantic engineering is how to adequately coordinate personal semantic interpretations of symbols [1]. What is missing, is a way of enabling that the individual semantic interpretation process, e.g., the naming and construction of perceivable bodies and qualities, can be coordinated in a group, given that constructing operators is creative or even fuzzy. The authors believe that such a process could rely on demonstrative acts like ostension or on an underlying mirror neuron mechanism. Second, the proposed formalism needs a full exposure. Defendable axioms have to be introduced (the authors have discussed a continuous version of an axiomatized theory in previous work [2]). Meta-logical properties, like expressivity, satisfiability, and reasoning capabilities of an appropriate finite first-order theory have to be discussed. And third, real application examples, e.g. for road network data [32] and hydrological qualities, will require extensions of the theory.

Acknowledgements

This manuscript owes much to the detailed comments of the anonymous reviewers. Our work is funded by the Semantic Reference Systems II project (DFG KU 1368/4-2) and the International Research Training Group on *Semantic Integration of Geospatial Information* (DFG GRK 1498).

References

[1] S. Scheider. The case for grounding databases. In *3rd Int. Conf. on GeoSpatial Semantics*, volume 5892 of *LNCS*, pages 44–62. Springer, Berlin, 2009.
[2] S. Scheider, K. Janowicz, and W. Kuhn. Grounding geographic categories in the meaningful environment. In M. Denis K.S. Hornsby, C. Claramunt and G. Ligozat, editors, *Spatial Information Theory, 9th Int. Conf., COSIT 2009, Proc.*, pages 69–87. Springer, Berlin, 2009.
[3] S. Harnad. The symbol grounding problem. *Physica D*, 42:335–346, 1990.
[4] L.C. Barsalou. Perceptual symbol systems. *Behavioral and Brain Sciences*, 22:577–660, 1999.
[5] W. Kuhn. Semantic engineering. In G. Navratil, editor, *Research Trends in Geographic Information Science*, volume 12 of *LNG&C*, pages 63–76. Springer, Berlin, 2009.
[6] J. Bentham. The theory of fictions. In C.K. Ogden, editor, *Bentham's Theory of Fictions*. Kegan Paul, Trench, Trubner, London, 1932.
[7] C.K. Ogden and I.A. Richards. *The Meaning of Meaning*. Harcourt, Brace & World, New York, 1923.

[8] W.V.O. Quine. On what there is. In *From a logical point of view. 9 logico-philosophical essays,2nd edition*. Harvard University Press, Cambridge, Massachusetts, 2nd edition, 1980.
[9] F. Neuhaus, P. Grenon, and B. Smith. A formal theory of substances, qualities and universals. In A. Varzi and L. Vieu, editors, *Proc. of the 3rd Int. Conf. on Formal Ontology in Information Systems (FOIS-04)*, pages 49–59. IOS Press, 2004.
[10] C. Masolo, S. Borgo, A. Gangemi, N. Guarino, and A. Oltramari. Wonderweb deliverable d18: Ontology library. Trento, Italy, 2003.
[11] F. Probst and M. Espeter. Spatial dimensionality as classification criterion for qualities. In B. Bennett and C. Fellbaum, editors, *Formal Ontology in Information Systems: Proc. of the 4th Int. Conf. (FOIS 2006)*, volume 150 of *Frontiers in artificial intelligence and applications*, pages 77–88. IOS Press, 2006.
[12] J. Bateman. Towards a generic foundation for spatial ontology. In *Formal Ontology in Information Systems: Proc. of the 3rd Int. Conf. (FOIS-2004)*, pages 237–248. IOS Press, Amsterdam, 2004.
[13] Z.W. Pylyshyn. *Things and Places. How the Mind Connects with the World*. The MIT Press, Cambridge, Massachusetts, 2007.
[14] E. von Glasersfeld. *Radical Constructivism: A Way of Knowing and Learning*. The Falmer Press, London, 1995.
[15] E. von Glasersfeld. An attentional model for the conceptual construction of units and number. *Journal for Research in Mathematics Education*, 12(2):83–94, 1981.
[16] R. VanRullen and C. Koch. Is perception discrete or continuous? *Trends in Cognitive Sciences*, 7(5):207–213, 2003.
[17] B.J. Scholl. Objects and attention: the state of the art. *Cognition*, 80:1–46, 2001.
[18] P.F. Strawson. *Individuals. An Essay on Descriptive Metaphysics*. Routledge, London, 1959.
[19] W. Köhler. *Gestalt Psychology. An Introduction to new Concepts in Modern Psychology*. Liveright, New York, 1992.
[20] J.J. Gibson. *The ecological approach to visual perception*. Houghton Mifflin, Boston, 1979.
[21] S. Borgo, N. Guarino, and C. Masolo. An ontological theory of physical objects. In L. Ironi, editor, *Qualitative reasoning. Proc. of the 11th Intern. Workshop on Qualitative Reasoning*, pages 223–231. Cortona, 1997.
[22] N. Burgess. Spatial cognition and the brain. *Ann. N. Y. Acad. Sci.*, 1124:77–97, 2008.
[23] P. Kay and C. McDaniel. The linguistic significance of the meanings of basic color terms. *Language*, 54(3):610–646, 1978.
[24] P. Kay and L. Maffi. Color appearance and the emergence and evolution of basic color lexicons. *American Anthropologist*, 101:743–760, 1999.
[25] D. Marr and H.K. Nishihara. Representation and recognition of the spatial organization of three-dimensional shapes. *Proc. of the Royal Society of London. Series B, Biological Sciences*, 200(1140):269–294, 1978.
[26] N. Guarino and C. Welty. Identity, unity and individuality: Towards a formal toolkit for ontological analysis. In W. Horn, editor, *ECAI 2000 Proc.*, volume 54 of *Frontiers in artficial intelligence and applications*, pages 219–223. IOS-Press, Amsterdam, 2000.
[27] W.V.O. Quine. Identity, ostension and hypostasis. In *From a logical point of view. 9 logico-philosophical essays*, pages 65–79. Harvard University Press, Cambridge, Massachusetts, 2nd edition, 1980.
[28] E.E. Savellos. On defining identity. *Notre Dame Journal of Formal Logic*, 31(3):476–484, 1990.
[29] H. Noonan. Identity (stanford encyclopedia of philosophy), 2009.
[30] T. Williamson. *Identity and Discrimination*. Blackwell, Oxford, 1990.
[31] R. Carnap. *Der logische Aufbau der Welt*. Felix Meiner Verlag, Hamburg, 1998.
[32] S. Scheider and W. Kuhn. Affordance-based categorization of road network data using a grounded theory of channel networks. *Int. J. Geogr. Inf. Sc.*, in press.
[33] R. Casati and A.C. Varzi. *Parts and places: The structures of spatial representation*. MIT Press, Cambridge, Mass., 1999.
[34] A. Tarski. What is elementary geometry. In P. Suppes L Henkin and A. Tarski, editors, *The axiomatic method. With special reference to geometry and physics*, pages 16–29. North-Holland Publishing, Amsterdam, 1959.
[35] B. Bennett, A.G. Cohn, P. Torrini, and S.M. Hazarika. A foundation for region-based qualitative geometry. In W. Horn, editor, *ECAI 2000 Proc.*, volume 54 of *Frontiers in artificial intelligence and applications*, pages 204–208. IOS-Press [u.a.], Amsterdam, 2000.
[36] P. Suppes. Finitism in geometry. *Erkenntnis*, 54:133–144, 2001.

Applications I

Formal Ontology in Information Systems
A. Galton and R. Mizoguchi (Eds.)
IOS Press, 2010

doi:10.3233/978-1-60750-535-8-147

On Building an Index Advisor for Semantic Web Queries

Lubomir Stanchev [a] Grant Weddell [b]
[a] *Indiana University - Purdue University Fort Wayne, USA*
[b] *University of Waterloo, Canada*

Abstract. Current optimization techniques for answering queries over Semantic Web data use realization to precalculate the individuals associated with every concept in the given ontology. However, this technique does not take into account the type of queries, written for example in nRQL or SPARQL-DL, that will arrive at the system. In this paper we propose how this additional knowledge can be used to create query-specific indices. We include experimental results that show how our approach can be used to improve the performance of the Pellet query engine for the popular LUBM benchmark.

1. Introduction

The Semantic Web and related terms have become buzz phrases in the last few years. For example, John Markoff coined the phrase Web 3.0 in the New York Times in 2006 referring to providing semantic capabilities that enhance the user experience. Although the World Wild Web Consortium (W3C) has attempted to standardize related languages (OWL, RDF, and SPARQL, to name a few), we are still far from realizing the dream of the Semantic Web because current algorithms for retrieving information from knowledgebases do not scale well for large data sources, such as the current size of the Internet. In this paper we try to address some of these scalability challenges by describing how search principles from relational database technology can be applied to knowledgebases. Specifically, relational database engines use index advisors to select indices that can optimize query workloads consisting of SQL queries. Here, we adopt a similar approach and describe how an index advisor can be used to construct *description indices* that can be used to optimize KIF-like queries ([1]) over an OWL-DL knowledgebase.

This is an important problem because without techniques for efficiently accessing knowledgebases their use will remain isolated to narrow domains, such as medical terms (e.g., the SNOMED ontology [2]). In most cases, the type of queries that will be asked from a knowledgebase are known upfront up to some parameters and therefore it is reasonable to create search data structures that can be used to efficiently answer the queries.

The problem that is addressed in this paper is intrinsically hard because conventional indexing techniques from relational databases fall short when it comes to querying knowledgebases. For example, consider a knowledgebase of chairs. For some chairs we may know that they are from the Medieval Period, while for other chairs we may know that they are from the European Renaissance, and there may be even chairs from the eighteenth century. Organizing these chairs into an index that is ordered relative to age is not a trivial task because additional knowledge of how these periods are related to each other is needed. Therefore, calls to a concept subsumption reasoner that can reason with additional data (called terminology) needs to be used when constructing or traversing an index.

Current solutions for solving the problem of indexing knowledgebases use realization to precompute the elements of each concept (see for example the Racer approach [3]). However, this is done independently of the type of input queries. For example, consider the following query, which is a modified version of a query from the LUBM benchmark ([4]), expressed in a KIF-like language.

(type Professor ?X) (type Department :P) (worksfor ?X :P) (order ?X by rank)

The query asks for all professors that work for a given department ordered by their rank. We have used $:P$ to denote a parameter to the query. In order to answer this query efficiently, we need to know all the professors in each department. The professors in a department need to be ordered relative to their subtype (e.g., full professors come first, followed by associate and assistant professors). An instance of the novel *description index* that is described in this paper will store the concept descriptions associated with every department individual. For each such individual, the index will also store the related professor individuals in the described order. Such a description index can be used to efficiently answer the example query. In contrast, such efficient access is not possible with existing techniques implemented in knowledgebase query engines such as Pellet ([5]) and Racer ([6]). The reasons are that: (1) existing engines do not create query specific indices and (2) they do not explore novel index types that are required for supporting knowledgebase queries.

On a related note, note that our approach is very different than the approaches taken by RDF databases, such as RDF3X ([7]), Hexastore ([8]) and LUPOSDATE ([9]). While these systems index RDF triplets, our approach indexes concept descriptions. As a result, a description index can store much richer information than an index on RDF triplets.

Our approach first examines each input query and considers possible plans for executing it (see for example [3]). Although different query plans can examine, for example, different join orders, they will have the same primitive queries as the building blocks. Efficient execution of these primitive queries is required for the efficient execution of the overall query. In this paper we consider primitive queries that have certain syntax. Such queries can be executed in the relational case in logarithmic time. When the input data is a knowledgebase, the retrieval time can be worse and will depend on the amount of uncertainty that is introduced in the data. Our final step is to create a description index for each primitive query. Note that the merging of description indices should also be investigated because it can potentially reduce the storage overhead without affecting the execution time of the input queries. However, index merging is beyond the scope of this paper and is left as a topic for future research.

One known limitation to our approach is that it relies on a query optimizer to break complex queries into simpler ones. However, we believe that this is unavoidable because an index advisor should be custom-fitted for the query optimizer that will use it (i.e., an index is only good if the query optimizer will use it). Another drawback of our approach is that indices with replicated data are created when the concept descriptions that describe the individuals in the knowledge are not descriptive enough (e.g., a person is defined as being older than twenty years of age). This can adversely affect both search and update time. One possible way to overcome this limitation is to consider index compression that will remove redundant copies of the same data. Similar to index merging, this research area is outside the scope of the paper and a topic for future investigation.

The main contributions of the paper are the new description index type that are described in Section 3 and the description index creation procedure that is presented in Section 4. Section 2 of the paper gives an overview of related research, while Section 5 outlines the results of our experimental evaluation.

2. Related Research

The Web Ontology Language - Description Logics (OWL-DL) [10] is introduced by the World Wild Web Consortium (W3C) as a standard for representing knowledgebases. While most existing research focuses on consistency checking using a tableau-based approach (Pellet [5], Fact++ [11], and Racer [6] are three popular implementations), there have been two notable proposal for SQL-like query languages over OWL-DL knowledgebases.

The first one is SPARQL-DL ([12]). The language is very expressive and the free variables can be not only individuals, but also concepts or relationships (i.e., the languages has capabilities that cannot be expressed in first-order logics). Notably, [13] describes how cost-best query optimization can be used to make query execution decisions, such as join-order selection. Currently, SPARQL-DL is supported by Pellet. The second language is nRQL and was created by the developers of Racer [14].

Papers, such as [3], explain how to use realization to precompute the elements of each concept in the terminology. Although this approach reduces the number of expensive calls to the reasoner, it can still leads to linear time complexity for answering certain queries, such as our example query. The reason is the lack of appropriate indices.

Ground breaking work in the area includes the papers [15,16]. They describe how to create an index that stores concept descriptions rather than individuals. The concept descriptions in the index are ordered relative to inferred values for some of the data properties. In this work we extend this research by describing how to create more complex indices that can support efficient execution of nested queries. (The two papers only address the problem of finding all the individuals that belong to a given concept description.)

3. Description Indices

In this section we introduce the concepts: *description tree index* and *description hash table*, which are the building blocks of a description index. The two artifacts correspond to search tree index and hash table, respectively, in the relational database sense.

A description tree index stores concept descriptions in a predefined order and allows for efficient range search and for retrieving the result relative to a predefined order. A description hash table stores concept descriptions that are clustered relative to inferred values of one or more properties and supports efficient answering of partial-match queries. We assume that the concept description are written in OWL-DL using the Manchester

(concept)	*(subsumed by)*
Full Professor	Professor **and** (*works for* **some** Organization)
Graduate Student	Student **and** (*advisor* **only** Professor)
Undergraduate Student	Student **and** (*takes course* **min** 2) **and** (*takes course* **max** 4)
Student	Undergraduate Student **or** Graduate Student

Table 1. Part of the LUBM Schema Expressed Using the Manchester OWL Syntax

OWL Syntax([17]). For completeness, we next present example expressions in this language, where the reader should refer to [10,17] for a complete overview.

3.1. The Manchester OWL Syntax

Our running example is based on the terminology of the LUBM benchmark. Part of the terminology, expressed using the Manchester OWL Syntax, is shown in Table 1, where bold is used for language reserved words, while properties (both data and object) are in italic.

The first subsumption states that if someone is a full professor, then they are a professor and they work for at least one organization. The second rule states that if someone is a graduate student, then they are a student and all their advisors are professors. The third rule states that undergraduate students must take between two and four courses. The last rule states that if someone is a student, then they must be either an undergraduate or graduate student.

Note that the first column of the table contains primitive concepts, while the second column contains *concept descriptions* (a primite concept is a special case of a concept description). A concept description describes all individuals that satisfy certain rules. For example, the concept description in the right column of the first row in Table 1 describes all professors that work for an organization. The relationship between the two columns of the table is *subsumption* (denoted as **SubClassOf**), that is, if an individual belongs to the primitive concept shown in the left column, then it must also belong to the set of individuals described by the concept description in the right column.

A set of subsumption rules form a *terminology* (i.e., the additional knowledge that is used when answering queries). The Manchester OWL Syntax is also used to describe the *individuals* in the knowledgebase. For example, a particular student may be described as follows.

is taking Calculus 101 **and** *is taking* Stats 101 **and** *member of* Computer Science Department **and** *age* **value** $[>= 20]$

This student takes Calculus 101 and Statistics 101, they are member of the Computer Science Department, and they are at least twenty years of age.

3.2. Description Tree Index

A formal definition of a description tree index follows.

Definition 1 (description tree index) *A description tree index has the syntax $\langle C, O\rangle$, where C is a concept description and O is an ordering description. The index will store* *all individuals* e *that have concept description* D *for which it can be inferred from the terminology* $\mathcal{T}$ *that* C *subsumes* D *(i.e.* $\mathcal{T}$ *implies* D ***SubClassOf*** C*). The ordering description* O *defines the order of the elements in the search tree.*

The definition relies on a way for defining ordering among concept descriptions, which is presented next.

Definition 2 (ordering description) *An ordering description* Od *has the following syntax.*

$$Od ::= \langle\rangle \mid \langle f\ \texttt{dir} : Od\rangle \mid \langle D_1 : Od_1, \ldots, D_m : Od_m\rangle$$

We have used $\langle\rangle$ *to denote an empty ordering,* `dir` *to denote* `asc` *or* `desc`*,* D *to denote a concept description, and* f *to denote a data property. In order for this ordering description to be valid relative to a terminology, it must be the case that "*D_i **and** D_j **SubClassOf EMPTY***" for* $1 \leq i \neq j \leq m$ *and "*D **SubClassOf** D_1 **or** $\ldots$ **or** D_m*" are both implied by the terminology, where* D *is a concept description that describes the set of individuals on which the order is defined (***EMPTY*** is used to denote the empty concept - i.e., bottom in description logics). We will say that the concept description* D *is before* E *relative to an ordering description* Od *and terminology* $\mathcal{T}$ *and write* $D \prec_{Od,\mathcal{T}} E$ *in the following cases (*x^* *is used to denote the renaming of* x *to* x^**):*

- *when* Od *is* $\langle f\ \texttt{dir} : Od_1\rangle$*:*
  - $\mathcal{T} \cup \mathcal{T}^*$ *implies* $(D$ **and** $E^*)$ **SubClassOf** $(f < f^*)$ *when* `dir=asc` *and* $(D$ **and** $E^*)$ **SubClassOf** $(f > f^*)$ *when* `dir=desc` *or*
  - $\mathcal{T} \cup \mathcal{T}^*$ *implies* $((D$ **and** $E^*)$ **SubClassOf** $(f = f^*))$ **and** $D \prec_{Od_1,\mathcal{T}} E$
- *when* Od *is* $\langle D_1 : Od_1, \ldots, D_m : Od_m\rangle$*:*
  - $\mathcal{T}$ *implies* $(D$ **SubClassOf** $D_i)$ **and** $(E$ **SubClassOf** $D_j)$ *for some* $i < j$ *or*
  - $\mathcal{T}$ *implies* $(D$ **or** $E)$ **SubClassOf** D_i *for some* i *and* $D \prec_{Od_i,\mathcal{T}} E$.

Note that we may omit some of the angle brackets in an ordering description when clear from the context. Similarly, when `dir` is `asc`, it may be omitted. Note that if f and g are data properties, then $f = g$ ($f > g$) represents the set of individuals that have the same value for the two properties (for which the value for the f property is bigger than the value for the g property).

An example of a description tree index is: ⟨Professor, ⟨*worksFor.name*: ⟨Full Professor : *age*, Associate Professor : *salary*, Assistant Professor: *publications*⟩⟩⟩. It denotes a search tree that contains all individuals that can be inferred to be professors. The ordering will be first relative to the name of the place of employment. In the same workplace, full professors will come first, followed by associate and assistant professors. Full professors in the same workplace will be ordered relative to age, associate professors - relative to salary, and assistant professors - relative to the number of publications.

Consider a query that asks for all associated professors with a given name (we will denote this name as :P) ordered by salary. To answer the query, we can do a search in the description tree index, where for simplicity we assume that the search tree is binary. For every node with concept description D we need to compare the concept descriptions D and "Associate Professor and $name$ = :P" relative to the ordering description of the description tree index. If D comes first, then we need to continue the search in the right subtree. If D comes second, then we need to continue the search in the left subtree. If the two concept descriptions are not comparable relative to the ordering description, then we need to check if the terminology implies "D **SubClassOf** (Associate Professor $\mathtt{and}$ $name$ = :P)". If this is the case, then we have found a concept description that belongs to the query result and we know that the other concept descriptions that belong to the result will be adjacent relative to an in-order traversal of tree. If the two concept descriptions are not comparable and the terminology does not imply this subsumption, then we need to check both the left and right subtrees of the current node. The reason is that in general an ordering description defines a partial order.

If we need the search to be always efficient (i.e., return each element of the query result in logarithmic time), then we need to enforce the following *descriptive sufficiency* property ([15]) for all concept descriptions in the description tree index. Note that the descriptive sufficiency property holds for the data that is generated from the LUBM benchmark.

Definition 3 (descriptive sufficiency) *A concept description D is sufficiently descriptive relative to an ordering description Od and terminology $\mathcal{T}$, written as $DS_{Od,\mathcal{T}}(D)$, if one of the following holds.*

- $Od = \langle\rangle$
- $Od = \langle f\ \mathtt{dir} : Od_1\rangle$, $DS_{Od_1,\mathcal{T}}(D)$, *and $\mathcal{T}$ implies D* **SubClassOf** $f = k$ *for some k*
- $Od = \langle D_1 : Od_1, \ldots, D_m : Od_m\rangle$, $DS_{Od_i,\mathcal{T}}(D)$, *and $\mathcal{T}$ implies "D* **SubClassOf** *D_i" for some i*

Next, consider a node in a description tree index with concept description C_1 that is "*age* **value** $[1, 8]$" and a left child node with concept description C_2 that is "*age* **value** $[5, 7]$". Suppose that the concepts in the tree are ordered relative to the ordering description $\langle age\rangle$. Now, if a new concept description C_3 with value "*age* **value** 3" is inserted in the knowledgebase, then it can be inserted either in the left or right child subtree of the root node because C_1 and C_3 are not comparable relative to the defined search tree order. However, inserting C_3 in the right subtree is obviously the wrong choice because $C_3 \prec_{\langle age\rangle,\mathcal{T}} C_2$. Therefore, when inserting a new element in a concept description index, we may need to consider both the left and right subtree of the current node if the descriptive sufficiency property does not hold for the indexed descriptions.

3.3. Description Hash Table

The general definition of a description hash table follows.

Definition 4 (description hash table) *A description hash table H has the syntax $\langle C, \{p_i\}_{i=1}^k\rangle$, where C is a concept description and $\{p\}_{i=1}^k$ are properties. It partitions all concepts descriptions that are subsumed by C using a hash function on the different values of $\{p\}_{i=1}^k$.*

Note that the second element of the syntax of a description hash table may be empty, in which case we will store all concept descriptions in a single bucket, that is, the description hash table will degenerate into a *description list*.

An example description hash table is: ⟨Graduate Student `or` Undergraduate Student, $\{advisor\}$⟩. It partitions the graduate and undergraduate students relative to their advisor. If the advisor of a student is not known, than this student could be placed in several hash buckets. For example, if the advisor of a student that is in the Computer Science Department is not known, but we know that students in the Computer Science department are supervised by professor from the Computer Science Department, then we only need to store the student in the hash buckets for Computer Science professors.

Searching in a description hash table is similar to searching in a regular hash table in the sense that the clustering allows us to prune buckets that do not contribute the query result. Since the same concept description can appear in multiple hash buckets, response time for search can degrade if the concept descriptions that are stored in the index are not descriptive.

3.4. Description Index

The definition of a description index follows.

Definition 5 (description index) *A description index can be represented as a rooted tree, which we will call the* definition tree *of the description index. The nodes in the tree can be either* hash nodes *or* tree nodes. *The label of a hash node is that of a description hash table, while the label of a tree node is that of a description tree index. The edges in the definition tree have labels that are object properties.*

A description index represents a set of description hash tables and description tree indices, where the connection between the data structures and their content is determined by the shape and labels of the definition tree.

Specifically, for a root node in the definition tree that is a hash node or a tree node, the corresponding description hash table or description tree index, respectively, is built. If the node n_1 is the child of the node n_2 and the edge between the two nodes has the label p, then a data structure is built for each concept description D stored in the data structure for n_2. Specifically, if n_1 is the tree node $\langle C, O\rangle$, then the description tree index $\langle C \texttt{ and } (p \texttt{ some } D), O\rangle$ is created. Alternatively, if n_1 is the hash node $\langle C, \{p_i\}_{i=1}^k\rangle$, then the description hash table $\langle C \texttt{ and } (p \texttt{ some } D), \{p_i\}_{i=1}^k\rangle$ is created.

An example description index is shown in Figure 1. Note that we have used *about* to denote the identifier of an element (it is represented as *rdf:about* in the LUBM benchmark data). The index contains a description hash table that stores all elements that can be inferred to describe a department. For each such element, a description tree index that stores all elements that can be inferred to be professors in the respective department is created, where the professors are ordered relative to their rank. Now, our example query from Section 1 can be answered by first finding the department with the specified value for *about* and then finding all the professors in this department using the corresponding description tree index.

4. Index Creation

In this section we explain how description indices are created from primitive queries.

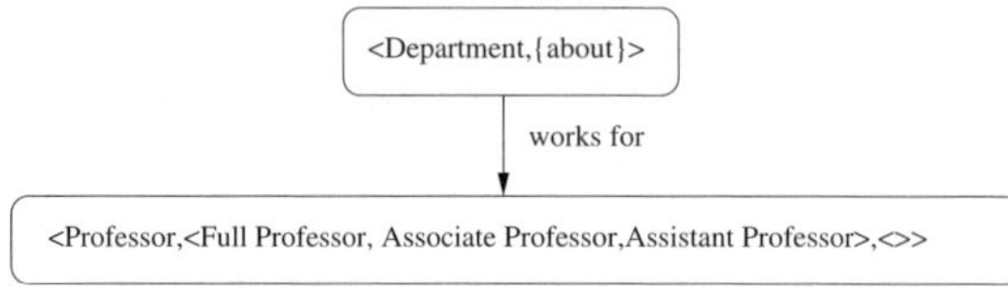

Figure 1. Definition tree of an example description index

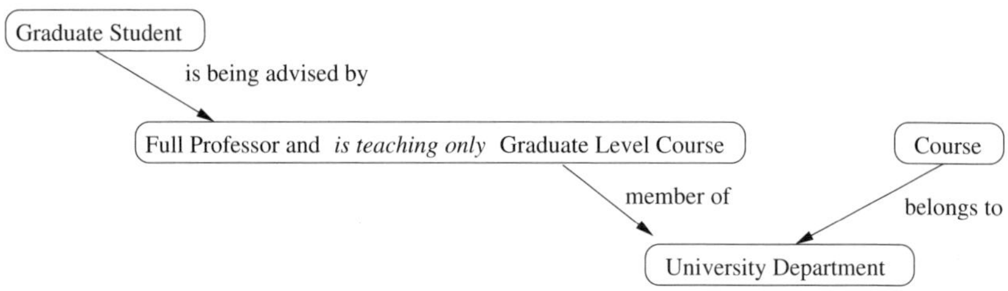

Figure 2. Example query graph

Definition 6 (primitive queries) *Primitive queries have a query graph that is in the shape of an inverse tree. Each node is labeled with a concept description, while edges are labeled with object properties. The query represented by the graph is a conjunction of KIF-like terms. For each node, the term "(type D_i $?x_i$)" is constructed, where D_i is the label of the node. For each edge between D_i and D_j labeled p_q the term "(p_q $?x_i$ $?x_j$)" will be created. In addition, KIF-like terms involving parameters can be specified on the concept description for the root node. This terms can be of form "(p_1 value :P_1)* **and** ... **and** *(p_k value :P_k)* **and** p_{k+1} `value` $[>=: P_{k+1}, <= P_{k+2}]$*", where the partial match terms or the range term may be missing. We postpone specifying the restriction on the ordering condition of the query.*

An example primitive query in this format is: "(**type** Graduate Student $?x_1$) (**type** Full Professor **and** *is teaching* **only** Graduate Level Course $?x_2$) (*is being advised by* $?x_1$ $?x_2$) (**type** University Department $?x_3$) (*member of* $?x_2$ $?x_3$) (*name* ?x3 :P1) (**type** Course $?x_4$) (*belongs to* $?x_4$ $?x_3$)", where the query graph is shown in Figure 2. The query asks for information about all graduate students who are advised by full professors that are members of a given department and who teach only graduate level courses. The query also asks about the courses in that department. The query will return information about the student, their advisor, the department of their advisor, and the all the courses in the department.

Given a primitive query that follows the described syntax, we create a description tree that has a definition tree that is the inverse tree of the query graph. In our example, the node for the university department will be the root node of the definition tree and the nodes for course and full professor will be its direct children. Note that the labels for the edges do not change, while the labels for the nodes change as described in the next paragraphs.

We will first explain how to construct the labels for the leaf nodes in the inverted tree of the query graph (the graduate student node in our example). If the leaf node is based on the concept D_1, then the node will be a hash node with label $\langle D, \{\}\rangle$ if no ordering is defined on the individuals that are subsumed by D. Alternatively, if an ordering condition is specified, then a tree node with concept description D and the ordering is created. For our example query, the hash node ⟨Graduate Student,{}⟩ will be created. Alternatively, if the query asked for the graduate students of the same advisor to be ordered by age, then the tree node ⟨Graduate Student,{*name*}⟩ will be created.

We next explain how the labels for the non-leaf and non-root nodes are created. If a node n has label D and no ordering condition is expressed on it, then the hash node $\langle D$ **and** $(p_1$ **some** $D_1)$ **and** $\ldots (p_k$ **some** $D_k), \{\}\rangle$ is created. In the expression, $\{D_i\}_{i=1}^k$ are concept descriptions for the child nodes in the definition tree that have already been constructed and $\{p_i\}_{i=1}^k$ are the respective inverse properties of the edges that connect the node to its children. In our example query, for the professor node will create the hash node ⟨Full Professor **and** *is teaching* **only** Graduate Level Course **and** *advises* **some** Graduate Student,{}⟩ because no ordering is defined on professors.

The label for the root node is defined similarly, with the addition that the parameterized predicate, when present, needs to be taken into account. Specifically, if the constraint "(p_1 value :P_1) **and** ... **and** (p_k value :P_k) **and** p_{k+1} `value` $[>=: P_{k+1}, <= P_{k+2}]$" is defined, then the tree node $\langle \ldots, \langle p_1, \ldots, p_{k+1}\rangle\rangle$ will be created. An ordering condition can also be specified in the query, where p_{k+1}, when a range predicate is defined, should be the first property in the ordering condition. If both an ordering condition and a range predicate are missing, then a hash node will be created. In our example, the hash node "⟨University Department **and** *offers* **some** Course **and** *has as member* **some** (Full Professor **and** *is teaching* **only** Graduate Level Course **and** *advises* **some** Graduate Student), {*name*}⟩" will be created.

We require that the ordering of the query is such that it follows the nodes of the definition tree of the description index. More precisely, the properties for each concept description must appear consecutively in the ordering and in the order of the definition tree. In our example, this means that the properties for the department should come first, potentially followed by properties of professor and graduate student, where the properties for the course can come any time after the properties for the department. Finally, if the ordering for a node with concept description D is not total, then there should be no ordering defined on the descendants of that node in the definition tree. In our example, ⟨Department.*name*, Professor.*salary*⟩ is a valid ordering as long as there are no two departments with the same name.

The so constructed description index can be used to answer the input query. The traversal will be efficient as long as the stored concept descriptions are sufficiently descriptive and all edges in the query graph are labeled with functional properties.

5. Experimental Results

Our experimental results are based on the LUBM benchmark([4]). We created a database that consists of twenty universities. The benchmark contains a program that generated data about each university (e.g., departments, students, professors, courses, etc.). The benchmark consists of fourteen queries. We executed each of the queries in two different modes. One way is using the description index structures that are described in the paper, were the indices were manually custom-built using our algorithm. The other way is by rewriting the queries in SQARQL-DL and executing them through Jena interface and using the Pellet reasoner. In both cases the heap was set to 1.5GB to avoid an out of

(query)	*(description index)*	*(Pellet)*
Q1	1	1076
Q2	47	3167
Q3	1	1263
Q4	1	1373
Q5	1	796
Q6	671	3619
Q7	1	1373
Q8	35	1966
Q9	51	4712
Q10	520	1404
Q11	31	1186
Q12	1	3213
Q13	35	858
Q14	468	2293

Table 2. Execution time for the LUBM queries in milliseconds

(query)	*(index size)*
Q1	5
Q2	4
Q3	3
Q4	3
Q5	14
Q6	13
Q7	14
Q8	21
Q9	15
Q10	14
Q11	1
Q12	1
Q13	14
Q14	10

Table 3. Size of indices for each query in MBs

space error. Both tests were executed on Sony VGN-NW150J laptop with 4GB of main memory and 2.10GHz CPU. The results of the experiments are shown in Table 2. We measured the time to compute and print the result, where the time to initially load the data was not measured. For example, Query 6 runs slowly in both scenarios because it asks for all the students and printing all students is time consuming. Conversely, Query 2 asks for all graduate students that are students in the university from which they got their undergraduate degree. Our solution performs an index join, which is significantly faster than the nested-loop join that is performed by Pellet.

We realize that there is a cost to pay for creating indexes. The obvious cost is the cost of storage. The size of the initial knowledgebase of twenty universities is 110MB. The amount of storage needed to store the indices for each query is shown in Table 3. As expected, indices bring slight storage overhead.

6. Conclusion

In this paper we described how to create description indices that can be used to index semantic web data. We believe the paper builds the foundation for creating an index advisor for SPARQL-DL queries over knowledgebases. Areas for future research include integrating the algorithm that is proposed in the paper in existing semantic query optimizers, extending description indices, and considering different description index merging strategies.

References

[1] Genesereth, M.R., Fikes, R.E.: Knowledge Interchange Format Version 3.0 Reference Manual. Standord Technical Manual http://www.ksl.stanford.edu/knowledge-sharing/kif/.
[2] International Health Terminology Standards Development Organization. http://www.ihtsdo.org/
[3] Haarslev, V., Möller, R.: Optimization Techniques for Retrieving Resources Described in OWL/RDF Documents: First Results (2004). In Ninth International Conference on the Principles of Knowledge Representation and Reasoning (KR) (2004)
[4] Pan, Z., Guo, Y., Heflin, J.: LUBM: A benchmark for OWL knowledge base systems. Journal of Web Semantics **3**(2) (2005) 158–182
[5] Sirin, E., Parsia, B., Grau, B.C., Kalyanpur, A., Katz, Y.: Pellet: A practical OWL-DL reasoner. Web Semantics: Science, Services and Agents on the World Wide Web **5**(2) (2007)
[6] Haarslev, V., Möller, R.: Racer: A Core Inference Engine for the Semantic Web. Second International Workshop on Evaluation of Ontology-based Tools (2003)
[7] RDF-3X. http://www.w3.org/RDF
[8] Weiss, C., Karras, P., Bernstein, A.: Hexastore:Sextuple Indexing for Semantic Web Data Management. VLDB2008
[9] Groppe, S., Groppe, J.: External Sorting for Index Construction of Large Semantic Web Databases. Proceedings of the 25th ACM Symposium on Applied Computing (ACM SAC 2010)
[10] OWL Web Ontology Language Guide. http://www.w3.org/TR/owl-guide/
[11] Tsarkov, D., Horrocks, I.: FaCT++ Description Logic Reasoner: System Description. Lecture Notes in Computer Science **4130** (2006) 292–297
[12] Sirin, E., Parsia, B.: SPARQL-DL: SPARQL Query for OWL-DL. 3rd OWL: Experiences and Directions Workshop (OWLED) (2007)
[13] Sirin, E., Parsia, B.: Optimizations for answering conjunctive abox queries: First results. In Proceeding of the International Description Logics Workshop (2006)
[14] Haarslev, V., Möller, R., Wessel, M.: Querying the semantic web with Racer + nRQL. In Proceedings of the KI-2004 International Workshop on Applications of Description Logics (2004)
[15] Pound, J., Stanchev, L., Toman, D., Weddell, G.E.: On ordering descriptions in a description logic. International Workshop on Description Logics (2007)
[16] Pound, J., Stanchev, L., Toman, D., Weddell, G.E.: On Ordering and Indexing Metadata for the Semantic Web. International Workshop on Description Logics (2008)
[17] Horridge, M., Drummond, N., Goodwin, J., Rector, A., Stevens, R., Wang, H.: The Manchester OWL syntax. OWL: Experiences and Directions (2006)

Formal Ontology in Information Systems
A. Galton and R. Mizoguchi (Eds.)
IOS Press, 2010

doi:10.3233/978-1-60750-535-8-158

A Categorization of KR&R Methods for Requirement Analysis of a Query Answering Knowledge Base

Vinay K. CHAUDHRI[a], Bert BREDEWEG[b], Richard FIKES[c], Sheila MCILRAITH[d], and Michael P. WELLMAN[e]
[a] *Artificial Intelligence Center, SRI International, Menlo Park, CA, USA 94025*
[b] *University of Amsterdam, Science Park 107, 1098 XG Amsterdam, The Netherlands*
[c] *Computer Science Department, Stanford University, Stanford, CA, USA 94305*
[d] *Department of Computer Science, University of Toronto, Toronto, Canada M5S 1A4*
[e] *Computer Science & Engineering, University of Michigan, Ann Arbor, MI 48109*

Abstract. Our long-term goal is to build a query answering system that can answer questions on a wide variety of topics and explain the answers. In such a situation, a designer faces the challenge of how to specify the KR&R requirements that are needed to answer questions. In this paper, we introduce a categorization of KR&R methods, and apply it to specifying the requirements for answering questions in six different domains: Physics, Chemistry, Biology, Environmental Science, Microeconomics, and U.S. Government & Politics. Drawing from the corpus of about 500 questions that we analyzed, we consider an example question in each domain and show the analytical process that we used to derive the requirements in terms of the KR&R categorization. We analyze the effectiveness of the current KR&R categorization, and identify directions for future work suggesting how this categorization can be further evolved by community participation.

Keywords. Domain Analysis, Knowledge Engineering, Query Answering, E-Science

Introduction

We examine the task of identifying the Knowledge Representation and Reasoning (KR&R) requirements for a query answering knowledge base (KB) designed to answer questions on a wide variety of topics. One possible approach for doing such an analysis is to assume a specific KR language and a system, and attempt to reduce each query answering task to the capabilities of that particular system. One could go to the extreme of actually implementing each question, and be very concrete in terms of the KR&R needs. The use of a specific KR language or system, however, is not desirable if one wants the results to be general across systems. Undertaking actual implementations can be far too expensive for the initial design and planning stage of a project. Motivated by these considerations, we focus in this paper on an analysis methodology to derive KR&R requirements from a set of questions to be answered by the KB. Our methodology is based on a categorization of KR&R methods. As a corpus of questions, we consider about 500 questions from Advanced Placement (AP)

Exams in the domains of Physics, Chemistry, Biology, Microeconomics, Environmental Science, and U.S. Government & Politics. We use an example question from each domain to show the analysis process for deriving the requirements, and then study the effectiveness of the KR&R categorization. Our analysis methodology and the use of KR&R categorization is a novel contribution, as a comparable analysis on a similar scale has never before been attempted.

This work is part of a larger effort called Project Halo that is staged, long-range research by Vulcan Inc. to develop a "Digital Aristotle" — a reasoning system capable of answering novel questions and solving advanced problems in a broad range of scientific disciplines and related human affairs (see http://www.projecthalo.com). We have connected this long-term goal to the grand challenge of representing a college-level textbook, and then answering questions at the back of that book [1, 2]. The AP exam is a college-level test administered in the United States (see http://www.collegeboard.com/student/testing/ap/about.html for more details). We chose the AP test as an evaluation criterion because it is a widely accepted standard for testing whether a person understands the content of a given subject.

1. A Categorization of KR&R Methods

Our approach for developing the categorization of KR&R methods was to review the proceedings of the recent international KR&R conferences for the topics of current research (http://www.kr.org) and standard textbooks on the subject [3, 4]. We used these resources to develop an initial inventory of KR&R categories. That inventory was refined by using it in the analysis of the six AP domains.

The KR&R categorization is divided into three broad subcategories: representation capabilities, built-in theories, and reasoning capabilities. The representation capabilities refer to the representation features of the KR language. The built-in theories refer to the capabilities that require special-purpose knowledge and reasoning methods. The reasoning capabilities refer to general-purpose inference or query answering methods supported by the system.

For this paper, we simply enumerate below the different KR&R categories. A more complete document with the definitions of each category is available online (http://www.ai.sri.com/halo/public/fois2010/).

- 1 Representation Capabilities
  - 1.1 Atomic Propositions
    - 1.1.1 Binary Relationships
    - 1.1.2 N-Ary Relationships
  - 1.2 Boolean Combinations of Atomic Propositions
  - 1.3 Quantification
    - 1.3.1 Universal and Existential Quantification over Objects
    - 1.3.2 Universal and Existential Quantification over Predicates
  - 1.4 Qualifying the Truth Value of Propositions
    - 1.4.1 Propositions qualified by "necessary" and "possible"
    - 1.4.2 Propositions qualified by "obligatory", "permitted", and "forbidden"
    - 1.4.3 Propositions qualified by "was", "will be", and "always"
  - 1.5 Structured Objects

- 1.6 Belief and Knowledge of Agents
- 1.7 Logic Programs
  - 1.7.1 Horn Logic Programs
  - 1.7.2 Ordinary Logic Programs
  - 1.7.3 Courteous Logic Programs
  - 1.7.4 Well-founded Semantics
- 1.8 Event-Condition-Action Rules
- 1.9 Contextualized Knowledge
- 1.10 Diagrams
- 1.11 Processes
  - 1.11.1 Discrete Processes
  - 1.11.2 Continuous Processes
  - 1.11.3 Hybrid Processes
- 1.12 Uncertainty
  - 1.12.1 Probabilities
  - 1.12.2 Vague Knowledge
  - 1.12.3 Approximate Values
- 1.13 Defaults
  - 1.13.1 Prioritized Defaults
- 1.14 Preferences
- 1.15 Qualitative Modeling
  - 1.15.1 Qualitative Physics
- 1.16 Aggregates
- 1.17 Teleology
- 1.18 Computational Knowledge
- 1.19 Causality

2 Built-In Theories
- 2.1 Continuous Dimensions
  - 2.1.1 Units of Measure and Quantities
  - 2.1.2 Points and Intervals
- 2.2 Clock Time and Calendar Dates
- 2.3 Spatial Models
- 2.4 Mathematics
  - 2.4.1 Real Numbers
  - 2.4.2 Elementary Algebra
    - 2.4.2.1 Elementary Algebra Representation
    - 2.4.2.2 Elementary Algebra Qualitative Reasoning
    - 2.4.2.3 Elementary Algebra Symbolic Reasoning
    - 2.4.2.4 Elementary Algebra Numeric Reasoning

3 Reasoning Capabilities
- 3.1 Theorem Proving
- 3.2 Query Answering
- 3.3 Satisfiability Testing
  - 3.3.1 Constraint Satisfaction
    - 3.3.1.1 Optimization
- 3.4 Inheritance Reasoning
- 3.5 Classification
- 3.6 Reasoning about Knowledge and Belief
- 3.7 Reasoning by Elimination

3.8 Reasoning with Uncertain Knowledge
  3.8.1 Reasoning with Probabilities
  3.8.2 Reasoning with Approximate Values
3.9 Defeasible Reasoning
  3.9.1 Default Reasoning
    3.9.1.1 Prioritized Default Reasoning
    3.9.1.2 Default Inheritance
  3.9.2 Abduction
  3.9.3 Making Assumptions
3.10 Reasoning about Processes
  3.10.1 Prediction
  3.10.2 Comparative Projection
  3.10.3 Planning
  3.10.4 Scenario Explanation
  3.10.5 Verification
  3.10.6 Process Description Analysis
3.11 Reasoning with Aggregates
3.12 Reasoning with Teleological Knowledge
3.13 Compare and Contrast
3.14 Description Comparison
  3.14.1 Determining Closeness of Match
3.15 Determination of Applicability
3.16 Detection and Resolution of Discrepancies
3.17 Generation of Reasonable Values
3.18 Identification of Essential Information
3.19 Explanation Generation
3.20 Reasoning about Preferences
3.21 Qualitative Reasoning
3.22 Equality Reasoning
3.23 Case-Based Reasoning
  3.23.1 Analogical Reasoning
3.24 Reasoning with Diagrams
  3.24.1 Reading Curves in a Diagram
  3.24.2 Recognizing Objects
  3.24.3 Determining Correspondence to an Equation
  3.24.4 Plotting an Equation
  3.24.5 Extracting Physical Models
  3.24.6 Matching Curves
3.25 Causal Reasoning
3.26 Reasoning with Examples

2. Requirement Analysis for Query Answering

We used the KR&R categorization in identifying the requirements for query answering for each of the six domains. We worked with one full-length AP Exam in each of these domains. The official descriptions of these exams and the course descriptions are available from the website of the College Board (http://www.collegeboard.com/student/testing/ap/subjects.html). Each practice exam was drawn from the *Princeton Review* guide (http://www.princetonreview.com/), which is commonly available test preparation material. A scanned copy of each sample exam, detailed answers to all questions of each sample exam, and a copy of our analysis of each complete example exam are available online (http://www.ai.sri.com/halo/public/fois2010/). Even a cursory review of these exams will reveal that the breadth of the topics covered (from Cell structure to laws of supply and demand) is enormous. The total number of questions on each exam that was analyzed is shown in Table 1. For our discussion, we will cover one question per domain.

	Multiple Choice	Free Response
Physics	70	6
Chemistry	75	8
Biology	100	4
Environmental Science	100	4
Microeconomics	60	3
U.S. Govt & Politics	60	4

Table 1: Number of questions analyzed in each domain

Since our goal was to derive KR&R requirements, the analyst should understand enough about the domain as well as KR&R to do an adequate job. In an initial iteration of the analysis that was limited to Physics, Chemistry and Biology, we tried to divide the work between a domain expert and a KR&R expert. Since that division was not very effective, for the current analysis we identified analysts with KR&R expertise who also knew enough about each domain to do the analysis.

Our analysis factors out the natural language processing of a question and focuses on the KR&R requirements for answering the question. We assumed that each question would be represented using predicates and functions that capture the logical content of the question, but not different ways to phrase the question using natural language. A separate analysis analyzing the natural language issues in understanding a question was undertaken and is available elsewhere [5]. Answering some questions can also require the use of open-ended knowledge about the world. Analyzing and specifying such world knowledge was also kept outside the scope, as we wanted to focus on knowledge that is explicitly written down and specified in a textbook.

2.1. Physics

In most Physics questions, a key challenge is to take a problem description and identify a suitable model to solve that problem – for example, choosing whether to use Newton's laws or equations of motion. This challenge is captured by the reasoning requirement labeled as determination of applicability (KR&R category 3.15).

Every question requires representing and reasoning with structured objects – in some cases, it is just an object and its properties, and in other cases it also includes a class-subclass hierarchy. This requirement is captured by KR category Structured Objects (KR&R category 1.5). Similarly, the use of units and measures (KR&R category 2.1.1) is required very frequently.

Equations are also used all across the domain and in at least three different ways: to make qualitative inferences (KR&R category 2.4.2.2), in numerical calculations (KR&R category 2.4.2.4), and for symbolic manipulation (KR&R category 2.4.2.3). As a specific example, consider question number 58 from the sample AP Physics test (The correct answer choice is shown in italics):

> How much force is required to lift a 50-newton object with an acceleration of 10 m/s^2?
>
> (A) 10 N
> (B) 50 N
> *(C) 100 N*
> (D) 150 N
> (E) 200 N

This question involves numeric solution of equations (KR&R category 2.4.2.4) and knowledge of units and measures (KR&R category 2.1.1). We also have to make a default assumption that the lifting action is vertical. This question requires establishing a free body diagram that can be thought of as a domain-specific micro-theory, which is a method used quite frequently in answering Physics questions.

2.2. Chemistry

Just like Physics, in most Chemistry questions a key challenge is to take a problem description and identify a suitable model to solve that problem. In many Chemistry questions, such model selection can be reduced to classification reasoning of the sort seen in description logics (KR&R category 3.5). Most questions also need to represent and reason with structured objects (KR&R category 1.5) and logic program rules (KR&R category 1.7). Many questions require the use of units and measures (KR&R category 2.1.1). As a specific example, consider the following question from the sample AP test:

> A 100 ml sample of 0.10 molar NaOH solution was added to 100 ml of 0.10 molar H3C6H5O7. After equilibrium was established, which of the ions listed below was present in the greatest concentration:
>
> *(A) $H2C6H5O7^-$*
> (B) $HC6H5O72^-$
> (C) $C6H5O73^-$
> (D) OH^-
> (E) H^+

Representing this question requires the use of structured objects (KR&R category 1.5), units and measures (KR&R category 2.1.1), and a representation for chemical formulas that are specialized forms of structured objects. Answering this question requires two problem-solving steps. (1) Determine how much of each solvent will be left after the neutralization reaction is over. In this case, the two solvents will completely neutralize each other. (2) Determine the remaining ions from the equation representation, which is usually a logic programming style rule (KR&R category 1.7). One can determine from the equation that the highest remaining concentration will be H2C6H5O7-. To represent the problem-solving steps, we need a representation of the problem-solving knowledge referred to as *computational knowledge* in our categorization (KR&R category 1.18).

2.3. Biology

Process descriptions are used heavily in Biology; nearly half the questions refer to processes in one way or other (KR&R category 1.11). The representations needed are almost always discrete and nonnumeric (KR&R category 1.11.1). Questions frequently ask about steps in a process, outcomes of a process (including products), roles of various entities in the process, and so on. Locations of processes and movement of entities in processes are also frequently considered.

Most process-oriented questions in Biology are answerable by inspection of process structure and characteristics or by relatively straightforward inference about them. Wherever the inspection requires process-specific special-purpose procedures, we refer to this reasoning as Process Description Analysis (KR&R category 3.10.6). Process-specific representational elements such as inputs, outputs, preconditions, and effects are needed for many of these questions. Most Biology questions require some form of semantic matching to match up question formulation with the appropriate content or problem-solving model in the KB (KR&R category 3.14). As a specific example, consider question number 6 from the sample AP Biology test:

> Which of the following is NOT a characteristic of bacteria?
>
> (A) Circular double-stranded DNA
> *(B) Membrane-bound cellular organelles*
> (C) Plasma membrane consisting of lipids and proteins
> (D) Ribosomes that synthesize polypeptides

In this question, we are asked which of the given characteristics does not apply to Bacteria. This question can be answered using a structured object representation of Bacteria. Since this question queries for negated information, either such information should be directly represented in the KB, or the system should provide a way to infer this information from a representation.

2.4. Environmental Science

The domain of Environmental Science requires rich representations of relevant qualitative processes (KR&R category 1.15, 1.11 & 3.10). Finding the appropriate set is typically achieved by classifying (KR&R category 3.5) a specific situation to match generic descriptions of structured objects (KR&R category 1.5). The notion of classification should be taken from a broad perspective, including all kinds of properties of concepts and manipulations. This reasoning is often a prerequisite for doing the 'real' analysis in terms of (*i*) establishing causal dependencies between different quantities resulting from different processes (concerning a single system state), (*ii*) determining behavior paths by finding transition from one state to another, and (*iii*) comparative analysis (KR&R category 3.13) to compare two or more possible behaviors (e.g., worse/better, more/less impact). There is some need for concepts of law and legal reasoning to represent issues that intend to regulate the behavior of humans in relation to the physical world that surrounds them. As a concrete example, consider question number 32 from a sample exam on Environmental Science:

> Which of the following organisms is the first to be adversely affected by thermal pollution in a stream?
>
> (A) Trees along the bank
> *(B) Insect larvae in the water*
> (C) Large fish migrating up stream
> (D) Birds drinking the water
> (E) Bacteria in the water

In a coarse representation for answering this question, one would define a class hierarchy for organisms, life stages, and so on (KR&R category 1.5). Young organisms would be situated as indicator species that are vulnerable to different kinds of pollution, including thermal. For this question, "Insect larvae in the water" would be the only case with a young life stage and hence the only indicator species being more vulnerable for (thermal) pollution. However, such a representation is brittle because it strongly depends on the correct wording of the organisms in the class hierarchy, and it does not capture much explanation of the phenomenon and therefore would limit the capabilities of the reasoner to explain the answer. A better solution is to have a generic class hierarchy of organisms, objects and substances, means to describe the structural organization of a subset of these in a particular context, qualitative descriptions of elementary processes capturing the possible causes of change (e.g., growth of species, heat exchange), and exogenous factors (such as polluters) [6]. This knowledge must be qualified with assumptions or perspectives that govern the inclusion (or exclusion) of certain details. In the case of solving the example question, organisms would first be positioned with respect to the water (e.g., in, above, next to) as well as how they use the water. Instantiating the applicable processes to the situation delivers the causal dependencies between the quantities involved (e.g., indicating a causal influence from the environment temperature on the growth rate of the populations). From the species actually affected by the polluter, comparative analysis reveals which organism is most vulnerable for thermal pollution. Some default reasoning may be required – e.g. to assume alternative water resources for ``Birds drinking the water'', and thereby exclude certain answer options as less plausible.

2.5. Microeconomics

Many questions in the Microeconomics domain call for reasoning about mathematical functions, and in particular about qualitative properties of these functions. The domain also requires the ability to move back and forth between analytic and geometric descriptions of the functions and relations – that is, between properties of functions and properties of their depiction on a graph. This is required for interpreting questions (many include graphs), understanding text (e.g., shifting a curve to the right corresponds to a positive monotone transform of the function), and producing graphs for the free-form questions. As a specific example, consider the following question from the sample AP test:

What are the effects on supply and demand curves for Frisbees if a new procedure reduces the cost of making a Frisbee®?

	Demand	***Supply***
(A)	Shifts right	Shifts right
(B)	No change	Shifts left
(C)	*No change*	*Shifts right*
(D)	Shifts left	Shifts right
(E)	Shifts right	Shifts left

This question posits a potentially causal factor, and asks separately for effects on supply and demand, two fundamental concepts in microeconomic analysis. A new procedure that reduces the cost of making a product (here, "Frisbees") would make a firm willing to supply more of the product, at any given price. This is the definition of a supply curve shift to the right. The question does not mention any factor that would affect the value of Frisbees to consumers, or influence any other known ingredient of demand. Thus, by default we would assume that there is no shift at all in the demand curve.

Each answer choice is a conjunction of effects on both the supply and demand curves. The reasoner would separately analyze what happens to supply and demand, and select the answer choice that contains the correct conjunction of these changes. The knowledge to perform this reasoning would be represented using structured objects (KR&R category 1.5), and basic axioms of supply and demand represented as condition-action causal rules (KR&R category 1.8).

We could also express this reasoning directly in terms of supply and demand as mathematical functions, specifying the quantity supplied or demanded at various prices. Expressed as curves on a graph, a shift in supply, for example, can be represented as the relation between two functions, the supply curve before and after. A shift to the right means that quantity supplied *after* is greater than *before* at every price, as noted above.

2.6. U.S. Government & Politics

Building an automated system that can be successful on an AP test for this domain seems to involve satisfying several requirements. First, since this domain uses a broad vocabulary, the system developers need to closely match the domain knowledge they build into the system with the domain knowledge that is likely to be asked about on an AP test (KR&R category 3.14). Second, the system needs to be capable of using heuristic methods to assess the likelihood that a suggested answer to a question is the correct answer, since in many cases the system may not have a sufficient understanding of either the question or the suggested answers to determine the correct answer with certainty. When such assessments determine that one or more of the suggested answers to a question are highly unlikely to be correct, it is advisable for the system to guess the correct answer by selecting one of the remaining suggested answers.

The reasoning required for this domain is primarily theorem proving (KR&R category 3.1) and description comparison that determines closeness of match (KR&R category 3.14.1). As a specific example, consider the following question from the sample AP test:

Which of the following correctly states the relationship between the federal and state judiciaries?

(A) Federal courts are higher courts than state courts and may overturn state decisions on any grounds.
(B) The two are entirely autonomous, and neither ever hears cases that originate in the other.
(C) The two are generally autonomous, although federal courts may rule on the constitutionality of state court decisions.
(D) State courts are trial courts; federal courts are appeal courts.
(E) State courts try all cases except those that involve conflicts between two states, which are tried in federal courts.

As an illustration, we consider here the detailed analysis of the answer option (A). There is no hierarchical relationship between state courts and federal courts. If a KB explicitly states that no hierarchical relationship exists, then one could trivially prove that the first clause of (A) is false. Otherwise, one could only fail to prove that the first clause of (A) is true, thus requiring negation as failure. Proving that the second clause of (A) is either true or false requires knowing whether or not there can be appeals of state court decisions that are not on constitutional grounds. If one knows that there can be, then the second clause of (A) can be proved to be false. The KB would need either an example of an appeal of a state court decision that is not on constitutional grounds (thus, reasoning from examples) or need an axiom stating that such appeals exist.

3. Evaluation of the KR&R Categorization

In reporting on two forms of evaluation of the KR&R categorization, we first analyze its usage in the context of the six domain analyses that we have presented in this paper. Second, we report on the implementations of query answering that were informed by the KR&R categorization.

3.1. Usage of KR&R Categorization in Domain Analyses

We used the KR&R categorization in analyzing the six domains. We analyzed each question in an exam, and stated the requirements using a KR&R category from our categorization. At the end of their analysis, we counted how frequently each category was used, as shown in Table 2. Some categories, such as structured objects (KR&R category 1.5), rules (KR&R category 1.7), and explanation generation (KR&R category 3.19), are so pervasive that almost every question requires them. Therefore, they are not shown in the table. The number in each column denotes the number of questions in a full-length exam that required that KR&R category for answering it. We can draw several general conclusions from this raw data.

First, only a fraction of the KR&R categories from the full categorization were used. That observation helps suggest a specific list of features that a system for answering AP questions for these six domains will need to support. It also helps focus attention on specific kinds of KR&R methods that should be studied more precisely and further detailed. The breadth of the KR&R categories used also suggests that any system capable of answering questions in these six domains will need to cover several different kinds of representation and reasoning methods.

Second, the data also help us see differences across the domains. Most strikingly, it is apparent that both Biology and Environmental Science make heavy use of process knowledge. Physics and Chemistry rely heavily on reasoning with equations. Computational knowledge is needed quite significantly in Chemistry. Such insights are useful in understanding the requirements for these domains and would not have been possible without the use of the KR&R categorization introduced in this paper.

Cat No	KR&R Category	P	C	B	E	G	M
1.10	Diagrams	30	7	14			8
1.11	Processes	3	4	44	72	1	
1.12.2	Vague knowledge						2
1.15	Qualitative modeling	3	20	6	72		
1.18	Computational knowledge		19	8			
2,1	Continuous dimension						6
2.3	Spatial relations and directions	4	1				
2.4	Mathematics						15
2.4.2.1	Simultaneous equations	1	6				
2.4.2.2	Qualitative reasoning with equations	18	5	1			6
2.4.2.3	Symbolic reasoning with equations	19	18	1			
2.4.2.4	Numerical solution of equations	24	4	2			
3.1	Theorem proving					9	
3.2	Query answering					17	
3.7	Reasoning by elimination	8	5	6			
3.9.2	Abduction			7			
3.9.3	Making assumptions	10	2				
3.10.3	Planning	2					
3.10.6	Process description analysis					1	
3.13	Compare and contrast			9	4	3	1
3.14	Description comparison					26	
3.21	Qualitative reasoning	2	19		30		15
3.25	Causal reasoning				30		

Table 2: Usage of KR&R Categorization. (P – Physics, C – Chemistry, B – Biology, E – Environmental Science, M – Microeconomics, G – U.S. Government & Politics)

Third, and most important, is the question of how uniformly and effectively the analysts were able to use this categorization? It is apparent that the usage of the categorization in the domains of Microeconomics, U.S. Government & Politics, and Environmental Science is sparser than in the domains of Physics, Chemistry, and Biology. We attribute this to the analysis approach in those domains. For example, it is quite obvious that some questions in each domain will require query answering and theorem proving, but those requirements were used only by the analyst in U.S.

Government & Politics. Another source for this difference could be that sometimes there is more than one way to answer a question, depending on what one assumes about what knowledge is represented in the KB versus what knowledge is derived. This limitation suggests a direction for further work to refine the methodology so that analysts can use these categories uniformly and consistently. Finally, the categories are overlapping. For example, for environmental science, wherever there was need for process representation (KR&R category 1.11), we needed to also use qualitative modeling (KR&R category 1.15), and wherever we needed causal reasoning (KR&R category 3.25), we also needed qualitative reasoning (KR&R category 3.21).

3.2. Implementations Informed by the KR&R Categorization

Informed by the results of the domain analysis, we have undertaken two different implementations of query answering. The first implementation is a system called AURA that is a mature prototype and has undergone significant testing and evaluation for the three science domains of Physics, Chemistry, and Biology [5, 7]. The second implementation is only preliminary, covering a small number of questions from each of the six domains, and is based on a representation language called SILK [8].

The current scope of AURA is to enable domain experts to construct KBs from 50 pages of a science textbook for each of Physics, Chemistry, and Biology in a way that another user can pose questions similar to those in an AP exam and get answers and explanations. In the near future, we will use AURA to represent a full textbook in one of the domains.

The overall concept of operation for AURA is as follows: a *knowledge formulation engineer* (KFE) with at least a graduate degree in the discipline of interest undergoes 20 hours of training to enter knowledge into AURA. A different person, called a *question formulation engineer* (QFE), with a high-school-level education undergoes 4 hours of training and asks questions of the system. Knowledge entry is inherently a skill-intensive task and therefore requires more advanced training in the subject as well as in using the system. A QFE is a potential user of the system, and the training requirement is low. KFEs do knowledge entry through a graphical user interface, and QFEs pose questions by converting them from original English into controlled English.

The current AURA system supports the KR&R categories of structured objects (KR&R category 1.5), rules (KR&R category 1.7), processes (KR&R category 1.11), equations (KR&R categories 2.4.2.1 and 2.4.2.4), process description analysis (3.10.1), query answering (KR&R category 3.2), compare and contrast (KR&R category 3.14), description comparison (KR&R category 3.14), and spatial relations and directions (KR&R category 2.3). Since the KR&R categories implemented in AURA are only a subset of all the required categories listed in Table 1, we do not expect the KBs authored by KFEs using AURA to be able to answer all the questions on a full-length AP exam.

In a recent evaluation, AURA was used by domain experts at SRI to construct KBs in the three domains from a 50-page syllabus, and these KBs were tested on a suite of questions known to the development team ahead of time. These KBs were able to correctly answer 79% of the questions in Physics, 73% of the questions in Chemistry, and 71% of the questions in Biology. The AURA system was also independently evaluated by having newly trained users construct KBs that were tested on novel questions. AURA was able to correctly answer 49% of the questions in

Biology, 42% in Physics, and 22% in Chemistry. Since the questions are posed through controlled English, QFEs usually introduce some simplifications, and therefore these results should not be viewed as an indication of the system's ability to answer questions posed in original English. These results, nonetheless, do demonstrate that the requirements analysis done using our described methodology did enable the construction of a system with a high degree of performance.

We recently started a small-scale project to prototype query answering using SILK with the goal to distribute some examples using a traditional logic programming framework. The implemented SILK examples are available online (see http://www.ai.sri.com/halo/public/fois2010/). These examples provide a concrete realization of the analysis work. For example, the SILK implementation of a Physics question shows how the logic programming rules can be used in combination with different approaches for stating defaults. While the domain analysis may suggest broad KR&R requirements, when it comes to actually producing an implementation; many much more specific decisions need to be made.

4. Related Work

Several researchers have investigated the problem of representing textbook knowledge and answering questions about that knowledge, for example, [9] [10] and [11]. No one has previously attempted to build a system that would function across the range of domains considered here. The six domains are different in many ways ranging from purely descriptive to highly mathematical. The query answering tasks range from lookup, to conventional rule-based or taxonomic reasoning, to qualitative reasoning and problem solving. In spite of these divergent requirements, our challenge has been to synthesize KR&R features that can be incorporated into a functional system. Such a task has never before been undertaken.

Work has been done on using competency questions to specify the requirements of a KB [12]. The problem we consider here is very different because of the sheer scope and diversity of the questions, and the need to assess the requirements much before reducing the task to a set of axioms.

The work most closely related to our KR&R Categorization is on information metrology, reasoning, and representation languages (IMRRL) done at NIST [13]. The NIST approach is similar to our KR&R categorization in that it studies the representation and the reasoning aspects separately. The NIST approach, however, is closely tied to very specific languages and logics – for example, Common Logic, description logic, RDF/S (Resource Description Framework Schema). The NIST approach also lacks the level of breadth and the coverage considered in our KR&R categorization, and it was done outside the context of a specific application need. We do believe, however, that there is considerable synergy between our categorization and IMRRL, and it will be promising to unify the two in our future work.

5. Summary and Conclusions

We considered the problem of specifying requirements for constructing a KB for answering questions in six diverse domains: Physics, Chemistry, Biology, Microeconomics, Environmental Science, and U.S. Government & Politics. The work is part of a larger effort to build a system to answer questions on a wide variety of topics and explain the answers. No established methodology helps a designer determine the features needed in such a system. The problem has been especially challenging because for answering some questions in these domains, the required methods are unresolved and topics of research. For requirements analysis, it is not realistic to expect a detailed design and implementation for each question. Therefore, we need a methodology that is coarse, yet serves as an informative analysis tool. Our analysis using the KR&R categorization presented here is a novel contribution because of its effectiveness in giving some quantitative measure of the KR&R needs across multiple domains, and by providing useful input in the design and implementation of AURA. The approach has several weaknesses, of course, as its usage by different analysts is not always consistent, the category definitions are sometimes overlapping, and more detailed guidelines and definitions need to be developed. The overall task, however, is too large for one group to undertake, and we hope to engage others in the community in further developing the categorization and the analysis methodology.

6. Acknowledgments

This work was funded by Vulcan Inc. under its Halo Advanced Research Program. We thank Bruce Porter and Ken Barker for conceptualizing the earlier drafts of the domain analysis framework. We thank Shirin Sohrabi, Hojjat Ghaderi, and David Martin for their contributions to the SILK implementations and domain analysis. We thank Benjamin Grosof for his inputs to the drafts of this work.

References

[1] Feigenbaum, E., Some Challenges and Grand Challenges for Computational Intelligence. *Journal of the Association of Computational Machinery,* 2003. 50(1): p. 32-40.

[2] Reddy, R., Three Open Problems in AI. *Journal of the Association of Computational Machinery,* 2003. 50(1).

[3] Brachman, R.J. and H.J. Levesque, *Knowledge Representation and Reasoning.* 2003, San Francisco: Morgan Kaufmann.

[4] Russell, S. and P. Norvig, *Artificial Intelligence: A Modern Approach.* 2003: Prentice Hall.

[5] Clark, P., et al. Capturing and Answering Questions Posed to a Knowledge-Based System. *International Conference on Knowledge Capture Systems (KCAP).* 2007. Whistler, Canada.

[6] Bredeweg, B. and P. Salles, eds. *Mediating Conceptual Knowledge Using Qualitative Reasoning. Handbook of Ecological Modeling and Informatics,* ed. S.V. Jorgensen, T.-S. Chon, and F.A. Recknagel. 2009, Wit Press: Southampton, UK. 351-398.

[7] Chaudhri, V.K., et al., Enabling Experts to Build Knowledge Bases from Science Textbooks, *International Conference on Knowledge Capture Systems (KCAP).* 2007: Whistler, Canada.

[8] Wan, H., et al. Logic Programming with Defaults and Argumentation Theories. *25th International Conference on Logic Programming.* 2009. Pasadena, CA.

[9] Bobrow, D.G. A Question-Answering System for High School Algebra and Word Problems. *Proceedings of the Fall Joint Computer Conference.* 1964. San Francisco, CA.

[10] Klenk, M. and K. Forbus, Analogical Model Formulation for Transfer Learning in AP Physics. *Artificial Intelligence,* 2009. 173(18): p. 1615-1638.

[11] Mukherjee, A. and U. Garain, A Review of Methods for Automatic Understanding of Natural Language Mathematical Problems. . *Artificial Intelligence Review,* 2008. 29: p. 93-122.

[12] Gruninger, M. and M.S. Fox, The Role of Competency Questions in Enterprise Engineering, *Proceedings of the IFIP WG 5.7 Workshop on Benchmarking – Theory and Practice. 1994.*

[13] Bock, C., et al., *Evaluating Reasoning Systems: Information Metrology, Reasoning, and Representation Languages.* 2006, National Institute of Standards and Technology.

Formal Ontology in Information Systems
A. Galton and R. Mizoguchi (Eds.)
IOS Press, 2010

doi:10.3233/978-1-60750-535-8-172

The Use of Ontology in Dental Restorative Treatment Decision Support System

Seon Gyu PARK[a], Sungin LEE[b], Myeng-Ki KIM[a] and Hong-Gee KIM[b, 1]
[a] *College of Dentistry, Seoul National University, South Korea*
[b] *Biomedical Knowledge Engineering Lab, Seoul National University, South Korea*

Abstract. Finding appropriate caries treatments is of paramount importance in dental decision making. That is, finding restorative treatment alternatives predicated on the dental disease and findings are advantageous and gainful in dental restorative decision making. The most immediate problem in clinical decision support systems in dentistry is to capture a doctor's clinical knowledge of treatments. This study is to specify the inter-relations among disease, anatomy, and treatment for restorative treatment decision support, and to conceptualize restorative treatment. As an explanatory example, we expound the developmental process of our ontology, and the formal approach used, for caries treatment.

Keywords. Biomedical Ontology, Clinical Decision Support, Dental Restorative Treatment, Dental Caries, Tooth Anatomy.

Introduction

An important ingredient in dental decision making process is to find an appropriate caries treatment. A treatment involves such considerations as caries location, caries depth, caries activity, and patient preferences (patient preferences are considered in treatment planning, and they are not differs from medical treatment planning [1]). Hence, it is beneficial and cost-effective for dental restorative decision making [2] to first find treatment alternatives, based on the disease of and findings for a patient, from which to narrow down to the best treatment satisfying patient preferences.

There have been numerous studies to employ clinical knowledge in Clinical Decision Support System (CDSS), which helps clinicians with medical decision making. And it has become quite common [3, 4] to use ontology to capture clinical knowledge and use it in the decision support system to solve medical problems. Reuse and sharing of the knowledge base ensures responsiveness to changes, and in order to achieve them, the ontology should be formal. A myriad of ontologies have been developed for particular applications without proper formalisms by individual researchers, rendering them non-reusable and unsharable, and spurring the needs of formal representation that give rise to upper, reference, and relation ontologies. Exemplary upper ontologies [5] include Basic Formal Ontology (BFO), the Descriptive Ontology for Linguistic and Cognitive Engineering (DOLCE), and the Suggested Upper Merged Ontology (SUMO). A reference ontology is an independent domain ontology catering to specific goals, and the Foundational Model of Anatomy (FMA) is

[1] Corresponding Author: Biomedical Knowledge Engineering Lab. #102 Bio Material Research bldg., College of Dentistry, Seoul National University, South Korea. E-mail: hgkim@snu.ac.kr

an example. The relations present in biomedical terminologies and ontologies were not clearly understood, let alone defined, until the Open Biomedical Ontology Relation Ontology (RO), which identifies ten logically defined relations: **is_a**, **part_of**, **located_in**, **contained_in**, **adjacent_to**, **transformation_of**, **derives_from**, **preceded_by**, **has_participant**, **has_agent**. These relations are tools required for the development and integration of biomedical ontologies. The Web Ontology Language (OWL) does not sufficiently represent RO's part-whole semantics: for example, reflexivity and anti-symmetricity of a property cannot be represented. One of the goals of OWL 2, a recommendation status recently approved by W3C, is to overcome such expressivity limitations.[2]

We developed a restorative treatment planning decision support system in which doctors' knowledge was captured using ontology in order to list up various treatment plans. The ontology used in our system is composed of the FMA reference ontology and a couple of medical terminologies, connected by RO on top of the BFO upper ontology base. These ontologies can help the system to present available restorative treatment options generated by medical reasoning processes. With the aid of the medically suitable restorative treatment options, the system leads doctors and patients to further narrow the options down to definitive restorative treatment plans based upon patient preferences and demographics.

In this paper, we will focus on the formal developmental process of the onotology for restorative treatment planning. The first task performed by the system is to find restorative treatment options based on the patient disease and oral anatomical locations. To generate the options, dental diseases/findings, oral anatomy, and dental restorative treatments are described as concepts in OWL2. The characteristics and semantic relationship of each concept is formally represented.

1. Ontological Foundations of the Dental Restoration Domain

There are 4 mutually disjoint categories, following closely to the distinctions made in BFO [6] : objects and processes are either continuants or occurrents predicated on time, or classes or individuals based on abstractness and concreteness. The class *Tooth* is a universal in the biomedical domain; an individual of this class is the particular tooth of a particular patient at a particular time and place. If an object exists regardless of time, it's a continuant; otherwise, an occurrent, such as a process, an activity, and an event. Examples of dental continuants are entities such as tooth and its surrounding organs. There are two families of continuants: dependent and independent. Qualities, roles, functions that require other entities for existence are dependent, and those that do not require other entities are independent. Dependent continuants require independent continuants as their bearers. Occurrents always are dependent on one or more independent continuants which are their participants such as agents, patients, and media.

Anatomic parts are obviously independent continuants, since their meanings are invariable, and their existence is acknowledged regardless of other entities. Disease is a different matter: it can be viewed as a process (i.e. occurrent) in which its state changes in time, or as a continuant that represents its medical conditions such as abnormal. This study takes the latter view of disease, that disease is a dependent continuant [22]. Treatments are entities that clarify themselves in consecutive stages or temporal parts,

[2] http://www.w3.org/TR/owl2-overview/

hence, occurrents. Table 1 shows these distinctions and their examples related to dentistry.

Table 1. Categories of the Dental Restoration related Concepts

	Occurrents	Dependent Continuants	Independent Continuants
Class	Amalgam Filling Composite Resin Filling Gold Inlay Restoration	Dentin Caries Enamel Caries Pulpitis	Tooth
Individual	Mr. Park's Amalgam Filling	Mr. Park's Pulpitis	Mr. Park's Tooth

We limit our discussion to classes related to treatment, since the purpose of this study is to generate treatment plans based on patient diseases and oral anatomical locations, to build an ontology to be used in the decision support system, and not to support dental record documentation for individual patients.

2. Construction of a unified disease-treatment-anatomy correlation

Instead of reinventing the wheel, we opted to use relevant ontologies and terminology systems, in our pursuit of building a comprehensive ontology that enables reuse and sharability and is suitable for discovering restorative treatment options. There are three main considerations of importance in designing an ontology for caries treatment plan generation: tooth anatomy including spatial relationship, disease and findings classification, and restorative treatment options. We imported existing reference ontologies and terminologies, as shown in Figure 1, to represent these considerations, and they work as the infrastructure for restorative treatment decision support system. It is our first attempt at developing a base ontology that includes concepts for dental diseases, restorative treatment, and tooth anatomy.

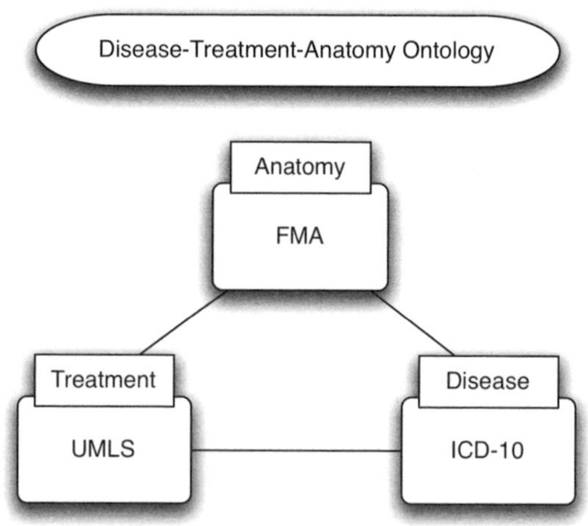

Figure 1. Disease, Treatment, and Anatomy Ontology Correlation.

FMA is a general anatomy-related biomedical ontology including comprehensive anatomical concepts [7]. Rigorous formal rules are applied to develop the taxonomical structure and partonomy among the terms in FMA, facilitating easy integration and realignment with other ontologies. At present, FMA is a reference ontology taken as the most suitable template to align existing ontologies in the medical domain. We used the tooth anatomy in FMA: 1) out of over eighty thousand concept classes, we imported only tooth-related concepts; 2) FMA uses frame-based formalism, and if we convert it to description logic based formalism, unintended conclusions or missing concepts may occur [8], hence, we didn't import slots (properties) in our study. There are several choices we have regarding disease classification: Medical Subject Headings (MeSH), NCI Thesaurus, International Classification of Disease (ICD-10). We adopted ICD-10 as the reference ontology of dental diseases, mainly because it's a well-known and documented classification system from which Korean Standard Classification for Diseases (KCD) has originated. There is to our best knowledge no comprehensive ontology related to treatment alternatives in general, and less chance to find a relatively complete classification system or ontology for restorative treatment alternatives. We, therefore, manually created treatment alternatives using concepts of Unified Medical Language System (UMLS) metathesaurus, which are used to generate clinical documents. The three perspectives – tooth anatomy, disease, and treatment – are semantically linked by relationships in OBO Relation Ontology (RO) [9]. Our final ontology is built by importing class concepts from the three perspectives interlinked by RO properties.

3. Concept Representation

Choosing a proper representation formalism is a very critical task in developing ontology. Many formalisms have been developed such as KIF, Ontolingua, Semantic Net, and Frames. In the Web arena, the Web-based Ontology Language (OWL) has emerged as a standard to semantically describe web resources. Also, it has been used to capture and represent clinical knowledge about diseases, findings, anatomy, and treatments in biomedical domain. OWL employs description logics, and is one of the most popular ontologies used in practice. Description logics has seen a significant amount of work for reasoning using it, and there are good editing tools such as Protégé[3] available. And since it affords consistency checking and inference computation, it's possible to consistently represent concepts. Hence, this study has chosen OWL2 as its representation formalism. Fig. 2 shows a part of our developed ontology.

OWL 2-based Manchester DL syntax[4] is used to show the caries treatment part of the restorative treatment ontology. Class is denoted in upper case italic, property in lower case bold. For example, all individuals included in the *Tooth* class are also included in the individuals of the class *Organ_with_organ_cavity*. We can represent this in OWL2 Manchester syntax as follows:

Class: *Tooth*
  SubclassOf: *Organ_with_organ_cavity*

[3] http://protege.stanford.edu
[4] http://www.w3.org/TR/owl2-manchester-syntax/

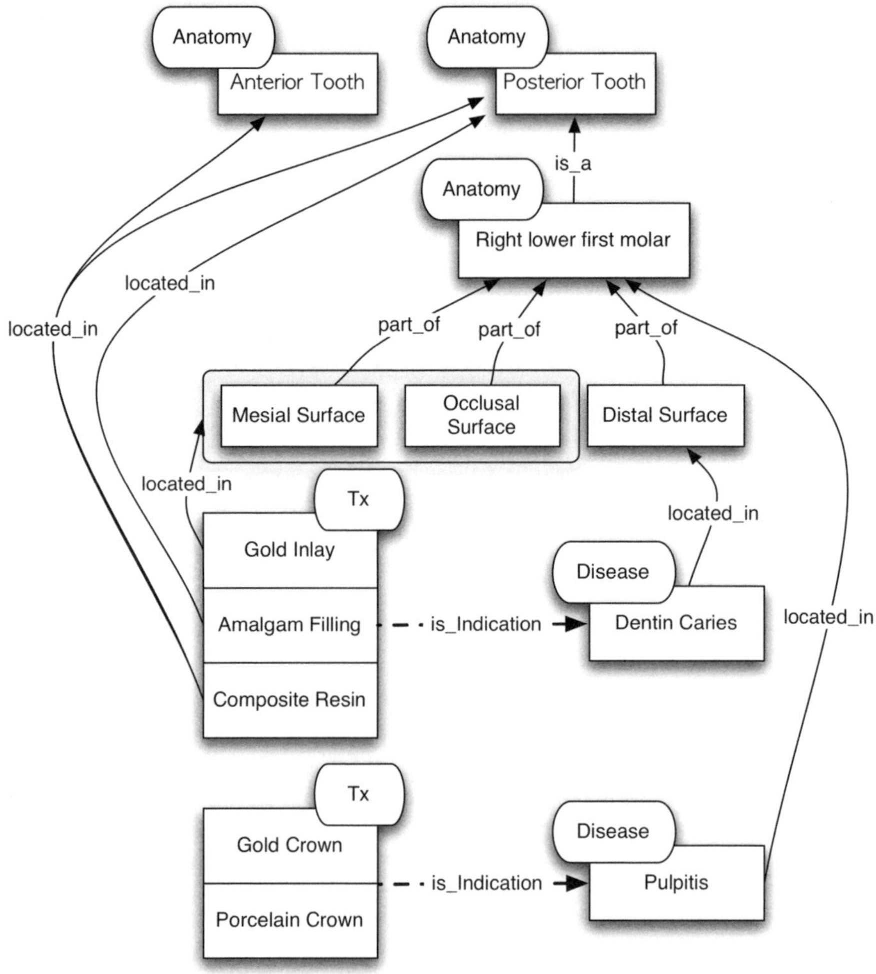

Figure 2. Example of our ontology.

This subsumption hierarchy is commonly referred to as **is_a** relation. Normally a human has 28 teeth, with additional four wisdom teeth. A tooth is either an anterior or posterior tooth. No tooth can be both anterior and posterior. This clinical knowledge can be expressed as:

Class: *Tooth*
  EquivalentTo: *Anterior_Tooth* or *Posterior_Tooth*

DisjointClasses: *Anterior_Tooth*, *Posterior_Tooth*

An anterior tooth is the one we expose when we smile, and anterior teeth usually include incisor and canine teeth. Posterior teeth are the ones involved chewing, and include premolar and molar teeth, and if wisdom teeth are present, they are also included. The way that each individual tooth, such as right upper first molar, falls into one of the two classes is explained in our previous study [10]. Each tooth has different functions, necessitating different treatments for them. We used the OBO RO's spatial relation **part_of** to represent part-whole relationships present in the dentin, one of the major tooth components.

ObjectProperty: **part_of**
  Characteristics: Transitive, Reflexive, AntiSymmetric
  SubPropertyOf: **located_in**

Class: *Dentin*
  SubclassOf: **part_of** some *Tooth*

Reasoning based on subsumption hierarchy is very intuitive and straightforward [11]. However, reasoning based on partonomy over formal ontologies is a challenging issue and has seen many studies devoted to it [12, 13]. One of the solutions uses artificial classes that separate the whole class from its proper part classes, effectively blocking unnecessary propagation of partonomic hierarchy to subsumption hierarchy [14]. This method is controversial because of the unclear meaning of the extra article class and additional extensive modifications to the original hierarchy. Therefore, this study has adopted the special treatment suggested by Schulz *et al* [15], where **located_in** is defined broadly enough to use it as a vehicle for partonomy propagation. For example, the located_in property and its related concepts can be represented as follows:

ObjectProperty: **located_in**
  Characteristics: Transitive, Reflexive

Class: *Dental_Caries*
  EquivalentTo: *Infectious_Disease* and **located_in** some *Tooth*

Class: *Dentin_Caries*
  EquivalentTo: *Infectious_Disease* and **located_in** some *Dentin*

The above says that dentin caries is an infectious disease located at a dentin as a whole or at any part of a dentin, because **part_of**, a sub-property of the **located_in** property, inherits the transitive and reflexive characteristics of **located_in**. In addition, since dentin is part of the tooth, it can be inferred that dentin caries is dental caries. The subsumption relationship between the **located_in** and **part_of** properties with the transitivity of these properties supports meaningful inference results.

A property in RO that can link treatment alternatives (occurrents) and diseases (dependent continuants) is **has_participant**. It can be used to link diseases and findings with a certain treatment process. However, in order to make the name more suitable to our domain, we designed a new application-specific property, **is_Indication**, based on **has_participant.**

The clinical knowledge that *Amalgam_Filling*, a restorative treatment, is a treatment candidate for dentin caries is represented as follows:

ObjectProperty: **is_Indication**
SubPropertyOf: **has_participant**
Domain: *Treatment*
Range: *Disease*

Class: *Amalgam_Filling*
SubClassOf: *Direct_Intracoronal_Restoration*
is_Indication some *Dentin_Caries,*
located_in some *Posterior_Tooth*
located_in some (not (*Esthetic_zone_of_oral_cavity*))

The metal color of amalgam dictates that amalgam is not to be used in esthetic zones and, hence, the location of amalgam should be limited to the posterior teeth. However, the posterior teeth do not always stand on the non-esthetic region of the oral cavity because of tooth migration to a missing site or congenital malposition. Thus, we add an axiom which constrains the positional candidates of non-esthetic dental materials, using the class Esthetic_zone_of_oral_cavity. It is the region containing all the biologic objects, exposed when one smiles, between the upper and lower lips. The **located_in** above not only represents a spatial relationship between biologic objects, but also a rather broad connection between occurrents and biologic objects, effectively contributing to the development of a concise ontology [15].

On the contrary, composite resin filling has a tooth color and can be used in both the anterior posterior teeth as shown below.

Class: *Composite_Resin_Filling*
SubClassOf: *Direct_Intracoronal_Restoration*
is_Indication some *Dentin_Caries,*
located_in some *Anterior_Tooth,*
located_in some *Posterior_Tooth*

We hope that restorative treatments based on location and disease help us to get appropriate answers we want.

Amalgam filling and composite resin filling are direct restorations; meaning that the fillings can be placed on the same day of the patient visit. If the dentist can 'manage' the depth and location of the caries, he can perform its removal and rehabilitation at the same time; otherwise, he takes an impression and fabricates a restoration such as inlays and crowns. Especially, if the caries is located between two teeth, saliva control and appropriate contact establishment become a challenge – all the more reasons for indirect restoration; a direct restoration in this case may result in bad prognosis.

We defined the dental surface and indirect restoration to include this kind of medical and mechanical knowledge in our ontology. The class *Surface_of_Tooth* is the anatomical concept to describe and refer to both the position of dental treatments and dental diseases. This class includes five different subclasses: buccal surface (the surface of a tooth adjacent to the cheeks), lingual surface (the surface of a tooth adjacent to the tongue), occlusal surface (the chewing surface of a tooth), mesial surface (the surface of a tooth adjacent to the front neighboring tooth), and distal surface (the surface of a tooth adjacent to the back neighboring tooth). *Surface_of_Tooth* captures conceptually the exposed surface of the tooth. However, we utilize this class as a good proxy for assessing where dental treatments or dental diseases are located.

Class: *Surface_of_Tooth*
EquivalentTo:*Buccal_Surface_of_Tooth* or
Occlusal_Surface_of_Tooth or
Lingual_Surface_of_Tooth or
Mesial_Surface_of_Tooth or
Distal_Surface_of_Tooth

Class: *Proximal_Surface_of_Tooth*
EquivalentTo: *Mesial_Surface_of_Tooth* or *Distal_Surface_of_Tooth*

Class: *Gold_Inlay_Restoration*
SubClassOf: **is_Indication** some *Dentin_Caries*
located_in some *Posterior_Tooth,*
located_in some *Proximal_Surface_of_Tooth*

Gold inlay, an indirect restoration, can only be located in the posterior tooth area because of its color. Also, if there is caries on the proximal surface of a posterior tooth, an indirect restoration, rather than such a direct restoration as amalgam filling, is preferred. Dental restorations can be further classified by restoration building process, and they differ in the applicable locations. In order to represent direct restoration more clearly, we defined another superclass, *Direct_Intracoronal_Restoration,* which includes *Amalgam_Filling* and *Composite_Resin_Filling* as its subclasses.

Class: *Direct_Intracoronal_Restoration*
SubClassOf:
located_in some (*Surface_of_Tooth* and (not *Proximal_Surface_of_Tooth* that **part_of** some *Posterior_Tooth))*

Proximal surface is not to be used with direct restoration and is specified as such in the ontology. This works as a constraint that limits the discovery of potential treatment alternatives for direct restoration.

Description Logics (DL) queries are used to retrieve restorative treatment alternatives suitable for patient context. For example, a DL query for a patient with dentin caries in right lower first molar is formulated as follows:

is_Indication some *Dentin_Caries* and **located_in** some
Right_Lower_First_Molar

The subclasses satisfying the above query are such classes as *Amalgam_Filling, Composite_Resin_Filling,* and *Gold_Inlay_Restoration.* If we use right upper canine, instead of right lower first molar, *Amalgam_Filling* and *Gold_Inlay_Restoration* will be excluded from the result. And if the query uses a more specific location identification such as 'its surface', instead of "right lower first molar", for the **located_in** property, a more proper set of restorative treatment options will be produced.

4. Discussion and Conclusion

This study shows the use of ontology in restorative treatment planning decision support, based on disease and caries location. The ontology explicitly specifies clinical knowledge by interlinking necessary medical concepts. The adopted formalism helped exclude unnecessary classes and properties from the ontology. Also, we reused existing ontologies, increasing the potential for sharability. Currently a component of our CDSS framework, the ontology can be used in other dental CDSSs [16] or dental Electronic Medical Record (EMR) systems. These systems are designed to provide help to the dentist in improving oral health status and to potentially reduce errors in practice [17].

A treatment decision is the result of bilateral communication between the doctor and the patient, and our goal is not to provide a definitive answer to treatment planning for dentists. The ontology is a CDSS component that helps produce context-sensitive lists of treatment plans. In order to generate such a list, we need at least a systematic, sophisticated, and formal way to represent patient contexts, such as disease and caries location. From a given list of treatment plans, the doctor chooses the most fitting treatment plan considering the patient preferences and his/her medical knowledge. Our ontology is designed to be simple and concise, while providing basis for simple medical reasoning over disease and location, and for generating a manageable number of potential restorative treatment plans for the doctor to employ in the task of decision making.

The use of ontology makes it possible to explicitly represent opaque medical knowledge, enabling presentation of clear and understandable information both to the dentist and the patient. Our ontology explicitly captures the process in which the dentist uses his implicit knowledge to generate a treatment plan, and as such, is a basis on which reuse and sharability of dental knowledge can be built upon. In terms of economical gains, our ontological approach for treatment planning can significantly save the dentist from searching on his own various treatment options from other resources [4].

The amount of medical knowledge needing to be covered in an application such as this is extensive and difficult to tease out and formalize, and as such has been a great challenge [18]. Also, alignment and mapping among terminology systems and ontologies is another difficult research issue [19, 20], along with the use of formal representation [21] to develop ontologies for common semantics in the medical domain.

Acknowledgements

This study was partly supported by a grant of the Korea Health 21 R&D Project, Ministry of Health & Welfare, Republic of Korea. (A050909)

References

[1] B. R. Johnson, A. Schwartz, J. Goldberg, A. Koerber, A chairside aid for shared decision making in dentistry: a randomized controlled trial. *Journal of dental education* **70** (2006), 133-141.

[2] B. A. White, G. Maupome, Clinical decision-making for dental caries management. *Journal of dental education* **65** (2001), 1121-1125.

[3] T. J. Bright, E. Y. Furuya, G. J. Kuperman, S. Bakken, Creating an ontology for an antibiotic prescribing decision support system. *AMIA Annu Symp Proc* (2008) 888.

[4] K. Farion, W. Michalowski, S. Wilk, D. O'Sullivan, S. Rubin, D. Weiss, Clinical decision support system for point of care use--ontology-driven design and software implementation. *Methods of information in medicine* **48** (2009), 381-390.

[5] O. Bodenreider, R. Stevens, Bio-ontologies: current trends and future directions. *Briefings in bioinformatics* **7** (2006), 256-274.

[6] P. Grenon, B. Smith, L. Goldberg, Biodynamic ontology: applying BFO in the biomedical domain. *Stud Health Technol Inform* **102** (2004), 20-38.

[7] C. Rosse, J. L. Mejino, A reference ontology for biomedical informatics: the Foundational Model of Anatomy. *Journal of biomedical informatics* **36** (2003), 478-500.

[8] C. Golbreich, S. Zhang, O. Bodenreider, The foundational model of anatomy in OWL: Experience and perspectives. *Web Semant* **4** (2006), 181-195.

[9] B. Smith, W. Ceusters, B. Klagges, J. Kohler, A. Kumar, J. Lomax, C. Mungall, F. Neuhaus, A. L. Rector, C. Rosse, Relations in biomedical ontologies. *Genome biology* **6** (2005), R46.

[10] S. G. Park, H. Kim, M. Kim, Tooth Positional Ontology Represented in OWL. In: Medinfo 2007: Proceedings of the 12th World COngress on Health (Medical) Informatics; Building Sustainable Health Systems (2007) 2288-2289.

[11] P. F. PatelSchneider, What's inheritance got to do with knowledge representation. portal.acm.org (1991).

[12] S. Schulz, U. Hahn, Part-whole representation and reasoning in formal biomedical ontologies. *Artificial Intelligence In Medicine* **34** (2005), 179-200.

[13] S. Schulz, A. Kumar, T. Bittner, Biomedical ontologies: What part-of is and isn't. *Journal of biomedical informatics* **39** (2006), 350-361.

[14] S. Schulz, M. Romacker, U. Hahn, Part-whole reasoning in medical ontologies revisited - Introducing SEP triplets into classification-based description logics. *Journal Of The American Medical Informatics Association* (1998), 830-834.

[15] S. Schulz, K. Marko, U. Hahn, Spatial location and its relevance for terminological inferences in bio-ontologies. *BMC Bioinformatics* **8** (2007), 134.

[16] S. G. Park, H. Kim, Dental decision making on missing tooth represented in an ontology and rules. *Lecture Notes in Computer Science* **4185** (2006), 322-328.

[17] E. A. Mendonça, Clinical decision support systems: perspectives in dentistry. *Journal of dental education* **68** (2004), 589-597.

[18] A. Yu, Methods in biomedical ontology. *Journal of biomedical informatics* **39** (2006), 252-266.

[19] S. Zhang, O. Bodenreider. Experience in aligning anatomical ontologies. *Int J Semant Web Inf* **3** (2007), 1-26.

[20] S. Schulz, M. Boeker, H. Stenzhorn, J. Niggemann, Granularity issues in the alignment of upper ontologies. *Methods of information in medicine* **48** (2009), 184-189.

[21] N. Guarino. Formal ontology, conceptual analysis and knowledge representation. *International Journal of Human Computer Studies* **43** (1995), 625-640.

[22] W. Ceusters, B. Smith. Referent tracking for treatment optimization in schizophrenic patients: A case study in applying philosophical ontology to diagnostic algorithms. *Journal of Web Semantics* **4** (2006), 229-236

Ontology Building

Formal Ontology in Information Systems
A. Galton and R. Mizoguchi (Eds.)
IOS Press, 2010

doi:10.3233/978-1-60750-535-8-185

A core ontology of instruments used for neurological, behavioral and cognitive assessments

Bénédicte BATRANCOURT[a], Michel DOJAT[b], Bernard GIBAUD[c], Gilles KASSEL[d, 1]

[a] *CRICM, UMR_S975, INSERM/CNRS, Pierre et Marie Curie Univ., Paris, France*
[b] *GIN, U 836, INSERM, Joseph Fourier University, Grenoble, France*
[c] *Visages, U 746, INSERM/INRIA/CNRS, University of Rennes 1, Rennes, France*
[d] *MIS, EA 4290, Jules Verne University of Picardie, Amiens, France*

Abstract. Neurosciences are progressively moving into a mass computational intensive era with the fusion of numerous large heterogeneous data sets from cellular to system level. To process and share this mass of information in a consistent and computational amenable form, computerized techniques – among them, ontologies - are currently designed to store, analyze and access this information. Recently, we proposed a multi-layered and multi-components ontology to deal with MR images and regions-of-interest that can be represented onto the images. In the present paper, we extend our initial ontology by adding a core ontology of subject data acquisition instruments modeling neuroclinical, neuropsychological and neurobehavioral tests used for neurological, behavioral and cognitive skills assessment. This ontology deals with instruments *per se* as specific artefacts, their variables and measured scores, and actions performed using instruments. In the paper, we underline the major aspects of our approach and emphasize its potential interest as a semantic reference for various neuroscience applications.

Keywords. Biomedical ontology, Artefact ontology, Knowledge Representation, Neuroscience, Brain

Introduction

Similarly to other biomedical scientists, neuroscientists collect facts, use knowledge (what they currently know about these facts) and then make inferences to produce new knowledge and facts [4]. As a consequence, there is a crucial need for computerized techniques to store, manage, analyze and share this information [1][36]. Alike bioinformatics with *in silico* experiments [33], neuroscience is progressively moving into a mass computational intensive era with fusion of various large heterogeneous data sets from cellular to system level [23]. These datasets are often disseminated in various medical centers and carried out in highly distributed environments such as grids [31][36]. Many research groups in various institutions make strong efforts to develop

[1] Corresponding Author. Fax: +33 3 22 82 76 68. E-mail addresses: benedicte.batrancourt@upmc.fr (B. Batrancourt), michel.dojat@ujf-grenoble.fr (M. Dojat), bernard.gibaud@irisa.fr (B. Gibaud), gilles.kassel@u-picardie.fr (G. Kassel).

federated and distributed infrastructures for biomedical imaging data [2][14][18]. To process the mass of information in a consistent and computational amenable form, ontologies have become recently very important in neurosciences [19][34]. The prominent effort in this direction is currently done via the Biomedical Informatics Research Network (BIRN) which proposes, based on an ontology-based vocabulary called BIRNLex a unified representation of the biomedical domains typically used to describe neuroscience data [5]. This ontological effort is driven by the OBO (Open Biomedical Ontologies) initiative that promotes shared biomedical ontologies[32].

In Neuroscience, imaging plays a central role providing information about brain structure and function. Among the different imaging modalities, Magnetic Resonance Imaging (MRI) strongly contributes to studying the healthy and the pathological brain, from both anatomical and functional perspectives and appears as the cornerstone of most cognitive studies [22]. In parallel with MRI images, questionnaires and batteries of tests are currently used to assess the neurological state of the subjects as well as their cognitive and behavioural performances. All these instruments focus on specific brain functions, which rely on specific anatomical structures or pathways, so they can be used in diagnosing brain dysfunction or damage and measuring intensity/severity of a subject's trait (e.g. behavioral, personality, psychological, psychopathological) [21]. Such tests and questionnaire-based interviews are complementary to MR images to investigate the correlation between measures of brain structure and function, derived from MR image analysis, and neurological, cognitive and behavioural traits, highlighted by test- and questionnaire-based assessments [9].

Recently, we proposed a multi-layered ontology (named OntoNeuroLOG) to deal with MR images and regions-of-interest that can be represented onto the images [34]. In the present paper, we extend our initial ontology by adding a new component to model the general characteristics of the neuroclinical, neuropsychological and behavioral tests and scores mostly used. To our knowledge, this significant effort represents the first attempt to model this kind of data. This core ontology is currently specialized for sharing data between four French neuroimaging centres through the federated NeuroLOG architecture[2], leading to the conceptualization of specific classes of instruments.

The paper is organized as follows: in the next section we remind of the most generic modules of OntoNeuroLOG onto which our Instrument ontology relies, especially the foundational ontology DOLCE[3] and a formal ontology of artefacts recently designed [17]. We then detail our main contribution, an ontology of subject data acquisition instruments, including instruments *per se* as specific technical artefacts, with their variables and scores associated, and actions performed using an instrument. In the Discussion section we underline the major aspects of our approach and emphasize in Conclusion its potential interest as a semantic reference for various neurosciences applications.

1. Methods: Our ontological reference framework

To define the OntoNeuroLOG ontology, we adopted a multi-layer and multi-components approach [35]. OntoNeuroLOG is organized into sub-ontologies (modules)

---

[2] see http://neurolog.polytech.unice.fr/doku.php

[3] http://www.loa-cnr.it/DOLCE.html

with different levels of abstraction. Schematically, three levels can be identified: at the most abstract level, the foundational DOLCE ontology [24] provides a set of abstract concepts (e.g. *physical object*, *event*, *quality*) and relations (e.g. *parthood*, *constitution*) for structuring (by specialization) any type of domain. At this level, DOLCE is supplemented by a few ontologies such as a formal ontology of artefacts [17]. At an intermediate level, "core" domain ontologies [12] define generic and central concepts in various domains such as medical images [34] or programs and software [20]. Lastly, at the most specific level, the previously mentioned ontologies are then specialized to define more specific concepts in the field of neuroimaging and image processing tools, respectively.

We adopt two different modeling languages for specifying our ontologies. At a developmental stage, modeling choices are specified – in the context of OntoSpec methodology [16] – by means of a semi-informal language which is semantically rich and includes temporally-indexed relations and meta-properties of the OntoClean methodology [13]. At run-time, the ontologies are encoded in a dialect of OWL – OWL-Lite augmented with rules – which is semantically much poorer than the former but allows for effective automatic inferences (the semantic search engine Corese [8] is currently used within the NeuroLOG project).

The new ontology of subject data acquisition instruments is situated at the intermediate level of core ontologies. Its definition relies on abstract primitives provided by generic ontologies (a list of these modules is presented in Table 1). Furthermore, it is used to model classes of specialized instruments (e.g. neuroclinical and neuropsychological instruments) which correspond to "domain" ontologies.

In the following part of this section, we remind of the main structuring principles and concepts provided by the modules of Table 1.

Table 1. Domains covered by most generic modules composing OntoNeuroLOG, along with the location of their OntoSpec manifestation (prefix=http://www.laria.u-picardie.fr/IC/Site/IMG/pdf)

Module	domains	Location of OntoSpec manifestation
Particular	Endurant, perdurant, quality, abstract	*prefix*/Particular-OS.pdf
Action	Deliberate action, intentional action, physical action, conceptual action	*prefix*/Action-OS.pdf
Participant role	Agent, substrate, consequent, result, instrument	*prefix*/Participant-role-OS.pdf
Function & artefact	Artificial object, functional object, artefact, technical artifact, social artefact	*prefix*/Function-artefact-OS.pdf
Inscription & Expression & Conceptualization	Support, inscription, Linguistic expression, concept, proposition	*prefix*/Inscription-OS.pdf

1.1 DOLCE

DOLCE's domain is that of `Particulars`[4], that is to say entities that cannot be instantiated (e.g. "my car") rather than *universals* (e.g. "being a car"). Four sub-domains of `Particulars` are distinguished (see Fig. 1):

[4] With respect to our notation, the informal labels on DOLCE's categories appear in the text in the `Courrier new` font with `First Capital Letters` for the concepts and a `javaLikeNotation` for relations. The same conventions apply for all the ontologies presented in the paper.

- Endurants are entities "enduring in time"[5]. Within Endurants, Physical Objects (e.g. a printed copy of an article) are distinguished from Non-Physical Objects (e.g. the contents of this article), this distinction corresponding to a difference between two realities or *modes* of existence for the entities. Basically, Non-Physical Objects exist insofar as agents speak about them. The domain of Non-Physical Objects covers entities whose existence depends on either an individual (for Mental Objects) or a community of agents (for Social Objects).
- Perdurants are entities "occurring in time" (e.g. your reading of this article) in which Endurants temporarily participate.
- Endurants and Perdurants have Qualities that we perceive and/or measure (e.g. the weight of the printed copy of an article, the time it takes for you to read this article). Note that these Qualities are inherent to the entity that bears them, since they are characteristic for it and they are present throughout the course of the entity's existence.
- Qualities take "values", called Quales (e.g. 25 grams, 20 minutes) within quality region spaces.

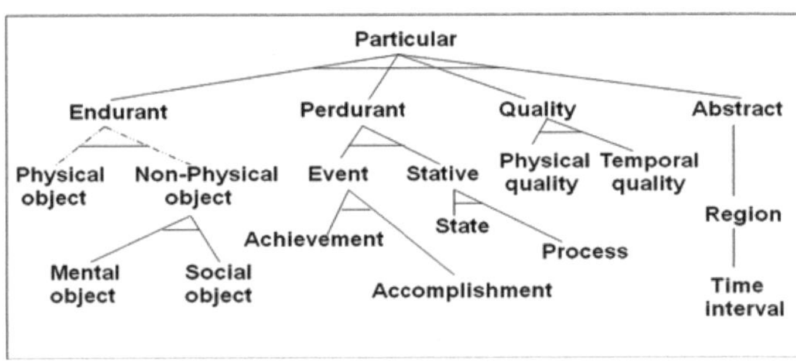

Figure 1. An excerpt of DOLCE's hierarchy of concepts. A solid line between two concepts represents a direct subsumption link. A dashed line reflects the existence of intermediate concepts. A line between two lines indicates that sibling concepts are incompatible

As a complement to DOLCE, our "Participation role" module specializes the participation relation to account for specific ways in which Endurants temporally participate in Perdurants (e.g. isAgentOfAt, isInstrumentOfAt, isResultOfAt) and such relations, in turn, are used to define *participation roles* specializing the concept Endurant (e.g. Agent, Instrument, Result).

Within the domain of Perdurants, Actions have been informally introduced into DOLCE-Lite-Plus as Accomplishments that "*exemplify the intentionality of an agent*" [24]. With the aim of conceptualizing the notion of *artefact* and subsequently the notion of *subject data acquisition instrument*, we introduced two specializations of these Actions. These specializations rely on a distinction between two kinds of *intentions*.

Following on from Searle [30], contemporary philosophers distinguish between two overall kinds of intention – a "prior intention" and "intention-in-action", to borrow

[5] Due to space limitations, we are only able to provide a very brief characterization of DOLCE's categories and we limit ourselves to categories of use in our ontology of instruments.

Searle's terms – which differ according to their temporality, role and content [27]. A *prior intention* consists in planning an action (prior to the realization of the action) and then rationally controlling the action. It relies on a conceptual representation of the type of action to be performed, comprising an objective (i.e. a goal) and, optionally, a means of achieving it (i.e. a plan). Once the action has been initiated, the *intention-in-action* consists in the continuous guidance and control of the initiated action by relying on a descriptive, context-sensitive representation of the said action.

Taking into account current knowledge on the phenomenology of actions [28], we first assimilate `Actions` to processes controlled by an intention (intention-in-action and/or prior intention); these contrast with `Happenings` which lack an intentional cause. We then introduce two specializations of `Actions`. Firstly, `Deliberate Actions` are initiated by a prior intention comprising a conceptual representation of the intended goal. Secondly, within `Deliberate Actions`, `Successful Actions` are carried out to completion and lead to their intended result.

1.2 I&DA

I&DA is a core ontology in the domain of information content entities and their physical materialization that was initially built for classifying documents by their contents [11]. I&DA extends DOLCE by introducing three main types of entities (see Fig. 2):

- `Inscriptions` (e.g. printed texts) are knowledge forms materialized by a substance (e.g. ink) and inscribed on a physical support (e.g. a sheet of paper, a hard disk). The peculiarity of these `Physical Endurants` lies in their intentional nature: `Inscriptions` count as other entities, `Expressions`.
- `Expressions` (e.g. texts, logical formulae) are non-physical knowledge forms ordered by a communication language. `Inscriptions` realize `Expressions` and, like `Inscriptions`, `Expressions` are intentional entities conveying contents for agents.
- `Conceptualizations` consist of the ultimate means by which agents can reason about a world. Two kinds of `Conceptualizations` are distinguished: `Propositions`, as a means of describing a state of affairs; and `Concepts`, as a means to classify entities. Note that, as for the practical semiotics introduced in the ontology SUMO [29], `Propositions` may encompass the content expressed by sentences, theories, books, and even libraries.

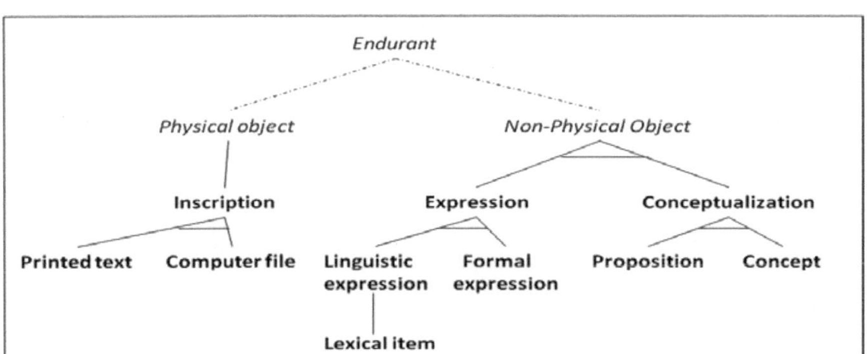

Figure 2. An excerpt of I&DA's hierarchy of concepts

We are going to see (in Section 3) that `Propositions` and `Concepts` correspond to the intrinsic nature of our instruments. Before that, we extend DOLCE in another way to account for the intentional nature of these instruments and their function.

1.3 Artefacts

The notion of *artefact* that we adopt elaborates on the common philosophical notion of an "*entity intentionally made or produced for some reason*" [15]. Analyzing the notions of *intention* and *reason*, this leads us to identify different classes of entities we find important to clearly distinguish and define [17] (see Fig. 3):

- Firstly, we contrast entities resulting from an action of production (`Producing Consequents`) with entities that are not intentionally produced (`Happening Consequents`). Among the latter figure `Experimental Artefacts` (which are unwanted results).
- Secondly, according to whether the intention of production is a prior intention or not, `Artefacts` are distinguished from `Non-Targeted Objects` (the latter result from `Non-Deliberate Actions` of production, e.g. routines).
- Thirdly, different kinds of reasons for producing `Artefacts` (hence different kinds of `Artefacts`) are considered: (i) conveying an emotion and being of aesthetic interest, for works of art, (ii) enabling their author (or another agent) to do something, for "functional" or `Technical Artefacts`. The latter are `Artefacts` to which a `Function` is ascribed, taking a `Function` to be an "*acknowledged capacity to enable the realization of a kind of action*" [17].

It is important to note that DOLCE's distinction between `Physical` and `Non-Physical Objects` transcends the domain of `Artefacts`. Indeed, the latter are defined by the *origin* of their existence (i.e. their intentional production) rather than a *mode* of existence. This difference explains why we are able to distinguish between physical artefacts (e.g. an oscilloscope, an image acquisition equipment) and non-physical artefacts (e.g. the content of an article, a subject data acquisition instrument).

To sum up, `Technical Artefacts` have – at least – a triple nature as entities (i) possessing an internal essence (be it physical, social or cognitive), (ii) having been intentionally (and successfully) produced, and (iii) having necessarily a `Function`.

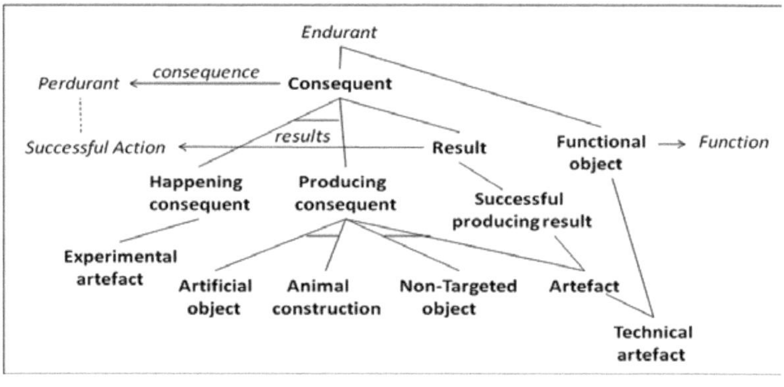

Figure 3. Core taxonomy of artefacts

With the modules presented in this section in hand, we now have at our disposal a minimal set of conceptual primitives which enables us to tackle the modeling of the domain of neurological, neuropsychological and behavioral instruments.

2. Our core ontology of instruments

In the core ontology we propose, instruments *per se* are considered as specific technical artefacts, with their own variables and scores associated, and actions performed using an instrument as specific conceptual actions.

2.1. Instrument-based assessments

An `Instrument-Based Assessment` action corresponds to an administration of an instrument or a 'testing' (to use the term recommended by [7]). The conceptualization of this action plays a pivotal role, linking together a large number of entities (cf. Fig. 4): a `Healthcare Professional` (for instance clinical neuropsychologist or neurologist), as `Agent`; the `Subject` about whom data are acquired and, more widely, the context in which this acquisition is performed (i.e. an `Examination` within a `Study`); the used instrument prescribing which data are to be acquired and how; results obtained following questions raised and/or tests performed.

These actions commonly take two forms according to whether they solicit an authentic production from the `Subject` (e.g., a reflex, a performance such as drawing, or a 500-meter walk), for `Test-Based Assessments`, or they consist in an interview, an inventory, for `Questionnaire-Based Assessments`. `Assessments` are then specialized according to the type of acquired data (e.g., psychological, behavioral, neuroclinical), mirroring in part the instruments taxonomy (cf. Fig. 5). The raison d'être of this specialization is to take into account specifications of the evidence of competence (knowledge, skills, abilities, specialties) that would be expected from someone seeking qualification as a test user.

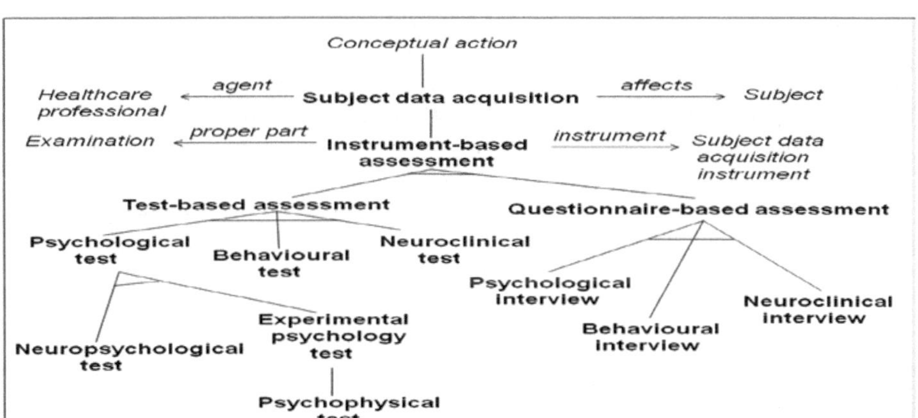

Figure 4. Taxonomy of `Instrument-based assessments.`

2.2. Subject data acquisition instruments

The instruments used to evaluate the state of subjects clearly are technical artefacts. For their conceptualization, we follow our theory of the threefold nature of technical artefacts [17]. This prompts to describe them as being:

- Intangible artefacts, i.e. propositional contents including "clearly defined methods and instructions for administration or responding, a standard format for data collection, and well-documented methods for scoring, analysis, and interpretation of results" [6].
- Technical artefacts allowing to explore entities related to the state of the subject – these categories of entities correspond to the `Domain(s)` of the instrument.
- Social artefacts intentionally created, adopted for use, then adapted and maintained by a community ascribing them the status of standard.

As the definition adopted from [6] indicates, we are faced to complex propositional contents. As an illustration of this complexity, some `Instruments` are explicitly composed of `Sub-instruments` exploring sub- or related domains (see Fig. 5). For example, to explore the multidimensional aspect of memory, the *General Memory Index* of the *Wechlser Memory Scale-III (WMS-III)* - a composite instrument designed to explore several memory abilities - is based on the delayed recall performances of several core "memory" tests, like the *Visual Memory Test* or the *Verbal Memory Test* [37]. Such a composition is also found for `Instruments` which assess a restricted set of cognitive functions. For example, the *Mini-Mental State (MMS)* [10], which is probably the most widely used instrument for dementia [21], is structured according to a set of several items such as the *MMS Orientation Test*, the *MMS Registration Test* or the *MMS Language Tests*. Moreover the *MMS Language Tests* consist of several items such as the *MMS Oral Order Language Test* or the *MMS Written Order Language Test*. This indicates that even an `Instrument` which addresses a relatively small domain may be structurally complex. Such a structure is important to model because, according to the context, only some parts of an instrument may be administrated.

The effects of brain disorders being rarely confined to a single behavioral dimension or functional system [21], `Instrument-Based Assessments` focus on different issues: neurological disorders (e.g. weakness, stiffness or visual impairments), cognitive impairments (e.g. aphasia, failure of judgment, lapse of memory), and other behavioral disorders (e.g. personality change, reduced mental efficiency or depression). Functionally, `Instruments` explore entities (their `Domain(s)`) which are of different ontological nature (e.g., states, abilities, cognitive functions, behaviors). For instance the memory is a cognitive function, while the depression is a Subject's pathological state. Moreover, an `Instrument` can be designed to explore one or several domains (`Mono-domain` *vs* `Multi-domain Instrument`). Generally, the goal with a `Multi-domain Instrument` is to integrate into one index the scores obtained by the patient while exploring different dimensions or functional systems. For instance, the MMS, which addresses the Global Cognitive efficiency, tries to obtain a global measure while exploring a whole set of domains: orientation, calculation, language, memory, praxia. Formally, a Domain is modeled as an individual concept which classifies classes of entities.

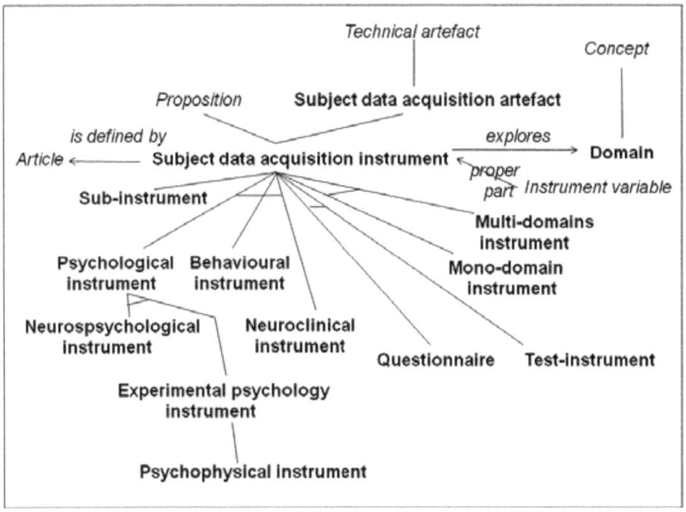

Figure 5. Taxonomy of `Subject data acquisition instruments.`

2.3. Instrument variables

`Instrument variables` are themselves `Subject data acquisition artefacts`. They carry two fundamental characteristics of the related instrument. First, they define what is being explored and measured using this instrument, represented by an explored `Domain` and a measured `Quality`, respectively. A distinction is introduced between `Main variables`, which explore the same `Domain` as the related instrument (i.e. same cognitive function or trait of the subject), and `Secondary variables`, which provide complementary information. `Variables` may also be categorized as `Sex dependent variables`, `Age dependent variables`, and `Cultural skill dependent variables`. When, for a variable, a typical value from a population of reference is available, the measured value can be standardized and stored in the corresponding score associated to the variable.

Second, `Instrument variables` define the range of allowed score values, with a basic distinction between `Coded variables`, which register `Coded scores`, and `Numerical variables` that register `Numerical scores`. The former are associated to a set of allowed `Coded variable values`, which are parts of the definition of the instrument. The latter, `Numerical variables`, can take any value in a certain range (which may be specified using min and max values). For instance, the MMS Calculation variable is a `Numerical variable` belonging to the range [0;5]. The Pessimistic thoughts variable of the *Montgomery-Asberg Depression Rating Scale (MADRS)* [26] is a `Coded variable` with the following `Coded variable values` {0 = 'No pessimistic thoughts', 2 = 'Fluctuating ideas of failure, self-reproach or self-depreciation', 3 = 'Persistent self-accusation, or definite but still rational ideas of guilt or sin. Increasingly pessimistic about the future', 6 = 'Delusions of ruin, remorse or irredeemable sin. Self-accusations, which are absurd and unshakable'}. `Values` are `Propositions` denoting, e.g., that "*the subject has no pessimistic thoughts as measured by the MADRS Pessimistic thoughts variable*". In the latter proposition, the term 'subject' does not refer to a particular individual, but to an abstract `Subject`.

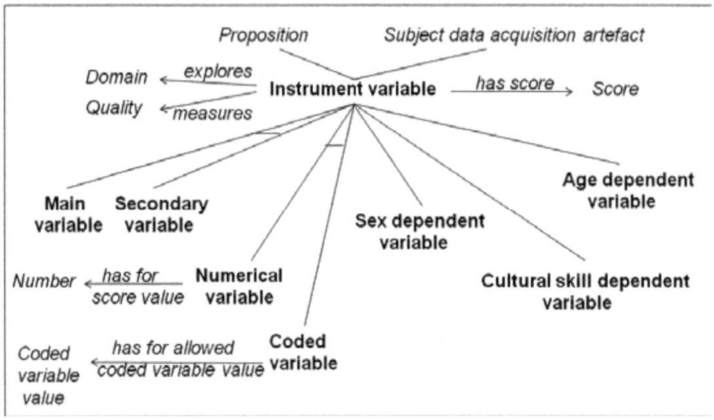

Figure 6. Taxonomy of `Instrument variables`.

2.4. Scores

`Scores` are `Propositions` that result from the recording of a particular `Subject`'s cognitive performance (e.g. calculation performance) or a particular `Subject`'s trait intensity (e.g. pessimistic thoughts intensity) during a particular `Instrument-based assessment`, in relation to a particular `Instrument Variable`. For instance a `Score` may correspond to the following propositions: *"During one MMS Calculation assessment, Patient X's Calculation performance is equal to 4 as measured by such MMS Calculation variable"* or "*During one MADRS assessment, Patient X has no pessimistic thoughts as measured by the MADRS Pessimistic thoughts variable*".

`Scores` are divided into `Coded scores` and `Numerical scores`. `Coded scores` specialize the `Coded variable values` allowed for a particular `Coded variable` by referring to a particular `Subject`.

`Numerical scores` are further categorized as `Raw scores`, `Corrected scores` and `Standardized scores` depending whether they result of the direct registering of the subject's performance, or result of some correction or standardization of such raw scores. One also distinguishes between `Scores with` (respectively `without`) `unit of measure`.

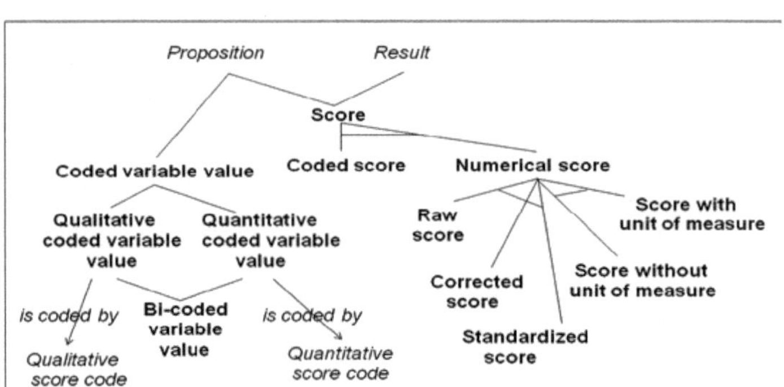

Figure 7. Taxonomy of `Scores`.

2.5. Codes

We have seen that `Variable values` and `Scores` are `Propositions`. To help synthesize these values and offer calculus facilities, these `Propositions` are usually coded. Let's take, for instance, the *Beck Depression Inventory (BDI-III)* [3], one of the most widely used instruments for measuring the severity of depression. One of its variables measures the sleeping dimension with values such as: "*The patient sleeps somewhat more than usual*" or "*The patient sleeps most of the day*". These `Propositions` are both qualitatively coded (by the respective `Qualitative Score codes`: 'Minimal' and 'Severe') and quantitatively coded (by the respective `Quantitative Score codes`: '1a' and '3a'). The latter `Codes` refer to a number (resp. 1 and 3), therefore enabling applying order relationships.

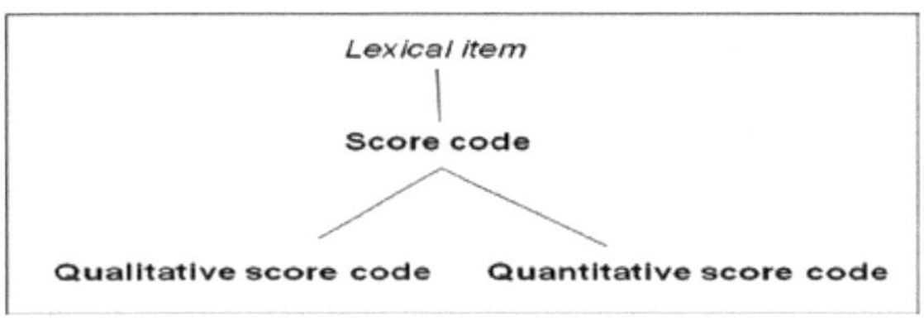

Figure 8. Taxonomy of `Score codes`.

3. Discussion

A central quest in current neuroscience is the understanding of relations, under normal or pathological conditions, between brain anatomy and brain function. Brain functions can be mainly explored by neuroimaging, such as functional MRI, and neuropsychology, when concerned with the behavioral expression of brain functions [19]. One of our goal, with the construction of the proposed core ontology, was to define a model supporting the investigation of correlations between MRI based findings and neuroclinical, behavioural and neuropsychological based findings. The latter can be assessed by scores, which register the subject's task ability, cognitive performance or trait intensity. These correlations will be investigated in mining a large collection of data via a federation of heterogeneous and distributed databases (NeuroLOG project). For instance in Alzheimer's disease (AD), Gray Matter (GM) loss in the temporal regions lobes seems correlated with a decrease in Global Cognitive Efficiency (GCE) score. The two widely used instruments to examine the cognitive changes that characterize AD are the Mini Mental State (MMS) and the Mattis Dementia Rating Scale (MDRS) [25]. Indeed, MMS and MDRS are multi-domains instruments because their sub-instruments screen a large set of cognitive skills: attention, orientation, calculation, language, memory, praxia. The MMS and MDRS main variables register a total score which is based on the scores obtained during each of their sub-instrument assessments. Depending on the clinicians habits or the context of the assessment, MMS or MDRS is considered to define the subject's GCE. NeuroLOG's platform allows to search for: "*all patients with a low GCE and with T1-weigthed images presenting a GM loss temporal lobes* ". Firstly, our core ontology allows (i) to retrieve all the `Instruments` (and their `Main variables`) that explore the `Domain`: Global Cognitive Efficiency, and (ii) to scan the entire set of related

`Scores`, while filtering those which have a value less than a cut-off value (the latter is provided by the user and is `Instrument` and research study dependent). Secondly, images of the patient are retrieved and a specific computational anatomy pipeline is processed to quantify the possible GM volume loss in temporal lobes in the selected images.

The definition of the present core ontology was based on the detailed examination of the common instruments routinely used in three neurology hospital departments in France. We consider this set of instruments as representative of the minimal core that core ontology should support via dedicated sub-ontologies.

Two important modeling choices should be emphasized. The first one concerns the conceptualization of `Instruments` and the fact that we chose to model specific standard `Instruments` (e.g. MMS, WMS-III) as classes and not instances. The reason is that, in some centers, administered `Instruments` do not strictly conform to the defined standard. To account for these variations, local `Instruments` are modeled as instances of classes, with the latter representing shared properties of standard `Instruments`. Such properties correspond to structural and functional properties presented in Section 2.2. As a consequence, our core ontology is specialized by sub-ontologies, each accounting for a specific `Instrument`. In some cases, however, variations become so important that this modeling is no longer adequate. A new standard is then built as a version of a previous one. Such a versioning relation is introduced between the two standards so that we can maintain the class/instances representation. The second modeling choice concerns the distinction between `Variable values` and `Scores`. As we have seen, the former are modeled as `Propositions` (referring to an abstract `Subject`) which pertain to the definition of `Instrument`, whereas the latter (referring to a particular `Subject`) are the result of an `Assessment`. We therefore have two different propositional contents which are linked by a specialization relation (thanks to this relation, information about `Score codes` is only attached to `Variable values`). It is important to note that `Scores` are moreover characteristic of `Assessments` (i.e. two `Assessments` do not share the same `Score`). This choice enlarges our model with a greater number of instances. However, when requesting to a given a `Score`, we directly obtain its specific context (`Subject`, `Examination` and `Study`).

4. Conclusion and perspectives

In this paper, we have proposed a core ontology of instruments which builds upon a conceptual framework comprising the foundational ontology DOLCE and a recently designed ontology of artefacts. Thanks to this building approach and the possibilities of mapping it offers with other biomedical ontologies (such as those based on BFO[6]), we would like to stress its potential interest as a semantic reference for various neurosciences applications.

Before it can be used, our core ontology must be complemented with ontologies modeling the actually shared `Instruments` (more precisely the common properties of shared `Instruments`, as stressed earlier). This work is in progress. Once these ontologies available, the next step will consist in aligning the different `Instruments'`

---

6 http://www.ifomis.org/bfo

instantiations (at the different clinical sites) to a common reference, thanks to the mediator used in the NeuroLOG system (Data Federator, SAP). This will enable to query the actual `Subjects' Scores` and to correlate such `Scores` with image findings, which is what the end-users are primarily interested in. A current limitation of our conceptualization of `Instruments` lies in our preliminary description of the `Domains` and `Qualities` respectively *explored* and *measured by* `Instrument variables`. Such `Domains` and `Qualities` are modeled as independent concepts, which strongly limits the kind of reasoning that can applied. Our intention is to define ontologies of brain functions and states, as well as ontologies of the `Qualities` that may be measured during `Instrument-based assessments`, that will certainly lead to enhanced querying and reasoning capabilities.

Acknowledgements

This work is funded by the French national research agency (ANR), NeuroLOG project, under contract number ANR-06-TLOG-024.

References

[1] G.A. Ascoli, Mobilizing the base of neuroscience data: the case of neuronal morphologies, *Nature Reviews Neuroscience* **7** (2006), 318-24.
[2] C. Barillot, H. Benali, M. Dojat, A. Gaignard, B. Gibaud, S. Kinkingnéhun, J. Matsumoto, M. Pélégrini, E. Simon, L. Temal, Federating Distributed and Heterogeneous Information Sources in Neuroimaging: The NeuroBase Project., In: V. Hernández, I. Blanquer, T. Solomonides, V. Breton and Y. Legré, eds., *Studies in Health Technology and Informatics: Challenges and Opportunities of HealthGrids*, IOS Press, 2006, pp. 3-13.
[3] A.T. Beck, R.A. Steer, G.K. Brown, Manual for Beck Depression Inventory II (BDI-II), San Antonio, TX, Psychology Corporation, 1996.
[4] O. Bodenreider, R. Stevens, Bio-ontologies: current trends and future directions, *Briefings in Bioinformatics* **7** (2006), 256-74.
[5] W.J. Bug, G.A. Ascoli, J.S. Grethe, A. Gupta, C. Fennema-Notestine, A.R. Laird, S.D. Larson, D. Rubin, G.M. Shepherd, J.A. Turner, M.E. Martone, The NIFSTD and BIRNLex Vocabularies: Building Comprehensive Ontologies for Neuroscience, *Neuroinformatics* **6(3)** (2008), 175-194.
[6] CDISC (Clinical Data Interchange Standards Consortium), CDISC Clinical Research Glossary Version 7.0, *Applied Clinical Trials* (2008), 12-58. Available at: ://www.cdisc.org/glossary/CDISC2008GlossaryVersion7.0.pdf
[7] CPTA (Committee on Psychological Tests and Assessment; American Psychological Association), Recent Developments Affecting the Disclosure of Test Data and Materials: Comments Regarding the 1996 Statement on the Disclosure of Test Data, 2007. Available at: ://www.apa.org/science/test-disclosure-statement.pdf
[8] O. Corby, R. Dieng-Kuntz, C. Faron-Zucker, Querying the Semantic Web with Corese Search Engine. In: Proceedings of the 15th ECAI/PAIS, Valencia, Spain, 2004.
[9] A.C. Evans, Brain Development Cooperative Group, The NIH MRI study of normal brain development, *NeuroImage* **30** (2006), 184-202.
[10] M.F. Folstein, S.E. Folstein, P.R. McHugh, Mini Mental State, *Journal of Psychiatric Research* **12** (1975), 189-198
[11] J.Y. Fortier, G. Kassel, Managing knowledge at the information level: an ontological approach, In: Proc. of the ECAI'2004 workshop on knowledge management and organizational memories, Valencia (Spain) (2004), pp. 39-45.
[12] A. Gangemi, S. Borgo (Eds.), Proceedings of the EKAW'04 Workshop on Core Ontologies in Ontology Engineering, Northamptonshire (UK), 2004, available at *://ceur-ws.org (Vol-118).*
[13] N. Guarino, C. Welty, An Overview of OntoClean. In: S. Staab, R. Studer (eds.), *Handbook on Ontologies*, Springer Verlag, 2004, pp. 151-171.

[14] U. Hasson, J.L. Skipper, M.J. Wilde, H.C. Nusbaum, S.L. Small, Improving the analysis, storage and sharing of neuroimaging data using relational databases and distributed computing, *Neuroimage* **39(2)**, (2008), 21:21.
[15] R. Hilpinen, Artifact. *Stanford Encyclopedia of Philosophy*, 2004, available at: ://plato.stanford.edu/entries/artifact/.
[16] G. Kassel, Integration of the DOLCE top-level ontology into the OntoSpec methodology, LaRIA Research Report 2005-08, 2005, available at: ://hal.ccsd.cnrs.fr/ccsd-00012203.
[17] G. Kassel, A formal ontology of artefacts, *Applied Ontology* (to appear).
[18] D.B. Keator, J.S. Grethe, D. Marcus, B. Ozyurt, S. Gadde, S. Murphy, S. Pieper, D. Greve, R. Notestine, H.J. Bockholt, P. Papadopoulos, BIRN Function, BIRN Morphometry, BIRN-Coordinating, A national human neuroimaging collaboratory enabled by the Biomedical Informatics Research Network (BIRN), *IEEE Trans Inf Technol Biomed* **12** (2008), 162-72.
[19] A.R. Laird, J.L. Lancaster, P.T. Fox, Lost in localization? The focus is meta-analysis, *NeuroImage* **48(1)** 2009, 18-20.
[20] P. Lando, A. Lapujade, G. Kassel, F. Fürst, An ontological investigation in the field of computer programs, In J. Filipe *et al.*, eds.: ICSOFT/ENASE 2007, *Software and Data Technologies*, Communications in Computer and Information Science, Springer-Verlag Berlin Heidelberg, 2008, vol. 22, pp. 371-383.
[21] M.D. Lezak, D.B. Howieson, D. W. Loring, H.J. Hannay, J.S. Fischer, Neuropsychological Assessment, Oxford University Press, 2004.
[22] N.K. Logothetis, What we can do and what we cannot do with fMRI, *Nature* **453** (2008), 869-78.
[23] M.E. Martone, A. Gupta, M.H. Ellisman, E-neuroscience: challenges and triumphs in integrating distributed data from molecules to brains, *Nat Neurosci.* **7(5)** (2004), 467-72.
[24] C. Masolo, S. Borgo, A. Gangemi, N. Guarino, A. Oltramari, L. Schneider, The WonderWeb Library of Foundational Ontologies and the DOLCE ontology. *WonderWeb Deliverable D18, Final Report*, vr. 1.0, (2003).
[25] S. Mattis, Mental status examination for organic mental syndrome in the elderly patient, in *Geriatric Psychiatry*. Edited by Bellack R, Karasu B. New York, Grune & Stratton, (1976), pp 77-121.
[26] S.A. Montgomery, M. Asberg, A new depression scale designed to be sensitive to change, *British Journal of Psychiatry* **134** (1979), 382-89.
[27] E. Pacherie, The content of intentions, *Mind and Language* **15** (2000), 400-432.
[28] E. Pacherie, The phenomenology of action: A conceptual framework, *Cognition* **107** (2008), 179-217.
[29] A. Pease, I. Niles, Practical Semiotics: A Formal Theory, Proc. of the International Conference on Information and Knowledge Engineering (IKE'02), (2002).
[30] J.R. Searle, *Intentionality*. Cambridge University Press, 1983.
[31] S.L. Small, M. Wilde, S. Kenny, M. Andric, U. Hasson, Database-managed grid-enabled analysis of neuroimaging data: the CNARI framework, *Int J Psychophysiol.* **73** (2009), 62-72.
[32] B. Smith, M. Ashburner, C. Rosse, J. Bard, W. Bug, W. Ceusters, L.J. Goldberg, K. Eilbeck, A. Ireland, C.J. Mungall, N. Leontis, P. Rocca-Serra, A. Ruttenberg, S.A. Sansone, R.H. Scheuermann, N. Shah, P.L. Whetzel, S. Lewis, The OBO Foundry: coordinated evolution of ontologies to support biomedical data integration, *Nat Biotechnol.* **25** (2007), 1251-1255.
[33] R. Stevens, M. Egana Aranguren, K. Wolstencroft, U. Sattler, N. Drummond, M. Horridge, A. Rector, Using OWL to model biological knowledge, *International Journal of Human - Computer Studies* **67** (2007), 583-94.
[34] L. Temal, M. Dojat, G. Kassel, B. Gibaud, Towards an ontology for sharing medical images and regions of interest in neuroimaging, *Journal of Biomedical Informatics* **41** (2008), 766-778.
[35] L. Temal, P. Lando, B. Gibaud, M. Dojat, G. Kassel, A. Lapujade, OntoNeuroBase: a multi-layered application ontology in neuroimaging, Proc. of the 2nd Workshop: Formal Ontologies Meet Industry (FOMI 2006), (2006), pp. 3-15.
[36] J.D. Van Horn, A.W.Toga, Multisite neuroimaging trials, *Curr. Opinion Neurol.* 22(4) (2009), 370-378.
[37] D. Wechsler, Weschsler Adult Intelligence Scale-III. San Antonio, TX: The Psychological Corporation, 1997.

Formal Ontology in Information Systems
A. Galton and R. Mizoguchi (Eds.)
IOS Press, 2010

doi:10.3233/978-1-60750-535-8-199

A Process-Centric Ontological Approach for Integrating Geo-Sensor Data

Anusuriya DEVARAJU[a] and Werner KUHN[a]
[a]Institute for Geoinformatics, University of Muenster
anusuriya.devaraju@uni-muenster.de, kuhn@uni-muenster.de

Abstract. We introduce a process-centric ontological approach to relate observed properties to geo-processes that influence those observations. These relations are used to handle semantic heterogeneities that impede the integration of geo-sensor data. Our approach comprises a process-centric hydrology ontology and its alignment with the DOLCE foundational ontology. We describe how DOLCE assists in classifying two hydrological processes and their participating entities. Our preliminary results indicate that the process-centric ontological approach can be used to resolve process and property naming ambiguity within a domain. We consider this as a first step toward a process-centric semantic integration of geo-sensor data.

Keywords. Semantic heterogeneities, sensor data, ontology, surface hydrological processes, DOLCE

1. Introduction

A Geo-Sensor Network (GSN) is a network of sensors that monitors the properties of natural environments in different locations at different times. Recent technological advances have facilitated GSNs as a new way to study the dynamics of geo-phenomena [1, 2]. For example, a geo-sensor *stream gauge* provides sequences of quantitative values of the time-varying observed property *water height*. These observations are influenced by a river flow process, which results from other processes such as surface runoff, rainfall and so on. The scenario in figure 1 indicates that facts about geo-processes can be inferred from sensor data. However, this is not easy to achieve due to the nature of sensors, which return huge amounts of data in different formats and semantics. Although sensor data can be made available via open standards (e.g., through OGC's Sensor Web Enablement (SWE) specifications), an effort is required to collate and interpret them, as the data schemas are developed independently and different semantics are used for the same or overlapping terms. Such semantic barriers pose a challenge to data consumers who need appropriate sensor data for forecast modeling and for generating environmental reports. What is currently missing is an approach to support the semantic integration of geo-sensor data.

To achieve semantic integration, the geo-sensor data must be interpreted from a common point of view. Such interpretation requires an understanding of the geo-processes that influence the sensor data. This paper introduces an ontological approach to represent the relations between observed properties and geo-processes. Guarino et al. (1995) define ontology as 'a logical theory which gives an explicit, partial account of a conceptualization'[3]. Ontology captures consensual knowledge of a domain; it describes the domain concepts and the constraints on their use explicitly.

Although the use of ontology for data integration is not new, the study introduces a *process-centric* ontological approach. Process-centric means that the ontology is developed by first identifying processes[1], entities and physical properties, followed by the relations between them. Entities are the physical objects, features, and amounts of matter that participate in a process and bear some physical properties. The goal of our process-centric ontology is to define the controlled terminologies that can be used to present a unified view over heterogeneous sensor data. Our current focus is to develop a DOLCE-aligned hydrology ontology to represent concepts of surface hydrology. The work presented in this paper is still in its early phase of development; we show the feasibility of applying process-centric ontology to integrate hydrological data. We believe our approach has the potential to play an important role in facilitating communication between and among producers and users of hydrological data.

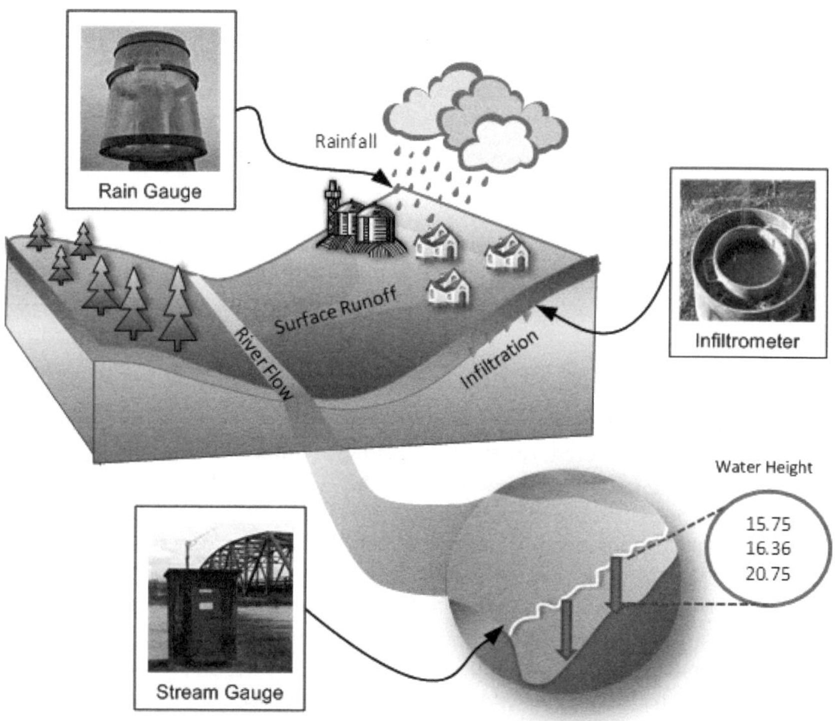

Figure 1. The relation between the observed properties and the hydrological processes

The remainder of the paper is organized as follows: Two challenges that motivate our research are given in section 2. Then, we present the related work in section 3. This is followed by an overview of the top-level distinctions for real world entities as specified in DOLCE. We introduce the basic ontological relations in section 5. Then, we de-

[1] The notion of 'processes' is used here rather broadly as it includes all kinds of perdurants, e.g., states, processes, events

scribe our process-centric ontological approach in section 6. In section 7, we discuss the contributions of the paper and the benefits of DOLCE basic categories for representing hydrological processes and the associated entities (i.e., physical objects, substance and physical properties).

2. Research Challenges

This section describes two research challenges that motivate our work: (a) the need for an approach to an explicit representation of geo-phenomena dynamics (b) finding out how this approach can resolve semantic heterogeneities that impede the integration of geo-sensor data. The two challenges are illustrated with examples from the hydrology domain.

2.1. Lack of principled ways of describing geographic events and processes

Galton (2008) explains the categorization of processes and events based on three main areas - Philosophy[4], Linguistics[5] and Artificial Intelligence[6]. The classification of process also has been pursued in other technical areas, for instance, a Process Model[2] has been developed as part of Operating Systems in computing field. Another example is the Business Process Model[3] to denote enterprise activities. The National Institute of Standards and Technology (NIST) developed the Process Specification Language (PSL)[4] – an interchange language to specify manufacturing, engineering and business processes. In event modeling, Bennett and Galton (2004) proposed a logical language called Versatile Event Logic (VEL) for representing events [7]; Pustejovsky, et al. (2003) developed TimeML - a specification language for event and temporal expressions in texts [8].

Galton (2008) pointed out that in Geographic Information Science, 'there is little consensus on exactly how dynamic entities like processes and events should be defined or differentiated from one another' [9]. The conceptual modeling of occurrences (i.e., processes and events) is typically based on specific applications and lacks the computational and reasoning viewpoints. Process modeling has mostly proceeded in ad hoc fashion, with no solid basis in theory [9]. Examples of the existing literature that deal with event and process modeling are [10-14].

The terminological inconsistencies have led to 'disagreements on classifying processes in relation to other categories such as state and event' [15]. For example, Yuan [10] and Claramunt [11] define an event as made of processes, whereas Dias [16] defines processes through the composition of events. Worboys [17] suggests that 'it is useful to view a process as a composite event'. Wang et al. [14] consider events and processes separately – 'events are things that happen to entities, while processes are the actions of entities when (during, after) events happen to them', which describe how the entities evolve. It is also possible to use the terms events and process loosely and interchangeably [15]. For example, Worboys [13] uses 'event' as a broad term to cover all kind of occurrents, including the processes. The author also states that 'one person's process is another's event, and vice versa'.

[2] http://www.cs.vu.nl/~ast/books/mos2/
[3] http://bpmn.org/index.htm
[4] http://www.mel.nist.gov/psl/

What is currently missing is a theory with well-defined vocabularies that allows an explicit representation of process, events, and their participants (e.g., physical objects and substance) to deal with geo-phenomena. This ontological theory would be useful for resolving process naming ambiguity. For example, the terms *infiltration* and *percolation* are often used interchangeably [18]. Infiltration moves water into soil, while percolation moves water through soil until it reaches and joins ground water. In a process-centric ontological approach, we can distinguish these processes based on their relations (i.e., a percolation is initiated by infiltration) and participants (i.e., unlike infiltration, percolation involves lower soil levels and ground water).

There are also cases where the same hydrological processes are named differently. *Surface runoff*, for example, is the water flow which occurs when soil is infiltrated to capacity and excess water, from rain, snowmelt, or other sources flows over the land[5]. *Overland flow* occurs when the amount of water falling on the ground is greater than the infiltration rate of the surface[6]. In many contexts, *overland flow* and *surface runoff* can be identified as the same process, as they are undistinguishable kinds of a 'runoff' process. They comprise the same phases – first, the precipitation rate exceeds the infiltration capacity of the soil and then the water accumulates on the surface and flows across it. Furthermore, they have the same participants such as the catchment, amounts of water, channels, vegetation, soil, etc. They may also have similar effects, for instance, causing soil detachment and sediment transport.

2.2. Enabling semantic integration of geo-sensor data

Several standards have been produced to cope with technical barriers (i.e., sensor data in multiple formats). Examples are the Observations and Measurements Encoding Standard[7] and the Sensor Markup Language (SensorML)[8], Common Alerting Protocol (CAP) and Emergency Data Exchange Language (EDXL)[9], Water Data Transfer Format (WDTF)[10], WaterML[11], Telescope Observation Mark-up Language (TOML)[12] and so on. These approaches allow for providing sensor data to potential applications in a standardized form. Although XML-based specifications have contributed to overcoming the syntax heterogeneities, they do not support the semantic integration of multiple data sources, as they generally do not place semantic constraints on the contents [19].

The following is an example of the usage of different terms to denote the same observed property, fully compatible with sensor data standards. In stream flow measurements, various names are used by hydrological data providers to identify gauge measurements. The USGS Surface-Water for the Nation (NWIS) standard calls it *gauge height*; the Washington State Department of Ecology identifies it as *raw stage*; the US Army Corps of Engineers calls it *stage*, and the Canadian Hydrographic Service Central and Arctic Region uses the term *water level*. There are also spatial and temporal semantic conflicts between sensor data and environmental models [20]. For instance,

---

[5] http://en.wikipedia.org/wiki/Surface_runoff
[6] http://www.eoearth.org/article/Surface_runoff
[7] http://www.opengeospatial.org/standards/om
[8] http://www.opengeospatial.org/standards/sensorml
[9] http://www.oasis-emergency.org/specifications
[10] http://www.bom.gov.au/water/WDTF_technical_information.shtml
[11] http://his.cuahsi.org/wofws.html
[12] http://omp.jach.hawaii.edu/schema/TOML/

'hydraulic conductivity is measured in the field at scales of the order centimeters to meters; the hillslope hydrology models, however, often include hydraulic conductivity as a parameter at scales of the order meters to kilometers' [21]. The aforementioned examples serve to illustrate how the semantic heterogeneity aggravates the difficulties in retrieving and combining sensor data into hydrological models.

3. Related Work

Semantic sensor data integration has become one of the most demanding topics in Sensor Web research. Broering et al. [22] introduced the vision of 'sensor plug & play' to support the on-the-fly integration of sensors. They discussed which challenges have to be overcome for such a seamless integration and how the lack of explicit semantics may lead to misinterpretations of sensor observations. They pointed out that geo-process representation within OGC's Sensor Web is still an open issue.

Kuhn [23] proposed a functional ontology to describe the act of observation as a process resulting in values. He introduced a generic notion of observer, as a role that can be played by human and technical sensors who observe properties of an entity. The work presented in this paper emphasizes geo-processes and their relations to observed properties.

Henson et al. [24] proposed an ontological representation of time series observations (based on Observation and Measurement in OWL) to allow conversion between event-based and interval-based observations. Henson's work includes the ontological representation of observed properties, features of interests, sampling time, and observation location; however, a geo-process representation is still missing.

Ordnance Survey developed a hydrology ontology to support the use of their data by customers and to enable semi-automatic processing of these data[13]. The ontology specifies inland hydrology features with functional, topological and mereological relations between them. However, it has no representation of hydrological processes and physical properties of hydro-features.

Bermudez et al. proposed a hydrology ontology that represents measurable properties, measurement types and medium, phenomena (i.e., hydrological processes) and physical endurants (i.e., features and substances)[14]. This ontology specifies a limited number of hydrological processes, but relations between the phenomena are missing. For example, there is no relation defined between physical endurants and phenomena.

Ram et al. [25] introduced an ontology-based integration framework called HyDSS to provide decision support and access to heterogeneous hydro-information sources. A schema for runoff modeling is developed to provide a logical description and set of relationships among multiple sources. In addition, a Semantic Conflict Resolution Ontology (SCROL) is used to resolve semantic conflicts (such as scaling and units) among those sources. Beran [26] developed 'Hydroseek' - an ontology-aided search engine for finding water quality and hydrological data from various agencies. The ontology specifies geo-processes and observed properties related to the environmental quality, surface, subsurface and atmospheric hydrology. In both Ram's and Beran's work, there is no categorical distinction between process, object, and quality[15]. Such a distinction is es-

[13] http://www.ordnancesurvey.co.uk/oswebsite/ontology/

[14] http://loki.cae.drexel.edu/~how/2004/09/hydrology

[15] In DOLCE terminology, the notion 'quality' is used instead of the notion 'property'

sential to identify cross-categorical relations as they can be used to derive from the sensor data an understanding of geo-processes occurring in the environment [9].

4. A Short Introduction to the DOLCE Foundational Ontology

We apply the general concepts from DOLCE to describe the surface hydrology domain concepts. We use the following typographical conventions to describe our ontological work:

- Categories and relations defined in DOLCE: **ENDURANT, HAS-PARTICIPANT…..**
- Categories at the domain level: `Precipitation, Lake, Soil…`

ENDURANT, PERDURANT, QUALITY and **ABSTRACT** are the four top level categories of DOLCE. Endurants are wholly present in each interval at which they exist [27], although they may change some or all of their attributes. **PHYSICAL OBJECT, AMOUNT OF MATTER, FEATURE** are kinds of **PHYSICAL ENDURANT** since they have direct spatial properties. On the other hand, **PERDURANTS** (i.e., **PROCESS, STATE, ACHIEVEMENT, ACCOMPLISHMENT**) are only partially present at any time at which they exist [27], i.e., some of their temporal parts (e.g., their previous or future phases) may not be present. **QUALITIES** are the entities we perceive or measure [27]. They depend on the entity they inhere in. Table 1 provides definitions of leaf categories in DOLCE which are related to our research.

Table 1. DOLCE Categories from [27]

Category	Definition	Examples
AMOUNTOFMATTER	Endurants with no unity; mereologically invariant - they change their identity when they change some parts.	Raindrops, Air, Soil
PHYSICALOBJECT	Endurants with unity; different types of objects have different unity criteria; objects do not depend on other objects for their existence.	Waterbody, Plant, Basin
PROCESS	Processes are (a) *cumulative* since the mereological sum of two instances of the same occurrence-type maintains the same occurrence-type (b) *weakly non-homeomeric* - some temporal parts of them are instances of the same most specific occurrent and some are not.	Precipitation, Wind, Infiltration
PHYSICALQUALITY	Physical qualities are dependent on the physical endurants in which they inhere. Physical endurants have a spatial location.	Volumetric flow rate, Depth and Slope of a River

The types of perdurants proposed in DOLCE resemble Vendler's verb classes in linguistics. Vendler [5] distinguishes between four kinds of verbs: verbs of *activity*, of *accomplishment*, of *achievement* and *stative* verbs. Similarly, DOLCE specifies the types of perdurants as **PROCESS, STATE, ACHIEVEMENT** and **ACCOMPLISHMENT**. The categories of perdurants are formed based on two aspects: *cumulativeness* and *homeomericity*. A perdurant type is *cumulative* if it holds of the mereological sum of two of its instances [27], and *homeomeric* if all its temporal parts can be described in the same way as the whole occurrence.

In this paper, we focus on the category **PROCESS**; the distinctions among other kinds of perdurants are therefore not explained. **PROCESS** is a kind of **PERDURANT** for which *cumulativity* and *weak non-homeomericity* hold. For example, *rain* is a process by which "water vapor in the atmosphere is returned to the Earth's surface as liquid drops" [18]. Thus, *rain* is classified as **PROCESS** because (a) the sum of two rain occurrences is still a rain occurrence, and (b) there are few temporal parts of rain occurrences which cannot be described in the same way used for a whole rain occurrence (consider an instant when ice crystals begin melting before they hit the ground; these instantaneous temporal parts of rain are not considered rain).

5. Basic Ontological Relations

The term *individual* (also called *particular*) refers to entities that cannot have instances (e.g., Lake St Clair in Tasmania), whereas the term *universal*[16] denotes entities that can have instances (e.g., the universal Forest may gain or lose instances, for example, due to deforestation). In this section, we describe the relations between the DOLCE categories **ENDURANT**, **PERDURANT,** and **QUALITY**, using examples from the hydrology domain.

5.1. Instantiation

The instantiation relation holds between individuals and universals. For example, 'South Esk River' is an instance of the universal `River` (a physical object), while 'Yesterday's Rain Showers' is an instance of the universal `Rain` (a process). The `River` is considered a kind of **PHYSICALOBJECT** since its instances, such as 'St Pauls River', are recognizable as single entities in hydrological sensor applications. `RiverFlow`, i.e., the movement of water in a river, is a kind of **PROCESS**.

5.2. Subsumption

In the subsumption relation between two universals, all individuals of a universal are necessarily individuals of another. For example, the universal `Stream` **SUBSUMES** the universal `Tributary`. This implies that to be a tributary the individual also needs to be a stream. Similarly for processes, the universal `Precipitation` (a process) **SUBSUMES** the universal `Snow` (a process).

5.3. Parthood

In DOLCE, parthood relations hold among concrete entities [27] (i.e., entities that exists at least in time such as objects, events, etc.). Two kinds of parthood relations can be differentiated. *Temporary parthood* is a relation between two **ENDURANTS** where one is part of the other at a particular time. For example, an individual endurant of kind `OrganicMatter` is **PART-OF** an individual endurant of kind `Soil` and this relation contains a reference to points in time. *A-temporal parthood* is a *time-independent* relation holding between two individuals of the categories **PERDURANT** or **ABSTRACT**.

[16] In DOLCE, the term 'universal' is reserved for those properties and relations whose instances are particulars [27]

For example, an individual perdurant `Melting` (i.e., a process of transformation of snowflakes into raindrops) is **PART-OF** an individual perdurant `Rain`.

5.4. Participation

In DOLCE, the **PARTICIPANT-IN** relation can only obtain between an **ENDURANT** and a **PERDURANT** and it is time-dependent [27]. The participation can be

- *Constant*: An individual endurant X participates in all parts of an individual perdurant Y. For instance, individual endurants `Water` and `PorousMaterial` participate in all parts of an individual perdurant `Percolation`.
- *Temporary*: An individual perdurant Y involves an individual endurant X in only some of its parts. For example, an individual endurant `River` participates in the final stage of an individual perdurant `Surface-Runoff`. It should be noted that the participating endurants are not part-of the perdurants. For instance, an individual endurant `Groundwater` is **PARTICIPANT-IN** a perdurant `Groundwater-Flow`; it is not part of it.

A process cannot occur without a participant. For example, *solar radiation* describes a process in which electromagnetic radiation emitted by the Sun filters through outer space and the Earth's atmosphere[17]. The participants of the process are the Sun, outer space, atmosphere, and particles or waves that carry the energy.

5.5. Inherence

A **PHYSICALQUALITY** can only **INHERE-IN** a **PHYSICALENDURANT** [27]. The inverse of this relation is the **HAS-QUALITY** relation. For example, individual physical qualities like `Depth, HydraulicRadius, Salinity` **INHERE-IN** an individual endurant `River`. An individual `River` has an individual **SPATIAL-LOCATION_Q** (a kind of the **PHYSICALQUALITY**) which identifies the position in space the object occupies. A **TEMPORALQUALITY** inheres in a **PERDURANT**. For example, an individual of `PrecipitationDuration` (a temporal property) inheres in an individual of `Precipitation` (a process).

6. Applying DOLCE to Surface Hydrological Processes

In this section, we identify two hydrological processes and then classify them in relation to the participating entities. The knowledge about these processes is extracted from standards [28-30], encyclopedias [18, 31] and glossaries [32, 33]. We align the domain concepts describing precipitation and evapotranspiration processes to the general categories defined in DOLCE. The result of our preliminary ontological work is available in OWL.[18] We focus here on the processes of precipitation and evapotranspiration, so that figures 2 and 3 only present the enduring entities and physical properties related to these two processes.

---

[17] http://en.wikipedia.org/wiki/Sunlight

[18] http://ifgi.uni-muenster.de/~a_deva01/publication.html

6.1. Precipitation Process

Figure 2 maps the precipitation process and its associated entities to basic categories in DOLCE. To be classified as precipitation, the liquid or solid form of water must both fall from the atmosphere and reach the ground [18]. Therefore, we classify `Rain`, `Snow`, `Drizzle`, `Sleet` and `Hail` as kinds of `Precipitation`. Virga is not a kind of precipitation since it evaporates before reaching the ground [18].

Each precipitation process involves several participants. For example, assuming instances of each process type have been specified, `Rain` involves **PHYSICALOBJECTS** such as `Land` (i.e., any portion of the earth's surface) as well as **AMOUNTSOFMATTER** such as `Cloud`, `RainDrops`, `SnowGrains`, and `SnowFlakes`. When an amount of snow grains and snowflakes falls into a layer of sufficiently warmer air, they melt into raindrops. `Cloud` is a kind of **AMOUNTOFMATTER** because it refers to the visible masses of water droplets and/or ice particles in the atmosphere.

Each of the enduring participants has physical properties. For example, `SnowFlakes` is a kind of **AMOUNTOFMATTER** which **HAS-QUALITY** such as `SnowAccumulation`, `SnowIntensity` and `SnowCover`. We classify the physical properties based on units relevant to hydrology in the SI system. `SnowAccumulation` is a kind of `LengthQ` since it refers to the depth of the snow on the ground accumulated either since the snow began falling or since a previous observation [32]. The `DimensionlessQ` specifies a physical property which has value without a physical unit and is thus a pure number. For example, `SnowCover` is a kind of `DimensionlessQ` (a physical quality) because it specifies the areal extent of snow-covered ground, expressed as percent of total area in a given region [32].

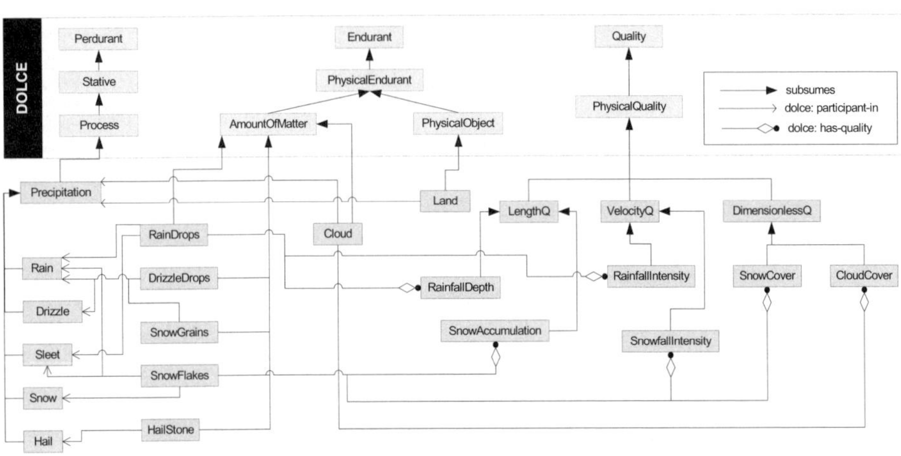

Figure 2. Precipitation process, its physical endurants and physical properties

The ontological work presented in figure 2 is useful to

a. retrieve the relevant geo-sensor data from multiple sources easily. For example, there can be various data sources capturing different types of precipitation, i.e., rain, snow over a region. These data may be stored in multiple locations and are not centralized into a single repository for easy access. In order to estimate the total volume of water delivered to a given region, the total precipitation within some period of time over a given region is required. The user then needs to identify the types of precipitation, query the data sources independently and combine the results. The relation between the precipitation data types and the precipitation process enables the user to retrieve all the precipitation-related data using a single query.

b. infer new facts. For instance, the user can identify the type of precipitation based on the **PHYSICAL QUALITY** `Diameter`. Rain drops have a diameter greater than 0.5mm while drizzle drops are considered to be less than 0.5mm [29].

6.2. Evapotranspiration Process

A perdurant is a proper part of another if it is part of it, but not vice versa. For example, evapotranspiration is a process that transports water into the atmosphere [31]. This process includes the evaporation process through which water is removed from wet surfaces (i.e., open water, soils and vegetation surfaces) and the transpiration process through which water is drawn up through the plant. Therefore, every instance of `evaporation` or `transpiration` is **PROPER-PART-OF** some instances of `evapotranspiration`. The participants of an evapotranspiration process include the participants of both evaporation and transpiration processes.

`Water` and `WaterVapour` are kinds of **AMOUNTOFMATTER** since none of them is an essential whole [27] (i.e they are not recognizable as isolated entities). On the other hand, `Reservoir` is kind of **PHYSICALOBJECT**[19] because it is an endurant with unity. `Reservoir` represents whole objects, since its instances like 'Lake Volta' are recognizable as single entities.

The individual endurant `Land` **HAS-QUALITY** `ActualEvapotranspiration` that is an individual physical quality. The actual evapotranspiration property belongs to the physical object `Land` since it refers to the water loss from a land surface due to the processes of evaporation and transpiration [31].The `EvaporationOpportunity` is a kind of `DimensionlessQ` since it specifies the ratio of the actual rate of evaporation from water surfaces to the potential evaporation under the existing conditions.

The term evapotranspiration is sometimes used interchangeably with evaporation, however, they differ in meaning[20]. Such process naming ambiguity can be resolved, for example, with the proper-parthood relation (Figure 3). This relation indicates that two processes are related, but not the same. Addressing only observed qualities, does not allow us to reason about when and where a process occurs. In DOLCE, since the temporal properties inhere in the perdurants and physical properties belong to the physical endurants, this allows flexibility in the query structure. For example, a user can construct a query like 'What is the amount of water lost through evaporation (a process) from a reservoir (a physical object) at a particular location (a physical property) on a specific day (a temporal property)?'

---

[19] In DOLCE, physical objects have no common unity criterion, since different subtypes of objects may have different unity criteria [27]

[20] http://www.bom.gov.au/climate/cdo/about/definitionsother.shtml

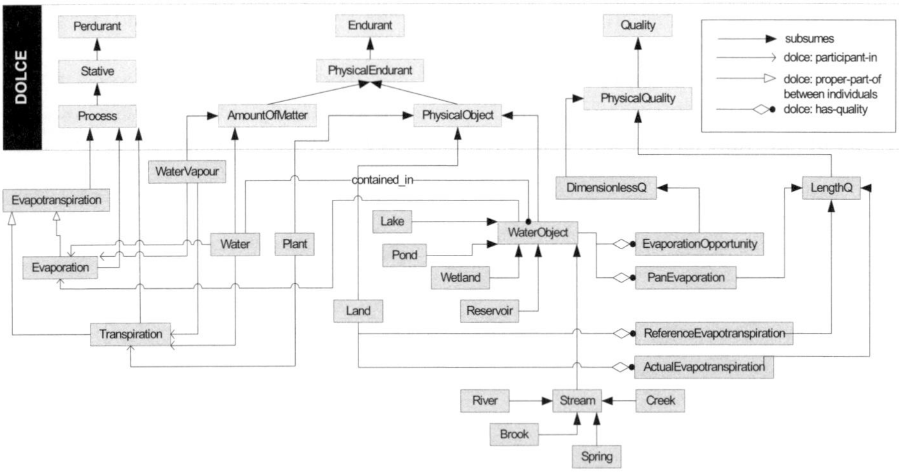

Figure 3. Evapotranspiration process, its physical endurants and physical properties

7. Discussion and Conclusions

Semantic heterogeneities in sensor data pose a challenge to users who want to use appropriate information for environmental modeling and forecasting. In this paper we claim that, to resolve them, it is essential to represent the processes that influence the observations. We have introduced a process-centric ontological approach to represent surface hydrology processes and their associated entities. We provide the ontological representation of two typical hydrological processes; they illustrate how a process-centric ontological approach can form a basis for integrating geo-sensor data as well as improve the understanding of processes in the environment. Specifically, our paper provides the following contributions:

a. We have shown that the DOLCE foundational ontology provides a useful framework by distinguishing occurrences, enduring entities, qualities, and their relations. We regard such distinctions as necessary in representing hydrological concepts. We have exemplified the alignment of concepts by describing two surface hydrological processes with DOLCE. These concepts are mapped to the basic categories in DOLCE using the subsumption, participation, inherence and parthood relations.
b. We have described how a process-centric ontological approach can be used to resolve process or property naming ambiguities. Thus, one process can be distinguished from other processes via participation relations with other entities. For instance, in contrast to the evaporation process, the transpiration process has different participants, such as plants which enable water to be transported through the stomata into the atmosphere.
c. We have shown that the relation between a process and its associated entities can be used to improve geo-sensor data retrieval. A hydro-process representation allows flexibility in the query structure (i.e., queries involving process, object and property). For example, the user is enabled to gain information on the duration of a precipitation process occurring in a region and on the amount of precipitation generated by the process.

During our ontology development, we have found several issues requiring further work:

a. The following are examples of temporary parthood (P) relations between two instances of endurants (assume that time is included) as depicted in the previous section. The parthood relation in DOLCE should be described by considering the three versions of parthood relations as advocated by [34].
   - Relation 1: P `(upstream, stream)`

   In this relation, every instance of `upstream` is part-of some instance of `stream`. Each instance of `stream` has an instance of `upstream` as its part.
   - Relation 2: P `(water well, aquifer)`

   Each instance of the `water well` stands in a part-of relation to some instance of `aquifer`. This relation claims that not each instance of `aquifer` has an instance of `water well` as a part.
   - Relation 3: P `(plant, wetland)`

   Each instance of `wetland` has some instance of `plant` as its part. This relation allows the fact that some instance of `plant` exists without being part-of the instance of `wetland`.

b. Although the relations at the level of individual (instance) are used to specify the relations of universals, it is vital to distinguish between individual-level and universal-level relations. Donnelly et al. [35] demonstrate that, in general, the logical properties of the universal-level relations do not match those of the instance-level relations.

c. Ongoing work focuses on a more detailed characterization of hydrological processes, specifying more of their participating endurants and related temporal and physical properties. This includes the representation of processes occurring in the upper soil zone such as surface runoff and infiltration.

d. In DOLCE, the parthood relation holds between two processes. For example, the `evapotranspiration` and `interception` processes are part of the `water loss` process. In representing hydrological processes, other types of relations between processes are also required besides the parthood relation. For example, a causal relation is needed to specify the relation between causal processes, i.e., the `precipitation` process *initiates* the `infiltration` process.

e. Another important direction for further work is to develop precise axiomatic characterizations of the relations depicted in the concept maps. Different kinds of participation relations between endurants and perdurants also will be investigated.

8. Acknowledgement

The research is funded through the International Research Training Group on Semantic Integration of Geospatial Information by the DFG (German Research Foundation), GRK 1498. The idea for this paper developed from the Summer Course 2009 - ‘Introduction to Formal and Applied Ontology’ taught by Thomas Bittner at the University of Muenster. We want to thank Thomas Bittner and our colleagues Krzysztof Janowicz and Jens Ortmann for fruitful discussions on our research topic. Reproduction of sensor figures from Wikipedia is also acknowledged.

References

[1] Kuhn, W., Geospatial Semantics: Why, of What, and How? , *Journal on Data Semantics III* **3534** (2005), 1-24.

[2] Hart, J.K. and K. Martinez, Environmental Sensor Networks: A revolution in the earth system science?, *Earth-Science Reviews* **78** (2006), 177-191.

[3] Guarino, N. and P. Giaretta, Ontologies and Knowledge Bases: Towards a Terminological Clarification, *Towards Very Large Knowledge Bases: Knowledge Building and Knowledge Sharing* (1995), 25-32.

[4] Steward, H., *The Ontology of Mind: Events, Processes, and States*, Oxford University Press, USA, 2000.

[5] Vendler, Z., *Linguistics in Philosophy*, Cornell University Press, Ithaca, 1967.

[6] James, F.A., Towards A General Theory of Action and Time, *Artificial Intelligence* **23**(2) (1984), 123-154.

[7] Bennett, B. and A. Galton, A Unifying Semantics for Time and Events, *Journal of Artificial Intelligence* **153**(1-2) (2004), 13-48.

[8] Pustejovsky, J., J. Castano, R. Ingria, R. Sauri, R. Gauzauskas, A. Setzer, and G. Katz, *TimeML: Robust Specification of Event and Temporal Expression in Text, IWCS-5, Fifth International Workshop on Computational Semantics*, 2003.

[9] Galton, A., *Processes and Events*, in *Encyclopaedia of GIS*, S. Shekhar and H. Xiong (eds.), Springer, 2008.

[10] Yuan, M., Representing Complex Geographic Phenomena in GIS, *Journal of Cartography and Geographic Information Science* **28** (2001), 83-96.

[11] Claramunt, C. and M. Theriault, *Toward semantics for modelling spatio-temporal processes within GIS, Proc. of International Symposiom on Spatial Data Handling (SDH'96)*, Netherlands, 1996.

[12] Galton, A. and M. Worboys, *Processes and Events in Dynamic Geo-Networks* In: A. Rodriguez, I. Cruz, Egenhofer, and L. M., S. (eds.): *Lecture Notes in Computer Science : Formal Representations for Geospatial Data*, pp. 45-59, Springer Berlin / Heidelberg, 2005.

[13] Worboys, M., Event-oriented approaches to geographic phenomena *International Journal of Geographical Information Science* **19**(1) (2005), 1-28.

[14] Wang, S., K. Nakayama, Y. Kobayashi, and M. Maekawa, *Considering events and processes within GIS: an event-based spatiotemporal data model*: In Proc. *IEEE International Symposium on Communications and Information Technology*, pp. 770 - 773 2004.

[15] Galton, A., Experience and History: Processes and their Relation to Events, *Journal of Logic and Computation* **18**(3) (2007), 323-340.

[16] Dias, T., G. Camara, F. Fonseca, and C. Davis, *Bottom-Up Development of Process-Based Ontologies, International Conference on Geographical Information Science (GIScience 2004)*, Washington, 2004.

[17] Worboys, M.F., *Modelling changes and events in dynamic spatial systems with reference to socio-economic units* In: A.U.R. Frank, J. and Cheylan (ed.): *Life and Motion of Socio-Economic Units (ESF GISDATA series)*, pp. 129-138, Taylor and Francis, 2001.

[18] Trimble, S.W., B.A. Stewart, and T.A. Howell, *Encyclopedia of Water Science (Second Edition)*, Taylor & Francis Group, 2008.

[19] Horsburgh, J.S., D.G. Tarboton, M. Piasecki, D.R. Maidment, I. Zaslavsky, D. Valentine, and T. Whitenack, An integrated system for publishing environmental observations data, *Environmental Modelling and Software* **24**(8) (2009), 879-888.

[20] Mackay, D.S., Semantic integration of environmental models for application to global information systems and decision-making, *SIGMOD Rec.* **28**(1) (1999), 13-19.

[21] Tague, C., *Heterogeneity in Hydrologic Processes: A Terrestrial Hydrologic Modeling Perspective*, In: G.M. Lovett, M.G. Turner, C.G. Jones, and K.C. Weathers (eds.): *Ecosystem Function in Heterogeneous Landscapes*, Springer New York, 2007.

[22] Broering, A., K. Janowicz, C. Stasch, and W. Kuhn, *Semantic Challenges for Sensor Plug & Play*, In: J.D. Carswell, S. Fotheringham, and G. McArdle (eds.): In Proc. *International Symposium on Web & Wireless Geographical Information Systems (W2GIS 2009)*, Maynooth, Ireland, pp. 72-86, Springer, 2009.

[23] Kuhn, W., *A Functional Ontology of Observation and Measurement*, In: K. Janowicz, M. Raubal, and S. Levashkin (eds.): In Proc. *Third Workshop on Geosemantics (GeoS 2009)*, Mexico City, pp. 26-43, Springer-Verlag Lecture Notes in Computer Science, 2009.

[24] Henson, C., H. Neuhaus, A. Sheth, K. Thirunarayan, and R. Buyya, *An Ontological Representation of Time Series Observations on the Semantic Sensor Web, 1st International Workshop on the Semantic Sensor Web 2009, collocated with the 6th European Semantic Web Conference (ESWC 2009)*, Herkalion, Greece, 2009.

[25] Ram, S., V. Khatrl, Y. Hwang, and S.R. Yool, Semantic modeling and decision support in hydrology, *Journal of Photogrammetric Engineering and Remote Sensing* **66**(10) (2000), 1229-1239
[26] Beran, B., *HYDROSEEK: An Ontology-Aided Data Discovery System for Hydrologic Sciences*, in *Department of Civil, Architectural and Environmental Engineering*, Drexel University, 2007.
[27] Masolo, C., S. Borgo, A. Gangemi, N. Guarino, A. Oltramari, and L. Schneider, *WonderWeb EU Project Deliverable D18: The WonderWeb Library of Foundational Ontologies*, Laboratory For Applied Ontology - ISTC-CNR, 2003.
[28] WMO, *Guide to Hydrological Practice - Data acquisition and processing analysis, forecasting and other applications (WMO-No. 168)*, World Meteorological Organization (WMO), 1994.
[29] WMO, *WMO Guide to Meteorological Instruments and Methods of Observation - WMO-No.8 (7th Edition)*, WMO, 2008.
[30] ISO/IEC, *Environmental Data Coding Specification* in *International Standard ISO/IEC 18025*, 2005.
[31] Cleveland, C.J. *Encyclopedia of Earth*. http://www.eoearth.org/
[32] AMS. *Glossary of Meteorology*. http://amsglossary.allenpress.com/glossary
[33] UNESCO, *International Glossary of Hydrology (Wmo/Omm/Vmo, No. 385)* 2nd Edition, Unipub, 1993.
[34] Bittner, T., M. Donnelly, and B. Smith, A Spatio-Temporal Ontology for Geographic Information Integration, *International Journal of Geographical Information Science* **23**(6) (2009), 765-798.
[35] Donnelly, M. and T. Bittner, *Spatial Relations Between Classes of Individuals*: *Spatial Information Theory*, pp. 182-199, 2005.

Formal Ontology in Information Systems
A. Galton and R. Mizoguchi (Eds.)
IOS Press, 2010

doi:10.3233/978-1-60750-535-8-213

A Well-Founded Software Measurement Ontology

Monalessa Perini BARCELLOS[a,b], Ricardo de Almeida FALBO[a] and Rodrigo DAL MORO[a]

[a] *Department of Computer Science, Federal University of Espírito Santo – Brazil*
[b] *COPPE, Federal University of Rio de Janeiro – Brazil*

Abstract. Software measurement is a relatively young discipline. As a consequence, it is not well defined yet, making the terminology used diverse. In order to establish a basic conceptualization regarding this domain, in this paper we present a Software Measur ement Ontology, developed grounded in the Unified Foundational Ontology.

Keywords. Domain Ontology, Foundational Ontology, Software Measurement Ontology

Introduction

Nowadays, software measurement is a key process for software project management and software process improvement. Measurement provides organizations with the objective information they need to make informed decisions that impact their business performance. Successful organizations use measurement as part of their day-to-day activities [1]. Depending on its maturity level, a software organization can perform measurement in different ways. In the initial maturity levels, such as the levels 2 and 3 of the Capability Maturity Model Integration (CMMI), the focus is on developing and sustaining a measurement capability that is used to support management information needs [2]. In high maturity levels, such as CMMI levels 4 and 5, measurement should be performed for the purpose of statistical process control, in order to understand the process behavior [3].

Considering this context, we started to work on a strategy to support organizations to obtain and maintain measurement repositories suitable for statistical process control, as well as to perform measurements appropriately in this context. This strategy is composed of two main components [4]: (i) *Instrument for Evaluating the Suitability of a Measurement Repository to Statistical Process Control*, which goal is to evaluate existing measurement repositories and to determine their suitability to statistical process control, identifying corrective actions, when necessary; and (ii) *Body of Recommendations for Software Measurement*, which aims to supply guidelines on how to perform measurement suitable for statistical process control. However, for both the instrument and the body of recommendations to be useful, people should agree on the same conceptualization regarding the software measurement domain. Thus, we added a third component to the strategy: a Software Measurement Ontology (SMO), which aims to capture the conceptualization involved in this domain, including traditional and high maturity aspects of software measurement. It should provide the basic vocabulary to be used in the other two components, also guiding their definition. Thus, we are looking for what Guizzardi [5] calls a domain reference ontology, i.e., an ontology that is constructed with the sole objective of making the best possible description of the domain in reality, with regard to a certain level of granularity and viewpoint.

A reference ontology is to be a special kind of conceptual model, an engineering artifact with the additional requirement of representing a model of consensus within a community. It is a solution-independent specification with the aim of making a clear and precise description of domain entities for the purposes of communication, learning and problem-solving. As a consequence, a reference ontology should be represented by an ontologically well-founded language [6]. Such a language must explicitly commit to fundamental ontological distinctions in their metamodels, given by a foundational ontology [6, 7]. Although recent research initiatives, such as [8, 9], have elaborated on the importance of foundational ontologies in the development of domain ontologies, such an approach has still not been broadly adopted.

Concerning the domain of software measurement, there are quite a few initiatives committed with ontology-based modeling and formalization of this domain, among them [10, 11]. Nonetheless, as a rule, such initiatives are not committed to the use of a foundational ontology as their basis, and, consequently, are obliged to rely on models of low expressivity.

For the reasons just mentioned, we decided to develop a Software Measurement Ontology (SMO), which is partially presented in this paper. In order to represent our ontology, we have used an ontologically well-founded UML modeling profile proposed in [7, 9]. This profile comprises a number of stereotyped classes and relations implanting a metamodel that reflects the structure and axiomatization of the Unified Foundational Ontology (UFO) [7, 9].

This paper is organized as follows: Section 1 provides a brief description of the software measurement domain; Section 2 introduces the ontological engineering approach employed in this work; Section 3 presents an overview of the SMO and presents in more details two of its sub-ontologies; Section 4 discusses related work; and finally, Section 5 concludes the paper.

1. A Brief Description of the Software Measurement Domain

Software Measurement is a primary tool for managing software life cycle activities, assessing the feasibility of project plans, and monitoring the adherence of project activities to those plans. It is also a key discipline in evaluating the quality of software products and the capability of organizational software processes [12].

The software measurement process includes, among others, the following activities: plan the measurement process, perform the measurement process, and evaluate measurement [12].

Software measurement should be driven by the information needs of the organization. Based on these information needs, first the organization has to define which entities (processes, products, resources and so on) will be the target of software measurement and which of their characteristics should be measured. Second, the organization has to define which measures are to be used to quantify those characteristics. Measures can be base measures, i.e., functionally independent of other measures, or derived measures, which are defined as a function of other measures. Once defined the measures, procedures for data collection, analysis and reporting should be defined. Finally, criteria for evaluating the collected data and the measurement process should be defined. Once the measurement is planned, it can be effectively performed. Measurement execution involves the application of the measurement procedures to get a value for each measure of a characteristic of an entity. Once data are collected, they should be analyzed using the analysis procedure, and the results should be communicated. Finally, the measurement process and its products should be evaluated in order to identify potential improvements.

Measurement provides the information required for decision making in several levels. Project managers, for instance, can use the information provided to perform a more efficient communication, to delineate the specific goals of the projects, to identify and solve problems in advance, and to make and justify key decisions. The organizations, in turn, can use the information provided to elaborate realistic plans for the projects, to compare the performance of the current projects with their plans, to guide the investments and process improvement decisions, and to aid to foresee if the ongoing projects will achieve the goals initially established [1].

As any relatively young discipline, software measurement is not well defined yet. When analyzing different proposal and standards, it becomes apparent that the terminology used is diverse. Many times, the same concept is designated by different terms in different proposals. Others, the same term refers to different concepts. In fact, the problem of terminology harmonization still needs to be solved [11]. In this context, a software measurement ontology, providing a set of coherent concepts, with the relations between them, and axioms constraining their interpretation, is of great value.

2. The Ontological Engineering Approach Employed

In order to develop the Software Measurement Ontology, partially presented in the next section, we have employed the SABiO (Systematic Approach for Building Ontologies) method [13, 14]. This method has been tested for the last ten years in the development of a number of domain ontologies in areas ranging from Harbor Management to Software Process to Electrocardiogram domain. SABiO prescribes an iterative process comprising the following activities: (i) *purpose identification and requirement specification* that concerns to clearly identify the ontology purpose and its intended uses, i.e., the competence of the ontology by means of competence questions; (ii) *ontology capture*, when relevant concepts, relations, properties and constraints should be identified and organized; (iii) *ontology formalization*, which comprises the definition of formal axioms in First-Order Logic; (iv) *integration of existing ontologies*, which involves the search for existing ontologies with reuse and integration in mind; (v) *ontology evaluation*, for identifying inconsistency as well as verifying the truthfulness with the ontology purpose; (vi) *ontology documentation*.

It is important to highlight that competence questions play a prominent role in this method by defining the scope and purpose of the domain conceptualization being developed, and serving as a testbed for ontology evaluation, since the competence questions are the questions the ontology is supposed to answer [13].

Another important feature of this method is that it suggests the use of a conceptual model written in a UML profile and a dictionary of terms to aid communication with domain experts. Concerning the UML profile, in this paper, we do not use the UML profile originally proposed by SABiO. Since our focus is on developing a domain reference ontology grounded in a foundational ontology, we have used an extension of the ontologically well-founded UML modeling profile proposed in [7, 9]. This profile comprises a number of stereotyped classes and relations implanting a metamodel that reflects the structure and axiomatization of the Unified Foundational Ontology (UFO) [7, 9]. UFO is a foundational ontology that has been developed based on a number of theories from Formal Ontology, Philosophical Logics, Philosophy of Language, Linguistics and Cognitive Psychology. It is composed by three main parts. UFO-A is an ontology of *endurants*. A fundamental distinction in UFO-A is between *Particulars (Individuals)* and *Universals (Types)*. Particulars are entities that exist in reality possessing a unique identity, while Universals are patterns of features, which can be realized in a number of different particulars [7]. UFO-B is an ontology of *perdurants* (events). The main distinction between perdurants and endurants is that endurants are wholly present or not, while perdurants happen in time [9]. UFO-C is an ontology of social entities (both endurants and perdurants) built on the top of UFO-A and UFO-B. One of its main distinctions is between *agents* and *objects*. Agents are capable of performing actions with some intention, while objects only participate in events [9].

A complete description of UFO falls outside the scope of this paper. However, in the sequel we give a brief explanation of its elements that are important for this paper. These elements are summarized in Figure 1.

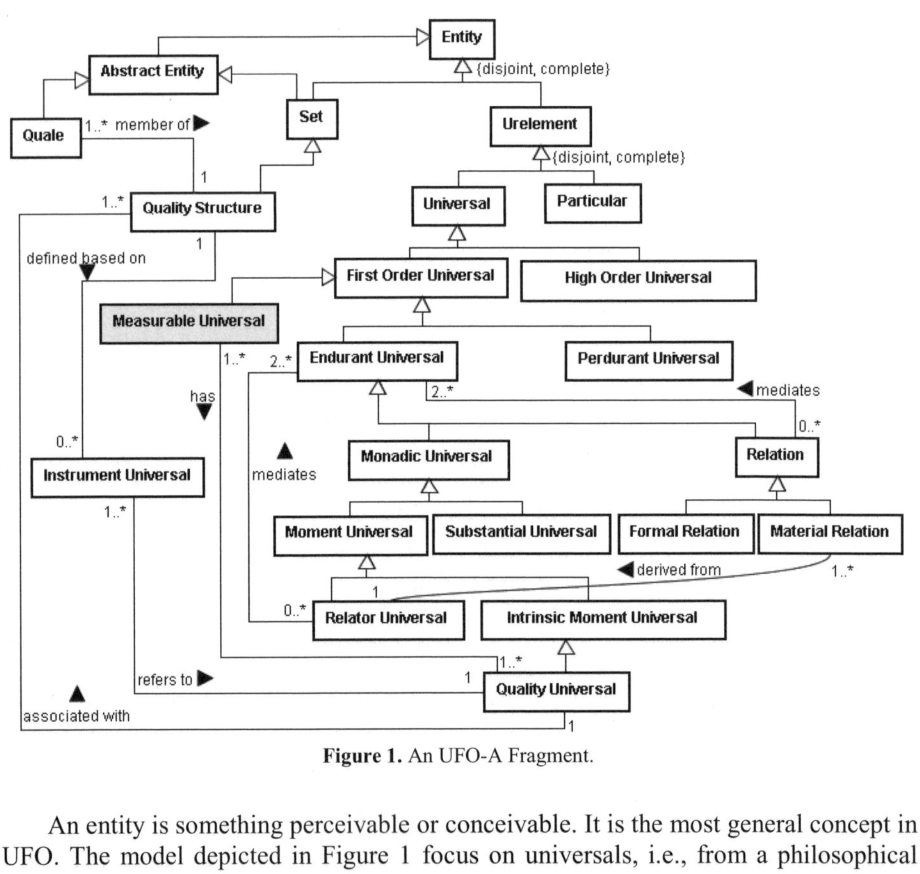

Figure 1. An UFO-A Fragment.

An entity is something perceivable or conceivable. It is the most general concept in UFO. The model depicted in Figure 1 focus on universals, i.e., from a philosophical standpoint, we are more interested in an ontology of universals, not in one of particulars. Universals are patterns of features, which can be realized in a number of different entities. They can be first order universals, i.e., universals whose instances are particulars, or high order universals, which are universals whose instances are also universals. Concerning first order universals, a fundamental distinction in UFO is the one between endurants and perdurants (events). Endurants persist in time maintaining their identity. Perdurants, in contrast, unfold in time with their multiple temporal parts.

Endurant universals can be monadic universals or relations. Monadic universals, in turn, can be further categorized into substantial universals and moment universals (properties). A moment is an endurant that is existentially dependent of another endurant, in the way, for example, that the color of an apple depends on the apple in order to exist. Existential dependence can also be used to differentiate intrinsic and relational moments. Intrinsic moments are dependent of one single endurant (e.g., color). Relators depend on a plurality of endurants (e.g., an employment) and, for this reason, provide the material connection between these endurants. In other words, we can say that they are the foundation for material relations such as "working at". Thus, material relations require relators in order to be established. Formal relations, in contrast, hold directly between individuals.

A quality universal is an intrinsic moment universal that is associated with a quality structure. Every quality universal is associated to a quality structure, which can be understood as a measurement structure (or a space of values) in which individual qualities can take their values. A quale is a point (a value) in a quality structure. For instance, the quality universal Weight is associated to a space of values that is a liner structure isomorphic to the positive half-line of the real numbers. For the same quality universal, there can be potentially many quality structures associated with it, but a quality structure is always associated with a unique quality universal. An instrument is used to associate a quality universal with values (qualia) in a quality structure. For a given quality universal, there can be different quality structures associated with different instruments.

In Figure 1, the concept Measurable Universal is shown detached in grey. It was introduced in UFO during this work to deal with the following situation: since both endurants and perdurants can be measurable entities, we introduce this concept as the class of entities that have some quality universal (i.e., an intrinsic moment that is associated with a quality structure).

Regarding substantial universals, as shown in Figure 2, while persisting in time, substantials can instantiate several substantial universals. Some of these types a substantial instantiates necessarily (i.e., in every possible situation) and define what the substantial is. These are the types named kind (for general substantials). There are, however, types that a substantial instantiates in some circumstances but not in other circumstances. These are named phases and roles. A phase is a type instantiated in a given time period but not necessarily in all periods. A role is a type instantiated in a given context, such as the context of a given event participation or a given relation. For instance, Person can be considered a kind, while Child and Adult would be phases of person, and Student would be a role that a person plays when enrolled in some educational institution. Finally, a category is a type that classifies substantials that belong to different kinds but that share a common essential property (i.e., a property that they must not lack). For instance, Rational Entity can be judge to represent an essential property that is common to all its instances and then it is a category.

Taking into account kinds, an important distinction in UFO is between agents and objects. According to UFO-C, an object kind is a non-agentive substantial universal. Its instances (objects) do not act. They can only participate in actions. Object kinds can also be further categorized into physical (e.g., Book) and social (e.g., Language). A normative description kind is a social object kind whose instances define one or more rules/norms recognized by at least one social agent (e.g., a method describing a set of directives on how to perform some activity within an organization).

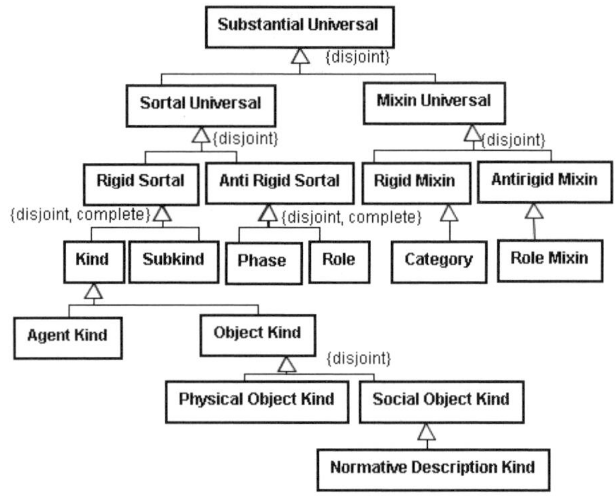

Figure 2. UFO´s Fragment related to Substantial Universals.

3. The Software Measurement Ontology (SMO)

According to SABiO, first we identified the SMO purpose. We want to capture the conceptualization involved in measurement in general, but also more specific aspects concerning measurement in high maturity levels. The main intended use of the SMO is to establish a common vocabulary to guide the definition of the strategy cited in the beginning of this paper. In this sense, the SMO should bring in a software measurement theory that is independent of specific applications. Although this is the main intended use of the SMO, we foresee its use also as a conceptual specification for developing and integrating supporting tools to the Measurement Process.

Since the software measurement domain is strongly related to the domains of software processes and organizations, we looked up to ontologies in these domains. We decided to use the software process ontology, which is grounded in UFO, described in [9]. In fact, the reuse of this ontology leads us to choose UFO as the foundational ontology to be use in our work. Concerning the domain of software organizations, we decided to reuse the software organization ontology proposed by Villela et al. [15]. This ontology, however, was not developed grounded in a foudational ontology, and thus, first, we reengineered it [16].

Since the scope of the SMO is very complex, we applied a decomposition mechanism allowing building the ontology in parts. The adopted strategy was to define sub-ontologies, starting from a core ontology, considering measurable entities and measures. From this core ontology, other five sub-ontologies were defined, each one treating some aspect as the way an organization performs measurement evolves. Thus the core ontology considers measurement in both initial and high maturity levels. The others sub-ontologies are more focused on aspects that are more important for measurement in high maturity levels. Figure 3 shows the sub-ontologies developed as UML packages, and their relationship as dependency relationships. In this figure the dependency relationships indicate that concepts and relations of a sub-ontology / ontology are used by another.

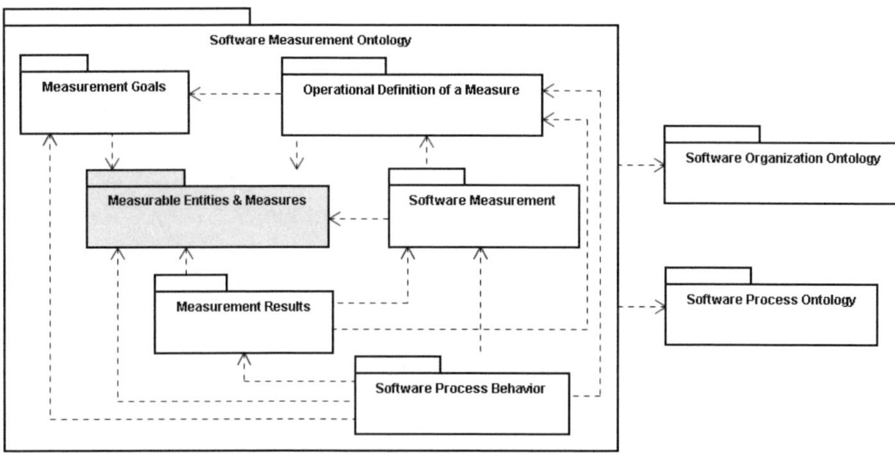

Figure 3. Sub-ontologies of the Software Measurement Ontology.

The Measurable Entities & Measures Sub-ontology treats the entities that can be submitted to measurement, their properties that can be measured and the measures used to measure them. As said before, it is the core of the SMO, and its concepts and relations are used by all the other sub-ontologies. The Measurement Goals Sub-ontology deals with the alignment of measurement to organizational goals. The Operational Definition of Measures Sub-ontology addresses the detailed definition of aspects related to measure collection and analysis established by an organization according with its measurement goals. The Software Measurement Sub-ontology refers to the measurement per se, i.e., collecting and storing data for measures. The Measurement Results Sub-ontology handles the analysis of the collected data for getting information supporting decision making. Finally, the Software Process Behavior Sub-ontology refers to applying the measurement results in the analysis of the behavior of the organizational software processes.

For each one of the sub-ontologies we accomplished the other steps of SABiO. As a result, the SMO ontology is composed of: (i) sets of competency questions, describing the sub-ontologies' requirements specification; (ii) structural conceptual models written in the ontologically well-founded UML profile defined based on UFO, capturing the concepts and relations of the sub-ontologies; (iii) a dictionary of terms, providing descriptions for each term in the ontology in natural language; and (iv) first order logic axioms, capturing constraints that are not captured by the conceptual models developed. With the sub-ontologies in hand, we needed to evaluate them. Since the SMO was not implemented in a programming language, such as OWL, we had to make the evaluation manually. For each competency question, we created an entry in a table showing the concepts, relations and axioms used to answer it. As a complementary way to evaluate the ontology, we also instantiate it with elements extracted from measure repositories of organizations.

Due to space limitation, in this paper it is not possible to present all sub-ontologies. Thus, in the rest of the paper we discuss part of the Measurable Entities & Measures Sub-ontology, presenting some of its competency questions, conceptual models and axioms. Also, part of its evaluation is shown. To this sub-ontology, several standards were considered, such as ISO/IEC 15939 [12], ISO/IEC 9126 [17], ISO/IEC 15504 [18], CMMI-Dev [2], Practical Software Measurement (PSM) [1], as well as other ontologies regarding the same domain, in special the one presented in [11].

As said before, the Measurable Entities & Measures Sub-ontology regards elements of entities (such as processes, artifacts and so on) that can be measured and the measures used to measure them. Basically, this sub-ontology should be able to answer, among others, the following competency questions:

- CQ1. Which are the types of entities that can be measured?
- CQ2. What is the type of a measurable entity?
- CQ3. Which are the measurable elements of a measurable entity?
- CQ4. Which are the measurable elements that characterize all measurable entities of the same type?
- CQ5. Which measurable elements can be directly measured?
- CQ6. From which other measurable elements can an indirectly measurable element be measured?
- CQ7. Which measures can be used to quantify a measurable element?
- CQ8. Which is the nature of a measure considering its dependency with others?
- CQ9. Which measures should be measured to compute a derived measure?
- CQ10. What is the scale of a measure?
- CQ11. What is the type of a scale?
- CQ12. Which are the values of a scale?
- CQ13. What is the measure unit of a measure?
- CQ14. Which are the measurement procedures that are applied to a measure?
- CQ15. Which are the measurement analysis procedures that are applied to a measure?
- CQ16. What are the calculation formulas used in a measurement procedure?
- CQ17. Which are the measures involved in a measure calculation formula?
- CQ18. Which measures are correlated to a given measure?

Figure 4 shows the conceptual model that addresses the competency questions CQ1 to CQ 12. In this figure, a **Measurable Entity** is anything that can be measure, such as processes, artifacts, projects and resources, and thus correspond to a *Measurable Universal* in UFO. Measurable entities can be classified according to types (**Measurable Entity Type**). For instance, process is a type of measurable entity. Although not shown in Figure 4, we use the Measure Entity Type as a specialization criterion, giving rise to a hierarchy of measurable entities. Thus, Measurable Entity Type is a *High Order Universal* in UFO, since its instances are, in fact, universals, more specifically subclasses of Measurable Entity.

As defined in UFO, *Measurable Universals* must have *Quality Universals*. In the case of SMO, these quality universals are **Measurable Elements**. All measurable entities of the same type should be characterized by the same measurable elements. For instance, projects can have their size measured. Thus, we say that a Measurable

Element characterizes a Measurable Entity Type, and the following axiom holds: If a measurable entity *men* is an instance of the measurable entity type *t* and *t* is characterized by the measurable element *mel*, then *mel* also characterizes *men* (**A1**).

$$(\forall men \in MeasurableEntity,\ t \in MeasurableEntityType,\ mel \in MeasurableElement)\ (instanceOf(men, t) \wedge characterizes(mel, t) \rightarrow characterizes(mel, men))$$

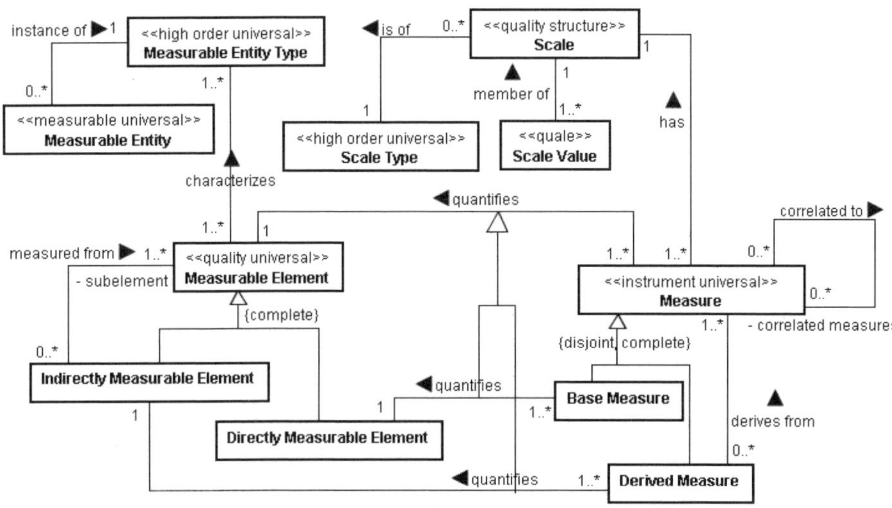

Figure 4. Fragment I of the Measurable Entities & Measures Sub-ontology.

Measurable Elements can be directly or indirectly measured. **Indirectly Measurable Elements** are measured by means of other measurable elements, said its sub-elements. The following axiom constrains the measurable elements that can be sub-elements of an indirectly measurable element: If a measurable element *mel* is sub-element of a indirectly measurable element *ime*, then *mel* and *ime* should characterize the same measurable entity type *t* (**A2**).

$$(\forall mel \in MeasurableElement,\ ime \in IndirectlyMeasurableElement)\ (subelement(mel, ime) \rightarrow (\exists t \in MeasurableEntityType)\ (characterizes(mel, t) \wedge characterizes(ime, t))$$

Moreover, the relation "*measured from*" is transitive, that is, if a measurable element *mel* is sub-element of an indirectly measurable element *ime1*, and *ime1* is sub-element of another indirectly measurable element *ime2*, then *mel* is also sub-element of *ime2* (**A3**).

$$(\forall ime1,\ ime2 \in IndirectlyMeasurableElement,\ mel \in MeasurableElement)\ ((subElement(mel, ime1) \wedge subElement(ime1, ime2) \rightarrow subElement(mel, ime2))$$

As discussed in Section 2, according to UFO, quality universals are associated with quality structures and instruments are used to associate a quality universal with values (qualia) in a quality structure. Based on this fragment of UFO, in the SMO, we consider a **Measure** as been an *Instrument Universal* that allows associating **Measurable Elements** (*Quality Universal*) with **Values** (*Quale*) of a **Scale** (*Quality Structure*). Thus a Measure quantifies a Measurable Element and has a Scale composed by Scale Values. Moreover, a Scale is of a **Scale Type**, which is a *High Order*

Universal, since its instances are, in fact, universals, more specifically subclasses of Scale (not shown in the model). Measures can be correlated to other measures, indicating, for instance, that they are related to the same goal, or that they have a cause-effect relationship and so on. Finally, Measures can be classified into **Base Measures**, which are functionally independent of other measures and used to quantify Directly Measurable Elements, and **Derived Measures**, which are defined as a function of other measures and used to quantify Indirectly Measurable Elements. Concerning the relationships between the subtypes of measures and measurable elements, the following axiom holds: If a derived measure *dme* quantifies an indirectly measurable element *ime* and *dme* derives from another measure *m*, then exists a measurable element *me* that is quantified by *m* and that is sub-element of *ime* (**A4**).

$$(\forall dme \in DerivedMeasure, m \in Measure, ime \in IndirectlyMeasurableElement)$$
$$(quantifies(dme, ime) \wedge derivesFrom(dme, m)) \rightarrow (\exists me \in MeasurableElement$$
$$(quantifies(m, me) \wedge subElement(me,ime)))$$

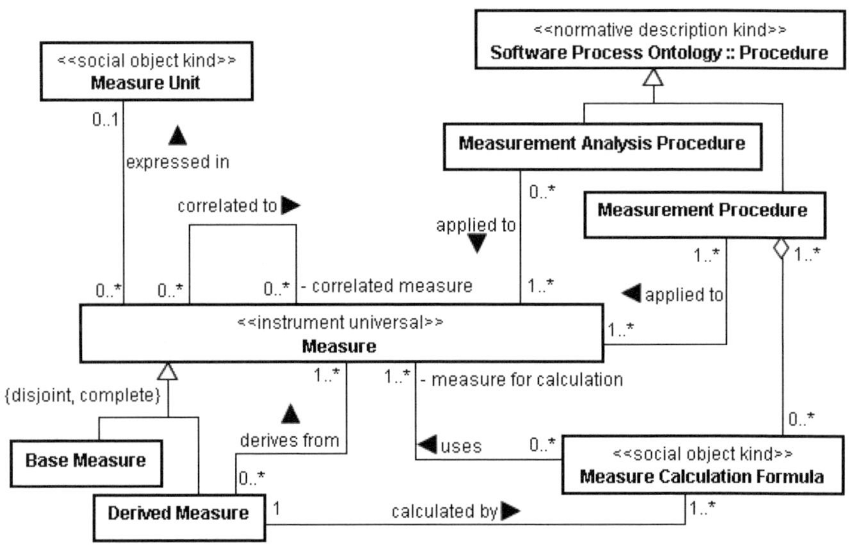

Figure 5. Fragment II of the Measurable Entities & Measures Sub-ontology.

Figure 5 shows the conceptual model that addresses the competency questions CQ13 to CQ 18. This figure shows that a **Measure** is expressed in a **Measure Unit**, which is a *Social Object Kind* in UFO. In order to guide measure collection and analysis, **Measurement Procedures** and **Measurement Analysis Procedures** are defined. Both are **Procedures** (a concept reused from the Software Process Ontology described in [9]), which is a *Normative Description Kind* in UFO, since a procedure defines one or more rules/norms recognized by at least the organization that adopts it. **Derived Measures** are calculated by **Measure Calculation Formulas**, which, in turn, uses other measures as measures for calculation. Those relations are constrained by the following axiom: if a derived measure *dme* is calculated by a measure calculation formula *mcf* that has a measure *m* as a measure for calculation, then *dme* is derived from *m* (**A5**).

$(\forall dme \in DerivedMeasure,\ m \in Measure,\ mcf \in MeasureCalculationFormula)$
$(calculatedBy(dme, mcf) \wedge measureForCalc(m, mcf) \rightarrow derivesFrom(dme, m))$

Concerning correlation between measures, when a derived measure *dme* is calculated by a measure calculation formula *mcf* that has another measure *m* as a measure for calculation, then *m* is a correlated measure of *dme* (**A6**).

$(\forall dme \in DerivedMeasure,\ m \in Measure,\ mcf \in MeasureCalculationFormula)$
$(calculatedBy(dme, mcf) \wedge measureForCalc(m, mcf) \rightarrow correlatedMeasure(m, dme))$

Finally, Measurement Procedures can aggregate Measure Calculation Formulas. Furthermore, if a derived measure *dme* is calculated by a measure calculation formula *mcf*, then there should be a measurement procedure *mp* applied to *dme* such as *mcf* is part of *mp* (**A7**).

$(\forall dme \in DerivedMeasure, mcf \in MeasureCalculationFormula)\ (calculatedBy(dme, mcf) \rightarrow (\exists mp \in MeasurementProcedure\ (appliedTo\ (mp,dme) \wedge partOf(mcf,mp))))$

As said before, to evaluate the ontology, we related the concepts, relations and axioms of the SMO to the competency questions answered by them, as well as we used individuals (extracted from measure repositories of organizations) to evaluate if the ontology was actually able to represent concrete situations of the real world. Table 1 shows part of the table developed to evaluate the ontology, considering competency questions CQ 6 and CQ 9.

Table 1. Evaluating the SMO

CQ	Concept 1	Relation	Concept 2	Axioms
6	Indirectly Measurable Element	is subtype of	Measurable Element	A2, A3
	Indirectly Measurable Element	measured from	Measurable Element (sub-element)	
	Measurable Element	characterizes	Measurable Element Type	
9	Derived Measure	derives from	Measure	A4
	Indirectly Measurable Element	is subtype of	Measurable Element	
	Directly Measurable Element	is subtype of	Measurable Element	
	Measure	quantifies	Measurable Element	
	Indirectly Measurable Element	measured from	Measurable Element	

Concerning CQ 6 – From which other measurable elements can be an indirectly measurable element measured? – the relation "*measured from*" is the main responsible for answering this question. However, this relation is constrained by the types of the indirectly measurable element and its sub-elements (A2). Also, axiom A3, which says that this relation is transitive, acts on the answer of this competency question.

Regarding CQ 9 – Which measures should be measure to compute a derived measure? – the relations "*derives from*" and "*quantifies*" (including its subtypes not shown in Table 1) are the main responsible for answering this question. These relations should respect axiom A4 that establishes a relationship between the measures used to compute a derived measure and the sub-elements from which the corresponding indirectly measurable element is measured from.

Finally, some instantiations were also used to evaluate the SMO. In this paper we discuss measurement aspects related to measuring an organizational Requirements Management Process. The Requirements Management Process of the Organization X (a Measurable Entity) is a Requirements Management Process (Measurable Entity Type), which is characterized, among others, by Requirements Stability (Indirectly Measurable Element). Requirements Stability is measured from Agreed Requirements and Changed Requirements (both Directly Measurable Elements). Requirements Change Rate is a Derived Measure used to quantify Requirements Stability. Its scale is the real interval ranging from 0 to 1 and, thus, it is a Ratio Scale (Scale Type). The Requirements Change Rate is derived from two base measures: Number of Agreed Requirements and Number of Changed Requirements, which in turn quantifies the elements Agreed Requirements and Changed Requirements, respectively. The Measure Calculation Formula applied to compute the Requirements Change Rate is: Requirements Change Rate = Number of Changed Requirements / Number of Agreed Requirements. Number of Agreed Requirements and Number of Changed Requirements are correlated measures of Requirements Change Rate. The measurement procedure used to measure Requirements Change Rate is to compute the measure calculation formula described above in the period comprised between two Requirements Specification Agreements. The measurement analysis procedure establishes that the value obtained should be analyzed in order to see if it diverges significantly from values obtained in similar projects of the organization. If this is true, the causes should be investigated and corrective actions should be accomplished.

4. Related Work

As said in the introduction of this paper, there are quite a few initiatives related to developing ontologies for the Software Measurement domain. The two most known are the one proposed by Martín and Olsina [10], called here MO-ontology, and the one proposed by Bertoa, Vallecillo and García [11], called here BVG-ontology. Our Measurable Entities & Measures Sub-ontology has many commonalities with these two ontologies, since they are inspired in some common sources, such as ISO/IEC 15939 [12]. Nevertheless, both initiatives are not committed to a foundational ontology.

Concerning the similarities, there are many common concepts, such as concepts related to measurable entities (entities in the MO and BVG-ontology), measures (metrics in the MO-ontology, and measures in BVG-ontology), measurable elements (attributes in the MO and BVG-ontology), scale and procedures (methods in the MO-ontology and approaches in the BVG-ontology). However, there are also many differences. Entities, both in MO and BVG-ontology, are considered to be composed of sub-entities. The whole-part relation used, however, is not in conformance with the whole-part theory discussed in UFO. Moreover, we do not agree with this relation. For example, people acting as a human resource role (role in the sense of UFO) can be considered a measurable entity. But they do not have sub-entities. Thus, in our SMO ontology we decided not to include this relation.

In MO-ontology, Numerical Scale (a subtype of Scale) is expressed in one or more Units. For us (and also in the BVG-ontology), measures are expressed in measure units, not scales. Further considering scales, UFO says that a quality structure has one or more qualia as members. Thus, since scales are quality structures, it is essential to model scale values as a concept in the SMO, what is not done in both MO and BVG-ontology.

Another problem is the concept of Indicator. In our view, although not discussed in this paper, an Indicator is a role (in the sense of UFO) that a measure plays when used to indicate the achievement of a goal. In MO-ontology, there is no relationship between measure and indicator. In BVG-ontology Indicator is considered a sub-type of Measure, but there isn't anything saying that it is a role. The consequence is that this conceptualization does not capture that all indicators must be associated to a goal, since it is this relationship that characterizes the role itself. Although not presented in this paper, in our SMO ontology, an Indicator is always associated with an Objective, which in turn is related to an Information Need. In the BVG-ontology, an indicator can be (or not) associated with an Information Need.

Both MO and BVG-ontologies use the concept of "Measurable Concept" with the following definition borrowed from ISO/IEC 15939: "Abstract relationship between attributes of entities and information needs". In our view, this definition does not make sense. In the best case, according to UFO, it would be a relator, since relators mediate the relata of a material relation. However, this concept is not clear, and thus we prefer not to include it in our SMO.

In our SMO we distinguish between directly and indirectly measurable elements. Both MO and BVG-ontologies do not do that. Moreover, considering the whole SMO (and not only its core sub-ontology), our SMO treats many other aspects that are not the target of those ontologies. Also, both MO and BVG-ontologies do not discuss constraints, and consequently axioms formalizing them.

In fact, there are several differences between our SMO and the MO and BVG-ontologies. Due to the limitations of space, in this paper it is not possible to discuss all of them in details. However, as a main conclusion, we claim that the use of UFO as a foundational ontology for supporting the development of a domain reference ontology was of great value and a distinction point of our work when compared with these two others. It allowed identifying several problems and drove the ontology engineering process, making explicit ontological commitments that were implicit and elucidating conceptual mistakes.

5. Conclusions

Although several researchers argue in favor of using a foundational ontology as a basis for developing domain ontologies, among them Guarino [19], Guizzardi and colleagues [9] and Fielding and colleagues [8], few works have explored this use. This is the case of the Software Measurement domain, which the proposed ontologies are in general lightweight ontologies, that are not grounded in foundational ontologies. In this paper we presented a Software Measurement Ontology (SMO) developed based on the Unified Foundational Ontology [7, 9]. UFO was chosen because it has been used to evaluate, re-design and integrate (meta) models of conceptual modeling languages, as well as to evaluate, re-design and give real-world semantics to domain ontologies [9].

The proposed ontology is used to establish a common vocabulary used in a strategy to support organizations to obtain and maintain measurement repositories suitable for statistical process control, as well as to perform measurements appropriately in this context. This strategy is composed of three components [4]: the SMO itself, an Instrument for Evaluating the Suitability of a Measurement Repository to Statistical Process Control, and a Body of Recommendations for Software Measurement. The instrument has already been evaluated by experts and used in real cases. The preliminary results point out to its usefulness and also for an agreement of the vocabulary used. The body of recommendations is ready and now it is being evaluated by experts. The feedback given by them will conclude our preliminary evaluation of the vocabulary used and, as a consequence, of the ontology.

As future work, we intend to use the proposed SMO as a conceptual specification for developing and integrating tools supporting the Measurement Process, both in initial and high maturity levels.

References

[1] J. McGarry, D. Card, C. Jones, B. Layman, E. Clark, J. Dean, F. Hall, *Practical Software Measurement: Objective Information for Decision Makers*, Addison-Wesley, Boston USA, 2002.

[2] CMMI Product Team, *CMMI for Development Version 1.2*, Software Engineering Institute, Pittsburgh USA, 2006.

[3] W.A. Florac, A.D. Carleton, *Measuring the Software Process: Statistical Process Control for Software Process Improvement*, Addison-Wesley, Boston USA, 1999.

[4] M.P. Barcellos, A.R.C. Rocha, R.A. Falbo, An Ontology-based Approach for Software Measurement and Suitability Measures Basis Evaluation to Apply Statistical Software Process Control in High Maturity Organizations, Proceedings of the ER2009 PhD Colloquium, Gramado, Brazil, 2009.

[5] G. Guizzardi, On Ontology, ontologies, Conceptualizations, Modeling Languages and (Meta)Models, In O. Vasilecas, J. Edler, A. Caplinskas (Org.). *Frontiers in Artificial Intelligence and Applications, Databases and Information Systems IV*. IOS Press, Amsterdam, 2007.

[6] V. Zamborlini, B. N. Gonçalvez, G. Guizzardi, Codification and Application of a Well-Founded Heart-ECG Ontology, Proceedings of the 3rd Workshop on Ontologies and Metamodels in Software and Data Engineering, Campinas, Brazil, 2008.

[7] G. Guizzardi, *Ontological Foundations for Structural Conceptual Models*, Universal Press, The Netherlands, 2005.

[8] J.M. Fielding, J. Simon, W. Ceusters, B. Smith, Ontological Theory for Ontology Engineering, Proceedings of the Ninth International Conference on the Principles of Knowledge Representation and Reasoning, Whistler, Canada, 2004.

[9] G. Guizzardi, R.A Falbo, R.S.S. Guizzardi, Grounding Software Domain Ontologies in the Unified Foundational Ontology (UFO): The case of the ODE Software Process Ontology. In Proceedings of the XI Iberoamerican Workshop on Requirements Engineering and Software Environments, 2008, 244-251.

[10] M.A.Martin, L. Olsina, Towards an Ontology for Software Metrics and Indicators as the Foundation for a Cataloging Web System, First Latin American Web Congress, 2003.

[11] M.F. Bertoa, A. Vallecillo, F. García, An Ontology for Software Measurement, In: C. Calero, F. Ruiz, M. Piatini (Eds.), *Ontologies for Software Engineering and Software Technology*, Springer-Verlag Berlin Heidelberg, 2006.

[12] ISO/IEC 15939, Systems and Software Engineering – Measurement Process, 2007.

[13] R.A. Falbo, C.S. Menezes, A.R.C. Rocha, A Systematic Approach for Building Ontologies. Proceedings of the 6th Ibero-American Conference on Artificial Intelligence, Lisbon, Portugal, Lecture Notes in Computer Science, vol. 1484, 1998.

[14] R.A. Falbo, Experiences in Using a Method for Building Domain Ontologies. In: Proc. of the 16th International Conference on Software Engineering and Knowledge Engineering, International Workshop on Ontology In Action. Banff, Canada, 2004.

[15] K. Villela, A.R. Rocha, G.H. Travassos et al., The Use of an Enterprise Ontology to Support knowledge Management in Software Development Environments. *Journal of the Brazilian Computer Society*, Brazil, 11(2): 45-59, 2005.

[16] M.P. Barcellos, R.A. Falbo, Using a Foundational Ontology for Reengineering a Software Enterprise Ontology. Proceedings of the Joint International workshop on Metamodels, Ontologies, Semantic Technologies, and Information Systems for the Semantic Web, 2009.

[17] ISO/IEC 9126, Software Engineering – Product Quality, 2001.

[18] ISO/IEC 15504, Information Technology – Process Assessment, 2003.

[19] N. Guarino, Formal Ontology and Information Systems. In Proceedings of International Conference in Formal Ontology and Information Systems, pp 3-15, 1998.

Formal Ontology in Information Systems
A. Galton and R. Mizoguchi (Eds.)
IOS Press, 2010

doi:10.3233/978-1-60750-535-8-227

SCOPE: A Situation Calculus Ontology of Petri Nets

Xing TAN [1]
Semantic Technologies Laboratory, Department of Mechanical and Industrial Engineering, University of Toronto

Abstract. By axiomatizing the semantics of Petri nets as a first-order (mostly) formal ontology called SCOPE, we propose in this paper a framework for the analysis of the structural and dynamical properties of Petri nets. More precisely, SCOPE is built as a Basic Action Theory in Reiter's version of situation calculus. In addition, we show the satisfiability of SCOPE, by virtue of the Relative Satisfiability Theorem. Fundamental structural and dynamical properties of Petri nets described in SCOPE are also presented, with two example uses of SCOPE given.

Keywords. Petri Nets, Situation Calculus, Basic Action Theory, Ontology, Model Characterization

Introduction

Petri nets as a powerful modeling tool have long been used to describe complex dynamical systems that involve concurrency, nondeterminism, asynchronism, and intense interactions between events and agents in these systems. The simple formalism that Petri nets offer has enabled unambiguous graphical representations of Petri nets and facilitated studies on the properties of Petri nets with mathematical rigor.

One recent application of Petri nets is within the context of the semantic Web, where, in contrast to the current Web, the semantics of the content and capability are well-defined such that they are machines-interpretable, enabling automation of a variety of different operations currently performed by human-beings in essence. In practice, Petri nets have shown to be quite handy in providing the operational semantics of certain class of Web services, i.e., Web-accessible service programs or devices. For example, in [4], in order to automatically describe, compose, simulate, and verify the Web service compositions, a Petri net formalism is employed to describe the operational semantics of DARPA Agent Markup Language-Services (DAML-S), a logic language describing Web services, after the descriptive semantics of DAML-S is first specified by situation calculus. Our thesis is that, Petri nets should have much broader applicability for the semantic Web. The rationale for this claim is that the logic action language situation calculus, particularly its variant as comprehensively studied by Reiter and et al. ([9], [10]), provides a simple but mathematically rigorous paradigm for axiomatization of dynamical systems, making it presumably an easy task to develop a situation-calculus-

[1]E-mail: xtan@mie.utoronto.ca.

based Petri nets action theory. As such, we propose in this paper SCOPE, a situation-calculus-based ontology of Petri nets.

SCOPE is introduced in Section 3 of this current paper. It adopts the simplicity of original Petri nets: it contains only one action type, namely, firing of transitions; whereas only one function value, namely the number of tokens at places, is subject to the change upon actions. We argue in this section the explicit applicability of certain assumption (the *causal completeness assumption*, to be precise) for the development of SCOPE. By proving that SCOPE satisfies both the unique formula requirement and the function consistency property, we show in addition that SCOPE is a Basic Action Theory, which qualifies the applicability of the Relative Satisfiability Theorem on SCOPE in Section 4.

In Section 4, we characterize a class of combinatorial structures and prove both the satisfiability theorem and the axiomatizability theorem for the class; that is, respectively, every structure in the class is a model for some subset of SCOPE axioms (including unique name axioms for actions and all axioms that are uniform in the initial state) and every model for the subset is isomorphic to some structure in the class. By applying the Relative Satisfiability Theorem, we also have that such a model can be extended to a model for all SCOPE axioms. In other words, SCOPE is satisfiable.

Other sections of this paper are as follows. Section 1 and Section 2 provide brief introductions to Petri nets and Reiter's situation calculus, respectively. Section 5 further provides a set of axiomatization to the structure constraints and mathematical properties of Petri nets and includes two examples of SCOPE use cases. Section 6 summarizes the paper.

1. Petri Nets

Petri nets and their markings are defined in Section 1.1, whereas several dynamical properties of Petri nets and structurally restricted subclasses of Petri nets are introduced in Section 1.2.

1.1. Basic Definitions

Definition 1 *A Petri net (PN) is a pair* (N, M_0) *where N is a triple* (P, T, F) *such that*

- P *is a finite set of node elements called places;*
- T *is a finite set of node elements called transitions;*
- *and* $F \subseteq (P \times T) \cup (T \times P)$ *consists of ordered pairs;*

and M_0 *is the initial marking, a mapping in the form* $M\colon P \to \mathcal{N}$*, indicating the initial assignment of a non-negative integer* k *to each place* p *in* P*. (In this case, we say that the place* p *is marked with* k *tokens.)*

In general, any marking M *for* N *in* PN *is defined as a vector* $(M(p_1), \ldots, M(p_m))$ *where* $p_1, \ldots, p_m$ *is an enumeration of* P *and* $M(p_i)$ *tokens are assigned to node* p_i*, for all* i *such that* $1 \leq i \leq m$*.*

The elements in $P \cup T$ are generically called nodes of PN. Given a node $u \in PN$, the set ${}^\bullet u = \{v|(v,u) \in F\}$ is the pre-set of u, where each v is the input of u, and the set $u^\bullet = \{v|(u,v) \in F\}$ is the post-set of u, where each v is the output of u. At any marking M, a place p is marked if $M(p) > 0$. A transition t is enabled in M if every place in ${}^\bullet t$ is marked in M. Enabled transition in M can occur (fire), leading to the successor marking M'.

Definition 2 *A marking transition from M to M' due to the firing of t (written as $M \stackrel{t}{\Longrightarrow} M'$) is defined by*

$$M'(p) = \begin{cases} M(p) - 1 & \textit{if } p \in {}^\bullet t \textit{ and } p \notin t^\bullet \\ M(p) + 1 & \textit{else if } p \notin {}^\bullet t \textit{ and } p \in t^\bullet \\ M(p) & \textit{otherwise} \end{cases}$$

for every place p.

Graphically, a Petri Net PN can be represented by a bipartite graph, where each place is represented by a circle, each transition is represented by a rectangle, the flow relation of the Petri net F is represented by arcs from places to transitions or from transitions to places, and k black dots will be placed into the rectangle for place p if it is marked with k tokens at M. Figure 1 (A) is a PN example where transitions T1 and T2 can be interpreted as *switch on* and *switch off*, respectively.

1.2. Petri Nets Properties

The concept of reachable marking is essential to the description and analysis of all properties (such as reachability, k-boundedness, and reversibility, as defined below) of Petri nets.

Definition 3 (reachable marking) *The transition (firing) sequence $\sigma = t_1, ..., t_m$ is a sequence of transition nodes in T; a σ is an occurrence sequence of a given Petri net $PN = (N, M_0)$ if $M_0 \stackrel{t_1}{\Longrightarrow} M_1$, ..., $M_{m-1} \stackrel{t_m}{\Longrightarrow} M_m$ (written as $M \stackrel{\sigma}{\Longrightarrow} M_m$). Also, we write $M \stackrel{*}{\Longrightarrow} M'$ and call M' is reachable from M if there exists a firing sequence σ such that $M \stackrel{\sigma}{\Longrightarrow} M'$. The set of all markings reachable from M is denoted by $R(N, M)$.*

Definition 4 (Reachability) *The reachability problem for Petri nets is the problem of finding, given a Petri net (N, M_0) and a marking M in it, if $M \in R(N, M_0)$.*

Definition 5 (k-boundedness) *Given a Petri net (N, M_0), the k-boundedness problem involves checking whether the number of tokens in each place does not exceed the integer k for any marking reachable from M_0. A 1-bounded Petri net is also said to be "1-safe".*

Definition 6 (Liveness) *A Petri net (N, M_0) is live if, for any marking $M \in R(N, M_0)$, there exists another marking M', such that $M \stackrel{*}{\Longrightarrow} M'$, i.e., M' is reachable from M.*

Definition 7 (Reversibility/Cycleness) *A Petri net (N, M_0) is reversible if M_0 is reachable from each $M \in R(N, M_0)$.*

Definition 8 (Coverability) *A Petri net (N, M_0) is coverable if there exists a marking $M' \in R(N, M_0)$ such that for any $p \in P$, $M'(p) \geq M_0(p)$.*

Definition 9 (Persistency) *A Petri net (N, M_0) is persistent if, for any $t_1 \in T$ and $t_2 \in T$, which are both enabled at any $M \in R(N, M_0)$, t_2 should still be enabled in M' where $M \stackrel{t_1}{\Longrightarrow} M'$.*

Given that Petri nets as a modeling language has rich expressive power, evaluating properties of a Petri net is often computationally expensive, if possible. However, the difficulty is largely reduced if we are dealing with certain subclasses of Petri Nets where their graphical structures are highly constrained. The properties of the subclasses of Petri nets defined as follows have been thoroughly studied.

Definition 10 *A Petri net $PN = (N, M_0)$, where N is (P, T, F), is an S-system if* $|{}^\bullet t| = |t^\bullet| = 1$ *for every* $t \in T$.

Definition 11 *A Petri net $PN = (N, M_0)$, where N is (P, T, F), is a T-system if* $|{}^\bullet p| = |p^\bullet| = 1$ *for every* $p \in P$.

Definition 12 *A Petri net $PN = (N, M_0)$, where N is (P, T, F), is a conflict-free system if* $p^\bullet \subseteq {}^\bullet p$ *for every place* p *with more than one output transition.*

Definition 13 *A Petri net $PN = (N, M_0)$, where N is (P, T, F), is a free-choice system if* $(p, t) \in F$ *implies* ${}^\bullet t \times p^\bullet \subseteq F$ *for every place* p *and every transition* t.

Later we will show, in Section 5.1, that all of these above properties or subclasses can be represented easily in SCOPE.

2. Reiter's Situation Calculus

2.1. Brief Introduction

The situation calculus is a logical language for representing changes upon actions in a dynamical domain; it is first proposed by McCarthy and Hayes in 1969 [6]. The language $\mathcal{L}$ of situation calculus as stated by [10] is a second-order many-sorted language with equality.

Three disjoint sorts: *action*, *situation*, *object* (for everything else in the specified domain) are included in the language $\mathcal{L}$. For example, *rain* denotes the act of raining, and $putdown(x, y)$ denotes the act of object x putdown y on the ground. A *situation* characterizes a sequence of actions in the domain. The constant situation S_0 is to denote the empty sequence of actions, whereas the function symbol *do* is introduced to construct the term $do(a, s)$, denoting the successor situation after performing action *a* (such as, in a weather simulation scenario, *rain*) in situation s. The situation term $do(sunshine, do(rain, s))$ denotes the situation resulting from first $rain$ and then $sunshine$, which distinguishes itself from the other situation term $do(rain, do(sunshine, s))$.

The binary predicate $\sqsubset$ specifies the order between situations. For example, $s \sqsubset s'$ stands for that the situation s' can be reached by performing one or several actions from s. $s \sqsubseteq s'$ is an abbreviation of $s \sqsubset s' \vee s = s'$. In addition, a predicate $Poss(a, s)$ is applied to specify the legality of performing action a in situation s, For example, $Poss(rain, s) \supset heavyCloudy$ says that it is possible to rain only if the sky is with heavy cloud.

In a particular domain, the language might contain situation independent relations, like $matchLocation(Toronto)$, and situation independent functions, like $size(Plot2)$.

However, in many of the more interesting cases, the values of relations and functions change between situations; accordingly, a relational fluent, or a functional fluent, in $\mathcal{L}$ is defined as a predicate, or a function, respectively, whose last argument is always a situation (e.g., $captain(John, do(catchFever, S_0))$ is a relational fluent, whereas $weight(John, do(recover, s))$ is a functional fluent).

A particular class of situation calculus theories called the Basic Action Theories is specified in [10] (also briefly presented in the subsequent section), where nice computational properties holds for operating regression on sentences satisfying certain conditions. For situation calculus at an introductory level, readers are referred to [2] and [1], where each includes a chapter of situation calculus. In-depth discussion is included in [10].

2.2. Basic Action Theories

The foundational axioms captures the concept of situation tree in a domain, whereas the Basic Action Theories are special situation calculus theories where nice theoretical and computational properties, such as the Relative Satisfiability Theorem, hold. (see [10] for more details.)

Definition 14 *The set $\mathcal{D}_f$ consists of four foundational axioms as follows*

$$do(a_1, s_1) = do(a_2, s_2) \supset a_1 = a_2 \wedge s_1 = s_2 \tag{1}$$

$$(\forall P).P(S_0) \wedge (\forall a, s)\big(P(s) \supset P(do(a, s))\big) \supset (\forall s)P(s) \tag{2}$$

$$\neg s \sqsubset S_0 \tag{3}$$

$$s \sqsubset do(a, s') \equiv s \sqsubseteq s' \tag{4}$$

Definition 15 *A basic action theory $\mathcal{D}$ is a collection of several sets of axioms as follows:*

$$\mathcal{D} = \mathcal{D}_f \cup \mathcal{D}_{ss} \cup \mathcal{D}_{ap} \cup \mathcal{D}_{una} \cup \mathcal{D}_{S_0}$$

where

- *$\mathcal{D}_f$ is the set of foundational axioms;*
- *$\mathcal{D}_{ss}$ is the set of successor state axioms for functional and relational fluents and*
  - ∗ *each relational fluent axiom is of the form*

    $$F(x_1, \ldots, x_n, do(a, s)) \equiv \Phi_F(x_1, \ldots, x_n, a, s)$$

    where $\Phi_F(x_1, \ldots, x_n, a, s)$ is uniform in s;
  - ∗ *each functional fluent axiom is of the form*

    $$f(x_1, \ldots, x_n, do(a, s)) = y \equiv \Phi_f(x_1, \ldots, x_n, y, a, s)$$

    where $\Phi_f(x_1, \ldots, x_n, y, a, s)$ is uniform in s;
  - ∗ *each functional fluent satisfies the consistency property (defined below);*
- *$\mathcal{D}_{ap}$ is the set of precondition axioms of the form*

  $$Poss(A(x_1, \ldots, x_n), s) \equiv \Pi_A(x_1, \ldots, x_n, s),$$

  where A is an n-ary action function symbol and $\Pi_A(x_1, \ldots, x_n, s)$ is uniform in s;

- $\mathcal{D}_{una}$ *is the action unique name axioms;*
- $\mathcal{D}_{S_0}$ *is a set of first-order sentences that are uniform in* S_0.

Definition 16 *A functional fluent* f *satisfies the consistency property if*
$\mathcal{D}_{una} \cup \mathcal{D}_{S_0} \models$
$(\forall \vec{x}).(\exists y)\phi_f(\vec{x}, y, a, s) \wedge \big((\forall y, y').\phi_f(\vec{x}, y, a, s) \wedge \phi_f(\vec{x}, y', a, s) \supset y = y'\big)$
and $f(\vec{x}, do(a, s)) = y \equiv \phi_f(\vec{x}, y, a, s)$ *is the corresponding successor state axioms for* f *in* $\mathcal{D}_{ss}$ *(Definition 4.4.5 in [10]) .*

The concept of the uniform formulas is formally defined in Definition 4.4.1 of [10]. Intuitively, the uniformity requirement for the precondition axioms and successor state axioms assure that the qualification of an action and the properties in the successor situation, respectively, are determined entirely by the current situation s.

One important theoretical result with respect to the Basic Action Theories is stated as follows. In Section 4, we will show its technical importance towards proving the satisfiability of SCOPE.

Theorem 1 (Relative Satisfiability) *A basic action theory* $\mathcal{D}$ *is satisfiable iff* $\mathcal{D}_{una} \cup \mathcal{D}_{S_0}$ *is (Theorem 4.4.7 in [10], and see [9] for the proof).*

3. SCOPE

SCOPE is formally defined in Sectin 3.1. In Section 3.2, we show that indeed SCOPE constructs a Basic Action Theory.

3.1. The Ontology

SCOPE is defined as a logical theory $\mathcal{S}$, which consists of several sets of axioms as follows:

$$\mathcal{S} = \mathcal{D}_f \cup \mathcal{S}_{ap} \cup \mathcal{S}_{ss} \cup \mathcal{S}_{una} \cup \mathcal{S}_{S_0}$$

where

- $\mathcal{D}_f$ is the foundational axioms;
- $\mathcal{S}_{ap}$ (Action Precondition Axioms)

$$Poss(fire(t), s) \equiv pre(p, t) \supset NumTkns(p, s) \geq 1$$

- $\mathcal{S}_{ss}$ (Successor State Axioms)
  $NumTkns(p, do(a, s)) = n \equiv$
  $\gamma_f(p, t, n, a, s) \vee (NumTkns(p, s) = n \wedge \neg(\exists n')\, \gamma_f(p, t, n', a, s))$, where [2]
  $\gamma_f(p, t, n, a, s) \stackrel{def}{=} \gamma_{f_a}(p, t, n, a, s) \vee \gamma_{f_b}(p, t, n, a, s)$,
  $\gamma_{f_a}(p, t, n, a, s) \stackrel{def}{=} ((\exists t).pre(t, p) \wedge \neg post(t, p) \wedge n = NumTkns(p, s) + 1 \wedge a = fire(t))$,
  $\gamma_{f_b}(p, t, n, a, s) \stackrel{def}{=} ((\exists t).pre(p, t) \wedge \neg post(p, t) \wedge n = NumTkns(p, s) - 1 \wedge a = fire(t))$.

[2] $\gamma_f(p, t, n, a, s)$, $\gamma_{f_a}(p, t, n, a, s)$, and $\gamma_{f_b}(p, t, n, a, s)$ are simply abbreviations.

- $\mathcal{S}_{una}$ (Unique Name Axioms) [3]

$$fire(t_1) = fire(t_2) \supset (t_1 = t_2)$$

- $\mathcal{S}_{S_0}$
  - $*$ $pre(p, t) \equiv post(t, p)$, which means that the place p is the input of the transition t if and only if t is the output of p;
  - $*$ for each arc from transition t to place p, define $pre(p, t)$; similarly, define $pre(t, p)$;
  - $*$ for each place p with initial marking k, define $NumTkns(k, S_0) = k$;

While modeling dynamical systems usually is a complicated task involving identifying complex networks of causal influences, axiomatizing Petri nets is performed directly on the abstract mathematical models and thus is free of this particular type of difficulty. In particular, we now address the relationship between the set of effect axioms $\mathcal{S}_{ef}$ for SCOPE and $\mathcal{S}_{ss}$ in SCOPE with respect to the Causal Completeness Assumption. In short, $\mathcal{S}_{ef}$ is not part of $\mathcal{S}$ but is entailed by $\mathcal{S}$.

Definition 17 *The set of effect axioms $\mathcal{S}_{ef}$ in SCOPE are defined as follows*

$$pre(t, p) \wedge \neg post(t, p) \supset NumTkns(p, do(fire(t), s)) = NumTkns(p, s) + 1,$$

$$pre(p, t) \wedge \neg post(p, t) \supset NumTkns(p, do(fire(t), s)) = NumTkns(p, s) - 1,$$

which is logically equivalent to

$$\gamma_f(p, t, n, a, s) \supset NumTkns(p, t, do(a, s)) = n. \qquad (5)$$

Given the clear definition on the transition rules in Petri nets, we know that we can make a causal completeness assumption (claim) from Equation 5; that is, it includes all the conditions under which the only action in the domain *fire* can cause the fluent *NumTkns* to have a value *n* in the successor situation. The Explanation Closure Axiom corresponding to this claim is

$$NumTkns(p, t, do(a, s)) \neq NumTkns(p, t, s) \supset (\exists t)\gamma_f(p, t, n, a, s) \qquad (6)$$

Theorem 2 *Equation 5 and Equation 6 together, are logically equivalent to the only successor state axiom in SCOPE*

$$NumTkns(p, do(a, s)) = n \equiv$$

$$\gamma_f(p, t, n, a, s) \vee (NumTkns(p, s) = n \wedge \neg(\exists n')\, \gamma_f(p, t, n', a, s))$$

Proof. see [10] for a proof on general cases. □

It is worth noting that the consistency of $\mathcal{S}_{ef}$ for SCOPE relies on the holding of the sentence

$$\neg(\exists p, t, n, n', a, s).\gamma_f(p, t, n, a, s) \wedge \gamma_f(p, t, n', a, s) \wedge n \neq n' \qquad (7)$$

[3] In general, for two distinct action a_1 and a_2, it is required in $\mathcal{S}_{una}$ that $a_1(\vec{x}) \neq a_2(\vec{y})$, but here they are not included as in SCOPE we have only one action "fire".

which in SCOPE states that the action *fire* cannot assign two different values to the fluent *NumTkns* to the successor situation whereas the sentence is simply entailed by applying $\mathcal{S}_{una}$.

3.2. A Basic Action Theory

Theorem 3 *SCOPE constructs a Basic Action Theory.*

Proof. It can be easily verified that the uniform requirement on the current situation s is satisfied in the precondition axioms, the successor state axioms, and the initial condition axioms of SCOPE.

The ontology contains one successor state axiom, for the only functional fluent $NumTkns$. Now we show the function consistency property as defined in Section 2 is satisfied with respect to the $NumTkns$.

The only successor state axiom in $\mathcal{S}_{ss}$ can be written in the form

$$NumTkns(p, do(a, s)) = n \equiv \phi_f(p, t, y, a, s)$$

where

$$\phi_f(p, t, y, a, s) \stackrel{def}{=} \gamma_f(p, t, n, a, s) \vee (NumTkns(p, s) = n \wedge \neg(\exists n')\, \gamma_f(p, t, n', a, s)).$$

Similar to the proof for Equation 7, we have

$$\mathcal{D}_{una} \models (\forall p, t, n, n', a, s).\ \gamma_f(p, t, n, a, s) \wedge \gamma_f(p, t, n', a, s) \supset n = n',$$

and from the definition of ϕ_f, we have

$$\mathcal{D}_{una} \models (\forall p, t, n, n', a, s).\ \phi_f(p, t, n, a, s) \wedge \phi_f(p, t, n', a, s) \supset n = n'.$$

Based on the definition of $\mathcal{S}_{S_0}$, we have

$$\mathcal{S}_{S_0} \models (\forall p, t)(\exists n)\phi_f(p, t, n, a, S_0)$$

Thus,

$$(\forall p, t, n, n', a, s)\ \phi_f(p, t, n, a, s) \wedge \phi_f(p, t, n', a, s) \supset n = n' \cup$$

$$(\forall p, t)(\exists n)\phi_f(p, t, n, a, s);$$

that is, informally, for every place p, there exists a unique value of token numbers n at initial situation S_0, and this uniqueness is maintained at every successor situations.

Hence, $\mathcal{D}_{una} \cup \mathcal{D}_{S_0} \models$
$(\forall p, t).(\exists n)\phi_f(p, t, n, a, s) \wedge (\forall n, n', a, s)(\phi_f(p, t, n, a, s) \wedge \phi_f(p, t, n', a, s) \supset n = n')$. □

4. Satisfiability of SCOPE

The bipartite incidence structure defined as follows is the building block for specifying the models of SCOPE.

Definition 18 *A bipartite incidence structure is a tuple* $\mathbf{B} = (\Omega_1, \Omega_2, \boldsymbol{in})$, *where* Ω_1, Ω_2 *are disjoint sets such that* $\boldsymbol{in} \subseteq (\Omega_1 \times \Omega_2)$. *Two elements that are related by* ***in*** *are called incident.*

Definition 19 *A Petri net structure* $\mathbf{P}^{ini}$ *is defined to include a 7-tuple in the form* $\langle P, T, F, \mathcal{N}, \boldsymbol{PtoT}, \boldsymbol{TtoP}, \boldsymbol{NumOfTkns}\rangle$ *where*

- P, T, F, $\mathcal{N}$ *are disjoint sets, presumably standing for places, transitions, fire actions, and natural numbers, respectively;*
- $\langle P, T, \boldsymbol{PtoT}\rangle$, $\langle T, P, \boldsymbol{TtoP}\rangle$, *and* $\langle P, \mathcal{N}, \boldsymbol{NumOfTkns}\rangle$ *are bipartite incidence structures;*

In addition, $\mathbf{P}^{ini}$ *contains,*

- *the unary function* ***fire*** $: \boldsymbol{T} \rightarrow \boldsymbol{F}$ *is defined such that, for any* $\langle t_1, f_1\rangle$ *and* $\langle t_2, f_2\rangle$ *in* ***fire***, $f_1 = f_2$ *only if* $t_1 = t_2$;
- *the relation set* ***pre*** $: (\boldsymbol{P} \cup \boldsymbol{T}) \times (\boldsymbol{P} \cup \boldsymbol{T})$ *is defined such that, for any two nodes* $n_1, n_2 \in (\boldsymbol{P} \cup \boldsymbol{T})$, $\langle n_1, n_2\rangle \in \boldsymbol{pre}$ *iff* $\langle n_1, n_2\rangle \in \boldsymbol{PtoT}$ *or* $\langle n_1, n_2\rangle \in \boldsymbol{TtoP}$;
- *the relation set* ***post*** $: (\boldsymbol{P} \cup \boldsymbol{T}) \times (\boldsymbol{P} \cup \boldsymbol{T})$ *is defined such that* $\langle n_1, n_2\rangle \in \boldsymbol{post}$ *iff* $\langle n_2, n_1\rangle \in \boldsymbol{pre}$.

Theorem 4 *Any structure in* $\mathbf{P}^{ini}$ *is a model of* $\mathcal{S}_{una\_S_0}$.

Proof. (Sketch.)
Suppose we have a $\mathbf{P} \in \mathbf{P}^{ini}$ ($\mathbf{P}^{ini}$ is obviously non-empty), it is easy to verify that each axiom in $\mathcal{S}_{una\_S_0}$ is satisfied by $\mathbf{P}$, that is:
$\mathbf{P} \models fire(t_1) = fire(t_2) \supset (t_1 = t_2)$ (by definition of **fire**)
$\mathbf{P} \models pre(p, t) \equiv post(t, p)$ (by definition of **pre** and **post**)
$\mathbf{P} \models pre(n_1, n_2)$ for each $pre(n_1, n_2) \in S_{S_0}$ (by **pre**),
$\mathbf{P} \models NumTkns(k, S_0) = k$ where $NumTkns(k, S_0) = k \in S_{S_0}$ (by definition of $\langle P, \mathcal{N}, \mathbf{NumOfTkns}\rangle$). □

Theorem 5 *Any model* $\mathcal{M}$ *of* $\mathcal{S}_{una\_S_0}$ *is isomorphic to a structure in* $\mathbf{P}^{ini}$.

Proof. (Sketch.) Let $\mathcal{M}$ be a many typed model of $\mathcal{S}_{una\_S_0}$, it is required that
$\mathcal{M} \models fire(t_1) = fire(t_2) \supset (t_1 = t_2)$
$\mathcal{M} \models pre(p, t) \equiv post(t, p)$
$\mathcal{M} \models pre(n_1, n_2)$ for each $pre(n_1, n_2) \in S_{S_0}$,
$\mathcal{M} \models NumTkns(k, S_0) = k$ where $NumTkns(k, S_0) = k \in S_{S_0}$,
which assures that $\mathcal{M}$ is an isomorphism to some $\mathbf{P}$ in $\mathbf{P}^{ini}$. □

To this end, we are able to obtain the following satisfiability theorem for SCOPE.

Theorem 6 *SCOPE is satisfiable.*

Proof. Since $\mathcal{S}_{una\_S_0}$ is satisfiable by any $\mathcal{M}$ corresponding to some $\mathbf{P} \in \mathbf{P}^{ini}$, $\mathcal{S}$ is also satisfiable, as by Pirri and Reiter's Relative Satisfiability Theorem ([9], [10]), $\mathcal{M}$ can be extended to some $\mathcal{M}'$, which is a model of $\mathcal{S}$. □

5. Applications of SCOPE

5.1. Axiomatization of SCOPE Subclasses

In this section, we provide an axiomatization (called $\mathcal{S}_{ps}$) to the subclasses and properties of Petri nets mentioned in Section 2. With $\mathcal{S}_{ps}$ and $\mathcal{S}$, two important tasks specified as follows, for the Petri nets Ontology designers, developers, and users can be performed: (1) to assure that the property say $\alpha \in \mathcal{S}_{ps}$ holds in the ontology to be developed; or (2) to check whether $\alpha \in \mathcal{S}_{ps}$ can be entailed from the existing ontology; that is, we can (1) check $\mathcal{S} \cup \alpha$ is satisfiable; or (2) check $\mathcal{S} \models \alpha$.

The specifications might use the following two abbreviations: [4]

$$enabled(t, s) \stackrel{def}{=} pre(p, t) \supset NumTkns(p, s) \geq 1$$

$$exec(s) \stackrel{def}{=} (\forall a, s).do(a, s) \sqsubseteq s \supset Poss(a, s).$$

Dynamical properties of Petri nets are defined as follows.

Cycle

$$(\exists s).\, exec(s) \wedge s \neq S_0 \wedge NumTkns(p, s) = NumTkns(p, S_0)$$

Reachability Given M_n, certain specified Marking on places, we have

$$(\exists s).\, exec(s) \wedge NumTkns(p_0, s) = n_0 \wedge \ldots NumTkns(p_i, s) = n_i,$$

where n_i is the specified number of tokens at the place p_i in the Marking M_n.

K-Boundedness

$$exec(s) \supset NumTkns(p, s) \leq k$$

Liveness

$$exec(s) \supset (\exists s_1).\, s \sqsubset s_1 \wedge exec(s_1)$$

Reversibility

$$exec(s) \supset (\exists s_1).\, s \sqsubset s_1 \wedge exec(s_1) \wedge NumTkns(p, s_1) = NumTkns(p, S_0),$$

where S_0 is the home situation corresponding the home marking of Petri nets.

[4] The second one is introduced as Equation 4.5 in [10].

Coverability (s_1 is covered by s_2)

$$(\exists s_1, s_2).\, exec(s_1) \wedge exec(s_2) \wedge NumTkns(p, s_1) \leq NumTkns(p, s_2)$$

Persistence

$$\neg(\exists s, t_1, t_2).\, exec(s) \wedge enabled(t_1, s) \wedge enabled(t_2, s) \wedge \neg enabled(t_1, do(fire(t_1), s))$$

Restricted classes of Petri nets are defined as follows.

S-systems

$$pre(p_1, t) \wedge pre(p_2, t) \supset p_1 = p_2,\ post(p_1, t) \wedge post(p_2, t) \supset p_1 = p_2$$

T-systems

$$pre(t_1, p) \wedge pre(t_2, p) \supset t_1 = t_2,\ post(t_1, p) \wedge post(t_2, p) \supset t_1 = t_2$$

Conflict-Free

$$\exists(t_1, t_2)\, post(p, t_1) \wedge post(p, t_2) \wedge t_1 \neq t_2 \supset pre(t_3, p) \wedge post(p, t_3)$$

Free-Choice

$$pre(p, t) \supset (\neg\exists p_1\, pre(p_1, t) \wedge p_1 \neq p) \vee (\neg\exists t_1\, pre(p, t_1) \wedge t_1 \neq t)$$

5.2. *Examples*

We now demonstrate the use of SCOPE by giving two examples. They are adapted from Figure 17 (h) of [5], which is a live, reversible, but 1-bounded Petri net instance, and Figure 17 (c) of [5], which is a non-live, irreversible, and 1-bounded Petri net instance. Their pictorial representations are shown in Figure 1 as (A) and (B). Also, the principle of induction for executable situations (PIES) as a consequence of $\mathcal{S}$ (see also [10]) turns out to be helpful:

$$(\forall P).P(S_0) \wedge (\forall a, s)\big(P(s) \wedge exec(s) \wedge Poss(a, s) \supset P(do(a, s))\big) \supset (\forall s).exec(s) \supset P(s).$$

Example 1 $\mathcal{S}_1 = \mathcal{D}_f \cup \mathcal{S}_{ap} \cup \mathcal{S}_{ss} \cup \mathcal{S}_{una} \cup \mathcal{S}_{S_0}$ *where*

$$\mathcal{S}_{S_0} = \{pre(p, t) \equiv post(t, p), pre(T_1, P_1), pre(P_1, T_2), pre(T_2, P_2), pre(P_2, T_1),$$

$$NumTkns(P_1, S_0) = 1, NumTkns(P_2, S_0) = 0.\}$$

1-boundedness: $\mathcal{S}_1 \models exec(s) \supset NumTkns(p, s) \leq 1.$
Proof. We prove 1-boundedness by showing
$exec(s) \supset [(NumTkns(P_1, s) = 1 \wedge NumTkns(P_2, s) = 0) \vee (NumTkns(P_2, s) = 1 \wedge NumTkns(P_1, s) = 0)]$.

Now define $\psi(s) \stackrel{def}{=} (NumTkns(P_1, s) = 1 \wedge NumTkns(P_2, s) = 0) \vee (NumTkns(P_2, s) = 1 \wedge NumTkns(P_1, s) = 0)$,

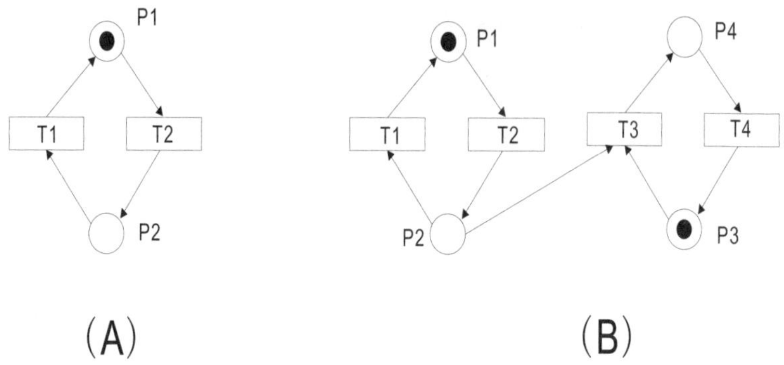

Figure 1. Two examples of Petri nets: (A) 1-bounded, live, and reversible; (B) 1-bounded, non-live, and irreversible.

thus $\psi(do(fire(t), s)) \stackrel{def}{=}$
$(NumTkns(P_1, do(fire(t), s)) = 1 \wedge NumTkns(P_2, do(fire(t), s)) = 0)$
$\vee(NumTkns(P_2, do(fire(t), s)) = 1 \wedge NumTkns(P_1, do(fire(t), s)) = 0)$.

$\psi(S_0)$ holds trivially, as $(NumTkns(P_1, S_0) = 1 \wedge NumTkns(P_2, S_1) = 0)$.

Now assume $\psi(s) \wedge exec(s) \wedge Poss(a, s)$ holds, we have two cases to consider

1. $(NumTkns(P_1, s) = 1 \wedge NumTkns(P_2, s) = 0)$
2. $(NumTkns(P_2, s) = 1 \wedge NumTkns(P_1, s) = 0)$

By using the SSA, for (1)
$(NumTkns(P_2, do(fire(t), s)) = 1 \wedge NumTkns(P_1, do(fire(t), s)) = 0)$
will be obtained, for (2)
$(NumTkns(P_2, do(fire(t), s)) = 0 \wedge NumTkns(P_1, do(fire(t), s)) = 1)$
will hold, obviously, (1) and (2) lead to the holdness of $\psi(do(fire(t), s))$; that is,
$(\forall a, s)[\psi(s) \wedge exec(s) \wedge Poss(a, s) \supset \psi(do(a, s))$.

By PIES, we have $(\forall s).exec(s) \supset \psi(s)$.
And finally, $exec(s) \supset NumTkns(p, s) \leq 1$. □

Liveness We also use the two cases. To prove $exec(s) \supset \exists s_1\ s \sqsubset s_1 \wedge exec(s_1)$ by proving

1. $exec(s) \wedge (NumTkns(P_1, s) = 1 \wedge NumTkns(P_2, s) = 0) \supset \exists s_1\ s \sqsubset s_1 \wedge exec(s_1)$;
2. $exec(s) \wedge (NumTkns(P_1, s) = 0 \wedge NumTkns(P_2, s) = 1) \supset \exists s_1\ s \sqsubset s_1 \wedge exec(s_1)$.

For (1), we will show that $do(fire(T_2), s)$ is such kind of s_1; similarly, for (2), we have $do(fire(T_1), s)$.

Reversibility We just show that any situation is the same as S_0 or its subsequent situation is S_0.

Example 2 $\mathcal{S}_2 = \mathcal{D}_f \cup \mathcal{S}_{ap} \cup \mathcal{S}_{ss} \cup \mathcal{S}_{una} \cup \mathcal{S}_{S_0}$ *where* $\mathcal{S}_{S_0} = \{pre(p,t) \equiv post(t,p), pre(T_1,P_1), pre(P_1,T_2), pre(T_2,P_2), pre(P_2,T_1),$
$pre(T_4,P_3), pre(P_3,T_3), pre(T_3,P_4), pre(P_4,T_4), pre(P_2,T_3),$
$NumTkns(P_1,S_0) = 1, NumTkns(P_3,S_0) = 1,$
$NumTkns(P_2,S_0) = 0, NumTkns(P_4,S_0) = 0.\}$

Observe, and also it is easy to see that the theory entails, that

- T_4 is possible to execute only if T_3 is executed;
- T_1 and T_2 execute in turn from initial situation S_0 before T_3 can execute;
- the number of tokens at both P_1 and P_2 will be zero after the execution of T_3;
- no successor situation after the execution of T_4 is executable.

Thus the non-liveness of $\mathcal{S}_{example}$ is entailed:
$\mathcal{S}_{example} \models \neg(exec(s) \supset \exists s_1 s \sqsubset s_1 \wedge exec(s_1)),$
as, for example, at the executable situation $do(fire(T_3), do(fire(T_2), S0))$ the transition T_1 is no longer live. Meanwhile, the irreversibility is implied from this non-liveness, for this example in particular.

In order to show the 1-boundedness, we can show that, after T_3 is executed, T_4 must be executed and deadlock is reached, whereas all places are bounded before T_3 is executed. More specifically, we can use PIES to show that at any of these executable situations, we have either $NumTkns(P_1,S_0) = 1 \wedge NumTkns(P_2,S_0) = 0,$
or $NumTkns(P_1,S_0) = 0 \wedge NumTkns(P_2,S_0) = 1.$

Thus the example is also 1-bounded:
$\mathcal{S}_{example} \models exec(s) \supset NumTkns(p,s) \leq 1.$

6. Summary

In this paper, we provide a formal (mostly in first-order logic) ontology called SCOPE for Petri nets. The design of SCOPE makes the full use of the strong correspondence between the situation s in situation calculus, which is a sequence of actions starting from the initial state S_0, and the marking M in Petri nets, which results from a sequence of transition firings starting from the initial marking M_0. Consequentially, SCOPE inherits completely the simplicity in formalism of Petri nets and their powerful expressive capability.

We define SCOPE as a Basic Action Theory of situation calculus such that we can take advantage of the Relative Satisfiability Theorem for Basic Action Theories and show in an easy and straightforward manner that SCOPE is satisfiable. This efforts endorses the qualification of SCOPE, to be an operational language describing Web service in semantic Web, or other use cases where unambiguous interpretations of operational semantics are strictly required.

Aside from the satisfiability of SCOPE, this paper introduces a combinatorial structure and uses it to fully characterize some core subset axioms ($\mathcal{S}_{una\_S_0}$) of SCOPE by providing the axiomatizability theorem and the satisfiability theorem for $\mathcal{S}_{una\_S_0}$. We will consider characterizing SCOPE completely in a future paper. Note that we often call $\mathcal{S}_{una\_S_0}$ as a *domain theory*, since, different from other sets in the ontology, it is domain dependent.

It is somewhat surprising how much reasoning tasks this small ontology can support. While it is the case that this benefit is largely empowered by applying second-order based foundational axioms, in reality, any concrete reasoning task can always use a replacement of a set of first-order axioms.

Major related work includes [7], and [3]. In [3], the semantics are first described by UML classes models, and then redirected into Protege, which is a logic-based ontology development tool, and finally presented in (Resource Description Framework) RDF and Web Ontology Language (OWL) formalisms. Given that the semantics of UML classes models have yet to be formally specified, model-theoretic results on this complicated semantic mapping process are not given in [3] and are intrinsically difficult to obtain indeed. Similarly, the Generic Process Model (GPM) semantic for Petri net, proposed in [7], lacks the arguments of the unique interpretations of GPM.

Future work on and beyond SCOPE can be divided into four categories as follows. One, extend SCOPE to include more features of high-level Petri nets; two, formally characterize several subclasses of SCOPE theories such that reasoning with specific queries are tractable; three, implement a stand-alone SCOPE reasoning system, preferably in the logic programming language Prolog; four, investigate SCOPE in concurrent or distributed systems, incorporating earlier work such as [8].

Acknowledgements

Technical guidance from Professor Michael Gruninger and the financial support of the NIST grant 60NANB7D6143 to this work are deeply appreciated. I am grateful to the anonymous reviewers for their detailed comments and suggestions.

References

[1] R. Brachman and H. Levesque, Knowledge representation and reasoning, Morgan Kaufmann, 2004.

[2] F. Lin, Situation Calculus, In F. Harmelen, V. Lifschitz, and B. Porter, editors, Handbook of Knowledge Representation, (2008), 649-669, Elsevier.

[3] D. Gasevic and V. Devedzic J. Davies, Reusing Petri nets through the semantic Web, *ESWS, LNCS 3053*,(2004), 284-298.

[4] S. Narayanan and S. McIlraith, Analysis and simulation of Web services, *Computer networks*, **42**, (2003), 675-693.

[5] T. Murata, Petri nets: properties, analysis and applications, *Proceedings of the IEEE*, **77(4)**, (1989), 541-580.

[6] J. McCarthy and P. Hayes, Some philosophical problems from the standpoint of artificial intelligence, In B. Meltzer and D. Michie, editors, *Machine Intelligence* (1969), 463-502, Edinburgh University Press, Edinburgh, Scotland.

[7] P. Soffer, M. Kaner, and Y. Wand, Assigning ontology-based semantics to process models: the case of Petri nets, *CAiSE, LNCS5074*, (2008), 16-31.

[8] M. Nielsen and V. Sassone, Petri Nets and Other Models of Concurrency. In: Lectures on Petri Nets I: Basic Models. (1998), 587-642.

[9] F. Pirri and R. Reiter, Some contributions to the metatheory of the situation calculus, *J. ACM*, **46(3)** (1999), 325-361.

[10] R. Reiter, Knowledge in Actioin: Logical foundations for describing and implementing dynamical systems, The MIT Press, 2001.

Biomedical and Chemical Ontologies I

Formal Ontology in Information Systems
A. Galton and R. Mizoguchi (Eds.)
IOS Press, 2010

doi:10.3233/978-1-60750-535-8-243

Foundational Process Relations in Bio-Ontologies

Atalay ÖZGÖVDE [a] and Michael GRÜNINGER [b]
[a] Department of Computer Science, University of Toronto
[b] Department of Mechanical and Industrial Engineering

Abstract. This paper aims to provide rigor to the process relations in the OBO relations ontology. We present a formal axiomatization of these relations in first order logic as a definitional extension of the Process Specification Language (PSL) Ontology. In particular, we formalize the process parthood, process specialization, process instantiation and instance level parthood relations of OBO. We also present a formal characterization of the models of our axiomatization and provide representation theorems showing the correctness of our characterization.

1. Introduction

Although a wide variety of biological and medical ontologies have been proposed, their axiomatizations in a logical language have often been insufficient for automated reasoning and semantic integration. In fact, many are not specified in a logical language, and even those which are axiomatized have not been evaluated with respect to their intended models.

The relations ontology (RO) ([10]) has been proposed as an upper ontology for the Open Bio-medical Ontologies (OBO) ([1], [7]) in order to ensure compatibility and consistency of OBO ontologies. The current version of the OBO Relation Ontology provides definitions for only class level relations which connect classes of entities such as the class of all genes, the class of all instances of DNA replication and so forth. Although the definitions of the class level relations rely on instance level relations, a formal characterization of the instance level relations is not provided. In ([2]), axiomatic specifications are given for logical properties of the instance level mereogeometrical relations in the Relation Ontology. In this paper we take a similar approach to characterize the process relations in the Relation Ontology. The primary motivation for this work is the recognition that the distinction between classes and instances alone is inadequate for characterizing the intended semantics of the relations for a process ontology.

Table 1 shows the process relations in the OBO Relation Ontology; since the same relation name is often used for both class-level and instance-level relations, we introduce some new relation names to allow us to distinguish between these two cases. The resulting nonlogical lexicon is also shown in Table 1, and we refer to the axiomatization of the intended semantics of this lexicon as the OBO Process Ontology. In this paper, we show that the OBO Process Ontology can be axiomatized as a definitional extension of the Process Specification Language (PSL) Ontology ([3], [4]) [1]. We specify translation definitions ([5]) for all of the relations in the nonlogical lexicon of OBO Process Ontology, which provides a first-order axiomatization. The OBO Process Ontology does not have an explicit axiomatization in a logical language. This paper is therefore not an exercise in ontology mapping, which presumes that both ontologies are axiomatized, but rather illustrates the methodology of augmenting an informally specified ontology with the axiomatization of a first-order ontology.

In addition to axiomatizing the intended semantics of the process terminology within the OBO Relation Ontology, we provide a formal specification of the models of the axiomatization. We also illustrate several propositions that are consequences of the axiomatization, demonstrating that the OBO Process Ontology is capable of supporting automated first-order reasoning with process descriptions.

RO Relation	1.arg	2.arg	3.arg	Nonlogical Lexicon
p instance_of P	instance	process	-	instance_of
p part_of p_1	instance	instance	-	subinstance
t earlier t_1	timepoint	timepoint	-	earlier
p has_participant c at t	process	continuant	timepoint	has_participant_at
p has_agent c at t	process	continuant	timepoint	has_agent_at
P is_a P_1	process	process	-	is_a
P part_of P_1	process	process	-	subprocess
p occurring_at t	instance	timepoint	-	occurring_at
p preceded_by p_1	instance	instance	-	preceded_by
t first_instant p	timepoint	instance	-	first_instant
t last_instant p	timepoint	instance	-	last_instant
p immediately_preceded_by p_1	instance	instance	-	immediately_preceded_by
P preceded_by P_1	process	process	-	preceded_by

Table 1. Process relations in the relation ontology and the corresponding lexicon used in this text. Parameter types: P - process class, C - continuant class, p - process instance, c - continuant instance, t - timepoint.

2. An example biological process

We will use the cell division process as the running example in order to clarify the axiomatic approach and its benefits. Cell division is a process that results in the division of a parent cell into two or more daughter cells. There are two types of cell division. Mitotic cell division is the process by which the parent nucleus divides to produce two new nuclei with the same number of chromosomes, identical to the parent nucleus; the purpose of mitotic cell division is the growth, repair and replacement of cells. Meiotic cell division results in four daughter cells, in which the number of chromosomes in the new cells are reduced by half; the purpose of meiotic cell division is sexual reproduction. Figure 1 shows the parthood and specialization structure of the cell division process; this is a representation of the structures which will be axiomatized by the process ontology.

[1]The PSL Ontology has been published as an international standard ISO 18629. The complete set of axioms for the PSL Ontology can be found at `http://www.mel.nist.gov/psl/psl-ontology/`.

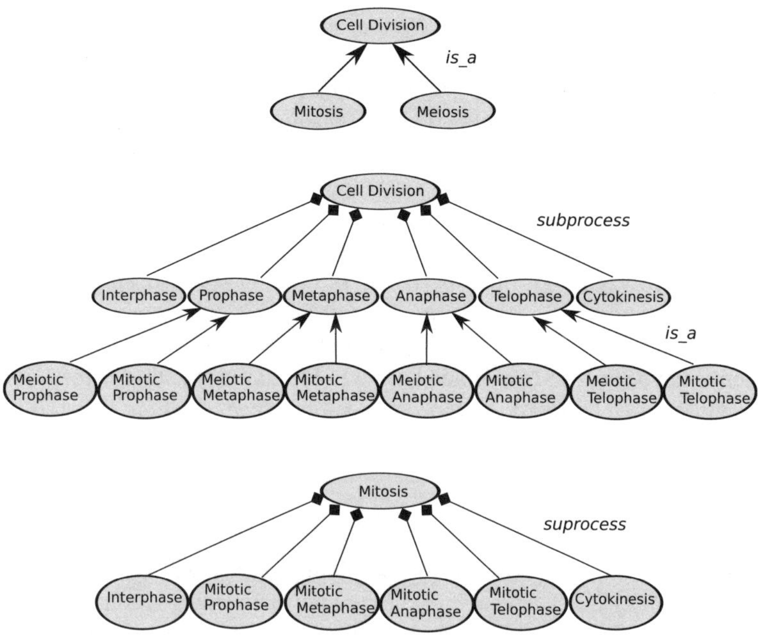

Figure 1. Diagrammatic view of the cell division process. Diamond arrows denote parthood, arrows denote specialization.

Cell division has six phases. During Interphase, cells carry out their normal function. At the later stages of interphase, cells prepare for mitosis or meiosis. During prophase, metaphase, anaphase and telophase the cytoplasm and nucleus of the dividing cell replicate and regroup into two sets in the opposite poles. Cytokinesis is the final stage where the cytoplasm and cell membrane splits into two. The example is a much simplified representation of cell division and provided for illustrative purposes; we will not attempt to fully axiomatize the cell division process.

3. Processes and Occurrences

Processes are repeatable behaviors whose occurrences cause continuants to undergo changes. It is important to distinguish between processes and process occurrences. Processes are neither endurants (continuants) nor perdurants (occurrents), since they do not change and they do not have temporal parts. Process occurrences are perdurants – they may have temporal parts (i.e. sub-occurrences such as changing the coffee filter while making coffee), and they have beginning and end timepoints.

The intuitive semantics of the RO process relations as described in ([10]) correspond very naturally to the ontological commitments made by the core theories in the PSL Ontology. The PSL Ontology axiomatizes the relationship between processes and process occurrences (instantiation), processes and subprocesses (process parthood) and process occurrences and subprocess occurrences (instance level parthood). In fact, one of the reasons for choosing the PSL Ontology as the basis for the axiomatization in this paper is that it is one of the few first-order ontologies in which both complex processes and their occurrences are elements of the domain.

The current version of the OBO relation ontology treats processes as classes and the *instance_of* relation as a counter part of the set-theoretic membership relation. In the PSL Ontology, processes and process instances are reified i.e. they are first class entities. In fact, most ontologies of action and change (see [8], [9] or [11]) favor reified represention for actions which allows actions to be arguments to relations and functions and expression of formulas that quantify over actions. This is also the approach taken in Thomas Bittner's Isabelle axiomatization of the mereogeometrical relations in the OBO Relations Ontology (See `http://isabelle.in.tum.de`).

Within the PSL Ontology, the *occurrence_of* relation associates processes with their occurrences. Each process occurrence is associated with a unique process, although processes can have multiple occurrences. We can characterize the *instance_of* relation of OBO in terms the *occurrence_of* relation of PSL. The axiomatization of the $instanceOf$ relation is closely tied to the formalization of activity specialization, which is addressed in Section 4.

3.1. Subactivities

Primitive processes are at the lowest level of granularity that a domain designer chooses to represent, and they are responsible for all the physical change in the world. A primitive process is specified in terms of the conditions that are necessary for its occurrence (preconditions) and the impact of its occurrences on the world (effects). Occurrences of complex processes correspond to sequences of occurrences of primitive processes; consequently, a complex process is specified in terms of dependencies and constraints among occurrences of its subprocesses.

Complex activity occurrences are also first class objects in the PSL ontology. The PSL ontology characterizes complex processes in terms of the relationship between occurrences of complex processes and occurrences of their subprocesses. Subprocesses occur during the occurrence of the process, however subprocesses can also occur externally. In other words, an occurrence of a subprocess during occurrence of a process may be coincidental. The PSL Ontology uses the *subactivity_occurrence* relation to associate complex activity occurrences with the occurrences of its subprocesses.

The OBO Process Ontology includes a composition relation that is defined on processes. The PSL Ontology uses the *subactivity* relation to capture the intuitions for process parthood. The $subactivity$ relation itself is a discrete partial ordering. An activity may have subactivities that do not occur and an activity may be a subactivity of multiple activities. Different subactivities may occur in different occurrences of an activity, with the requirement that subactivity occurrences are occurrences of subactivities. The axiomatization of the $subactivity$ relation in the PSL Ontology allows models where processes that share subactivities do not co-occur.

Process parthood is a class level relation in the current version of OBO Relation Ontology. Formal definitions for class level relations are given in terms of their instance level counter parts in the ontology. Process parthood definition is also given in the same style. Based on the discussion above, one could write the definition of process parthood in the OBO Relation Ontology as follows:

$$\forall a, a_1 . subProcess(a_1, a) \equiv \forall o_1 . occurrence\_of(o_1, a_1) \supset$$
$$\exists o . occurrence\_of(o, a) \wedge subactivity\_occurrence(o_1, o)$$

However, this definition requires every instance of a subprocess be part of an instance of the process it is part of. Consider the cytokinesis phase of the cell cycle. Cytokinesis is a subProcess of both mitosis and meiosis. The definition above amounts to saying that whenever cytokinesis occurs, both mitosis and meiosis must occur such that the cytokinesis occurrence is part of their occurrences. Cytokinesis may also be part of other processes such as cancerious cell division. Occurrence of cytokinesis indicates occurrence of one of mitosis, meiosis or a cancerious growth mutually exclusively.

Following this discussion, we can introduce the translation definitions for OBO Process Ontology relations associated with $partOf$:

$$\forall a, a_1 . subProcess(a_1, a) \equiv subactivity(a_1, a) \quad (1)$$

$$\forall s, o . subinstance(s, o) \equiv subactivity\_occurrence(s, o) \quad (2)$$

Note that the constraints between the *subactivity* and *subactivity_occurrence* relations in PSL do not require that processes that share subactivities necessarily co-occur.

3.2. Orderings over Occurrences and Time

The next set of relations in the OBO Process Ontology focus on the ordering relations on process occurrences and the timepoints at which processes occur. Some approaches ([6], [9]), do not distinguish between timepoints and process occurrences, so that process occurrences form a subset of timepoints, and the ordering relations are conflated to the ordering over timepoints. Nevertheless, it is important to maintain a distinction between timepoints and process occurrences; although each occurrences is associated with a beginning and ending timepoints, occurrences have preconditions and effects, whereas timepoints do not.

In the PSL Ontology, timepoints are distinct objects from activities and activity occurrences and they form an infinite linear ordering corresponding to the *before* relation. This allows us to specify the following translation definition for the ordering over timepoints in the OBO Process Ontology:

$$\forall t_1, t_2 . earlier(t_1, t_2) \equiv before(t_1, t_2) \quad (3)$$

In addition to the ordering over timepoints, the PSL Ontology axiomatizes an ordering over process occurrences known as an occurrence tree; this is a discrete partially ordered set of primitive activity occurrences containing all sequences of activity occurrences [2]. Since not all of these sequences will intuitively be physically possible within a given domain, we consider the subtree of the occurrence tree that consists only of possible sequences of activity occurrences, which we refer to as the legal occurrence tree. The $legal(o)$ relation specifies that the primitive activity occurrence o is an element of the legal occurrence tree. The PSL Ontology uses the *precedes* relation to axiomatize the partial ordering of the occurrences in the legal occurence tree, leading to the following translation definition for the OBO Process Ontology ordering relation over process occurrences:

[2]Occurrence trees are similar to the situation trees that are models of Reiter's axiomatization of the situation calculus ([8]).

$$(\forall p, p_1)\ preceded\_by(p, p_1) \equiv (\exists o, o_1)\ root\_occ(o, p) \wedge leaf\_occ(o_1, p_1) \wedge precedes(o_1, o) \tag{4}$$

Since each branch of the occurrence tree is a discrete linear ordering of process occurrences, the PSL Ontology uses the $successor$ function to denote the next occurrence of a particular process within the tree; this captures the intended semantics of the following relation in the OBO Process Ontology:

$$(\forall p, p_1)\ immediately\_preceded\_by(p, p_1) \equiv (\exists a)\ (p_1 = successor(a, p)) \tag{5}$$

Occurrences along a branch of the occurrence are linearly ordered and the $begin\_of$ and end_of functions in map occurrences to the underlying timeline; this corresponds to the following OBO Process Ontology relations:

$$(\forall p, t)\ first\_instant(t, p) \equiv (t = beginof(p)) \tag{6}$$

$$(\forall p, t)\ last\_instant(t, p) \equiv (t = endof(p)) \tag{7}$$

Interestingly, the relations within the OBO Process Ontology that associates objects and occurrences with the different timepoints over which the process is occurring is identical in name to the corresponding relation in the PSL Ontology:

$$(\forall o, t)\ occurring\_at(o, t) \equiv occurring\_at(o, t) \tag{8}$$

$$(\forall a, x, t)\ has\_participant(a, x, t) \equiv (\exists o)\ occurrence\_of(o, a) \wedge participates\_in(x, o, t) \tag{9}$$

Occurrences of complex processes are not part of the occurrence tree. Figure 2, shows a possible model of occurrences of mitosis and meiosis processes, $o_1^{mitosis}$ and $o_2^{meiosis}$ respectively. In the figure occurrences are enumerated to distinguish distinct occurrence objects, and superscripts are the associated processes; for example, $s_1^{interphase}$ denotes the particular occurrence, s_1, in the model that is an occurrence of the interphase process. The dotted arrows indicate the *subactivity_occurrence* relation. The occurrences s_1, s_9, s_{10}, s_{378}, s_{380} and s_{381} are subactivity occurrences of $o_1^{mitosis}$ and they are part of the occurrence tree.

The OBO Relation Ontology includes an ordering relation $preceded\_by$ over processes, in addition to process occurrences. Unfortunately, partial ordering relations over processes are not well-defined in cases where there are multiple occurrences of the same processes.

4. Process specialization

A specialization of an activity is one way in which the activity can occur. The axiomatization of the OBO Process Ontology therefore treats specialization as a special kind of nondeterminism, since complex processes capture the different ways of aggregating primitive process occurrences. Intuitively, the more general the process, the more nondeterministic it is, while processes become more deterministic as they get more specialized. In this approach, a specialization of a process is a nondeterministic subprocess, so that occurrences of a specialized process correspond to a subset of the occurrences of the more general process. Consider the cell division example. An occurrence of cell division

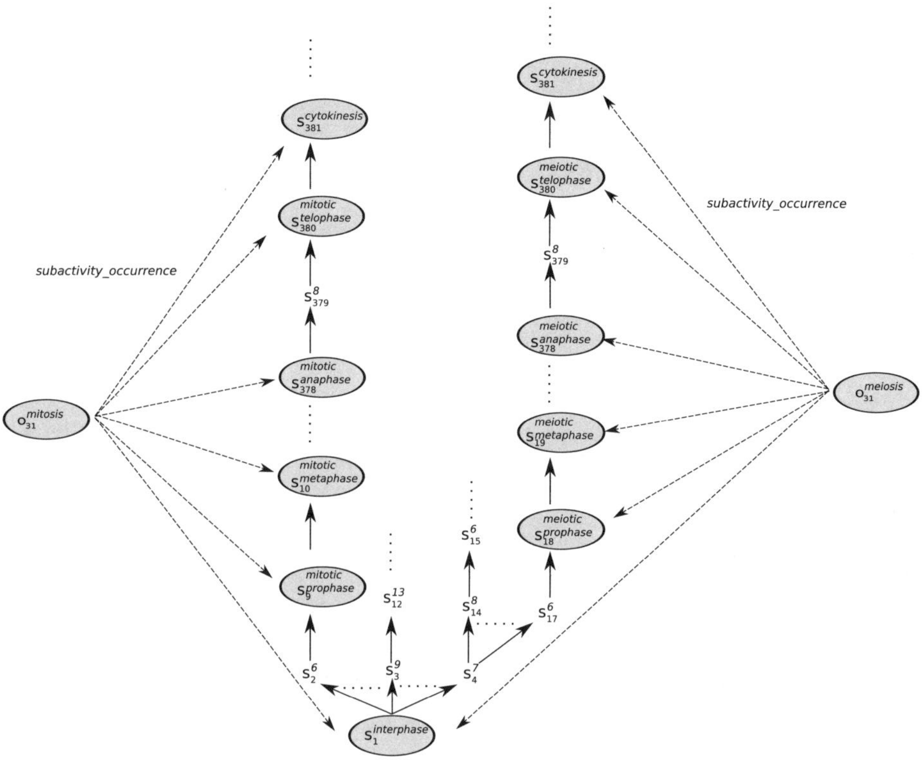

Figure 2. A fragment of a possible PSL model of occurrences of mitosis and meiosis. Note that s_x^y denotes an occurrence of process y.

corresponds to the occurrence of one of mitosis or meiosis; either of these is a specialization of cell division. In addition, an occurrence of cell division involves an occurrence of prophase, which can be mitotic or meiotic depending on which specialization of cell division occurs.

4.1. Axiomatization

Recall that the notion of process occurrence in PSL is distinguished from the notion of a process instance. For example, when mitosis occurs there is also an occurrence of cell division; however these two occurrences are distinct even though one process is a specialization of the other. What is common between these two occurrences is that they share the same primitive subprocess occurrences. We call such occurrences *coextensive*, and introduce the following conservative definition using the PSL Ontology.

$$\forall o_1, o_2.coextensive(o_1, o_2) \equiv activity\_occurrence(o_1) \wedge activity\_occurrence(o_2) \wedge$$
$$(\forall s.legal(s) \supset (subactivity\_occurrence(s, o_1) \equiv subactivity\_occurrence(s, o_2))) \quad (10)$$

Using this notion, we can axiomatize the isA relation in terms of coextensive process occurrences, with the additional property that specializations of a process do not occur outside occurrences of the more general processes:

$$\begin{aligned}&\forall a_1, a_2.isA(a_1, a_2) \equiv \\ &activity(a_1) \wedge activity(a_2) \wedge subactivity(a_1, a_2) \wedge \\ &(\forall o_1.occurrence\_of(o_1, a_1) \supset \exists o_2.occurrence\_of(o_2, a_2) \wedge \\ &coextensive(o_1, o_2) \wedge subactivity\_occurrence(o_1, o_2))\end{aligned} \tag{11}$$

The isA relation can therefore be seen as a restriction of the $subactivity$ relation in the PSL Ontology; we can define a corresponding restriction to the $occurrence\_of$ relation:

$$(\forall o, a)\ instanceOf(o, a) \equiv \exists a_1.isA(a_1, a) \wedge occurrence\_of(o, a_1) \tag{12}$$

4.2. Consequences

Let T_{obo} be the set of axioms 1 - 12 and T_{psl} be the set of axioms in the PSL Ontology. the following results are the consequences of the axioms [3].

Theorem 1

$$\begin{aligned}T_{obo} \cup T_{psl} \models [(\forall a, b) isA(a, b) \equiv ((\forall o_1)\ instanceOf(o_1, a) \supset \\ ((\exists o_2)\ instanceOf(o_2, b) \wedge ((\forall s)\ partOf(s, o_1) \equiv partOf(s, o_2))))]\end{aligned}$$

Informally, the next theorem follows from the *subactivity_occurrence* relation being reflexive, transitive and antisymmetric and the *coextensive* relation being an equivalence relation.

Theorem 2 *The isA relation is reflexive, transitive and antisymmetric:*

$$\begin{aligned}&T_{obo} \cup T_{psl} \models (\forall a)\ isA(a, a) \\ &T_{obo} \cup T_{psl} \models (\forall a_1, a_2, a_3)\ isA(a_1, a_2) \wedge isA(a_2, a_3) \supset isA(a_1, a_3) \\ &T_{obo} \cup T_{psl} \models (\forall a_1, a_2)\ isA(a_1, a_2) \wedge isA(a_2, a_1) \supset (a_1 = a_2)\end{aligned}$$

We can next show that our characterization of the *isA* relation respects the way the *isA* relation defined in the OBO Relation Ontology.

Theorem 3

$$T_{obo} \cup T_{psl} \models (\forall a, b)\ isA(a, b) \equiv ((\forall o)\ instanceOf(o, a) \supset instanceOf(o, b))$$

Proof $\Rightarrow$: Let a, b be such that $isA(a, b)$ holds also let o be such that $instanceOf(o, a)$ holds. Then there exists a_1 such that $isA(a_1, a)$ and $occurrenceOf(o, a_1)$. By theorem 2, $isA(a_1, b)$ also holds. Then by the definition of the instanceOf relation, $instanceOf(o, b)$ follows.

$\Leftarrow$: Let $\forall o.instanceOf(o, a) \supset instanceOf(o, b)$ and let o, a be such that $occurrenceOf(o, a)$. By the definition of the *instanceOf* relation and theorem 2, $instanceOf(o, a)$ holds. Then we also have that $instanceOf(o, b)$. Since every occur-

[3] Due to space limitations, we do not include proofs of these two theorems in this paper, although proofs have been generated automatically using the Prover9 theorem prover.

rence is an occurrence of a unique activity, using the definition of the instanceOf relation again we conclude that $isA(a, b)$. □

Finally, we can prove that the translation definitions for several of the OBO Process Ontology relations are logically equivalent to straightforward transcriptions of their intended semantics as discussed in [10]:

Theorem 4 $T_{obo} \cup T_{psl} \models$

$$occurring\_at(o,t) \equiv \exists t_1, t_2, s_1, s_2.root\_occurrence(s_1, o) \wedge leaf\_occurrence(s_2, o) \wedge begin\_of(s_1) = t_1 \wedge end\_of(s_2) = t_2 \wedge (earlier(t_1, t) \vee t_1 = t \vee earlier(t, t_2))$$

$$preceded\_by(p, p_1) \equiv \forall t_1, t_2, occurring\_at(p, t) \wedge occurring\_at(p_1, t_1) \supset earlier(t_1, t)$$

$$first\_instant(t, p) \equiv occurring\_at(p, t) \wedge \forall t_1.earlier(t_1, t) \supset \neg occurring\_at(p, t_1)$$

$$last\_instant(t, p) \equiv occurring\_at(p, t) \wedge \forall t_1.earlier(t, t_1) \supset \neg occurring\_at(p, t_1)$$

5. Reasoning with processes

Subprocesses and associated specialization hierarchy do not completely characterize a process. Two processes that share the same set of subprocesses and parents may be distinct in terms of dependencies and dynamics among their subprocess occurrences. In order to fully represent a process, a description must be given that specifies the subprocesses that occur as part of its occurrences as well as constraints on the subprocess occurrences. For example, the description of the mitosis process can be specified as:

Process Description $\Sigma_{mitosis}$ (The mitosis process):

$$\forall o, instance\_of(o, mitosis) \supset \exists s_1, s_2, s_3, s_4, s_5, s_6.$$
$$instance\_of(s_1, interphase) \wedge instance\_of(s_2, mitoticProphase) \wedge$$
$$instance\_of(s_3, mitoticMetaphase) \wedge instance\_of(s_4, mitioticAnaphase) \wedge$$
$$instance\_of(s_5, mitoticTelophase) \wedge instance\_of(s_6, cytokinesis) \wedge$$
$$subinstance(s_1, o) \wedge subinstance(s_2, o) \wedge subinstance(s_3, o) \wedge$$
$$subinstance(s_4, o) \wedge subinstance(s_5, o) \wedge subinstance(s_6, o) \wedge$$
$$preceded\_by(s_2, s_1) \wedge preceded\_by(s_3, s_2) \wedge preceded\_by(s_4, s_3) \wedge$$
$$preceded\_by(s_5, s_4) \wedge preceded\_by(s_6, s_5)$$

One of the advantages of designing a first-order logic based theory is that one can use an off-the-shelf generic first-order theorem prover such as Prover9 or Vampire to validate the theorems of the theory or to do automated reasoning at the domain level. For example, we can express the property that whenever *mitosis* occurs there are occurrences of *mitotic_metaphase* and *mitotic_anaphase* such that the occurrence of *mitotic_anaphase* is preceded by the occurrence of *mitotic_metaphase*; moreover, this is a consequence of Process Description for mitosis, together with the axioms of the ontology:

$$T_{obo} \cup T_{psl} \cup \Sigma_{mitosis} \models (\forall o) instance\_of(o, mitosis) \supset (\exists s_1, s_2)\, instance\_of(s_1, mitotic\_metaphase) \wedge instance\_of(s_2, mitotic\_anaphase) \wedge preceded\_by(s_2, s_1)$$

Suppose we included a description for the *meiosis* process similar to the one given for the *mitosis* process. Furthermore, suppose we also added constraints for the *subprocess* and *is_a* relations to capture the cell division process as depicted in Figure 1, $is\_a(mitosis, cell\_division)$, $subprocess(mitotic\_prophase, mitosis)$, $is\_a(meiotic\_telophase, telophase)$ and so forth. Then we could also prove the following property:

$$T_{obo} \cup T_{psl} \cup \Sigma_{mitosis} \models (\forall o)\, instance\_of(o, cell\_division) \supset (\exists s_1, s_2)\, instance\_of(s_1, metaphase) \wedge instance\_of(s_2, anaphase) \wedge preceded\_by(s_2, s_1)$$

Note that a description for the cell division process is not required to prove the property above. Also note that *metaphase* and *anaphase* are abstract processes that occur only through their mitotic or meiotic specializations.

Reasoning with the OBO Process Ontology is not limited to reasoning about the static structure of complex processes. Making predictions about the future and explanations about the past often involve the state of the world and how processes change the state. PSL includes a sub-theory that is intended to capture the basic intuitions about states and their connections to processes.

A state is intuitively a set of fluents and fluents are parameters of a domain that are subject to change through occurrences processes. The effect axioms of processes describe how their occurrences change fluents. Temporal mereogeometrical relations axiomatized in ([2]), such parthood, location and connection relations would be fluents in an integrated theory. For example, the effect axioms for the *cytokinesis* process would describe how the spacial properties of the participating cell change as a result of the occurrence of the process.

6. Verification of the Ontology

In this section, we provide a formal characterization of the models of the axiomatization of the OBO Process Ontology, and propose theorems that demonstrate that the models of the axioms are equivalent to the models in the characterization. Although a complete characterization has been done for all of the axioms in the ontology, space restrictions only allow us to specify the models of the axioms for the isA and $instanceOf$ relations in this paper.

The ontology is verified by providing a complete characterization of all models of the axioms up to isomorphism. One approach to this problem is to use representation theorems – we evaluate the adequacy of the ontology with respect to some well-understood class of mathematical structures (such as partial orderings, graph theory, and geometry) that capture the intended interpretations of the ontology's terms. Given the definition of some class of structures $\mathfrak{M}$, we prove that the class exists and is nonempty, which also provides a characterization of the structures in the class up to isomorphism. We prove that every structure in the class is a model of the ontology and that every countable model of the ontology is isomorphic to some structure in the class.

6.1. Models of the PSL Ontology

The models of the axioms of the PSL Ontology have been characterized up to isomorphism [3]. We first review some of the underlying intuitions before defining the fundamental structures that constitute the models of the PSL Ontology.

6.1.1. Intuitions

The basic structure that characterizes occurrences of complex activities within models of the ontology is the activity tree, which is a subtree of the legal occurrence tree that consists of all possible sequences of primitive subactivity occurrences; the relation $root(s, a)$ denotes that the subactivity occurrence s is the root of an activity tree for a, and relation $leaf(s, a)$ denotes that the subactivity occurrence s is the leaf of an activity tree for a. The $min\_precedes(s_1, s_2, a)$ relation is used to denote that subactivity occurrence s_1 precedes the subactivity occurrence s_2 in occurrences of the complex activity a. Elements of an activity tree are ordered by the $min\_precedes$ relation; each branch of the activity tree is a linearly ordered set of occurrences of subactivities of the complex activity.

In a sense, an activity tree is a microcosm of the occurrence tree, in which we consider all of the ways in which the world unfolds in the context of an occurrence of the complex activity. Different subactivities may occur on different branches of the activity tree – different occurrences of an activity may have different subactivity occurrences or different orderings on the same subactivity occurrences.

6.1.2. Basic Structures for Models of the PSL Ontology

To formalize the intuitions in the previous section, we provide the following definitions for the structures which are used to specify models of the PSL Ontology; they will also be used to specify the models of the OBO Process Ontology in the next section.

The structure that corresponds to the $subactivity$ relation is the following partial ordering:

Definition 1 *A subactivity ordered set $\mathcal{A} = \langle A, \prec \rangle$ is a discrete partial ordering over the set of activities A.*

The subactivity ordered set specifies how complex activities can be decomposed into subactivities; the activity tree specifies how occurrences of a complex activity correspond to occurrences of its subactivities.

Definition 2 *An activity tree τ for an activity $\mathbf{a}$ is a subtree of a legal occurrence tree such that*

- *all elements of τ are occurrences of primitive subactivities of $\mathbf{a}$;*
- *τ contains a unique element if $\mathbf{a}$ is primitive.*

Definition 3 *A complex activity structure $\mathcal{C}$ is the union of all activity trees for all activities in the subactivity ordered set $\mathcal{A}$.*

In addition, there is a one-to-one correspondence between occurrences of complex activities and branches of the associated activity trees, which is captured by the following mapping:

Definition 4 *Let $\mathcal{C}$ be a complex activity structure. Let $\mathcal{B}$ be the set of branches in activity trees in $\mathcal{C}$, and let O be the set of activity occurrences of complex activities.*

A complex mapping $\beta : \mathcal{B} \rightarrow O$ is a bijection such that if $\mathbb{B}$ is a branch of an activity tree for a complex activity $\mathbf{a}$, *then* $\langle \beta(\mathbb{B}), \mathbf{a} \rangle \in \mathbf{occurrence\_of}$

The axioms for $subactivity\_occurrence$ relation guarantee that the branches of the activity trees for a subactivity are contained in the branches of the activity tree for the complex activity.

6.2. Models of OBO Process Ontology

6.2.1. Mappings on Activity Trees

Before we define the class of structures that formalizes the notion of activity specialization, we first need to specify a mapping that captures the relationships between activity trees, and consequently the relationships between the occurrences of the activities. Given the definition of activity trees, any mapping that preserves the activity tree needs to preserve the orderings over the elements of the activity trees and it must also preserve the relationship between elements of the activity trees and occurrences of subactivities of $\mathbf{a}$.

Definition 5 *Let τ_1, τ_2 be activity trees for the activities* $\mathbf{a_1}$, $\mathbf{a_2}$, *respectively.*

A mapping $\varphi : \tau_1 \rightarrow \tau_2$ is a full embedding iff

1. $\langle \mathbf{s_1}, \mathbf{s_2}, \mathbf{a_1} \rangle \in \mathbf{min\_precedes} \Leftrightarrow \langle \varphi(\mathbf{s_1}), \varphi(\mathbf{s_2}), \mathbf{a_2} \rangle \in \mathbf{min\_precedes}$;
2. $\langle \mathbf{s_1}, \mathbf{s_2}, \mathbf{a_1} \rangle \in \mathbf{leaf} \Leftrightarrow \langle \varphi(\mathbf{s_1}), \varphi(\mathbf{s_2}), \mathbf{a_2} \rangle \in \mathbf{leaf}$.

6.2.2. Classes of Structures

We begin by defining a partial ordering on the sets of activity trees.

Definition 6 *Let $\mathcal{C}$ be a complex activity structure.*

$\langle \mathcal{C}^s, \subseteq \rangle$ is a partial ordering on the set of activity trees in $\mathcal{C}$ such that $\tau_i \subseteq \tau_j$ iff there is a full embedding of τ_i into τ_j.

One intuition behind activity specialization is that an activity does not occur outside of an occurrence of any of its generalizations. This is formalized as the requirement that all activity trees for the activity are embedded within the activity trees of the generalized activities. A second intuition is that an activity's specializations correspond to the different ways in which an activity can occur, so that specialized activities are subactivities of the general activities. These two considerations lead us to the following definition of the structure which will ultimately be used to characterize the extension of the $\mathbf{isA}$ relation:

Definition 7 *Let $\mathcal{A}$ be a subactivity ordered set, let $\mathcal{C}$ be a complex activity structure, and let $\varphi : \mathcal{C} \rightarrow \mathcal{A}$ be a surjective mapping such that $\varphi(\tau) = \mathbf{a}$ iff τ is an activity tree for the activity $\mathbf{a}$.*

A substructure $\mathbb{S} \subseteq \mathcal{A}$ is specialized subactivity ordered set iff φ maps ideals in $\langle \mathcal{C}, \subseteq \rangle$ to ideals in $\mathbb{S}$.

The ideal of an activity in the partial ordering is equal to the set of all activities that are generalizations of the activity. If $\mathbf{a}$ is an activity in the specialized subactivity ordered set and τ is an activity tree for $\mathbf{a}$, then the set of activity trees containing τ (i.e. the ideal in $\langle \mathcal{C}, \subseteq \rangle$) is mapped to the set of activities containing $\mathbf{a}$ as a subactivity (i.e. the ideal in $\mathcal{A}$). This guarantees that there are no activity trees for an activity that are not subtrees of the activity trees for its generalizations.

The second class of structures represents the extension of the $\mathbf{instanceOf}$ relation.

Definition 8 *Let (A, O, E) be a bipartite graph consisting of activities A and activity occurrences O.*

Suppose $N(\mathbf{a_i}) = \{\mathbf{o} : (\mathbf{o}, \mathbf{a}) \in E\}$.

$\mathbb{I} = \langle A, O, E \rangle$ is an instance graph iff $(\bigcup_i N(\mathbf{a_i}), \subseteq) \cong \mathbb{S}$ where $\mathbb{S}$ is the specialized subactivity ordered set.

6.2.3. Introducing $\mathfrak{M}^{obo}$

Definition 9 *Let $\mathfrak{M}^{obo}$ be the class of structures such that $\mathcal{M} \in \mathfrak{M}^{obo}$ we have*

1. *$\mathcal{M} = \mathcal{N} \cup \mathbb{S}$ such that*
   - *(a) $\mathcal{N}$ is a model of T_{psl};*
   - *(b) $\mathbb{S} = \langle A, \sqsubseteq \rangle$ is a specialized subactivity ordered set.*
   - *(c) $\mathbb{I} = \langle A, O, E \rangle$ is an instance graph.*
2. *$\langle \mathbf{o_1}, \mathbf{o_2} \rangle \in \mathbf{coextensive}$ iff $\beta^{-1}(\mathbf{o_1}) = \beta^{-1}(\mathbf{o_2})$.*
3. *$\langle \mathbf{a_1}, \mathbf{a_2} \rangle \in \mathbf{isA}$ iff $\mathbf{a_1} \sqsubseteq \mathbf{a_2}$.*
4. *$\langle \mathbf{o}, \mathbf{a} \rangle \in \mathbf{instanceOf}$ iff $(\mathbf{o}, \mathbf{a}) \in E$.*

If $T_{special}$ is the subtheory of T_{obo} containing the axioms for isA and $instanceOf$, then we can then prove the following characterization theorems:

Theorem 5 *Any structure $\mathcal{M} \in \mathfrak{M}^{obo}$ is a model of $T_{special} \cup T_{psl}$ and any countable model of $T_{special} \cup T_{psl}$ is isomorphic to a structure $\mathcal{M} \in \mathfrak{M}^{obo}$.*

7. Summary

In this paper, we have provided a first-order axiomatization of the intended semantics of the process relations within the OBO Relations Ontology. We did this by specifying translation definitions using the PSL Ontology, so that the axioms which constitute the OBO Process Ontology form a definitional extension of the PSL Ontology. We also characterized the models of the resulting axiomatization, thereby demonstrating the formal verification of the ontology.

With the axioms of the OBO Process Ontology and the PSL Ontology, we can specify process descriptions for biological processes, which cannot be done with existing ontologies. For example, the Biological Process Ontology of the Gene Ontology cannot represent biological pathways since biological processes in the ontology are specified only in terms of the associated molecular functions.

The OBO Process Ontology can also be used to define classes of queries associated with more traditional reasoning problems within knowledge representation, such as temporal projection, planning, (e.g. biochemical synthesis) and plan verification. This opens up new avenues for research in the application of automated reasoning to biomedical ontologies.

References

[1] Obo: Open biomedical ontologies. `www.obo.sourceforge.net/`.

[2] Thomas Bittner. Logical properties of foundational mereogeometrical relations in bio-ontologies. *Appl. Ontol.*, 4(2):109–138, 2009.

[3] M Grüninger. Guide to the ontology of the process specification language. In S Staab, editor, *Handbook of Ontologies in Information Systems*. Springer-Verlag, 2003.

[4] M Grüninger and C Menzel. Process Specification Language: Principles and applications. *AI Magazine*, 24(3):63–74, 2003.

[5] Michael Gruninger and Joseph B. Kopena. Semantic integration through invariants. *AI Mag.*, 26(1):11–20, 2005.

[6] P Hayes. A catalog of temporal theories. *Artificial Intelligence Technical Report UIUC-BI-AI-96-01*, 1996.

[7] Christopher J. Mungall. Obol: integrating language and meaning in bio-ontologies: Conference papers. *Comp. Funct. Genomics*, 5(6-7):509–520, 2004.

[8] Raymond Reiter. *Knowledge in Action: Logical Foundations for Specifying and Implementing Dynamical Systems*. MIT Press, 2001.

[9] Murray Shanahan. The event calculus explained. *Lecture Notes in Computer Science*, 1600:409–430, 1999.

[10] Barry Smith, Werner Ceusters, Bert Klagges, Jacob Köhler, Anand Kumar, Jane Lomax, Chris Mungall, Fabian Neuhaus, Alan L. Rector, and Cornelius Rosse. Relations in biomedical ontologies. *Genome biology*, 6(5):R46+, 2005.

[11] Heinrich Wansing. Agency and deontic logic, j.f. horty. *J. of Logic, Lang. and Inf.*, 13(3):379–381, 2004.

Formal Ontology in Information Systems
A. Galton and R. Mizoguchi (Eds.)
IOS Press, 2010

doi:10.3233/978-1-60750-535-8-257

What are chemical structures and their relations?

Janna HASTINGS [a,1], Colin BATCHELOR [b], Christoph STEINBECK [a] and Stefan SCHULZ [c]

[a] *European Bioinformatics Institute, Hinxton, UK*
[b] *Royal Society of Chemistry, Thomas Graham House, Cambridge, UK*
[c] *Institute of Medical Biometry and Medical Informatics, University Medical Center Freiburg, Germany*

Abstract.
In chemistry, advances in computational technologies have allowed research into molecules that have not been synthesized yet, and may never be, to become widespread. These are described in terms of their structures, which are expressed as chemical graphs. Chemical graphs are a representational artifact, and as such are of a different ontological nature than the molecular entities which they describe.

ChEBI (Chemical Entities of Biological Interest) is an ontology of chemical entities such as atoms, ions and molecules. ChEBI is being developed within a realist framework, explicitly incorporating only those entities which are known to exist. However, its molecular entities are described with chemical graphs, and ChEBI makes use of two IUPAC 'derivation' relations, which are defined partly in terms of chemical graphs and names rather than real molecules. Many modern chemical databases do not make explicit a distinction between the structures of chemical entities which do not exist (predicted molecules) and those which do exist (experimentally verified molecules), with both similarly described by chemical graphs.

We therefore here analyse the ontological nature of these chemical graphs and the relations which hold between them. We interpret chemical graphs as representations of mathematical "connectivity" objects that can be used to precisely and exhaustively define many classes of molecule based on known properties of the connection of parts within molecules. We furthermore scrutinize the contentious relations in ChEBI and address their formal definitions both in terms of the graphs which represent their structures, and in terms of the molecular entities themselves. Finally, we show how these relations can be expressed using description logics.

Keywords. chemistry, ontology, chemical graph, information

Introduction

Chemical Entities of Biological Interest (ChEBI) is a database and ontology of molecular entities such as atoms, ions, groups, and molecules [1,2], which are either products of nature or synthetic products used to intervene in the processes of living organisms. The ChEBI ontology includes a structure-based classification under a root term 'molecular

[1]To whom correspondence should be addressed. European Bioinformatics Institute, Hinxton, UK CB10 1SD; E-mail: hastings@ebi.ac.uk.

structure', and a classification of the activities which molecular entities may exhibit in biological or chemical processes under a root term 'role'.

Following IUPAC [3], ChEBI defines 'molecular entity' as

> Any constitutionally or isotopically distinct atom, molecule, ion, [...] etc., identifiable as a separately distinguishable entity.

That is, fixed configurational molecular variations like tautomers and stereoisomers are represented as separate ChEBI entities, in contrast to conformations of molecules which are free to rotate around a bond, as they are impossible to isolate in practice.

1. Problem

In chemistry, *in silico* methods in drug discovery and chemical synthesis are increasingly being used, where computable plans of molecules are submitted to computer simulations. The result of such experiments (e.g. how well a molecule is predicted to attach to a receptor protein) may then trigger the synthesis of a 'real' molecule in the lab. In other cases the existence of a postulated molecule is speculative, and the research question of whether corresponding molecules exist in nature or can be chemically synthesized, remains open [4].

These predicted molecules are described in terms of their structures, which are expressed as chemical graphs. Chemical graphs are a kind of representational artifact, and as such are of a different ontological nature than the molecular entities which they describe. They are encoded in various computable formats and displayed as graph pictures. Many modern chemical databases do not make explicit a distinction between the structures of chemical entities which do not exist (predicted molecules)[2] and those whose existence has been experimentally verified.

The ChEBI ontology subscribes to the realist framework of much work in modern biomedical ontology including the Open Biomedical Ontologies (OBO) Foundry [6], explicitly incorporating only entities which are known to exist. However, its molecular entities are described with chemical graphs where possible. Furthermore, ChEBI makes use of two IUPAC 'derivation' relations, *has_parent_hydride* and *has_functional_parent*, which do not have a straightforward realist interpretation in terms of chemical entities, even where these entities exist, as these relations are defined partly in terms of graphs and names. The IUPAC Gold Book [3] defines a 'parent hydride' as

> A [...] structure having a semisystematic or trivial name to which only hydrogen atoms are attached.[3]

Note the reference to 'structure', which implies the chemical graph rather than the chemical entity, and the reference to 'name' which is also an information entity[4]. The situation is similar for the IUPAC definition of 'functional parent' as

[2]For a large collection of such predicted molecules, see the GDB [5].

[3]`http://goldbook.iupac.org/P04405.html`

[4]The word 'parent' in both cases denotes that the name of the target of the relationship has been used to derive the name of the child.

> A structure the name of which implies the presence of one or more characteristic groups [...] [5]

It is clear that chemists happily interchange the two concepts of structures (graphs) and molecular entities without much concern, resulting in much confusion in the terminology used in chemical discourse[6].

We therefore here analyse chemical graphs and these relations and address the following problems:

1. What is the ontological nature of chemical graphs and their relationship to chemical entities, real or predicted?
2. Which ChEBI relations
   (i) range over chemical entities and which range over graphs; and
   (ii) range over individuals and which range over classes?
3. How can these relations be specified using standard description logics?

2. Background

We analyze chemical graphs and their relation to real molecular entities according to the principles of formal ontology, especially following the precept of the Basic Formal Ontology (BFO) [7,8,9], and the Open Biomedical Ontologies (OBO) [6]. Here, we give relevant background to the discussion which follows.

2.1. Realism and Ontology

The realist background to much modern work in biomedical ontology holds that ontology in the biomedical sciences should be devoted to the representation of entities as they exist in reality [10]. Furthermore, reality neatly divides between *individuals* (tokens, particulars), the specific individual objects which exist in space and time, and universals (types, kinds), which represent everything that is common to a group of individuals *of the same kind*, thus delineating classes. Examples of individuals are the person Bob Smith, the cat Frodo, and Mary's digestion process after lunch this afternoon. Examples of universals are *Human*, *Feline*, and *Digestion*. In chemistry, the individuals are the atoms, ions and molecules which constitute all matter in the world; the universals are the types of atoms, ions and molecules, representing what is common in a group of individuals.

We find it useful to differentiate Aristotelian realism from Platonist realism. Both schools admit universals as entities, however, in Aristotelian realism, universals are *in* real things, observable (directly or indirectly) by the senses, whereas Platonist universals are "abstract", unable to be perceived [11]. Furthermore, Aristotelian universals existentially depend on their individuals, while Platonist individuals existentially depend on their universals. Franklin [12] differentiates between "this-worldly", or strict, Aristotelianism, in which uninstantiated universals do not exist in any way; and "Platonist Aristotelianism", in which universals exist, but we can know about more universals than

[5] `http://goldbook.iupac.org/F02556.html`

[6] This confusion is exemplified in the present name 'molecular structure' of the root of the ChEBI classification of chemical entities.

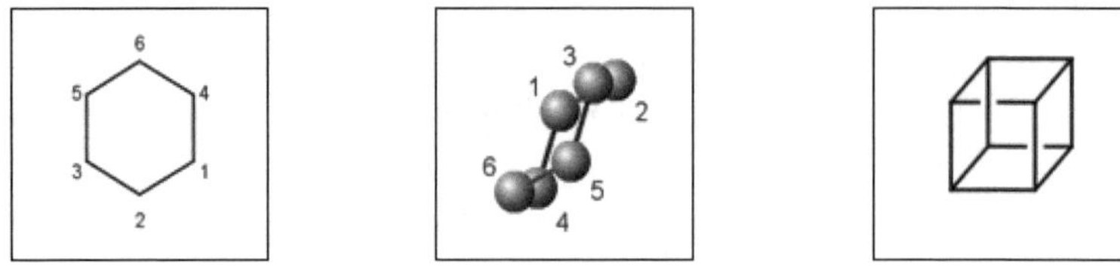

(a) 2D cyclohexane (b) 3D cyclohexane (c) Impossible cubane

Atom,	Atom,	Type
2	1	1
3	2	1
4	1	1
5	3	1
6	4	1
5	6	1

(d) Connection table

x	y	z
0.71	-0.41	0.00
0.00	-0.82	0.00
-0.71	-0.41	0.00
0.71	0.41	0.00
-0.71	0.41	0.00
0.00	0.82	0.00

(e) 2D coordinates

x	y	z
0.52	0.42	-1.34
-0.98	0.15	-1.11
-1.22	-0.86	0.03
1.22	0.86	-0.03
-0.52	-0.42	1.34
0.98	-0.15	1.11

(f) 3D coordinates

Figure 1. Chemical graphs

actually do exist, and it is a contingent, or empirical, matter which of the universals we can know about are instantiated and which are not.

However, the representational framework increasingly used in biomedical ontologies, Description Logics (DL) [13] does not distinguish between universals and non-universals. DL terminology admits classes and individuals, but with no restriction that a class should extend a universal. We can easily introduce classes that do not correspond to universals. For instance, we can create a class *Human* as the extension of the universal *Human*, but the defined class *not Human* does not represent any universal (since there is nothing in common with the entities so described), and the class *Human or Plant* is logically sound but ontologically unsound.

2.2. Graph theory and chemistry

The objects of graph theory are mathematical entities (as numbers are), dealing with the way in which objects are connected. The principal object of graph theory is a graph, which consists of a set of objects and the binary relations between them. Graph theory has found many applications in chemistry and is used to represent many different chemical objects including molecules, reactions, crystals and clusters [14]. The particular type of chemical graph with which we here concern ourselves is the molecular graph which represents the constitution of a molecule in terms of nodes (atoms) and edges (bonds). For practical purposes, chemical databases that store these as adjacency matrices extend this to include two-dimensional and three-dimensional coordinates.

Figure 1 illustrates examples of chemical graphs, 2D and 3D coordinates, and the corresponding visualisations as are common in chemistry. Note that Hydrogen nodes are suppressed in Figure 1, as is common in representation of chemicals by graphs. Hydrogen-suppressed graphs are termed skeleton graphs. Coordinates are given in "co-ordinate space" with respect to the axes of the images, that is, they are unitless.

Chemical graphs simplify the complex nature of a molecule, allow schematic representation of molecules, and enable many useful predictions to be made about physical and chemical properties of molecules which are based on connectivity. They thus neatly extend the domain of chemistry discourse by allowing for the representation of processes and molecules, the existence of which is only hypothesized or predicted.

However, chemical graphs can also be constructed for molecules which *cannot* exist, such as the impossible figure in Figure 1 (c)[7]. This molecule is infeasible because the bonds depicted cannot physically exist. Another kind of chemical impossibility is to have too many bonds to a particular atom. Chemists, and to a certain extent computational tools, are able to validate a chemical graph to assess whether it corresponds to a molecule which is chemically feasible[8].

Much of chemistry can be expressed using the graph formalism, but chemical graphs do not describe everything in chemistry. They do not work for non-pairwise bonding as found in metal coordination compounds, ionic bonding as found in minerals, and hydrogen bonding which is responsible for base pairing in DNA and RNA. It is also impossible to draw a chemical graph that defines broad types of chemical entity such as 'organic molecule', or 'carbohydrate', or most of the families of naturally-occurring chemical compounds. Furthermore, there are molecules such as D-glucose that rapidly interconvert (tautomerize) between forms with very different (ring-like and chain-like) chemical graphs.

2.3. Relations between chemical entities

Subsumption

The *is_a* relation is used throughout the ChEBI ontology to link classes to their taxonomic parents, as illustrated in Figure 2 (a). We can interpret the *is_a* relation straightforwardly as representing the taxonomic hierarchy of chemical entities. With respect to the chemical graphs illustrated, we can interpret the *is_a* relation only through recourse to chemistry-specific constructs which imply, by definition, hierarchy: the 'R' groups used to define the structure of chemical classes, the implicit hierarchy of bond types in which a stereospecific bond (up or down) is a specialisation of a stereounspecified bond.

Mereology

The *has_part* relation, illustrated in Figure 2(b), is used in ChEBI in the following, semantically distinct, cases:

- to link salts with individual ions;
- to link atoms and molecules with subatomic particles;
- to link molecules with atoms; and
- to link whole molecules with groups and other molecule parts.

Parthood is also implied by the *is_substituent_group_from* relation, although in the opposite direction. This relation links a group, residue or ring to the molecule from which it is principally composed. Thus, we can say that *A is_substituent_group_from*

[7]http://metallome.blogspot.com/2009/02/impossible-figures.html

[8]Note that chemical feasibility varies with respect to conditions, since it is possible to create otherwise infeasible molecules by, for example, keeping them at low temperatures in a helium matrix; and at high enough temperatures and pressures in collapsing stars, all molecules become infeasible.

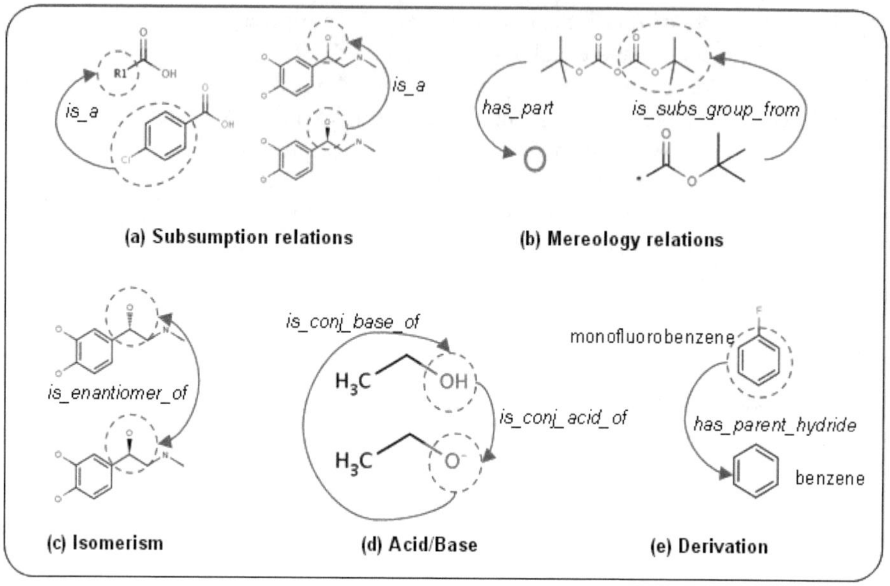

Figure 2. Relations between chemical entities

B implies that *B has_part A*, but also that the parthood in this case is somehow maximal. Also, the domain of *is_substituent_group_from* is restricted to molecular parts (groups/residues/rings/skeleta) while the domain of the *has_part* relation is across all chemical entities in ChEBI.

With respect to chemical entities, parthood relations can be interpreted as denoting composition. However, forming a whole usually alters the shape and/or charge distribution of the part, as electron orbitals are rearranged in the bonds and interactions which allow the molecule to exist as a whole. With respect to chemical graphs, parthood denotes that the graph of the part is a *subgraph*[9] of the graph of the whole.

Isomerism

ChEBI includes two relationships for isomerism, namely *is_tautomer_of* to link tautomers, which are isomers that readily interconvert by a chemical reaction called tautomerization, which results in the relocation of a hydrogen atom (proton); and *is_enantiomer_of* to link enantiomers, as illustrated in Figure 2 (c), which are mirror images of each other. Note that ChEBI does not explicitly include relationships for other forms of isomerism, either structural isomerism or stereoisomerism, which are however equally valid candidates for relations holding between chemical entities in a chemical ontology.

Tautomers are so named because they are able to be interconverted by tautomerization reactions. It is often the case that enantiomers interconvert in solution. However, some forms of isomerism are not readily interconverted, and thus can best be thought of as a relationship based on similarity in constitution between molecules. With respect to chemical graphs, various algorithms exist for detecting isomeric graphs, but these are

[9] A subgraph of a graph G is a graph whose node set is a subset of that of G, and whose adjacency relation is a subset of that of G restricted to this subset of nodes [http://en.wikipedia.org/wiki/Subgraph].

non-trivial.

Acid/Base relations

Is_conjugate_base_of and *is_conjugate_acid_of* are the relations used between a conjugate base and acid, illustrated in Figure 2 (d), in which the acid is able to donate a proton to the base in an acid/base reaction. ChEBI does not explicitly include relations for reactions in which more than one proton is donated. With respect to chemical graphs, as with tautomers, algorithms do exist which are able to detect this relationship between graphs in some, but not all, cases.

IUPAC nomenclature relations

Has_functional_parent and *has_parent_hydride* are relations introduced by IUPAC to illustrate the derivation of correct nomenclature for molecules. They do have a structural meaning – in the case of *has_functional_parent*, a functional group has been added, removed or modified between the two structures linked with the relation; and in the case of *has_parent_hydride*, as illustrated in Figure 2 (e), the target structure has the principal skeleton of the source, bonded only to hydrogens. However, not all structures which differ only by the addition / removal of functional groups can be termed functional parents, and not all structures which consist of carbon skeletons bonded only to hydrogen can be termed parent hydrides. The choice of which structures to term parent hydrides and which structures to term functional parents is partly for historical reasons, and has to do with the system of nomenclature, whereby the names of chemical entities are derived from positional substitution of the names of other chemical entities.

2.4. Information Artifacts

The Information Artifact Ontology (IAO) [15] is an ontology of information entities such as the files on computers and the information content of books and publications. The root term is 'information content entity', which is defined as being generically dependent on some artifact (the bearer of the information, such as a book, or computer) and about some entity (for example, a name is about the entity that it is a name of). This "aboutness" is encoded in the relation *is_about* which links information entities to non-information entities. Note that the inverse of the *is_about* relation is problematic from a realist perspective, since information is not a property of the thing it is about.

A special type of information described in IAO is that which encodes a plan specification, that is, the information content specifies a process which has to be followed in order to bring about some goal or objective. In this case, we can link the material output of the process that follows the plan specification, if such exists, with the *has_specification* relation to the plan specification itself.

3. What are chemical graphs?

The first question that we have set ourselves regards the ontological nature of chemical graphs and their relationship to chemical entities. Recall that chemical graphs are representations of chemical entities, but that chemical graphs may exist for chemical entities which *do not* (or are not known to) exist, and for chemical entities which *cannot* exist. Chemical universals (CU)[10] exist in their individuals, i.e. if there is no such individual then there is no such CU. An individual of a CU is a single molecule, and CUs are arranged in subtype hierarchies. For each CU there are one or more chemical graphs (CG).

We here propose several approaches for how to interpret chemical graphs in an ontology, and discuss their pros and cons. We use **bold** face for individuals and relations between individuals, *Italics with leading capital* for universals and relations between universals or between individuals and universals, and *lower case italics* for classes. Each of the following proposals include defined classes, which do not necessarily entail the existence of an individual.

3.1. Chemical graphs as individuals with information content

In this proposal, we interpret chemical graphs as individuals of a *chemical graph* subtype of the IAO class *information content entity*. As information entities, chemical graphs are generically dependent on some material information bearer (such as a computer or a book) and specifically dependent on the entity that they are information about. The relationship between a CG and the CU it describes is the *is_about* relation. For example,

Beta-farnesene $\sqsubseteq$ *Farnesene*
beta-farnesene-CG $\in$ *CG* $\sqsubseteq$ *InformationContentEntity*
beta-farnesene-CG $\in$ (*CG* $\sqcap \forall$ **is_about**.*Beta-farnesene*)

As individuals, CGs do not reflect the hierarchy of their related CUs. For each CU we can construct at least one CG. However, there may be CGs for which no CUs exist, as in the case of predicted molecules in computational experiments, and speculative molecules in theoretical chemistry research. In these cases we cannot use **is_about** to relate the CG to a CU, since the latter does not exist. However, for each CG individual we can define a class of chemical entities regardless of the theoretical consideration of the existence of individuals belonging to that class. Given the CG **a-CG**, the corresponding defined class *a* is the equivalent to the expression $\exists$ **has_specification**.{**a-CG**}, where **has_specification** is being used to imply a liberal interpretation of a chemical graph as a plan specification of a possible molecule.

This approach has the advantage that for speculative CUs we can create fully defined classes, and in a DL ontology there is no difference between classes that extend universals and classes that do not, although this may be specified in an annotation property. On the downside we have to accept that because CGs are individuals, no hierarchical relationships between CGs can be asserted, and the intuitive sense that a chemical graph is still "about something" (even if the CU does not exist) is not taken into account. We also have difficulty dealing with situations in which there are multiple CGs for a CU.

3.2. Chemical graphs as information types

Rather than considering chemical graphs as individuals of the *chemical graph* information entity type, we can regard chemical graphs as information entity types themselves. A CG is thus a type (universal) which is instantiated by the specific files which are the bearer of that information content on computers, or the sketches on whiteboards in

[10]We regard 'universal' here as synonymous with 'type' or 'kind', deferring as far as possible philosophical questions about the nature of universals.

chemists' offices. Thus, using the same example as before, we end up with the following hierarchy:

Beta-farnesene-CG $\sqsubseteq$ *Farnesene-CG* $\sqsubseteq$ *CG* $\sqsubseteq$ *InformationContentEntity*

Furthermore, chemical graphs can lead to the generation of synthesis plan specifications (which involves steps like adding such and such an amount of a given precursor to a certain volume of other material dissolved in a solvent, heating, cooling, evaporating, and so forth).

As per the first proposal, we can create defined classes for CUs based on these CGs. Furthermore, this approach allows us to express the hierarchy of CGs as a hierarchy of information entities. We can also account for the "aboutness" of those CGs which are generated as part of a pre-synthesization planning process. However, we still cannot account for what a CG is about if it represents a molecule for which a synthesis would not be feasible given currently available technology, nor one that is chemical infeasible.

3.3. Chemical graphs as mathematical entities

In both of the previous proposals we have regarded chemical graphs as nothing more than information about molecules, on a par with other forms of information about molecules such as names, database references and literature citations. However, this categorisation seems to underexplain the chemical graph. It is certainly the case that a chemical graph does encode information about a molecule, but the information which is encoded is a very special type of information – the connectivity of the molecule – which seems an essential structural feature of the molecule.

A graph is a mathematical entity, and thus, as is the case for all mathematical objects, it seems to enjoy only an abstract kind of existence. Plato spoke of immaterial and abstract forms which had no causal relationship to the material world that we inhabit and perceive. Aristotelian realists, on the other hand, seem committed to reject mathematical objects as universals, and BFO has heretofore not made any commitments with regard to mathematical objects. However, it is possible to synthesize Aristotelian realism with mathematical objects by regarding the mathematical objects as dependent entities which inhere in material entities by virtue of the *numeric and structural relationships* between the material entities [12].

In the case of chemical graphs, the connectivity described by the graph is the structural, mathematical property of connection between separate parts of a whole in a chemical entity. As such, the connectivity represented by the graph is a mathematical entity that represents what is common in collections of distinct parts connected in exactly that way. The existence of a particular connectivity is determined by the existence of parts connected in that way, and larger connectivities can be built up out of smaller connectivities by means of creating further connections which themselves exist in that way[11].

Note that, for a given CU, we now have three ontologically interesting categories:

1. the CU, which has instances individual chemical entities;
2. the connectivity[12], which exists in many individual molecules;
3. the chemical graph representation of the connectivity, which is an information artifact, concretized in a particular file on the computer.

[11] We here adopt the "Platonist Aristotelian" approach to universals.

[12] Similarly, we can extend our mathematical conception of connection to include spatial relations such as being above or below, thus incorporating chirality.

We can now deal with chemical graphs for which no corresponding molecular entities exist via the intermediate, mathematical, connectivity object. Connectivity is a property that is grounded in the existence of parts and the existence of connections between parts of that type, rather than being grounded in the properties of a specific molecule. And if we take chemical graphs to be "about" connectivity, rather than "about" CUs, because of the properties of compositionality of connectivities, we find that the actual existence of a CU which matches a CG becomes less relevant. However, we do have a toolkit for evaluating the feasibility of a given CG to correspond to a real molecule, because the connectivity represented by a particular graph can be evaluated. If it is found that instances of that connectivity do not exist, such as for the impossible molecule illustrated in Figure 1 (c), then we know that the graph represents an invalid connectivity and thus does not correspond to a feasible CU.

We now have the mechanism to address all of the shortcomings of our earlier formulations. As before,

Beta-farnesene $\sqsubseteq$ *Farnesene*

Beta-farnesene-CG $\sqsubseteq$ *InformationContentEntity*

However, the "aboutness" of the CG is rather to the connectivity mathematical entity (ME):

Beta-farnesene-CG $\sqsubseteq \forall$ **is_about**.*Beta-farnesene-connectivity-ME*

But nevertheless the CG remains a specification for a class of chemical entities (CUs)

$\exists$ **has_specification**.*Beta-farnesene-CG*

And in this case, we know via experimental evidence that the extension of this class is non-empty:

Beta-farnesene $\equiv \exists$ **has_specification**.*Beta-farnesene-CG*

4. Which relations do graphs participate in?

We now address the problem of the interpretation of the chemical relationships presented earlier. One question we need to answer is how to assert relationships between predicted or speculative molecules, given that the standard logical expression of relationships between individuals requires the existence of individuals in order for the relationship to be asserted. We will approach this through the definition of equivalent *graph* relations.

Subsumption

We can interpret the subsumption relation *is_a* as used in ChEBI as ranging over CUs. However, we should be wary of this straightforward interpretation, both for the case of speculative molecules, and since structural classes in ChEBI may not exhibit functional or dispositional unifying characteristics. In chemistry, a universal groups chemical entities that exhibit a shared functional disposition which is grounded in a shared aspect of the molecular structure. Amino acids, having the disposition to polymerize to form proteins, regardless of their chirality, are definitely a universal. A stereounspecified parent, as in Figure 2(a), however, has no such interesting dispositions.

Thus, given the requirement for subsumption relations between classes which do not correspond to universals, we further define a relation between connectivities (MEs), *is_graph_specialization_of*, which can be determined via standard mathematical graph manipulation techniques, which can operate on CGs as representations of MEs. Where two CUs exist, if an *is_graph_specialization_of* relation holds between the two MEs, and the CUs are equivalent to the defined classes corresponding to the CGs which are about those MEs, then we can conclude that the *is_a* relation holds between the CUs.

Mereology, Isomerism and Acid/Base relations

The situation is similar for the *has_part* and *is_substituent_group_from* relations used in ChEBI. Here, the relevant graph relation is *is_subgraph_of*. For the isomerism and acid/base relations, we can define equivalent graph relations, but should bear in mind that these graph relations are very specific to chemistry.

IUPAC derivation relations and nomenclature

As expected, the situation becomes more complex when dealing with the IUPAC derivation relations. The definitions of the *has_functional_parent* and *has_parent_hydride* relations supplied by IUPAC refer to derivation of one 'structure' from another and to the contribution of the name of the parent to the name of the child. The implied derivation of one entity from another may correspond to an actual derivation process, that is, it may be possible to derive a molecule from its parent hydride or functional parent by a controlled functional modification reaction; but in many cases this is not the case, and it is not required for the relationship to hold true. We therefore propose that the *has_functional_parent* and *has_parent_hydride* relations are best understood as ranging over graphs and chemical nomenclature.

A chemical name is an information entity similarly to a chemical graph. We can differentiate between trivial and systematic names. Trivial names are those which are in common use for certain chemical entities. Systematic names are generated based on the chemical structure, *i.e.* the connectivity. For trivial names, it is possible for the structure of the entity so named to be wrong (as was often the case in the early days of chemical structure determination) and to be updated as greater accuracy in structure determination became available, without the name changing. However, it is not possible for a systematic name to be wrong in this way, since if the structure changes, necessarily so must the name. We therefore propose that trivial names are about chemical entities (CUs) while systematic names are about connectivity (MEs).

The names which form part of the definitions of the IUPAC derivation relations, however, are trivial or semi-systematic, thus fall into the former category. Thus, the formalization of the ChEBI relation *is_parent_hydride* is something like the conjunction of:

Fluorobenzene-name ≡ (*Name* ⊓ ∀ **is_about**.*Fluorobenzene*);
Benzene-CG ≡ (*CG* ⊓ ∀ **is_about**.*Benzene-connectivity-ME*);
Fluorobenzene-CG ≡ (*CG* ⊓ ∀ **is_about**.*Fluorobenzene-connectivity-ME*);
Fluorobenzene-name ⊑ ∃ **is_derived_from**.*Benzene-name*; and
Benzene-CG ⊑ ∃ **is_hydride_graph_of**.*Fluorobenzene-CG*

5. Simplified Representation in Description Logics

We here attempt to represent all ChEBI relations in DL, bearing in mind the above discussion about the interpretation of chemical graphs and relations. We aim at (i) coherence with philosophical theory, (ii) intuitiveness, (iii) parsimony, (iv) graceful evolution (little lack of compatibility with the current representation in ChEBI), and (v) DL compatibility. One criterion to assess this approach is to what extent the current ChEBI relations can be used without violating one of these precepts. Description logics impose the following restrictions:

1. The only relation between classes is the taxonomic subsumption relation $\sqsubseteq$;
2. The only relation between individuals and classes is the membership relation $\in$;
3. All other relations are relations between individuals. For their use in class descriptions they need to be quantified by the $\exists$ or $\forall$ quantifier;
4. The internal structure of a CG may not be expressible in a DL in such a way as to preserve decidability, because it may be cyclic.

We therefore have to make a distinction between (i) the whole ontological framework, and (ii) its practical DL implementation. Here is our proposal:

1. Each CG defines a class. The relation between the CG and the defined class is implicit in ChEBI;
2. These classes are DL classes. They are not fully defined in DL, but are, implicitly, by their underlying CG specification;
3. The fact that two different CGs correspond to two different classes does not preclude that they be co-extensional because they extend the same universal;
4. Whether these classes extend universals can be captured by using the labels in IAO that distinguish universals from mere defined classes;
5. The existing ChEBI class-to-class relations are expressed in DL as follows:
   A is_a B $=_{def}$ $A \sqsubseteq B$
   A has_part B $=_{def}$ $A \sqsubseteq \exists$ **has_part**.*B*
   A has_role B $=_{def}$ $A \sqsubseteq \exists$ **has_role**.*B*
   A is_tautomer_of B $=_{def}$ $A \sqsubseteq \forall$ **is_tautomer_of**.*B*
   A is_enantiomer_of B $=_{def}$ $A \sqsubseteq \forall$ **is_enantiomer_of**.*B*
   A is_conjugate_base_of B $=_{def}$ $A \sqsubseteq \forall$ **is_conjugate_base_of**.*B*
   A is_conjugate_acid_of B $=_{def}$ $A \sqsubseteq \forall$ **is_conjugate_acid_of**.*B*
   A has_functional_parent B $=_{def}$ $A \sqsubseteq \forall$ **has_functional_parent**.*B*
   A has_parent_hydride B $=_{def}$ $A \sqsubseteq \forall$ **has_parent_hydride** *B*.
   A is_substituent_group_from B $=_{def}$ $A \sqsubseteq \forall$ **is_substituent_group_from**.*B*
   A is_conjugate_acid_of B $=_{def}$ $A \sqsubseteq \exists$ **is_conjugate_acid_of**.*B*

The use of the value restriction ($\forall$) prevents unintended models, because it does not create an ontological dependence. Using $\exists$ instead would, e.g., require that for each molecule that instantiates one stereoisomeric type there must be some instance of the corresponding enantiomer. This is inadequate from a chemical standpoint because there are situations where we need to express relations between predicted or speculative entities.

However, we are aware that value restrictions are rather a surrogate for relations between classes or universals we cannot represent. If we state that *A* implies $\forall$ **is_enantiomer_of**.*B*, we express that for each molecule of the type *A* – if there is some enantiomer, then it must be of the type *B*. This is not the full story, but it comes close.

6. Discussion

The problem of asserting relations between classes or universals, and the difficulty to translate this into a simple and computable logic, is a constant issue for biomedical ontologies and has been much discussed in the context of the OBO Foundry. Originally developed for the Gene Ontology, the OBO Format [16] proposes relationships between "concepts", only part of which can be straightforwardly translated into description logics. The use of OWL Full was suggested by Hoehndorf et al. (2008) [17], with classes and universals represented separately. Universals are represented in the same manner as individuals, which allows the use of OWL object properties to express inter-universal relationships.

Although the differentiation between classes and universals is crucial from a philosophical standpoint, we do not recommend that ChEBI introduces this distinction for parsimony reasons. It would be hardly communicable to ChEBI users why they would have to choose, e.g. between Glucose (universal) and Glucose (defined class based on a given chemical graph). For the same reason the representation of information entities in parallel is not an option, because here, users would be confronted with Glucose (universal/class) on the one hand and Glucose (CG) on the other hand. Chemical graphs are included in ChEBI at present only as annotations against the core terms.

Our proposal is that the connectivity gives a full definition for certain classes of molecules (naturally excluding all classes of molecules which fall outside of the scope of the chemical graph formalism, as described). It is this mathematical entity which is represented in chemical graph files, patent claims, and so on. We can therefore consciously deviate from the principle that all nodes in DL ontologies should represent universals only. Instead, we allow them to represent both classes that extend universals and classes that are merely fully defined by means of other universals, viz. chemical graphs.

7. Conclusion

The fact that chemists need to define not only existing chemical entities but also some molecules which are speculative or predicted, described with chemical graphs, raises the problem of defining the ontological nature of the chemical graphs. We have discussed the ontological status of chemical graphs using principles of formal ontology, and concluded that, besides molecules and information there is another type, viz. the connectivity as a mathematical entity. Furthermore we analyzed the different kinds of relations and concluded that there are ChEBI relations that hold between molecules and other ones that hold between information entities.

Driven by practical need we then broke down this philosophical framework to be compatible with a non-disruptive and parsimonous evolution of ChEBI, obeying architectural constraints such as the use of description logics. This has led to several compromises. On the one hand we refrained from the use of higher-level relations, but we were able to represent their meaning at least partly by DL value restrictions. On the other hand we did not blow up the ontology by adding information entities and mathematical universals as separate constructs. Rather, we considered connectivity as specifications that allow for fully specifying DL classes.

We understand this work as an contribution to the ongoing discussion on the representation of "non-existing" entities and information, and argue for the use of defined classes in addition to classes that extend universals.

Acknowledgements

This work was partly funded by the European Commission under SLING, grant agreement number 226073 (Integrating Activity) within Research Infrastructures of the FP7 Capacities Specific Programme, and by the BBSRC, grant agreement number BB/G022747/1 within the "Bioinformatics and biological resources" fund. The authors wish to thank Kirill Degtyarenko, Alan Ruttenberg, Larry Hunter and Martin Boeker for helpful discussions, and the reviewers of an earlier version of this manuscript whose comments substantially contributed to the end result.

References

[1] Degtyarenko, K.; de Matos, P.; Ennis, M.; Hastings, J.; Zbinden, M.; McNaught, A.; Alcantara, R.; Darsow, M.; Guedj, M.; Ashburner, M. ChEBI: a database and ontology for chemical entities of biological interest. *Nucl. Acids Res.* **36** (2008), D344–D350.

[2] De Matos, P.; Alcantara, R.; Dekker, A.; Ennis, M.; Hastings, J.; Haug, K.; Spiteri, I.; Turner, S.; Steinbeck, C. Chemical Entities of Biological Interest: an update. *Nucl. Acids Res.* **38** (2010), D249–D254.

[3] International Union of Pure and Applied Chemistry, [http://www.iupac.org/], last accessed Feb 14, 2010.

[4] Dasent, W.E. *Non-existent Compounds*, Marcel Dekker, New York, 1965.

[5] Blum L. C.; Reymond J.-L. 970 Million Druglike Small Molecules for Virtual Screening in the Chemical Universe Database GDB-13. *J. Am. Chem. Soc.* **131(25)** (2009), 8732–8733.

[6] Smith, B.; Ashburner, M.; Rosse, C.; Bard, J.; Bug, W.; Ceusters, W.; Goldberg, L.J.; Eilbeck, K.; Ireland, A.; Mungall, C.J.; The OBI Consortium; Leontis, N.; Rocca-Serra, P.; Ruttenberg, A.; Sansone, S.A.; Scheuermann, R.H.; Shah, N.; Whetzel, P.L.; Lewis, S. The OBO Foundry: coordinated evolution of ontologies to support biomedical data integration. *Nature Biotechnology* **25** (2007), 1251–1255.

[7] Grenon, P. and Smith, B. SNAP and SPAN: Towards Dynamic Spatial Ontology. *Spatial Cognition and Computation: An Interdisciplinary Journal*, **4(1)** (2004), 69–104.

[8] Smith B. and Grenon P. The Cornucopia of Formal-Ontological Relations. *Dialectica* **58(3)** (2004), 279–296.

[9] Smith, B. and Grenon, P. Basic Formal Ontology. [http://www.ifomis.uni-saarland.de/bfo/], last accessed Feb 14, 2010.

[10] Smith, B. (2004) Beyond Concepts: Ontology as Reality Representation. In: Varzi, A., Vieu, L. (Eds.), Formal Ontology and Information Systems. Proceedings of the Third International Conference (FOIS 2004), IOS Press, Amsterdam. 73–84.

[11] Brown, J. R. *Philosophy of Mathematics: A contemporary introduction to the world of proofs and pictures.* Second Edition. Routledge, New York, NY 10016.

[12] Franklin, J. (2009) Aristotelian Realism. Chapter in *The Philosophy of Mathematics*, ed. A. Irvine (Handbook of the Philosophy of Science series, North-Holland Elsevier, 2009), 101–153.

[13] Baader, F.; Calvanese, D.; McGuinness, D.L.; Nardi, D.; Patel-Schneider, P.F., editors. *The Description Logic Handbook. Theory, Implementation, and Applications*, Cambridge, U.K.: Cambridge University Press, 2007.

[14] Trinijastic, N. *Chemical Graph Theory*. CRC Press, Florida, USA, 1992.

[15] Information Artifact Ontology. [http://code.google.com/p/information-artifact-ontology/] Last accessed Feb 14, 2010.

[16] Day-Richter, J. The OBO Flat File Format Specification, version 1.2 [http://www.geneontology.org/GO.format.obo-1_2.shtml], last accessed Feb 14, 2010.

[17] Hoehndorf, R.; Loebe, F.; Poli, R.; Herre, H.; Kelso, J. GFO-Bio: A biological core ontology. *Applied Ontology* **3(4)** (2008), 219–227.

Formal Ontology in Information Systems
A. Galton and R. Mizoguchi (Eds.)
IOS Press, 2010

doi:10.3233/978-1-60750-535-8-271

Ontological dependence, dispositions and institutional reality in chemistry

Colin BATCHELOR [a,1], Janna HASTINGS [b] and Christoph STEINBECK [b]
[a] *Royal Society of Chemistry, Thomas Graham House, Cambridge, UK CB4 0WF*
[b] *European Bioinformatics Institute, Hinxton, UK CB10 1SD*

Abstract. Biochemical 'small molecules' are involved in all living processes across all biological domains. Chemical ontologies provide structured chemical data and thereby support cross-disciplinary and integrative research across systems biology, chemogenomics and metabolomics. Efforts are underway to align ChEBI with upper level ontologies such as BFO, but confusion persists as to the ontological status of the ChEBI 'role' entities, which refer to continuants which inhere in chemical entities by virtue of the activity of the chemical entities. We provide a formal classification of these 'role' entities according to the continuants and endurants on which they ontologically depend, discuss the nature of chemical dispositions and the relevance of institutional reality, and address granularity issues in modelling chemical activity.

Keywords. chemistry, ontology, disposition

Introduction

Biochemical 'small molecules' are involved in all living processes across all biological domains. Chemical ontologies provide structured chemical data and thereby support cross-disciplinary and integrative research across systems biology, chemogenomics and metabolomics. ChEBI[2] (Chemical Entities of Biological Interest) [1] is an ontology of molecular entities such as molecules, groups, rings and atoms, apart from those that have been directly encoded by the genome such as proteins. All entities in ChEBI are manually annotated with multiple synonyms, useful references and, where applicable, a molecular structure.

Molecular entities in ChEBI are primarily classified according to their molecular structure. The classification of molecules according to formal operations on their structures is well established and documented at length in publications such as the IUPAC Gold, Red and Blue Books [2,3,4]. However, many of the groupings of molecular entities which are relevant to chemists and systems biologists are not primarily structure-based, but rather function-based, with the relevant criterion for a grouping being the bioactivity, chemical reactivity, physiological effect or other intended use by humans of the chemical entity.

[1]To whom correspondence should be addressed. Royal Society of Chemistry, Thomas Graham House, Cambridge, UK CB4 0WF; E-mail: BatchelorC@rsc.org.
[2]Available at `http://www.ebi.ac.uk/chebi`.

ChEBI captures these properties of the activity of chemical entities in a classification beneath a root term 'role', with chemical entities being linked to particular roles by means of the *has_role* relationship. Within this ontology we find entities representing bioactivity such as 'agonist' and 'inhibitor' as well as entities representing chemical reactivity such as 'acid' and physiological effect such as 'cardiotoxic agent'.

Problem

The classification of roles has hitherto been *ad hoc* and not grounded in formal ontological principles. The importance of formal ontological analysis as a component in creating usable, relevant, and interoperable structured data, is becoming widely recognised within the life sciences ontological community [5,6,7,8]. Without such a grounding, the possibilities for different interpretations by human readers is vast, and the plurality of possible interpretations hinders the use and interoperability of the classification. We have identified the following shortcomings with the ChEBI 'role' ontology:

- Multiple terms proliferate for similar-sounding things such as 'neurotoxic agent' and 'neurotoxin'; 'bronchodilator agent' and 'bronchodilator drug'.
- Definitions indicate confusion between these similar-sounding things, such as receptor agonist and antagonist terms which have definitions which begin with 'a drug'.
- Granularity distinctions which apply to the interpretation of different 'role' terms are not made explicit.
- The reliance on a single root term 'role' and related relationship *has_role* serves to give the false impression that the entities classified under this root form a homogeneous ontological category.

We address these shortcomings through a formal analysis and re-classification of the ChEBI 'role' terms, provide clarification on the nature of chemical dispositions and the relevance of institutional reality to some forms of chemical activity, and address granularity issues.

About this paper

The remainder of this document is organised as follows. First, we present some background information and useful definitions. We then examine the terms in the ChEBI 'role' ontology and discuss their properties from the point of view of formal ontology, with specific reference to the entities on which they ontologically depend and the conditions under which we can ascribe aspects of institutional reality to them. We propose an algorithm for classification of chemical activity which can be applied to a re-classification of the ChEBI 'role' ontology. Finally we explain the semantics of the different categories. As part of the OBO Foundry [5], ChEBI is committed to using the Basic Formal Ontology (BFO) [9,10] as an upper-level ontology. We thus give a mapping to BFO, though our approach will be suitable for any upper-level ontology that distinguishes categorical from dispositional properties, such as DOLCE [11] and GFO [12].

Background

Formal ontology

We shall work here in the realist context of much modern work on biomedical ontology, distinguishing between *instances*, which are real entities that actually exist, and *universals*, which are the types into which instances may be categorised, with the essence of the universal constituted by what is common between all the instances of that universal [13].

We take properties to exist only if they can be instantiated as the properties of some material entity. In the language of BFO [9,10], properties are *specifically dependent continuants*, in that they are entities which endure in time (continuants), they cannot exist without the existence of their bearer (dependent), and cannot be transferred from one bearer to another (specifically dependent). An example of a specifically dependent continuant is the brownness of Fred's hair, since it cannot exist without Fred's hair, and neither can it be transferred to someone else's hair.

We find it useful to distinguish between *one-sided dependence*, in which the dependent entity stands to its bearer in a relation of existential dependence but the converse relation of existential dependence does not hold (the brownness of Fred's hair depends on Fred's hair, but Fred's hair will persist despite his dyeing it purple), and *mutual dependence*, in which both entities stand in a relation of existential dependence on one another [14,15]. However, the distinction in BFO between independent and dependent continuants is not merely one of existential dependence, but one of *inherence*, that is, dependent continuants are properties of independent continuants.

A further relevant distinction is that between *non-realizable* dependent continuants (qualities), which are fully present in their bearers at all times [9], such as hair colour; and *realizable* dependent continuants, which inhere in their bearers by virtue of what would happen to the bearer should a particular set of circumstances obtain [10], such as the disposition of a glass to break if hurled at a brick wall. Realizable properties are realized as processes, and are referred to in common language by various names such as 'disposition', 'tendency', 'role' and 'function'.

For clarity, we shall insist that realizable properties be realized as *alienable processes*. An alienable process is one which has no mutual ontological dependence on its bearer. An example of an inalienable process is the life of a frog, which depends existentially upon the frog just as the existence of the frog depends existentially on its life. By contrast, an example of an alienable process is the frog's reproduction, since the frog can go its whole life without reproducing, thus, the life of the frog is not ontologically dependent on the frog's reproduction.

The 'role' terms in ChEBI

We use release 59 of ChEBI in this analysis, in which there are approximately 500 'roles', organized under 'biological role', 'application' and 'chemical role'. They all refer to the realizable activities of chemical entities. First, biological roles refer to such activities within a living system. An example of a ChEBI entity classified as a biological role is 'enzyme inhibitor'.[3] The role is realized by the molecule binding to the active site of an

[3]Given the root term is named 'role', it would be clearer to name this class 'enzyme inhibitor role'.

enzyme and rendering it inactive. Applications are the uses to which a chemical entity can be put by humans, such as a pesticide, describing the use of a chemical entity for the purpose of killing insects. Finally, chemical roles describe the activity of molecular entities in the context of other molecular entities, such as being a proton donor in a chemical reaction. We shall see that this intuitive division will prove to, in most cases, have a sound ontological basis.

The ChEBI 'roles' are linked to the specific chemical entities in which the role inheres, by means of the *has_role* cross-ontology relationship. Thus, the chemical entity 'paracetamol' (CHEBI:46195) *has_role* 'cyclooxygenase 2 inhibitor' (CHEBI:50629). Note that for a particular instance of the chemical entity, the realizable may never be realized. A particular molecule of paracetamol may, along with the rest of the tablet it is packaged with, end up being discarded into a refuse bin such that it never acts as a COX inhibitor. Nevertheless, the paracetamol universal has the 'role' COX inhibitor because a particular molecule which instantiates that universal *would* realize that function if it came into the correct *circumstances* (*i.e.* proximity to a COX enzyme).

During the early years of the development of the ChEBI ontology, the *is_a* relationship was used both to link chemical entities to structural classes and to role classes. For example, 'caffeine' (CHEBI:27732) was classified as *is_a* 'central nervous system stimulant' (CHEBI:35337) in addition to *is_a* 'trimethylxanthine' (CHEBI:27134). This was problematic for several reasons [16] and was corrected late in 2008 with the introduction of the *has_role* relationship to link molecular entities to realizables. However, the terminology 'role' that was adopted is potentially misleading with respect to an alignment with BFO since 'role' in BFO is defined primarily with respect to *social context*.

Granularity

We distinguish between chemical *substances*, such as a portion of water in a jug, and *molecular entities*, such as individual water molecules. (There is a deeper point here—Lucas [17] argues that quantum mechanical entities such as electrons and atoms, being indistinguishable ([18]), are not themselves substances, as they have no haecceity or thisness.) Individual molecules form the *granular parts* of a portion of substance. A useful granular part in the case of a salt or elemental crystal is the smallest spatial region which characterises the structure of the crystal—the unit cell. A case which is difficult to categorise for purposes of granularity is that of covalently bound macroscopic molecules, such as diamonds and nanotubes, in which a single molecule is a substance in its own right. However, for most purposes the intuitive granular division into individual molecules and portions of substance will apply.

We additionally find it useful to distinguish levels of granularity in the realizable entities which can inhere in chemical entities. We use *bulk granularity* when a realizable entity inheres in a portion of chemical substance, and *molecular granularity* when a realizable entity inheres in a single molecule, or countably small[4] set of molecular entities. For example, dispositions such as 'inhibitor', 'agonist', and 'blocker' are realised by a single molecule binding to a single enzyme active or regulatory site, thus have molecular granularity; on the other hand the 'analgesic' role can only be realized

[4]We use 'countably small' to indicate that we still consider at molecular granularity scenarios where a specific count, such as two or even fifteen, of molecules of a particular type are required to cause the realization; but not a vague amount such as hundreds or thousands.

on the level of an entire organism, thus has bulk granularity. Ultimately, each bulk granularity realizable can be viewed as being grounded in granular parts of one or several corresponding molecular granularity realizables, just as the chemical substance which the bulk realizable inheres in is grounded in grains of individual molecules. An example of a chemical entity in ChEBI to which realizables have been associated at both levels of granularity is 'caffeine' (CHEBI:27732), which *has_role* 'central nervous system stimulant' (CHEBI:35337) (bulk granularity) and *has_role* 'ryanodine receptor modulator' (CHEBI:38809) (molecular granularity).

Previous related work

Early work on the ontology of functions was done in the EcoCyc project [19] to facilitate function-based querying of biological data; and in the development of the Gene Ontology [20] 'molecular function' ontology. Karp [19] differentiates between the *local function* of a molecular entity, understood as the immediate individual interactions within a living organism; and the *integrated function* which is the broader, organism-specific process in which the interactions of many molecular entities come together towards a biological goal. This seems to parallel the distinction between the GO 'molecular function' and 'biological process'.

Building on this, Burek and Herre et al. [21] presented a formal ontology of functions and proposed it be used to systematically add explicit links between molecular functions and biological processes in GO. They also and introduced the relations *IsRealization* and *HasFunction* for relating functions to processes, and individuals to functions, respectively. They define a function in a biological context as
"the abstraction of biological processes or other entities towards a goal: when X has the function Y with the goal Z, then X is supposed to cause or otherwise bring about the state of the world Z, thus realizing Y." Also, "A biological entity (such as a process) is a realization of a function if it mediates between two states of the world, one satisfying the requirements, the other satisfying the goal." [21]

Much recent work [22,23,24] has aimed to clarify the distinction between a role, a function, and a disposition, with reference to a biological or social context. Common to all realizable entities are inherence in a continuant (the bearer), and realization in a process in which the bearer is a participant. Arp and Smith [22] (incorporated into BFO) distinguish between

- a *function*, which occurs in virtue of the bearer's *physical makeup*, which the bearer possesses because of how it *came into being*; further subdivided into artefactual (created by humans) and biological (created by genetic expression within an organism);
- a *role*, which occurs in some special natural, social, or institutional set of circumstances *not* by virtue of the bearer's physical structure; roles are best described as being *played* by the bearer;
- a *disposition*, which is realized in a process that is *invariably* caused by its bearer when the bearer is introduced into specific *circumstances*, by virtue of the bearer's physical structure.

Dumontier [25] proposes an OWL-based approach to modelling the ways in which molecular entities can participate in biochemical reactions, identifying predicates for the derivation of one entity from another (*derivesFrom*); and the realization of a biochemical role (*realizes*). Dumontier argues that the distinction between a role and a function may be irrelevant at the molecular level.

Hoehndorf [23], following Searle [26], adds clarification of the distinction between function acquired by causality, in which the bearer of a function exists because it causes a specific process to occur, and function acquired by social ascription, in which a particular social and cognitive context forms the circumstances 'framing' a process in such a way as to ascribe a function to a particular participant. Lord [24] grounds the definition of biological function in evolution, and specifically in evolutionary homology.

We will follow Hoehndorf and Lord in distinguishing between socially-ascribed functions and functions ascribed to endogenous biological molecules according to their causal powers in an organism. However, the focus on mainly biological molecules such as enzymes, and the broader context of living organisms, has ensured that none of the previous work that we are aware of provides a comprehensive treatment of realizable entities for small molecules. For example, it is not clear in any of the previous work to what extent small, *i.e.* non-biological, molecules can be said to have evolved, since they are not directly encoded by the genome. We will address this point later in this paper, and also address points that previous work has not addressed at all, such as dispositions involving chemical reactivity outside of a biological context, and the definition of pharmaceutical roles.

Analysis of ChEBI 'roles'

The authors analysed the entities in the ChEBI 'role' ontology, and assigned them to the children of 'dependent continuant' according to our independent understandings of BFO. We then compared our findings, concentrating on cases of disagreement, resulting in the following analysis. We have not attempted a proper interannotator agreement study because so many of the terms are descendants of a common and completely determining parent such as 'drug' or share headwords such as 'agonist' or 'inhibitor', meaning that any subset of the 500 would be far from strictly independent.

Biological role

Many biologists are wary of function talk as sounding teleological, however a biological function can be thought of as being realized in some process in the broader context of prolonging the life of, or effecting the reproduction of, some organism, as a result of *selection pressure* among the organism's ancestors. This seems to be the case for nearly all of the entities beneath 'biological role' in ChEBI. We argue that the selection process has resulted in the molecule being the way it is to have the disposition to participate in or effect a given process, and that this is sufficient for the ascription of biological function, regardless of whether the function is realized in the original organism. Hence a molecule that was evolved as a kinase inhibitor in one organism, if ingested in sufficient amounts by a different organism that has sufficiently similar kinase molecules, will still have the biological function realized as inhibition of kinase activity in the second organism.

Application

The 'application' hierarchy splits neatly between those species (we say 'species' in order to defer questions of granularity and efficacy) that have a brute function and those that have an institutional 'status' function [26]. Brute functions, those functions that are realized as mind-independent processes such as changing colour (or, for sticklers, changing the frequencies at which something absorbs or reflects electromagnetic radiation) or killing bacteria, here correspond to BFO's notion of an artefactual function. The species in question have been designed by human beings or selected from a broader set of species in order to realize a particular function. An example of such a brute function in ChEBI is 'fluorochrome'. By contrast, drug compounds only count as drugs in complicated institutional contexts such as clinical trials and medical treatments, and hence realize status functions in the same way as the physicians that prescribe them and the pharmacists that make them up. This is not to say that their efficacy is due to social or institutional fiat, except of course for placebos; the biological function and corresponding status function are far from mutually exclusive, and in the case of a molecule whose physiological effects are well understood will coincide. Status functions that are realized as processes (there are other forms of status function in Searle) fall under BFO's notion of a role. An example of such a drug role in ChEBI is 'tranquilizing drug'.

Chemical role

The 'chemical role' hierarchy for the most part identifies only simple processes, such as gaining a proton or emitting a photon, that are realized in simple contexts. As such they can be described as dispositions. Some of these, such as being an acid, are *mutual* dispositions, as being an acid depends existentially on there being a base, just as being a proton donor depends existentially on there being a proton acceptor, as we shall explain in greater detail below. These processes are mind- and institution-independent and hence do not count as roles in the archetypal sense. Furthermore, the participation in the simple processes, at molecular granularity, fundamentally changes the molecular structure of the molecules involved. For example, once a molecule in an acid-base reaction has donated or gained a proton, the same molecule is no longer able to donate or accept the same proton again, and can only participate in a different mutually dependent reaction. Thus these dispositions cannot be defined as roles, since role is clearly defined within BFO to be 'not such that, if it ceases to exist, then the physical make-up of the bearer is thereby changed'.

Non-realizable properties

A fourth, significantly more troublesome, category, examples of which are scattered throughout ChEBI as a whole, is that of the non-realizable property. The problematic ones are not the monadic qualities, such as being cyclic or linear or having a particular shape, but rather the ones with multiple dependence. For example, a molecule is a secondary metabolite not by virtue of its constitution but by virtue of having been created within an organism as the result of certain sorts of metabolic process. This is different in a key way from being active in an organism by virtue of participating in that organism's metabolic process, in that the molecule in question, as an output, does not actually participate at all in the relevant process.

Being a secondary metabolite is a special case of being a natural product, but currently secondary metabolite is in the 'biological role' hierarchy while certain other natural products are in the main 'molecular structure' hierarchy. Representing natural products in the structure-based ontology is clearly unsatisfactory, since there is no core structural feature which determines that a particular molecule is a natural product. However, representing natural products as realizables is also unsatisfactory for reasons already described. Thus, there are two ways of representing this within the ontology:

1. to add a new relational quality hierarchy and a *has_quality* relationship that connects the molecule to its relational quality. Note that this is necessarily an all–only[5] relation, since the quality of being a secondary metabolite applies equally to those instances which in reality have been synthesised through the relevant metabolic process, as well as those instances structurally identical to the former but which have been synthesised by a human in a laboratory.
2. to treat 'natural product' and 'metabolite' as 'defined classes' in the manner of the Ontology for Biomedical Investigations (OBI) [27]. The relevant molecules will have an *output_of* relation (again necessarily all–only) to some biological process.

Algorithm for classifying properties of molecules

Among the dependent continuants we now have the following structure:

- Quality
- Realizable entity
    - ∗ Disposition
    - ∗ Status function (role)
    - ∗ Artefactual function (application)
    - ∗ Biological function
- Defined class (for those things that are not universals but can be defined in terms of universals)

We propose the following decision tree for classification of molecular realizables:

1. Is it realizable as an alienable process?
   If YES go to 3.
   If NO go to 2.
2. Is it by virtue of the molecule alone?
   If YES then it is a monadic quality.
   If NO then it is a defined class. Write out, as far as you can, and using the Relationship Ontology where possible, a logical definition for it.
3. Has it been selected for by evolution?
   If YES then it is a biological function.
   If NO then go to 4.
4. Does it realize its processes in an institutional context?
   If YES then it is a status function (role)
   If NO then go to 5.

[5]Alan Ruttenberg, personal communication

5. Has it necessarily been produced (synthesized or chosen) in order to carry out a particular function?
   If YES then it is an artefactual function.
   If NO then it is a disposition.

Mappings to other ontologies

All realizables which inhere in chemical entities are realized in processes. Furthermore, most of them are realized only when certain relevant conditions obtain. Specifying the processes and conditions under which a particular realizable may be realized allows a semantic definition to be formalised. There is a wide range of different types of processes and conditions which may apply, which clarifies differences in the nature of the realizable entities.

Gene Ontology

Integral to the formal semantics of the ChEBI realizable entities which we have classified as biological functions (*i.e.*, most of those currently classified under the term 'biological role') is that they are realized in processes which we can map to the Gene Ontology. We can further specialise the nature of the participation of the chemical entity in the process, into

- *causation*, when the chemical entity causes the process,
- *positive regulation*, when the chemical entity increases the rate of the process, and
- *negative regulation*, when the chemical entity decreases the rate of the process.

Biological functions may be realized in GO biological processes. However, we regard the terms in the Gene Ontology 'molecular function' ontology as single-step (or concerted) processes, that is, 'enzyme inhibitor activity' (GO:0004857) should be interpreted as a part of enzyme inhibition. We therefore allow for biological functions to be realized in GO molecular functions. There is a very close parallel between some of the biological functions defined in ChEBI and the activities defined in GO, however, this should not be interpreted as semantic identity: the function, in ChEBI, is a realizable dependent continuant which inheres in a small molecule, while the activity, in GO, is an occurrent. The difference is between a ChEBI *function* and a GO *functioning*.

Table 1 gives some example mappings from ChEBI realizables to GO biological processes and molecular functions. Note that these functions are all realized at the molecular granularity.

In some cases there is both a molecular function and a biological process for a particular biological function. In these cases, we recommend mapping to the GO molecular function, as the smallest process which characterises the function being described. Care, however, must be taken to avoid seemingly attractive mappings, which lead to a situation of circularity in definition. An example of such would be toxin (CHEBI:27026), which we may wrongly assert is realized in 'response to toxin' (GO:0009636). The problem here is that 'response to toxin' is itself defined by the function toxin. Clearly, in this case the correct definition for toxin would refer to any response which has a deleterious effect on an organism.

Table 1. Mapping biological functions to GO

Function	Functioning	Form of participation
enzyme inhibitor (CHEBI:23924)	'enzyme inhibitor activity' (GO:0004857)	causation
glycoside hydrolase inhibitor (CHEBI:52424)	'anhydrosialidase activity' (GO:0033995)	negative regulation
provitamin (CHEBI:50188)	'vitamin biosynthetic process' (GO:0009110)	causation (by virtue of being a necessary input)
cholinergic agonist (CHEBI:38324)	'synaptic transmission, cholinergic' (GO:0007271)	positive regulation
cholinergic antagonist (CHEBI:48873)	'synaptic transmission, cholinergic' (GO:0007271)	negative regulation
photosystem-I inhibitor (CHEBI:26088)	'negative regulation of photosynthetic electron transport in photosystem I' (GO:0009773)	negative regulation
cytokinin (CHEBI:23530)	'cytokinin mediated signaling or - receptor activity' (GO:0009736)	causation

Some examples of biological functions which do not map to biological processes or molecular functions in GO are

- 'synthetic auxin' (CHEBI:26841). Here, the term implies not only a function, but also a particular form of derivation (synthetic production). In this case we propose that this term be dealt with as per our earlier recommendation for natural products and metabolites.
- 'gamma secretase modulator' (CHEBI:48668). In this case, although 'gamma secretase complex' (GO:0070765) is a GO cellular component, no GO biological processes or molecular functions are defined which operate on this complex. We propose that the particular processes which operate on this complex be defined.
- 'volatile oils' (CHEBI:27311). Here, the term doesn't imply a function that can inhere in a molecular entity at all, but rather seems to refer to a class of substances, rather than molecular entities. We propose this term be deprecated in ChEBI.
- 'photobiochemical role' (CHEBI:52216). Here, a straightforward mapping to GO is not available because there is no common parent in GO for all light-involving processes, chiefly because from the perspective of biology, they do not constitute a natural kind. If this term is to be more than just an index heading, this function ought to be defined as a disjunction (and hence a defined class) of the available GO light-involving processes.

Molecular processes

The 'chemical roles' in ChEBI are realized in molecular processes, such as those described in the molecular process ontology (MOP), which complements the continuants in ChEBI with occurrents[6]. Chemical roles provide paradigmatic examples of mutually-dependent dispositions. Let us take the simplest case, which is of a Brønsted acid (CHEBI:39141), better known as a proton donor, and a Brønsted base (CHEBI:39142). The dependence relations go something like this:

[6] Available at `http://www.rsc.org/ontologies/`.

> The disposition D to donate a proton depends specifically on the molecule M it inheres in, and generically on the protons within that molecule.

It also generically depends on some other molecule M' and that molecule's disposition D' to accept a proton. D' specifically depends on M' and generically on those atoms within M' with which any of the protons originally in M can form bonds. D and D' are both realized as proton transfer (MOP:0000680). This is the situation expressed at its most general. In practice not all protons in the proton donor are equal and nor are all proton-accepting atoms in the proton acceptor, and in a solution that completely surrounds the solvent, the most acidic proton will be donated first.

This brings us to acids and bases. The school definitions of acid and base are couched in terms of pH and reflect the disposition, at room temperature and atmospheric pressure at sea level, to donate a proton to water, producing an H_3O^+ ion or receive a proton, leaving an OH^- ion. The acid and base definitions used by chemists are slightly different. There is in fact a hierarchy of them. The most general definition, and the least helpful, is the Usanovich definition, where an acid has the disposition to receive negative charge and a base has the disposition to receive positive charge. The two in ChEBI are the Lewis definition, which involves Lewis bases "transferring" electron pairs ('electron pair transfer', MOP:0000679) to Lewis acids, and the Brønsted–Lowry definition, which is the same as the proton donor/acceptor definition above. Because geology is dominated by the Earth's oxidising atmosphere, geochemists use the Lux–Flood definition, whereby an acid is something that receives an oxide ion (O^{2-}) donated by a base. The best way to proceed, though it is unsatisfactory, is to define acids and bases disjunctively such that the disposition to behave as an acid is the disposition to behave as a Lewis acid, a Usanovich acid, a Lux–Flood acid or a Brønsted acid, and the same holds for the disposition to behave as a base. Other examples of mutual dispositions are a solvent and the solute that dissolves in it, a chelator and the chelate it chelates, and a deaminating agent and the amine donor it deaminates.

Disease, Anatomy, Taxonomy and Preparation

A 'drug' role in ChEBI always inheres in a small molecule, and as such is really the role played by the *active ingredient* in a pharmaceutical formulation, because drugs are complicated substantial entities containing not only the active ingredient but a matrix (usually chalk), stabilizers, flavourings and many other sorts of molecule. We also do not need to consider placebos and non-medical treatment such as acupuncture in our formalism of drug roles. However, a general treatment of drug roles in the context of a drug ontology would also need to consider these, as well as other useful information such as the countries in which a particular drug may be approved, and the dosage information.

Important to note is that the granularity of realization of a drug role is at the bulk level of granularity, considering the organism as a whole—the human being (or dog, cow or cat) who is the subject of the treatment using that drug. Although we might be tempted to say that this is not the case, for example, for the antibiotic drug role, we find on closer analysis that the term antibiotic splits neatly into the antibiotic drug *role*, which is realized when particular substances are *approved* for treatment of bacterial conditions in humans, and the antibiotic *biological function*, which is realized at the level of granularity at which a particular portion of substance kills or inhibits the growth of at least one bacterium in physiological conditions.

The following ChEBI drug roles are all status functions, with the exception of mode of action.

- the particular disease or *symptom* for which they are targeted as *treatment*.
- the *anatomical location* which is the site of targeted operation of the substance, such as 'central nervous system drug' (CHEBI:35470). These should be mapped to the FMA [28].
- the *organism* which the drug is targeted against, such as 'antitreponemal drug' (CHEBI:36050). These should be mapped to the NCBI Taxonomy [29].
- the *mode of action*, such as 'partial prostacyclin agonist' (CHEBI:51577). These should be treated in the same way as the biological functions above.
- the preparation *mode of delivery* such as 'inhalation anaesthetic' (CHEBI:38870) and 'oral contraceptive' (CHEBI:49325). These describe *substances* and hence are outside the scope of ChEBI.

Artefactual functions

The artefactual functions which inhere in chemical entities—*i.e.* synthetic chemicals—are often realized in processes undertaken in the context of biomedical investigations, and therefore we propose in this case a mapping to OBI, the Ontology of Biomedical Investigations. Examples of these are 'fluorochrome' (CHEBI:51217) and 'swelling agent' (CHEBI:51267).

There are various artefactual functions which provide the brute function of organism-specific targeted killing: 'disinfectant' (CHEBI:48219), 'fungicide' (CHEBI:24127), 'insecticide' (CHEBI:24852), 'herbicide' (CHEBI:24527), and others. The mechanism is unimportant, therefore we propose these be mapped to the organism itself (via a taxonomy).

Like drug roles, artefactual functions such as these apply at the bulk granularity level rather than individual molecules.

Structural features

Some 'role' terms contain a 'role'-like descriptor combined with structure-like descriptors. Examples of this are

- alicyclic antibiotic (CHEBI:22309)
- xenobiotic organic ether (CHEBI:27334)

We propose that these be treated with defined classes consisting of the intersection of the relevant structural class (e.g. alicyclic molecule) and *has_role* the relevant role class (e.g. antibiotic). Thus,

- alicyclic antibiotic $\equiv$ alicyclic molecule $\cap$ has_role (some antibiotic).
- xenobiotic organic ether $\equiv$ organic ether molecule $\cap$ has_role (some xenobiotic).

Discussion and Conclusion

In this paper we have analysed the ChEBI 'roles' in the light of recent work on roles and dispositions, as well as Searle's work on social reality. As ChEBI is an OBO Foundry ontology we are particularly interested in aligning its 'roles' with the realizable entity branch of the Basic Formal Ontology BFO. Our most important result is a methodology for determining what category a property of a molecule belongs to. We have used this methodology to put forward a set of definitions for ChEBI's realizable entities in terms of processes described by other ontologies, in particular the Gene Ontology, and *vice versa.*

We anticipate that our analysis will be particularly useful for a better ontological description of pharmaceuticals, formal descriptions of which have hitherto been hopelessly confused. Many realizable entity terms in ChEBI describe the modes of action of pharmaceuticals; our approach enables us to distinguish those that are dispositional (such-and-such a molecule really does bind to such-and-such a pocket in a protein) from those that are status functions (such-and-such a pharmaceutical product is prescribed "as" an antidepressant in the context of a clinical consultation).

Our focus in this paper has been on molecules; in future we will extend this work to cover dependent continuants that inhere in substantial entities at other granularities.

Acknowledgements

This work was partly funded by the European Commission under SLING, grant agreement number 226073 (Integrating Activity) within Research Infrastructures of the FP7 Capacities Specific Programme, and by the BBSRC, grant agreement number BB/G022747/1 within the "Bioinformatics and biological resources" fund. The authors wish to thank Stefan Schulz, Alan Ruttenberg, Michel Dumontier, Robert Hoehndorf and Barry Smith for comments and helpful discussions, as well as the reviewers of an earlier version, whose comments helped to significantly improve the paper.

References

[1] de Matos, P.; Alcántara, R.; Dekker, A.; Ennis, M.; Hastings, J.; Haug, K.; Spiteri, I.; Turner, S.; and Steinbeck, C. (2010) Chemical Entities of Biological Interest: an update. Nucl. Acids Res. 2010 38: D249–D254.

[2] McNaught, A.D.; Wilkinson, A. (1997) Compendium of Chemical Terminology, 2nd edition. Blackwell Science, 1997 [ISBN 0-86542-6848]

[3] Connelly, N.G; Damhus, T.; Hartshorn, R.M.; Hutton, A.T. (2005) Nomenclature of Inorganic Chemistry - IUPAC Recommendations 2005. The Royal Society of Chemistry, 2005 [ISBN 0 85404 438 8]

[4] Panico, R.; Powell, W.H; Richer, J-C. (1993) A Guide to IUPAC Nomenclature of Organic Compounds, Blackwell Science, 1993 [ISBN 0-63203-4882], Corrections published in Pure Appl. Chem., Vol. 71, No. 7, pp.1327-1330, 1999.

[5] Smith, B.; Ashburner, M.; Rosse, C.; Bard, C.; Bug, W.; Ceusters, W.; Goldberg, L.J.; Eilbeck, K.; Ireland, A.; Mungall, C.J.; The OBI Consortium; Leontis, N.; Rocca-Serra, P.; Ruttenberg, A.; Sansone, S-A.; Scheuermann R.H.; Shah, N.; Whetzel, P.L.; Lewis, S. (2007) The OBO Foundry: coordinated evolution of ontologies to support biomedical data integration, Nature Biotechnology 25, 1251 - 1255.

[6] Simon, J.; Fielding, J.; Dos Santos, M.; Smith, B. (2005) Formal Ontology for Natural Language Processing and the Integration of Biomedical Databases, International Journal of Medical Informatics, 75 (3-4), 2005, 224-231.

[7] Smith, B. (2008) New Desiderata for Biomedical Terminologies, in K. Munn and B. Smith (eds.), Applied Ontology: An Introduction, Frankfurt/Lancaster: ontos, 2008, 83-109.

[8] Schulz, S.; Stenzhorn, H.; Boekers, M.; Smith, B. (2009) Strengths and Limitations of Formal Ontologies in the Biomedical Domain, Electronic Journal of Communication, Information and Innovation in Health (Special Issue on Ontologies, Semantic Web and Health), 2009.

[9] Grenon, P.; Smith, B. (2004) SNAP and SPAN: Towards Dynamic Spatial Ontology. Spatial Cognition & Computation: An Interdisciplinary Journal, Vol. 4, No. 1. (2004), pp. 69-104.

[10] Smith, B.; Grenon, P. (2004) The Cornucopia of Formal-Ontological Relations. Dialectica, Vol. 58, No. 3. (2004), pp. 279-296.

[11] Gangemi, A.; Guarino, N.; Masolo, C.; Oltramari, A.; Oltramari, R.; Schneider, L. (2002) Sweetening Ontologies with DOLCE, Springer, 2002.

[12] Herre, H. (2009) General Formal Ontology (GFO) : A Foundational Ontology for Conceptual Modelling, In Theory and Applications of Ontology, Springer, 2009.

[13] Smith, B. (2004) Beyond Concepts: Ontology as Reality Representation. In: Varzi, A., Vieu, L. (Eds.), Formal Ontology and Information Systems. Proceedings of the Third International Conference (FOIS 2004), IOS Press, Amsterdam. pp. 73–84.

[14] Smith, B. (1998) The basic tools of formal ontology. In Formal Ontology in Information Systems, Frontiers in Artificial Intelligence and Applications, pages 19–28, Amsterdam, Oxford, Tokyo, Washington, DC, IOS Press.

[15] Lowe, J. E. (2009) Ontological Dependence, The Stanford Encyclopedia of Philosophy (Fall 2009 Edition), Edward N. Zalta (ed.), [http://plato.stanford.edu/archives/fall2009/entries/dependence-ontological/]

[16] Batchelor, C. (2008) An Upper-Level Ontology for Chemistry. In Proceeding of the 2008 conference on Formal Ontology in Information Systems.

[17] Lucas, J. R. (2006) Quantum Mechanics, chapter 11 in Reason and Reality. [http://users.ox.ac.uk/∼jrlucas/reasreal/quanchp3.pdf], last accessed Oct 29, 2009.

[18] French, S. (2008) Identity and Individuality in Quantum Theory, The Stanford Encyclopedia of Philosophy (Fall 2008 Edition), Edward N. Zalta (ed.), [http://plato.stanford.edu/archives/fall2008/entries/qt-idind/].

[19] Karp, P. D. (2000) An ontology for biological function based on molecular interactions. Bioinformatics 16(3) 2000.

[20] Gene Ontology Consortium (2000) Gene ontology: tool for the unification of biology. Nat. Genet. May 2000; 25(1):25-9.

[21] Burek, P.; Hoehndorf, R.; Loebe, F.; Visagie, J.; Herre, H.; Kelso, J. (2006) A top-level ontology of functions and its application in the Open Biomedical Ontologies. Bioinformatics Vol. 22(14), pp. e66–e73.

[22] Arp, R.; Smith, B. (2008) Function, Role and Disposition in Basic Formal Ontology. In Proceedings of the 11th Annual Bio-ontologies SIG meeting, July 20, 2008, Colocated with ISMB 2008, Toronto, Canada.

[23] Hoehndorf, R.; Kelso, J.; Herre, H. (2009) Contributions to the formal ontology of functions and dispositions: an application of non-monotonic reasoning. In Proceedings of the 12th Annual Bio-Ontologies SIG meeting, June 28, 2009, Colocated with ISMB 2009, Stockholm, Sweden.

[24] Lord, P. (2009) An evolutionary approach to Function. In Proceedings of the 12th Annual Bio-Ontologies SIG meeting, June 28, 2009, Colocated with ISMB 2009, Stockholm, Sweden.

[25] Dumontier, M. (2008) Situational modeling: Defining molecular roles in biochemical pathways and reactions. In OWLED 2008, 2008.

[26] Searle, J. (1995) The Construction of Social Reality. Harmondsworth: Penguin.

[27] Soldatova, L.; The OBI Consortium (2008) Modelling biomedical experimental processes with OBI, in Proceedings of the 12th Annual Bio-Ontologies SIG meeting, June 28, 2009, Colocated with ISMB 2009, Stockholm, Sweden.

[28] Rosse, C.; Mejino, J. V. L. (2003) A reference ontology for biomedical informatics: the Foundational model of Anatomy, J. Biomed. Inform., 2003, 36:478–500.

[29] Sayers, E.W.; Barrett, T.; Benson, D.A.; Bryant, S.H.; Canese, K.; Chetvernin, V.; Church, D.M.; DiCuccio, M.; Edgar, R.; Federhen, S.; Feolo, M.; Geer, L.Y.; Helmberg, W.; Kapustin, Y.; Landsman, D.; Lipman, D.J.; Madden, T.L.; Maglott, D.R.; Miller, V.; Mizrachi, I.; Ostell, J.; Pruitt, K.D.; Schuler, G.D.; Sequeira, E.; Sherry, S.T.; Shumway, M.; Sirotkin, K.; Souvorov, A.; Starchenko, G.; Tatusova, T.A.; Wagner, L.; Yaschenko, E.; Ye, J. (2009) Database resources of the National Center for Biotechnology Information. Nucleic Acids Res. 2009 Jan;37(Database issue):D5-15. Epub 2008 Oct 21.

Products and Functions

Formal Ontology in Information Systems
A. Galton and R. Mizoguchi (Eds.)
IOS Press, 2010

doi:10.3233/978-1-60750-535-8-287

Towards an Ontology of Products

Massimiliano Vignolo[1]
University of Trento

Abstract. We speak of types of products and of instances of products. I argue that the ontological status of types of products is the same as that of material stuffs, like water and gold, which have a non-particular level of existence. I also argue that the relationship between types of products and their instances is logically similar to the relation of constitution, which holds between, say, gold and a ring made of gold. On my view types of products are concrete entities that can be created in space and time and undergo complete destruction as well as instances of products.

Keywords. Ontology, Products, Type, Token, Instance

Introduction

We speak of products in two distinct senses. One (henceforth "product$_1$") is the sense in which a product can have many particular objects as its instances. The other (henceforth "product$_2$") is the sense in which a particular object falling under a sortal concept is an instance of a product$_1$. To make the distinction clear, consider the following example. The car driven by Sean Connery in *Goldfinger* is an instance of the Aston Martin DB5. As a particular object falling under the sortal concept *car*, that car is a product$_2$. The Aston Martin DB5 of which the car driven by Sean Connery is an instance is a product$_1$.

One philosophical problem concerns the ontological status of products$_1$ and their relation to products$_2$. Typically products$_2$ are particular objects and their ontological status does not give rise to deep conceptual difficulties, at least to the extent that three-dimensionalism is accepted. By contrast, the ontological status of products$_1$ gives rise to conceptual concerns. In our everyday parlance we say that products$_1$ are created or made as well as products$_2$ are. For example, we say that the Aston Martin DB5 was created in 1963 and produced until the 1965 by the Aston Martin factory in Tickford Street, Newport Pagnell, UK, and that the Aston Martin DB5 is not widespread in Mongolia, etc. When we make these assertions we locate the Aston Martin DB5 as product$_1$ in certain spatiotemporal regions. Taken at face value, our common parlance presents products$_1$ as entities that possess spatiotemporal properties and, due to the criterion that divides entities in concrete and abstract depending on whether they possess spatiotemporal properties or not, we speak of products$_1$ as of concrete entities. In my account I focus mainly upon this commonplace characteristic of products$_1$ and

[1] Department of Information Engineering and Computer Science, University of Trento, Italy; e-mail: maxi@nous.unige.it. This work is supported by the FP7 EU Large-scale Integrating Project OKKAM-Enabling a Web of Entities (no. 215032). For more details, visit http://www.okkam.org/. I am grateful to Andrea Bianchi and Claudio Masolo for their helpful comments on an early draft of this paper.

try not only to preserve this characteristic but also to argue that the alternative views calling for a revision of it are much less palatable than my proposal.

In this paper I argue that $products_1$ have the same ontological status as the ontological status that according to some philosophers material stuffs have, like water and gold. The entities that have such ontological status possess a *non-particular* level of existence. My proposal preserves the intuition that $products_1$ are concrete entities with spatiotemporal properties, but it also encourages the conclusion that the relation between $products_1$ and $products_2$ is logically similar to the relation of constitution which holds between material stuffs and the objects made up of material stuffs, like for example a ring and the gold that constitutes that ring.

The plan of the paper is the following. In section 1 I frame the conceptual problem raised by the ontological status of material stuff. In section 2 I present the formalization of one solution to that problem. In section 3 I recapitulate the main lines of the suggested solution on the ontology of material stuffs. In section 4 I extend that picture to the ontology of $products_1$. In section 5 I discuss the advantages of my picture over some alternative views.

1. Conceptual concerns on the ontology of material stuff

Some philosophers[2] put in question the view that reality is ontologically structured in a hierarchy starting with particular objects and going on with properties (or kinds) of particular objects, properties (or kinds) of properties of particular objects and so on. They hold that some entities have a non-particular level of existence, and take material stuffs like water and gold to be entities of that kind. What does it mean that material stuffs have a non-particular level of existence? Those philosophers move their analysis from a tension they detect in Peter Strawson's reflections on the subject.[3]

Strawson turned his attention to what he called "feature-placing sentences", i.e. sentences like "there is water in the basement". Strawson held that such sentences do not imply quantification over particular objects of any sort. Strawson claimed that such sentences make reference to *incidences* of a general feature as opposed to *instances* of sortal concepts. In other words, such sentences locate a general feature in a given spatiotemporal region instead of introducing some particular object of one sort or another in that region. In general, the introduction of particular objects is accomplished by means of sortal concepts involving criteria of identity, conditions of persistence and principles of individuation for the objects falling under them. If, for instance, we consider a material stuff like gold, individual objects can be introduced by adding expressions like "bit", "piece" etc. When we utter the sentence "there is a piece of gold in this room", we quantify over particular objects, i.e. pieces of gold. Pieces of gold have identity criteria, persistence conditions and principle of individuation. However, a piece of gold is not an instance of the concept *gold* but an instance of the sortal concept *piece of gold*. A piece of gold has identity criteria, persistence conditions and individuation principle different from those of the gold that it is made of. The gold that is contained in this piece of gold might persist even if this piece of gold ceases to exist by being divided in smaller pieces or even reduced to dust of gold.

---

2 See, for example, Laycock [6] [7] [8], Burke [3] [4].

3 Cf. Strawson [14].

The divide between *incidences* of material stuffs and particular objects that are *instances* of sortal concepts is grounded in the fact that whenever a feature-placing sentence is true, we are not able to find a logically equivalent sentence that implies quantification over particular objects falling under a sortal concept. For example, the sentence "there is water in the basement" might be true because some water has been poured in a jug in the basement, or because there is a puddle of water on the floor of the basement. However, neither "there is a jug of water in the basement" nor "there is a puddle of water in the basement" is logically equivalent to "there is water in the basement". "There is water in the basement" might continue to be true even if the water in the jug is poured into ten glasses, or the water in the puddle is collected and poured into a bottle or even turns into water vapor. The problem is that it is impossible to find a sortal concept F such that sentences of the form "there is water…" are logically equivalent to sentences of the form "there is a F…" which imply quantification over Fs.[4] The divide between incidences of stuffs and particular objects that are instances of sortal concepts captures a distinction in basic ontological categories: the category of incidences of material stuffs and the category of particular objects falling under sortal concepts.

Strawson, however, did not push his analysis far enough to introduce an ontological category of entities that are concrete but have a non-particular level of existence, which is different from the existence of particular objects. The limit of Strawson's analysis is his adherence to the ontological primacy of particular objects, which made it impossible for him to recognize a basic ontological category different from that of particular objects and led him to construe the use of sentences like "there is water in the basement" as responding to a defective pre-particular level of thought instead of being the proper descriptions of a non-particular level of existence.[5] In other words, the fact that we think of material stuffs in terms different from those in which we think of particular objects appeared to Strawson as the result of the imperfection of our thought and not the right application of a sound ontological category distinct from that of particular objects.

Some philosophers who try to elaborate Strawson's insights treat material stuffs as belonging to a genuine ontological category of entities different from the category of particular objects. In the next section I present the formalization of the solution advocated by those philosophers. In section 4 I argue that types of products belong to the same ontological category as that of material stuff.

2. Semantics and formalization

Strawson spoke of *incidences* of stuffs as opposed to *instances* of sortal concepts. Speaking of incidences of stuffs as the presence of a general feature and opposed to instances of sortal concepts as the presence of particular objects is little more than a metaphorical way of speaking. The point that needs to be explained is what makes a

[4] Cartwright [5] proposes quantification over quantities of stuff, in a sense of "quantity" according to which the gold in Jane's ring now might be the same quantity of gold as the quantity that was in her mother's earrings some years ago. Laycock [7] criticizes Cartwright's view and holds that, say, the water in the basement constitutes a quantity of water but cannot be identified with a quantity of water, and it does not fall under the concept quantity of gold. The water in the basement is not an F of any kind, not even a quantity of water, hence it is not a particular object.

[5] For an assessment of Strawson's view see Laycock [6].

sentence like, say, "there is water in the basement" true, when it is true. There must be something in the basement that makes that sentence true. But what might it be, if not the presence of a particular object?

Henry Laycock [6] elaborates Strawson's intuition and argues that material stuffs, like water and gold, has a *non-particular* level of existence. According to Laycock, feature-placing sentences do not imply quantification over particular objects falling under sortal concepts like, say, quantities, bits, pieces, portions, pools, drops etc. of water and gold. A mass noun occurring in a feature-placing sentence functions as neither a definite nor an indefinite *singular* term making reference to one particular object. Rather, a mass noun occurring in a feature-placing sentence functions as a *plural* referring term, making reference collectively to a plurality of objects. It is worth stressing that a plurality of objects is not a plural object, i.e. one entity of a special sort like a set, a mereological sum or an aggregate. A plurality of objects is not *one* object but *many* objects. Thus, to say that there is water in the basement is certainly to assert the existence of something in the basement, upon which the truth value of the sentence depends, but not to assert the existence of *one* particular object falling under a sortal concept. Laycock holds that in saying that there is water in the basement we assert the existence of a plurality of water-elements in the basement. It is not the task of philosophical analysis to tell what stuff-elements are. That is the task of science, which tells us that water-elements are H_2O molecules.

George Boolos in his articles from the 1980s[6] introduced plural first order logic, in which beside singular terms and singular variables referring to and taking single particular objects as values, there are plural terms and plural variables referring collectively to and taking many objects as values at once. In plural first order logic the predicate "∠" is introduced as a logical predicate standing for the relation of being one of a plurality of objects. By applying plural first order logic to Laycock's picture, mass nouns function as plural terms referring collectively to pluralities of stuff-elements. Feature-placing sentences, then, imply quantification over pluralities of stuff-elements. Quantification over pluralities is not singular quantification over entities of a new sort – pluralities – but quantification of a new sort – plural quantification – over individuals. Let us consider some examples:

The sentence

(a) There is water in the basement

can be analyzed into

(a') $\exists xs(\forall y(y \angle xs \rightarrow (\text{Water-element}(y) \wedge @\text{the\_basement}(y))))$

To read: there is a plurality of objects xs such that for any object y, y is one of them only if y is a water-element and is in the basement.

The sentence

(b) Water is widespread in G

can be analyzed into

[6] See Boolos [1][2]. See also Lynnebo [9], Lynnebo and Nicolas [10], Rayo [12][13].

(b') $\exists xs(\forall y(y\angle xs \rightarrow \text{Water-element}(y)) \wedge \text{Widespread\_in\_G}(xs))$

To read: there is a plurality of object xs such that for any object y, y is one of them only if y is a water-element and xs are widespread in G.

The sentence

(c) Water is colorless

can be analyzed into

(c') $\forall x(\exists ys(\forall z(z\angle ys \rightarrow \text{Water-element}(z)) \wedge Cysx) \rightarrow \text{Colorless}(x))$

To read: for any object x, if there is a plurality of object ys such that for any object z, z is one of them only if z is a water-element and ys constitute x, then x is colorless.

The analysis of sentence (c) involves a complication. It requires a notion of constitution as a relation between pluralities of objects and particular objects.[7] Constitution can be defined as follows:

$$Cxsy \equiv_{def} \forall z(z\angle xs \rightarrow z<y) \wedge \forall w(w<y \rightarrow \exists o(o\angle xs \wedge Oow))$$ [8]

To read: the objects xs constitute the object y if and only if for any object z, z is one of the xs only if z is a proper part of y and for any object w, if w is a proper par of y, then there exists an object o such that o is one of the xs and o and w overlap.

The sentence

(d) The water in the bottle is frozen

can be analyzed into

(d') $\exists xs(\forall y(y\angle xs \leftrightarrow \text{Water-element}(y) \wedge @\text{bottle}(y)) \wedge \forall z(Cxsz \rightarrow \text{Frozen}(z))$[9]

---

[7] One might look for an alternative analysis avoiding the notion of constitution. For example, one might analyze (c) into (c''): $\forall y(\text{Water-element}(y) \rightarrow \text{Colorless}(y))$. I prefer (c') to (c''), since we do not say that a water-molecule is colorless. Alternatively, one might analyze (c) into (c'''): $\forall xs(\forall y(y\angle xs \rightarrow \text{Water-element}(y)) \rightarrow \text{Colorless}(xs))$. But then "colorless" is either distributive or non-distributive. If it is distributive, we are forced to say that a water molecule is colorless. On the other hand, I have no clear intuition about what being collectively colorless is for water molecules. Moreover, the analysis (c') accords with the idea that what is true of all individual objects that are (correctly, or in normal conditions) constituted by A-elements plays a decisive role in determining what can be truly predicated of the stuff A. The idea is that there is a systematic relation between the property designated by a predicate when it is truthfully predicated of objects constituted of A-elements and the property designated by that predicate when truthfully predicated of the stuff A. In general, for any predicate P that can be predicated of stuff A, if there is some property P' which P stand for and is such that it is impossible that something is (correctly, or in normal conditions) constituted of A-elements and lack the property P', then P is true of stuff A. In other words, to say that water is liquid amounts to saying that every object that is constituted (correctly , or in normal conditions) of water is liquid.

[8] One might take constitution and parthood to be temporal indexed relations: $C_txsy \equiv def\ \forall z(z\angle xs \rightarrow z<_ty) \wedge \forall w(w<_ty \rightarrow \exists o(o\angle xs \wedge O_tow))$. To read: the objects xs constitute the object y at t if and only if for any object z, if z is one of the xs then z is a proper part of y at t and for any object w, if w is a proper part of y at t, then there exists an object o such that o is one of the xs and o and w overlap at t.

[9] See footnote 7 on the need for the notion of constitution.

To read: there is a plurality of object xs such that for any object y, y is one of them if and only if y is a water-element and is in the bottle, and for any object z if xs constitute z then z is frozen.[10]

In the next section I recapitulate the main lines of Laycock's picture on the ontology of material stuffs.

3. The ontology of material stuffs

On Laycock's picture, the existence of stuffs consists in the existence of pluralities of stuff-elements and their essential property of combining one another to constitute particular objects with certain chemical and physical characteristics. The reality of material stuffs is more basic than the reality of the particular objects that are constituted of material stuffs. A plurality of stuff-elements is an incidence of stuff, not an instance of a sortal concept. In fact, incidences of material stuffs do not possess principles of individuation, identity criteria and persistence conditions that are peculiar of particular objects that are instances of sortal concepts.

Laycock[11] offers an incisive illustration of the impossibility of individuating incidences of stuffs. Imagine an enclosure A containing two pigs at t_1. At t_2 one pig enters another enclosure B and the other pig enters a different enclosure C. At t_1 nobody can know which pig will enter which enclosure at t_2. However, at t_1 the pig which will enter the enclosure B can be denoted by the singular definite description "the pig that will enter the enclosure B", even though it cannot be picked up as such. The same holds for the pig that will enter the enclosure C. Although at t_1 we can identify neither pig as the one that will enter one or the other of the two enclosures, we certainly can identify both of them simply as different pigs. This is to say that there is a procedure – related to the application of the sortal concept *pig* – for dividing the population of the enclosure A at t_1 in such a way that one of the pigs is the pig that will *de facto* enter the enclosure B and the other is the pig that will *de facto* enter the enclosure C, even if at t_1 we cannot know which one is the pig that will enter which enclosure. The existence of such procedure is the result of the fact that *pig* is a sortal concept being associated to a principle of individuation for the things that fall under it.

Cases involving particular objects falling under sortal concepts contrast with cases involving incidences of material stuffs. Laycock offers the example of a jug A containing some water at t_1. At t_2 the water contained in the jug A is poured into two glasses, B and C. At t_1 A contains the water that will be poured in B and the water that will be poured in C at t_2, which can be denoted respectively by the plural descriptions "the water that will be poured into glass B at t_2" and "the water that will be poured into glass C at t_2". Neither of them, however, can be identified at t_1, not even as simple incidences of water, because at t_1 there is no procedure – related to the application of the concept *water* – for dividing the water contained in A into two quantities of water in such a way that in virtue of the sole application of the concept *water* we are guaranteed that one quantity is the incidence of water that will *de facto* be poured in glass B at t_2 and the other quantity is the incidence of water that will *de facto* be poured in glass C at t_2. Of course, it might happen *by chance* that at t_1 one divides the water contained in the jug A in two smaller quantities and that one of them is the incidence of

[10] Here the object z might be a quantity in Cartwright's sense. See [5].
[11] Cf. Laycock [7] p. 435.

water that will be poured into B and the other the incidence of water that will be poured into C at t_2. The point is that such division would not be the logical consequence of the application of the concept *water*, in contrast with the application of sortal concepts, like the case of the concept *pig*.

Some considerations on the identity and persistence conditions of material stuffs, too, suggest that incidences of material stuffs are not – and cannot be – particular objects. Consider the ice forming an ice cube in a gyn&tonic.[12] We tend to think that the ice cannot survive any change in its amount, but also that only when all of the ice that constitutes the cube has melted, the ice ceases to exist. It is important to note that when we say that the ice persists identical only if it does not change in its amount, we mean that all of the ice persists under that condition, and when we say that the ice ceases to exist when it disappears, we mean that the ice ceases to exist only if none of it has left. This much would be plainly paradoxical if the ice that constitutes the ice cube in the gyn&tonic were treated as a particular object. As a matter of fact, to say both that some particular object persists identical only so long as it remains the same amount of material stuff, and also that it does not cease to exist until all that stuff has disappeared, gives rise to contradiction, because if an object loses identity it ceases to exist, and so long as it keeps on existing it cannot fail to persist and to keep its identity. The invited conclusion is that it makes no sense at all to apply the persistence and identity conditions of particular objects to incidences of material stuffs. It makes no sense to do so, because incidences of material stuffs are not particular objects. Incidences of material stuffs are pluralities of objects. When we refer to the ice in the gyn&tonic, we refer to a plurality of objects, not to a particular object. That is the reason why after an amount of ice has melted, we can say that the ice is not identical, although we cannot say that the ice has ceased to exist. It is false that all the ice has persisted identical through the melting of some of its amount, and it is false that none of the ice has left. As noted above, this conclusion would be plainly paradoxical, were the ice in the gyn&tonic a single object.

This ontological picture of material stuffs is in contrast with the doctrine that everything that is concrete must be particular. Material stuffs are concrete and non-particular. Our common intuition takes material stuffs to be concrete, if anything is. We speak as if material stuffs has spatiotemporal properties. We regard sentences like "there is no water on the moon", "petroleum is decreasing on the earth", "there was no steel in 5000 b.C. on the earth" as true. We assert such sentences in order to locate the presence of material stuffs in determinate places at determinate (intervals of) times. Although material stuffs are not particular objects, they cannot be treated as universal entities. If we want to take our parlance at face value, we cannot treat material stuffs as universal entities, since universals are abstract entities, and abstract entities do not possess spatiotemporal properties. The view that material stuffs possess a non-particular level of existence allows us to keep faith to our everyday parlance and to think of material stuffs as concrete entities.

We also say that material stuffs are created and can undergo destruction. For instance we say that penicillin was created by Alexander Fleming in 1928. Material stuffs can also be destroyed. We can imagine a scenario in which a crazy scientist builds a machine for electrolyzing each water molecule without incurring contradiction. Suppose that water is present only on earth. At the end of the process of electrolysis no water would remain. All water would be destroyed. After long time, some aliens find

[12] I borrow this example from Laycock [8] pp. 22-24.

out a method for synthesizing atoms of oxygen and hydrogen to build up water molecules. At that time water would be recreated and brought into existence for a second time. This case is instructive because it shows that material stuffs might have an intermittent existence. Material stuffs can be brought into and go out of existence. The water on earth and the water synthesized by the alien scientist would not be two different substances. They would be one and the same material stuff. Some philosophers have tried to apply the notion of intermittent existence to particular objects.[13] They claim that when a clock is disassembled for repairing, the clock ceases to exist and starts to exist again only when it is reassembled. I will not argue in favor or against that view, but I will insist on an important difference between disassembled particular objects and material stuffs. The intermittent existence of particular objects requires that the parts of the particular objects that are reassembled persist identical throughout the time the particular objects are disassembled. On the contrary, the intermittent existence of material stuffs does not demand such a strict condition to be met, as the water molecules synthesized by the alien scientists might be totally new.

The relation between material stuffs and the particular objects into which material stuffs can be divided is the relation of constitution, which holds between concrete entities as it has been defined in the previous section. The relation of constitution holds between pluralities of stuff-elements and particular objects. Thus, particular objects can be said to divide a given material stuff not because they fall under a certain sortal concept but because they are constituted by stuff-elements. As said above, the presence of material stuffs implies the presence of pluralities of stuff-elements, no matter what particular objects falling under what sortal concepts those stuff-elements constitute. For instance, the existence of the gold which constitutes this ring does not imply the existence of the ring, nor does it imply the existence of a piece, a lump etc. of gold, since the same gold might exist even in the form of dust scattered in some places.

Constitution, then, is the key to the solution to the problem of the relationship between material stuffs and particular objects. Alternative proposals are all to be rejected. The relations of instantiation and exemplification hold between kinds and properties and particular objects. The point is that kinds and properties are universal entities and, thereby, abstract entities. Any picture that treats material stuffs as abstract entities sounds highly counterintuitive, since, for instance, abstract entities cannot undergo creation and destruction. For the very same reason, the relation of membership cannot do. Material stuffs are not to be identified with set-theoretic entities, i.e. with sets of all and only those particular objects having certain chemical structures in common. Sets are abstract entities too and cannot have spatiotemporal properties. Strictly speaking, we could not say that there is no water on the moon, were we to identify water with the set of all aqueous particular objects, for sets have no spatiotemporal locations. Alternatively, the relation of parthood might preserve the concreteness of material stuffs. Water would be the mereological sum of all aqueous particular objects. Contrary to set-theoretic entities, mereological sums are concrete entities. However, the identification of material stuffs with mereological sums gives rise to conceptual difficulties. Indeed, the idea that water is the mereological sum of all aqueous objects misrepresents the nature of water. The fact is that there is no spatiotemporal connection between all those aqueous parts that might give justification to the claim that they are all parts of one particular object. When a particular object is disassembled, its parts stand in a certain spatiotemporal relation to one another. They

[13] See, for example, Burke [3].

are parts of a single larger object in virtue of that spatiotemporal relation. On the contrary, an aqueous object is not part of water in virtue of a spatiotemporal relation to all other aqueous objects. Aqueous objects are not aqueous in so far as they are parts of a larger particular object, but because they are constituted by water-elements.[14]

In the following section I argue that $products_1$ have the same ontological status as that of material stuffs. They are entities possessing a non-particular level of existence.

4. The ontology of $products_1$

Laycock interprets the presence of incidences of material stuffs not as presence of instances of sortal concepts but as presence of pluralities of stuff-elements and then analyzes the existence of material stuff in terms of existence of pluralities of stuff-elements. The water in the basement is not *one* object, falling under a sortal concept like *pool*, *drop*, *quantity*, etc. and having identity and persistence conditions peculiar of particular objects, but *many* objects, i.e. water-elements. My proposal is to extend Laycock's idea to the ontology of $products_1$. The existence of a $product_1$ does not imply the existence of particular objects, i.e. $products_2$ that are its instances, all falling under a unique sortal concept. The existence of a $product_1$ consists in the existence of pluralities of objects, more precisely pluralities of $product_1$-elements. In general, given a $product_1$ A, the notion of A-element can be defined as follows:

> For any x, x is an A-element if and only if there exist a plurality of objects ys and x is one of them and ys are assemblable according to some procedure to form an object falling under the sortal sort G with properties $P_1 \ldots P_n$. (where for any object o, o is an instance of product A if and only if it is a G and has the properties $P_1 \ldots P_n$).

While science discovers what the elements of stuffs are, artifacts do not have a hidden essence to be discovered. What count as elements of a given $product_1$ depend on the procedure for assembling them to form its instances. Hence, the elements of a $product_1$ can be defined by listing them from the assemblage procedure. I leave it open the question of what an assemblage procedure is, whether a blueprint, or a plan, a project, or a technical/engineering design, and the question of the manner in which the intentions of the authors, designers, executors contribute to the existence of assemblage procedures, and hence to the existence of $products_1$. All the questions on the intentionality of artifacts give rise to very important metaphysical issues. However, I put them aside, because they have no direct bearing on the question as to whether $products_1$ have a non-particular level of existence and what the relation between them and $products_2$ is. Of course, the sortal G and the properties $P_1 \ldots P_n$ in the above definition depend on the assemblage procedure. Applying the definition to the aston_martinDB5-elements, we obtain:

$$\text{Aston\_martinDB5-element}(x) \equiv_{def} \exists ys(x \angle ys \wedge AMys)$$

[14] Here I draw on Laycock [6] p. 24.

(here "AM" stands for the property of being assemblable according to some procedure to form an object that is a car with properties $P_1 \ldots P_n$ – where $P_1 \ldots P_n$ are the properties that all and only cars of the model Aston Martin DB5 exemplify).

We can treat names of products$_1$ as mass nouns like water and gold and adopt the following formalization. The sentence

(a) The Aston Martin DB5 is widespread in G

can be formalized into

(a') $\exists xss(\forall ys(ys \angle xss \rightarrow AMys) \wedge Widespread\_in\_G(xss))$

To read: there is a superplurality[15] of object xss such that for any plurality of objects ys, if ys are among xss, then ys can be assembled according to some procedure in order to form a car with the properties $P_1 \ldots P_n$ and xss are widespread in G.[16]

The sentence

(b) The Aston Martin DB5 is a sports car

can be formalized into

(b') $\forall x(\exists ys(AMys \wedge Cysx) \rightarrow Sports\_car(x))$

To read: for any object x if there is a plurality of objects ys such that ys can be assembled according to some procedure in order to form a car with the properties $P_1 \ldots P_n$ and ys constitute x, then x is a sports car.

The sentence

(c) John's car is an Aston Martin DB5

can be formalized into

(c') $\exists xs(AMxs \wedge CxsJohn's\_car)$

To read: there is a plurality of object xs such that xs can be assembled in order to form a car with properties $P_1 \ldots P_n$ and xs constitute John's car.

We can adapt Laycock's example on the impossibility of individuating incidences of material stuffs to the case of incidences of products$_1$. Suppose a large number of aston_martinDB5-elements are stored in a warehouse at t_1. Suppose the aston_martinDB5-elements are sold to customers who, then, assemble them by their own. John and Jim want to buy two pluralities of aston_martinDB5-elements for assembling two cars at t_2. Certainly, both the plurality that will constitute John's car

[15] A superplurality is a plurality of pluralities, i.e. a plurality to which pluralities belong. Quantification over superpluralities is not singular quantification over a new kind of entities, nor is it plural quantification over pluralities. Rather it is a new kind of quantification – superplural – over individuals. See Rayo [13] and Linnebo and Nicolas [10].

[16] I am not claiming that "widespread" is always superplural, i.e. takes always superpluralities as arguments. Obviously, "widespread" can take pluralities as arguments too.

and the plurality that will constitute Jim's car at t_2 are stored in the warehouse at t_1. We can denote them respectively as "the aston_martinDB5-elements that will constitute John's car at t_2" and "the aston_martinDB5-elements that will constitute Jim's car at t_2". But we cannot individuate them simply as incidences of the Aston Martin DB5 at t_1. There is no procedure – related to the application of the concept *Aston Martin DB5* – for singling them out of the plurality of all the aston_martinDB5-elements stored in the warehouse at t_1. The conclusion follows that the concept *P*, where P is a $product_1$, has no principle of individuation.[17] Pluralities of $products_1$-elements are incidences and not instances of sortal concepts. $Products_1$ have the same non-particular level of existence as that of material stuffs.

I take the following analogies between $products_1$ and material stuffs to shed more light on the nature of $products_1$ and to strengthen the view that $products_1$ and material stuffs have the same ontological status. For instance, we can assert sentences like "the Aston Martin DB5 has never been sold in Ulan Bator", "the Aston Martin DB5 has never been produced after 1965" to locate the presence of the Aston Martin DB5 in space and time. The view that $products_1$ possess a non-particular level of existence preserves the commonplace idea that $products_1$ are concrete entities. We also say that the Aston Martin DB5 was created in 1963 and might undergo complete destruction. We might also hypothesize a scenario in which the Aston Martin DB5 first undergoes complete destruction and then is brought back into existence. Suppose human life comes to an end on earth and all human beings and all their artifacts go out of existence. In that scenario the Aston Martin DB5 ceases to exist. After long time, an alien community develops the technology for building cars and alien engineers design the Aston Martin DB5 and start a line of production of cars of that model. When the first stock of aston_martinDB5-elements is delivered by the line of production, the Aston Martin DB5 is brought into existence as $product_1$ for a second time. The Aston Martin DB5 produced in Tickford Street since 1963 and until 1965 and the Aston Martin DB5 produced by the aliens would be one and the same $product_1$.[18]

In addition, the presence of $products_1$ implies the presence of $products_1$-elements, not of $products_2$ as particular objects falling under a unique sortal concept. Imagine the following scenario. The factory in Tickford Street manufactured only the aston_martinDB5-elements and sold them to customers, who then assembled their cars by their own. If the factory in Tickford Street had produced only the aston_martinDB5-elements, no car would have been produced in Tickford Street. In that scenario, the factory in Tickford Street would still have produced the Aston Martin DB5 from 1963 to 1965, without producing any car.

In the next section I discuss and reject some alternative accounts on the ontology of $products_1$.

[17] It must be noted that very often both material stuff and products1 are packaged in specific forms due to human interests, or even other natural reasons. So we speak of "one beer", "two beers", "three rocks", and "one Aston Martin DB5", "two Aston Martin DB5". My claim is that when we use such expressions we mean one bottle of beer, two pints of beer, three lump of rock, one car of the model Aston Martin DB5 (= one car constituted of the Aston Martin DB5), etc. This point is stressed in Laycock [6] p. 18.

[18] Though fundamental in many other fields, questions about copyrights, intellectual properties, legal monopolies etc. do not have any bearing on the ontological status of both products1 and material stuff.

5. Advantages over alternative views

The first account I intend to reject identifies $products_1$ with set-theoretic entities whose members are all and only those $products_2$ that are their instances. The Aston Martin DB5 is reduced to the set of all cars produced by the Aston Martin factory since 1963 and until 1965. The relation between $products_1$ and $products_2$ is reduced to the membership relation.

This account contrasts with the commonplace view that $products_1$ are created and might undergo complete destruction. The difficulty for the view that identifies $products_1$ with set-theoretic entities stems from the fact that we do not say that sets are created and destroyed. Sets are abstract entities and abstract entities are not created nor destroyed. Yet, we are strongly inclined to say that the Aston Martin DB5 was created by manufacturing wheels, engines and brakes and whatever else is needed for the construction of cars of that model. We are strongly inclined to say that at the moment in which the first set of components of the Aston Martin DB5 was finished, the Aston Martin DB5 was brought into existence as $product_1$. This line of reasoning against the identification of $products_1$ with set-theoretic entities rests on our everyday parlance. One might object that our everyday parlance is in need of revision. Maybe there is a sense in which one might be said to create and destroy a set by creating and destroying its members[19] or, rather, we ought to abandon the idea that $products_1$ are created and destroyed. Only $products_2$ can undergo such processes. Accordingly, it would not be true that in 1963 the Aston Martin DB5 was created. It would instead be true that since 1963 and until 1965 a certain number of cars were manufactured by the factory in Tickford Street, all belonging to a given set of things responding to certain physical properties.

The identification of $products_1$ with sets of $products_2$, however, suffers from a more serious difficulty that makes such identification untenable. The difficulty stems from the fact that the identity of a set depends on the identity of its members. In general, to say that the identity of x depends on the identity of y is to say that which thing y is determines which thing x is.[20] If a set depends for its identity on its members, then a set could not be the set it is, unless it has just the members it does have. In other words, given a set, the change of even one of its members produces the change of the set itself. However, a $product_1$ A might have had different and more or fewer $products_2$ as its instances than it actually does have. Despite that, our intuition contrasts with the idea that the $product_1$ A would have been different if some of its instances had been numerically different or more or fewer in number. Since the fact that the identity of a set depends on the identity of its members is a direct consequence of the axiom of extensionality which explains that in which the identity of sets consists, the conclusion follows that we cannot identify $products_1$ with set-theoretic entities because they have different identity criteria.

The second account I want to discuss identifies $products_1$ with patterns that are exemplifiable by $products_2$. Patterns might be thought of as conjunction of properties. Accordingly, the Aston Martin DB5 would be the conjunction of the properties that are exemplified by all and only those cars produced by the factory in Tickford Street since

---

19 Although sets are abstract entities and outside space and time, one might introduce special properties that sets might have in virtue of having members with certain physical, spatiotemporal properties, to the extend that a set of, say, pieces of gold might be said, in a certain sense, to be located where its members are located.

20 Here I draw on Lowe [11].

1963 and until 1965. At first sight, also this view contrasts with our everyday linguistic practice of saying that $products_1$ are created and might undergo complete destruction. In fact, properties are commonly regarded as universal entities, and universals are atemporal, uncaused and abstract. It would follow that those people who cooperated to the production of the Aston Martin DB5 did not create it but discovered it and created only its instances. In other words, neither the engineers nor anybody else who contributed to its production brought the Aston Martin DB5 into existence as $product_1$. If $products_1$ are patterns, then they exist timelessly. At most people can select $products_1$, but never create or destroy them. For example, an engineer who is projecting a car can be described as operating a selection among properties, not as cooperating to the creation of a $product_1$ as a novel entity

It must be admitted that there is something odd in the idea that $products_1$ exist timelessly, waiting to be discovered and selected. One might object that this sense of oddity is simply the result of our custom of everyday parlance and, then, invite a revision of our parlance. However, there is a major flaw in the idea that $products_1$ are patterns. One consequence of the reduction of $products_1$ to patterns is that the logic between $products_1$ and $products_2$ is reduced to the universal/particular scheme. This has a very counterintuitive effect on the epistemology of $products_1$. The fact is that we have experience of the Aston Martin DB5 as $product_1$, which would be impossible, were the Aston Martin DB5 a universal entity. Of course, we might experience several cars of that model. Each time, however, we experience the *same* $product_1$, namely the Aston Martin DB5. It is sufficient for us to encounter the Aston Martin DB5 just once in order to experience it fully. And each time we experience one car of that model, though we might be experiencing a different car, we experience the *same* thing, always identical in all individual cars. This would be impossible if the Aston Martin DB5 were a universal, since we can experience only concrete entities, and universals are abstract entities. If $products_1$ are patterns and patterns are conjunctions of properties, then we cannot experience $products_1$. The cognitive contact with properties is commonly accounted for in terms of abstraction. We separate in thought that which is held in common by various objects. Even on radical nativist theories, it is agreed that we need several encounters with something exemplifying a certain property in order to trigger the innate module for structuring the corresponding concept, which is our mind's link to the property in question. In general, then, we do not experience properties, but only objects exemplifying properties. After experiencing those objects, we form the concept we need to think of the property held in common by the experienced objects. Thus, if the Aston Martin DB5 were reduced to a pattern of properties, we could not enjoy it by watching a car of that model just once, the same way we can enjoy Beethoven's *Fifth* by listening to just one performance of it, or taste the Coca Cola by having just one sip of it, or touch the consistency of snow by touching it just once. Rather, we would be able to enjoy the Aston Martin DB5 only after experiencing many cars of that model. This conclusion contrasts with our intuitions about the epistemology of $products_1$.

The third account I want to discuss identifies $products_1$ with the mereological sums of all $products_2$ that are their instances. Thus, suppose that only 10 cars were manufactured by the factory in Tickford Street. The Aston Martin DB5 would be the mereological sum of all and only those 10 cars. This view has the advantage of preserving the idea that $products_1$ are concrete entities. The relation between mereological sums and their parts is different from the relation between sets and their members. Sets can persist through the destruction of one or more of their members, while mereological sums cannot persist through the destruction of one or more of their parts. The relation between mereological sums and their parts is similar to some extent to the relation between a physical object and its component elements like, say, my desk and the top of my desk. My desk cannot persist through the destruction of its top. My desk ceases to be a desk at all without its top. It must be noted, however, that the relation between mereological sums and their parts is much stronger than the relation between physical objects and their component parts. A physical object might not persist identical through the destruction of some of its parts, but it might persist identical through the destruction *and* the replacement of those parts. My desk ceases to exist without its top. However, the top of my desk can be replaced with a qualitative identical top and my desk remain identical through that replacement. On the contrary, the mereological sum of the components of my desk cannot persist identical through the replacement of any of its parts. According to some philosophers, this shows that my desk is not identical with the mereological sum of its components. But it also shows that the identification of $products_1$ with the mereological sums of $products_2$ suffers from the very same difficulty that affects the identification of $products_1$ with set-theoretic entities. The fact is that mereological sums depend for their identity on the identity of their parts. Thus, had the factory in Tickford Street manufactured more or fewer cars than those that actually manufactured, the Aston Martin DB5 would have been a different entity. This conclusion contrasts with our intuition that the identity of a $product_1$ is independent of the identity of its instances. I find this objection decisive against the identification of $products_1$ with mereological sums of $products_2$.

References

[1] G. Boolos, "To Be Is To Be a Value of a Variable (or to Be Some Values of Some Variables", *Journal of Philosophy* 81 (1984): 430-450.
[2] G. Boolos, "Nominalist Platonism", Philosophical Review 94 (1985): 327-344.
[3] M.B. Burke, "Cohabitation, Stuff and Intermittent Existence", *Mind* 89 (1980): 391-405.
[4] M.B. Burke, "Coinciding Objects: Reply to Lowe and Denkel", *Analysis* 57 (1997): 11-18.
[5] H.M. Cartwright, "Quantities", *Philosophical Review*, 79 (1970): 25-42.
[6] H. Laycock, "Some Questions of Ontology", *The Philosophical Review* 81 (1972): 3-42.
[7] H. Laycock, "Theories of Matter", *Synthese* 31 (1975): 411-442.
[8] H. Laycock, *Words without Objects*, Oxford University Press, Oxford, 2006.
[9] Ø. Lynnebo, "Plural Quantification Exposed", *Nous* 37 (2003): 71-92.
[10] Ø. Lynnebo and D. Nicolas, "Superplurals in English", *Analysis* 68 (2008): 186-197.
[11] E.J. Lowe, *The Possibility of Metaphysics: Substance, Identity, and Time*, Clarendon Press, Oxford, 1998.
[12] A. Rayo, "Words and Objects", *Nous* 36 (2002): 436-464.
[13] A. Rayo, "Beyond Plurals", in A. Rayo and G. Uzquiano (eds), *Absolute Generality*, Oxford University Press, Oxford, 2006, pp. 220-254.
[14] P.F. Strawson, *Individuals*, Methuen, London, 1959.

Formal Ontology in Information Systems
A. Galton and R. Mizoguchi (Eds.)
IOS Press, 2010

doi:10.3233/978-1-60750-535-8-301

Characterizing Functions based on Ontological Models from an Engineering Point of View

Yoshinobu KITAMURA[a,1] and Riichiro MIZOGUCHI[a]
[a] *The Institute of Scientific and Industrial Research, Osaka University, Japan*

Abstract. The purpose of this paper is to characterize some definitions of function in engineering and philosophy from an engineering point of view. To do this, this paper firstly discusses some fundamental kinds of function based on ontological distinctions. Next, based on them, we characterize our definition with justifications from the engineering view and present an ontological model of artifact function along the product life-cycle. Then, we try to characterize a philosophical definition of biological organs using the model. Next, we discuss function of a non-biological (non-organic) natural thing. Lastly, we characterize functions of an artifact, a biological organ and a non-biological natural thing based on another ontological model along the evolution of creatures.

Keywords. an ontology of function, functions of artifacts, biological organs, and natural things, interoperability of functional knowledge

Introduction

This paper discusses some ontological issues on functionality. Much research has been carried out on the notion of function in several research areas. In engineering design [1]-[6], artificial intelligence [7]-[10] and value engineering [11], representation of artifact function for computer-supported design has been investigated. In philosophy [12]-[17], what is function of mainly biological organs has been extensively discussed.

The problem here is that there are many definitions of function without clear relationship among them [4][6][15]. Especially, there is a large gap between definitions of functions in engineering and those in philosophy. For example, in engineering, Umeda *et al.* define a function as "a description of *behavior* abstracted by human through recognition of the behavior in order to utilize it" [3]. In this definition, a function is directly related with a physical process performed by an artifact when it is used. The perception similar to this can be found in many definitions in engineering (e.g., [2][5][7][8]). On the other hand, in philosophy, a function is typically a special feature of a thing [15]. For example, in the causal-role function analysis [13] and ICE theory [17], a technical (artifact) function is regarded as a special kind of capacity to be ascribed to an artifact. Thus, according to the former definition in engineering an artifact *performs* a function, while an artifact *has* a function as a property or a function is *attributed* to an artifact according to the latter definition in philosophy. Then, we could say "a function exists *outside* an artifact" according to the former *or* "a function

[1] Corresponding Author: 8-1, Mihogaoka, Ibaraki, Osaka 567-0047, Japan; kita@ei.sanken.osaka-u.ac.jp

exists *inside* an artifact" according to the latter. As you see, there are large ontological gaps between them, even if we compare two definitions of artifact functions only.

In this paper, we aim at characterizing some definitions of function in engineering and in philosophy based on two ontological models of functions. The consideration is made from an engineering point of view based on our long experiences in ontological research on function in engineering design. The authors have established a suite of ontologies of artifact function and an ontology-based functional modeling framework for engineering design [18]-[21]. The framework has been successfully deployed in some manufacturing companies [20]. Those practical experiences provide real engineering basis for the consideration in this paper.

We first discuss some ontological distinctions and fundamental kinds of function based on our previous consideration [20]-[24] with comparisons to some definitions of function in the literature. Next, Section 2 characterizes our definition of artifact function [20][22][24] using those kinds of function and explains its justifications from the engineering point of view. In addition, we present an ontological model of artifact function proposed in [23], which is a macroscopic temporal model along a product life-cycle. Then, in Section 3, we try to account a philosophical definition of function of biological organs proposed by Johansson *et al.* [25] by extending (and specializing) that model. We also make a comparison between our definition and the definition of function in Basic Formal Ontology (BFO) [26]. In addition, Section 4 discusses functions of non-biological (non-organic) natural things and then compares our view with the definition of artifacts proposed by Borgo and Vieu [27]. Lastly, we characterize those functions of artifacts, biological organs and non-biological natural things based on another ontological model of function along the evolution of creatures.

Our motivations for information systems to clarify the notion of function and the relationships among definitions of function are an explicit viewpoint for describing functional knowledge in the information systems and its interoperability [21]. In practice, engineers tend to describe functional knowledge such as functional decomposition [2] based on an implicit perception of function in an ad hoc manner [20]. As a consequence of inconsistency of the implicit perceptions, it is difficult to share and reuse the functional knowledge. Moreover, the interoperability between functional knowledge based on different definitions of function in the literature is difficult due to the lack of the clear relationship among those definitions. Thus, the ontological investigation in this paper will contribute toward providing engineers some differentiated viewpoints for consistent functional modeling. The clarification of relationship among several definitions in the literature contributes to interoperability.

1. Ontological Distinctions of Function

In this section, we discuss some fundamental kinds of function based on ontological distinctions of function. Those distinctions except that between function and behavior discussed in Section 1.2 are orthogonal to each other. The target of the discussion here is mainly function of artifacts[2], while the similar distinctions can be made for biological organs and non-biological natural things as discussed later.

---

[2] In this paper, we regard an artifact as a physical object that exists in the spatial-temporal space and consists of devices (components) as a system based on a device-oriented ontology [20][24]. We use term 'device' for both artifacts and components. We treat not the artistic aspect but only the physical and functional aspects of an artifact. We discuss our view on artifacts in Section 4.

1.1. Actual Function and Capacity Function

As discussed in the introduction, one of the large differences between the definitions of functions in engineering and those in philosophy is when and where a function exists. In many definitions in engineering (e.g., [2][5][7][8]), a function is directly related to a process performed by an artifact when the artifact is used. On the other hand, in many definitions in philosophy, a function is a special feature of an artifact [15] and what the artifact has or is ascribed to an artifact.

For distinctions of these two senses of function, in this paper, we call the former *actual function*. We regard the latter sense of function as a *capacity to perform the actual function* and then we call the latter *capacity function*. There are deep ontological differences between them. A capacity function is a thing (property) that a device *has* (or is *ascribed* to a device), *exists inside* the device, and is *dependent* on the device. On the other hand, an actual function is a thing that a device *performs (cannot have)*, exists *outside* the device and is *less dependent* on the device. A capacity function is based on a set of appropriate properties (e.g., physical attributes, structure, geometry and material) for realization of the corresponding actual function. A capacity function represents a possibility to perform an actual function and thus is potential and hidden in a device. Then, it is induced by a user at the use phase according to context of use (as discussed in the next sub-section). Thus, when we say "a device has a function", the function referred to is a capacity function.

In philosophy, Boorse [28] makes a similar distinction in terms of a "weak function statement" and a "strong function statement", which roughly correspond to the actual function and the capacity function, respectively. The distinction between *function* and *functioning* in [25] is also similar and they roughly correspond to the capacity function and the actual function. The capacity function is also similar to the notion of *disposition* in [25]. We will revisit these topics in Section 3.

As an exceptional definition in engineering design, Hubka and Eder [1] define functions as follows: "The function is a property of the technical system, and describes its ability to fulfill a purpose, namely to convert an input measure into a required output measure under precisely given condition." In this definition, a purpose represents intended effects as output effects, while a function is the *ability* for an internal task of the technical systems. Thus, the purpose and the function in their definition [1] roughly correspond to the actual function and the capacity function, respectively.

1.2. Function and Behavior

For the actual function performed by an artifact, the distinction between function and *behavior* is important. In both engineering and philosophy, this distinction is extensively discussed. In many definitions in engineering, a function is defined as behaviors *intended* by a user (and/or designer) and is regarded as a subset of behaviors. Such the intention-relatedness is captured in the literature as "aims-means" [1], "means and ends" [8], F-B relationship [3] and in value engineering [9].

We capture an actual function based on context-dependency. We define *behavior of a device* as the changes in the attribute values of the operands which the device affects [20][24]. When a behavior type is identified as the behavior of a device, its instances can play different functions (as *roles* as discussed below) according to teleological contexts, which we call *function contexts (FC)* and we will discuss in Section 1.3. For example, when we identify "to exchange (transfer) heat" as the behavior type of a heat exchanger, which is described as temporal changes of the temperatures of the fluids, an instance of the heat-exchange behavior type can play either of the following functions; (1) "to give heat" function when the heat exchanger is used as a heater with a turbine in a power plant, (2) "to remove heat" function when it is used as a radiator with an engine in a car.

Thus, we define an *actual function* as "a role played by a (device-oriented) behavior in a teleological (function) context" [20]. We call this just 'function' as discussed in Section 2. A role concept cannot be defined without a context and the existence of a role concept depends on the existence of the context [29]. Strictly speaking, a function is a composite of a function-role concept and the behavior playing the function-role concept, which is a kind of a thing called a role-holder [29]. Thus, a function is not a selected behavior. Based on the definition, we say that "a behavior plays a function role". If a device performs a behavior and the behavior plays a function role in a context, then the device plays a *function-performer role* in the context.

In some philosophical considerations [13][17][28], function is regarded as a role, though the role is played by a function-performer. According to the categorization of definitions of function in [15], our definition is a kind of 'goal-contribution theory' in 'recent past backward-looking reductionist category', because our definition is 'goal-directed' (see the next subsection) and we need 'reach back into history as far as the establishment of the goal' [15]. The general characteristics of roles have been extensively investigated such as 'externally-founded', 'anti-rigid' and 'dynamic/multiple' [29][30]. We have shown that function satisfies those generic characteristics [20]. On the other hand, in [2][5][7], function is not distinguished explicitly from behavior based on the intention-relatedness. Some researchers distinguish purpose from function (e.g., [31][32]), whereby the purpose represents a human-intended goal. Chandrasekaran and Josephson discuss an environment function as an effect on the environment [9]. While the effect of the function in our definition is local within the device performing the function, the environment function and the purpose capture the effects on the environment or human perception, which are consequences in causal or enabling relations of the local effect. Borgo *et al.* [33] investigate a formal account of the definitions of function and behavior in [9].

1.3. External Function and Component Function

An artifact performs an actual function when it is used externally by a user. A component in a system performs such a function that contributes to the whole goal of the system. We distinguish these functions as *external function* and *component function* according to the distinctions of the function context as explained below.

The *external function* is performed by the largest and outermost device as the whole system under an *external function context* which depends directly on the user's intention, i.e., how the artifact is used by a user externally. By the word "external" here, we mean that its *context* is *external* to the device when the device is seen as the whole system. Thus, all the performances of external functions are directly intended by a user[3]. An artifact has generally some capacities to perform the external functions (i.e., capacity functions) as discussed in Section 1.1. Among those possible functions, an external function is performed according to a specific user's intention. For example, a screwdriver can be used for performing a screwing (exerting rotational force on a

[3] Note that the success of the actual function and its validation by a user are different problems.

screw) function or a hitting (exerting linear force on something) function using the tail part of the screwdriver. Some of such capacities are intentionally designed by the designer, as discussed in the next section.

The *component function* is performed by a component embedded in a system under a *system function context* which is determined by a *functional structure* in which the system's whole function is hierarchically achieved by a sequence of (relatively finer-grained) components' functions. The functions of the heat exchanger discussed above are examples of this type. When the heat exchanger is embedded in a power plant, under the system function context which consists of the whole function "to convert heat energy to electricity" and the functions of other components in that plant, the heat-exchange behavior plays "to give heat" as the component function. Such a functional structure is called "degree of complexity" [1], function decomposition [2], or function achievement relation [20]. The causal-role function analysis [13] also captures the relationship between the whole function and the component functions as contribution. The constituent function [34] also is similar to the component function.

This distinction is related to the issue of what a function depends on. The external function depends primarily on a user's intention (I-goals [24]), while a component function depends directly on a functional structure of the system. For an artifact, the possible component functions are determined by a designer. When it is used, component function actually performed is selected according to the external function of the system based on the user's intention. In this sense, the actual component function of an artifact *indirectly* depends on the user's intention as well. For a biological organ in an organism, as we will discuss in Section 3, its component function contributes to the function of the organism as the whole system in the same manner as that of an artificial component. It depends *only* on the functional structure of the system, because there is no external use of the system. Based on this same nature, we can separate the user's intention from the system function context of the component function and thus we could regard that the component function depends on the system (NI-goals [24]). Note that an actual function (either component or external function) depends not only on its context but also on a behavior and a device's capacity (capacity function).

Vermaas and Houkes emphasize that functions are features that are ascribed by agents to artifacts relative to use plans and human beliefs on capacity [17]. Our external function context depends on such a "use plan," though such agent's beliefs are implicit in our definition. Garbacz points out that a function is a state of affairs, which represents a connection between objects and processes [35]. Our definition tries to define the connection in terms of the context from the device-oriented point of view.

1.4. Essential Function and Accidental Function

The function context is categorized also according to whether it is essential to a specific device or not. In the example of the screwdriver discussed above, the screwing external function is intended by its designer. The screwdriver is designed and manufactured (i.e., is made to exist) for performing this function. Such an external function is regarded as an *essential external function* under a *designed function context*. On the other hand, the hitting function of the screwdriver is intended *not* by the designer *but only* by the user. Such an external function is regarded as an *accidental external function* under an *accidental use function context*. This distinction is relative with respect to a device. For example, the screwing function could be performed by a key as its accidental function. The hitting function is an essential function of a hammer. As discussed in Sections 3 and 4, the external functions of a physical entity which is not intentionally designed (e.g., biological organs and non-biological natural things) are regarded as *accidental*.

Whether a component function embedded in a system is regarded as essential or accidental depends on the equality of the functions of the component between *function*$_1$ intended by a designer of the component and *function*$_2$ intended (used) by a designer of the system. Usually, the *function*$_2$ is the same as the *function*$_1$ and then is essential[4]. If not, the *function*$_2$ is regarded as *accidental* to the component. For example, slurry containing diamond powder is manufactured for improving cutting efficiency. However, in a cutting machine, the slurry is also used for cooling the cutting blade. In such a case, from the viewpoint of the intention of the designer of the slurry as a component, the slurry performs a cooling function as an accidental component function. If there is no designer of a system (e.g., an organism), its component functions can be regarded as *essential* as discussed in Section 3, because they are developed in nature (e.g., by natural evolution). If there is a designer of a system and no designer of a component (e.g., an artifact has a natural thing as its part), the component function of the component is regarded as *accidental* in the same manner of the external function.

In the discussion above, the actual function of a device is discussed. Both essential and accidental functions require the device's capacity to perform the function. We call the capacity function to perform an essential actual function of a device as an *essential capacity function*. For an accidental actual function, we call an *accidental capacity function*. For an essential actual function of a device, the physical properties necessary for the capacity to perform that function are intentionally designed by a designer and are manufactured. An accidental capacity function of a device is not intended but potentially inheres in the device. When an appropriate context and appropriate inputs for the corresponding accidental actual function are given to the device, that accidental capacity function is induced and is exhibited as an actual function. In the example of the screwdriver, the screwdriver has the screwing essential capacity function and the hitting accidental capacity function based on its shape and hardness.

1.5. Actual function and Specification of Function

So-called *required function* in engineering design exists in nature as a *specification of function*, which specifies what type of actual functions is required to be realized in spatiotemporal space at the use phase. By specification, we here mean a *proposition* that specifies a thing in the real world[5] [36] independently of whether it is explicitly written or not. Before designing, an instance of the *required function at design phase* is usually given as a part of a design requirement. Before using, a user intends an instance of the *required function at the use phase* as an implicit (not-written) instance of specification of function.

The capacity function also has the sense of *specification* that specifies what type of actual functions the device can perform at the use phase, though it has the sense of 'possibility' as well. In the same manner, we can consider *specifications of device, behavior and function context*. A specification of a device is typically produced as the result of designing and specifies the physical properties of the device to be manufactured (see Section 2.2).

---

[4] We can make other distinctions such as mandatory and optional (supplementary).

[5] Note that class definitions in ontologies are *meta*-specifications, because they include classes which specify specifications. We do not discuss such *meta*-specifications here.

2. A Definition and an Ecological Model from an Engineering Point of View

2.1. A Definition of "Function" from an Engineering Point of View

In this section, we explain justification of our definition of function in Section 1 from an engineering point of view. Firstly, our primary definition of "function" is not a capacity function but an actual function. Its first justification is the importance of *actual effects* and values for users from the engineering viewpoint. In engineering, what type of actual effects a user can obtain is of importance. It is represented as an instance of a specific type (class) of the actual function (e.g., "to give heat").

The second justification is the definition of those types of function. Such a definition (e.g., "giving-heat function" class) refers to a behavior as a role-player (heat-flow between two entities) and a function context as a role context (the teleological focus on the heat-receiving entity). Thus, it is defined as a sub-type of the actual function. Each capacity function cannot be defined without referring to those types of actual functions. For example, the heat-exchanger has two capacity functions which are the capacities to perform the giving-heat actual function and the removing-heat actual function. In addition, the required function in engineering design refers to those types of the actual function in the same manner. In the design phase, there is no *instance* of the actual function to be realized but its *type* exists before almost all designs start[6].

The third justification is from the realization-independence of function. A specific required function can be realized by different artifacts with different physical features. This engineering requirement justifies our definition of functions as an actual function detached from artifacts.

As a consequence, the existence of an instance of an (actual) function is *dynamic*. It exists dependently on a specific function context such as a user's intention and its existence is supported by a realized behavior of a device and the device's capacity to perform the function. This dynamism fits in well with the function's properties; those are, dependence on contexts and realization-independence. On the other hand, the instance of an essential capacity function exists during the whole period of the device's existence (we will examine this topic in Section 4). Thus, its existence is *stable*. This difference is the result of the detachment of function from a device.

Our definition of function includes accidental functions as well as essential functions. An accidental use is distinguished from a (proper) function in many philosophical writings (e.g., [12][15][16]). Such accidental use is called "function-as." We regard an accidental effect as a function if it is recognized in a specific function context. If not, it is a behavior. The first justification for our use of the term 'function' here is the effect-oriented definition from the engineering viewpoint. As actual effects, an essential function and an accidental function can have the same intended effect for users[7]. The second justification is that our primary definition of function is an actual function, which is different from the capacity function inhering in a device which is mainly discussed in philosophy.

---

[6] One might think so-called innovative design invents a new type of function. We think many of such designs invent not a type of function but a new *way of function achievement* ("how to achieve a function") [20] for an existing type of function or new application of an existing function to a different operand. This is a benefit of our detachment of function from the way of function achievement [20].

[7] By the "same effect", we here mean the same type (class) of the function. The level of optimization of function's performances such as efficiency, accuracy and reliability is different between that of the essential function and that of the accidental function.

2.2. An Ecological Model of Function

We have proposed an ontological model of artifact function along a product life-cycle [23]. This section briefly overviews that model which is called an *ecological* model of function. Figure 1 shows its portion. It shows macroscopic temporal changes of the individuals (instances) of function and function-related concepts where the time flows from left to right. Each of Figure 1(a), (b), (c) ... shows a thing that appears at a *phase* in a time interval or at a time point. The transition between those phases (depicted as a dark-gray arrow) is made by an activity such as designing, manufacturing and use.

As the first phase (a), the *specification* (in the sense discussed in Section 1.5) of a *function context* of anticipated use and that of an *actual function* to be realized are given as a part of the design requirement. The latter is called the *required function at the design phase*. At the phase (b) after the designing activity, there are the *specifications* of a function and a device, which are determined for satisfying the design requirements and are to be realized in the real world. The former is called *specification function*, which satisfies the required function in the successful design.

The manufacturing activity is to make a device to exist in the real world at the phase (c) according to the specification of the device. The device has (at least) an *essential capacity function*, which satisfies the specification function in the design result. In addition, a device can have other accidental capacity functions as the derived (and unintended) results of the designing and the manufacturing.

Figure 1(d) shows a situation where a user intends to realize a specific function in a specific *external function context*. The intended specific function is represented as a *specification of function* and is called a *required function in the use phase*.

As shown in Figure 1(e), when a device is used in the intended function context and the device has the capacity to perform a function satisfying the required function in the use phase, the device performs a behavior instance and the behavior plays the actual function instance as a role in the function context. This is a result of a user's activity to select such a device that has a capacity function which can satisfy the required function. The capacity function is either essential or accidental to the device. When the device is broken and then loses the capacity function (or when the capacity is insufficient due to the wrong selection), the actual function disappears. If the lost capacity function is essential, it might sometimes affect the device's identity as discussed in Section 4.

This ecological model of function explains what kinds of function (discussed in Section 1) exists in what phase in the product life-cycle. It clarifies the relationships among those kinds of functions. Please refer to [23] for the detail. Using this model, we can characterize functions of biological organs and non-biological natural things as discussed in the following sections.

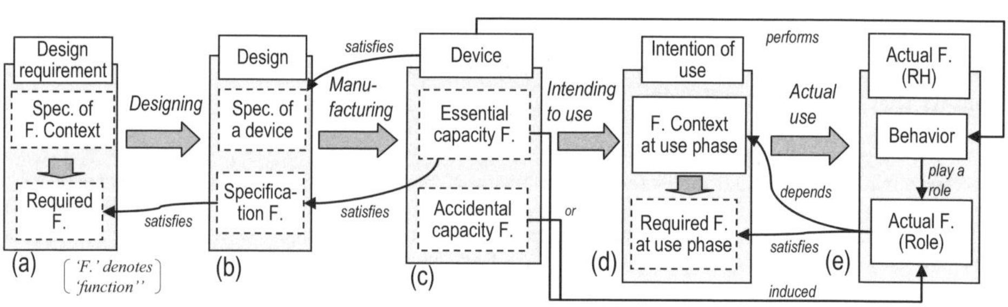

Figure 1. An ecological model of function

3. Characterizing a Philosophical Definition of Function of Biological Organs

In philosophy, function of biological organs has been extensively investigated [15]. Typically, a function of a biological organ inheres to the organ (called a *function bearer*) and is an *objective non-relational property* as pointed out in [37]. The differences between functions of biological and artificial functions are extensively discussed in the book of [37]. Here we try to characterize a philosophical definition of biological function by Johansson *et al.* [25] using the model discussed thus far.

Johansson *et al.* define a function of a biological organ as "a disposition to act in a certain way to contribute to the realization of [a ...] larger function on the part of that whole organism which is its host."[25] This definition can be represented as a special case of the model of artifact function presented in Section 2 with extensions of the definitions introduced in Section 1 in which the function performer is generalized from an artifact to a physical entity without intentional designing/manufacturing. Figure 2 shows the example of a heart. The function of the heart, "to increase pressure of the blood", is performed (realized) in the *system function context*, that is, the functional structure of the blood circulation system (and of the body as the whole). Its performance relies on the heart's capacity to perform that function. This is the same as that of a pump embedded in a fluid circulation system. Thus, the notions of "function" and "functioning" defined in [25] roughly correspond to the *capacity function* and the *actual function*, respectively, There is, however, neither designer's intention nor *external function context* based on user's intention of external use. Thus, we can classify the function in this definition as *essential and component capacity-function*. In the case of biological function, in addition, the system function context is fixed to the organ and does not change. Thus, the relationship between the organ's capacity function and the actual function performed by the organ is *static* unlike the component functions of engineering artifacts. This seems to be one of the reasons of the definition of function as a capacity function, which makes sense in the case of biological function.

We, however, think that the biological organs can perform *external functions* as well. For example, a heart can perform a sound-making (heart sounds) function as an external function under the context of medical diagnosis whereby a medical doctor listens to heart sounds. This function is regarded as *accidental*, because there is no designer's intention for external use of the biological organ. Many philosophers reject this as a function of a heart (e.g., [12]). We would also reject it under their definitions. As discussed in Sections 2.1, our justification for the acceptance of the sound-making as an accidental external function of a heart is the effect-oriented viewpoint of engineering. Moreover, the typical discussion of the rejection in philosophy is about

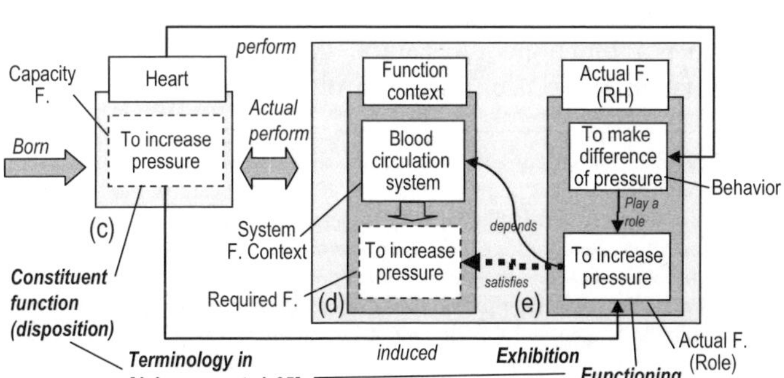

Figure 2. A model of biological function

component functions of the heart, which we do not discuss here. In addition, we do not discuss external function of the *organisms* (e.g., human) as the whole system.

Arp and Smith recently propose a sophisticated definition of functions including both artifact function and biological function in BFO [26]. According to that paper, a (generic) function is a *realizable entity* ("realizable dependent continuant"), which has a *realization*(s) as a process in which its bearer is participant. The realization occurs in virtue of the bearer's physical makeup, which that bearer possesses because of how it came into being. An artifact function is defined under this generic definition as such a function that the bearer's physical makeup for the function is realized by intentional designing and manufacturing to function in a certain way and the function bearer does indeed reliably function in that way. This definition of function is also similar to the *capacity function*, while its realization corresponds to the *actual function*. This definition of artifact function roughly corresponds to the *essential capacity function* and does not include the *accidental function*. The definition includes the notion of reliability, though we think that the reliability is a relative issue of optimization of the function's performance and thus our definition of function does not include the reliability. In [26], a biological function also is redefined under that generic definition. That definition includes the component function only in the same manner as the above.

4. Artifact Function and (non-biological) Natural-thing Function

In this paper, we intuitively regard an artifact as "a physical thing that is intentionally designed and manufactured based on intention about function to be used". Usually, an engineering artifact is based on designer's intention about function to be used by potential users. Thus, this view of an artifact is not based on the user's intention at the use phase but the designer's intention at the design phase. As discussed in Section 1.4, an artifact is designed and manufactured for performing its essential actual function and thus it has appropriate physical properties as the corresponding essential capacity function. When the artifact loses its essential capacity function permanently, the artifact is not regarded as the same subtype of artifacts any more[8]. Thus, for an artifact, having the essential capacity function is an *essential property* of the artifact. By the *essential property* of a thing, we here mean such a property that provides the thing's *identity* [36]. For example, the essential property of a screwdriver is to have the screwing capacity function. When a screwdriver loses this capacity permanently, it is not regarded as a screwdriver anymore. Note that the actual performance of an essential function (as an actual function) is *not* an essential property of an artifact. Even if a screwdriver is used for hitting a nail as an accidental function, we can say that it is still a screwdriver.

We can consider a function of a natural thing[9], which is neither intentionally designed nor manufactured for use[10]. When a physical thing is regarded as a natural

[8] Malfunction of an artifact can be defined with respect to its *specification function* (defined in Section 2.2) determined by a designer. We think there are the following three cases of malfunction according to the levels of the loss of capacity; (1) the artifact's capacity to perform a function is *insufficient*, so that the level of the performance of an actual function (e.g., the output temperature of a heating-function) is insufficient with respect to the specification, (2) the capacity is *temporarily lost*, so that the artifact temporarily cannot perform an actual function of the same type required in the specification, and (3) the capacity is *permanently lost* (e.g., an artifact is fatally broken and thus it cannot be repaired). Only in the last case (3), the artifact loses its identity and thus ceases to belong to the same subtype of artifacts. In the case (1) or the case (2), malfunctioning artifacts keep its identity and remain belonging to the same type.

[9] We exclude biological things, organic things and living things from the natural things discussed here.

thing and it is used under a teleological intention, it is regarded as that it performs an *accidental external function*. For example, let us consider a situation where a pebble as a natural thing is used by a user as a paper-weight. In our view, the pebble performs the "to exert vertical force on a piece of paper" function as an accidental external actual-function. The pebble potentially has a capacity to perform that function as an accidental capacity function based on its weight and the shape of its bottom. It is induced by the use as a paper-weight. It is regarded as *accidental*, because there is no designer's intention for external use as a natural thing. It is impossible to enumerate all the capacity functions of a natural thing like the accidental capacity functions of an artifact.

Next, let us consider a situation where an agent cuts the bottom of the pebble and then make its surface flat, intending to make the pebble to hold the paper stably (i.e., with intention to improve performance of the pebble's function). Thus, if we can regard that cutting act as a manufacturing activity, we can regard that manufactured pebble as an artifact, which has the exerting-force function as its *essential* function. In this case, there is no explicit design phase but we can regard that an implicit design activity has been done simultaneously with the manufacturing activity.

Lastly, let us consider a situation where an agent selects a pebble with a flat bottom from many natural pebbles in a dry riverbed. This act is regarded not as a manufacturing activity but as a selection activity to select an appropriate function-performer based on the required function at the use phase. This is the same as the act performed in the transition from the phase (d) to the phase (e) in the model for artifacts shown in Figure 1. For example, a user can select either a screw driver or a key for the screwing function. Thus, in this situation, the selected pebble is not an artifact but a natural thing, which can perform the function as an accidental function.

Borgo and Vieu deeply investigate an ontological definition of 'artifact' [27]. In their definition, an artifact is the result of "intentional acts" of an agent called a *creator*, which are selection of a physical object and attribution of some capacities to it. In the example of the pebble, by those *creator*'s acts, a paperweight made of a pebble comes into existence. According to their definition, even if a user only selects an object and attributes a capacity to it, the object can be regarded as an artifact (like the example of "a piece of coal to write on a board" in [27]). In this case, it is based on the user's intention at the use phase (the phase (d)) and the capacity[11] (the phase (c)) in our model shown in Figure 1. Their definition includes the case where a designer is the *creator* of artifacts as well ("a commercial pen"), though the designing process includes other important activities besides the intentional selection and the capacity attribution.

Our view on artifacts requires designer's intention (the phases (a) and (b)), a designing activity and a manufacturing activity (the phase (c)) as well as the user's intention. It captures the change inherent in a thing, which is made by intentional designing/manufacturing activities. This observation leads us to a distinction between two kinds of the notion of an artifact, say, a *weak artifact* which can be recognized even if there is only the user's intention and a *strong artifact* which requires the designer's (and manufacture's) intention as well. We might be able to consider that it is a terminological problem which of them is called just an 'artifact'.

---

[10] Our goal here is neither to define notions of artifact and natural thing nor to define the designing and manufacturing activities that change a natural thing to an artifact. We discuss functions of them, when a physical thing is regarded as an artifact or a (non-biological) natural thing.

[11] In [27], the capacity is *attributed* to an artifact by an agent. The artifact does not always have the capacity in reality. Precisely speaking, our capacity function represents a real capacity that an artifact has.

In addition, there is notion of 'product' which is similar to an artifact. We regard a product as "a produced or manufactured thing". It is a role played by an output (resultant) thing of the manufacturing activity. An artifact plays the product role in the context of the manufacturing activity. The notion of artifacts in this paper depends on a designing activity and a manufacturing activity with designer's intention. Thus, the context of the notion of a product is narrower than that of an artifact.

Note that the term 'product' has different meanings such as 'for sale' and 'to be offered to a market'. Indeed, WordNet defines two senses; "commodities offered for sale" and "an artifact that has been created by someone or some process". Our view corresponds to the latter sense. Borgo and Vieu define 'product' based on 'exchange purpose' which has wider sense than the former sense 'for sale' [38].

5. Characterizing Functions along the Evolution of Creatures

In this section, we try to explain the differences among the definitions of functions of artifacts, biological organs and non-biological natural things discussed thus far. Our approach is to characterize those differences based on an ontological model along the evolution of creatures using the ontological distinctions discussed in Section 1.

In the pre-human era, there were only the *component functions* under the *system function context*, because there was no external use of biological organs. As discussed in Section 3, the relationship between the *actual function* and the *capacity function* is static in a biological system. Such core notion of function at this era roughly corresponds to the philosophical definitions of biological organs in [25][26], where a function is defined as the *essential and component capacity-function*.

In human era, humans *use* a physical thing externally with an intentional goal. Thus, the notions of the *external function* based on the external use, *the required function at the use phase* and the *accidental function* appeared in this era. Using these notions, we can represent intentional use of a non-biological natural thing and its function as *accidental external function*. The function in the case where a user is a creator of an artifact in the definition of an artifact in [27] roughly corresponds to the notion of function at this era. The function context of a component function of a sub-part of the non-biological natural thing is a functional structure which is the same as that of the biological system. The whole goal of the functional structure of the biological system, however, inheres in itself, while that of the non-biological natural thing in the external use depends on the intention of an external user. Therefore, although definition of biological function as a kind of *essential and component capacity-function* makes sense in pre-human era, it is not successful in explaining *accidental and external function* that appeared in the human era.

Moreover, in order to improve quality of the performance of the functions, humans started to do the designing activity and the manufacturing activity under their intentions of use. At this phase, the notion of the *required function at the design phase* and the *specification function* in engineering design came into existence. In our view, the notion of an *artifact* appeared based on such designer's intention. Our functional model presented in Section 2 includes all these notions.

In this model, we understand that the notion of function has evolved along with the evolutional history of creatures. We can characterize the functions of biological organs and of non-biological natural things in external use at the initial and intermediate eras in the evolutional process for the artifact function at the last era.

6. Concluding Remarks

In this paper, aiming at clearer understanding of the notion of function, we pointed out ontological differences of some definitions of functions of an artifact, a biological organ and a non-biological natural thing. It is based on ontological models using the fundamental kinds of functions with the ontological distinctions. Using them, some important differences and their relationships were explicated.

Our aim here is not standardization of definition of function but interoperability of different definitions of function. For this, we had proposed some upper-level types of function as a reference ontology of function [21]. The kinds of function in this paper are more fundamental and will be integrated into the reference ontology.

Of course, we do not claim that the ontological distinctions in this paper are sufficient for explaining all the differences among functions of an artifact, a biological organ and a non-biological natural thing. The contribution of this paper is to point out some important distinctions from the engineering point of view. There are other important aspects for the difference [16] such as the social aspect in artifact function [38] and the evolutional aspect for biological organs (e.g., reproduction). Lastly, a formal account of the distinctions like that in [33] is expected.

Acknowledgements: A part of the consideration in this paper is affected by the discussions with Barry Smith (University at Buffalo), Stefano Borgo, Laure Vieu, Nicola Guarino (ISTC-CNR) and Pieter Vermaas (TU Delft). The authors are most grateful to them. This does not imply that they agree on the contents of this paper.

References

[1] Hubka, V. and Eder, W.E., 1988, *Theory of Technical Systems*, Springer-Verlag.

[2] Pahl, G. and Beitz, W., 1996, *Engineering Design - a Systematic Approach*, Springer-Verlag.

[3] Umeda, Y., Ishii, M., Yoshioka, M., Shimomura, Y., and Tomiyama, T., 1996, "Supporting Conceptual Design based on the Function-Behavior-State Modeler", *Artificial Intelligence for Engineering Design, Analysis and Manufacturing (AI EDAM)*, **10**, pp. 275-288.

[4] Hubka, V. and Eder, W.E., 2001, "Functions Revisited", In *Proc. of the Int'l Conf. on Eng. Design 01.*

[5] Hirtz, J., Stone, R.B., McAdams, D.A., Szykman, S., and Wood, K.L., 2002, "A Functional Basis for Engineering Design: Reconciling and Evolving Previous Efforts", *Research in Engineering Design*, **13**, pp. 65-82.

[6] Stone, R. B. and Chakrabarti, A. (eds.), 2005, "Special Issues: Engineering Applications of Representations of Function", *AI EDAM*, **19** (2 and 3).

[7] Chandrasekaran, B., Goel, A. K. and Iwasaki, Y, 1993, "Functional Representation as Design Rationale", *Computer*, **26** (1), pp. 48-56.

[8] Lind, M., 1994, "Modeling Goals and Functions of Complex Industrial Plants", *Applied Artificial Intelligence*, **8**, pp. 259-283.

[9] Chandrasekaran, B. and Josephson, J.R., 2000, "Function in Device Representation", *Engineering with Computers*, **16** (3/4), pp. 162-177.

[10] Goel, A. K., Rugaber, S., and Vattam, S., 2009, "Structure, Behavior, and Function of Complex Systems: the Structure, Behavior, and Function Modeling Language", *AIEDAM*, **23** (1), pp. 23-35.

[11] Miles, L. D., 1961, *Techniques of Value Analysis and Engineering*, McGraw-hill.

[12] Wright, L., 1973, "Functions", *Philosophical Review*, **82**, pp. 39-168.

[13] Cummins, R., 1975, "Functional Analysis", *The Journal of Philosophy*, **72** (20), pp. 741-765.

[14] McLaughlin, P., 2001, *What Functions Explain: Functional Explanation and Self-Reproducing Systems*. Cambridge University Press.

[15] Perlman, M., 2004, "The Modern Philosophical Resurrection of Teleology", *The Monist*, **87** (1), pp. 3-51.

[16] Wouters, A., 2005, "The Function Debate in Philosophy", *Acta Biotheoretica*, **53**, pp. 123-151.

[17] Vermaas, P.E. and Houkes, W., 2006, "Technical Functions: A Drawbridge between the Intentional and Structural Natures of Technical Artefacts", *Studies in History and Philosophy of Science*, **37**, pp. 5-18.

[18] Sasajima, M., Kitamura, Y., Ikeda, M., and Mizoguchi, R., 1995, "FBRL: A Function and Behavior Representation Language". In *Proc. of IJCAI-95*, pp. 1830-1836.

[19] Kitamura, Y., Sano, T., Namba, K., and Mizoguchi, R., 2002, "A Functional Concept Ontology and Its Application to Automatic Identification of Functional Structures". *Advanced Engineering Informatics,* **16**(2), pp. 145-163.

[20] Kitamura, Y., Koji Y., and Mizoguchi, R., 2006, "An Ontological Model of Device Function: Industrial Deployment and Lessons Learned", *Applied Ontology*, **1**(3-4), pp. 237-262.

[21] Kitamura, Y., Takafuji, S. and Mizoguchi, R., 2007, "Towards A Reference Ontology for Functional Knowledge Interoperability", In *Proc. of the ASME 2007 Int'l Design Eng. Technical Conferences & Computers and Information in Engineering Conference (IDETC/CIE 2007)*, DETC2007-35373.

[22] Kitamura, Y. and Mizoguchi, R., 2009, "A Device-Oriented Definition of Functions of Artifacts and Its Perspectives", *Functions in Biological and Artificial Worlds: Comparative Philosophical Perspectives*, MIT Press, pp. 203-221.

[23] Kitamura, Y. and Mizoguchi, R., 2009, "Some Ontological Distinctions of Function based on the Role Concept", In *Proc. of the ASME IDETC/CIE 2009,* DETC2009-87168.

[24] Mizoguchi, R. and Kitamura, Y., 2009, "A Functional Ontology of Artifacts", *The Monist*, **92** (3), pp. 387-402.

[25] Johansson, I., Smith, B., Munn, K., Tsikolia, N., Elsner, K., Ernst, D., and Siebert, D., 2005, "Functional Anatomy: A Taxonomic Proposal", *Acta Biotheoretica*, **53**(3), pp. 153-66.

[26] Arp, R. and Smith, B., 2008, "Function, Role, and Disposition in Basic Formal Ontology", In *Proc. of Bio-Ontologies Workshop (ISMB 2008)*, pp. 45-48.

[27] Borgo, S. and Vieu, L., 2009, "Artefacts in Formal Ontology", *Handbook of Philosophy of Technology and Engineering Sciences*, Meijers, A., (ed), Elsevier, pp. 273–308.

[28] Boorse, C., 2002, "A Rebuttal on Functions", *Functions: New Essays in the Philosophy of Psychology and Biology*, Oxford Univ. Press, pp. 63-112.

[29] Mizoguchi, R., Sunagawa, E., Kozaki, K. and Kitamura, Y., 2007, "The Model of Roles within an Ontology Development Tool: Hozo", *Applied Ontology*, **2**(2), pp. 159-179.

[30] Masolo, C., Vieu, L., Bottazzi, E., Catenacci, C., Ferrario, R., Gengami, A. and Guarino, N., 2004, "Social Roles and their Descriptions", In *Proc. of the 9th Int'l Conf. on the Principles of Knowledge Representation and Reasoning (KR2004)*, pp. 267–277.

[31] Chittaro, L., Guida, G., Tasso, C., and Toppano, E., 1993, "Functional and Teleological Knowledge in the Multimodeling Approach for Reasoning about Physical Systems: A Case Study in Diagnosis", *IEEE Transactions on Systems, Man, and Cybernetics*, **23**, pp. 1718–1751.

[32] Rosenman, M. A. and Gero, J. S., 1998, "Purpose and Function in Design: From the Socio-cultural to the Technophysical", *Design Studies*, **19**, pp. 161–186.

[33] Borgo, S., Carrara, M., Garbacz, P. and Vermaas, P. E., 2009, "A Formal Ontological Perspective on the Behaviors and Functions of Technical Artifacts". *AIEDAM*, **23**(1), pp. 3-21.

[34] Johansson, I., 2006, "The constituent function analysis of functions", *Science—A Challenge to Philosophy?,* Peter Lang , pp. 35–45.

[35] Garbacz, P., 2006, "Towards a Standard Taxonomy of Artifact Functions". *Applied Ontology*, **1**(3/4), pp. 221-236.

[36] Mizoguchi, R., 2003, 2004, "Tutorial on ontological engineering - Part 1-3", *New Generation Computing*, **21**(4) and **22**(1-2).

[37] Vermaas, P., 2009, "On Unification: Taking Technical Functions as Objective (and Biological Functions as Subjective)", *Functions in Biological and Artificial Worlds*, MIT Press, pp. 69-87.

[38] Borgo, S. and Vieu, L., 2006, "From Physical Artefacts to Products", In *Proc. of FOMI 2006 - Formal Ontologies Meet Industry*, pp. 85-99.

Verification and Evaluation

Formal Ontology in Information Systems
A. Galton and R. Mizoguchi (Eds.)
IOS Press, 2010

doi:10.3233/978-1-60750-535-8-317

Ontology Verification with Repositories

Michael GRÜNINGER [a], Torsten HAHMANN [b], Ali HASHEMI [a], Darren ONG [a]
[a] *Department of Mechanical and Industrial Engineering, University of Toronto, Toronto, Ontario, Canada M5S 3G8*
[b] *Department of Computer Science, University of Toronto, Toronto, Ontario, Canada M5S 3G8*

Abstract. In this paper we show how the relationships between first-order ontologies within a repository can be used to support ontology verification. We discuss the use of representation theorems and classification theorems to characterize the models of an ontology, and then show how such results can be obtained from notions such as relative interpretation.

Keywords. ontology repository, ontology evaluation, first-order logic, representation theorems

1. Ontology Verification

Verification is concerned with the relationship between the intended models of an ontology and the models of the axiomatization of the ontology. In particular, we want to characterize the models of an ontology up to isomorphism and determine whether or not these models are equivalent to the intended models of the ontology. This relationship between the intended models and the models of the axiomatization plays a key role in the application of ontologies in areas such as semantic integration and decision support.

We can say that two software systems are semantically integrated if their sets of intended models are equivalent. However, systems cannot exchange the models themselves – they can only exchange sentences in the formal language that they use to represent their knowledge. We must be able to guarantee that the inferences made with sentences exchanged in this way are equivalent to the inferences made with respect to the system's intended models – given some input the application uses these intended models to infer the correct output.

In the area of decision support, the verification of an ontology allows us to make the claim that any inferences drawn by a reasoning engine using the ontology are actually entailed by the ontology's intended models. If an ontology's axiomatization has unintended models, then it is possible to find sentences that are entailed by the intended models, but which are not provable from the axioms of the ontology.

Unfortunately, it can be quite difficult to characterize the models of an ontology up to isomorphism. Ideally, since the classes of structures that are isomorphic to an ontology's models often have their own axiomatizations, we should be able to reuse the characterizations of these other structures. In this paper we show how the relationships between first-order ontologies within a repository can be used to support ontology design and evaluation. Throughout the paper, we will focus on the role that model-theoretic properties play in the application of an ontology repository. In particular, we will address the following challenges:

- How can we identify and characterize the classes of structures that are isomorphic to the models of ontologies?
- What is the weakest theory that is required to axiomatize the intended models of an ontology?
- How can the design of new ontologies be driven by investigating the properties of the models of existing ontologies?

All of these questions are being investigated in the context of the COLORE (Common Logic Ontology Repository) project, which is building an open repository of first-order ontologies that serve as a testbed for ontology evaluation and integration techniques, and that can support the design, evaluation, and application of ontologies in first-order logic. All ontologies are specified using Common Logic (ISO 24707), which is a recently standardized logical language for the specification of first-order ontologies and knowledge bases. At the lowest level are theories of general mathematical structures, such as algebraic structures (e.g. semigroups, groups, rings, vector spaces), and combinatorial structures (e.g. orderings, lattices, graphs). These ontologies serve as the basis for the representation theorems for generic ontologies currently within the repository, such as processes, time, mereotopology, and geometry. Future work will design new ontologies for manufacturing standards (such as ISO 10303 STEP (Standard for the Exchange of Product data) and ENV 12204 (Constructs for Enterprise Modelling)), which will extend and integrate the generic ontologies.

The fundamental insight of this paper is that we can use the relationships between ontologies to assist us in the characterization of the models of the ontologies. The objective of the work is the construction of the models of one ontology from the models of another ontology by exploiting the relationships between these ontologies and their modules in the repository.

2. Relationships Between Ontologies

We begin with the relationship between ontologies and their subtheories within the repository. Theories within the repository will be referred to as modules. An ontology is a theory that consists of one or more modules, so that relationships between ontologies can be defined with respect to the relationships between their modules. We first introduce the set of relationships between ontologies and their modules within a repository, and then show how we can use these relationships to characterize the models of the ontologies.

2.1. Extensions

The simplest relationship between ontologies is that of extension, In particular, the notion of conservative extension has played a key role in the study of modular ontologies ([8], [9]):

Definition 1 *Let T_1 be a first-order theory with language $\mathcal{L}(T_1)$ and let T_2 be a first-order theory with language $\mathcal{L}(T_2)$.*

T_2 is a conservative extension of T_1 iff $\mathcal{L}(T_1) \subset \mathcal{L}(T_2)$ and for any formula $\Phi \in \mathcal{L}(T_1)$, we have $T_2 \models \Phi$ iff $T_1 \models \Phi$.

Several results ([15]) illustrate how conservative extensions of theories are related to extensions and substructures of models of the theories. In particular, if for every model $\mathcal{M}_1 \in Mod(T_1)$ there exists a model $\mathcal{M}_2 \in Mod(T_2)$ such that $\mathcal{M}_1 \subset \mathcal{M}_2$, then T_2 is a conservative extension of T_1. Alternatively, if T_2 is a conservative extension of T_1 then for any model $\mathcal{M}_2 \in Mod(T_2)$ there exists a model $\mathcal{M}_1 \in Mod(T_1)$ such that $\mathcal{M}_1 \subset \mathcal{M}_2$.

Since our goal is to construct the models of an ontology by using the models of theories that are already in the repository, these propositions tell us how to capture and reuse existing constructions. If we have constructed the models of one theory by extending models of the other theory, then this is captured in the repository as a conservative extension relationship. If we know that one theory is a conservative extension of another (e.g. by proof-theoretic means), then we know that models of the theory can be constructed from models of the other.

2.2. Relative Interpretation

Different ontologies within the same language can be compared using the notions of satisfiability, extension, and independence. More difficult is to compare ontologies that are axiomatized in different languages; in such cases, we need to determine whether or not the nonlogical lexicon of one ontology can be interpreted in the nonlogical lexicon of the other ontology. In this section, we review the basic concepts from model theory that will supply us with the techniques for comparing ontologies in different languages.

We will adopt the following definition from [5]:

Definition 2 *An interpretation π of a theory T_0 with language L_0 into a theory T_1 with language L_1 is a function on the set of parameters of L_0 such that*

1. *π assigns to $\forall$ a formula $\pi_\forall$ of L_1 in which at most the variable v_1 occurs free, such that*

$$T_1 \models (\exists v_1)\, \pi_\forall$$

2. *π assigns to each n-place relation symbol P a formula π_P of L_1 in which at most the variables $v_1, ..., v_n$ occur free.*
3. *For any sentence σ in L_0,*

$$T_0 \models \sigma \Rightarrow T_1 \models \pi(\sigma)$$

Thus, the mapping π is an interpretation of T_0 if it preserves the theorems of T_0.

Definition 3 *An interpretation π of a theory T_0 into a theory T_1 is faithful iff there exists an interpretation π of T_0 into T_1 and*

$$T_0 \not\models \sigma \Rightarrow T_1 \not\models \pi(\sigma)$$

for any sentence $\sigma \in \mathcal{L}(T_0)$.

Thus, the mapping π is a faithful interpretation of T_0 if it preserves satisfiability with respect to T_0. We will also refer to this by saying that T_0 is faithfully interpretable in T_1.

For example, the work in [10] shows that the PSL-Core theory within the PSL Ontology [11] is interpretable by Reiter's axiomatization of situation calculus, but that this is not a faithful interpretation, since there are sentences consistent with PSL-Core that are not consistent with situation calculus.

Definable equivalence is a generalization of the notion of logical equivalence between ontologies with the same language.

Definition 4 *Two ontologies T_1 and T_2 are definably equivalent iff T_1 is faithfully interpretable in T_2 and T_2 is faithfully interpretable in T_1.*

Similarly, faithful interpretations are a generalization of the notion of conservative extension.

Theorem 1 *T_1 is faithfully interpretable in T_2 iff there is theory T_3 such that T_1 is definably equivalent to T_3 and T_2 is a conservative extension of T_3.*

2.3. Definability

Relative interpretations specify relationships between theories; we are also interested in specifying relationships between models of the theories. We begin with the notion of definable sets within a structure.

Definition 5 *Let $\mathcal{M}$ be a structure with domain M and language L.*

A set $X \subseteq M^n$ is definable in $\mathcal{M}$ iff there is a formula $\varphi(v_1, ..., v_n)$ of L such that $X = \{\langle a_1, ..., a_n\rangle \in M^n \ : \ \mathcal{M} \models \varphi(\langle a_1, ..., a_n\rangle)\}$.

Using this definition, we can adopt the following approach from [17]:

Definition 6 *Let $\mathcal{N}$ be a structure in $\mathcal{L}_0$ and let $\mathcal{M}$ be a structure in $\mathcal{L}$. We say that $\mathcal{N}$ is definable in $\mathcal{M}$ (equivalently, $\mathcal{M}$ defines $\mathcal{N}$) iff we can find a definable subset X of M^n and we can interpret the symbols of $\mathcal{L}_0$ as definable subsets and functions on X so that the resulting structure in $\mathcal{L}_0$ is isomorphic to $\mathcal{N}$.*

Since we will also be interested in characterizing the models of an ontology's axiomatization up to elementary equivalence, we will need a generalization of the notion definability:

Definition 7 *A structure $\mathcal{M}$ is weakly definable in $\mathcal{N}$ iff there exists a structure $\mathcal{K}$ such that $\mathcal{N}$ is elementary equivalent to $\mathcal{K}$ and $\mathcal{M}$ is definable in $\mathcal{K}$.*

The relationship between relative interpretations of ontologies and definability of structures is captured in a straightforward way by the following theorem:

Theorem 2 *If there exists a faithful interpretation of an ontology T_1 into an ontology T_2, then every model of T_2 defines some model of T_1.*

Using techniques that characterize the definable sets within a model, this result can be used to show when relative interpretations between theories do not exist (see [10]).

2.4. Classes of Theories

The notion of definability allows us to distinguish between different kinds of subtheories of an ontology. We will later see how this distinction impacts the verification of ontologies.

Definition 8 *A theory T_2 is a definitional extension of a theory T_1 iff every constant, function, and relation in any model of T_2 is definable in some model of T_1.*

It is easy to see that a definitional extension of a theory T is also a conservative extension of T, although the converse is not true; that is, there are conservative extensions of theories which are not definitional extensions.

Definition 9 *Two theories T_1 and T_2 with disjoint nonlogical lexicons are synonymous iff there exists a theory S in the language formed by taking the union of the lexicons of T_1 and T_2 such that S is a conservative extension of both T_1 and T_2.*

The notion of logical synonymy is stronger than definable equivalence, and it allows us to explicitly axiomatize the mapping between the ontologies as conservative definitions:

Theorem 3 *T_1 and T_2 are synonymous theories iff there exists a set of conservative definitions Σ_{12} with respect to T_1 such that*

$$T_1 \cup \Sigma_{12} \models T_2$$

and there exists a set of conservative definitions Σ_{21} with respect to T_2 such that

$$T_2 \cup \Sigma_{21} \models T_1$$

For example, the alternative axiomatizations of lattices as posets and as algebras demonstrate that these are synonymous theories.

Definition 10 *A module T_{core} in the repository is a core theory iff no function and no relation in models of T_{core} is definable in the models of any other theory unless that theory is synonymous.*

Core theories are the modules that are the building blocks of the repository. The relations that are axiomatized in a definitional extension are those which are definable in a core theory, and in Section 4 we will see how the definitional extensions are related to the models of the core theories.

Definition 11 *A core hierarchy is a set of core theories $T_1, ..., T_n$ such that $\mathcal{L}(T_i) = \mathcal{L}(T_j)$, for all i, j.*

For example, the theories that axiomatize classes of partial orderings form a core hierarchy – all theories have the same language (i.e. the ordering relation $\leq$) and all are extensions of the theory that contains the three axioms for a partial ordering (transitivity, reflexivity, and antisymmetry).

By the following theorem, theories in the same core hierarchy are related by non-conservative extension.

Theorem 4 *If T_1 and T_2 are core theories in the same core hierarchy, then*

$$T_1 \subset T_2 \Leftrightarrow Mod(T_2) \subset Mod(T_1)$$

In other words, models of a core theory in a core hierarchy are models of its subtheories that are modules in the same core hierarchy; extensions only restrict the sets of models, not the structures of the models themselves. This is not in general the case for all core theories; for example, the core theories in the PSL Ontology do not form a core hierarchy, since each theory expands the nonlogical lexicon; as a result, the models of a core theory in the PSL Ontolgy are constructed by extending models of other core theories.

2.5. Related Work

The use of relative interpretations between first-order axiomatized theories as a means to combine smaller theories has been implemented by the Interactive Mathematical Proof System (IMPS). IMPS is a mathematical theorem prover that utilizes a repository of axiomatized mathematical theories linked to each other through relative interpretations using the little theories approach to mechanize traditional tools of classical mathematical reasoning [7]. The use of relative interpretations by IMPS provide the means to transport a theorem from the theory it was proved in to any other theory linked with an interpretation. The IMPS repository is organized around the relative interpretations available between stored theories. Furthermore, IMPS guarantees the consistency of generated proofs based on the notion of relative consistency between theories. Within IMPS there is a set of theories deemed *foundational*, meaning they are regarded or known to be consistent. Since all proofs begin with a foundational theory and any theory developed from another is a conservative extension of the original theory, all theories developed are consistent relative to the original foundational theory [6]. Although the use and definitions of theory interpretations and relative consistency in IMPS are specific to the purpose of theorem proving, it nonetheless shows how such relationships can be utilized to relate and combine theories. Unfortunately, relative consistency proofs alone are insufficient to verify an ontology. Strictly speaking, we only need to show that a model exists in order to demonstrate that a theory is satisfiable. However, in the axiomatization of domain theories, we need a complete characterization of the possible models.

The Information Flow Framework, an application of category theory to knowledge representation, uses theory interpretations for sharing ontologies in distributed settings [16]. Instances of two different ontologies are linked if they share the same *type* subsumption hierarchy. Finding equivalent *types* between those ontologies are done using theory interpretations through a common upper ontology. A virtual ontology is then formed as a fusion of all participating ontologies and used as the complete system through which the sharing of information occurs [16].

Using $\mathcal{E}$-connections for modularization of OWL ontologies has been explored for both the decomposition of existing ontologies [8] and for ontology design [9]. The $\mathcal{E}$-connection language is a formalism that allows the combination of decidable logics in a way that preserves decidability while adding expressiveness [9]. An $\mathcal{E}$-connection is a set of $\mathcal{E}$-connected ontologies that each model a different application domain, while the $\mathcal{E}$-connection itself models the union of all the domains [8]. In the case of using $\mathcal{E}$-connections to decompose a large ontology into modules (a collection of axioms), each module encapsulates some terms of the original ontology. In [8] the definition of semantic encapsulation is given as a component that preserves a basic set of entailments of a term in an ontology. This leads to the partitioning of a large ontology into a collection of modules that are conservative extensions of one another. The relationship of conservative extensions between modules ensures that each module can be reused independent of the rest while retaining the original semantics of its contained terms. An algorithm for partitioning an OWL ontology into $\mathcal{E}$-connected ontologies is provided in detail in [8]. The major limitation of using $\mathcal{E}$-connections is that the use of such modules as a means of refining an ontology (non-conservative extensions of a theory) becomes impossible.

3. Ontology Verification: Core Theories

Any ontology can be partitioned into a set of core theories and a set of definitional extensions to the core theories. We therefore approach the problem of ontology verification from two perspectives. First, we consider the verification of core theories through representation theorems, and then we consider the verification of definitional extensions through classification theorems. In both cases, we show how the relationships between ontologies within the repository can be used to specify properties of the models of the ontologies.

3.1. Representation Theorems

We can evaluate the adequacy of the application's ontology with respect to some class of structures that capture the intended meanings of the ontology's terms by proving that the ontology has the following two fundamental properties:

- Satisfiability: every structure in the class is a model of the ontology.
- Axiomatizability: every model of the ontology is elementary equivalent to some structure in the class.

The purpose of the Axiomatizability Theorem is to demonstrate that there do not exist any unintended models of the theory, that is, any models that are not specified in the class of structures. In general, this would require second-order logics; however, if we assume that the ontology supports interoperability among first-order inference engines which exchange first-order sentences, then we do not need to restrict ourselves to elementary classes of structures when we are axiomatizing an ontology. Since the applications are equivalent to first-order inference engines, they cannot distinguish between structures that are elementarily equivalent. Thus, the unintended models are only those that are not elementary equivalent to any model in the class of structures.

Classes of structures for theories within an ontology are therefore axiomatized up to elementary equivalence – the theories are satisfied by any model in the class, and any model of the core theories is elementarily equivalent to a model in the class.

In this section, we are interested in constructing models of one ontology by combining models of ontologies in repository, or by decomposing the models of the ontology into models of other ontologies in the repository. We will consider two motivating examples – the mereotopology RT and the core theories PSL-Core and Occurrence Trees from the PSL Ontology.

3.2. Relationship to Interpretability

In this section, we show how representation theorems for ontologies are captured by the relationships between modules within the repository. We begin by a model-theoretic definition for the key property that underlies the Satisfiability and Axiomatizability Theorems:

Definition 12 *A class of structures $\mathfrak{M}$ can be represented by a class of structures $\mathfrak{N}$ iff there is a bijection $\varphi : \mathfrak{M} \rightarrow \mathfrak{N}$ such that for any $\mathcal{M} \in \mathfrak{M}$, $\mathcal{M}$ is weakly definable in $\varphi(\mathcal{M})$ and $\varphi(\mathcal{M})$ is weakly definable in $\mathcal{M}$.*

Note that representation is up to elementary equivalence rather than up to isomorphism, since we are using the notion of weak definability between models.

Theorem 5 *A theory T_1 is definably equivalent with a theory T_2 iff the class of models $Mod(T_1)$ can be represented by $Mod(T_2)$.*

We can use this result in two ways – if we have specified Satisfiability and Axiomatizability Theorems for a particular ontology, we can capture this in the repository by identifying the theories that axiomatize the classes of structures that are elementary equivalent to the models of the ontology. Alternatively, if we are attempting to prove the Satisfiability and Axiomatizability Theorems for the ontology, then we can use the relationships between theories in the repository to identify any other theories that are definably equivalent to the ontology; the models for these other theories will provide the classes of structures that characterize the models of the ontology.

The notion of representability allow us to specify the weakest theory required to axiomatize the intended models of an ontology. For example, some process ontologies may represent a timeline as the real numbers, yet the intended models for the timeline simply require a dense linear ordering. Since the theories in the repository are combined to specify a theory that is definably equivalent to the ontology, eliminating any axioms would result in unintended models.

3.3. Examples from Mereotopology

Within formal ontologies, spatial ontologies are amongst the most widely studied ontologies. Our environment is saturated with spatial and spatio-temporal information. Hence, every upper ontology contains some definitions and axioms dealing with spatial information. Within spatial ontologies, mereotopologies capturing topological (contact) and mereological (parthood) relations between regions of space have been most widely studied. First-order ontologies of mereotopologies are in particular interesting because a large set of possible axioms and their interactions can be studied in a clearly defined setting. In the study of mereotopologies, representation theorems helped to establish the relationship between different ontologies. Lattices in general and, more specifically, contact algebras consisting of a lattice and a binary contact relation satisfying certain axioms have proven useful as representations of Whiteheadian mereotopology [14]. Here, we only summarize some of the results to exemplify the usefulness of representation theorems for verifying ontologies.

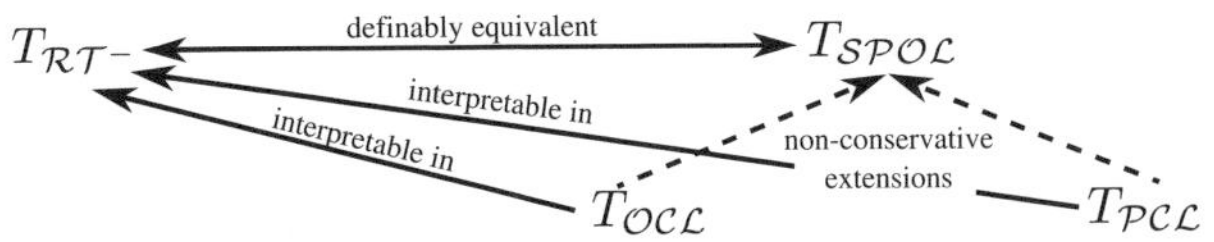

Figure 1. The ontologies and modules $T_{\mathcal{RT}^-}$, $T_{\mathcal{SPOL}}$, $T_{\mathcal{OCL}}$ and $T_{\mathcal{PCL}}$ and their relationships.

For example, the models of the first-order ontology of mereotopology $T_{\mathcal{RT}^-}$ (a generalization of the ontology from [1]) can be represented by the definably equivalent ontology of Stonian p-ortholattices (Stonian, pseudocomplemented, orthocomplemented lattices) $T_{\mathcal{SPOL}}$. The axiomatization of $T_{\mathcal{RT}^-}$ and the precise structure of Stonian details are not important here, but can be found in [13] together with the details of the representation theorem. The main point here is that Stonian p-ortholattices are a natural class of lattices that is definable as the ontology $T_{\mathcal{SPOL}} = T_{\mathcal{OCL}} \cup T_{\mathcal{PCL}} \cup \{S1\}$ consisting of a module for orthocomplemented lattices $T_{\mathcal{OCL}}$ and a module for pseudocomplemented lattices $T_{\mathcal{PCL}}$ strengthened by the Stone identity $(S1)$ $(x+y)^{**} = x^* + y^*$ where * denotes the pseudocomplementation operation. Of course, $T_{\mathcal{OCL}}$ and $T_{\mathcal{PCL}}$ are themselves ontologies; both of them are non-conservative extensions of the ontology of bounded lattices. As mentioned before, these lattices are definable in terms of $\leq$ and thus form a core hierarchy. From the knowledge that $T_{\mathcal{RT}^-}$ is definably equivalent to $T_{\mathcal{SPOL}}$, we can then, for example, deduce that the each of the ontologies $T_{\mathcal{OCL}}$ and $T_{\mathcal{PCL}}$ are interpretable in $T_{\mathcal{RT}^-}$, but not faithfully interpretable in $T_{\mathcal{RT}^-}$. All these classes of lattices have been studied for half a century in lattice theory and are well-understood, cf. [2]. Hence, giving representation theorems for a not-well understood ontology in terms of a better-understood mathematical theories (and their first-order ontologies) helps to verify whether the mereotopology captures the intended models.

Perhaps more well-known is the representation of the models of the popular mereotopology Region Connection Calculus (RCC) [3] by Boolean Contact Algebras (BCA), the latter structures denoted by $\langle A, C\rangle$. For the RCC, we use in the following the theory $T_{\mathcal{RCC}}$ as axiomatized by (RCC1)-(RCC8) from [4]. BCAs, in turn, consist of a standard Boolean algebra $A = \langle A; 1; 0;'; +; \cdot\rangle$ with a bottom element 0, a top element 1 and the sum and intersection operations $+$ and $\cdot$ for which many definably equivalent first-order theories can be found, e.g., in [19]. We denote any such theory based on the single predicate $\leq$ by $T_{\mathcal{BA}}$. Another definition of a Boolean algebra established in [13] is that of a distributive Stonian p-ortholattice. Furthermore, BCAs require a binary contact relation C that is reflexive, anti-symmetric, and extensional as captured by the first-order theory $T_{\mathcal{C}} = \{C1, C2, Ext\}$. For details see e.g. [20]. The axioms (P) and (O) which define the pivotal mereotopological relations of parthood P and overlap O are definitional extensions of $T_{\mathcal{C}}$.

(C1) $x \neq 0 \rightarrow C(x, x)$ (Reflexivity)
(C2) $C(x, y) \leftrightarrow C(y, x)$ (Symmetry)
(Ext) $\forall z(C(x, z) \rightarrow C(y, z)) \leftrightarrow x = y$ (Extensionality)
(P) $P(x, y) \leftrightarrow \forall z(C(x, z) \rightarrow C(y, z))$ (Parthood)
(O) $O(x, y) \leftrightarrow P(x, y) \vee P(y, x)$ (Overlap)

(C0) $\neg C(0, x)$ (Null disconnectedness)
(C3) $C(x, y) \wedge y \leq z \rightarrow C(x, z)$ (Monotonicity of C with respect to $\leq$)
(C4) $C(x, y + z) \rightarrow C(x, y) \vee C(x, z)$ (Topological sum)
(Con) $(x \neq 0 \wedge x \neq 1) \rightarrow C(x, x')$ (Connectedness of x and x')

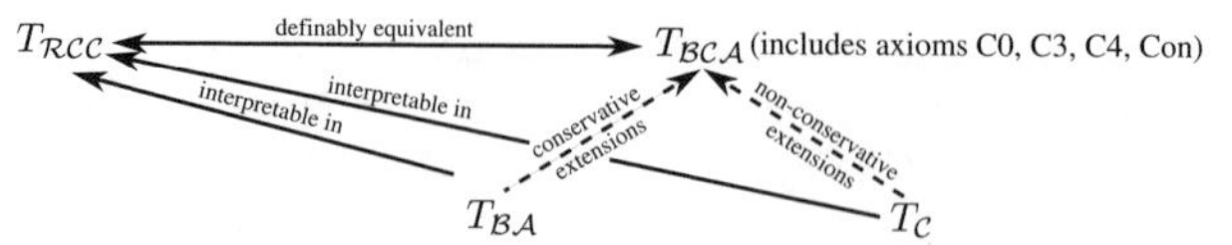

Figure 2. The ontologies and modules $T_{\mathcal{RCC}}$, $T_{\mathcal{BCA}}$, $T_{\mathcal{BA}}$ and $T_{\mathcal{C}}$ and their relationships.

In addition, the axioms $C0, C3, C4, Con$ govern the interplay between the Boolean algebra and the relation C. Notice that in these axioms all relations apart from C, and allfunctions and constants are defined in the Boolean algebra. This results in the theory $T_{\mathcal{BCA}} = T_{\mathcal{BA}} \cup T_{\mathcal{C}} \cup \{C0, C3, C4, Con\}$ being definably equivalent to, for details see $T_{\mathcal{RCC}}$ [20,4]. The mapping between the two theories is defined by three equivalences: $P(x, y) \leftrightarrow x \leq y$ $\quad \neg C(x, y) \leftrightarrow x < y$ $\quad O(x, y) \leftrightarrow x \cdot y \neq 0$

Due to (C0), (C3), (C4), and (Con), we cannot choose arbitrary models from $T_{\mathcal{BA}}$ and $T_{\mathcal{C}}$ and combine them into a model of the theory $T_{\mathcal{BCA}}$. We can however select an arbitrary Boolean algebra and choose a model from $T_{\mathcal{C}}$ accordingly so that we obtain a model of $T_{\mathcal{BCA}}$. In particular, we have to make sure that the equivalence $\neg C(x, y) \leftrightarrow x < y$ is satisfied. The reverse, i.e. taking an arbitrary model of $T_{\mathcal{C}}$ and constructing a model of $T_{\mathcal{BCA}}$ accordingly, is not guaranteed to work.

Both these examples show how representation theorems can be used to obtain several relationships between different ontologies and their modules (see Figures 1 and 2). The first example of the theory T_{RT^-} demonstrated how the intersection of two theories is captured, while the second example of the theory T_{RCC} shows how a module (T_{BA}) can be supplemented by another module (T_C) to build an ontology definably equivalent to another ontology. In these examples, we exploited the relationships between the models of the different theories to characterize the relationships between the ontologies and modules. They also demonstrate that there are different ways in which models of multiple ontologies can be combined to construct complex ontologies. The next section formalizes one special case thereof with especially well-behaved properties.

3.4. Reducibility

Suppose that we wish to provide representation theorems for some new theory T. Even if there is no single ontology (i.e. set of modules) in the repository that is definably equivalent to T, we can still use the models of repository theories to specify a representation of $Mod(T)$. We want to capture the following intuition: the representation of $Mod(T)$ is reducible to the representations of $Mod(T_1)$, ..., $Mod(T_n)$ for some set of modules $T_1, ..., T_n$ in the repository. Moreover, we want to characterize this notion of reducibility by using the relationships among modules in the repository. The question is therefore how we can use the representations of the $Mod(T_i)$ to specify the representation of $Mod(T)$.

As we did with the notion of representation, we begin with a model-theoretic definition of the relationship:

Definition 13 *A class of structures $\mathfrak{M}$ is reducible to the classes of structures $\mathfrak{N}_1, ..., \mathfrak{N}_n$ iff there is a set of surjections $\varphi_i : \mathfrak{M} \rightarrow \mathfrak{N}_i$ such that if $\mathcal{M} \in \mathfrak{M}$ and*

$$\mathcal{M} = \mathcal{M}_1 \cup ... \cup \mathcal{M}_n$$

then $\mathcal{M}_i$ is weakly definable in $\varphi_i(\mathcal{M}_i)$ and $\varphi_i(\mathcal{M}_i)$ is weakly definable in $\mathcal{M}_i$.

As we did with representability, we can show how the model-theoretic notion of reducibility can be characterized by the relationships between modules in the repository:

Theorem 6 *Let T be a theory and let $T_1, ..., T_n$ be a set of modules in the repository.*
$Mod(T)$ is reducible to $Mod(T_1), ..., Mod(T_n)$ iff

- *T faithfully interprets each theory T_i, and*
- *$T_1 \cup ... \cup T_n$ is definably equivalent to a subtheory $T' \subset T$ such that*

$$Mod(T) \subset Mod(T')$$

If a theory T is reducible to a set of theories, then from any model $\mathcal{M}_i \in Mod(T_i)$, we can construct a model $\mathcal{M}$ of T; each such model is isomorphic to a substructure of $\mathcal{M}$. The axioms in $T \setminus T'$ are expressed in the same language as T; in this sense, they are not satisfied by new classes of structures, but instead specify *how* the substructures $\mathcal{M}_i \in Mod(T_i)$ are assembled to construct a model $\mathcal{M}$ of T. If a theory T is not reducible to a set of theories, then there exist models of one theory which cannot be combined with models of other theories to construct a model of T. In this case, T is not a faithful interpretation of one of the theories. For example, the theory $T_{\mathcal{RCC}}$ from the previous section is not reducible to the theories $T_{\mathcal{BA}}$ and $T_{\mathcal{C}}$. The next section gives an example of a reducible theory.

3.5. Examples from the PSL Ontology

The models of the PSL-Core theory [18] provide an example of reducibility. In particular, we can identify three classes of structures that can be combined to construct models of PSL-Core. Two of these are classes of incidence structures which are represented by the decomposition of graphs:

Definition 14 *Let $G = (V, E)$ be a directed graph with no nontrivial cycles, and let $P(E)$ be a partitioning of the edges in G.*
A partitioning incidence structure is the tripartite incidence structure of rank 3:

$$\mathbb{I} = (P(E), E, V, \in)$$

A graph incidence structure is the bipartite incidence structure of rank 2:

$$\mathbb{I} = (E, V, \in)$$

Theorem 7 *Let T_{linear} be the theory of linear orderings, let $T_{partition}$ be the theory of partitioning incidence structures, and let $T_{graph-incidence}$ be the theory of graph incidence structures.*
$T_{pslcore}$ is reducible to $T_{linear} \cup T_{partition} \cup T_{graph-incidence}$.

Thus, any linear ordering, partitioning incidence structure, and graph incidence structure can be combined to construct a structure that is isomorphic to a model of $T_{pslcore}$. The additional axioms in $T_{pslcore}$ specify how the substructures are combined by constraining the mapping of timepoints, activity occurrences and objects to the linear ordering.

3.6. Foundational Theories

The methodology proposed in this section leads to some obvious questions. If all core theories in the repository have representation theorems, how do we avoid infinite regress? Do there exist theories which are foundational in the sense that the models of all other theories are represented using the models of the foundational ones? If so, how can we characterize the models of such foundational theories?

There are three techniques that can be used to address these questions. First, there are some theories that are so general that they can be used to represent the models for a wide range of theories. For example, graphs (symmetric binary relations) and preorders (transitive, reflexive relations) are used to specify the structures for ontologies such as [21], yet we do not provide representation theorems for graphs and preorders. Also note that powerful theories such as Peano Arithmetic do not play the role of foundational theories in this sense, since representability requires that the models of the two theories are equivalent, whereas the models of Peano Arithmetic properly contain many other classes of models as substructures.

In some cases, we can use the notion of mutual interpretability, in which two different theories are definably equivalent so that both can be used as foundational. For example, classes of lattices are often characterized by topological representations.

A third technique is to use structure theorems to specify the models of a theory. In this case, we provide representation theorems for a small class of structures and then specify how all models can be constructed from such "building block" structures. This approach is taken for theories such as linear orderings, groups, rings, and modules.

4. Ontology Verification: Definitional Extensions

The evaluation of the definitional extensions within an ontology is based on the notion of definable sets and the particular property of such sets that they are preserved by automorphisms of the underlying models.

4.1. Classification Theorems

Many ontologies are specified as taxonomies or class hierarchies, yet few ever give any justification for the classification. If we consider ontologies of mathematical structures, we can classify models by using properties of models, known as invariants, that are preserved by isomorphisms. For some classes of structures, invariants can be used to classify the structures up to isomorphism; for example, vector spaces can be classified up to isomorphism by their dimension. For other classes of structures, such as graphs, it is not possible to formulate a complete set of invariants. Nevertheless, even without a complete set, invariants can still be used to provide a classification of the models of a theory. In a sense, classification theorems provide an alternative approach to characterizing the models of a core theory – if a model can be reconstructed up to isomorphism from the invariants alone, then the invariants provide an implicit representation of the models.

This approach can also be justified by the application of ontologies to support semantic integration. If the ontologies of two software applications have the same language, then the applications will be interoperable if they share the semantics of the terminology in their corresponding theories. Sharing semantics between applications is equivalent to sharing models of their theories, that is, the theories have isomorphic sets of models. We therefore need to determine whether or not two models are isomorphic, and in doing so, we can use invariants of the models.

4.2. Relationship to Interpretability

Following this methodology, the set of models for a core theory can be partitioned into equivalence classes defined with respect to the set of invariants of the models. Each equivalence class in the classification of the core theory's models is axiomatized using a definitional extension of the core theory. In particular, each definitional extension of the core theory is associated with a unique invariant for the models of the theory. The different classes and relations that are defined in the extension correspond to different properties of the invariant. In this way, the terminology of an ontology arises from the classification of the models of the core theories with respect to sets of invariants.

Invariants for models may also be related to invariants of their substructures. For example, definitional extensions of PSL-Core axiomatize classes of activity occurrences that arise from the automorphism group of the occurrence structure within a model of PSL-Core, and classes of timepoints arise from the automorphism group of the timeline structure. Other examples of invariants for the PSL Ontology were first discussed in [12]. The most prevalent class of occurrence constraints is that of *markovian* activities, activities whose preconditions depend only on the state prior to their occurrences (e.g., to withdraw money from a bank account, there must be sufficient funds in the account). The class of markovian activities is defined in the PSL definitional extension $state\_precond.def$. In this case, the substructure of a model of PSL characterizes the relations between states and activity occurrences. The invariant that corresponds to this extension is the automorphism group and the classes that are defined in the extension correspond to different classes of groups.

5. Ontology Design

The design of new core theories can be driven by investigating the properties of the models of existing ontologies within the repository. For example, models of existing mereotopologies are represented by classes of lattices (e.g. Boolean lattices and Stonian p-ortholattices). It is possible to design new mereotopology ontologies by searching for other classes of lattices axiomatized within the repository which can be used to represent alternative ontological choices with respect to the parthood and connection relations.

Definitional extensions of a core theory T axiomatize the classes of models in $Mod(T)$. Since the class of models of a core theory is a restriction of the class of models of other theories in the same core hierarchy, nonconservative extensions of a core theory T are often related to the classification of the models of T with respect to invariants.

Another approach to the design of new ontologies is to consider the definability of invariants. Definitional extensions arise when the invariants for models of T are definable in T. In some cases, however, the invariants for models of a theory T may not be definable in T, but rather may be definable in a core theory which is an extension of T.

6. Summary

The concepts and methods discussed in this paper, in particular the relationships of relative interpretation together with conservative and nonconservative extension, can be used to organize the theories within an ontology repository. We have shown how to use these relationships between ontologies to assist us in the characterization of the models of the ontologies. In particular, we can use the notion of interpretability to specify representation theorems, and use the notion of reducibility of structures to construct the models of one ontology from the models of another ontology by exploiting the relationships between these ontologies and their modules in the repository.

References

[1] Asher, N. and Vieu, L. (1995) Toward a geometry of common sense: a semantics and a complete axiomatization for mereotopology. In *Proc. of the 14th Int. Joint Conf. on Artificial Intelligence (IJCAI'95)*, pp. 846–852. Morgan Kaufmann, 1995.

[2] T. S. Blyth. *Lattices and Ordered Algebraic Structures*. Springer London, 2005.

[3] Cohn, A.G., Bennett, B., Gooday, J.M., and Gotts, N.M. (1997) RCC: a calculus for region based qualitative spatial reasoning. *GeoInformatica*, 1:275–316, 1997.

[4] Düntsch, I., Wang, H., and McCloskey, S. (1999) Relation algebras in qualitative spatial reasoning. *Fundamenta Informaticae*, 39(3):229–248, 1999.

[5] Enderton, H. (1972) *Mathematical Introduction to Logic*,Academic Press.

[6] Farmer, W. M. (2000) An Infrastructure for Intertheory Reasoning. In: CADE-17, *Lecture Notes in Computer Science (LNCS)*, D. McAllester, ed., p. 1831:115-131.

[7] Farmer, W. M., Guttman, J. D., Thayer, F. J. (1992) Little Theories. In: CADE-11, *Lecture Notes in Computer Science (LNCS)*, D. Kapur, ed., p. 607:567-581.

[8] Grau, B., Parsia, B., Sirin, E., Kalyanpur, A. Automatic Partitioning of OWL Ontologies Using E-Connections, *Proc. of Description Logic Workshop (DL)*, 2005.

[9] Grau, B., Parsia, B., Sirin, E. (2009) Ontology Integration Using E-connections, pp.293-320, *Modular Ontologies*, Stuckenschmidt et al. (eds.). Springer-Verlag, Berlin.

[10] Gruninger, M. (2009) Definability and Process Ontologies, *Ninth International Symposium on Logical Formalizations of Commonsense Reasoning*, Toronto, Canada.

[11] Gruninger, M. (2009) Process Ontologies, pp. 419-421, *Handbook of Ontologies, 2nd Edition*, S. Staab (ed.). Springer-Verlag, Berlin.

[12] Gruninger, M. and Kopena, J. (2004) Semantic Integration through Invariants, *AI Magazine*, 26:11-20.

[13] Hahmann, T., Winter, M., and Gruninger, M. (2009) Stonian p-ortholattices: A new approach to the mereotopology RT_0. *Artificial Intelligence*, 173:1424–1440, 2009.

[14] Hahmann, T., and Grüninger, M. (2010) Region-based theories of space: Mereotopology and beyond. In *Qualitative Spatio-Temporal Representation and Reasoning: Trends and Future Directions*. IGI Publishing. in press.

[15] Hodges, W. (1993) *Model Theory*. Cambridge University Press.

[16] Kent, Robert E. (2000) The Information Flow Foundation for Conceptual Knowledge Organization. In: Dynamism and Stability in Knowledge Organization. Proceedings of the Sixth International ISKO Conference. Advances in Knowledge Organization 7 (2000) 111-117. Ergon Verlag, Wurzburg.

[17] Marker, D. (2002) *Model Theory: An Introduction*. Springer Verlag.

[18] Menzel, C. and Gruninger, M. (2001) A formal foundation for process modeling, *Second International Conference on Formal Ontologies in Information Systems*, Welty and Smith (eds), 256-269.

[19] Padmanabhan, R. and Rudeanu, S. (2008) *Axioms for Lattices and Boolean Algebras*. World Scientific, 2008.

[20] Stell, J.G. (2000) Boolean connection algebras: a new approach to the Region-Connection Calculus. *Artificial Intelligence*, 122:111–136, 2000.

[21] Troquard, N., Trypuz, R., Vieu, L. (2006) Towards an ontology of agency and action: From STIT to ONTOSTIT+, pp. 179-192, *Proceedings of the Fourth International Conference on Formal Ontology in Information Systems*, B. Bennett and C. Fellbaum (eds.) Baltimore. IOS Press.

Formal Ontology in Information Systems
A. Galton and R. Mizoguchi (Eds.)
IOS Press, 2010

doi:10.3233/978-1-60750-535-8-331

Evaluating Ontologies with NLP-Based Terminologies – A Case Study on ACGT and Its Master Ontology

Gintarė GRIGONYTĖ[a,1], Mathias BROCHHAUSEN[b], Luis MARTÍN[c], Manolis TSIKNAKIS[d], Johann HALLER[e]

[a] *Department for Applied Linguistics, Translation and Interpreting, Saarland University, Germany*
[b] *Institute for Formal Ontology and Medical Information Science, Saarland University, Germany*
[c] *Biomedical Informatics Group, Artificial Intelligence Laboratory, School of Computer Science, Universidad Politécnica de Madrid, Spain*
[d] *Foundation for Research and Technology Hellas (FORTH), Institute of Computer Science, Greece*
[e] *Institute of the Society for the Promotion of Applied Information Sciences at the Saarland University, Germany*

Abstract. Natural language processing (NLP) plays a major role in knowledge engineering. However, NLP's usage is traditionally being seen as a means of extracting knowledge required for building knowledge resources, i.e. ontologies, knowledge bases. When it comes to the evaluation of these knowledge artefacts, then general trends are: expert reviewing, evaluating against existing ontologies and democratic ranking. We propose a new approach for evaluating domain coverage of application ontologies which is based on NLP techniques. The latter can be seen as one way of bridging the gap between terminologies and ontologies in order to create user-understandable expert systems.

Keywords. Ontology evaluation, domain terminology, glass box evaluation, biomedical ontology, NLP.

Introduction

Ontology-based clinical systems and environments raise severe questions with respect to the strategies employed to evaluate them. These problems are due to multiple layers of techniques addressing users from various backgrounds, namely clinicians, medical informaticians, bioinformaticians, and software engineers. Coming up with a sound strategy to evaluate the ontology or ontologies these systems utilize is of key importance. Distinguishing between glass box and black box evaluation techniques [1, 2] provides the first step to disentangle the multiple agents seen as users on different levels of the systems integration and use.

---

[1] Corresponding Author: Gintarė Grigonytė, Department for Applied Linguistics, Translation and Interpreting, Saarland University, Campus D-66123, Saarbrucken, Germany; E-mail g.grigonyte@hmf.vdu.lt

In this paper we will provide an overview of the scope of ontology-based engineering in the ACGT project (Advancing Clinico-Genomic Trials on Cancer) and present the strategies used for evaluating the ACGT Master Ontology (MO). We show how thesauri extracted from domain specific scientific publications can be used to provide the basis to evaluate domain coverage. Furthermore, we will show how this technique supports the choice of either class names or rdf labels in order to make the ontology more accessible and understandable for domain experts.

The main thesis is that ontology development and NLP-based term extraction should go hand in hand. The thesauri in this approach is not used to populate the ontology, but to test and ensure domain coverage.

1. The ACGT project

The ACGT integrated project aims to address the obstacles created by the flood of multilevel datasets (from the molecular, to the organ, to the individual level), the lack of a common infrastructure for clinical research institutions and the creators of molecular data. As a result of this situation, very few cross-site studies and multi-centric clinical trials are performed, and in most cases it is not possible to seamlessly integrate multi-level data. Moreover, clinical researchers and molecular biologists often find it hard to take advantage of each other's expertise due to the absence of a cooperative environment which enables the sharing of data, resources, or tools for comparing results and experiments, and of a uniform platform supporting the seamless integration and analysis of disease-related data at all levels [3]. ACGT's endeavour is to overcome these obstacles by setting up a semantic grid infrastructure in support of multi-centric, post-genomic clinical trials [4].

The system which the project aims for will facilitate the horizontal transfer of laboratory findings data to the clinical management and treatment of patients database systems. This goal can only be achieved if state-of-the-art semantic technologies are part of the IT environment. In order to meet this goal, the ACGT project needed an ontology to be utilized in the context of the selected Local-As-View (LAV) database integration strategy [5]. In such integration strategy the ontology plays the role of a global schema, to which all local schemata are mapped, solving the different data heterogeneities present in the integrated sources. To this end, the ontology is needed to cover both, unified terminology and independent schema construct meanings. The ACGT project achieves the integration of heterogeneous biomedical databases through a grid service oriented semantic mediation software layer that makes use of the ACGT-MO [6, 7]. However, before building a new terminology resource the state of the art in semantic representation of cancer research and management was assessed to prevent unnecessary developments.

The ACGT Semantic Mediation Layer (ACGT-SM) is comprised by a set of tools and resources that collaborate in the processes of Database Integration and Semantic Mediation (Figure. 1). The ACGT-MO plays a main resource role in this system, acting as Global Schema – i.e. global framework for semantic homogenization -, representing the needed homogenized formalization of the domain knowledge. The ACGT-SM database integration approach is based in a Local as View Query Translation solution, coping with the problem of heterogeneous database integration. Data is not actually integrated, but a virtual repository accessible to the users is offered with the shape of a unique view of a database. This repository can be accessed using a uniform interface that is consistent with the information provided by the ACGT-MO, i.e. queries are formulated in the "ontology language", retrieving information from the underlying databases. The virtual repository has the shape of an RDF database, and the language selected for performing queries is SPARQL [8].

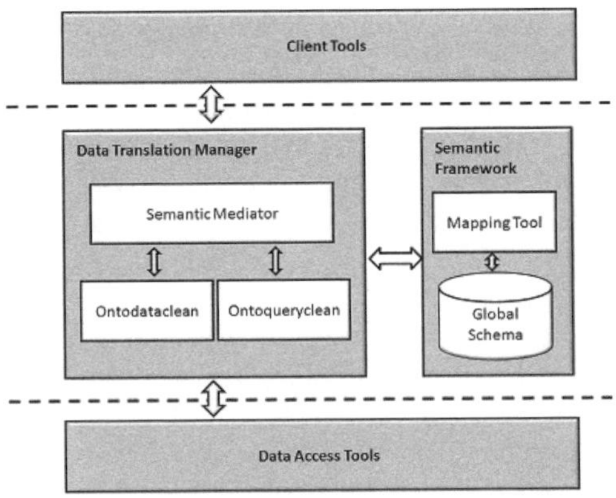

Figure 1. ACGT Semantic Mediator Layer architecture.

The ACGT-SM architecture is shown in Figure 1. The different components that comprise it are devoted to address singular problems within database integration, such as schema level heterogeneities and instance level conflicts both at the query and data levels. The Semantic Mediator acts as the coordinator of these tools that are independently designed as web services. The system also includes a tool designed to help in the process of building mappings. This mapping tool is able to show ontology and schema structures, providing a means to navigate and find elements in order to find the correspondences to be registered.

The ACGT-SM offers its data services using an OGSA-DAI [9] grid based interface. The OGSA-DAI middleware allows easy access and integration of data via the grid. However, in the case of the ACGT-SM no grid infrastructure is needed to access these services. The minimum requirement is having web access. The ACGT-SM offers two main services, namely 1) launching a query (subsequently receiving results), and 2) browsing repository schema. The latter shows a subset of the ACGT-SM underlying RDF schema. This subset is built taking into consideration user's needs.

This software system has been tested with clinical relational and image databases [10], obtaining promising results. Ultimately, a final user query tool has been developed by the consortium, aiding non-technical users in the processes of building and launching SPARQL queries.

2. Evaluating Ontologies – General Trends and Obstacles

Evaluation of ontologies is becoming a key interest in ontology-driven computing. The spread of ontological engineering over the last years fostered the development of a multitude of ontologies. On the one hand, it is good to see that ontologies are becoming more and more a common solution for interoperability problems. On the other hand, the vast number of artefacts leaves potential engineers interested in utilizing ontologies with the problem of identifying the quality of resources available for his concerns. Yet, the development of shared standards to evaluate ontologies seems to be rather slow.

[1] provides a key source with respect to ontology evaluation describing four different methodologies in that field. Yet, when it comes to evaluating the usability of the methods themselves the authors are merely checking whether or not a methodology is actually in use, regardless of the outcome it produces.

It is widely accepted that there is a central distinction traditionally drawn between two different evaluation strategies namely "glass box" or "component" evaluation and "black box" or "task based" evaluation. This distinction does apply to evaluation processes regarding ontologies and ontology-driven systems as well [1, 2]. The two strategies must be seen as complementary each providing testing for different kinds of qualities.

Glass box evaluation is used for those evaluation methods which aim at a direct evaluation of the ontology as such. It covers aspects like domain coverage, fitness of the ontology for a given task, and everything that has to do with logical and structural virtues of the artefact at hand, plus an assessment of the modules of which the ontology at hand is build from [2].

Black box evaluation measures the performance of an ontology-driven application and is typically carried out using the same interfaces that the end-users are going to employ [1]. [2] gives user-friendliness and agreement of domain experts as quintessential measurements to be done in black box evaluations. Naturally, black box evaluation can be done by end-users. In this paper we concentrate on reporting a glass box evaluation technique used on the ACGT MO and its results.

Hartmann *et al.* stress that glass box evaluating should start in the preparation phase for creating an ontology (type 1) and it should accompany the entire development process (type 2) and should continue after the release of the ontology (type 3). Typically, type 1 and type 2 evaluations are done by the ontology engineer developing the artefact in question, whereas type 3 consists of activities typical for ontology experts outside the project [1]. Notably, there are no domain experts or end-users involved in those activities.

For the ACGT project four main aspects of glass box evaluation have been identified:

- Logical soundness
- Task orientation
- Re-use of existing ontologies
- Domain coverage

3. Glass Box Evaluation of ACGT MO

3.1. Logical soundness

In order to assess the logical soundness of the ACGT MO it has been continuously checked for logical consistency during the development process using the Pellet reasoner [11].

3.2. Task orientation

Task orientation provides a problem for the ACGT MO ontology since there is not only one task for which it is to be used in the ACGT system. The two main components relying on the MO are, of course, the mediator and ObTiMA. Yet, from the very beginning of the development, it was clear that the ACGT MO would be an artefact between an application ontology and a domain ontology [12].

Nevertheless, the developers of the ontology-driven software components provide feedback on how the MO fits in and whether it serves all needs of the applications.

3.3. Re-use of existing ontologies

The ACGT MO re-uses three ontologies of the OBO Foundry [13] which is a library of ontologies built to meet the same quality criteria and to provide ontological reference of different domains of the life sciences [14]. The three ontologies are:

- Basic Formal Ontology (BFO) [15]
- Relation Ontology (RO) [16, 17]
- Foundational Model of Anatomy (FMA) [18, 19].

Whereas the OWL implementations of BFO and RO are directly imported into the owl.file of the ACGT MO, this was not possible with respect to the FMA. The reason for this was the size of the FMA in its entirety. The developers of the MO decided just to include anatomical entities as they occurred in the documentation serving as a blueprint for the targeted studies and represent it in formal is_a classes using the FMA as a model. The whole upper structure of the ontological representation of anatomical entities is taken from the FMA.

3.4. Domain coverage

The major aspect that can be evaluated with a glass box approach is completeness of domain coverage of the ontology. Domain coverage takes into consideration two aspects of ontologies:

- An ontology represents entities from a specific domain. By evaluating domain coverage it is possible to address whether the ontology makes a right distinction for its domain. In our approach it is ensured by experts choosing the suitable register of text of the domain, i.e. scientific publications, reports, specific domain documents like clinical trials, and using this text register for domain specific knowledge extraction. This plays along with the point of view of knowledge engineering - domain specific knowledge can be captured from domain specific texts.
- An ontology is subject of continuous change. Therefore, its evaluation should be flexible in assessing changes in the domain. This aspect can be addressed by simply extending the register of the domain texts. For instance, adding new scientific publications into the domain corpus.

We use domain specific register of texts and NLP techniques to acquire a domain specific terminology and arrange it into domain thesaurus. We assume that terms used in the register of the domain reflect the concepts of the domain present in the domain ontology. Therefore mapping between domain thesaurus terms and ontology concepts results on assessment of two key ideas:

a) How well does the ontology provide reference to the domain specific terminology?
b) What parts of the ontology refer to the explicitly available domain knowledge?

These two questions do not entirely govern ontology evaluation but can assist either experts evaluating domain ontologies or users evaluating task-driven usability of ontologies.

4. Evaluating domain coverage utilizing automatically acquired domain thesauri

Our strategy for evaluating the coverage of the ACGT MO is based upon combining techniques of corpus linguistics and terminology extraction. We use a corpus of the domain as a source reflecting the knowledge of the domain. Domain specific terms which we can automatically acquire are going to be used for evaluating the completeness and coverage of the domain with respect to their relation to concepts present in the ACGT MO ontology.

Pursuing this strategy we need to be aware of the essential differences between a thesaurus and an ontology. The thesaurus contains terms and gives specific relationships between them, whereas an ontology is a representational artefact that consists of the universals or classes to which terms refer to and the relationships between those entities [20]. Thus, the relations between the entities in the ontology are those between the universals and classes represented by the ontology. The relation between *term* and the representation of an *entity* in an ontology as shown in Figure 2.

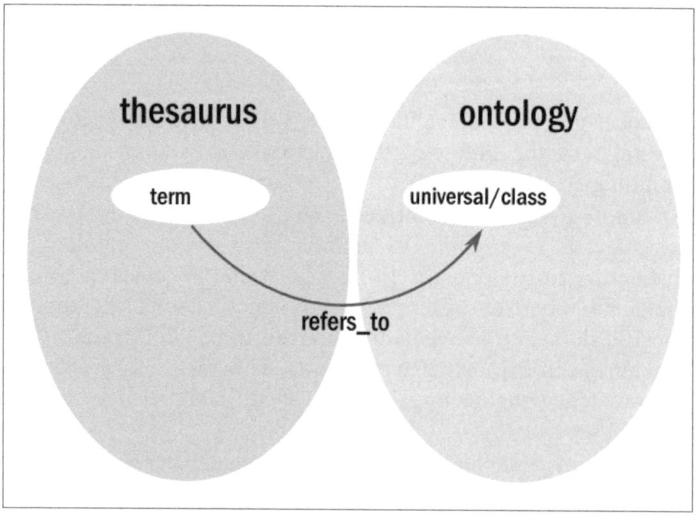

Figure 2. Relation between *term* in a thesaurus and *entity* in an ontology.

The starting point of this approach is collecting a corpus of the domain. A corpus can contain any domain specific texts, namely, scientific publications, project reports, books, medical notes, etc. The most important feature of a corpus is that it has to be balanced for the task it will be used for. This issue is addressed by ensuring diversity, a correspondence to the domain register and a reasonable quantity of texts. Textual data comes in a variety of forms, and as far as text mining concerns, the most challenging texts are unstructured language texts. The analysis of such texts usually involves linguistic heuristics.

The judgement on completeness of the ontology is done by acquiring a list of terms, arranging them into the thesaurus of the domain and identifying which of them maps to the ontology at hand.

In order to acquire a list of terms that are **actively used** in the domain and are **specific** for the domain, we have applied a [21] methodology for terminology extraction. The process of term extraction is depicted in Figure 3. It encompasses the main stages of terminology extraction: morphological analysis, shallow parsing, rule based detection of noun phrases (NPs), term candidate extraction, termhood assessment and building a term list hierarchy.

With regard to the ACGT project, we started with collecting 3334 domain specific abstracts of scientific publications. In general, the domain of the ACGT MO is cancer research and management. Due to the focus of the project the ontology is concentrated on three types of cancer: mammary carcinoma, nephroblastoma (Wilms' tumour) and rhabdoid tumour. The corpus of 3334 abstracts consists of tree registers – 1500 abstracts from Pubmed [http://www.ncbi.nlm.nih.gov/pubmed/] concerned with mammary carcinoma and nephroblastoma, and 334 for rhabdoid tumour. The small number of abstracts on rhabdoid tumour reflects Pubmed's publication situation on the topic. Obviously, there does not exist a high number of publications dealing specifically with this tumour.

We are aware of the fact that the literature basis used in this analysis can only be an approximation to the final use case for the ACGT MO, but since real clinical data is hard to acquire we decided to test the usability of our approach with a textual basis from publications.

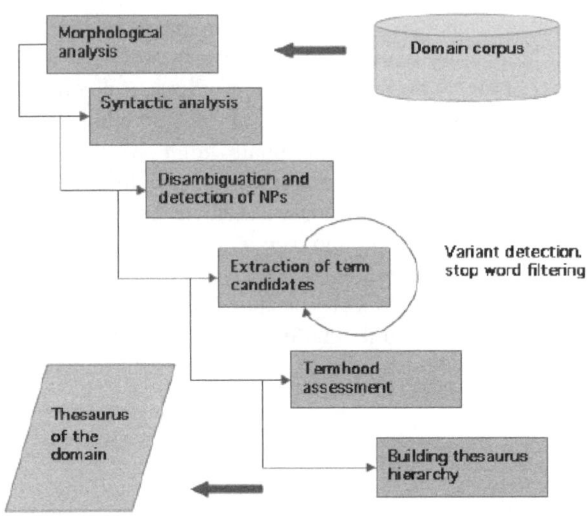

Figure 3. The process of acquiring a domain specific term list and arranging it into the thesaurus of the domain.

Morphological analysis is the first and a major step in the linguistic processing pipeline (see Figure 3.). Unstructured texts are preprocessed and information for the following stages of the process are gathered. The MPRO morphological tagger [22] was used for this task. The aim of this step is to analyze each word and acquire information such as lemma, part of speech, morphological derivation, possible semantic class etc. The acquired information is then sent to a syntactic parser for syntactic phrases to be marked in the text. For the task of term extraction only noun phrases (NPs) are taken into consideration. NPs usually are single word terms, multi word terms, acronyms or proper names. These specific structures of NPs are referred to as **candidate terms**. We have used the AUTOTERM [23] tool to extract grammatically correct single word terms and multi word. However, in natural language the NP structure is an essential and frequently used one. Naturally, it raises the need of distinguishing between domain specific NPs and NPs of general use. We approach this problem by using a couple of techniques.

The first one is linguistic filtering, which is finding variants and non-basic forms of a term. For instance, *relapse-free survival* and *relapse free survival*, or *tumor* and *tumour* are obviously referring to the same concept, and therefore should be marked as variants. Usually linguistic filtering includes a stop-word filtering technique, which assures that arbitrarily selected words will not appear in the extracted term list.

The second one is statistic filtering also known as a **termhood assessment.** The idea behind it is that the importance of a term can be calculated from the statistics (frequency) of a word and its context. For instance, by calculating Inverse document frequency (IDF) measure we can check whether a term is not too general or too specialized [21]. However, since any reasonable statistics measurement has to do with a reliable data volume, and our experiment corpus was rather small, next to IDF values we have used a corpus from other register - British National Corpus [24] (BNC) - 100 million word collection of samples of written and spoken language from a wide range of topics.

The method of contrasting two different registers is well known in corpus linguistics. We have used BNC to provide some means of validation, within respect of contrasting how frequently words constituting term are used in different registers, i.e. domain specific corpus and general language corpus. Adjectives and adverbs were of special interest, as if these words are frequent nor-related register, i.e. in BNC, it gives information about how good term candidate might be. For instance, adjectives like *specific, significant* or *national* appear very frequently in BNC and can be used as stop-words. That eases the detection of vague candidate terms like *significant criterion* and *specific part*. In contrast, *bilateral* and *renal* are very domain specific words, which do not appear frequently in general language registers.

After acquiring the statistical measures on how relevant terms are to the experiment domain, we have built shallow hierarchies of terms, based on their vertical hypernym-hyponym relationship, which distinguishes between specific and more abstract terms:

```
tumour
| Wilms tumour
| | bilateral Wilms tumour
| | unilateral Wilms tumour
| | necrotic Wilms tumour
| rhabdoid tumour
| | malignant rhabdoid tumour
| | renal rhabdoid tumour
| | congenital rhabdoid tumour
```

The evaluation strategy is to check whether terms of the domain terminology list are present in the domain ontology. In order to expedite the evaluation process, mappings between ontology concepts and thesaurus terms are established. Figure 4 shows a term *metastasis* taken from an automatically acquired domain thesaurus and how it relates to an ACTG MO ontology snippet.

5. Results

In this chapter we will concentrate on the results of using a thesaurus to validate the domain coverage of the ACGT MO.

The main strategy for establishing mappings concerns mainly two targets: first, finding out what ontological entities are reflected in the extracted term list, and second, what term list sections are not reflected in the ontology. For instance, in figure 4 we show how a part of domain terminology compares to a snippet of ACGT MO ontology. A mapping between terminology's *metastasis* and ontology's *metastasis* can be established. In doing this we are always aware of the fact that the terminology merely provides terms, whereas the ontology consists of the representation of entities which names are chosen more or less arbitrarily[2]. Regarding the ACGT MO, however, the use of natural language terms as class names was established to make the ontology more easily accessible to clinical project partners in ACGT for review purposes.

We need to be aware that if it turns out that a domain specific, highly used term has no referent in the ACGT MO, the ontology can be extended with other types of *metastasis* represented in the terminology list.

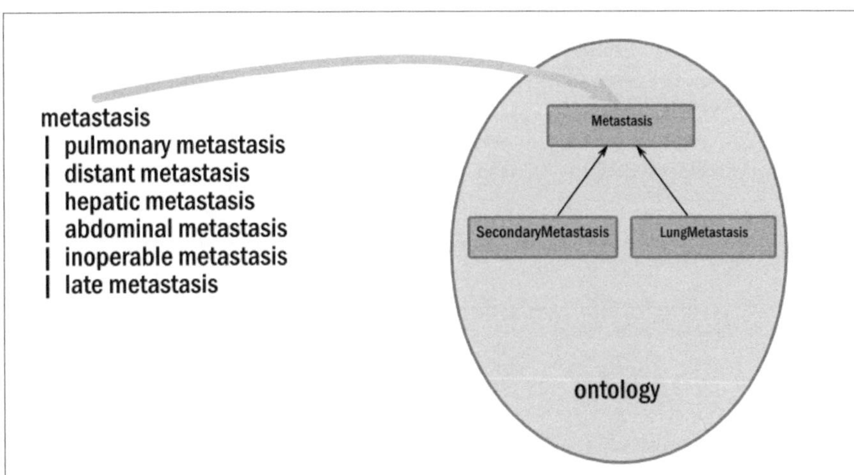

Figure 4. "Metastasis": a part of the domain terminology list and a part of ontology.

Another important aspect of the process is noticing synonymous relationships between the ontology's entities and terms. For instance, *LungMetastasis* and *pulmonary metastasis* are synonymous. *LungMetastasis* is an arbitrary name and is not present in domain corpus. *Pulmonary metastasis* is a frequent term in the domain texts

[2] In fact, there are quite a few ontologists who advocate the use of numbers as class names.

(found 69 times), but it is not present in ontology. The decision of which one is to be used in the ontology is entirely domain expert dependent. However, this glass box evaluation technique can be helpful in pointing out terms used in 'real life', thus facilitating interaction between domain experts on the one hand and ontologists or the ontology on the other.

The evaluation of ACGT MO with respect to the coverage of the domain showed that 53% of ontology concepts map directly to domain thesaurus terms.

Some of the mappings related issues are presented in Tables 1-4.

Table 1. Domain term is morphologically equivalent to ontology concept.

Ontology class	Thesaurus term	Term count in domain corpus
RenalVein	renal vein	2
NephrogenicRest	nephrogenic rest	2
TreatmentCycle	treatment cycle	3
ClinicalTrial	clinical trial	17
SurgicalApproach	surgical approach	1
PartialNephrectomy	partial nephrectomy	3
BacterialInfection	bacterial infection	2
ViralInfection	viral infection	2
CongenitalSyndrome	congenital syndrome	3
LateEffect	late effect	5
TumorRegression	tumor regression	4

Table 2. Domain term partly maps to ontology concept.

Ontology class	Thesaurus term	Term count in domain corpus
StandardPartialNephrectomy	partial nephrectomy	3
ChronicViralInfection	viral infection	2
ImmatureTeratomaGCTDisease	immature teratoma	4

Table 3. An example of ontology concepts that remain unmapped.

Ontology class
EndOfBloodPressureMeasuringProcess
pN2a
FeverGrade4
ECOGPerformanceRating

The examples in Table 3. are clearly indicating problematic practices in ontology development. Especially the fact that "pN2a" cannot be mapped stresses that ontologists should refrain from using abbreviations or acronyms as class names. The last two classes are presenting specific gradings which do not frequently occur in publications, but may well occur in patient documentation which is one focus of the ACGT MO.

Table 4. An example of thesaurus terms that were found in the domain text register, but are not present in ontology.

Thesaurus term	Term count in domain corpus
cortical lesion	1
contralateral biopsy	3
intracranial hemorrhage	2
survival	414

Mappings of thesaurus terms to the ontology can be problematic since the aim of an ontology is not to provide one class per term. Retrieving the knowledge about these kind of missing mappings can however serve to raise the awareness of ontologists to possible data loss, given that the knowledge behind the terms cannot be expressed by the ontology.

6. Conclusions and Future Work

The results presented here show that using domain thesauri to validate domain coverage of an ontology is a highly promising approach. Especially checking the ontologies for class names or labels that are actually used by domain experts is a highly important step since it fosters accessibility and usability of the ontology to the domain experts. The latter is a crucial aspect in the development and maintenance of clinical ontologies. The domain experts are the only group that can effectively guide the maintenance in a way that secures future usefulness to the actual clinical situation with its specific points of view and restrictions.

The impact of the analysis regarding the modification and improvement of the ACGT MO are twofold: First, the clarification of term usage in the clinical field will lead to changes with respect to the class names used, or at least to additional labels supplied within the ontology. Secondly, the developers of the ontology are hinted to missing classes in their representation of the domain. Together with the domain experts active in building the ontology decisions can be taken which of the areas identified by the present study are of relevance to the use case and ought to be represented by the ontology

We hold, that the result achieved should not be used to change or extend the taxonomy of the ontology, since terminological subsumptions do not necessarily indicate ontological subsumption.

The results we achieved for the coverage of the ACGT MO clearly hint to the fact that in order to optimize the accuracy of the testing, the corpora should be enhanced with texts from real patient documentation, since this is a key issue in the applications of the ACGT MO. First steps in this direction have been taken, but the results are not yet available.

Acknowledgements

The work on ACGT and the ACGT ontology was co- funded by the EU (FP6-IST-026996). Gintare Grigonyte was funded by DAAD (Deutscher Akademischer

Austausch Dienst) scholarships A/07/92317. Authors want to thank IAI (Institute of the Society for the Promotion of Applied Information Sciences at the Saarland University) for providing software assisting terminology extraction.

References

[1] Hartmann J., Spyns P., Giboin A., Maynard D., Cuel R., Suárez-Figueroa M.C., and Sure Y., Methods for ontology evaluation, Knowledge Web Deliverable D1.2.3, 2004.
[2] Gangemi A., Catenacci C., Ciaramita M., Lehmann J., Modelling Ontology Evaluation. In Proceedings of the Third European Semantic Web Conference Berlin, Springer, 2006, pp. 140-154.
[3] K. H. Buetow, Cyberinfrastructure: Empowering a 'Third Way,' Biomedical Research, Science Magazine, vol. 308, no. 5723 (2005), pp. 821-824.
[4] M. Tsiknakis, M. Brochhausen, J. Nabrzyski, J. Pucaski, G. Potamias, C. Desmedt and D. Kafetzopoulos, "A semantic grid infrastructure enabling integrated access and analysis of multilevel biomedical data in support of post-genomic clinical trials on Cancer", IEEE Transactions on Information Technology in Biomedicine, Special issue on Bio-Grids, March 2008, Vol. 12, No. 2, pp. 205-217.
[5] Cali, "Reasoning in Data Integration Systems: Why LAV and GAV Are Siblings," Proceedings ISMIS 2003, Lecture Notes in Computer Science 2871, London, Springer 2003, pp 562-571.
[6] http://www.ifomis.org/acgt/1.0
[7] M. Tsiknakis et al., Building a European Biomedical Grid on Cancer, Challenges and Opportunities of HealthGrids: Procs. of the HealthGrid 2006 conference, pp. 247-258, Valencia, Spain, 2006.
[8] SPARQL Query Language for RDF. Available at: http://www.w3.org/TR/rdf-sparql-query.
[9] The OGSA-DAI Project. Available at: http://www.ogsadai.org.uk.
[10] L. Martín, E. Bonsma, A. Anguita, J. Vrijnsen, M. García-Remesal, J. Crespo, M. Tsiknakis, V. Maojo, "Data Access and Management in ACGT: Tools to Solve Syntactic and Semantic Heterogeneities Between Clinical and Image Databases", in Advances in Conceptual Modeling – Foundations and Applications, Lecture Notes in Computer Science, 2007, pp. 24-33.
[11] http://clarkparsia.com/pellet.
[12] Guarino, N., Formal Ontology in InformationSystems. In: Guarino N. (ed.): 1st International Conference on Formal Ontology in Information Systems (FOIS '98), Trento, Italy. IOS Press, MAmsterdam, 3-15.
[13] http://www.obofoundry.org.
[14] Smith B., Ashburner M., Rosse C., et al., The OBO Foundry: Coordinated Evolution of Ontologies to Support Biomedical Data Integration. Nature Biotechnology, 25 (11), November, 1551-5.
[15] http://www.ifomis.org/bfo.
[16] http://www.obofoundry.org/ro.
[17] Smith B, Ceusters W, Klagges B, et al., Relations in Biomedical Ontologies. Genome Biology, 2005, 6:R46.
[18] http://sig.biostr.washington.edu/projects/fm.
[19] Rosse C, Mejino JVL., A reference ontology for biomedical informatics: the Foundational Model of Anatomy. J Biomed Inform. 2003, 36:478-500.
[20] Smith B., Kusnierczyk W., Schober D., Ceusters W. (2006) "Towards a Reference Terminology for Ontology Research and Development in the Biomedical Domain", Proceedings of KR-MED, 2006, 57-66.
[21] Avizienis, A., Grigonyte, G., Haller, J., von Henke, F., Liebig, T., Noppens, O. „Organizing Knowledge as an Ontology of the Domain of Resilient Computing by Means of Natural Language Processing - An Experience Report". Artificial Intelligence Research Society Conference, 2009, Florida.
[22] Rösener, Ch., Theofilidis, A., Maas, D. 2009. Morphosyntactical and semantical analysis of text: The MPRO tagging procedure, in proceedings of State of the Art in Computational Morphology Workshop on Systems and Frameworks for Computational Morphology, SFCM 2009, Zurich, Switzerland, p. 76-87.
[23] Hong, M.; Fissaha, S.; and Haller, J. 2001. Hybrid Filtering for Extraction of Term Candidates from German Technical Texts. Nancy: Proceedings of Terminology & Artificial Intelligence, 2001, 223-232.
[24] http://www.natcorp.ox.ac.uk/

Applications II

Formal Ontology in Information Systems
A. Galton and R. Mizoguchi (Eds.)
IOS Press, 2010

doi:10.3233/978-1-60750-535-8-345

Towards a formal ontology for history of church administration

Pawel GARBACZ [a,1], Robert TRYPUZ [a], Bogumil SZADY [b], Piotr KULICKI [a], Przemyslaw GRADZKI [a] and Marek LECHNIAK [a]

[a] *John Paul II Catholic University of Lublin, Faculty of Philosophy*
[b] *John Paul II Catholic University of Lublin, Faculty of Humanities*

Abstract. The paper presents preliminary results in the area of ontological engineering for historical research. Historical information systems are still in the initial stage of development. Our experience hitherto shows that the decisive stage in the development of such systems is a conceptual model and ontological engineering seems to be the right tool to build it. Our particular aim is to develop a database system for the history of the administrative structure of the Catholic Church in Central-Eastern Europe in the so-called pre-statical period, i.e. roughly from XII to XIX century. We use DOLCE as a foundational ontology, especially its part concerning social objects. We build an axiomatic system that formally defines the basic notions of those structures and may be interpreted as the conceptual scheme of this database.

Keywords. ontology of social objects, databases in historical sciences, administrative structure, church history

Introduction

History is not a favourite domain in ontological engineering. Perhaps one of the reasons is the fact that historical information systems are still in the initial stage of development and the issues of data integration and sharing are still some way ahead. That fact, however, may be interpreted as a motive for preparatory work in formal ontologies for history. So, instead of creating heterogenous systems that will need to be later re-integrated, we suggest that we should start with the ontologically-based sharable architectures. This paper presents some initial results in that area.

Our aim is to develop a database system to store information on history of the administrative structure of the Catholic Church in Central-Eastern Europe. Our initial experience with the subject shows that the decisive stage in the development of the system is a conceptual model of the objects and processes involved. It turns out that the domain in question is surprisingly complex, so we focused in this paper only on a selection of such entities. Namely, we present an axiomatic system that is supposed to formally define the following notions, which are considered in historical research as salient to the aforementioned domain:

1. beneficium ecclesiaticum together with its parts dos and officium

[1]Corresponding Author: Pawel Garbacz.

2. parochia and beneficium parochialis
3. plebanus, patronus, and parochianus
4. territorium parochiae

We decided to stick to the Latin names because the English translations tend to change their semantic content and connotations. Table 1 provides the reader with the approximate translations.

Latin	English	German
institutiones ecclesiasticae	ecclesiastical institutions	Kirchliche Institutionen
parochia	parish	Pfarrei
beneficium ecclesiasticum	benefice	Kirchliche Benefizium
beneficium parochialis	parish benefice	Pfarrbenefizium
dos	endowment	Kirchenvermögen
officium	duty	Pflicht
ecclesia	church	Kirche
plebanus	parish priest	Pfarrer
parochianus	parishoner	Pfarrkind
territorium parochiae	parish territory	Pfarrkreis
ecclesia parochialis	parish church	Pfarrkirche
patronus	patron	Patron

Table 1. Bilingual translations of the Latin terms

Although the above selection is rather sparse, we needed 24 definitions and 21 axioms to characterise them with a medium degree of adequacy. The axiomatic system presented in this paper is envisaged as a small part of the more comprehensive formal ontology of sacral objects. We use the term "sacral object" without any prejudice to such ideological questions as the epistemic values of religious beliefs, social impact of religions, aesthetics of sacral art, and so on. A sacral object is understood here as an entity that is considered by some organised religious group as related to their beliefs in the supranatural being(s). In the case of more institutionalised religions some of these objects pertain to the administrative dimensions of these groups. This is our focus in this paper.

Obviously, the envisaged formal ontology of sacral objects (SacrOnt) will be a domain ontology. In order to avoid reinventing the wheel, we choose to "stitch" it up to a top-level ontology. After several unsuccessful attempts we found out that at the current stage of development the most suitable framework is provided by the DOLCE ontology - however, in section 5 we describe other possibilities.

The structure of the paper is as follows. First we briefly describe the current developments in historical databases. Section 2 summarises DOLCE's perspective on social entities and section 3 gives informal description of a place of sacral objects in that ontology. The next section is central to the paper as it presents in a formal manner our view on the sacral objects. Section 5 explains the reasons for choosing DOLCE as our top-level ontology and outlines other options. Finally section 6 presents the use of the SacrOnt formal ontology to construct a database schema to be populated with data from the ecclesiastical resources.

1. Databases in Historical Research

Applications of databases in the historical sciences have a tradition dating back to the 80s of the twentieth century. Major historical and geographical initiatives have shifted from the collection of data files to databases or networks of distributed databases (e.g., the U.S. National Historic Geographic Information System, Great Britain Historical GIS, The Belgium Historical GIS, China Historical GIS (CHGIS), The Electronic Cultural Atlas Initiative (ECAI), HGIS Germany – cf. [7]). However, most of the data collections concern the "statistical period" (XIX and XX century), where the quality of data is high, and does not go further into the past.

Such data collections are supported by systems known as HDBMS (*Historical Database Management System*) or TDBMS (*Temporal Database Management System*). Recent developments in geographical information systems have lead to the introduction of spatiotemporal databases (STDBMS). Their main advantage is the ability to record, store, analyze and share basic types of geometric attributes, including temporal descriptions. One of the most important research initiatives in Europe related to STDBMS was Chorochronos research project, which was funded by the European Commission in the late 1990s ([9]). One of the results of this project was a spatiotemporal extension of the Unified Modeling Language (UML) to support modelling of the historical phenomena. Also most of the modern database tools, both commercial and open source, enable the user to record spatiotemporal data (Oracle Spatial, PostgreSQL PostGIS, MySQL).

The existing solutions are optimised for collecting data at the time they appear (like live transactions or current statistical data) and for tracing their history. The approach to the past in historical research seems to be different. Past events are reconstructed from sources that are different from those available now. Consequently, the information collected is incomplete, uncertain and heterogenous, which makes it difficult to be stored in a database. Also, hardly any of the available systems have the capacity of representing intentional phenomena that prevail in human history. Our paper is one of the early contributions in this area.

2. Social Objects in DOLCE

DOLCE is a foundational ontology of particulars with a clear cognitive bias. In fact, its aim is to capture the ontological categories underlying natural language and human commonsense. For this reason the categories introduced in DOLCE are thought by its developers as "cognitive artifacts ultimately depending on human perception, cultural imprints and social conventions" [10, p. 13]. The categories are obtained by the analysis of the surface structure of language and cognition. In consequence, DOLCE's categories are at the so-called mesoscopic level, the level of the middle-sized objects we, as humans, perceive. This makes DOLCE particularly suitable as a basis for the domain ontology for history.

DOLCE provides a total of about 40 categories and 100 relations which are axiomatized by 80 axioms (see Figure 1). Each node in the graph is a category of the ontology. One category is a subcategory of another if there is a path in the graph from the former to the latter. The class of subcategories of a given category forms a partition except where dots are inserted.

The domain of discourse, i.e., of quantification, is restricted in here to particulars (see the top node of Figure 1), which means that universals themselves are not organized but only used for organizing and characterizing particulars.

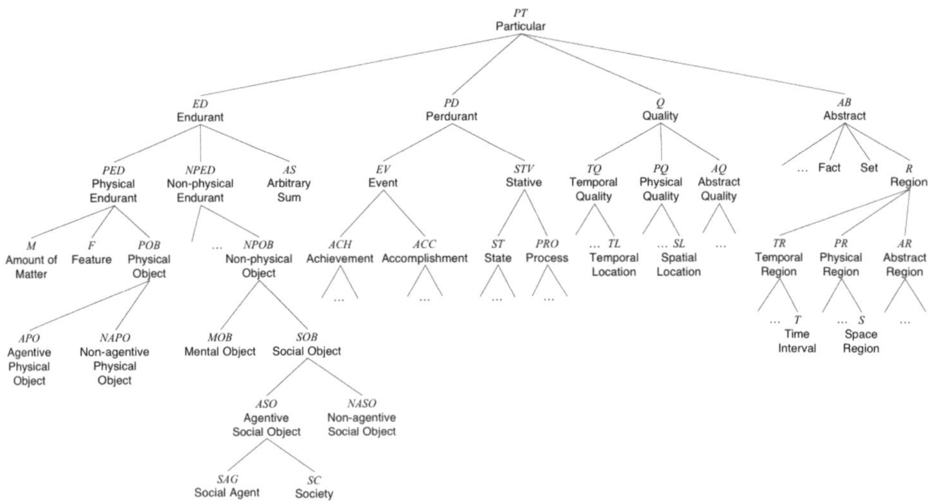

Figure 1. DOLCE taxonomy

Abstract entities are characterised as "existing neither in space nor in time", e.g., facts, sets, temporal and physical regions. On the other hand, concrete entities: endurants (e.g., a book), perdurants (e.g., my writing) and qualities (e.g., the weight of this object) "exist at least in time".

The categories of *endurants* (ED) and *perdurants* (PD) play here prominent roles. Endurants are entities that exist in time and all their parts are present at any time of their existence, whereas perdurants are entities that happen in time, and may be only partially present in the moment of time in which they exist. The main relationship between endurants and perdurants is *participation* (PC)—for any endurant there is always a perdurant in which it participates, and vice versa.

Applying DOLCE to history, we focused on non-physical endurants that depend in their existence on intentional phenomena or, strictly speaking, on social conventions. Object of that kind are dubbed the social objects (cf. [11,1]). DOLCE mentions three categories of social objects which we shall briefly describe below: *social concepts* (including the category of *role*) like theater, money, priest, *social descriptions* (i.e. the social conventions), and *social individuals* (including the category of *organization*) like NOKIA or The National Theatre in Warsaw.

Social concepts (CN) are those social objects that are defined (DF) by social descriptions (DS). Their main function is to classify (CF) other objects. If an entity is classified by a social concept (at some time) it means that (at this time) it satisfies all the constraints stated in the description of the classifying social concept (e.g. the piece of paper on my desk is classified as ten-zloty banknote because it satisfies all the constraints a ten-zloty banknote should satisfy in order to be considered as such). It is assumed that one entity can be classified by different concepts in the same time. What is important to note is that social concepts do not change during their life, i.e. cannot change their definitions. It means that new descriptions define new concepts.

[11] restricts the domain of classified objects to endurants, however it also mentions the possibility of lifting this restriction. Indeed, [8] provides social concepts that classify perdurants and some abstract objects.

Social concepts that are anti-rigid (roughly, that are not necessary properties) and founded (roughly, that are definitionally dependent on other objects) are called *social roles* (RL). Everything that has been written above about concepts applies to roles as well.

Social descriptions are created by communities of intentional agents at the time of their first encoding in a language. They have a unique semantic content, however their internal structure can be complex: they can be decomposed into simpler descriptions. Descriptions must be encoded in some physical medium. They are usually accepted (adopted) by (communities of) intentional agents, but a description can exist even if no one accepts it, as long as it remains encoded. So, descriptions cease to exist when their last physical support ceases to exist. For the purposes of our formalisation, it is important to note that each social concept is defined by exactly one description[2]. A description must use at least one concept; obviously, one concept can be used by different descriptions. During their life, they always define and use the same concepts. Descriptions are usually created 'in the scope of' social individuals. As emphasised in [1], in order for a description to be *valid* for a social individual, a necessary condition is the occurrence of a social event in which both the social individual and the description participate.

Social individuals, similarly to concepts, are defined and can be used in descriptions, but they do not classify entities. The most interesting social individuals are agentive. They can create and accept descriptions, i.e. make them valid. It is often the case that one description defines both an agentive social individual (i.e., an organization) and a related social role. The agentive social individual acts "through" certain agents that are classified by this role.

3. SacrOnt as embedded in DOLCE

The ecclesiastic categories aforementioned in the introduction are embedded in the legal system and practice of the Catholic Church.[3] Obviously, their ontological content is not explicitly stated there and needs to be re-engineered, so to speak, from these sources. We started from the following definitions:

> Parochia stricte et proprie est certus territorii dictrictus per papam vel episcopum determinatus, habens unum rectorem stabilem, cum potestate populum ibidem existentem regendi et iudicandi, eique sacramenta aliqua divina administrandi. [2, p. 51][4]

[2]It is because in the extension of DOLCE on social objects [11] it is assumed that each description is defined by at least one description and that descriptions defining the same concepts are DF-extensional.

[3]We should rather say that they *were* embedded as the whole structure changed in the twentieth century, in particular after the Second Vatican Council.

[4]A parish is, in the strict and proper sense, a certain territory that is determined by a bishop or pope and has a constant governor who entertains the executive and judicatory powers and the power of administering divine sacraments to its inhabitants.

Beneficium ecclesiasticum, de quo hic est sermo, est ius perpetuum percipiendi fructus ex bonis ecclesiasticis ratione spiritualis officii personae ecclesiasticae auctoritate Ecclesiae constitutum. [3, p. 1804][5]

Unde iuspatronatus [...] sumptum definitur, quod sit ius seu potestas nominandi sive praesentandi clericum promovendum ad beneficium ecclesiasticum vacans. Est in re communis. Seu iuspatronatus est ius honorificum, onerosum et utile, alicui (1) competens in ecclesia, eo quod de Ordinarii consensu eam construxerit, fundaverit vel dotaverit; aut id a suis antecessoribus factum fuerit. [4, p. 1227] [6]

After several discussions with our SME (*subject domain expert*) in history on the actual content of these descriptions we established that the closest ontological category for the following notions are DOLCE's roles:[7]

1. beneficium ecclesiaticum (axiom 1) - in SacrOnt represented as BenEccl,
2. dos and officium (axiom 3) - in SacrOnt represented as, respectively, Dos and Officium,
3. parochia (axiom 2) - in SacrOnt represented as Parochia.

Moreover beneficium parochialis is also a role as a subcategory of beneficium ecclesiaticum.

The pivotal category here is beneficium ecclesiasticum. Definitions 8 and 9 imply that beneficium ecclesiasticum is construed as the mereological sum of two roles, i.e. Dos and Officium, that are defined by parts of the ecclesiastical description that erects institutiones ecclesiasticae.

Employing the notion role allows us to treat all aforementioned in the introduction categories of the administrative structure of the Church we selected as *sui generis* classifiers:

1. dos and officium classify plebani and patroni. To be more specific, we model beneficium ecclesiaticum as the composition of (exactly one) dos and (exactly one) officium (definition 8) and then within a single beneficium parochialis:

   (a) plebanus is classified *both* by dos and officium (definition 13):

   - SacrOnt categories Dos and Officium classify jointly through relation parochiaePlebanus certain non-physical agentive objects as plebani.

   (b) patronus is classified by dos but *not* by officium (definition 14):

   - SacrOnt category Dos classifies through relation parochiaePatronus certain non-physical agentive objects as patroni.

---

[5]A parish benefice, which is defined here, is the perpetual right to benefits from ecclesiastical properties because of the performed ecclesiastical duty, whose right has been constituted by the ecclesiastical authority.

[6]Thus, the law of patronage may be defined as the right of power to nominate or present a priest for a vacating parish benefice. It follows from the common law that the law of patronage is a honorary, comendable, and useful right that belongs to a person in a church [building] because this person has built, funded or furnished it according to the bishop's permission or because its ancestors did that.

[7]Table 2 mentions all concepts SacrOnt borrows from DOLCE.

2. Moreover, dos classifies certain concrete objects as ecclesiastical endowments (definition 11) and officium classifies certain events as actions that are considered obligatory for certain agents (definition 12).
3. parochia classifies parochianus (definition 15) and territorium parochiae (definition 16):
   - SacrOnt category Parochia classifies through relation parochiaeGens certain non-physical agentive objects as parochiani,
   - SacrOnt category Parochia classifies through relation parochiaeTerr certain features as parochiae territorii.

However this schema constitutes the point of departure from DOLCE. Axiom A11 in [11] implies that all objects classified by social concepts are endurants. This constraint is too strong for our domain where dos may classify both endurants (e.g., a windmill) and perdurants (e.g., certain services). In order to emphasise this difference, we use the symbol $\mathtt{CF}^*$ (instead of CF) to represent this extended relation of classification. Although $\mathtt{CF}^*$ classifies now also perdurants, for the sake of uniformity, we keep its temporal parameter.

Axioms 13–18 express the various aspects of the uniqueness of the ecclesiastical classifications.

Since in DOLCE roles depend on descriptions, so we include the so called ecclesiastical descriptions (EcclDS) that contain

- descriptions that define dos (EndDS) via relation fundatio,
- descriptions that define officia (EcclNorm) via relation creatio,
- descriptions that define institutiones ecclesiasticae (ErecDS) via relation erectio.

In fact, we crafted our ontology so that these descriptions are the only primitive notions - all other terms are defined with the help of the DOLCE categories. The three aforementioned relations, i.e. fundatio, creatio, and erectio are subtypes of DOLCE's DF. Note that the domain of church administration requires that besides DOLCE constraint to the effect that each concept is defined by (DF) at most one description we should also have other constraints that concern our subtypes of DF - see axioms 8–10.

We should note that our formal-ontological analysis revealed the ontological ambiguity of the term "officium" as used in the church documents. It turned out that the term denotes both the *role* that classifies certain actions and the *description*, or more specifically a norm, that defines the aforementioned role. Other terms, e.g., "parochia", suffer from the similar problems.

The full formalism is presented in the next section. Table 3 lists all specific categories of SacrOnt. We should emphasise that the current formalism constitutes only a small fragment of the whole ontology. Consequently, we included certain notions that we will use in the more comprehensive subsequent version, e.g., institutiones ecclesasticae.

4. Formalism

In the formalism below all universal quantifications over whole formulas are left implicit. We make use of the standard priorities between connectives to avoid unnecessary bracketing. Terms with index "$_f$" are function symbols.

Expression	Meaning
$\mathtt{APO}(x)$	x is an agentive physical object
$\mathtt{CF}^*(x, y, t)$	x is classified by y at t where x can be *any* particular
$\mathtt{CP}(x, y)$	x is a permanent part of y
$\mathtt{DF}(x, y)$	x is defined by y
$\mathtt{DS}(x)$	x is a description
$\mathtt{ED}(x)$	x is an endurant
$\mathtt{Event}(x)$	x is an event
$\mathtt{F}(x)$	x is a feature
$\mathtt{lf}(x)$	life of x
$\mathtt{NAPO}(x)$	x is a non-agentive physical object
$\mathtt{P}(x, y)$	x is part of y
$\mathtt{PC}(x, y, t)$	x participates in y at t
$\mathtt{PP}(x, y, t)$	x is a proper part of y at t
$\mathtt{Pre}(x, t)$	x is present at t
$\mathtt{RL}(x)$	x is a role
$x + y$	the mereological sum of x and y

Table 2. DOLCE concepts used in SacrOnt

4.1. Salient definitions

Ecclesiastical subtypes of DF

(D1) $\mathsf{erectio}(x, y) \triangleq \mathtt{DF}(x, y) \wedge \mathsf{ErecDS}(y)$.
(D2) $\mathsf{fundatio}(x, y) \triangleq \mathtt{DF}(x, y) \wedge \mathsf{EndDS}(y)$.
(D3) $\mathsf{creatio}(x, y) \triangleq \mathtt{DF}(x, y) \wedge \mathsf{EcclNorm}(y)$.

Ecclesiastical subtypes of RL

(D4) $\mathsf{InstEccl}(x) \triangleq \exists y\ \mathsf{erectio}(x, y)$.
(D5) $\mathsf{Parochia}(x) \triangleq \exists y\ [\mathtt{DF}(x, y) \wedge \mathsf{ParDS}(y)]$.
(D6) $\mathsf{Dos}(x) \triangleq \exists y\ \mathsf{fundatio}(x, y)$.
(D7) $\mathsf{Officium}(x) \triangleq \exists y\ [\mathtt{DF}(x, y) \wedge \mathsf{EcclNorm}(y)]$.
(D8) $\mathsf{erectio}(x, y) \rightarrow \exists y_1, y_2, z_1, z_2\ \{[\mathtt{CPP}(y_1, y) \wedge \mathsf{fundatio}(z_1, y_1)] \wedge [\mathtt{CPP}(y_2, y) \wedge \mathsf{creatio}(z_2, y_2)] \equiv \mathsf{benEccl_f}(x, z_1, z_2) \triangleq z_1 + z_2\}$.

8 is an implicit definition of $\mathsf{benEccl_f}$. That is to say, it specifies what it means that x is a beneficium ecclesiasticum that consists of dos z_1 and officium z_2, i.e., $\mathsf{benEccl_f}(x, z_1, z_2)$. Namely, z_1 and z_2 need to be defined by parts (respectively, y_1 and y_2) of the description (y) that defines x. The consistency of 8 is guaranteed by axioms 9–12.

(D9) $\mathsf{BenEccl}(x) \triangleq \exists y, z_1, z_2\ [x = \mathsf{benEccl_f}(y, z_1, z_2)]$.
(D10) $\mathsf{BenParoch}(x) \triangleq \exists y, z_1, z_2\ [x = \mathsf{benEccl_f}(y, z_1, z_2) \wedge \mathsf{Parochia}(y)]$.

Expression	Meaning	Status
$\mathsf{benDos}(x, y, t)$	x is classified as an (insititutionis) dos by y at t	defined
$\mathsf{BenEccl}(x)$	x is a beneficium ecclesiastice	defined
$\mathsf{benEccl_f}(x, y, z)$	beneficium ecclesiastice for (institutio ecclesiastice) x consisting of (dos) y and (officium) z	defined
$\mathsf{benEventum}(x, y)$	x is an event in the life of (beneficium ecclesiastice) x	defined
$\mathsf{benOfficium}(x, y, t)$	x is classified as an (beneficiorum) officium by y at t	defined
$\mathsf{BenParoch}(x)$	x is a beneficium parochialis	defined
$\mathsf{benVita}(x)$	life of (beneficium ecclesiastice) x	defined
$\mathsf{creatio}(x, y)$	(officium) x is established by y	defined
$\mathsf{Dos}(x)$	x is a dos	defined
$\mathsf{EcclesiaAedificium}(x)$	x is an ecclesia	primitive
$\mathsf{EcclDS}(x)$	x is an ecclesiastical description	primitive
$\mathsf{EcclNorm}(x)$	x is an ecclesiastical set of norms	primitive
$\mathsf{EndDS}(x)$	x is an ecclesiastical endowment description	primitive
$\mathsf{ErecDS}(x)$	x is a description erecting a church institution	primitive
$\mathsf{erectio}(x, y)$	(institutiones ecclesiasticae) x is established by y	defined
$\mathsf{InstEccl}(x)$	x is an institutiones ecclesiasticae	defined
$\mathsf{fundatio}(x, y)$	(dos) x is established by y	defined
$\mathsf{Parochia}(x)$	x is a parochia	defined
$\mathsf{Officium}(x)$	x is an officium	defined
$\mathsf{ParDS}(x)$	x is a description erecting a parochia	primitive
$\mathsf{parochiaeEcclesia}(x, y, t)$	x is classified as an ecclesia parochialis by y at t	defined
$\mathsf{parochiaeGens}(x, y, t)$	x is classified as a parochianus (ordinarius) by y at t	defined
$\mathsf{parochiaeMembrum}(x, y, t)$	x is classified as a parochiae membrum by y at t	defined
$\mathsf{parochiaePatronus}(x, y, t)$	x is classified as an (parochiae) patronus by y at t	defined
$\mathsf{parochiaePlebanus}(x, y, t)$	x is classified as a plebanus by y at t	defined
$\mathsf{parochiaeTerr}(x, y, t)$	x is classified as a territorium parochiae by y at t	defined
$\mathsf{parochEventum}(x, y)$	x is an event in the life of (parochia) x	defined
$\mathsf{parochVita}(x)$	life of (parochia) x	defined

Table 3. SacrOnt specific predicates and terms

Ecclesiastical subtypes of $\mathtt{CF}^*$

(D11) $\mathsf{benDos}(x, y, t) \triangleq [\mathtt{ED}(x) \vee \mathtt{PD}(x)] \wedge \mathtt{CF}^*(x, y, t) \wedge \mathsf{Dos}(y)$.

(D12) $\mathsf{benOfficium}(x, y, t) \triangleq \mathtt{Event}(x) \wedge \mathtt{CF}^*(x, y, t) \wedge \mathsf{Officium}(y)$.

(D13) $\mathsf{parochiaePlebanus}(x, y, t) \triangleq \mathtt{APO}(x) \wedge \mathsf{BenParoch}(y) \wedge [\mathtt{CF}^*(x, \mathsf{dos_f}(y), t) \wedge \mathtt{CF}^*(x, \mathsf{officium_f}(y), t)]$.

(D14) $\mathsf{parochiaePatronus}(x, y, t) \triangleq \mathtt{APO}(x) \wedge \mathsf{BenParoch}(y) \wedge [\mathtt{CF}^*(x, \mathsf{dos_f}(y), t) \wedge \neg\mathtt{CF}^*(x, \mathsf{officium_f}(y), t)]$.

(D15) $\mathsf{parochiaeGens}(x, y, t) \triangleq \mathtt{APO}(x) \wedge \mathtt{CF}^*(x, y, t) \wedge \mathsf{Parochia}(y)$.

(D16) $\mathsf{parochiaeTerr}(x, y, t) \triangleq \mathtt{F}(x) \wedge \mathtt{CF}^*(x, y, t) \wedge \mathsf{Parochia}(y)$.

Ecclesiastical perdurants

(D17) $\mathsf{Parochia}(x) \rightarrow \mathsf{parochVita}(x) \triangleq \mathtt{lf}(x)$.

(D18) $\mathsf{parochEventum}(x, y) \triangleq \mathtt{P}(x, \mathsf{parochVita}(y))$.

(D19) $\mathsf{BenEccl}(x) \rightarrow \mathsf{benVita}(x) \triangleq \mathtt{lf}(x)$.
(D20) $\mathsf{benEventum}(x, y) \triangleq \mathtt{P}(x, \mathsf{benVita}(y))$.

4.2. Auxiliary definitions

(D21) $\mathtt{CPP}(x, y) \triangleq \mathtt{CP}(x, y) \wedge x \neq y$.
(D22) $\mathsf{dos_f}(x) = y \triangleq \exists z, v\ x = \mathsf{benEccl_f}(v, y, z)$.
(D23) $\mathsf{officium_f}(x) = y \triangleq \exists z, v\ x = \mathsf{benEccl_f}(v, z, y)$.
(D24) $\mathsf{parochiaeMembrum}(x, y, t) \triangleq \mathsf{parochiaePlebanus}(x, y, t) \vee \mathsf{parochiaeGens}(x, y, t)$.

The consistency of definitions 22 and 23 is guaranteed by axiom 19.

4.3. Bridging axioms

(A1) $\mathsf{BenEccl}(x) \rightarrow \mathtt{RL}(x)$.
(A2) $\mathsf{InstEccl}(x) \rightarrow \mathtt{RL}(x)$.
(A3) $\mathsf{Dos}(x) \vee \mathsf{Officium}(x) \rightarrow \mathtt{RL}(x)$.
(A4) $\mathsf{EcclDS}(x) \rightarrow \mathtt{DS}(x)$.
(A5) $\mathsf{EcclesiaAedificium}(x) \rightarrow \mathtt{NAPO}(x)$.

4.4. Proper axioms

Subsumption axioms

(A6) $\mathsf{BenParoch}(x) \rightarrow \mathsf{BenEccl}(x)$.
(A7) $\mathsf{ErecDS}(x) \vee \mathsf{EndDS}(x) \vee \mathsf{EcclNorm}(x) \rightarrow \mathsf{EcclDS}(x)$.

Ecclesiastical definition uniqueness constraints

(A8) $\mathsf{erectio}(x_1, y) \wedge \mathsf{erectio}(x_2, y) \rightarrow x_1 = x_2$.
(A9) $\mathsf{fundatio}(x_1, y) \wedge \mathsf{fundatio}(x_2, y) \rightarrow x_1 = x_2$.
(A10) $\mathsf{creatio}(x_1, y) \wedge \mathsf{creatio}(x_2, y) \rightarrow x_1 = x_2$.

Mereological axioms for beneficia ecclesiastice

(A11) $\mathsf{ErecDS}(x) \rightarrow$
$[\mathtt{CPP}(y_1, x) \wedge \mathsf{fundatio}(z_1, y_1) \wedge \mathtt{CPP}(y_2, x) \wedge \mathsf{fundatio}(z_2, y_2) \rightarrow y_1 = y_2]$.
(A12) $\mathsf{ErecDS}(x) \rightarrow$
$[\mathtt{CPP}(y_1, x) \wedge \mathsf{creatio}(z_1, y_1) \wedge \mathtt{CPP}(y_2, x) \wedge \mathsf{creatio}(z_2, y_2) \rightarrow y_1 = y_2]$.

Ecclesiastical classification uniqueness constraints

(A13) $\mathsf{parochiaeTerr}(x, y_1, t) \wedge \mathsf{parochiaeTerr}(x, y_2, t) \rightarrow y_1 = y_2$.
(A14) $\mathsf{parochiaeTerr}(x_1, y, t) \wedge \mathsf{parochiaeTerr}(x_2, y, t) \rightarrow x_1 = x_2$.
(A15) $\mathsf{parochiaeMembrum}(x, y_1, t) \wedge \mathsf{parochiaeGens}(x, y_2, t) \rightarrow y_1 = y_2$.
(A16) $\mathsf{parochiaeEcclesia}(x, y_1, t) \wedge \mathsf{parochiaeEcclesia}(x, y_2, t) \rightarrow y_1 = y_2$.
(A17) $\mathsf{parochiaeEcclesia}(x_1, y, t) \wedge \mathsf{parochiaeEcclesia}(x_2, y, t) \rightarrow x_1 = x_2$.
(A18) $\mathsf{benDos}(x, y_1, t) \wedge \mathsf{benDos}(x, y_2, t) \rightarrow y_1 = y_2$.

Other axioms

(A19) $\mathsf{benEccl_f}(x_1, y_1, z_1) = \mathsf{benEccl_f}(x_2, y_2, z_2) \rightarrow x_1 = x_2 \wedge y_1 = y_2 \wedge z_1 = z_2$.
(A20) $\mathsf{parochiaePlebanus}(x, y, t) \rightarrow \neg\mathsf{parochiaeGens}(x, y, t)$.
(A21) $x = \mathsf{benEccl_f}(y, z_1, z_2) \rightarrow \mathtt{CPP}(x, y)$.

5. SacrOnt **outside** DOLCE

SacrOnt	CIDOC CRM	SUMO	DOLCE
InstEccl	E73.Information_Object	Organization	RL
BenEccl			
Dos	E73.Information_Object	RegionalLaw / Contract	RL
Officium			
EcclesiaAedificium	E22.Man-Made_Object	Building	NAPO
EcclDS	E31.Document	RegionalLaw	DS
erectio	P67.refers_to	represents	DF
fundatio			
creatio			
parochiaeGens	shortcut/concatenation of P141.was_assigned by and P42.assigned	Classifying	CF*
parochiaeTerr			
parochiaeEcclesia			
parochiaePatronus			
benDos			
benOfficium			
parochiaePlebanus	shortcut/concatenation of P141.was_assigned by and P42.assigned	occupiesPosition	CF*
parochEventum	E5.Activity	IntentionalProcess	PD
benEventum			

Table 4. SacrOnt outside DOLCE

Our model of administrative structure of the Catholic Church is based on DOLCE. The main reason for this choice is its fragment that represents social objects. We found it useful that we could easily describe the following facts:

1. a document encodes a (social) description,
2. a description defines a (social) concept,
3. a concept classifies other objects.

In our opinion, this allowed us to simplify the structure of the resulting database mainly due to the use of the subtypes of DF we defined in SacrOnt.

Still, it is possible to locate SacrOnt's central categories also within other top-level ontologies. Table 4 shows this possibility for CIDOC CRM and SUMO. For most of SacrOnt concepts it has been rather difficult to find the adequate proper parent category in CIDOC CRM and SUMO, since in many places they are incompatible with DOLCE, which has determined our ontological choices. Although we tried to identify the most suitable concepts, these mappings are rather imprecise. For some concepts (e.g., InstEccl, BenEccl) they are bound to change completely their meaning provided by the axioms and definitions of SacrOnt. On the other hand, some categories of CIDOC CRM might be seen as more suitable for our current formalism than DOLCE framework, e.g., E22.Man-Made_Object.

In sum, it turned out that in this case the efforts to keep the ontological neutrality of a given domain ontology from top-level ontologies are not as painless as in other cases (cf. [6]).

6. SacrOnt Database

SacrOnt **ontology**	**DB application**
APO	APO table
F	TERRITORIUM table
PC	table relationship
Parochia	PAROCHIA table
BenParoch	BENEFICIUM_PAROCHIALIS table
benEventum	BEN_PAROCHIALIS_EVENTUM table
parochEventum	PAROCHIAE_EVENTUM table
EcclesiaAedificium	ECCLESIAE_AEDIFICIUM table
parochiaePlebanus	(mediated) table relationship
parochiaeGens	(mediated) table relationship
parochiaeTerr	(mediated) table relationship
parochiaeEcclesia	(mediated) table relationship
parochiaePatronus	(mediated) table relationship
benDos	(mediated) table relationship

Table 5. SacrOnt database schema elements

We defined the above portion of SacrOnt with the aim to construct a database schema to be populated with data from the ecclesiastical resources. To this end, we selected a number of "leaf" nodes in the SacrOnt taxonomy together with the respective relationships - see table 5.

In order to deal with the temporal parameter of some of those relationships, we follow the method suggested in [5] and use perdurants as the so-called temporal pivots. Roughly speaking, in order to express the fact that, say, a certain agentive physical object is classified as plebanus at a certain time by a certain role, we find the relevant part of the life of this role, whose temporal boundaries coincide with this time, and use this role as our classifier. So it is not a role that classifies a certain object at a certain time, but a perdurant in which this role participates atemporally classifies this object.

The logical model (entity relationship diagram) of the resulting database is presented in figure 2, the physical model (server model diagram) is shown in figure 3. Both models where created using Oracle Designer and finally implemented in a Postgres database.

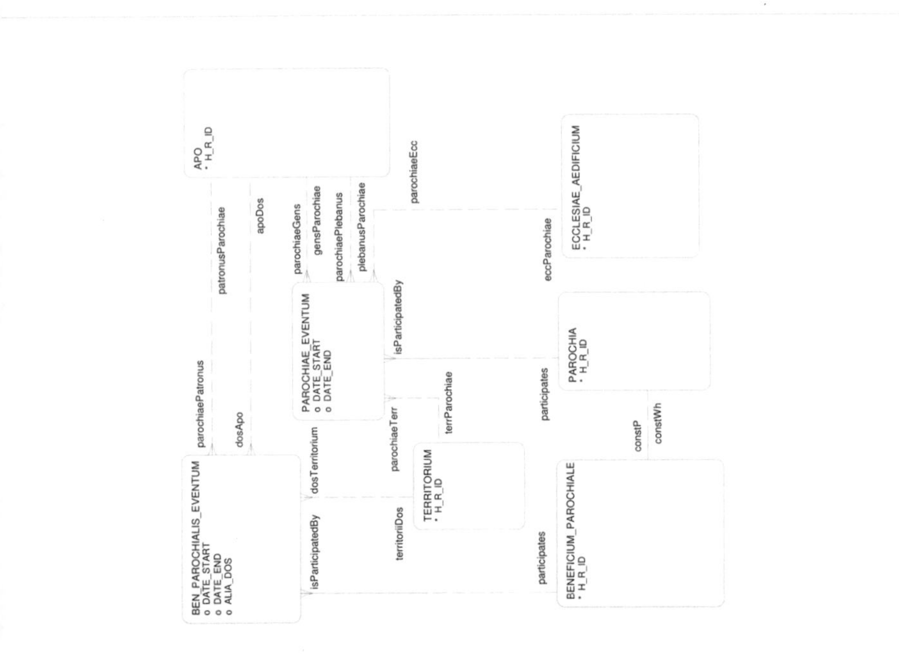

Figure 2.: SacrOnt database logical model

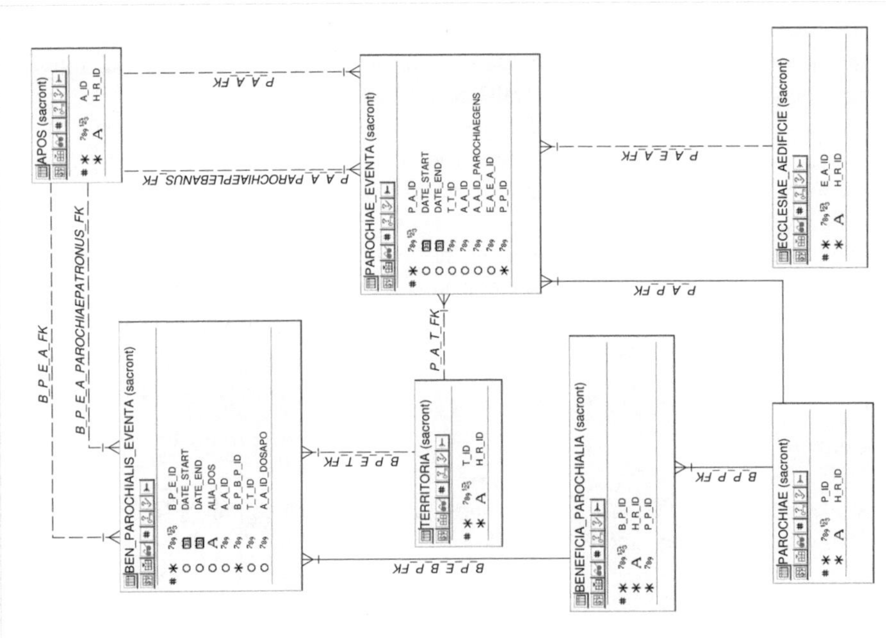

Figure 3.: SacrOnt database physical model

7. Further work

The formal system presented in this paper is just a tiny part of the domain ontology that is needed to support the design of the database system for the history of the administrative structure of the Catholic Church in Central-Eastern Europe. The domain is broader and more complex than it appears at first. However, even our restricted study revealed the benefits of the formal-ontological approach. The conceptual framework we employed turned out to be subtle enough to disambiguate different meanings of such historical terms as "parochia" or "officium".

Besides adding new domain-specific concepts to the ontology (e.g., episcopus) we intend to extend it so that it would include concepts needed for spatio-temporal identifications. After all, we aim to provide a historian with a tool by means of which we would be able to locate such objects parochie in space and time.

Acknowledgements

Pawel Garbacz and Robert Trypuz were partially supported by the grant N N101 150037 from the Ministry of Science and Higher Education.

References

[1] E. Bottazzi and R. Ferrario. Preliminaries to a DOLCE Ontology of Organizations. *International Journal of Business Process Integration and Management*, 2008.

[2] L. Ferrariis, *Prompta Bibliotheca Canonica, Juridica, Moralis, Theologica, Ascetica, Polemica, Rubristica, Historica*, vol 7., Venetiis 1782.

[3] L. Ferrariis, *Prompta Bibliotheca Canonica, Juridica, Moralis, Theologica, Ascetica, Polemica, Rubristica, Historica*, vol 1., Paris 1863.

[4] L. Ferrariis, *Prompta Bibliotheca Canonica, Juridica, Moralis, Theologica, Ascetica, Polemica, Rubristica, Historica*, vol 4., Paris 1853.

[5] P. Grenon, *Temporal Qualification and Change with First–Order Binary Predicates*. In B. Bennett, Ch. Fellbaum. (eds.): Proceeding of the 2006 conference on Formal Ontology in Information Systems, pp. 155–166, 2006.

[6] P. Garbacz, M. Lechniak, P. Kulicki, R. Trypuz, *Do you still want to vote for your favorite politician? Ask Ontobella!*, In R. Ferrario, A. Oltramari. (eds.): Formal Ontology Meets Industry, pp. 102-113, 2009.

[7] I. Gregory, R. Healey, *Historical GIS: structuring, mapping and analyzing Geographies of the past*, Progress in Human Geography 31(5), 2007, pp. 638-653.

[8] A. Gangemi, M.-T. Sagri, D. Tiscornia, *A Constructive Framework for Legal Ontologies*. In V.R. Benjamins et al. (eds.): Law and the Semantic Web, 3369, pp. 97, 2005.

[9] M. Koubarakis et al. (eds), *Spatiotemporal Databases: The Chorochronos Approach*, Berlin: Springer-Verlag, 2003.

[10] C. Masolo, S. Borgo, A. Gangemi, N. Guarino, and A. Oltramari, *WonderWeb Deliverable D18, Ontology Library (final)*. Technical report, LOA-ISTC, CNR, 2003.

[11] C. Masolo, L. Vieu, E. Bottazzi, C. Catenacci, R. Ferrario, A. Gangemi and N. Guarino, *Social roles and their descriptions*. In D. Dubois, C. W., editor, Proceedings of the Ninth International Conference on the Principles of Knowledge Representation and Reasoning (KR2004), pp. 267–277, Whistler, Canada. M.A. Williams, 2004.

Formal Ontology in Information Systems
A. Galton and R. Mizoguchi (Eds.)
IOS Press, 2010

doi:10.3233/978-1-60750-535-8-359

Using the cDnS ontology as upper-level for a Scholarly Debate Ontology

Neil BENN [1]

Knowledge Media Institute, The Open University, Walton Hall, Milton Keynes, United Kingdom, MK7 6AA

Abstract. There is an active area of research concerned with designing tools that support quantitative and qualitative analysis of academic knowledge domains. Knowledge Domain Analysis (KDA) research investigates computational support for users who desire to understand and/or participate in the scholarly inquiry of a given academic knowledge domain. KDA technology supports this task by allowing users to identify important features of the knowledge domain such as the predominant research topics, the experts in the domain, and the most influential researchers. However, a key limitation of work to date is its inability to provide machine-readable models of the *debate* in academic knowledge domains. This paper argues that KDA technology should support users in understanding the features of scholarly debate as a prerequisite for engaging with their chosen domain. To this end, the paper proposes a Scholarly Debate Ontology which specifies the formal vocabulary for representing debate in academic knowledge domains. The ontology is designed with reference to an upper-level ontology that specifies the generic elements of any domain, such as academic domains, where knowledge is collectively constructed and modified by social agents.

Keywords. top-level vs. application-level ontologies, ontology-based application systems, argumentation, knowledge modelling, ontology design patterns.

Introduction

Knowledge Domain Analysis (KDA) research (e.g. [1] [2] [3] [4] [5]) investigates computational support for users who desire to understand and/or participate in the scholarly inquiry of a given academic knowledge domain. KDA technology supports this task by allowing users to identify important features of the knowledge domain such as the predominant research topics, the experts in the domain, and the most influential researchers. However, one limitation of the existing research is its inability to support users in understanding the features of *scholarly debate* as a prerequisite for engaging with their chosen domain. KDA tools need to be able to reason over formal models of the debate in academic knowledge domains.

To this end, this paper proposes a *Scholarly Debate Ontology*, which specifies the formal vocabulary for constructing representations of debate in academic knowledge domains. In accordance with best practices for ontology design, the paper presents a design process that involves using an upper-level ontology as the basis for selecting the essential

[1]E-mail: n.j.l.benn@open.ac.uk

elements of the world to be represented, thus ensuring that the design process adheres to the principle of *minimal ontological commitment* [6].

The paper begins by characterising knowledge domains as settings for the collective construction of knowledge, thus motivating the reuse of an *upper-level constructivist ontology*. The paper then defines the *Scholarly Debate Ontology*, which specifies the essential elements of debate in academic domains. The upper-level ontology acts as a design aid for selecting the essential elements of scholarly debate to be specified in the SDO.

1. The cDnS ontology: codifying social constructivism

The *Constructivist Descriptions and Situations (cDnS)* ontology "provides the expressivity to talk about the contexts (social, informational, circumstantial, and epistemic), in which collectives make and produce sense" [7]. In other words, cDnS can be characterised as an ontology of collective sensemaking. "Collective sensemaking" or "collective knowledge construction" is a useful way of characterising the key activity of knowledge domains, thus the cDnS ontology provides a suitable vocabulary for describing the portion of reality that is of current interest—in this case, the setting of academic knowledge domains.

Most significantly, the key knowledge domain activities of representing and communicating knowledge constitute *semiotic* processes. Semiotics is the study of signs and their use in the representation and communication of meaning. In Charles Sanders Peirce's prominent theory of semiotics [8], the basic structure of signs in semiotic processes consists of three components: the *sign-vehicle*, which is the entity perceived by the senses; the *object* referred to by the sign-vehicle, which may include imaginary objects and ideas; and the *interpretant*, which is the mental representation that links the sign-vehicle to the object in the mind of some conceiving agent. As will be discussed later in the section, these semiotic components correspond to key elements of the cDnS ontology. Indeed, a core configuration of elements within the cDnS ontology[2] can be used to describe any generic semiotic process where an agent conceives some description (or representation) about entities in the world and communicates this description via some object for conveying information.

Although the design approach is to reuse this constructivist ontology, this paper attempts to remain neutral with respect to the perennial philosophical debate about whether we can only *construct* reality via our subjective and socially-mediated representations of it (a *constructivist* viewpoint) or whether we can *derive* true representations of a single objective reality that exists independently of our conceptualisation of it (a *realist* viewpoint). That philosophical debate is beyond the scope of this paper, which, for the purposes of selecting a suitable upper-level reference ontology, is concerned with characterising knowledge domains as settings for conducting intellectual inquiry through its production of texts as the primary means of representing and communicating knowledge (cf. [9]). This is irrespective of whether or not the "representations of knowledge" that are produced and communicated via published texts correspond to true facts in reality.

[2] In the cDnS ontology's original form as the DOLCE+DnS ontology this configuration of ontological categories was sometimes referred to as the *Semiotic Ontology Design Pattern*

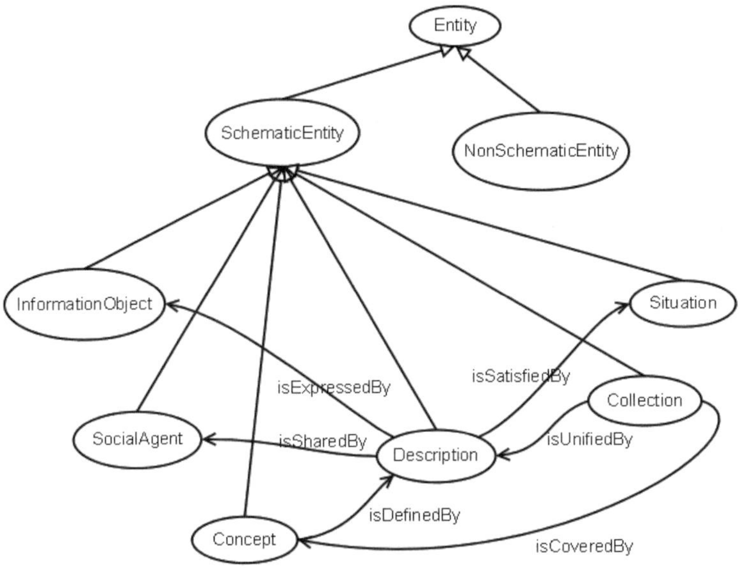

Figure 1. The cDnS ontology.

As the authors of [10] note, a view of knowledge as socially constructed and socially negotiated does not logically imply an *anti*-realist position.

The cDnS ontology is depicted in Figure 1. The core[3] cDnS ontology consists of the following main classes: cdns:Entity, cdns:InformationObject, cdns:Description, cdns:Situation, cdns:Concept, cdns:SocialAgent, and cdns:Collection. These, along with the main relations in the ontology, will be described in more detail in the remainder of this section[4]. As each class is described, an analysis is made of how, as upper-level classes, they can be interpreted in the context of academic knowledge domains, as a way of demonstrating the suitability of the cDnS ontology for the design task at hand.

1.1. Entity

Entity is "the class of everything that is assumed to exist in some domain of interest for any possible world" [11]. In the cDnS ontology, the *cdns:Entity* class is specified as the uppermost class in the hierarchy from which all other cDnS classes are sub-classed. There are two main categories of Entity: *SchematicEntity* (typically social entities like organisations and information), and *NonSchematicEntity* (for example, time intervals and spatial coordinates). However, the main development on the cDnS ontology has focussed on "axiomatising" the former type of Entity—i.e. *SchematicEntity*.

[3]There are two extended versions of the cDnS ontology that are not treated here.

[4]The description of the cDnS ontology that follows is based on two main publications, [11] and [7]. There are some peripheral modifications made in the cDnS ontology between [11] and [7], which demonstrates that the ontology is still a work in progress. Nonetheless, the core elements of the ontology have become stable enough to be suitable for the purposes of the present work.

1.2. InformationObject

"Information objects" are the vehicles for communicating semantic content or meaning between agents; they are the *expression* of semantic content, or to use Peircean terminology, they are the *sign-vehicle* in a given semiotic process, where *cdns:Entity* plays the role of the "object" in the semiotic process—i.e. an information object in the cDnS sense can be about any other entity. Any unit of information can be treated as an instance of *cdns:InformationObject*, and this is independently of how the information (as something which is abstract) is realised in a physical medium. However, according to [11], information objects must have a physical realisation so that their informational content is perceivable by some agent. Based on this characterisation a single information object can have multiple physical realisations or modalities—e.g. a newspaper article can have a paper and an electronic realisation[5].

In the context of academic domains, the most typical examples of information objects are publications, which are the main vehicles for representing and communicating knowledge. A single publication, taken as a whole, can be considered to be an information object. Furthermore, a single publication is composed of clauses and sentences (*verbal* expressions of knowledge), as well as tables, graphs, and figures (hybrid, i.e. both verbal and *non*-verbal, expressions of knowledge). Each of these components of a publication can be considered to be an information object in its own right. This corresponds with the view of [12] that academic publications, particularly scientific publications are semiotic hybrids.

1.3. Description

A Description is the abstract, communicable semantic content or meaning that is expressed by an information object. In Peircean terminology, a Description is the "interpretant" that is formed in the mind of some conceiving agent. According to [13], different information objects, possibly even in different languages, can be associated with the same description or semantic content.

In the context of academic domains, just as there are different types of information objects, there are different types of descriptions. For example, a single scholarly publication can be regarded as an information object that expresses a *thesis*, in much the same manner as a novel can be regarded as an information object that expresses a *plot*. The thesis of a scholarly publication is therefore an example of a description in the cDnS sense. Furthermore, each clause or sentence that makes up a publication can be characterised as an information object that expresses either some *propositional* content (as is the case with declarative sentences that may represent some theory conceived by an agent) or some *non-propositional* content (as is the case with interrogative sentences—i.e. questions). Therefore, the propositional or non-propositional content of individual clauses and sentences are also examples of Descriptions.

[5]There is an issue here with the ontological status of different modalities or modes of expression. For example, is an orally-delivered speech the same expression as the written speech but just a different modality or are they two entirely different expressions? The intuitive answer seems to be to treat the orally-delivered speech and the written speech as the same abstract conceptual work, in which case the cDnS characterisation is appropriate—i.e. a single information object can have multiple realisations.

1.4. Situation

A situation is said to provide a setting for other entities, including other situations. A situation, in the cDnS sense, represents a state of affairs that is observable by some agent. A situation is said to *satisfy* a description. Inversely, a description is said to represent an agent's conceptualisation of a particular situation. The constructivist nature of the cDnS ontology suggests that situations do not exist independently of descriptions—i.e., a state of affairs requires an agent to conceive of it. However, the reverse is not necessarily true—that is descriptions are not dependent on situations, since there exist descriptions that do not describe a particular situation.

1.5. Concept

Concepts are *defined by* and *used by* Descriptions. Concepts are used to classify and name other entities. So, for example, in the American constitution, there is an article (i.e. a Description in the cDnS sense) which defines the concept of "US President". This concept of "US President" can then be said to classify the entity "Barack Obama". Furthermore, a concept can classify different entities at different times—e.g. the concept "US President" has classified "Bill Clinton" and also "George Bush"—while a concept can also classify different entities at the same time—e.g. "British MP" classifies a number of persons currently sitting in the British Parliament.

In the context of academic domains, concepts correspond to elements of the specialised vocabulary or conceptual system of a particular domain. These domain concepts are typically defined and used by the theories and statements (i.e. the descriptions in a cDnS sense) that are shared and communicated among the agents in the domain.

1.6. SocialAgent

An Agent is required to interpret a given Information Object. When an Agent *interprets* an Information Object, the agent is said to *conceive* the Description that is *expressed by* that particular Information Object.

In the context of academic domains, persons involved in the production of scholarly texts can be characterised as social agents. Also, in the context of knowledge domains, one particularly important feature of agents and their relationship to information objects is that it is possible for two agents (e.g. an author and a reader) to *interpret* an Information Object differently, thereby conceiving of different descriptions [14]. These different descriptions can even sometimes be contradictory, even though ostensibly they have been derived from the same information object.

1.7. Collection

The collection class captures the intuitive notion of such entities as groups, teams, and associations. A Collection has at least two entities as its members and is said to "emerge" out of its member entities such that, "while retaining their identity, unity, and physical separation, [member entities] are 'kept together' in order to form a new entity" [15]. Note however, that the members of collection can change or be substituted during the life of a collection without affecting the identity of the collection. This is one feature of cDnS collections that helps to differentiate them from mathematical sets. Furthermore, mathematical sets can be empty or singletons, but no empty or singleton collections are allowed in the cDnS "axiomatisation".

In the context of academic domains, the community of researchers in a given knowledge domain can be thought of as a collection of agents that share one or more descriptions[6]—these descriptions are said to unify the collection [7]. The "collection of agents" characterisation also applies to such entities as organisations, research groups or teams, and conference committees.

With this upper-level semiotic and constructivist framework in place, the paper proceeds to describe the design of the Scholarly Debate Ontology, which will define the vocabulary for representing debate in academic knowledge domains. As will be shown in the next section, the cDnS ontology just described will be used to illuminate some of the design choices in the Scholarly Debate Ontology.

2. The Scholarly Debate Ontology: codifying dialectical exchange

The Scholarly Debate Ontology builds on the debate mapping approach of Robert Horn et al.[16], who, in landmark argumentat modelling work, created seven paper-based, wall-mountable debate maps for analysing the history and current status of scholarly debate about whether computers can think. Horn's work is directly relevant here because he also recognises that when it comes to the task of analysing knowledge domains, it is important to understand how all the arguments fit together in that knowledge domain. He is particularly interested in representing dialectical exchange between scholars so as to be able to answer the question: *"Where can I get an overview of the history of the arguments so I can decide which I want to read?"*

What has emerged from Horn's work is a theory of the structure of scholarly debate, which has subsequently been articulated by his colleague in the creation of the maps, Jeffrey Yoshimi, in what he calls a "logic of debate" [17]. Whereas most argument modelling research concentrates on the microstructure of arguments (e.g. modelling the schemes of inference that link premises to conclusions), the concern of a logic of debate is how arguments themselves are "constituents in macro-level dialectical structures" ([17]). This section describes how the basic elements of this logic of debate are implemented as classes and relations in the Scholarly Debate Ontology, all within the semiotic and constructivist framework outlined in the previous section.

2.1. Issue

In the Horn debate mapping approach, argumentative exchange between two or more scholars is depicted as occurring within the context of a particular issue[7]. Figure 2 shows the definition of the *Issue* class. In the context of academic domains, issues typically correspond to the research questions expressed in individual academic publications. Thus, the Issue class is defined as an indirect subclass of the cDnS class *cdns:Description* via another new class for the Scholarly Debate Ontology, *NonPropositionalContent*[8].

---

[6] [7] uses the term "knowledge community" to label such a collection of agents.

[7] Indeed, the approach taken by Horn is sometimes referred to as *issue mapping*.

[8] As explained in the previous section, descriptions found in scholarly publications represent either some propositional content (expressed in declarative sentences in the publication) or some non-propositional content (expressed in interrogative sentences—i.e. questions—in the publication).

```
(def-class NonPropositionalContent (#_cdns:Description))

(def-class Issue (NonPropositionalContent)
   ((verbalExpression :type String)
    (#_cdns:isExpressedBy :type Publication)))

(def-relation relatedIssueOf (?iss1 ?iss2)
   :constraint (and
                 (Issue ?iss1)
                 (Issue ?iss2)))
```

Figure 2. The specification of the Issue class: Issue is defined as a subclass of NonPropositionalContent, which in turn is a subclass of cdns:Description. The Issue class inherits the cdns:isExpressedBy attribute from cdns:Description, and specialises it so that it holds values of Publication, another class defined in the ontology. The relatedIssueOf relation is defined as holding between two Issue instances.

Therefore, as a subclass of *cdns:Description*, an Issue inherits the *cdns:isExpressedBy* attribute, and specialises this attribute so that it holds values of type *Publication*, another class defined in the ontology. The Issue class is specified with another attribute—*verbalExpression*—which allows an arbitrary text string to be associated with a given *Issue* instance. The *verbalExpression* attribute is introduced here primarily because of pragmatic argument modelling, to make the manual process of representing real debates more tractable for a human modeller. The composition[9] of the text string that appears as the value of the *verbalExpression* attribute has no impact on the reasoning of the system. Indeed, it is the case that an issue could be expressed in a non-textual manner, in which case the *verbalExpression* attribute might be replaced by a *nonVerbalExpression* attribute. Note, however, that this paper does not suggest that all verbal and non-verbal forms of expression in scholarly text are directly interchangeable. As discussed previously, scholarly texts consist of both verbal expressions (e.g. sentences and paragraphs) and non-verbal expressions (e.g. graphs and figures). According to [12] "no verbal description can construct the same meaning as a picture", which suggests that non-verbal expressions cannot be directly reduced to corresponding verbal expressions. However, [12] also explains that we learn to count different abstractions as the same for some restricted purposes. Finally, the listing shows that the *Issue* class is also specified with one new relation—*relatedIssueOf*—which allows one issue to be asserted as related to another issue. This is intended currently as all-compassing, generic relation that can be specialised in future research that determines the key relationships between Issues.

Indeed, following the ontology-design principle of minimal ontological commitment, only the essentials of the *Issue* class for the purposes of representing scholarly debate, have been specified in the ontology. However, it is possible that in future iterations of the ontology design it may be desirable to extend the definition of the *Issue* class to incorporate explicit constraints on issues such as whether a given issue allows a closed

[9]Even though the text string itself can have an arbitrary composition, it is useful to express the text-string in a grammatically well-formed manner even if it means that the text string no longer corresponds verbatim with the original source from which it has been taken.

```
(def-class PropositionalContent (#_cdns:Description))

(def-class Proposition (PropositionalContent)
   ((verbalExpression :type String)
    (#_cdns:isExpressedBy :type Publication)))

(def-class Argument (PropositionalContent)
   ((hasPremise :type Proposition
                :min-cardinality 1)
    (hasConclusion :type Proposition
                   :max-cardinality 1)))
```

Figure 3. The definition of the Proposition and Argument classes: Both classes are subclasses of PropositionalContent, which in turn is a subclass of cdns:Description.

set of answers (e.g. only "Yes" or "No" answers) or an open set of answers to be offered in response to a given issue.

2.2. Proposition and Argument

In addition to issues, the logic of debate consists of propositions and arguments, thus two classes, *Proposition* and *Argument*, are introduced into the ontology. As shown in Figure 3, both the *Proposition* class and the *Argument* class are defined as subclasses of the class *PropositionalContent*, which in turn is a specialisation of the cDnS class *cdns:Description*. As with the *Issue* class described previously, the *verbalExpression* attribute is introduced here for the *Proposition* class primarily because of pragmatic argument modelling reasons. Here the conceptualisation of *Argument* corresponds to a collection of propositions, one of which is a conclusion and the rest of which are premises. Thus the *Argument* class is defined with attributes *hasPremise* and *hasConclusion*, both of which have values of type *Proposition*. Note also that the *Argument* class is defined with the constraint of having at least one (:min-cardinality 1) premise and at most one (:max-cardinality 1) conclusion. In Yoshimi's logic of debate, the distinction between propositions and arguments is one of a matter of scale—he suggests that it is possible to condense the representation of an entire argument down to a single declarative sentence and that furthermore, for argument visualisation, it is useful to do so.

On Horn's debate maps, the propositions and arguments depicted as part of an issue region can be said to "address" that particular issue. The *addresses* relation is one that is implicit in Horn's representation scheme but which is now made explicit in the Scholarly Debate Ontology.

Horn's representation scheme then defines two main relations—*is supported by* and *is disputed by*—that hold between arguments. [17] offers three examples of types of support between any arguments A1 and A2: (1) logical—i.e. A2 supports[10] A1 if A2

[10] In detailing the terminology of his logic of debate, Yoshimi uses the active form of the verbs "supports" and "disputes". In contrast the terminology of the Horn debate mapping scheme uses the passive form "is supported by" and "is disputed by", with the reason being that this allows the map reader to visualise the arguments from left to right. With respect to representing the relation in a formal knowledge base, the distinction between the

```
(def-relation supports (?p1 ?p2)
  :constraint (and
              (PropositionalContent ?p1)
              (PropositionalContent ?p2))
  :sufficient (and
              (Argument ?a)
              (hasConclusion ?a ?p2)
              (hasPremise ?a ?p1)))

(def-relation disputes (?p1 ?p2)
  :constraint (and
              (PropositionalContent ?p1)
              (PropositionalContent ?p2)))

(def-relation addresses (?p ?iss)
  :constraint (and
              (PropositionalContent ?p)
              (Issue ?iss)))
```

Figure 4. The specification of the "supports", "disputes", and "addresses" relations.

strengthens the conclusion of A1, (2) historical—i.e. A2 supports A1 if A2 is an earlier argument that A1 draws on, and (3) specialization—i.e. A2 supports A1 if A2 is a more specific version of A1. In terms of disputation, according to the logic of debate, argument A2 disputes argument A1 if the conclusion of A2 is the negation of some statement in A1. In the logic of debate, both supports and disputes are irreflexive, asymmetric, and non-transitive. Figure 4 shows the definition of the *addresses*, *supports*, and *disputes* relations in the Scholarly Debate Ontology. The *:sufficient* component of the supports relation definition specifies that the relation between premise and conclusion is also a special case of the supports relation.

2.3. *Position and ViewpointCluster*

The final element of the logic of debate is position, which [17] informally defines as a "family of mutually complementary arguments" relative to a debate. More formally, a position is defined as a collection of arguments related by the supports relation, forming what the author refers to as an "aggregated support path". The author gives example positions such as Materialism in the Philosophy of Mind and Utilitarianism in Ethics.

According to [17], positions are important elements of the logic of debate because they provide additional information that is essential to understanding the structure of debate. This view about the informational value of positions or philosophical camps[11] is echoed by [18] and [19], which have identified that one of the difficult aspects of under-

active and passive form is not a fundamental one, and it is typical to have both forms specified in the ontology (as inverses of each other). The choice is then left to the modeller as to which form to use when representing a particular relation instance.

[11]The term "philosophical camp" is used by [18] to describe the same debate phenomenon.

```
(def-class Position (#_cdns:Collection)
  ((hasViewpoint :type PropositionalContent)
   (associatedPerson :type Person)
   (hasOpposingPosition :type Position)))

(def-class ViewpointCluster (#_cdns:Collection)
  ((hasViewpoint :type PropositionalContent)
   (associatedPerson :type Person)
   (hasOpposingClusterWeak :type ViewpointCluster)
   (hasOpposingClusterStrong :type ViewpointCluster)))
```

Figure 5. The specification of the Position and ViewpointCluster classes, both as a subclasses of the cdns:Collection class.

standing debates is that the protagonists come from quite different worldviews, bringing vastly different assumptions about the nature of reality. So in order to provide support for learners in gaining insight into why particular arguments take place, the debate maps created by [16] include a description of all the major camps from which scholars enter the debate.

The specification of the *Position* class is shown in Figure 5. This specification shows that the *Position* class is defined as a subclass of the *cdns:Collection* class in the cDnS ontology. The specification also includes the attributes hasViewpoint (which links instances of the *PropositionalContent* class to a given position), *associatedPerson* (which links instances of *Person* to a given position) and *hasOpposingPosition* (which links one position to another when the two positions clash with each other in the context of a particular issue).

Specifying the *Position* class in the ontology allows for top-down representation of existing intellectual groupings in a scholarly debate. However, it is noted here, and argued further elsewhere [20] that supporting the bottom-up detection of similar intellectual groupings should be a major aim of any technology that purports to enable representing and reasoning about debates in knowledge domains. As described in [20], combining ontology-based analysis with graph-based cluster analysis is one viable approach to enabling bottom-up detection of coherent groups of argument. Thus, Figure 5 also introduces an ontological specification for these debate structures that can be automatically detected. This specification is introduced to be able to distinguish ontologically between what is explicitly represented in a top-down manner and what can be detected in a bottom-up manner. The class *ViewpointCluster*[12] is introduced to account for the latter. The ontology specifies that two *ViewpointCluster* instances can be opposed to each other. The assumption here is that opposition between *ViewpointCluster* instances can be determined based on the occurrence of *disputes* relations between individual *Argument* instances that are part of each *ViewpointCluster* instance. Two intuitive criteria have been trialled in [20] for detecting opposing *ViewpointCluster* instances. Using the first criterion, the system infers an opposition relation between two *ViewpointCluster* instances if at least one viewpoint in one cluster has a *disputes* relation with at least one viewpoint

[12]The rationale behind the name is that "viewpoint" is used in [7] as a synonym for "Description", and "Cluster" indicates the central role played by cluster analysis to this task.

```
(def-class Person (#_cdns:SocialAgent))

(def-class Publication (#_cdns:InformationObject)
  ((hasAuthor :type Person)
   (hasTitle :type String)
   (hasYear :type #_time:Year-In-Time)))

(def-class DomainConcept (#_cdns:Concept)
  ((#_cdns:isDefinedIn :type #_cdns:Description)))
```

Figure 6. The specification of the Person, Publication, and DomainConcept classes as subclasses of the cdns:SocialAgent, cdns:InformationObject, and cdns:Concept classes, respectively.

in the other cluster. This criterion is labelled as "weak opposition". Using the second criterion, the system infers an opposition relation between two clusters if more than half (i.e. the majority) of the viewpoints in one cluster have a *disputes* relation with the viewpoints in the other cluster. This criterion is labelled as "strong opposition". Weakly and strongly opposed clusters are related to the appropriate *ViewpointCluster* instance via the *hasOpposingClusterWeak* and *hasOpposingClusterStrong* attributes respectively.

2.4. Person, Publication, and DomainConcept

These classes do not correspond directly to elements of the logic of debate. However, these classes correspond to what [17] refers to as "argument classifiers"—i.e. additional information within the debate, such as who made a particular argument or in what year and publication was the argument put forward, which is useful for the debate map reader. Yoshimi also recognises the special relevance that such additional information may have for computable representations of the debate, where a user may want to query a system to find (e.g.) all the arguments made by a particular author or in a particular journal. Figure 6 shows the specification of *Person* (which is defined as a subclass of *cdns:SocialAgent*), *Publication* (which is defined as a subclass of *cdns:InformationObject*), and *DomainConcept* (which is defined as a subclass of *cdns:Concept*).

Figure 7 shows a semantic-network-like visualisation of the Scholarly Debate Ontology. The figure shows the relationship between classes in the SDO ontology and upper-level classes of the cDnS ontology.

Conclusion and Future Work

This paper described the design of an ontology for representing and reasoning about scholarly debate in academic knowledge domains. The ontology has been used to represent and reason about actual scholarly debates as described in more detail elsewhere [20]. However, what this paper focussed on was the design considerations for the ontology. The paper began by characterising academic domains as settings for the collective construction of knowledge, thus motivating the reuse of the upper-level cDnS ontology. This upper-level ontology acted as a framework for ensuring the design process captured

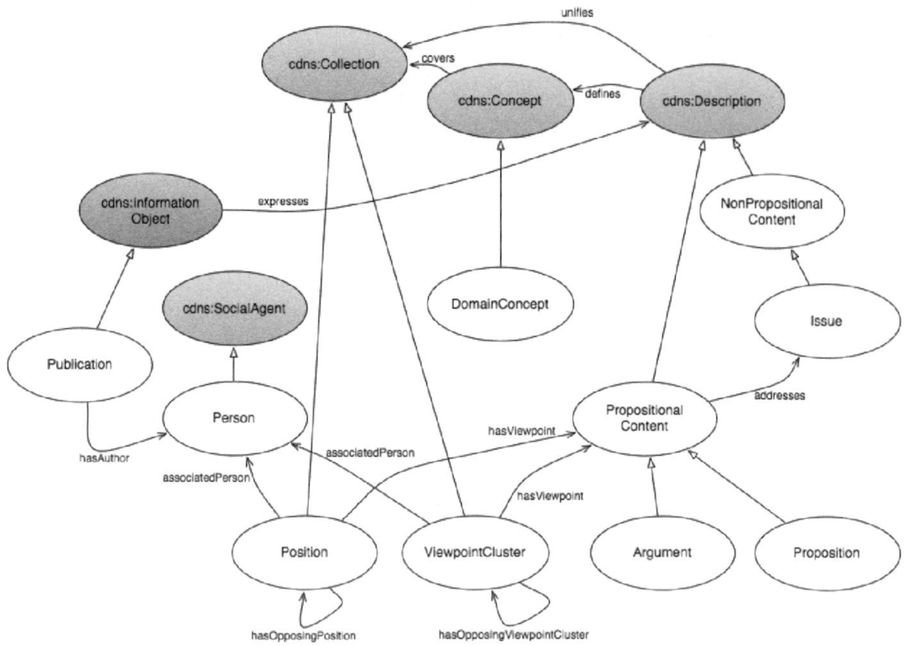

Figure 7. The Scholarly Debate Ontology

the essential elements of debate in knowledge domains. Finally, the paper specified the classes and relations in the Scholarly Debate Ontology.

For the short-term, pragmatic concerns of building an example application, the ontology-based modelling described in [20] was conducted in a centralised, single-person setting, as this enabled rapid prototyping of the proposed approach to knowledge domain analysis. However, in the longer term, decentralised, mass modelling of scholarly material would be necessary to allow the technology to be widely deployed. The scenario of distributed, mass modelling is likely to involve individual authors submitting representations of their papers. Indeed, it is not overly ambitious to envisage a future scenario where authors submit a formal representation of their paper along with the actual paper itself, in much the same manner that they currently submit abstracts as meta-descriptions of the paper. However, it is likely that other users of such a system would contribute models of literature where they are not the original authors. Thus distributed annotation itself presents a conceptual challenge—i.e. the challenge of determining how to deal with multiple, possibly contradictory representations of the same source material. It is clear that in a scholarly discourse there can be competing conceptualisations (descriptions) of reality AND we can have competing interpretations (descriptions) of a publication that expresses conceptualisations of reality. The ideal solution is to explicitly represent both but make a clear ontological distinction between them. The cDnS ontology, with its formal treatment of *situations*, provides a comprehensive framework for solving this problem. As mentioned previously, one instance of *cdns:Situation* can provide the setting or context for another *cdns:Situation* instance. This means that situations can be layered, with one situation having the other within its scope. Future work will seek to exploit the cDnS ontology in this way.

Finally, future work will seek to extend the Scholarly Debate Ontology with a more thorough treatment of intellectual groupings in knowledge domains. In this regard, one extension of the cDnS ontology that gives an extensive treatment of "collectives" could prove beneficial.

Acknowledgements

The work presented here is part of the PhD thesis of the author [20]. Thus the author would like to thank the supervisors of that PhD—Dr. Simon Buckingham Shum, Prof. John Domingue, and Dr. Clara Mancini—for their tireless support of this research endeavour.

References

[1] Chen, C. (2006). "CiteSpace II: Detecting and Visualizing Emerging Trends and Transient Patterns in Scientific Literature." *Journal of the American Society for Information Science and Technology* 57(3): pp. 359–377.

[2] Haase, P., J. Broekstra, M. Ehrig, M. Menken, P. Mika, M. Olko, M. Plechawski, P. Pyszlak, B. Schnizler, R. Siebes, S. Staab and C. Tempich (2004). *Bibster—A Semantics-Based Bibliographic Peer-to-Peer System.* Third International Semantic Web Conference (ISWC 2004), Hiroshima, Japan, 07–11 November 2004, Springer: pp. 122–136.

[3] Kampa, S. (2002). Who are the experts? E-Scholars in the Semantic Web. Department of Electronics and Computer Science, University of Southampton. PhD Thesis.

[4] schraefel, m. c., N. R. Shadbolt, N. Gibbins, S. Harris and H. Glaser (2004). *CS AKTive space: representing computer science in the semantic web.* 13th International Conference on World Wide Web, WWW 2004, New York, NY, USA, 17–22 May 2004, ACM: pp. 384–392.

[5] Buckingham Shum, S., V. Uren, G. Li, B. Sereno and C. Mancini (2007). "Modeling Naturalistic Argumentation in Research Literatures: Representation and Interaction Design Issues." *International Journal of Intelligent Systems, Special Issue on Computational Models of Natural Argument* (Editors: Chris Reed and Floriana Grasso) 22: pp. 17-47.

[6] Gruber, T. R. (1995). "Toward Principles for the Design of Ontologies Used for Knowledge Sharing." International Journal of Human-Computer Studies 43(5–6): pp. 907–928.

[7] Gangemi, A., J. Lehmann and C. Catenacci (2007). *Norms and plans as unification criteria for social collectives.* Normative Multi-agent Systems, Germany, March 18-23, 2007, Internationales Begegnungs- und Forschungszentrum für Informatik.

[8] Atkin, A. (2007). Peirce's Theory of Signs. *The Stanford Encyclopedia of Philosophy (Fall 2007 Edition).* E. N. Zalta, URL = <`http://plato.stanford.edu/archives/fall2007/entries/peirce-semiotics/`> (last accessed on 13 November 2007).

[9] Knorr-Cetina, K. D. (1981). *The Manufacture of Knowledge: An essay on the constructivist and contextual nature of science*, Pergamon Press, ISBN 0080257771.

[10] Driver, R., H. Asoko, J. Leach, E. Mortimer and P. Scott (1994). "Constructing Scientific Knowledge in the Classroom." *Educational Researcher* 23(7): pp. 5–12.

[11] Gangemi, A. (2008). "Norms and plans as unification criteria for social collectives." *Journal of Autonomous Agents and Multi-Agent Systems* 17(1): pp. 70–112.

[12] Lemke, J. L. (1998). Multiplying Meaning: Visual and Verbal Semiotics in Scientific Text. *Reading Science.* J. R. Martin and R. Veel. London, Routledge: pp. 87-113.

[13] Masolo, C., L. Vieu, E. Bottazzi, C. Catenacci, R. Ferrario, A. Gangemi and N. Guarino (2004). *Social Roles and their Descriptions.* Ninth International Conference on the Principles of Knowledge Representation and Reasoning (KR2004), Whistler, Canada, 02–05 June 2004, AAAI Press: pp. 267–277.

[14] Behrendt, W., A. Gangemi, W. Maass and R. Westenthaler (2005). *Towards an Ontology-Based Distributed Architecture for Paid Content.* The Semantic Web: Research and Applications, 2nd European Semantic Web Conference (ESWC 2005), Heraklion, Crete, Greece, 29 May–01 June 2005, Springer-Verlag: pp. 257–271.

[15] Bottazzi, E., C. Catenacci, A. Gangemi and J. Lehmann (2006). "From collective intentionality to intentional collectives: An ontological perspective." *Cognitive Systems Research* (7): pp. 192–208.

[16] Horn, R. E., J. Yoshimi, M. Deering, R. McBride, D. Fleischman, T. DiDonna and J. Wedel (1998). *Mapping great debates: Can computers think? 7 maps and a Handbook.* Bainbridge Island, WA, MacroVU Press, ISBN 1-892637-08-1.

[17] Yoshimi, J. (2004). "Mapping the Structure of Debate." *Informal Logic* 24(1): pp. 1–21.

[18] Horn, R. E. (1998). *Using Argumentation Analysis to Examine History and Status of a Major Debate in Artificial Intelligence and Philosophy.* Fourth International Conference of the International Society for the Study of Argumentation, Amsterdam, Netherlands, 16–19 June 1998: pp. 375–381.

[19] Horn, R. E. (2003). Infrastructure for Navigating Interdisciplinary Debates: Critical Decisions for Representing Argumentation. *Visualizing Argumentation.* P. Kirschner, S. Buckingham Shum and C. Carr. London, Springer: pp. 165–184.

[20] Benn, N.J.L. (2009). "Modelling Scholarly Debate: Conceptual Foundations for Knowledge Domain Analysis Technology." PhD Thesis, available as: Technical Report KMI-09-04, Knowledge Media Institute, The Open University, UK. URL=<http://kmi.open.ac.uk/publications/pdf/kmi-09-04.pdf>

Formal Ontology in Information Systems
A. Galton and R. Mizoguchi (Eds.)
IOS Press, 2010

doi:10.3233/978-1-60750-535-8-373

Ontologies for Distributed Command and Control Messaging

Duc N. NGUYEN [a], Joseph B. KOPENA [a], Boon Thau LOO [b], William C. REGLI [a,1]
[a] *Drexel University, Philadelphia, PA, USA*
[b] *University of Pennsylvania, Philadelphia, PA, USA*

Abstract. This paper presents the development of a set of ontologies for use in messaging systems within military and emergency first responder command and control applications. These ontologies are used to annotate and subscribe to messages within a content delivery and service discovery middleware connecting sensors, services, and agents on the network. Ontologies serve an important role in this middleware in providing for flexible addressing and querying that increases the decoupling between senders and receivers afforded by the middleware. This is particularly important in the target applications, which feature heterogenous components and software versions spanning development organizations and deployment time. Discussed here are application uses, development methodology, evaluation criteria, and other notes on these ontologies and their creation. The goal of this paper is to provide useful input to others engaged in similar development efforts.

1. Introduction

Although arguably tantalizingly close to real world, commonplace use, computerized, handheld, mobile command and control systems for dismounted warfighters—troops on the ground—as well as for emergency first responders—police, fire, and emergency medical personnel—are still largely open areas of research and development. These applications aim to improve collaboration and situational awareness among such users by providing tools for geopositioning, map annotation, messaging, plan development and monitoring, media sharing, and other tasks. Many prototype systems have been developed and even deployed, but many hurdles remain to be overcome.

Among these are the challenging, dynamic environments in which these systems must operate, with minimal maintenance, reconfiguration, or deployment overhead. Great emphasis in developing such systems has been placed on the disruption prone nature of the wireless communication technology needed to meet mobility and platform requirements. High latency, low bandwidth, and frequent link disruptions are commonplace and require continual adaptation. Systems must also tolerate frequent hardware and other failures, as well as incorporation of dynamically introduced nodes and components.

Less commonly addressed but as important are issues of interoperability. Particularly in the case of first responder applications, it must be expected that systems must incorporate and work alongside components and systems developed by a number of ven-

[1] `dn53@drexel.edu`, `tjkopena@cs.drexel.edu`, `boonloo@cis.upenn.edu`, `regli@drexel.edu`

dors and configured and deployed by a variety of authorities, all with differing structure, policies, and procedures. Similarly, in many cases systems must conceivably interoperate with components developed and deployed well before the lifetime of current elements, such as sensor or communication infrastructure emplaced years before use.

The authors' OntoNet [8] project aims to address many of these issues through content delivery and service discovery middleware. By providing for message publishing and subscription, OntoNet intends to provide a flexible, abstract platform for connecting sensors, services, and agents on the network. Such middleware eases system development by reducing the need for application developers to directly address and develop protocols and techniques for networking in disruption prone environments.

OntoNet also promotes flexibility via a knowledge-based approach to message addressing and matching. Messages are tagged with metadata in the Resource Description Framework (RDF) [10], while subscriptions are registered and matched as Web Ontology Language (OWL) [4] class expressions. Sets of ontologies are used to structure that metadata and queries, providing supports for the messages, services, and other entities of particular application domains.

This paper describes the development of ontologies for use in OntoNet for military and first responder command and control applications. These applications are briefly presented, along with development methodology, evaluation criteria, and other notes on these ontologies and their creation. The goal of this paper is to provide useful input to others engaged in similar development efforts.

2. Motivating Scenarios

Although many elements of the OntoNet project are fairly generic, particular focus is given to supporting mobile, handheld command and control (C2) systems. Both settings share many similarities in terms of feasible computing platforms, challenging networking environments, and other aspects. Although different, they also share many core structures in their underlying data and messaging patterns, and consequently the ontologies developed to support messaging in those arenas. Both settings are briefly described here.

2.1. Military Command and Control

According to the Military Decision Making Process [7], the military planning process typically starts with a commander issuing orders to staff to gather data, intelligence, and issuing warning orders to lower level units involved in the operation. During this information gathering phase, the commander incorporates data and other information sources such as unit strength and readiness, terrain information, enemy capabilities, civilian areas, and past enemy activities. This usually requires collaboration among command staff and lower echelons along with querying external data sources. Upon completion of the planning phases, the orders are disseminated to subordinate units to be executed.

During operations monitoring, commanders monitor the situation from information flowing up from subordinate units and other information sources. As the operation evolves, commanders monitoring the situation collaborate between the echelons and issue updates and new orders. An alert such as an IED detection or enemy ambush issued from individual dismount soldiers is sent up to their superior commanders. Such alerts may necessitate a change in the plan and commanders will update subordinates accordingly. Events from external sources and higher echelons such as missile reports also get filtered down to lower echelons and may cause changes to plans.

Similarly, lower echelon units may exchange their own collaboration messages and situation update information among themselves. This may be as simple as automated, GPS-based position updates and vital statistics reports, or as complex as ad hoc plan annotations on common map displays, shared media such as video feeds,

2.2. Emergency First Responders

Many organizations maintain response teams for chemical, biological, or radiological (CBR) incidents, such as industrial or transport accidents. Unfortunately, current best practices largely use non-integrated and redundant tools applied via manual processes. Even among well provisioned teams, critical data collection is frequently performed via clipboard and pen—a difficult task in full protective suits. Automating these processes may significantly improve team performance and efficiency but faces several challenges.

Among these are basic network connectivity and management issues. A mix of mobile and fixed nodes may be in use, fielded by a number of different organizations and potentially using low power, low cost radios. Importantly, team members must be able to operate and work together before infrastructure may be deployed, as well as in environments where disconnections are frequent and they must operate independently. These constraints may imply complex, heterogenous network topologies spanning organizations and employing mobile ad hoc and mesh networking techniques as necessary while also utilizing infrastructure such as base stations as available to gain higher performance and wider resource accessibility.

2.3. Command and Control Relationship

A key aspect of OntoNet's approach is that sensors or software generate messages with associated metadata which is used to deliver those messages to the appropriate destination(s). This functionality can be used to support many tasks such as data and alert dissemination, service requests, and content retrieval. By addressing messages and destinations via declarative, ontology driven languages, the above interoperability challenges may be met with flexible, extensible, formal reasoning mechanisms. Applying that query based messaging paradigm in distributed, robust middleware also decouples message senders and receivers to a great degree, promoting rapid system integration and improved manageability.

3. Background and Related Work

This section details related work on the development of ontologies for their respective domains. Military Ontologies have been created and incorporated into upper and mid-level ontologies. Sensor network ontologies are being developed to augment existing data formats for better automated inference in support for discovery, matching, composition, and search. These domains, while different, have similar qualities with regard to the command hierarchy, communications infrastructure, and data flows.

3.1. Military Ontologies

Anderson *et. al*[1] present an ontology of the basic categories and relationships needed to represent modern military organization. The key features of the modern military organization ontology is the echelon structure and the subordination properties associated with a modern military organization. This ontology was merged into the Suggested Upper Merged Ontology (SUMO) [11].

The typical *is_a* relationship implies a hierarchy of concepts. When applied to a modern military organization, the colloquial usage does not apply for creating hierarchies of military echelons. Military echelons are related using a *subEchelon* relationship. The *subEchelon* relationship state one object is a subechelon of another, for example, a Company is a *subEchelon* of a Battalion. Furthermore, there are military units that are considered equivalent levels in the military echelon. For example, Regiments (found in French brigades) are typically equivalent in size and function as Battalions, *i.e.*, regiments and battalions are both sub-echelons of a Brigade. There are also differences in terminology; *e.g.*, a Russian infantry division is different in strength than a US infantry division. Figure 1 depicts this subechelon structure and composition of the modern military organization from the division to the squad/section levels.

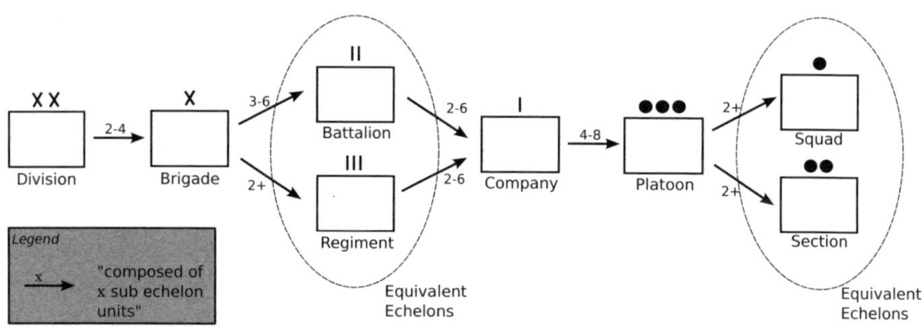

Figure 1. The military echelon structure from division to squad/section.

The resulting knowledge-base created by Bowman *et. al* [3] to aid commanders in developing courses of action with respect to principles of war and military operations. The goal for this work was to construct a full ontology to determine the focal point of an opposing force, termed the "center-of-gravity" of the enemy. This is accomplished with a large enough ontology such that sufficient inferences can be made. The goal of OntoNet is to provide reasoning capabilities that balance complexity and robustness of queries.

3.2. First Responder and Governmental Formats

There are several standardization efforts to create a data format for inter-agency emergency messages that span local, state, federal and non-governmental organizations. EDXL[2] is a suite of OASIS standards for emergency response messaging between multiple juristictions and organizational levels. The suite includes standards for distribution

[2] `http://xml.coverpages.org/edxl.html`

(EDXL-DE[3]), message standards (EDXL-RM[4]), hospital status (EDXL-HAVE), and alerting protocols (CAP). The US Department of Justice is sponsoring an effort to provide a common interchange format between jurisdictions with the Global Justics XML Data Model[5]. These messaging formats were created so that agencies have a common standard for interoperability. These message standards do not, however, enable automated understanding and composition of the messages without a richer ontology backing the formatting.

The OpenGIS Sensor Model Language (SensorML) [2] is a specification for geometric, dynamic and observational characteristics of sensors and sensor systems. While the goal is to provide a data format for specifying sensors, sensor systems, and processes, SensorML can be encoded for the Semantic Web.

The Universal Core (UCore)[6] is a data model set forth by the U.S. government for intelligence and Department of Defence (DoD) agencies. The primary goal of UCore is to facilitate interoperability through common data formats and ontologies between government agencies. It provides a messaging framework for packaging data for dissemination. The key piece of UCore is the shared basic concepts of who, what when and where in the domain of usage. This format does include basic representations for core types and relationships between them. A limitation with this format is the lack a richer representation that describes the relationships and entity types. For instance, without context a "father-son" *HasFamilialRelationTo* relationship type does not have any difference than a "uncle-nephew" *HasFamilialRelationTo* relationship.

3.3. Sensor Network Ontologies

The interchange formatting community is not in the dark about backing data formats with descriptive meaning. There are efforts that aim to incorporate a backing ontology or including expressivity into the data models.

Leveraging the descriptive power of ontologies in a sensor networks and systems dates dates back to 2003 with IrisNet [5]. This work envisioned heterogeneous sensors being deployed worldwide and accessed via the web. The key feature of this architecture is the ability to collect and query data received from the sensors from a single interface.

More recently, Sheth *et. al* [13] are working to combine the efforts of the Open Geospatial Consortium and the W3C's Semantic Web activities to create a Semantic Sensor Web. This integration effort adds RDF annotations to sensor data which is then consumed and visualized in a single application interface.

4. Methodology

This section describes the process for developing the ontologies used for OntoNet's applications. The goal is to provide an ontology that balances expressivity and complexity with a bias towards reducing expressivity (where possible) in favor of minimizing complexity. The approach to developing these ontologies roughly follows the procedures outlined by Grüninger and Fox [6] and Noy and McGuinness [12].

[3]`http://docs.oasis-open.org/emergency/edxl-de/v1.0/EDXL-DE\_Spec\_v1.0.pdf`

[4]`http://docs.oasis-open.org/emergency/edxl-rm/v1.0/EDXL-RM-SPEC-V1.0.pdf`

[5]`http://it.ojp.gov/default.aspx?area=nationalInitiatives\&page=1013`

[6]`https://ucore.gov`

4.1. Competency Questions

The competency questions defined in [6] and [12], provide a starting point for developing an ontology. These questions could be considered *use cases* for the application of the ontologies. The scenarios described above in Section 2 describes the application domain of the ontologies for OntoNet. From these scenarios two generic competency questions arise pertaining to the delivery of messages and the organizational structure of the source and destinations of the messages:

- Given the characteristics of the contents of the message, where should these messages be delivered?
- Given the characteristics of the host and the contents of the message, what messages should the host subscribe to?

Domain dependent, specific questions focus on the characteristics of the messages and the senders and recipients of the messages. During an operation, units at the lower echelons (*e.g.*platoons and dismounted soldiers) provide updates of their current position and status to their peers and superior units (*e.g.*battalion command). These position reports and messages are sent as multicast messages where units interested in these types of messages would subscribe to messages of this type. A corresponding competency question for battalion command to subscribe to these messages would be:

- What position reports are from my subordinate units?

Additionally, battalion command and company commanders may request to receive messages of higher priority such as those alerting of events such as ambushes or course corrections. Questions corresponding to these requests would be:

- Which alert messages are about attacks on units part of the First Battalion?
- Which alert messages are about improvised explosive device detections?

The above competency questions cover subscribing to classes of messages from certain units. There are situations where a dismount soldier would issue a request for specific services such as a medevac for wounded soldiers or field maintenance on damaged vehicles. Competency questions for these situations would revolve around describing the event and the units issuing the request and the descriptions of the units at the destination.

- Which medevac units can evacuate wounded soldiers?
- What unit can provide artillery support for location X?
- What kind of unit can provide field maintenance to damaged vehicles?

From these competency questions, the ontologies developed for OntoNet will include information on different of source and destinations based on characteristics of the units such as the roles they play and their capabilities. Furthermore, the ontologies will include information on the characteristics of the messages being transmitted throughout the system.

4.2. Terminology

The classes of the ontologies in OntoNet describe the kinds of messages and the units (the source and destinations of these messages). Instances of these classes correspond to the specific entities in the applications.

Senders and receivers in the military domains correspond with units along the military hierarchy. The military mid-level ontologies in SUMO provide terms and descriptions for units in the military hierarchy including: *Division*, *Brigade*, *Battalion*, *Company-Military*, *Platoon*. The units will also have specific roles and functionality assigned to them such as infantry, mechanized , engineers, medical support, field maintenance, etc.

The messages are classified by type of message: *Orders*, *Reports*, *Requests*, and *Alerts*. The properties of the messages include information about the message such as the time, the sender, and a description of the message. The descriptions of messages pertain to events such as ambushes, artillery fire, wounded soldiers, evacuation requests, and so on.

5. Ontology

The terminology used in the OntoNet ontologies leverage existing upper and mid-level ontologies: SUMO and OpenCyc [7]. Not only does this approach simplify development of the ontology, but it also aids in integration with other products using the same ontologies. The mid-level ontologies provide an abstract subsuming representation for the domain dependent ontologies and instances. The structure of the entire ontology advances the notion of a *background ontology* and a *specific ontology*.

The background ontology is the ontology that specifies the basic unit hierarchy and its roles. The OntoNet military ontology has the concepts, brigade, battalion, company, platoon, squad, etc. which are subsumed by the Unit concept. This ontology is based on the military ontology incorporated into SUMO.

The specific ontology refers to the individuals and instances of units used in the application. For example, the 4th Infantry Brigade is a subechelon of the 7th Division, and the Medical Company is a subechelon of the 235 Support Battalion are instances of Brigade and Battalion.

5.1. Concepts and Concept Relationships.

The unit concepts and relationships uses the ModernMilitaryOrganization ontology developed in [1] and subsequently included in SUMO. The OWL version of the SUMO defines the subEchelon as a subproperty of subOrganization. The subOrganization property is classified as a TransitiveProperty in OWL. The subEchelon relationship defines a unit as a subOrganization of another.

Unit Ontology: This organizational classification defines the hierarchy of the oranization based on scenario specific characteristics, *e.g.*military chain of command, communications chain of command. This characterization can be used for defining source and/or destination of messages. MilitaryUnits, depicted in Figure 2a, represent the ontology of units from division down to squad. The *is-a* relationship between units denotes that every Echelon in the military hierarchy is a Unit class. Where there are cycles between Classes (*e.g.*Regiment, Squadron, Battalion), these units are equivalent classes. Different command hierarchies have different names for equivalent sized unit structures. For example, the Regiment is a command structure typically used by the

[7] http://opencyc.org/

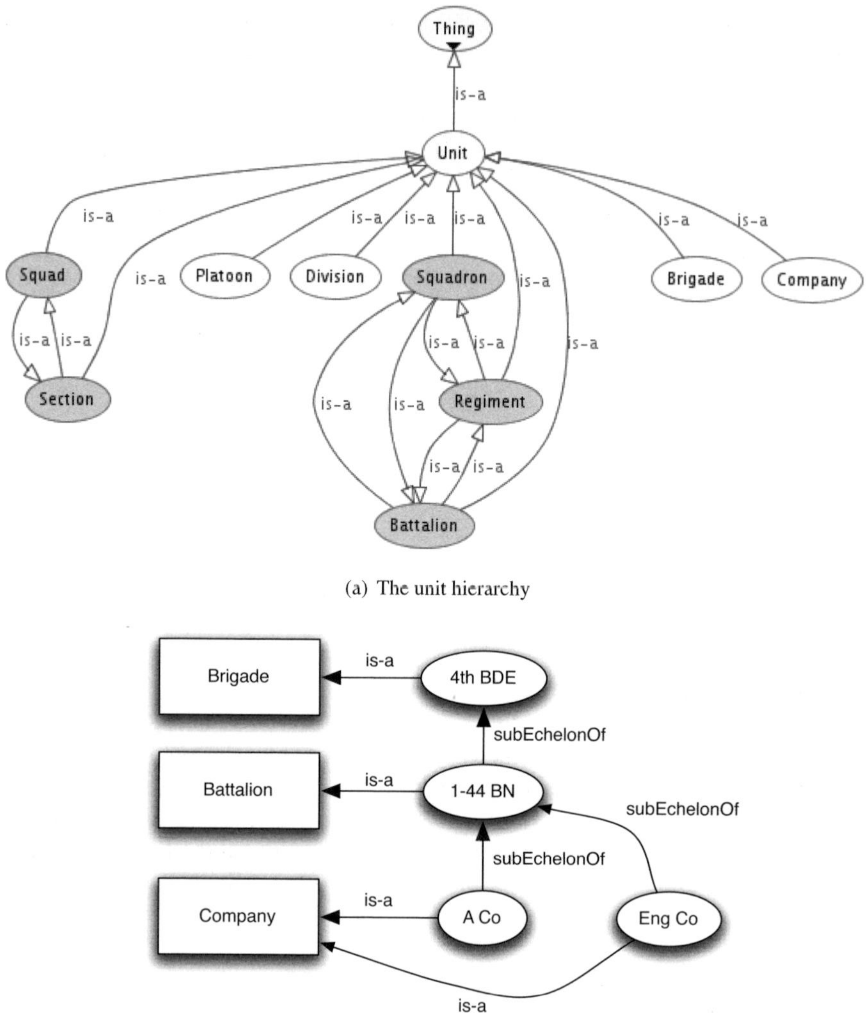

(a) The unit hierarchy

(b) An excerpt of the unit ontology

Figure 2. The unit hierarchy and an excerpt of the unit ontology demonstrating the *subEchelon* structure.

French Military and has roughly the same size and structure as a Battalion (US Army) and Squadron (US Navy). The unit instances are related to one another via the *subEchelon* Transitive Property. An excerpt of the unit ontology is shown in Figure 2b. The `1-44 BN` is a battalion instance and a *subEchelon* of the `4th BDE`, a brigade. Additionally, `A Co` and `Eng Co` are companies and are *subEchelons* of the `1-44 BN`.

Unit Type Ontology: This is a taxonomy of the types of units in the organization. Rather than defining the structure of communications, this type ontology is used to describe the units themselves. For example, a unit can be a medical support unit in a military organization or a HazMat team for emergency responders organization.

Unit Capabilities Ontology: This ontology specifies the capabilities of units. It provides a structure for reasoning over specific capabilities of units. For example, a re-con unit in a military organization can provide a target for fire support and a medevac helicoptor can evacuate an injured person to a hospital.

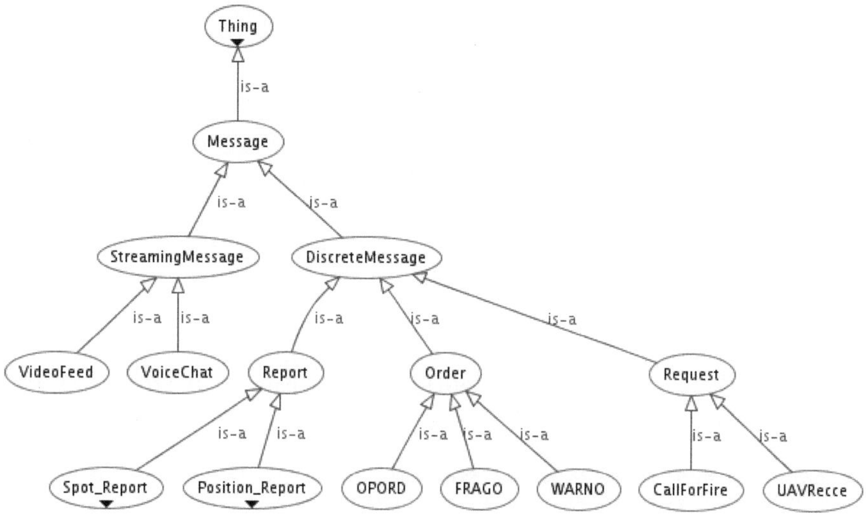

Figure 3. The message hierarchy

Message Type Ontology: This ontology describes the various types of messages sent and received in the system. For example, a request for fire or position or spot report. The classes of messages (Figure 3) are broken down into discrete and streaming messages, and further into the types of messages: Orders, Requests, and Reports.

Message Contents Ontology: This ontology describes the contents of the messages such as position information, CBR payloads, and enemy movement events. Events are part of the message type and message contents ontologies. They describe the type of event that the message is reporting about. The messages have associated descriptions. In general, all messages will have a sender, intended receiver (if a direct message), a description of the type of message, a description of the message contents.

5.2. Queries

With the ontology described above, we can now formally state the comptetancy questions in the form of description logic queries. OntoNet [9] supports multiple matching models based on the three components: Messages, destinations, and ontologies. *Receiver querying* is the typical message model where destinations publish queries that are matched against message descriptions. An example query based on the military command and control ontologies would enable battalion headquarters to monitor the locations and status of subordinate units at the company and platoon levels.

The following description matches position reports from direct subordinates, *i.e.* the companies directly below the `1-44 Battalion` and not from the platoons.

$$BNPosRptQuery \equiv PosRpt \sqcap \exists sender.(Company \sqcap \exists subEchelon.\{\text{1-44\_IN\_BN}\})$$

Battalion command units would also subscribe to Spot Report messages about various events. The most general would be subscribing to receive all Spot Reports, *i.e.* from companies as well as platoons.

$$SpotRpt\_ArmoredVehicle \equiv Spot\_Report \sqcap \exists subEchelon.\{\text{1-44\_IN\_BN}\}$$

On the other hand, a medevac unit interested in being alerted of wounded soldiers in the field would subscribe to messages where units are attacked.

$$SpotRpt\_Attacks \equiv Spot\_Report \sqcap \exists activityAbout.EnemyEvent \sqcap$$

Likewise, a field maintenance unit with the role of reparing and retrieving damaged vehicles is only interested in receiving Spot Reports about attacks on armored vehicles:

$$SpotRpt\_ArmoredVehicle \equiv Spot\_Report \sqcap \exists activityAbout.EnemyEvent \sqcap \exists sender.(\exists hasRole.ArmoredArtilleryRole)$$

Conversely, with *message querying* the messages have include queries that match the descriptions of the destinations. There are situations where a specific message would not be covered by a receiver query. For example, a message calling for a medevac might not be a spot report but rather, just a position report with metadata to deliver the message to units that can provide medical evacuations. The metadata describing the receiver would look like this:

$$Receiver \equiv Unit \sqcap \exists hasRole.MedicalRole$$

Likewise, specific requests would need to be delivered to units with certain capabilities. An example spot report message of a company from the `1-44 Battalion` contains an alert of an ambush by the enemy. This message query states the message needs to be delivered to superior units and also units that can provide fire support.

$$FireSupportReqMsgQuery \equiv Unit \sqcap \exists hasRole.ArmoredArtilleryRole$$

6. Application Examples

To demonstrate the use of the OntoNet ontologies consider the following application for Command and control during a military patrol. The command hierarchy consists of a battalion with 4 infantry companies, a reconnaissance troop, a squadron of tanks, a medical support company, and a field maintenance crew. This hierarchy is defined as a set of OWL individuals. For example, an abbreviated description of the battalion is shown in OWL in Figure 4.

```
<Battalion rdf:about="#1-44_IN_BN">
  <rdf:type rdf:resource="&owl;Thing"/>
  <subEchelon rdf:resource="#4_IBCT_US"/>
  <hasRole rdf:resource="#InfantryRole"/>
</Battalion>
```

Figure 4. An example 1-44 Infantry Battalion description.

During the planning phase of the operation the commander of the battalion will need to gather readiness and capabilities of units under his command. Commander constructs standing queries to be alerted of events via Spot Reports and position reports.

The support companies also construct standing queries to receive reports such, for example, the company medic requires spot reports for the wounded and the field maintenance company requires spot reports for attacks on vehicles.

Once the planning is complete and the communications infrastructure is in place, the operation commences. During the patrol, the units in the field automatically send continuous status updates in the form of position reports. These updates are broadcasted to their unit commander, *e.g.*the platoons send their positions to the company leader which are combined to form a single position report for the company to be delivered to the battalion CP.

A unit will issue a Spot Report for events such as attacks or changes in course. The spot report would contain metadata describing the sender, receiver, and content of the message. The OntoNet middleware will deliver the messages to units subscribed to those message classes. The messages are also delivered to the destinations described in the receiver. An example full Spot Report of a unit being attacked is shown in Figure 5. This message will be delivered to the battalion CP, and the company medic because those units subscribed to those messages. The message is also delivered to any unit that has the role of being armored artillery as specified by the `receiver` property.

```
<Spot_Report rdf:about="#Msg_SpotRpt_ArmoredInd">
  <rdf:type rdf:resource="&owl;Thing"/>
  <sender rdf:resource="#SP_BTRY_4-4_FA_BN_4_IBCT_US_"/>
  <activityAbout rdf:resource="#EnemyAmbushEvent_i"/>
  <receiver rdf:resource="#RcvrDesc"/>
  <hasLocation rdf:resource="#position3"/>
</Spot_Report>

<owl:Thing rdf:about="#RcvrDesc">
  <rdf:type>
    <owl:Class>
      <owl:intersectionOf rdf:parseType="Collection">
        <rdf:Description rdf:about="#Unit"/>
        <owl:Restriction>
          <owl:onProperty rdf:resource="#hasRole"/>
          <owl:someValuesFrom rdf:resource="#ArmoredArtilleryRole"/>
        </owl:Restriction>
      </owl:intersectionOf>
    </owl:Class>
  </rdf:type>
</owl:Thing>
```

Figure 5. An example Spot Report with a description of the intended destinations.

7. Conclusion

OntoNet's knowledge-based approach to message addressing and matching significantly increases the potential decoupling between message senders and receivers enabled by such middleware. This is particularly important in the target military and first responder settings, which may include many diparate components and ad hoc interactions over time. Knowledge-based reasoning does incur additional computational costs over simpler addressing schemes, but this downside is more than matched by improvements in rapid reconfiguration, system extension, and interoperability that this approach supports. Future work in OntoNet includes determining the exact extent of these costs, particularly on hardware platforms typical for these applications, and possibilities in leveraging the structure of both the core ontologies and reasoning requirements to optimize reasoning.

References

[1] W. Anderson and B. Peterson. An ontology of modern military organizations and their structure. In *Workshop on the IEEE Standard Upper Ontology (IJCAI01)*, 2001.
[2] M. Botts. OpenGIS sensor model language (SensorML) implementation specification. Technical Report 07-000, Open Geospatial Consortium, Jul 2007.
[3] M. Bowman, A. Lopez Jr, and G. Tecuci. Ontology Development for Military Applications. In *Proceedings of the SouthEastern Regional ACM Conference, Atlanta, GA*. Citeseer, 2001.
[4] M. Dean, G. Schreiber, et al. OWL Web Ontology Language reference. World Wide Web Consortium (W3C), February 2004. `http://www.w3.org/TR/2004/REC-owl-ref-20040210/`.
[5] P. B. Gibbons, B. Karp, Y. Ke, S. Nath, and S. Seshan. Irisnet: An architecture for a worldwide sensor web. *IEEE Pervasive Computing*, 2(4), October–December 2003.
[6] M. Grüninger and M. Fox. Methodology for the Design and Evaluation of Ontologies. In *The Workshop on Basic Ontological Issues in Knowledge Sharing*, 1995.
[7] Headquarters. Army planning and orders production. Technical Report FM 5-0, Department of US Army, January 2005.
[8] J. B. Kopena and B. T. Loo. Ontonet: Scalable knowledge based networking. In *In Proceedings of the 4th International Workshop on Networking Meets Databases*, 2008.
[9] J. B. Kopena, W. C. Regli, and B. T. Loo. Message models and aggregation in knowledge based middleware for rich sensor systems. In *In Proceedings of the 6th International Workshop on Data Management for Sensor Networks*, 2009. .
[10] O. Lassila, R. Swick, et al. Resource Description Framework (RDF) Model and Syntax Specification. World Wide Web Consortium (W3C), 1999. `http://www.w3.org/TR/1999/REC-rdf-syntax-19990222/`.
[11] I. Niles and A. Pease. Towards a standard upper ontology. *International Conference on Formal Ontology in Information Systems*, October 2001.
[12] N. F. Noy and D. L. McGuinness. Ontology development 101: A guide to creating your first ontology. Technical Report KSL-01-05, Stanford University Knowledge Systems Laboratory, March 2001.
[13] A. Sheth, C. Henson, and S. S. Sahoo. Semantic sensor web. *IEEE Internet Computing*, 12(4):78–83, July–August 2008.

Biomedical and Chemical Ontologies II

Formal Ontology in Information Systems
A. Galton and R. Mizoguchi (Eds.)
IOS Press, 2010

doi:10.3233/978-1-60750-535-8-387

Realism for scientific ontologies

Michel Dumontier [a,1] and Robert Hoehndorf [b,c]
[a] *Department of Biology, Institute of Biochemistry and School of Computer Science, Carleton University*
[b] *European Bioinformatics Institute*
[c] *Institute for Medical Informatics, Statistics and Epidemiology (IMISE), University of Leipzig*

Abstract. Science aims to develop an accurate understanding of reality through a variety of rigorously empirical and formal methods. Ontologies are used to formalize the meaning of terms within a domain of discourse. The Basic Formal Ontology (BFO) is an ontology of particular importance in the biomedical domains, where it provides the top-level for numerous ontologies, including those admitted as part of the OBO Foundry collection. The BFO requires that all classes in an ontology are actually instantiated in reality. Despite the fact that it is hard to show whether entities of some kind exist or do not exist in reality (especially for unobservable entities like elementary particles), this criterion fails to satisfy the need of scientists to communicate their findings and theories unambiguously. We discuss the problems that arise due to the BFO's realism criterion and suggest viable alternatives.

Keywords. Realism, biomedical ontology, philosophy of science

1. Introduction

Science aims to better understand reality through a variety of rigorously empirical (observation and experimentation) and formal methods (mathematics, statistics and logic). Reality, however, is hard to investigate due to intrinsic stochasticity in addition to unknown, inaccessible, and multiple levels of complexity. To reduce this complexity, contemporary scientists develop tractable experimental or computational models of reality that provide a slightly more controlled environment in which experiments may be carried. Indeed, scientific models of reality provide great insight into otherwise complex real world entities, and more importantly, may predict the existence of yet unobserved entities with detailed descriptions of their innate structure, qualities and roles and functions.

Increasingly in the last decade, scientists have engaged in the building of ontologies for the specific purpose of knowledge management and knowledge discovery – that through common understanding of terms, scientific data and findings could be consistently annotated thus promoting data integration and exchange across heterogeneous representations, and support advanced methods for symbolic and numeric data mining. The Basic Formal Ontology (BFO) [16] is one of several foundational ontologies that is guiding the development of dozens of biomedical domain ontologies. Formal ontology aims

[1]Corresponding Author: Michel Dumontier, michel_dumontier@carleton.ca.

to provide a specifcation of the meaning of terms within a vocabulary [18]. Ontologies that use the BFO as its upper level ontology may be considered for inclusion into the OBO Foundry [44], provided that the ontology is orthogonal to other candidate ontologies. A key criterion for BFO-compliant ontologies is that they employ a particular form of realism, termed here *BFO-realism*, which, among other things, insists that classes in the ontologies must have instances in reality.

Leaving philosophical debate aside, we must ask ourselves whether the criteria for realist ontologies used in the OBO Foundry lead to ontologies that are useful for scientific applications and for scientific communication. In particular, we believe that scientific hypotheses, categories of objects which cannot (yet) be shown to exist, and specifications of categories of objects are used in communications amongst scientists and should be represented and formally described in ontologies. Ontologies that are exclusively built upon classes that have instances in reality face the problem of representing these issues and fail to support interoperability.

Here, we discuss the kind of realism employed by the BFO and by the OBO Foundry ontologies with regard to its adequacy for scientific research, and propose an alternative to solve some of the problems we identify.

2. Realism

In its simplest form, realism corresponds to the belief that "there is a real world existing independently of us" [41], a world constituted of objective facts. These facts exist independently of our minds and independently of the representations we create of them, they exist completely independent of us.

Realism is not identical with or implies a theory of truth. In particular, realism is not identical to the correspondence theory of truth. Realism is not an epistemic theory, nor does realism prefer a form of representing reality. "Realism does not say how things are but only that there is a way that they are" [41].

Realism can be contrasted with idealism, which is the philosophical view that the nature of reality depends on human minds and perception. Idealism is often derived from the observation that the only epistemic basis we have for claims about the external world are our perceptual experiences, or that "[a]ny cognitive state occurs as part of a set of cognitive states and within a cognitive system" [41]. Various arguments for idealism in the context of formal ontology have already been discussed and rejected [41,43], and we will not add to this discussion here. Instead, we will focus the discussion on realism about universals and its role in the construction of formal ontologies.

Depending on what kind of object is assumed to exist, different kinds of realism can be distinguished. Realism about universals exerts the belief that universals (entities that may be instantiated in many things) exist. A universal is an entity which "is of such a nature as to be predicated of many subjects" [3]. They are the things to which the general terms in utterances correspond. Whether universals *exist* is an old problem in philosophy [27].

Two major forms of realism about universals can be distinguished, Platonic and Aristotelian realism. In Platonic realism, universals exist in a realm of their own, are not tied to space and time, and only some of these universals are actually instantiated in our world.

According to Aristotelian realism, universals exist *in re*, i.e., in their instances. Therefore, according to Aristotelian realism, universals are in space and time. For example, the universal *Chair* (or chair-ness) is present in all chairs which existed in the past, exist now and will exist in the future. In Aristotelian realism, universals and their instances share a symbiotic relationship; one cannot exist without the other. In particular, there are no universals which have no instance in reality.

For example, *Unicorn* is not a universal in the Aristotelian sense, because it has no instances in reality (to the best of our knowledge, because only depictions and descriptions of the unicorn can be found, and the unicorn is understood to be a creature of fantasy). As Aristotelian universals exist in their instances, and no instances exist, the universal *Unicorn* does not exist.

In its defense of realism against idealism and other anti-realist philosophies, Smith [43] proposes the principle to use Aristotelian universals as a basis for building ontologies:

> Bad ontologies are (*inter alia*) those whose general terms lack the relation to corresponding universals in reality, and thereby also to corresponding instances.
> Good ontologies are reality representations, and the fact that such representations are possible is shown by the fact that, as is documented in our scientific textbooks, very many of them have already been achieved, though of course always only at some specific level of granularity and to some specific degree of precision, detail and completeness.

In physics, the Higgs boson [21] is a fundamental particle predicted by the Standard Model of physics [35], and since no instances are known, *Higgs boson* may not be an Aristotelian universal. In chemistry, molecules that are not known to exist, but are described through chemical specifications may also not qualify as Aristotelian universals. The consequences of applying this principle to the development of ontologies is, that categories such as *Higgs boson* or chemicals which are not believed to exist (yet), must not be included in a scientific ontology [46]:

> Designer drugs are conceived, modeled, and described long before they are successfully synthesized, and the plans of pharmaceutical companies may contain putative references to the corresponding chemical universals long before there are instances in reality. But again: such descriptions and plans can be perfectly well apprehended even within terminologies and ontologies conceived as relating exclusively to what is real. Descriptions and plans do, after all, exist. On the other hand it would be an error to include in a scientific ontology of drugs terms referring to pharmaceutical products which do not yet (and may never) exist, solely on the basis of plans and descriptions. Rather, such terms should be included precisely at the point where the corresponding instances do indeed exist in reality, exactly in accordance with our proposals above.

This principle has subsequently been adopted by the OBO Foundry ontologies built on the Basic Formal Ontology (BFO) [16], and is being followed, to the extent possible, by ontologies still under development such as the Ontology of Biomedical Investigations (OBI) [7] and the Information Artifact Ontology (IAO) [14]. These ontologies must only contain classes and use relations that are based on Aristotelian universals. BFO-based ontologies cannot have classes which have no instances in reality.

3. Applications of ontologies in science

To understand whether BFO's criterion to use Aristotelian universals for building ontologies indeed leads to *good* ontologies, we must answer the question whether the use of this principle leads to ontologies that are better suited to solve the problems that ontologies are designed to solve.

Biomedical ontologies have been pursued to increase the accuracy of capturing biological knowledge, whether through the semantic annotation of data, or by representing the outcomes of biological experiments. Over 150 controlled vocabularies and ontologies are now available through the NCBO BioPortal [6] and include ontologies to describe scientific processes such as experimentation, the formulation and testing of hypothesis, and the reporting of scientific results in publications or scientific databases. Ultimately, ontologies serve as a means for knowledge management and knowledge discovery, exemplified by formalized domain-specific languages that are in use in various disciplines, in particular chemistry [9] or molecular biology [23], and sophisticated knowledge representation for model organism biology [47], or in capturing the specific response to drugs based on genetic background [11].

3.1. Database interoperability

Ontologies such as the Gene Ontology (GO) [4] have been designed to facilitate interoperability between different research communities, each of which used a slightly different terminology. This required tedious and potentially erroneous mappings to be created and maintained. Established in 1998, the Gene Ontology Consortium has pursued the development of an ontology to formally and consistently specify the meaning of terms used to describe the processes, functions and cellular locations of gene products. Teams of curators in different model organism projects link gene products to their corresponding function, localization and biological process. Having a common terminological basis has certainly helped improve the progress of bioinformatics in function prediction by identifying putative relations across new or integrated experimental data [37].

Where GO terms refer to categories whose existence has been demonstrated in scientific reports, the criterion of using Aristotelian universals is adequate. However, with more than 25,000 categories in the GO, it is unclear whether all GO categories have been demonstrated to have instances. Even if this were the case, the Gene Ontology and other OBO Foundry [44] ontologies are increasingly being used for other purposes, including hypothesis generation [38] or literature retrieval [10]. As discussed below, these tasks put new and unexpected demands on the ontologies.

3.2. Scientific discourse and hypotheses

Scientific discourse deals with the written or spoken communication of scientific investigation including hypothesis, evidence, physical and computational experiments, materials and methods, data and results including charts and figures. Consider a hypothesis a clever idea or a proposed explanation for some observable phenomenon which may be expressed as a mathematical model or as a logical proposition. But what if the entities described within the hypothesis are not known to exist? This is, after all, a major motivation for, in the very least, biological research. The BFO-realists would balk at including such unknown or debatable entities into a scientific ontology, yet it is obviously critical in not only accurately describing scientific models and theories, but also in being truly innovative and thinking outside already established and accepted scientific knowledge.

For example, the elementary particle *Higgs boson* [21] is predicted by the Standard Model in particle physics [35]. However, so far no instances of this predicted entity have been found, despite considerable efforts [48]. Consequently, within BFO's realist framework, there is no space for an ontological category of *Higgs boson*s, because there may not be any instances of such a category. Yet clearly there is a need amongst scientists to communicate information about Higgs bosons, their properties and especially their potential to enter into causal relations. Furthermore, there is a need to specify what a Higgs boson is (or would be if there is one) in information systems that store, process or retrieve information about elementary particles. So we must answer the question how the nature of hypothetical entities such as *Higgs boson*s can be specified through BFO-realism.

3.3. Information artifacts and the aboutness problem

Hypotheses (as written propositions), theories (as collections of propositions) and written specifications (as documents describing how to represent information) are Information Content Entities (ICEs) in the domain of the Information Artifact Ontology (IAO) [14]. In the IAO, ICEs are generically dependent continuants (GDCs) – these depend on the existence of some material object of a certain kind. They are always *about* [40] some entity in reality. For example, a datum of temperature measurement is generically dependent on a physical representation of the datum, and it is *about* a temperature quality of some entity.

The IAO is represented using OWL-DL [31,36], the description logic variant of the Web Ontology Language (OWL). OWL-DL is a decidable fragment of first order logic, which extends the semantics of the *SROIQ* description logic [25] with datatypes and punning.

The axiom corresponding to the aboutness of information content entities (ICE) is the following description logic statement:

$$ICE \sqsubseteq \exists is\_about.Entity \tag{1}$$

The class *Entity* refers to BFO's top-level class. As BFO is an ontology of particulars, instances of *Entity* must be particulars, too; either continuants or occurrents. *Entity* does not include ontological categories in its extension.

With exceptions (such as a hypothesis about the existence of a planet or asteroid), hypotheses in empirical sciences are about *categories* of particulars. Kinds of hypothetical particles in physics are a consequence of the Standard Model [35] (or other theories). Yet no particular particles are predicted, but rather categories of particles, characterized by their mass, spin and other properties. Limited by the BFO, which includes only particulars in their domain of discourse, the IAO currently fails to represent *about* what information entities referring to categories are.

At least three options exist how to represent theories and hypotheses, or, more generally, information entities, about categories in a BFO compliant way:

1. Using higher-order relations in OWL permits to relate particulars (GDCs) to OWL classes (which represent categories of entities).
2. Adding a new top-level distinction between *Universals* and *Particulars* in BFO. Instances of the OWL class *Universal* are universals, while the current BFO taxonomy can be kept as a sub-category of the *Particular* class. This approach is illustrated in Figure 1.
3. Representing categories as GDCs that are existentially dependent on a universal requires no change to the BFO.

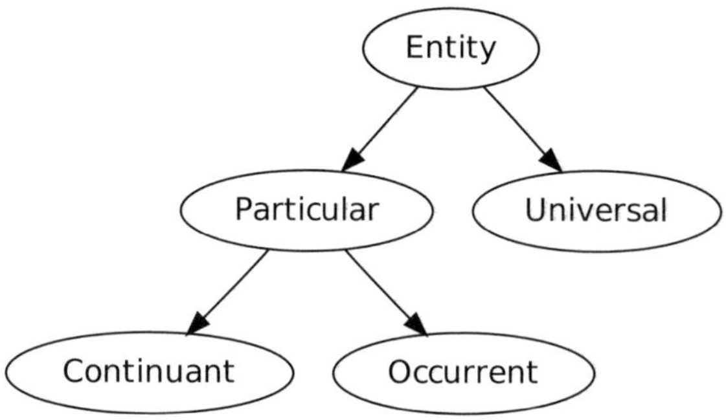

Figure 1. Modified top-level of BFO.

The first option would require no changes to the BFO, yet necessitates the use of an undecidable logic, OWL-Full. The second option is already implemented in the OBO Relationship Ontology (RO) [45] where instances of both categories are related using an explicit **instance-of** relation, and the third option reflects the classification of universals as a classification of GDCs.

However, whichever option is selected to represent information about universals in the BFO, all approaches fail to represent the meaning of terms which refer to categories of beings for which we are not certain that instances exist in this world, because these categories may not be universals, and, consequently, no class corresponding to the category will be included in a BFO-based ontology. Although the BFO has the capability to represent the features of theories or hypotheses, it fails to capture what these theories are about. However, these hypothetical categories are of high importance for the progress of the sciences, and the failure to include them in formal scientific ontologies hinders the ability of scientists to communicate about their theories, and may potentially hinder the progress of science. So far, we have demonstrated this using an example from physics, discussing theories of *Higgs bosons*. Yet the restriction employed by the BFO does not only limit current scientific progress, but fails to serve already established disciplines such as chemistry, where borderline cases and impossibility results are vital for the understanding of particular phenomena and domains.

3.4. Molecules and molecular specifications

Molecules are material entities in that they are maximally connected, spatially extended, retain their identity in time and are the bearer of qualities. Molecules themselves are composed of atoms that are connected through stable covalent bonds, and the three-dimensional arrangement of the atoms that constitute a molecule is called molecular structure. Molecular structure determines several properties including reactivity, polarity, color, magnetism, and biological activity.

Over 80 chemical specification languages exist to capture and represent knowledge about molecules. Molecular graphs (atoms, connectivity and stereochemistry) can be represented by the Simplified Molecular Input Line Entry Specification (SMILES) [1], the IUPAC International Chemical Identifier (InCHI) [32], and extended with other knowledge representation languages such as the XML-based Chemical Markup Language (CML) [34]. More recently, an OWL-based chemical structure ontology [28] has been developed. Since multiple chemical specification languages can be used to specify the same molecule, it is important to provide an ontological foundation for these languages. Furthermore, there is a need to describe information about molecules, particularly the values obtained by a calculation or a measurement protocol. This goal is being addressed in a collaborative effort to develop an ontology of chemical information [13]. The important aspect of encoding this knowledge is that the information content is *about* a molecule or a class of molecules. This viewpoint is critical for the OBO Foundry ontologies IAO and the chemical information ontology: that there exists a relation between the information entities and the real world entities they describe.

Thus, a major challenge for the BFO-realists is how to represent molecular structures that have been designed, but for which no instances are yet known to exist. It has been argued [15] that molecular structure is in fact a "non-effective specification", in contrast to an "effective specification" which details how one might actually execute the procedure by which one realizes the objective. These specifications should *not* hold an aboutness relation to real world entities until, of course, the real world entity has been demonstrated to exist. It is further argued that any properties that we might derive from the structure are simply predictions, and don't really describe the real world entity.

Yet, it is entirely unsatisfying that we cannot examine a glyph, diagram or sequence of characters, conforming to one of the molecular structure specification languages and acknowledge that this description in fact corresponds to a specific category of molecules, independent of whether we know it to exist. Moreover, whether the specified molecules exist or not, the properties we compute are also information about the specific molecules. Instances of the category of molecules would indeed have all the normal properties and characteristics of molecules, and they are studied under that aspect.

It is routine science for chemists to investigate chemicals that do not yet exist. During the course of their investigation, they specify the target molecule's structure and put forward biosynthetic strategies. Increased due diligence could include a computational study to assess the compound's stability, so as to better understand under which conditions it may be synthesized. For example, de Silva and Goodman [8] pursue a computational chemistry approach to answer the question of which saturated acyclic alkanes can never be made under normal conditions. They identify two molecules, illustrated in Figure 2, which have never been synthesized and are unlikely to exist except perhaps briefly under extremely low temperatures. It is clear that their study provides information about

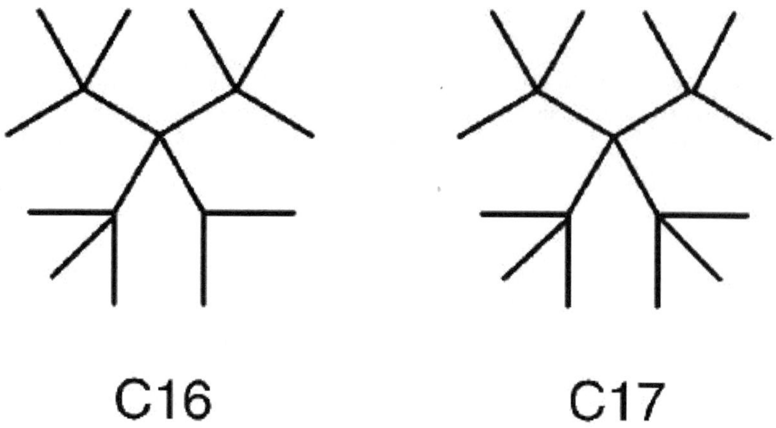

Figure 2. The smallest acyclic alkanes that could not naturally exist.

a class of chemical compounds for which there is no *known* physical evidence of their existence, and the scientific contribution is exactly the impossibility result, as outlined in the study's conclusion [8]:

> The strain energy analysis and the DFT calculations suggest that the limit of stability lies either at C15 or C16, and so the smallest alkane that can never be made will be either C16 or C17, except perhaps at very low temperatures for a short time. We are confident that C17 could never be made and suggest that C16 is the smallest saturated alkane that cannot be made.

While BFO-based ontologies can represent the properties and features of the *specification* of a class of molecules, it fails to represent the properties and features of the class of specified objects – independent from whether or not instances of the specified class of objects exist.

3.5. Perpetual motion

Perpetual motion and perpetual motion machines are discussed in science for centuries. They have served to test the boundaries of scientific theories and hypotheses [2] and continue to do so [20].

A perpetual motion machine is a machine that runs forever. Perpetual motion machines violate either the first or the second law of thermodynamics [12]. Perpetual motion machines of the first kind create energy from nothing (and violate the first law of thermodynamics about the conservation of energy). Perpetual motion machines of the second kind are able to extract energy at some point, use it for work, and have everything return to an original state at the end of the cycle (violating the second law about increasing entropy). Using other criteria, several other classes of perpetual motion machines can be distinguished [26].

The notion of perpetual motion and perpetual motion machines continues to be useful to test the limits of scientific theories and challenge new discoveries. Hence, a scientific classification (or ontology) of perpetual motion machines has been developed. It is precisely the fact that these machines are considered to be impossible that makes them useful for science [5]. Consequently, they are useful in scientific communication and information systems in scientific domains, and therefore an important notion for scientific ontologies.

3.6. Alternatives to BFO's realism

So, are there alternatives to the use of Aristotelian universals for building ontologies? There are, and they are quite common in the formal ontology community outside the biomedical domain [18,17]. It is the view of ontology as a specification of a conceptualization of a domain, as a formal theory specifying the *meaning* of terms in a vocabulary – a vocabulary containing all the relevant terms within the domain to be covered. In this view, an ontology is not concerned with the question whether one of its classes has an instance *in this world* (or in "reality"), but rather with specifying the properties and characteristics of the instances *if there are any*.

The importance of *impossibility* results in science such as the apparent impossiblity of perpetual motion or certain chemical structures has some important consequences for constructing scientific ontologies. When formal ontologies for science specify the necessary properties of a category's instances (i.e., the properties of the instances in every possible world in which the category does have instances), the laws of nature must be seen as contingent, because these laws are the subject matter of the domain modeled. Scientific ontologies are intended to support the communication between scientists and must, by their very nature, be able to accommodate different scientific views. Restricting the categories in scientific ontologies by the natural laws themselves would make it impossible to use these ontologies for the discovery, discussion or communication of novel results that may contradict any of the established scientific theories, because the choice of the ontology would already preclude the possibility of such results.

It may still be desirable to know whether a majority of scientists *believe* some theory to be true or false, or some category to have instances or not. For this purpose, OWL meta-modelling [33] can be used to add epistemic information to an ontological class, e.g., with attributes such as *predicted*, *hypothetical* or *confirmed*.

4. Discussion

The criterion employed by the BFO to base ontologies on universals that are instantiated fails to satisfy the needs of scientists in various illustrative cases that are representative of a larger set of more general problems. It must be emphasized that, within the BFO, no definition or axiomatic characterization of "universal" is currently available. The closest to a definition of "universal" in the BFO is the statement [43]:

> A universal is defined as anything that is instantiated, and an instance as anything that instantiates some universal. The relation of instantiation is hereby taken as primitive, and it is specified axiomatically that it holds exclusively between instances and universals (in that order).

However, this does not help us to determine if an entity is a universal or an instance of a universal, or even whether instances and universals are disjoint or may overlap.

Yet it has been argued that BFO's criterion of using only Aristotelian universals for classes in an ontology leads to better ontologies, because it helps to prevent various mistakes. In particular, false **is-a** assertions are claimed to be prevented through the use of the criterion.

However, it is hard to see how the use of universals contributes to avoiding the identified mistakes [43]. The argumentation in [43] seems entirely focused on the benefits of using universals over *concepts*. The notion of concept is, it is claimed [43,42], not well-defined, and should be replaced by the notion of "universal". Yet, within the BFO, "universal" is only specified as something that has instances, making it a weak notion rarely more adequate than "concept". It is therefore unclear why **is-a** relations such as

- dog **is-a** dog or apple,
- dog and mammal **is-a** dog or apple,
- dog **is-a** non-cat

are apparently excluded with the use of universals instead of concepts. Since axioms or definitions for "universal" are not provided in the BFO, no option remain to determine whether "dog or apple" is a universal or not – except by reference to an ontological authority.

We focus on the BFO here due to its importance in constructing ontologies in the biomedical and related domains. However, other ontologies are used within these domains as well, in particular DOLCE [29] in the BioTop project [39] and the GFO [19] in the GFO-Bio project [24].

Neither DOLCE nor the GFO have a restriction similar to the BFO in that their classes must correspond to Aristotelian universals. As a consequence, neither faces the challenges in representing scientific theories, hypotheses or specifications we discussed so far. Furthermore, each explicitly includes some form of representing ontological categories. The DOLCE contains, in an extension [30], a way of constructing *concepts*.

The GFO is designed from the beginning as an ontology not only of individuals, but also of ontological categories. GFO permits the inclusion of multiple kinds of categories, including mind-independent categories (universals) and mind-dependent categories (concepts).

5. Conclusions

We discussed a form of realism that is promoted by the Basic Formal Ontology and is being employed throughout biomedical ontologies that are candidates for inclusion in the OBO Foundry. This form of realism states that the classes and relations in these ontologies must be instantiated in reality. In particular, categories of entities which are not assumed or *known* to exist cannot be included in ontologies exemplifying this form of realism. This includes a number of entities predicted by current theories in physics such as *Higgs boson*, and also the referents of chemical specifications, in particular molecules.

The form of realism employed by the BFO and the OBO Foundry ontologies is inadequate for numerous tasks that ontologies are being used for, in particular for the capture and communication of scientific discourse, the representation of the referents of specifications and, in general, the contents of scientific theories. While BFO's realism criterion is intended to facilitate the construction of "good" ontologies, it hinders at the same time the development of more useful ontologies for science. We show that other criteria which are more common in the formal ontology community, such as the use of the axiomatic method [22] and the specification of the meaning of every term necessary within a domain or application, suffice to avoid the problems BFO's realism criterion tries to address, and apply it to uninstantiated classes such as the referents of scientific theories, chemical specifications and impossibility results.

Acknowledgements

We thank Nico Adams for interesting and helpful discussions about realism and chemicals that cannot exist. We thank two anonymous reviewers for valuable comments on an earlier draft of this manuscript.

References

[1] E. Anderson, G.D. Veith, and D. Weininger. Smiles: A line notation and computerized interpreter for chemical structures. Technical report.

[2] Stanley Angrist. Perpetual motion machines. *Scientific American*, 218(1):115–122, 1968.

[3] Aristotle. *De Interpretatione*, chapter 7. Electronic Text Center, University of Virginia Library, 2001.

[4] M. Ashburner, C. A. Ball, J. A. Blake, D. Botstein, H. Butler, J. M. Cherry, A. P. Davis, K. Dolinski, S. S. Dwight, J. T. Eppig, M. A. Harris, D. P. Hill, Issel L. Tarver, A. Kasarskis, S. Lewis, J. C. Matese, J. E. Richardson, M. Ringwald, G. M. Rubin, and G. Sherlock. Gene ontology: tool for the unification of biology. The Gene Ontology Consortium. *Nat Genet*, 25(1):25–29, May 2000.

[5] John D. Barrow. *Impossibility : The Limits of Science and the Science of Limits*. Oxford University Press, 1998.

[6] Ncbo bioportal. `http://bioportal.bioontology.org/`.

[7] Mélanie Courtot et al. The owl of biomedical investigations. In Catherine Dolbear, Alan Ruttenberg, and Ulrike Sattler, editors, *OWLED*, volume 432 of *CEUR Workshop Proceedings*. CEUR-WS.org, 2008.

[8] K. M. Nalin de Silva and Jonathan M. Goodman. What is the smallest saturated acyclic alkane that cannot be made? *J. Chem. Inf. Model.*, 45(1):81–87, 2005.

[9] K. Degtyarenko, P. Matos, M. Ennis, J. Hastings, M. Zbinden, A. McNaught, R. Alcantara, M. Darsow, M. Guedj, and M. Ashburner. ChEBI: a database and ontology for chemical entities of biological interest. *Nucleic Acids Research*, 2007.

[10] A. Doms and M. Schroeder. GoPubMed: exploring PubMed with the Gene Ontology. *Nucleic Acids Res*, 33(Web Server issue):783–786, Jul 2005.

[11] Michel Dumontier and Natalia Villanueva-Rosales. Towards pharmacogenomics knowledge discovery with the semantic web. *Briefings in bioinformatics*, February 2009.

[12] Enrico Fermi. *Thermodynamics*. Dover Publications, New York, 1956 [1936].

[13] `http://code.google.com/p/semanticchemistry/`.

[14] `http://code.google.com/p/information-artifact-ontology/`, 2009.

[15] `http://groups.google.com/group/bfo-discuss/browse_thread/thread/93d960b1f3deee39`.

[16] Pierre Grenon. Bfo in a nutshell: A bi-categorial axiomatization of BFO and comparison with DOLCE. Technical report, University of Leipzig, Leipzig, 2003.

[17] Thomas R. Gruber. Toward principles for the design of ontologies used for knowledge sharing. *International Journal of Human-Computer Studies*, 43(5-6), 1995.

[18] Nicola Guarino. Formal ontology and information systems. In Nicola Guarino, editor, *Formal Ontology in Information Systems: Proceedings of the First International Conference (FOIS'98), Trento, Italy, 6-8 June 1998*, volume 46 of *Frontiers in Artificial Intelligence and Applications*, Amsterdam, June 1998. IOS Press.

[19] Heinrich Herre, Barbara Heller, Patryk Burek, Robert Hoehndorf, Frank Loebe, and Hannes Michalek. General Formal Ontology (GFO) – A foundational ontology integrating objects and processes [Ver-

sion 1.0]. Onto-med report, Research Group Ontologies in Medicine, Institute of Medical Informatics, Statistics and Epidemiology, University of Leipzig, Leipzig, 2006.
[20] Paul R. Heyl. Perpetual motion in the twentieth century. *The Scientific Monthly*, 22(2):143–145, 1926.
[21] P. W. Higgs. Broken symmetries, massless particles and gauge fields. *Physics Letters*, 12:132–133, September 1964.
[22] David Hilbert. Axiomatisches denken. *Mathematische Annalen*, 78:405–415, 1918.
[23] Robert Hoehndorf, Janet Kelso, and Heinrich Herre. The ontology of biological sequences. *BMC Bioinformatics*, 10(1):377+, 2009.
[24] Robert Hoehndorf, Frank Loebe, Roberto Poli, Janet Kelso, and Heinrich Herre. Gfo-bio: A biological core ontology. *Applied Ontology*, 2008. in press.
[25] Ian Horrocks, Oliver Kutz, and Ulrike Sattler. The even more irresistible sroiq. In *In KR*, pages 57–67. AAAI Press, 2006.
[26] Kevin T. Kilty. Perpetual motion. `http://www.kilty.com/pmotion.htm`, 1992.
[27] Gyula Klima. The medieval problem of universals. In Edward N. Zalta, editor, *The Stanford Encyclopedia of Philosophy*. Winter 2008 edition, 2008.
[28] Mykola Konyk, Alexander De Leon, and Michel Dumontier. Chemical knowledge for the semantic web. In *Proceedings of Data Integration in the Life Sciences (DILS2008)*, page Lecture Notes in Bioinformatics (LNBI). Springern, 2008.
[29] Claudio Masolo, Stefano Borgo, Aldo Gangemi, Nicola Guarino, and Alessandro Oltramari. WonderWeb Deliverable D18: Ontology library (final). Technical report, Laboratory for Applied Ontology, ISTC-CNR, Trento, Italy, 2003.
[30] Claudio Masolo, Laure Vieu, Emanuele Bottazzi, Carola Catenacci, Roberta Ferrario, Aldo Gangemi, and Nicola Guarino. Social roles and their descriptions. In *Proceedings of the Ninth International Conference on the Principles of Knowledge Representation and Reasoning (KR2004), Whistler, Canada, June 2-5, 2004*, 2004.
[31] Deborah L. Mcguinness and Frank van Harmelen. OWL Web Ontology Language overview. W3C recommendation, World Wide Web Consortium (W3C), February 2004.
[32] Alan McNaught. The iupac international chemical identifier:inchl. *Chemistry International*, 28(6), 2006.
[33] Boris Motik, Peter F. Patel-Schneider, and Bernardo Cuenca Grau. Owl 2 web ontology language: Direct semantics. Technical report, W3C, 2009.
[34] P. Murray-Rust and H. S. Rzepa. Chemical markup, xml and the worldwide web. part 4. cml schema. *Journal of Chemical Information and Modeling*, pages 757–772, 2003.
[35] Cheng Ta Pei and Li Ling Fong. *Gauge Theory of Elementary Particle Physics*. Oxford, 1984.
[36] Peter, Patrick Hayes, and Ian Horrocks. Owl web ontology language – semantics and abstract syntax. urlhttp://www.w3.org/TR/owl-semantics/, February 2004.
[37] Kay Prufer, Bjoern Muetzel, Hong-Hai Do, Gunter Weiss, Philipp Khaitovich, Erhard Rahm, Svante Paabo, Michael Lachmann, and Wolfgang Enard. Func: a package for detecting significant associations between gene sets and ontological annotations. *BMC Bioinformatics*, 8:41+, February 2007.
[38] S. A. Racunas, N. H. Shah, I. Albert, and N. V. Fedoroff. Hybrow: a prototype system for computer-aided hypothesis evaluation. *Bioinformatics*, 20 Suppl 1, August 2004.
[39] Stefan Schulz, Elena Beisswanger, Joachim Wermter, and Udo Hahn. Towards an upper-level ontology for molecular biology. *AMIA Annu Symp Proc*, 2006, 2006.
[40] John R. Searle. *Intentionality: An essay in the philosophy of mind*. Cambridge University Press, 1983.
[41] John R. Searle. *The Construction of Social Reality*. Free Press, January 1997.
[42] B. Smith. From concepts to clinical reality: an essay on the benchmarking of biomedical terminologies. *J Biomed Inform*, 39(3):288–298, June 2006.
[43] Barry Smith. Beyond concepts: Ontology as reality representation. In Achille Varzi and Laure Vieu, editors, *Proceedings of FOIS 2004*, 2004.
[44] Barry Smith, Michael Ashburner, Cornelius Rosse, Jonathan Bard, William Bug, Werner Ceusters, Louis J. Goldberg, Karen Eilbeck, Amelia Ireland, Christopher J. Mungall, Neocles Leontis, Philippe Rocca-Serra, Alan Ruttenberg, Susanna-Assunta Sansone, Richard H. Scheuermann, Nigam Shah, Patricia L. Whetzel, and Suzanna Lewis. The obo foundry: coordinated evolution of ontologies to support biomedical data integration. *Nat Biotech*, 25(11):1251–1255, November 2007.
[45] Barry Smith, Werner Ceusters, Bert Klagges, Jacob Köhler, Anand Kumar, Jane Lomax, Chris Mungall, Fabian Neuhaus, Alan L. Rector, and Cornelius Rosse. Relations in biomedical ontologies. *Genome*

Biology, 6(5), 2005.

[46] Barry Smith, Waclaw Kusnierczyk, Daniel Schober, and Werner Ceusters. Towards a reference terminology for ontology research and development in the biomedical domain. In *Proceedings of KR-MED 2006*, 2006.

[47] Natalia Villanueva-Rosales and Michel Dumontier. yowl: An ontology-driven knowledge base for yeast biologists. *J. of Biomedical Informatics*, 41(5):779–789, 2008.

[48] W. M. Yao et al. Searches for higgs bosons. *Journal of Physics G: Nuclear and Particle Physics*, 33(1), 2006.

Formal Ontology in Information Systems
A. Galton and R. Mizoguchi (Eds.)
IOS Press, 2010

doi:10.3233/978-1-60750-535-8-400

Dispositions and the Infectious Disease Ontology

Albert GOLDFAIN [a,1], Barry SMITH [b] and Lindsay G. COWELL [c]

[a] *Blue Highway, Syracuse, NY, USA*
[b] *University at Buffalo, Buffalo, NY, USA*
[c] *Duke University Medical Center, Durham, NC, USA*

Abstract. This paper addresses the use of dispositions in the Infectious Disease Ontology (IDO). IDO is an ontology constructed according to the principles of the Open Biomedical Ontology (OBO) Foundry and uses the Basic Formal Ontology (BFO) as an upper ontology. After providing a brief introduction to disposition types in BFO and IDO, we discuss three general techniques for representing combinations of dispositions under the headings *blocking dispositions*, *complementary dispositions*, and *collective dispositions*. Motivating examples for each combination of dispositions is given along with a specific use case in IDO. Description logic restrictions are used to formalize statements relating to these combinations.

Keywords. infectious disease ontology, basic formal ontology, dispositions

1. Introduction: IDO, BFO, and OGMS

The Infectious Disease Ontology (IDO) is designed to provide a consistent terminology, taxonomy, and logical representation for the domain of infectious diseases. IDO consists of a core ontology (henceforth "IDO Core") intended to cover terms common to all infectious diseases (e.g., 'host', 'pathogen', 'infection', 'immunity'), and a suite of extension ontologies for specific diseases (e.g., Influenza, HIV, Malaria). The purpose of the IDO Core is to ensure that the extension ontologies created in its terms are interoperable. IDO Core is designed to be disease- and pathogen-neutral and to represent entities and relations across three dimensions: (1) *biological scale*: gene, cell, organ, organism, population (2) *disciplinary perspective*: clinical, biological, epidemiological, (3) *host, pathogen, and vector organism type*: e.g., human, rat, pig, maize, HIV, influenza, mosquito. Both the IDO Core and its extensions will adhere to the guidelines and best practices of the OBO (Open Biomedical Ontology) Foundry ontologies. As such IDO depends on the Basic Formal Ontology[2] (BFO) as its upper ontology.

[1]Corresponding Author: Albert Goldfain, Blue Highway LLC, 2-212 Center for Science & Technology Syracuse, New York 13244-4100; E-mail: agoldfain@blue-highway.com.
[2]`http://www.ifomis.org/bfo`

A key feature of the infectious disease domain that must be captured in IDO is the nature of the ability and tendency for entities to participate in certain kinds of processes. Thus, BFO dispositions are of central importance to IDO. The philosophical literature is rich with analyses of dispositions, elements of which we believe can be fruitfully applied in developing ontologies that capture relations between biological entities which involve an element of ability or tendency.

This paper is a preliminary step in the formalization of dispositions for IDO. In the next two sections, we describe the treatment of dispositions in BFO and IDO and present a simple conditional analysis of dispositions. We spend the remainder of the paper describing and formalizing different types of relations between dispositions.

2. Dispositions in BFO and IDO

BFO embraces a distinction between categorical properties (e.g., triangularity) and dispositional properties (e.g., fragility). BFO makes this distinction by partitioning specifically dependent continuants (i.e., individual entities that depend for their existence on a specific bearer) into qualities (categorical properties) and realizable entities (including dispositional properties and roles). The relevant BFO definitions (from [3]) are:

> **Quality** $=_{def}$ A specifically dependent continuant that is exhibited if it inheres in an entity or entities at all.

> **Realizable Entity** $=_{def}$ A specifically dependent continuant that inheres in independent continuant entities and is not exhibited in full at every time in which it inheres in an entity or group of entities.

> **Realization** $=_{def}$ A process in which a realizable entity is exhibited or manifested.

For the present paper, the only realizable entities we will concern ourselves with are dispositions[3], defined in BFO as follows:

> **Disposition** $=_{def}$ A disposition is a realizable entity which is such that, if it ceases to exist, then its bearer is physically changed, and whose realization occurs in virtue of the bearer's physical make-up when this bearer is in some special circumstances.

Unlike roles, dispositions are not optional for the entities that bear them. If an entity has a certain structure in the present, then it has a certain disposition, and if it ceases to have that structure in the future, then it loses that disposition. In other words, a disposition is a realizable entity that is a reflection of the in-built or acquired physical make-up of the independent continuant that is its bearer, and it may be lost because the parts of its bearer have changed in some way. A disposition is thus also known as an internally-grounded realizable entity.

By making both qualities and dispositions first-class entities, BFO implicitly rejects both categorical monism, the view that all properties are categorical, and dispositional monism, the view that all properties are dispositional. We embrace the view that a dispo-

[3]Dispositions are further subdivided into capabilities and functions in BFO; anything said about dispositions in this paper also applies to the subtypes.

sition will only inhere in a bearer at a given time in virtue of the qualities of the bearer at that time: every disposition is in need of some categorical base. Collectively, it is certain qualities inhering in parts the entity has (for example molecular structure) which form the physical basis for each given disposition, and we can say that they confer the disposition on the bearer. Reference to both qualities (such as mass and temperature) and dispositions (such as solubility) has explanatory value in scientific theories, and the conferring qualities are a good way to differentiate dispositions from one another. Thus, a change in qualities (in physical structure) may imply a change in, gain, or loss of a disposition. Also, dispositions may be borne without ever being manifested.

As part of its realist orientation, BFO attempts to avoid treatments of modality (necessity, possibility) in terms of special entities such as possible worlds in favor of a focus on objects existing in the present, actual world. Dispositions provide a formal mechanism for taking account of future manifestations (BFO occurrents) in terms of what is true of the underlying independent continuants in the present; roughly, dispositions say how something *is* in terms of *what it has the built-in potential to do or suffer.*

IDO subscribes to a dispositional characterization of disease provided by the Ontology for General Medical Science[4] (OGMS). In OGMS, every disease is a disposition towards pathological processes whose physical basis is a disorder and whose realization is a disease course. Some but not all manifestations of the disease disposition become clinically significant in the sense that they occur with signs and symptoms accessible to the patient or the clinician[1]. IDO inherits these relationships between entities as illustrated in Figure 1:

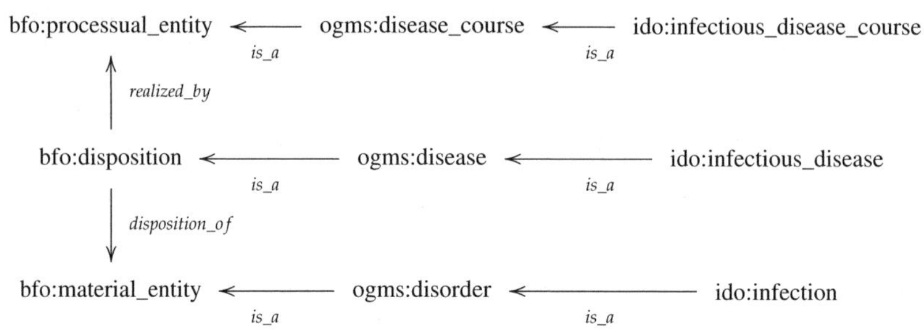

Figure 1. Relations between IDO and OGMS.

The relevant OGMS definitions are as follows:

Disorder $=_{def}$ A disorder is a material entity which is clinically abnormal and part of an extended organism. Disorders are the physical basis of disease.

Disease $=_{def}$ A disposition (i) to undergo pathological processes that (ii) exists in an organism because of one or more disorders in that organism.

Disease Course $=_{def}$ The totality of all processes through which a given disease instance is realized.

[4] `http://code.google.com/p/ogms/`

And the relevant IDO definitions hanging from these OGMS terms are as follows:

Infection $=_{def}$ A disorder that has as part a clinically abnormal infectious agent colony which causes the elevated risk for pathological processes associated with the disorder.

Infectious Disease $=_{def}$ A disease whose physical basis is an infection.

Infectious Disease Course $=_{def}$ A disease course that is the realization of an infectious disease.

Taking diseases to be dispositions highlights the fact that they can be present without being manifested and that they can be realized in multiple different sorts of manifestations (dependent for example on presence or absence of symptom-suppressant drugs). Resort to dispositions thus allows us to describe what an object *can* do and to have this description still be correct even if relevant realizing processes never take place. This is obviously a great advantage in an area such as immunology, where the object of our study involves structures in the body designed precisely to *prevent* certain categories of processes. Diseases inhere in organisms with disorders, not solely in the disorders, since there may be parts of the organism aside from the disorder that participate in the disease course. For infectious diseases in particular, we do not localize the disease in the disorder since the infection is actually not a part of the diseased organism.

Diseases, like all dispositions, are often detected and understood through the examination of their manifestation. Beyond the infectious disease course, IDO recognizes several subprocesses of host-pathogen interaction, each of which can be seen as the realization of some disposition. A disposition D is only added to IDO Core when D picks out a biologically recognized property and we are able to specify the IDO process type for manifestations of its instances. Even though biological reality may be such as to contain a disposition towards any logical combination of processes, we feel that IDO should only contain those sparse dispositions most relevant to capturing the important dynamics of infectious diseases.

In what follows, the use of IDO dispositions is formalized using description logic restrictions. Ultimately, the full IDO suite of ontologies will require a more expressive logic for comprehensive reasoning[5], but we would like to deploy description logic wherever possible since it is the foundation of the decidable reasoning in OWL DL. Wherever possible, relations from the OBO Relation Ontology (RO) or the proposed extension of this ontology[6] (RO-Proposed) are used in order to avoid the proliferation of new relations and to remain compatible with OBO ontologies. Unless otherwise specified, all relations used in this paper relate universals (types).

The syntax and semantics of the description logic expressions we will use for DL concept descriptions C, D (classes in OWL, universals in BFO), DL role R (property in OWL, type-level OBO relation in BFO), interpretation $\mathcal{I}$, and domain of interpretation $\Delta^{\mathcal{I}}$ are as follows:

[5]Most likely, IDO axioms will need a suitable rule language and second-order logic

[6]`http://www.obofoundry.org/ro/`

Name	Syntax	Semantics
Intersection	$C \sqcap D$	$C \cap D$
Union	$C \sqcup D$	$C \cup D$
Existential Quantification	$\exists\mathbf{R}.C$	$\{a \in \Delta^{\mathcal{I}} \mid \exists b.(a,b) \in \mathbf{R}^{\mathcal{I}} \wedge b \in C^{\mathcal{I}}\}$
Empty Concept	$C = \perp$	$C = \emptyset$
Concept Inclusion	$C \sqsubseteq D$	$C^{\mathcal{I}} \subseteq D^{\mathcal{I}}$
Concept Equality	$C \equiv D$	$C^{\mathcal{I}} = D^{\mathcal{I}}$

Table 1. DL syntax and semantics used in this paper.

3. The Conditional Analysis of Dispositions

A starting point for the logical analysis of dispositions is the simple conditional analysis. Such an analysis attempts to logically explicate the causal link between a stimulus and a manifestation via a subjunctive/counterfactual conditional. Bird presents the simple conditional analysis as follows ([5] p. 24): Let '$D_{(S,M)}$' abbreviate 'x is disposed to manifest M in response to stimulus S, and '$\Box\!\!\rightarrow$' symbolize the subjunctive/counterfactual conditional, so that $Sx \Box\!\!\rightarrow Mx$ if x were S then it would be M. The (simple) conditional analysis of dispositions may then be symbolized:

$$D_{(S,M)}x \leftrightarrow Sx \Box\!\!\rightarrow Mx \tag{1}$$

The simple conditional analysis fails in two ways. In the case of what are called *finkish dispositions*[7], the categorical basis for the disposition is removed after the stimulus Sx is applied, but before manifestation Mx can occur, thus violating the counterfactual. Dispositions frequently take time to manifest after the stimulus is applied, so there is a chance that the disposition may be lost during this time. Bird provides a relevant example: "Some food might become infected with the bacterium Clostridium botulinum and thereby become poisonous. It can lose that disposition [to poison] by cooking or irradiation" [4]. The simple conditional analysis also fails in the case of *antidotes* (or *masks*) to a disposition. In this case the disposition is left intact after the stimulus is applied, but the manifestation fails to occur because of external conditions. Bird puts it as follows: "When an antidote is present an object can have a disposition to M when S yet fail to yield M when given stimulus S, because the conditions that, in conjunction with the disposition's causal basis, would normally bring M about, have been interfered with" [4]. For example, a small forest fire that is contained by firefighters still bears the disposition to burn down the entire forest, but it cannot manifest that disposition because it is contained.

In the philosophical literature on dispositions, it is customary to discuss such background conditions, circumstances, contexts, or laws of nature. Mumford makes an important distinction between two types of background conditions:

> *α-conditions*: being *conditions that prevent the manifestation of a disposition though the disposition itself remains*, for example: lack of oxygen prevents a struck match from lighting though it remains flammable; the lack of a mate prevents a man from breeding though he remains fertile; placing a vase in a sturdy glass prevents it from being broken though it remains fragile.

β-conditions: being *conditions that prevent something from having a disposition*, for example: a match being wet stops it being flammable; a zero or low sperm count stops a male from being fertile; a strengthening process stops a vase from being fragile ([9] p. 86).

These conditions correspond nicely to antidotes and finkish dispositions respectively.

While this machinery is often used only to discredit the simple conditional analysis, it can also be used to describe relationships between dispositions. Background conditions, external circumstances, and laws of nature can all be construed in a dispositional way. Sometimes these dispositions block each other, complement each other, or are manifested in a collective way. We will spend the remainder of the paper examining these dispositional relationships.

4. Blocking Dispositions

Special emphasis must be placed on the fact that what is often preventing the manifestation of a disposition is the manifestation of another disposition. We will call the latter a *blocking disposition*. For example, a particular carnivorous predator with a disposition to eat a particular prey animal blocks predators of the same type from manifesting the same type of disposition (assuming that the particular prey animal is the only one readily available). In general, if D_1 is a disposition and D_2 is a blocking disposition for D_1, then it must be the case that the manifestation of D_2 prevents the manifestation of D_1. A blocking disposition might be understood in different ways:

1. **Incompatible occurrents**: The manifestation of D_1 and the manifestation of D_2 are somehow incompatible occurrents, meaning either that they cannot co-occur or that one negatively regulates[7] the other.
2. **Incompatible qualities**: The manifestation of D_2 results in a continuant's acquring a quality that is incompatible with some quality that the same continuant would have acquired through the manifestation of D_1. That is, we have two qualities that cannot be simultaneously exhibited (e.g., a square circular object).

We utilize reference to blocking dispositions in IDO as a means to describe the general phenomena of protective resistance. By giving resistance a positive characterization, in which we describe what dispositions are actively manifested, descriptions of resistance can play a more explanatory role in explanations and query answering. The current IDO Core definition of protective resistance is as follows:

Protective Resistance$=_{def}$ is a disposition that inheres in a material entity (x) by virtue of the fact that the entity has a part (e.g. a gene product), which itself has a disposition (1) to ensure a physiologic response of a certain degree to an entity of type Y with the capability to damage x, or (2) to prevent the completion of some process caused by an entity of type Y with the capability to damage x. The realization of the disposition protects x from or mitigates the damaging effects of Y. The protective resistance disposition is realized in a biological process.

By convention, lowercase variables range over instances and uppercase variables range over types. The prevented process referred to in clause (2) must be critical to how the damaging entity would damage x. For example, there may be several processes caused

[7]The RO Proposed relation P_1**negatively_regulates**P_2 holds between processes P_1 and P_2 when the unfolding of P_1 decreases the frequency, rate, or extent of P_2.

by an infectious organism that are prevented by the host, but this prevention does not result in resistance because the completion of these processes is not necessary. It is only certain critical processes whose prevention results in resistance.

An example of protective resistance is the resistance of MRSa to the antibiotic methicillin. Without blocking dispositions, we can describe this resistance by noting the lack of affinity to methicillin (a disposition) in the penicillin-binding protein of MRSa (PBP2a): MRSa is resistant to methicillin because one of its parts lacks an affinity for it. As an explanation of *why* MRSa is resistant, however, invoking the lack of affinity to methicillin seems to be begging the question. The same situation can be described in a positive (active) way by considering the disposition of PBP2a to synthesize peptidoglycan (an essential component of the bacterial cell wall) as a blocking disposition for the disposition of methicillin to bind to penicillin-binding proteins.[8] In this way, protective resistance is seen as an active response to methicillin. We discuss at length the benefits of representing such dispositions using an active and positive characterization in [6].

In this situation, we can argue for incompatible occurrents: the process of cell wall construction (as a manifestation of the typical disposition of PBP) is incompatible with the process of methicillin binding (which is the manifestation of affinity to methicillin that PBP2a lacks). We could also argue for incompatible qualities: for a particular peptidoglycan molecule, being part of a lattice is incompatible with being bound by methicillin.[9] As a result, the molecular structure of a well-formed bacterial cell wall (i.e., a peptidoglycan lattice) is incompatible with the molecular structure of a compound bound to methicillin.

Cell wall construction is something a bacteria will participate in when no methicillin is present. In order to see this typical cellular process as an active response, we need the machinery of blocking dispositions. Protective resistance to methicillin is exhibited by MRSa in the process of cell wall construction by blocking the disposition of methicillin to bind to PBP.

It is easiest to formulate blocking dispositions in a description logic schema with variables D_1 and D_2 and the RO_Proposed relation **negatively_regulates**

$$D_2\_blocking\_disposition\_of\_D_1 \equiv \exists\mathbf{realized\_by}.(\exists\mathbf{negatively\_regulates}.\exists\mathbf{realizes}.D_1 \sqcap \exists\mathbf{realizes}.D_2) \tag{2}$$

But we may also describe the inability for D_1 and D_2 to co-occur at time T using:

$$\exists\mathbf{realizes}.D_1 \sqcap \exists\mathbf{realizes}.D_2 \sqcap \exists\mathbf{occurs\_at}.T = \bot \tag{3}$$

Description logic does not provide schema variables, so each such disposition must be fleshed out in concrete terms by the relevant IDO extension ontologies. In the case of MRSa, for example, the disposition of PBP2a to construct a cell wall is a **blocking_disposition_of** the disposition to bind to methicillin, because constructing a cell wall negatively regulates binding to methicillin in the case of PBP2a. In the case of MSSa (Methicillin-*susceptible* Staph aureus), the disposition of PBP to bind to me-

[8]Note that since we are dealing with the impossibility of co-occurrence, we could also take the disposition to bind PBP as a blocking disposition for the disposition to synthesize peptidoglycan.

[9]This could also be framed as an incompatibility of spatial co-location.

thicillin is a **blocking_disposition_of** the disposition to construct a cell wall, because binding to methicillin negatively regulates cell wall construction.

Such an analysis is not without its problems. One minor concern is that calling something a blocking disposition may be considered too perspectival, biasing the ontological term towards D_1 being blocked by rather than blocking D_2. A more serious problem is how can we empirically distinguish between something not happening to a specific continuant as the result of (1) an external blocking disposition or (2) as the result of its own internal makeup.

A further worry involves the identity criteria for blocking dispositions. *Storm*-resistant walls on a particular house are most likely also *lemonade*-resistant, but in virtue of the same underlying structure (i.e., categorical properties). So is the particular lemonade resistance inhering in those walls identical to the particular water resistance inhering in those walls? It seems counterintuitive to say so, but if we say these are not identical we open the door to a combinatorial explosion of resistance dispositions. Similarly, penicillin binding protein has an affinity to penicillin (as its name suggests) which is conferred by the same qualities that yield methicillin resistance, but we do not want to say that these forms of resistance are identical because some staph aureus may be susceptible to methicillin but resistant to penicillin. The standard answer to such worries from the realist ontology camp is that terms are included in an ontology in reflection not of what is combinatorially possible but rather of the actual needs of biologists who are describing real biological phenomena. Whether dispositions referred to by such terms are or are not identical will need to be decided on a case-by-case basis, but such a decision is then not in principle more problematic for dispositions than for entities of other sorts.

5. Complementary Dispositions

In addition to blocking each other, dispositions can also manifest in complementary ways. This is most evident with those dispositions that happen to be functions. Man-made tools have certain functions because they were designed for complementary manifestation with the functions of other tools (e.g., the functions of hammers and nails, locks and keys). Biological functions, like artifactual functions, evolve in complementary dependence upon each other (e.g., the functions of sperm and egg cells).

A certain key K has a disposition D_K to unlock a certain lock L, while the lock L has a disposition D_L to be unlocked by K. Both D_K and D_L are manifested in the same process, namely, K's unlocking of L. What underlies these complementary dispositions is the key's disposition to transmit torque when rotated, the lock's disposition to release when unlatched, and a relation between the qualities (i.e., shapes) of the lock and key that confers these dispositions (i.e., the key's fitting the lock). In order to see that D_K and D_L are not the same disposition, we can consider the different ways in which the unlocking process might fail. The key's shape may erode and no longer fit the lock, in which case D_K is lost, but D_L remains. The lock may rust to such a degree that D_L is lost, but D_K remains.

Martin uses the phrase 'reciprocal disposition partners for mutual manifestation' to describe such paired dispositions and advocates the use of such pairs to replace cause and effect in scientific explanation [2]. Bird suggests that dispositions might always come in reciprocal pairs [5]. Under these analyses, there are two distinct dispositions in our example, one inhering in the key and the other inhering in the lock, but they are both manifested in the same process (instance). However, other analyses are possible:

1. **Whole with a Single Disposition**: A mereological whole W which has parts K and L has a single disposition D. For example, if $W = K + L$ (where '+' denotes mereological sum) then we can say W has the disposition to undergo an unlocking process (in virtue of an *intrinsic* quality of W (i.e., the relative shapes of its parts K and L). We do not prefer this analysis because there may be many key copies (and indeed many lock copies) made such that all keys fit all locks. We then would have a generic dependence involving a relative shape quality whose bearer would be very difficult to specify.
2. **Whole with a Collective Disposition**: A mereological whole $W = K + L$ in which K has disposition D_K and L has disposition D_L and the whole has disposition $D = D_K +_d D_L$. Of course, such an account would need to define a mereological sum '$+_d$'for dispositions since parthood between dispositions is less clearly defined than parthood between independent continuants and parthood between occurrents. We will discuss something similar in the next section, but we can think of this account treating D as the total manifestation of D_K and D_L.

The terminology of complementary dispositions is useful in representing symbiotic relationships between organisms. It is used by IDO to describe the properties of interacting hosts and infectious organisms. 'Host', 'pathogen', 'infectious agent[10]', 'mutualist', and 'commensal' are all BFO roles in IDO.

The dispositional relationship between a host and an infectious agent works very much like a lock and key in that the success of a host-pathogen interaction process (e.g., transmission, symbiosis, or colonization) depends on the possession and manifestation of certain dispositions. Two such dispositions are the 'infectious disposition' and the 'capability to play the host role'. The relevant IDO definitions are as follows:

Pathogenic Disposition$=_{def}$ The disposition to initiate processes that result in a disorder.

Infectious Disposition $=_{def}$ A pathogenic disposition to be transmitted from one organism to another and to establish a clinically abnormal colony in the second organism.

Capability to Play the Host Role $=_{def}$ A disposition to participate in symbiosis as host with another organism of a certain type.

Infectious Organism Role $=_{def}$ A parasite role borne by an organism in virtue of the fact that it has the infectious disposition towards its partner in symbiosis.

Host Role $=_{def}$ A symbiont role borne by an organism in virtue of the fact that it provides an environment supportive for the survival and reproduction of its partner in symbiosis.

The infectious disposition and the capability to play the host role are complementary dispositions realized during symbiosis. Like the unlocking process above, a symbiosis process may fail if, for example, the host cannot provide enough nutrients for the infectious organism to ensure its survival or because the host is immune.

[10]There are subtle distinctions between the pathogen role and the infectious agent role, but since our primary concern here is dispositions, we will ignore these distinctions for simplicity.

Description logic does not permit a perspicuous representation of complementary dispositions in terms of the dispositions themselves. In order to capture two dispositions oriented "towards" each other with a potential for mutual manifestation, we must place restrictions on the continuants and occurrents involved. We represent complementary dispositions inhering in continuants C_1 and C_2 whose mutual manifestation process is P using the following restriction on P:

$$P \equiv \exists \textbf{realizes}.\exists \textbf{disposition\_of}.C_1 \sqcap \exists \textbf{realizes}.\exists \textbf{disposition\_of}.C_2 \quad (4)$$

P is equivalent to the type of process that is the realization of dispositions of both C_1 and C_2. In IDO, this establishes a network-of-restrictions representation for complementary dispositions. For example, a process in which an infectious agent colonizes its host is a realization of complementary dispositions of both the infectious agent and host, such processes are captured in DL for IDO as follows:

$$\begin{aligned} &Colonization\_of\_Organism\_Process \sqsubseteq \\ &\quad \exists \textbf{realizes}.\exists \textbf{disposition\_of}.\exists \textbf{has\_role}.Infectious\_Organism \sqcap \quad (5) \\ &\quad\quad \exists \textbf{realizes}.\exists \textbf{disposition\_of}.\exists \textbf{has\_role}.Host \end{aligned}$$

Both (4) and (5) express necessary, but not sufficient descriptions of complementary dispositions.

It may be asked whether there is a complementary disposition for *every* disposition in an ontology, since every process involving the interaction of two continuants might be viewed from the perspective of either participant. Certainly it seems possible to model any interaction in this way, but for practical reasons, we do not add such an axiom in IDO. Whether we add a complementary disposition in specific cases depends on user needs – if scientists using IDO find it necessary to use a complementary disposition term for annotation, then this term will be added to IDO.

6. Collective Dispositions

A natural generalization of the ideas developed above is to move from a focus on two dispositions towards a consideration of processes involving the collective manifestation of arbitrarily large aggregates of dispositions. Collectives acquire dispositions not possessed by their individual constituents. This is most clearly seen when we consider dispositions as capabilities. A crowd has the collective capability to do the wave in virtue of each individual crowd member's capability to stand at the appropriate time. Two people have the collective capability to lift a w pound weight in virtue of the first person's capability to lift w_1 pounds and the second person's capability to lift w_2 pounds, where $w = w_1 + w_2$. Sometimes collectives are identified by their capabilities. For example, a mob of people is identified by a collective ability (and intent) to do damage. Such collective phenomena involve dispositions inhering in an aggregate of material entities.

BFO makes a three way distinction between material entities: 'fiat object part', 'object', and 'object aggregate', and utilizes the theory of granular partitions to handle issues of truth and reference at different granularities. What counts as an 'object' for a particular investigation is a matter of scale and is usually determined by the perspective of the investigator:

> For a partition to do its work, it needs to have cells large enough to contain the objects that are of interest in the portion of reality which concerns the judging subject, but at the same time these cells must somehow serve to factor out the details which are of no concern. [11] (p. 27)

The same material entity may be considered as an object or an aggregation of (potentially heterogeneous) parts. To reason correctly in a certain context, it is often essential to commit to one or the other perspective. This is evident with the infectious disease domain, where, for example, an infection can be thought of as a unified object in a clinical context, or as a collection of microorganisms in a microbiological context.

To support broad reasoning at different granularities, we either need an ontology of collectives (cf. [12]) or a formulation of which granular partitions are in use. We do not claim that there are a fixed level of granularities or a fixed number of granular partitions:

> Sperm and eggs are both cells, but much of what we have to say about eggs pertains to individual eggs, whereas much more that we have to convey about sperm concern the collective, although we need a mechanism to cross levels of collectivity to speak of a single sperm fertilizing a single egg. Indeed, one of the issues in fertility research is to determine which factors depend on the collective of sperm and the fluids in which they are swimming, and which depend on the individual sperm cells themselves. Hence, we explicitly reject any notion of a fixed set of levels of granularity[10], (p. 336).

Here we will only focus on the differences between dispositions inhering in objects of a certain type and those inhering in aggregates of those types of objects, and the impact of these differences on reasoning. The RO does not have a specific relation for membership in an aggregation, which is a very specific mereological relation, so we will recruit the **proper_part_of** relation for our purposes. The mereology of independent continuants and occurrents is more developed than that of dependent continuants. We hold the view that any parthood relation between dispositions (dependent continuants) must be couched in parthood relations of their bearers (independent continuants) or in parthood relations of their manifestations (occurrents). Each independent continuant may serve a different role in the collective (e.g., a CEO and an assembly line worker are both part of the same collective in different roles), but in IDO we are primarily interested in organism populations of the same type of organism.

The realization of a collective disposition need not involve the realization of the individual dispositions in unison, rather, complex behaviors may be described in terms of complex patterns of realization. Also, we cannot assume that transitivity of parthood implies a compositionality of dispositional properties. A certain population may have a certain collective disposition but may lose that disposition with the addition or removal of members (of the same type) to that population. With these issues in mind, we formulate a definition of collective disposition as follows:

> **Collective Disposition** $=_{def}$ A disposition inhering in an object aggregate *OA* in virtue of the individual dispositions of the constituents of *OA* and that does not itself inhere in any part of *OA* or in any larger aggregate in which *OA* is a part.

The definition purposefully underspecifies the relationship between the individual dispositions. The individual dispositions do not have to complement one another (indeed, they may even block each other) in order for a collective disposition to inhere in the aggregate.

An example of the use of collective dispositions in IDO is the definition of the term 'herd immunity':

> **Herd Immunity** $=_{def}$ A collective disposition that inheres in an organism population by virtue of the fact that a sufficient number of members of the population have immunity to

an infectious agent thereby reducing transmission and protecting non-immune members from the infectious agent population.

The organism population in which an instance of herd immunity inheres is determined by its spatiotemporal arrangement. This population is composed of members that are organisms of the same type, X, have the capability to play the host of infectious agent role in symbiosis with an organism that has the infectious disposition relative to X, and are frequent participants in processes that would transmit the infectious agent between members of the population. Herd immunity is an example of a collective disposition that may be lost if more members are added to the population (in roughly the same spatiotemporal region), specifically if non-immune members are added.

In order to represent collective dispositions in description logic, we first need to consider whether a single disposition can cross scales of aggregates. More formally, we need to consider the range of the **disposition_of** relation and the domain of its inverse relation **has_disposition**. Given X **has_disposition** D we need to decide whether any of X's parts or anything in which X is a part can have the same disposition type D. Formally,

$$\exists\textbf{has\_disposition}.D \sqcap (\exists\textbf{proper\_part\_of}.X \sqcup \exists\textbf{has\_proper\_part}.X) \stackrel{?}{=} \bot \qquad (6)$$

We favor a view in which the same disposition type can inhere at different levels of granularity, but the same disposition instance cannot. Under this view, no subpopulation S of an organism population P with herd immunity has the *same* herd immunity, and no larger population L in which P is a subpopulation has the *same* herd immunity.

An object aggregate C has collective disposition D if, assuming for all $1 \leq i \leq n$, P_i is part of the process aggregate that realizes D

$$P_i \in \exists\textbf{proper\_part\_of}.\exists\textbf{realizes}.D \qquad (7)$$

and there is a member of C with a disposition to manifest each P_i

$$\exists\textbf{proper\_part\_of}.C \sqcap \exists\textbf{has\_disposition}.\exists\textbf{realized\_by}.P_i \neq \bot \qquad (8)$$

If both conditions are satisfied then we can describe the constituents of C by:

$$\begin{aligned}\exists\textbf{proper\_part\_of}.C \sqcap (&\exists\textbf{has\_disposition}.\exists\textbf{realized\_by}.P_1 \sqcup \\ &\exists\textbf{has\_disposition}.\exists\textbf{realized\_by}.P_2 \sqcup \\ &\vdots \\ &\sqcup \exists\textbf{has\_disposition}.\exists\textbf{realized\_by}.P_n)\end{aligned} \qquad (9)$$

This restriction lets us reason over the parts of the aggregate that bears the collective disposition.

7. Conclusion

We have discussed the various ways in which individual dispositions interact in their mutual realization and provided examples of how this characterization is used within IDO. Any ontology of infectious diseases must provide the basis for data integration and reasoning across organism types, disciplines, and scales, and these three dimensions play a central role in our characterization of dispositions. In particular, blocking dispositions and complementary dispositions are used to represent the relationships between the organisms bearing the roles (e.g. host, pathogen, vector) needed to perpetuate a chain of infection. Collective dispositions are used to relate dispositions and their realizations observed at the level of populations to dispositions and their realizations observed at the level of individuals, something of importance in the clinical and biological domains, but of particular importance for connecting entities in these domains to epidemiological entities.

Independent continuants may appear not to interact at all (or only to interact to a small degree) because their constituent parts are in a state of dynamic equilibrium. Dynamic equilibria are pervasive in biomedicine and involve many pairwise blocking and pairwise complementary dispositions being realized simultaneously at a smaller scale than the scale of observation. The disposition relationships presented in this paper may be used to further study dynamic equilibria from an ontological perspective.

While the present work is an initial step in formalizing dispositional interactions for IDO, it is still somewhat fragmented. At present, OWL-DL restrictions are being constructed for the textual definitions presented in this paper. Further work is required to express all such restrictions and axioms in a single representational framework. We believe such a framework must include expressive higher-order logics to enable sufficiently powerful reasoning in the infectious disease domain.

Acknowledgements

This work was funded by the National Institutes of Health through Grant R01 AI 77706-01. Smith's contributions were also funded through the NIH Roadmap for Medical Research, Grant 1 U 54 HG004028 (National Center for Biomedical Ontology). Cowell's contributions were also funded by a Burroughs Wellcome Fund Career Award at the Scientific Interface. We would like to acknowledge the useful feedback from three anonymous reviewers.

References

[1] R. Scheuermann, W. Ceusters, and B. Smith, Toward an Ontological Treatment of Disease and Diagnosis, *Proceedings of the 2009 AMIA Summit on Translational Bioinformatics* (2009), 116–120.

[2] D. Armstrong, C. Martin, and U. Place, *Dispositions: A Debate*, Routledge, London 1995.

[3] R. Arp and B. Smith, Function, Role, and Disposition in Basic Formal Ontology, *Proceedings of Bio-Ontologies Workshop (ISMB2008)*, 45–48.

[4] A. Bird, Antidotes All the Way Down?, *Theoria* **19** (2004), 259–269.

[5] A. Bird, *Nature's Metaphysics: Laws and Properties*, Clarendon Press, Oxford, 2007.

[6] A. Goldfain, L. Cowell, and B. Smith, Towards and Ontological Representation of Resistance: The Case of MRSa, *Proceedings of the First International Conference on Biomedical Ontology* (2009), 61–64.

[7] C. B. Martin, Dispositions and Conditionals, *The Philosophical Quarterly* **44**(1994), 1–8.
[8] G. Molnar, *Powers: A Study in Metaphysics*, Oxford University Press, Oxford, 2003.
[9] S. Mumford, *Dispositions*, Oxford University Press, Oxford, 1998.
[10] A. Rector, J. Rogers, and T. Bittner, Granularity, Scale, and Collectivity: When Size Does and Does Not Matter, *Journal of Biomedical Informatics* **39** (2006), 333–349.
[11] B. Smith and B. Brogaard, A Unified Theory of Truth and Reference, *Logique et Analyse* **43** (2003), 49–93.
[12] Z. Wood and A. Galton, A New Classification of Collectives, *Formal Ontology in Information Systems: Proceedings of the Fifth International Conference* (2008).

Formal Ontology in Information Systems
A. Galton and R. Mizoguchi (Eds.)
IOS Press, 2010

doi:10.3233/978-1-60750-535-8-414

Segmenting and Merging Domain-specific Ontology Modules for Clinical Informatics

Chimezie Ogbuji [a,b], Sivaram Arabandi [b], Songmao. Zhang [c], and Guo-Qiang Zhang [b]
[a] *Cleveland Clinic, Cleveland OH, USA*
[b] *Case Western Reserve University, Cleveland OH, USA*
[c] *Chinese Academy of Sciences, Beijing, P. R. China*

Abstract. A significant set of challenges to the use of large, source ontologies in the medical domain include: automated translation, customization of source ontologies, and performance issues associated with the use of logical reasoning systems to interpret the meaning of a domain captured in a formal knowledge representation. SNOMED-CT and FMA are two reference ontologies that cover much of the domain of clinical informatics and motivate a better means for re-use. In this paper, we present a method for segmenting and merging modules from these ontologies for a specific domain that preserve the meaning of the anatomy terms they have in common.

Keywords. Ontology, SNOMED-CT, Segment, Module, Clinical Informatics

1. Introduction

The role of ontology is increasingly being recognized for small and medium-sized clinical data integration projects. There is a critical need to construct portable, domain-specific ontologies to support not only data curation after the completion of a study, but also on-going activities of clinical research.

For example, PhysioMIMI [22] is a NCRR funded informatics infrastructure for collecting, managing and analyzing diverse sleep-related data types across institutions. It is an ongoing effort for which the hope is that novel markers of disease can be identified, leading to new approaches for screening, diagnosing and treating illnesses. It is being used with a Sleep Domain Ontology (SDO) which covers data for sleep studies (Polysomnograms).

Within the larger medical informatics community, there is a growing consensus on two medical terminologies that leverage formal knowledge representation: SNOMED Clinical Terms (SNOMED-CT) and the Foundational Model of Anatomy (FMA). Despite the increased importance of SNOMED-CT, it is quite large and the use of logical inference systems to process it is hampered by performance issues. Even the most sophisticated description logic inference engines run into memory exhaustion when attempting to classify (i.e., compute all the subsumption relationships between concepts)

SNOMED-CT in its entirety [1]. In some cases within its content, SNOMED-CT has issues with definitions that are sometimes inconsistent or incomplete [2][3][4][5].

This paper proposes a general segmentation method for constructing fragments of well-delineated ontologies for specific domains or applications. It starts with a set of SNOMED-CT terms provided by the user (representing a particular domain) and extracts a subset of SNOMED-CT terms. During this extraction, whenever terms having a corresponding FMA corollary are reached, they are replaced by terms that preserves their original meaning. These FMA terms are used as seeds to extract a corresponding subset of the FMA.

Our segmentation method provides a clinical investigator and informatician with the flexible choice of either using such an extract as is, extending it to incorporate additional terms that are not covered a priori by composing them anew via post-coordination, or integrating the modules into their own ontologies. It also gives an investigator the ability to work around inconsistent and/or incomplete definitions while permitting the re-use of those aspects of the source ontologies that are not problematic.

The rest of the paper is as follows. First, we give an overview of two reference ontologies: SNOMED-CT and the FMA. We discuss the current challenges in re-using source ontologies. We review a recent alignment [10] between the two ontologies and define the problem of ontology extraction. We then present our combined method and indicate how it can provide a way to connect a researcher to a reference ontology in an incremental manner. Finally, we demonstrate the value of such an approach via an example.

2. Background

In this section, we introduce the source ontologies relevant to our method (SNOMED-CT and FMA), discuss the extraction of a standard description logic representation from the SNOMED-CT distribution, and summarize related work.

2.1. Source Material

SNOMED-CT [6] resulted from a merge of SNOMED Reference Terminology (SNOMED RT) developed by the College of American Pathologists and Clinical Terms version 3 (CTV3) developed by the National Health Service (NHS) of the United Kingdom. It is a comprehensive terminological framework of content for clinical documentation and reporting. It provides a foundation for semantic interoperability to code, retrieve, and analyze clinical data. The scope of its almost half a million concepts covers much of healthcare, including: clinical findings, procedures, body structures, organisms, substances, pharmaceutical products, specimens, quantitative measures, and clinical situations.

One of the challenges in using SNOMED-CT is in the nature of its primary distribution format. Although it appeals to an underlying description logic, it is distributed in a relational format that encodes its logical content in a manner that is both redundant and non-standard.

The expressive power of $\mathcal{EL}$ (the description logic underlying SNOMED-CT terminology [23]) has proven to be sufficient for SNOMEDT-CT terminology [3]. The Ontology Web Language (OWL) has emerged as a cross-industry ratified standard for representing description logic theories for RDF, the foundation of the Semantic Web. $\mathcal{EL}$ is a subset of the description logic underlying OWL-DL. In this manner, the SNOMED-CT terminology can be manipulated and serialized as OWL documents.

The SNOMED-CT manual describes [6] two methods for generating *normal forms* that facilitate complete and accurate retrieval of SNOMED CT expressions. It leverages the underlying description logic of SNOMED-CT for this purpose an. The normal form extraction routine is recursive and all concepts referred to from a target concept are also *replaced* with their appropriate normal forms. The *short normal form* is appropriate for predicate expressions and is also the most concise of the two normal forms described in the "Transforming Expressions to Normal Forms" section of the SNOMED-CT manual. It is the one used in our implementation.

SNOMED-CT uses a method in the anatomical part that reifies *part-of* relations. For every proper SNOMED anatomy concept, called *entity* class, there are two auxiliary classes, the *structure* class and the *part* class [7]:

> The main idea underlying the SEP-triplet approach is to represent a part-whole relationship between two entity classes not by a part-of link between the entity class, but rather by an inclusion link between the structure class of the *part* and the part class of the *whole*.

For the sake of space, we refer the reader to [7],[8], and [23] for more information regarding the use of description logic notation for SNOMED-CT.

The Foundational Model of Anatomy is an evolving ontology developed at the University of Washington since 1994. Its objective is to conceptualize the physical objects and spaces that constitute the human body [9]. The underlying model is a frame-based knowledge representation covering over 75,000 concepts including macroscopic, microscopic and sub-cellular canonical anatomy. The FMA is regarded as foundational for two reasons: anatomy is fundamental to all biomedical domains and the anatomical concepts in the FMA generalize to all biomedical domains.

Concepts in the FMA are connected by several relations from mereology (the formal theory and study of part-whole relationships). For the purpose of what we describe here, we are only concerned with the *part_of* and *has_part* relationship between anatomy. The FMA adheres to a very strict, Aristotelian ontological modeling paradigm that ensure the definitions used are consistent and state the essence of anatomical entities in terms of their characteristics.

The version of the FMA we used in our method was a 2006 OWL translation from the Open Biomedical Ontology (OBO) format for ontologies that are part of the OBO foundary. This is different from other existing versions of the FMA in OWL such as that of Goldbreich et al. [26] which is the result of a direct translation of the FMA in its original format into OWL DL.

2.2. Prior Work

2.2.1. The Alignment of FMA and SNOMED-CT

There is significant overlap between the anatomical terms in both SNOMED-CT and the FMA. Bodenreider and Zhang [10] exploit the alignment of anatomical entities in these two systems to analyze and characterize the differences between them. They leveraged both lexical analysis as well as structural analysis to identify some 7500 concepts in SNOMED-CT that have a counter part in the FMA.

In [10] Concept and relations were extracted from each ontology as well as the synonyms for these terms. The names of these concepts and relations were normalized and analyzed for similarity as the basis for identifying equivalent concepts. A second step validates the results of this initial lexical analysis. The transitive closure of subsumption (*is a*) and partitive relationships as well is used to identify structural similarity among the terminological anchors in both the FMA and SNOMED-CT. The result is a 1-1 association between subsets of anatomical concepts in the FMA and in SNOMED-CT.

This mapping is key to the general applicability of our method in the domain of clinical medicine.

2.2.2. Re-using Standard, Source Ontologies: Challenges and Methods

There is a recognized need for standardized controlled vocabularies in clinical research informatics. In addition, the re-use of formal ontologies or controlled vocabularies is widely considered a best practice in contemporary medical terminology methods and guidelines [11]. Bontas and Tolksdorf [2] provide an analysis of the challenges related to the process of re-using ontologies. They define *ontology re-use* as the process in which available ontological knowledge is used as input to generate new ontologies.

In addition, they emphasize the difference between *ontology merging* and *ontology integration*. The former is a process for building a *target ontology* in a particular subject while re-using content from *source ontologies* within the same subject. In the latter case, the new ontology and the source ontology are from non-overlapping subjects [11]. For the purpose of the method we present here, we will focus primarily on ontology merging where the broader subject in common to both the new ontology and its source is clinical medicine.

Cimino [12], gives an influential overview of desiderata for controlled vocabulary systems, which includes criteria that helps to emphasize the challenges in re-using controlled vocabularies for specific purposes. He identifies a critical need for a formal, explicit, and reproducible method for recognizing and filling (domain-specific) gaps in the content of medical terminologies.

Rector [13] investigates the requirements and conflicts that make developing comprehensive, re-usable terminology challenging. He argues that clinical terminology systems need to be able to extend smoothly and quickly in response to changes to the demands of the end users. As a result, a fixed enumerated list of concepts can never be complete and the process of attempting to enumerate such a list a priori results in an intractable, combinatorial explosion of terms. This approach is often referred to as *pre-coordination* and is in contrast to an approach that attempts to enumerate all the atomic components of a set of terms such that users can combine and create new terms from these components on demand. This is called *post-coordination.*

Rector [14] also proposes a set of normalization criteria and an approach for decomposing an ontology into independent disjoint taxonomies (or modules), which can then be recombined using definitions and axioms to represent the relationships between them explicitly. The goal is for modules[1] to be identified with trees of primitives and for the boundaries between those trees to be identified with definitions involving primitives.

[1]The term *module* as it is used there is different from the way we use it later in this paper. Whereas Rector emphasizes *differentia*, we later use the term to emphasize the preservation of meaning for terms shared with a domain-specific ontology and the modules our method produces.

He gives a rationale for the criteria of their normal form (*minimizing implicit differentia*):

> The essence of the requirement for independent homogeneous taxonomies of primitives is that there be exactly one implicit differentiating notion per primitive concept, thus confining implicit information to its irreducible minimum. All other differentiating notions must be explicit and expressed as *restrictions* on the relations between concepts.

As a result of the challenges, there is a lack of complete coverage for specific domains [12]. This is usually overcome in a variety of ways. On the one hand, ontology developers with a need for content in a particular domain can create new, isolated ontologies. On the other hand, they can re-use an existing, standard medical ontology in its entirety, post-coordinating new terms to fill the gaps in content for the new domain. For example, in the case of SNOMED-CT, it can be used as-is for a particular domain. However, applications that re-use a standard medical ontology such as SNOMED-CT in its entirety will inherit those idiosyncratic definitions that are sometimes inconsistent or incomplete [2][3][4][5].

Alternatively, a semi-automated framework can be used to facilitate the incremental, coordinated re-use of source ontologies in the creation of new ones. This is the approach used in PROMPT, a formalism-independent algorithm outlined by Noy and Musen [15]. It attempts to automate the process of merging and alignment as much as possible. However, where merging and alignment cannot be automated, it guides the user, suggests possible actions, identifies conflicts, and proposes solutions to these conflicts. It also relies on a lexical match between term names in order to facilitate both the automated portion of the algorithm and the user feedback loop.

Noy and Musen's approach is also the one used by Bontas and Tolksdorf [2] in both of their use cases. In addition to using an initial, user-specified list of matches between the target and source ontologies, they also rely on the ability to extract sections of the source ontologies by following semantic connections starting from the original terms. Unfortunately, they do not describe this extraction process in any reproducible detail.

Bontas and Tolksdorf conclude (in at least the medical terminology use case) that the benefits of re-use were outweighed by the engineering costs. The major challenges they identify are: automated translation of source ontologies into a common knowledge representation format, customization of the source ontologies, and scalability issues.

d'Aquin et al. [25] demonstrate how existing modularization techniques can be adapted to address the requirements of their application. They use a modularization algorithm based on a traversal paradigm and provide a set of criteria for evaluating the effectiveness of their method. They describe three major, generic steps of the *dynamic knowledge selection algorithms*: the selection of relevant ontologies, the modularization of the selected ontologies by a particular algorithm, and the merging of the relevant ontology modules in a meaningful way.

3. Method

We want to generate anatomy and clinical terminology modules that make use of principled normal forms, are minimal in size, and preserve the meaning of re-used symbols across multiple ontologies as much as is computationally feasible. We also want the process to be automated as much as possible to take advantage of a common, well-specified knowledge representation format, and to have the ability to facilitate the customization of a large source ontology.

In particular we want a procedure that:

1. Helps to identify and fills gaps in clinical terminology systems,
2. Uses normalized OWL representations,
3. Has sufficient expressive power for bio-medical domain,
4. Re-uses as much of FMA as possible.

We achieve these requirements by (respectively): providing a way for an informatician to control the amount of the modules that are extracted, taking advantage of normal form transformations to emphasize explicit differentia, leveraging a more expressive description logic language than the one underlying current SNOMED-CT, and use a set of rules to maximize the amount of FMA re-used to reify SEP triplets.

In order to define such a method, we need to provide an appropriate lexicon for discussing the semantics of the problem and briefly discuss an efficient segmentation algorithm originally used for segmenting GALEN [17] that we will use in concert with the normal form extraction procedures included with the SNOMED-CT documentation.

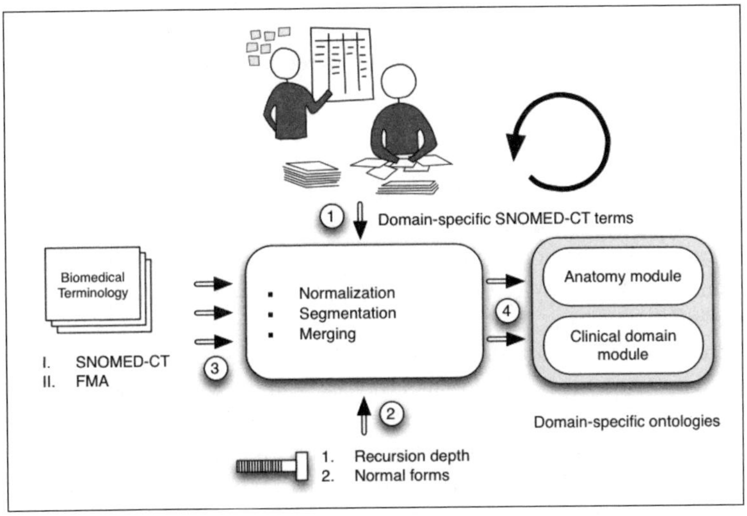

Figure 1. Method overview

3.1. Preliminary

The sizes of major medical ontologies are quite large and push the limits of the deductive reasoning systems that benefit from the use of formal logic to represent medical terminology. In our setting of controlled medical vocabulary, however, the more significant challenge as a result of the size of these ongologies has less to do with reasoning complexity and more to do with ontology engineering considerations such as the management and maintenance of terms. As a result, there has been some investigation into formally specified algorithms for segmenting such large ontologies into more manageable chunks.

Grau et.al. [16] define a formal relationship between description logic ontologies called a *deductive, conservative extension.* The intuition behind this relationship is motivated by a scenario where we are developing an ontology $\mathcal{P}$ and want to reuse a set of symbols from a foreign ontology $\mathcal{Q}$ without changing their meaning. If $\mathcal{P}$ does not change the meaning of the symbols it has in common with $\mathcal{Q}$, we can say that $\mathcal{P} \cup \mathcal{Q}$ is a conservative extension of $\mathcal{Q}$.

Definition (Deductive conservative extension) 1 *For any two ontologies $\mathcal{O}$ and $\mathcal{O}_1$ that share the same description logic language $\mathcal{L}$ and symbols from a common set of terms* **S** *(or a* signature*) from that language and $\mathcal{O}_1 \subseteq \mathcal{O}$,*[2] *$\mathcal{O}$ is considered a deductive, conservative extension to $\mathcal{O}_1$. if every logical consequence of $\mathcal{O}$ is already a logical consequence of $\mathcal{O}_1$.*

Definition (Module) 2 *An ontology $\mathcal{O}'_1$ is a* module *for $\mathcal{O}$ in $\mathcal{O}'$ with respect to $\mathcal{L}$ if $\mathcal{O}'_1 \subseteq \mathcal{O}'$ if $\mathcal{O} \cup \mathcal{O}'$ is a deductive, conservative extension of $\mathcal{O} \cup \mathcal{O}'_1$ for some signature within $\mathcal{L}$.*

The intuition here is that when answering an arbitrary query involving the terms in $\mathcal{O}'$ (its signature), importing the module $\mathcal{O}'_1$ (a more manageable fragment of $\mathcal{O}$ *connected* through the terms it has in common with $\mathcal{O}'$) should give exactly the same answers as if the whole ontology $\mathcal{O}$ had been imported instead.

3.2. Web Ontology Segmentation

Seidenberg and Rector [17] describe an ontology segmentation algorithm that starts with a normalized ontology and a set of terms and creates an extract around those terms and related concepts using the underlying formal representation to navigate the relationships between concepts. Their method traverses up the *is a* links from the given set of terms towards the ontological root.

In addition, other relationships (called role restrictions in description logics) are traversed and the concepts reached in this way are also the basis for an extraction of their *is a* relationships. However, this lateral traversal is limited by a user-specified recursion depth. This allows the user to fine-tune the amount of the original ontology extracted.

The modularization algorithm of d'Aquin et al. [25] is inspired by that of Seidenberg and Rector. Likewise, in our procedure we re-use this ontology segmentation algorithm to extract a relevant, manageable subset of the FMA.

While this method is in contrast to the module extraction procedures given by Grau et.al. that compute modules for ontologies with respect to a signature, it scales well with respect to complex, large ontologies [17]. Grau et.al do not perform any empirical comparison between their sound methods and that of Seidenberg and Rector, however they summarize the data complexity for the problem of deciding conservative extensions for a range of description logic languages. The problem of deciding deductive, conservative extensions with respect to a signature using algorithms with tractable (sub-exponential) data complexity for $\mathcal{EL}$ is an open research problem [16].

[2]Note, we inherit the abuse of notation from [16] in using $\subseteq$ to indicate both the normal description logic notation for inclusion between concepts as well as to denote syntactic subsumption between two ontologies where the axioms in one exist in the other

3.3. Procedure

Having given a lexicon for the semantics of creating ontology modules and an efficient hueristic for doing so, we now describe our procedure for extracting domain-specific normal forms from SNOMED-CT. During this extraction, whenever terms that have a corresponding the FMA corollary (as identified by Bodenreider and Zhang) are reached, they are replaced appropriately. The FMA terms that are reached this way are used as seeds for the Seidenberg and Rector segmentation algorithm to extract a corresponding subset of the FMA.

Below, we give definitions for the SEP-triplet classes that we later use:

Definition (E_{class}) 3 *We define E_{class} as the set of SNOMED-CT anatomy concepts that represent an entire anatomical entity.*

Definition (P_{class}) 4 *We define P_{class} as the set of SNOMED-CT anatomy concepts that represent a part of an anatomical entity.*

Definition (S_{class}) 5 *We define S_{class} as the set of SNOMED-CT anatomy concepts that represent either an entire anatomical entity or a part thereof.*

Using the previously introduced notation, we can specify the semantics of the *ideal* extraction more formally. We refer to the common set of terms (or signature) that correspond to the mapped anatomy terms from SNOMED-CT and the FMA as $\mathbf{S}_{\text{anatomy}}$. For each term in $\mathbf{S}_{\text{anatomy}}$ there is a pair $(A_{\text{sct}}, A_{\text{fma}})$ that represents the mapping between anatomy terms of the two terminologies where A_{sct} is a component of an SEPtriplet and A_{fma} is the corresponding FMA term.

We use $\mathcal{O}_{\text{snomed}}$ to denote the short normal form of a subset of SNOMED-CT generated using the $\mathcal{EL}$ extraction algorithm, starting with a user-specfied set of SNOMED-CT concepts. $\mathcal{O}_{\text{fma}}$ is the FMA ontology.

Definition (Anatomy Module for a Clinical Domain) 6 *$\mathcal{O}'_{snct\text{-}fma}$ is a* module *for $\mathcal{O}_{snomed}$ in $\mathcal{O}_{fma}$ with respect to $\mathbf{S}_{anatomy}$.*

Definition (Clinical Domain Module for Anatomy) 7 *$\mathcal{O}'_{fma\text{-}snct}$ denotes a* module *for $\mathcal{O}_{fma}$ in $\mathcal{O}_{snomed}$ in with respect to $\mathbf{S}_{anatomy}$.*

We import $\mathcal{O}'_{\text{snct-fma}}$ into $\mathcal{O}'_{\text{fma-snct}}$, resulting in a domain-specific, merged subset of both SNOMED-CT and the FMA. We will refer to this merged subset as $\mathcal{O}_{\text{merged}}$.

Definition (Cross-module Definitions) 8 *$A_{\text{inter-module}}$ are the SNOMED-CT concepts in $\mathcal{O}'_{snct\text{-}fma}$ defined by existential role restrictions where the filler class involve FMA terms from $\mathbf{S}_{anatomy}$ placed using any of our rules.*

These cross-module boundary terms represent the kind of explicit definitions that the normalization procedure given by Rector attempts to support. In some cases, as we will later show, these definitions are augmented by virtue of their connection to the FMA and therefore permit additional, richer entailments.

These module definitions capture the ideal case since, for instance, the Seidenberg and Rector algorithm is a heuristic and does not necessarily produce deductive, conser-

Table 1. Rules that maximize the usage of the FMA concepts for reifying SEP triplets

If	Then
$A_{\text{sct}} \in E_{\text{class}}$	1. If $A_{\text{sct\_s}}$ is the S_{class} in the SEP triplet of A_{sct}, then for every restriction where $A_{\text{sct\_s}}$ is the filler of a *site* existential role restriction, replace with $A_{\text{fma}} \sqcup \exists part\_of.A_{\text{fma}}$ 2. If $A_{\text{sct\_p}}$ is the P_{class} in the SEP triplet of A_{sct}, then for every restriction where $A_{\text{sct\_p}}$ is the filler of a *site* existential role restriction, replace with $\exists part\_of.A_{\text{fma}}$
$A_{\text{sct}} \in P_{\text{class}}$	1. If $A_{\text{sct\_s}}$ is the S_{class} in the SEP triplet of A_{sct}, then for every restriction where $A_{\text{sct\_s}}$ is the filler of a *site* existential role restriction, replace with $A_{\text{fma}} \sqcup \exists part\_of.A_{\text{fma}}$

vative extensions. The tradeoff is expedience for completeness[3]. We also note that the signature we use will not be the entire 7500 mappings from SNOMED-CT to the FMA (i.e, $\mathbf{S}_{\text{anatomy}}$) but rather only those mappings for SNOMED-CT terms that are reached during the short normal form extraction of $\mathcal{O}_{\text{snomed}}$.

Having outlined the general idea, we now need to provide a mechanism for replacing A_{sct} terms with the corresponding A_{fma} in a way that preserves the general intent of the SEP anatomy scheme by transcribing them into a more expressive description logic. The notion of a module assumes that the common signature is completely shared by both original ontologies. However, in our case, although we have a 1-1 mapping for some of the anatomy terms in both ontologies, the SNOMED-CT axioms regarding anatomy refer only to the A_{sct} terms.

We use a set of rules to determine how we replace the A_{sct} term in a mapping with class descriptions involving the FMA anatomy term instead (i.e., A_{fma}). The form used depends on the nature of A_{sct}.

The process is driven by the mappings from A_{sct} terms in $\mathcal{O}'_{\text{snct-fma}}$ to the corresponding A_{fma}. For every such entry in the mapping, we use the rules listed on Table 1 to determine how the axioms where A_{sct} is the *filler* class in an existential role restriction of *site*[4], is replaced. In addition to the replacements given in rules, we also replace A_{sct} with A_{fma} in all axioms, including those of the form $\texttt{Concept} \sqsubseteq A_{\text{sct}}$ and $\texttt{Concept} \equiv (A_{\text{sct}} \sqcap \cdots)$.

Note that one existential role restriction on site could be changed to the disjunction ($\sqcup$) over instantiations of its replacement. We address the verbosity via the following transformation:

This replacement should apply uniformly to all of $\mathcal{O}'_{\text{snct-fma}}$.

$$\frac{\exists site.\text{A1} \sqcup \exists site.\text{A2}}{\exists site.(\text{A1} \sqcup \text{A2})}$$

For the details regarding how to identify the S_{class} or P_{class} of the SEP triplet associated with a particular A_{sct}, we refer the reader to [19].

[3]By completeness we mean that not all entailments from the combination of SNOMED-CT and FMA in their entirety will follow in the modules.

[4]We follow the convention of Rector and Brandt [18] in using a *site* relation as a shorthand for either of procedureSite or findingSite from SNOMED-CT.

4. Sleep Domain

Having described our method, we now present the SDO as an example domain demonstrating its usage. Thirty nine SNOMED-CT terms of interest from the sleep domain were identified as seeds. The diagram below provides an overview of the categories of concepts selected for extraction. It consists of a crop circle visualization [20] of the SDO modules with an overlay of screen shots from the existential outline view plugin[5] in Protege 4.

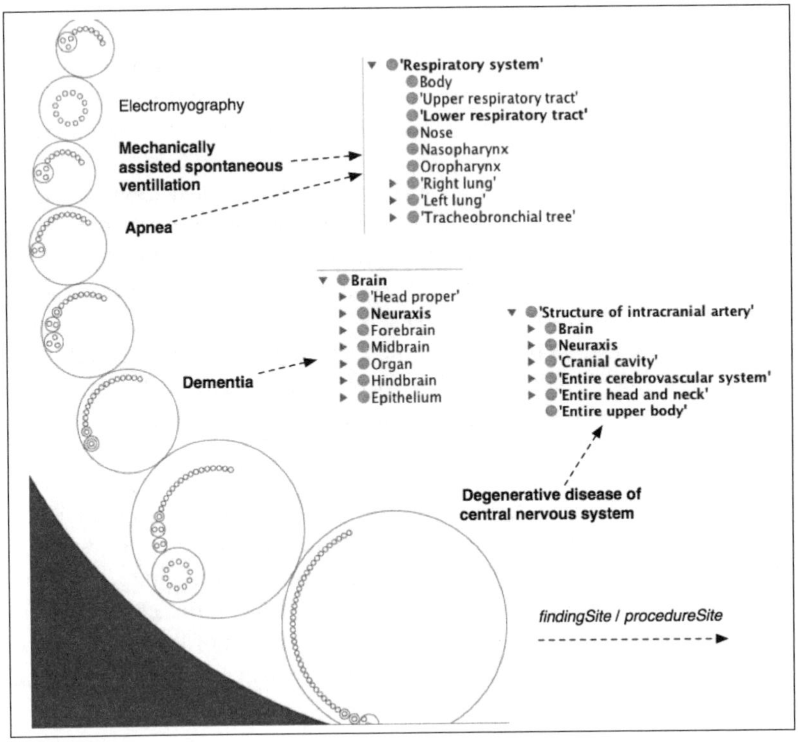

Figure 2. SDO Overview

We use *Glaucoma* as an example concept. Wordnet defines glaucoma as:

> An eye disease that damages the optic nerve and impairs vision (sometimes progressing to blindness)

In the original (normalized) SNOMED-CT definition, the finding site of glaucoma is OpticDiscStructure, which only has an E_{class} subordinate term: EntireOpticDisc. The former was mapped to the FMA concept *Intra-ocular part of optic nerve* from synonymy and the latter to the FMA concept of *Optic disc*. So after the replacement, the finding site of glaucoma has changed to IntraOcularPartOfOpticNerve$_{\text{fma}}$ and (OpticDisc$_{\text{fma}}$ $\cup$ $\exists part\_of$.OpticDisc$_{\text{fma}}$), following the rules for S_{class} and E_{class}.

In the following section, we will look more closely at another sleep domain concept and its placement in the module our method produces.

[5] http://code.google.com/p/co-ode-owl-plugins/wiki/OutlineView

5. Analysis

In order to demonstrate that we have met the quality criteria for module extraction given in section 3, we analyze the results from the SDO domain. In the following steps, we discuss the number of classes that reside at the periphery due to the given depth of recursion. This will indicate how the method can proceed incrementally by adding these classes to the list of FMA classes to extract. We load the result in Protege in order to demonstrate portability via the use of a standard ontology format (OWL). Finally, we examine the proportion of classes extracted from FMA that were used in SNOMED-CT axioms.

The method was implemented in Python using a library for manipulating the OWL representation of the ontologies called InfixOWL [21], the rdflib[6] RDF library, and a library for managing a MySQL database where the SNOMED-CT distribution was loaded called MySQLdb[7].

This implementation was used to extract the SDO-related terms as modules of SNOMED-CT and the FMA or and without the use of normal forms for a more compressed SNOMED-CT theory.

The Seidenberg and Rector algorithm was set to a recursion depth of 2. As a result of running the implementation with these inputs, we obtain an OWL document consisting of 1726 (*1366*)[8] classes, and 33 object properties. The combined SDO modules ($\mathcal{O}'_{\text{snct-fma}}$) are comprised of 825 (*718*) classes and 3 object properties. 81 (*53*) related SNOMED-CT anatomy concepts (a subset of $\mathbf{S}_{\text{anatomy}}$) were replaced with their FMA counterpart. Amongst these, 43 (*35*) were members of S_{class}, 37 (*17*) were members of E_{class}, and one was an instance of the P_{class}.

The ontology was loaded into Protege version 4.0 and the Pellet plugin was installed for use as a classifier. There were no inconsistencies after classifying the ontology. In order to demonstrate the way in which the extract can act as a bridge, we examine the SNOMED-CT concept of *CorticobasalDegeneration*. The extracted module describes Corticobasal Degeneration as a special kind of degeneration of the central nervous system or any part thereof. In particular, it is a disease of the cerebral cortex and the Basal ganglia or a part thereof:

$$
\begin{aligned}
&\text{CorticobasalDegeneration} \equiv \text{Disease} \sqcap \\
&\qquad (\exists associatedMorphology.\text{Degeneration}) \sqcap \\
&\qquad (\exists site.(SetOfBasalGanglia_{\text{fma}} \sqcup \exists part\_of.SetOfBasalGanglia_{\text{fma}})) \sqcap \\
&\qquad (\exists site.CerebraCortex_{\text{fma}})
\end{aligned}
$$

The extraction from and alignment to the FMA provides partitive axioms that *connect* the cerebral cortex to up to 100 other subordinate anatomical entities as well as a

[6]http://code.google.com/p/rdflib/

[7]http://sourceforge.net/projects/mysql-python/

[8]The numbers in parenthesis correspond to modules where the SNOMED-CT extract is based on the normal form extraction.

few ancestral anatomical entities. So, we can infer, for instance, that the cerebral cortex is also a kind of cortex of neuraxis, component of external gray matter, and organ component of the neuraxis.

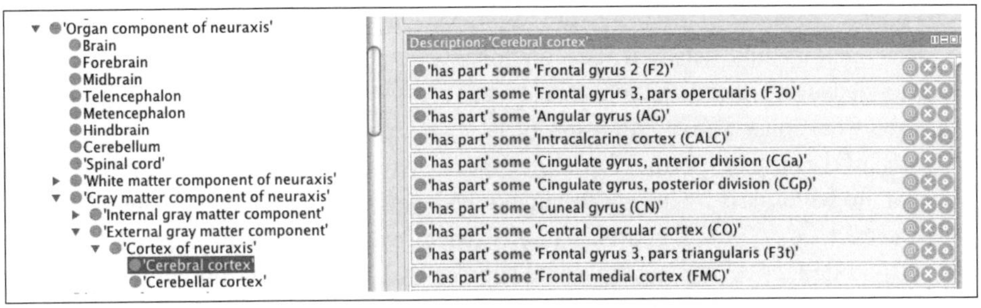

Figure 3. Cerebral cortex in Protege

Among the sleep domain related classes, 366 (*85*) of them are disorders or procedures defined by their relationships to anatomic parts via *site*. Within these, 23(*4*) involve FMA concepts from $\mathbf{S}_{\text{anatomy}}$. Intuitively, these correspond to the $A_{\text{inter-module}}$ terms for the sleep domain. They codify pathology and clinical management theories using the shared anatomy signature. 266 (*232*) FMA classes reside at the edge of the segmentation extraction and correspond to candidates for subsequent FMA extractions in order to incrementally expand the scope of the domain by connections to related parts of human anatomy.

6. Concluding Remarks

The motivation behind the development of d'Aquin et al.'s modularization method is similar to ours. However, we further demonstrate the general value of ontology modularization and merging through its applicability to the challenges of managing biomedical terminology and in filling gaps using existing reference ontologies in a coordinated way. d'Aquin et al. claim that anything that can be entailed from a source ontology can still be entailed from the modules produced by their method. However, they do not show how this characteristic is guaranteed. In our case, it is sacrificed in order to ensure that the segmentation process is tractable.

A few challenges were encountered in our investigation. First, our approach in reifying the semantics of the SEP anatomy terms is problematic in at least one way. The use of $\sqcup$ for anatomical structures introduces the need for a more expressive description logic than $\mathcal{EL}^+$ [24] (which does not include support for concept disjunctions) such as $\mathcal{ALC}$ [16]. Essentially, the target language is $\mathcal{EL}^+$ with the addition of $\sqcup$.

In implementing the extraction heuristic of Seidenberg and Rector, we only traversed up *is a* links. As a result, the connected FMA terms did not have their more specific subordinate terms included in the extracted modules. We found in practice that such a downward extraction had a significant impact on the size of the resulting modules. Seidenberg and Rector faced a similar problem and thus chose not to extract subordinate terms of classes reached via lateral traversal [17].

The use of a more expressive description logic to reify SEP-Triplets is similar to the approach of Suntisrivaraporn [7] where they transcribe the triplets by re-using the SNOMED-CT terms. Instead, we use terms from a reference ontology of anatomy. Still, their use of relation inclusion axioms is needed to ensure that axioms such as *a disease of the part is a disease of the whole* properly propagate up the *site* relation.

The relationships between the components of the modules we generate can be characterized using the deductive, conservative extension relationship. SNOMED-CT is a deductive, conservative extension of $\mathcal{O}_{\text{snomed}}$, because $\mathcal{O}_{\text{snomed}}$ is an extraction of SNOMED-CT using the normal form rules specified in the SNOMED-CT manual, which are meant to be lossless by design. As mentioned earlier, the segmentation algorithm we use to extract $\mathcal{O}'_{\text{fma-snct}}$ is a heuristic in the general case and thus it is unclear whether $\mathcal{O}'_{\text{fma-snct}}$ is a deductive, conservative extension of $\mathcal{O}_{\text{merged}}$. The determination of whether that algorithm produces deductive, conservative extensions for either $\mathcal{EL}$, $\mathcal{EL}^+$, or the extension of the latter with $\sqcup$ is beyond the scope of this work.

Finally, $\mathcal{O}'_{\text{snct-fma}}$ is a deductive, conservative extension of $\mathcal{O}_{\text{merged}}$ since every axiom of the form $A_{\text{fma}} \sqsubseteq B_{\text{fma}}$ (where A_{fma} is a FMA class and B_{fma} is composed of the FMA classes and properties only) in $\mathcal{O}_{\text{merged}}$ also holds in the original FMA. This is the case regardless of whether or not the extraction algorithm produces deductive, conservative extensions since the reification of the SEP-Triplets in $\mathcal{O}'_{\text{snct-fma}}$ take advantage of the truth-preserving nature of the SNOMED-CT to FMA mappings.

This basically means (keeping in mind the caveats regarding the segmentation algorithm used) that any application that uses the FMA can still use our merged ontology without any inconsistency. On the other hand, for an application that uses SNOMED-CT, when incorporating our merged ontology, an informatician has to be aware that the same disease may have two sites where one is a SNOMED-CT class and the other is a FMA class.

The method we present addresses automated translation, customization of source ontologies, and performance issues. It is meant to be generally applicable to situations where a specific domain that is not well-covered by SNOMED-CT can be conceptualized by extending or directly re-using an ontological framework aligned with both SNOMED-CT and the FMA in a semi-automated manner. Third-party applications that use this framework can provide feedback to the user regarding additional terms to consider as a source for incrementally extracting aligned modules. So, it meets a critical need to fill gaps in the content of medical ontologies and provides a clinical informatician with a powerful tool in the process.

7. Acknowledgement

This work was sponsored by the Choose Ohio First Scholarship and Tomas & Evelyn James Fellowship Biomedical Informatics, MADIS of the Chinese Academy of Sciences, the Case Western Reserve University / Cleveland Clinic CTSA Grant UL1 RR024989 from the National Center for Research Resources (NCRR), and NCRR Grant NCRR-94681DBS78.

References

[1] Baader, F., Lutz, C., and Suntisrivaraporn, B., Is tractable reasoning in extensions of the description logic EL useful in practice, *Proceedings of the 2005 International Workshop on Methods for Modalities* (2005), pp. 5.

[2] Bontas, E.P., Mochol, M., and Tolksdorf, R., Case studies on ontology reuse, *Proceedings of the 5th International Conference on Knowledge Management IKNOW05* (2005).

[3] Bodenreider, O., Smith, B., Kumar, A., and Burgun, A., Investigating subsumption in SNOMED CT: An exploration into large description logic-based biomedical terminologies, *Artificial intelligence in medicine* **39** (2007), pp. 183–195.

[4] Ceusters, W., Smith, B., Kumar, A., and Dhaen, C., Ontology-based error detection in SNOMED-CT, *Studies in health technology and informatics* **107** (2004), pp. 482.

[5] Rector, A.L. and Brandt, S., Why do it the hard way? The case for an expressive description logic for SNOMED, *Journal of the American Medical Informatics Association* **15** (2008), pp. 744–751.

[6] SNOMED–CT, User Guide–January 2007 release http://www. ihtsdo. org/fileadmin/user_upl oad/Docs_01, *Technical_Docs/snomed_ct_ user_guide. pdf.*

[7] Suntisrivaraporn, B., Baader, F., Schulz, S., and Spackman, K., Replacing SEPtriplets in SNOMED CT using tractable description logic operators, *Proceedings of AIME, LNCS* (2007).

[8] Schulz, S., Markó, K., and Suntisrivaraporn, B., Complex occurrents in clinical terminologies and their representation in a formal language, *Proc. 1st European Conference on SNOMED CT (SMCSâĂŹ06)* (2006).

[9] Rosse, C. and Mejino, J.L.V., A reference ontology for biomedical informatics: the Foundational Model of Anatomy, *Journal of Biomedical Informatics* **36** (2003), pp. 478–500.

[10] Bodenreider, O. and Zhang, S., Comparing the representation of anatomy in the FMA and SNOMED CT, *AMIA Annual Symposium Proceedings* (2006), pp. 46.

[11] Pinto, H.S. and Martins, J.P., A methodology for ontology integration, *Proceedings of the 1st international conference on Knowledge capture* (2001), pp. 131–138.

[12] Cimino, J.J., Desiderata for controlled medical vocabularies in the twenty-first century, *Methods of information in medicine* (1998).

[13] Rector, A.L., Clinical terminology: why is it so hard?, *Methods of information in medicine* **4/5** (1999), pp. 239–252.

[14] Rector, A.L., Modularisation of domain ontologies implemented in description logics and related formalisms including OWL, *Proceedings of the 2nd international conference on Knowledge capture* (2003), pp. 121–128.

[15] Noy, N.F. and Musen, M.A., PROMPT: Algorithm and tool for automated ontology merging and alignment, *Proceedings of the Seventeenth National Conference on Artificial Intelligence (AAAI-2000)* (2000).

[16] Grau, B. C., Horrocks, I., Kazakov, Y., Sattler, U., Modular Reuse of Ontologies: Theory and Practice, *Journal of Artificial Intelligence Research* **31** (2008), pp. 273–318.

[17] Seidenberg, J. and Rector, A., Web ontology segmentation: Analysis, classification and use, *Proceedings of the 15th international conference on World Wide Web* (2006), pp. 13–22.

[18] Rector, A.L. and Brandt, S., Why do it the hard way? The case for an expressive description logic for SNOMED, *Journal of the American Medical Informatics Association* **15** (2008), pp. 744–751.

[19] Schulz, S., Romacker, M., and Hahn, U., Part-whole reasoning in medical ontologies revisited–introducing SEP triplets into classification-based description logics., *Proceedings of the AMIA Symposium* (1998), pp. 830.

[20] Wang, T.D. and Parsia, B., Cropcircles: topology sensitive visualization of owl class hierarchies, *Lecture Notes in Computer Science* **4273** (2006), pp. 695.

[21] Ogbujic, C., InfixOWL: An Idiomatic Interface for OWL, *OWLED* (2008).

[22] Anoymous, Three New Informatics Pilot Projects to Aid Clinical and Translational Scientists Nationwide, *NIH News* (2009) . http://nih.gov/news/health/jan2009/ncrr-26.htm

[23] Schulz, S., Marko, K., and Suntisrivaraporn, B., Formal representation of complex SNOMED CT expressions, *BMC Medical Informatics and Decision Making* **8** (2008), pp. S9.

[24] Baader, F., Lutz, C., and Suntisrivaraporn, B., Efficient reasoning in EL+, *Proceedings of DL2006* **189** (2006).

[25] d'Aquin, M., Sabou, M., and Motta, E., Modularization: a key for the dynamic selection of relevant knowledge components, *Proceedings of the ISWC 2006 Workshop on Modular Ontologies* (2006).

[26] Golbreich, C., Zhang, S., and Bodenreider, O., The foundational model of anatomy in OWL: Experience and perspectives, *Web Semantics* **4** (2006), pp. 181–195.

Formal Ontology in Information Systems
A. Galton and R. Mizoguchi (Eds.)
IOS Press, 2010

Subject Index

Formal Ontology in Information Systems
A. Galton and R. Mizoguchi (Eds.)
IOS Press, 2010

Author Index